Islam and Ecology

Publications of the Center for the Study of World Religions, Harvard Divinity School

General Editor: Lawrence E. Sullivan
Senior Editor: Kathryn Dodgson

Religions of the World and Ecology

Series Editors: Mary Evelyn Tucker and John Grim

Cambridge, Massachusetts

Islam and Ecology

A Bestowed Trust

edited by

RICHARD C. FOLTZ

FREDERICK M. DENNY

and

AZIZAN BAHARUDDIN

distributed by

Harvard University Press

for the

Center for the Study of World Religions

Harvard Divinity School

Printed in the United States of America

Grateful acknowledgment is made for permission to reprint the following:

Kaveh L. Afrasiabi, "Toward an Islamic Ecotheology," *Hamdard Islamicus*, vol. 18, no. 1, pages 33–49.

L. Clarke, "The Universe Alive," in *Thinking about the Environment*, edited by Thomas M. Robinson and Laura Westra. Lanham, Md.: Lexington Books, 2002. Reprinted by permission of Rowman & Littlefield Publishers, Inc.

S. Nomanul Haq, "Islam and Ecology: Toward Retrieval and Reconstruction." Reprinted by permission of *Dædalus*, Journal of the american Academy of Arts and Sciences, from the issue entitled, "Religion and Ecology: Can tthe Climate Change?" Fall 2001, vol 130, no. 4.

Mawil Y. Izzi Dien, "Islam and the Environment: Theory and Practice," *Journal of Beliefs and Values*, 1997, vol. 18, no. 1, pages 47–58. Reprinted by permission of Taylor and Francis Ltd.; http://www.tandf.co.uk/journals.

James L. Wescoat, Jr., "Landscape of Religion," *Landscape Research*, 1995, vol. 20, no. 1, pages 19–29. Reprinted by permission of Taylor and Francis Ltd.; http://www.tandf.co.uk/journals.

Cover art: 1960.117.4.2.1. Attributed to Mahesh. It's the Day for the Garden! Folio 173a from a Divan of Anvari. 1588. Indian. Mughal Period, 932–1274/1526–1588. Ink, opaque watercolor and gold on paper. 13.97 cm. x 7.62 cm. Folio. Courtesy of the Arthur M. Sackler Museum, Harvard University Art Museums, Gift of John Goelet, formerly in the collection of Louis J. Cartier. Photo credit: Katya Kallsen.

Cover design: Patrick Santana

Cataloging-in-Publication Data available from the Library of Congress

ISBN 0-945454-39-2 (hardcover)
ISBN 0-945454-40-6 (paperback)

Acknowledgments

The series of conferences on religions of the world and ecology took place from 1996 through 1998, with supervision at the Harvard University Center for the Study of World Religions by Don Kunkel and Malgorzata Radziszewska-Hedderick and with the assistance of Janey Bosch, Naomi Wilshire, and Lilli Leggio. Narges Moshiri, also at the Center, was indispensable in helping to arrange the first two conferences. A series of volumes developing the themes explored at the conferences is being published by the Center and distributed by Harvard University Press under the editorial direction of Kathryn Dodgson.

These efforts have been generously supported by major funding from the V. Kann Rasmussen Foundation. The conference organizers appreciate also the support of the following institutions and individuals: Aga Khan Trust for Culture and Tom Kessinger, for his special assistance with the Islam and Ecology conference, Association of Shinto Shrines, Nathan Cummings Foundation, Dharam Hinduja Indic Research Center at Columbia University, Germeshausen Foundation, Harvard Buddhist Studies Forum, Harvard Divinity School Center for the Study of Values in Public Life, Jain Academic Foundation of North America, Laurance Rockefeller, Sacharuna Foundation, Theological Education to Meet the Environmental Challenge, and Winslow Foundation. The conferences were originally made possible by the Center for Respect of Life and Environment of the Humane Society of the United States, which continues to be a principal cosponsor. Bucknell University, also a cosponsor, has provided support in the form of leave time from teaching for conference coordinators Mary Evelyn Tucker and John Grim as well as the invaluable administrative assistance of Stephanie Snyder. Her thoughtful attention to critical details is legendary. Then President William Adams of Bucknell University and then Vice-President for Academic Affairs Daniel Little have also granted travel funds for faculty and students to attend the conferences. Grateful acknowledgment is here made for the advice from key area specialists in shaping each conference and in editing the published volumes. Their generosity in time and talent has been indispensable at every step of the project. Special thanks are given to Fazlun Khalid, founder director of the Islamic Foundation for Ecology and Environmental Sciences, for his assistance in planning the Islam conference with John Grim. Throughout this process, the support, advice, and encouragement from Martin S. Kaplan has been invaluable.

Contents

Series Preface

LAWRENCE E. SULLIVAN

Religion distinguishes the human species from all others, just as human presence on earth distinguishes the ecology of our planet from other places in the known universe. Religious life and the earth's ecology are inextricably linked, organically related.

Human belief and practice mark the earth. One can hardly think of a natural system that has not been considerably altered, for better or worse, by human culture. "Nor is this the work of the industrial centuries," observes Simon Schama. "It is coeval with the entirety of our social existence. And it is this irreversibly modified world, from the polar caps to the equatorial forests, that is all the nature we have" (*Landscape and Memory* [New York: Vintage Books, 1996], 7). In Schama's examination even landscapes that appear to be most free of human culture turn out, on closer inspection, to be its product.

Human beliefs about the nature of ecology are the distinctive contribution of our species to the ecology itself. Religious beliefs—especially those concerning the nature of powers that create and animate—become an effective part of ecological systems. They attract the power of will and channel the forces of labor toward purposive transformations. Religious rituals model relations with material life and transmit habits of practice and attitudes of mind to succeeding generations.

This is not simply to say that religious thoughts occasionally touch the world and leave traces that accumulate over time. The matter is the other way around. From the point of view of environmental studies, religious worldviews propel communities into the world with fundamental predispositions toward it because such religious worldviews are primordial, all-encompassing, and unique. They are *primordial* because they probe behind secondary appearances and stray thoughts to rivet human attention on realities of the first order: life at its source, creativity in its fullest manifestation, death and destruction at their origin, renewal and salvation in their germ. The revelation of first things is compelling and moves communities to take creative action. Primordial ideas are prime movers.

Religious worldviews are *all-encompassing* because they fully absorb the natural world within them. They provide human beings both a view of the whole and at the same time a penetrating image of their own ironic position as the beings in the cosmos who possess the capacity for symbolic thought: the part that contains the whole—or at least a picture of the whole—within itself. As all-encompassing, therefore, religious ideas do not just contend with other ideas as equals; they frame the mind-set within which all sorts of ideas commingle in a cosmology. For this reason, their role in ecology must be better understood.

Religious worldviews are *unique* because they draw the world of nature into a wholly other kind of universe, one that appears only in the religious imagination. From the point of view of environmental studies, the risk of such religious views, on the one hand, is of disinterest in or disregard for the natural world. On the other hand, only in the religious world can nature be compared and contrasted to other kinds of being—the supernatural world or forms of power not always fully manifest in nature. Only then can nature be revealed as distinctive, set in a new light startlingly different from its own. That is to say, only religious perspectives enable human beings to evaluate the world of nature in terms distinct from all else. In this same step toward intelligibility, the natural world is evaluated in terms consonant with human beings' own distinctive (religious and imaginative) nature in the world, thus grounding a self-conscious relationship and a role with limits and responsibilities.

In the struggle to sustain the earth's environment as viable for future generations, environmental studies has thus far left the role of religion unprobed. This contrasts starkly with the emphasis given, for example, the role of science and technology in threatening or sustaining the ecology. Ignorance of religion prevents environmental studies from achieving its goals, however, for though science and technology share many important features of human culture with religion, they leave unexplored essential wellsprings of human motivation and concern that shape the world as we know it. No understanding of the environment is adequate without a grasp of the religious life that constitutes the human societies which saturate the natural environment.

A great deal of what we know about the religions of the world is new knowledge. As is the case for geology and astronomy, so too for religious studies: many new discoveries about the nature and function of religion are, in fact, clearer understandings of events and processes that began to unfold long ago. Much of what we are learning now about the religions of the world was previously not known outside of a circle of adepts. From the ancient history of traditions and from the ongoing creativity of the world's contemporary religions we are opening a treasury of motives, disciplines, and awarenesses.

A geology of the religious spirit of humankind can well serve our need to relate fruitfully to the earth and its myriad life-forms. Changing our habits of consumption and patterns of distribution, reevaluating modes of production, and reestablishing a strong sense of solidarity with the matrix of material life—these achievements will arrive along with spiritual modulations that unveil attractive new images of well-being and prosperity, respecting the limits of life in a sustainable world while revering life at its sources. Remarkable religious views are presented in this series—from the nature mysticism of Bashō in Japan or Saint Francis in Italy to the ecstatic physiologies and embryologies of shamanic healers, Taoist meditators, and Vedic practitioners; from indigenous people's ritual responses to projects funded by the World Bank, to religiously grounded criticisms of hazardous waste sites, deforestation, and environmental racism.

The power to modify the world is both frightening and fascinating and has been subjected to reflection, particularly religious reflection, from time immemorial to the present day. We will understand ecology better when we understand the religions that form the rich soil of memory and practice, belief and relationships where life on earth is rooted. Knowledge of these views will help us reappraise our ways and reorient ourselves toward the sources and resources of life.

This volume is one in a series that addresses the critical gap in our contemporary understanding of religion and ecology. The series results from research conducted at the Harvard University Center for the Study of World Religions over a three-year period. I wish especially to acknowledge President Neil L. Rudenstine of Harvard University for his leadership in instituting the environmental initiative at Harvard and thank him for his warm encouragement and characteristic support of our program. Mary Evelyn Tucker and John Grim of Bucknell University coordinated the research, involving the direct participation of some six hundred scholars, religious leaders, and environmental specialists brought to Harvard from around the world during the period of research and inquiry. Professors Tucker and Grim have brought great vision and energy to this enormous project, as has their team of conference convenors. The commitment and advice of Martin S. Kaplan of Hale and Dorr have been of great value. Our goals have been achieved for this research and publication program because of the extraordinary dedication and talents of Center for the Study of World Religions staff members Don Kunkel, Malgorzata Radziszewska-Hedderick, Kathryn Dodgson, Janey Bosch, Naomi Wilshire, Lilli Leggio, and Eric Edstam and with the unstinting help of Stephanie Snyder of Bucknell. To these individuals, and to all the sponsors and participants whose efforts made this series possible, go deepest thanks and appreciation.

Series Foreword

MARY EVELYN TUCKER and JOHN GRIM

The Nature of the Environmental Crisis

Ours is a period when the human community is in search of new and sustaining relationships to the earth amidst an environmental crisis that threatens the very existence of all life-forms on the planet. While the particular causes and solutions of this crisis are being debated by scientists, economists, and policymakers, the facts of widespread destruction are causing alarm in many quarters. Indeed, from some perspectives the future of human life itself appears threatened. As Daniel Maguire has succinctly observed, "If current trends continue, we will not."[1] Thomas Berry, the former director of the Riverdale Center for Religious Research, has also raised the stark question, "Is the human a viable species on an endangered planet?"

From resource depletion and species extinction to pollution overload and toxic surplus, the planet is struggling against unprecedented assaults. This is aggravated by population explosion, industrial growth, technological manipulation, and military proliferation heretofore unknown by the human community. From many accounts the basic elements which sustain life—sufficient water, clean air, and arable land—are at risk. The challenges are formidable and well documented. The solutions, however, are more elusive and complex. Clearly, this crisis has economic, political, and social dimensions which require more detailed analysis than we can provide here. Suffice it to say, however, as did the *Global 2000 Report*: ". . .once such global environmental problems are in motion they are difficult to reverse. In fact few if any of the problems addressed in the *Global 2000*

Report are amenable to quick technological or policy fixes; rather, they are inextricably mixed with the world's most perplexing social and economic problems."[2]

Peter Raven, the director of the Missouri Botanical Garden, wrote in a paper titled "We Are Killing Our World" with a similar sense of urgency regarding the magnitude of the environmental crisis: "The world that provides our evolutionary and ecological context is in serious trouble, trouble of a kind that demands our urgent attention. By formulating adequate plans for dealing with these large-scale problems, we will be laying the foundation for peace and prosperity in the future; by ignoring them, drifting passively while attending to what may seem more urgent, personal priorities, we are courting disaster."

Rethinking Worldviews and Ethics

For many people an environmental crisis of this complexity and scope is not only the result of certain economic, political, and social factors. It is also a moral and spiritual crisis which, in order to be addressed, will require broader philosophical and religious understandings of ourselves as creatures of nature, embedded in life cycles and dependent on ecosystems. Religions, thus, need to be reexamined in light of the current environmental crisis. This is because religions help to shape our attitudes toward nature in both conscious and unconscious ways. Religions provide basic interpretive stories of who we are, what nature is, where we have come from, and where we are going. This comprises a worldview of a society. Religions also suggest how we should treat other humans and how we should relate to nature. These values make up the ethical orientation of a society. Religions thus generate worldviews and ethics which underlie fundamental attitudes and values of different cultures and societies. As the historian Lynn White observed, "What people do about their ecology depends on what they think about themselves in relation to things around them. Human ecology is deeply conditioned by beliefs about our nature and destiny—that is, by religion."[3]

In trying to reorient ourselves in relation to the earth, it has become apparent that we have lost our appreciation for the intricate nature of matter and materiality. Our feeling of alienation in the modern period has extended beyond the human community and its patterns of material exchanges to our interaction with nature itself. Especially in technologically sophisticated urban societies, we have become removed from the recognition of our dependence on nature. We no longer know who we are as earthlings; we no longer see the earth as sacred.

Thomas Berry suggests that we have become autistic in our interactions with the natural world. In other words, we are unable to value the life and beauty of nature because we are locked in our own egocentric perspectives and shortsighted needs. He suggests that we need a new cosmology, cultural coding, and motivating energy to overcome this deprivation.[4] He observes that the magnitude of destructive industrial processes is so great that we must initiate a radical rethinking of the myth of progress and of humanity's role in the evolutionary process. Indeed, he speaks of evolution as a new story of the universe, namely, as a vast cosmological perspective that will resituate human meaning and direction in the context of four and a half billion years of earth history.[5]

For Berry and for many others an important component of the current environmental crisis is spiritual and ethical. It is here that the religions of the world may have a role to play in cooperation with other individuals, institutions, and initiatives that have been engaged with environmental issues for a considerable period of time. Despite their lateness in addressing the crisis, religions are beginning to respond in remarkably creative ways. They are not only rethinking their theologies but are also reorienting their sustainable practices and long-term environmental commitments. In so doing, the very nature of religion and of ethics is being challenged and changed. This is true because the reexamination of other worldviews created by religious beliefs and practices may be critical to our recovery of sufficiently comprehensive cosmologies, broad conceptual frameworks, and effective environmental ethics for the twenty-first century.

While in the past none of the religions of the world have had to face an environmental crisis such as we are now confronting, they remain key instruments in shaping attitudes toward nature. The unintended consequences of the modern industrial drive for unlimited economic growth and resource development have led us to an impasse regarding the survival of many life-forms and appropriate management of varied ecosystems. The religious traditions may indeed be critical in helping to reimagine the viable conditions and long-range strategies for fostering mutually enhancing human-earth relations.[6]

Indeed, as E. N. Anderson has documented with impressive detail, "All traditional societies that have succeeded in managing resources well, over time, have done it in part through religious or ritual representation of resource management."[7]

It is in this context that a series of conferences and publications exploring the various religions of the world and their relation to ecology was initiated by the Center for the Study of World Religions at Harvard. Coordinated by Mary Evelyn Tucker and John Grim, the conferences involved some six hundred scholars, graduate students, religious leaders, and environmental activists over a period of three years. The collaborative nature of the project is intentional. Such collaboration maximizes the opportunity for dialogical reflection on this issue of enormous complexity and accentuates the diversity of local manifestations of ecologically sustainable alternatives.

This series is intended to serve as initial explorations of the emerging field of religion and ecology while pointing toward areas for further research. We are not unaware of the difficulties of engaging in such a task, yet we have been encouraged by the enthusiastic response to the conferences within the academic community, by the larger interest they have generated beyond academia, and by the probing examinations gathered in the volumes. We trust that this series and these volumes will be useful not only for scholars of religion but also for those shaping seminary education and institutional religious practices, as well as for those involved in public policy on environmental issues.

We see such conferences and publications as expanding the growing dialogue regarding the role of the world's religions as moral forces in stemming the environmental crisis. While, clearly, there are major methodological issues involved in utilizing traditional philosophical and religious ideas for contemporary concerns, there are also compelling reasons to support such efforts, however modest they may be. The world's religions in all their complexity and variety remain one of the principal resources for symbolic ideas, spiritual inspiration, and ethical principles. Indeed, despite their limitations, historically they have provided comprehensive cosmologies for interpretive direction, moral foundations for social cohesion, spiritual guidance for cultural expression, and ritual celebrations for meaningful life. In our search for more comprehensive ecological worldviews and more effective environmental ethics, it is inevitable that we will draw from the symbolic and conceptual resources of the religious traditions of the world. The effort to do this is not without precedent or problems, some of which will be signaled below. With this volume and with this series we hope the field of reflection and discussion regarding religion and ecology will begin to broaden, deepen, and complexify.

Qualifications and Goals

The Problems and Promise of Religions

These volumes, then, are built on the premise that the religions of the world may be instrumental in addressing the moral dilemmas created by the environmental crisis. At the same time we recognize the limitations of such efforts on the part of religions. We also acknowledge that the complexity of the problem requires interlocking approaches from such fields as science, economics, politics, health, and public policy. As the human community struggles to formulate different attitudes toward nature and to articulate broader conceptions of ethics embracing species and ecosystems, religions may thus be a necessary, though only contributing, part of this multidisciplinary approach.

It is becoming increasingly evident that abundant scientific knowledge of the crisis is available and numerous political and economic statements have been formulated. Yet we seem to lack the political, economic, and scientific leadership to make necessary changes. Moreover, what is still lacking is the religious commitment, moral imagination, and ethical engagement to transform the environmental crisis from an issue on paper to one of effective policy, from rhetoric in print to realism in action. Why, nearly fifty years after Fairfield Osborne's warning in *Our Plundered Planet* and more than thirty years since Rachel Carson's *Silent Spring,* are we still wondering, is it too late?[8]

It is important to ask where the religions have been on these issues and why they themselves have been so late in their involvement. Have issues of personal salvation superseded all others? Have divine-human relations been primary? Have anthropocentric ethics been all-consuming? Has the material world of nature been devalued by religion? Does the search for otherworldly rewards override commitment to this world? Did the religions simply surrender their natural theologies and concerns with exploring purpose in nature to positivistic scientific cosmologies? In beginning to address these questions, we still have not exhausted all the reasons for religions' lack of attention to the environmental crisis. The reasons may not be readily apparent, but clearly they require further exploration and explanation.

In discussing the involvement of religions in this issue, it is also appropriate to acknowledge the dark side of religion in both its institutional expressions and dogmatic forms. In addition to their oversight with regard to the environment, religions have been the source of enormous manipulation of power in fostering wars, in ignoring racial and social injustice, and in promoting unequal gender relations, to name only a few abuses. One does not want to underplay this shadow side or to claim too much for religions' potential for ethical persuasiveness. The problems are too vast and complex for unqualified optimism. Yet there is a growing consensus that religions may now have a significant role to play, just as in the past they have sustained individuals and cultures in the face of internal and external threats.

A final caveat is the inevitable gap that arises between theories and practices in religions. As has been noted, even societies with religious traditions which appear sympathetic to the environment have in the past often misused resources. While it is clear that religions may have some disjunction between the ideal and the real, this should not lessen our endeavor to identify resources from within the world's religions for a more ecologically sound cosmology and environmentally supportive ethics. This disjunction of theory and practice is present within all philosophies and religions and is frequently the source of disillusionment, skepticism, and cynicism. A more realistic observation might be made, however, that this disjunction should not automatically invalidate the complex worldviews and rich cosmologies embedded in traditional religions. Rather, it is our task to explore these conceptual resources so as to broaden and expand our own perspectives in challenging and fruitful ways.

In summary, we recognize that religions have elements which are both prophetic and transformative as well as conservative and constraining. These elements are continually in tension, a condition which creates the great variety of thought and interpretation within religious traditions. To recognize these various tensions and limits, however, is not to lessen the urgency of the overall goals of this project. Rather, it is to circumscribe our efforts with healthy skepticism, cautious optimism, and modest ambitions. It is to suggest that this is a beginning in a new field of study which will affect both religion and ecology. On the one hand, this process of reflection will inevitably change how religions conceive of their own roles, missions, and identities, for such reflections demand a new sense of the sacred as not divorced from the earth itself. On the other hand, environmental studies can recognize that religions have helped to shape attitudes toward nature. Thus, as religions themselves evolve they may be indispensable in fostering a more expansive appreciation for the complexity and beauty of the natural world. At the same time as religions foster awe and reverence for nature, they may provide the transforming energies for ethical practices to protect endangered ecosystems, threatened species, and diminishing resources.

Methodological Concerns

It is important to acknowledge that there are, inevitably, challenging methodological issues involved in such a project as we are undertaking in this emerging field of religion and ecology.[9] Some of the key interpretive challenges we face in this project concern issues of time, place, space, and positionality. With regard to time, it is necessary to recognize the vast historical complexity of each religious tradition, which cannot be easily condensed in these conferences or volumes. With respect to place, we need to signal the diverse cultural contexts in which these religions have developed. With regard to space, we recognize the varied frameworks of institutions and traditions in which these religions unfold. Finally, with respect to positionality, we acknowledge our own historical situatedness at the end of the twentieth century with distinctive contemporary concerns.

Not only is each religious tradition historically complex and culturally diverse, but its beliefs, scriptures, and institutions have themselves been subject to vast commentaries and revisions over time. Thus, we recognize the radical diversity that exists within and among religious traditions which cannot be encompassed in any single volume. We acknowledge also that distortions may arise as we examine earlier historical traditions in light of contemporary issues.

Nonetheless, the environmental ethics philosopher J. Baird Callicott has suggested that scholars and others "mine the conceptual resources" of the religious traditions as a means of creating a more inclusive global environmental ethics.[10] As Callicott himself notes, however, the notion of "mining" is problematic, for it conjures up images of exploitation which may cause apprehension among certain religious communities, especially those of indigenous peoples. Moreover, we cannot simply expect to borrow or adopt ideas and place them from one tradition directly into another. Even efforts to formulate global environmental ethics need to be sensitive to cultural particularity and diversity. We do not aim at creating a simple bricolage or bland fusion of perspectives. Rather, these conferences and volumes are an attempt to display before us a multiperspectival cross section of the symbolic richness regarding attitudes toward nature within the religions of the world. To do so will help to reveal certain commonalities among traditions, as well as limitations within traditions, as they begin to converge around this challenge presented by the environmental crisis.

We need to identify our concerns, then, as embedded in the constraints of our own perspectival limits at the same time as we seek common ground. In describing various attitudes toward nature historically, we are aiming at *critical understanding* of the complexity, contexts, and frameworks in which these religions articulate such views. In addition, we are striving for *empathetic appreciation* for the traditions without idealizing their ecological potential or ignoring their environmental oversights. Finally, we are aiming at the *creative revisioning* of mutually enhancing human-earth relations. This revisioning may be assisted by highlighting the multiperspectival attitudes toward nature which these traditions disclose. The prismatic effect of examining such attitudes and relationships may provide some necessary clarification and symbolic resources for reimagining our own situation and shared concerns at the end of the twentieth century. It will also be sharpened by identifying the multilayered symbol systems in world religions which have traditionally oriented humans in establishing relational resonances between the microcosm of the self and the macrocosm of the social and natural orders. In short, religious traditions may help to supply both creative resources of symbols, rituals, and texts as well as inspiring visions for reimagining ourselves as part of, not apart from, the natural world.

Aims

The methodological issues outlined above were implied in the overall goals of the conferences, which were described as follows:

1. To identify and evaluate the *distinctive ecological attitudes,* values, and practices of diverse religious traditions, making clear their links to intellectual, political, and other resources associated with these distinctive traditions.

2. To describe and analyze the *commonalities* that exist within and among religious traditions with respect to ecology.

3. To identify the *minimum common ground* on which to base constructive understanding, motivating discussion, and concerted action in diverse locations across the globe; and to highlight the specific religious resources that comprise such fertile ecological ground: within scripture, ritual, myth, symbol, cosmology, sacrament, and so on.

4. To articulate in clear and moving terms *a desirable mode of human presence with the earth;* in short, to highlight means of respecting and valuing nature, to note what has already been actualized, and to indicate how best to achieve what is desirable beyond these examples.

5. To outline the most significant areas, with regard to religion and ecology, in need of *further study;* to enumerate questions of highest priority within those areas and propose possible approaches to use in addressing them.

In this series, then, we do not intend to obliterate difference or ignore diversity. The aim is to celebrate plurality by raising to conscious awareness multiple perspectives regarding nature and human-earth relations as articulated in the religions of the world. The spectrum of cosmologies, myths, symbols, and rituals within the religious traditions will be instructive in resituating us within the rhythms and limits of nature.

We are not looking for a unified worldview or a single global ethic. We are, however, deeply sympathetic with the efforts toward formulating a global ethic made by individuals, such as the theologian Hans Küng or the environmental philosopher J. Baird Callicott, and groups, such as Global Education Associates and United Religions. A minimum content of environmental ethics needs to be seriously considered. We are, then, keenly interested in the contribution this series might make to discussions of environmental policy in national and international arenas. Important intersections may be made with work in the field of development ethics.[11] In addition, the findings of the conferences have bearing on the ethical formulation of the Earth Charter that is to be presented to the United Nations for adoption within the next few years. Thus, we are seeking both the grounds for common concern and the constructive conceptual basis for rethinking our current situation of estrangement from the earth. In so doing we will be able to reconceive a means of creating the basis not just for sustainable development, but also for sustainable life on the planet.

As scientist Brian Swimme has suggested, we are currently making macrophase changes to the life systems of the planet with microphase wisdom. Clearly, we need to expand and deepen the wisdom base for human intervention with nature and other humans. This is particularly true as issues of genetic alteration of natural processes are already available and in use. If religions have traditionally concentrated on divine-human and human-human relations, the challenge is that they now explore more fully divine-human-earth relations. Without such further exploration, adequate environmental ethics may not emerge in a comprehensive context.

Resources: Environmental Ethics Found in the World's Religions

For many people, when challenges such as the environmental crisis are raised in relation to religion in the contemporary world, there frequently arises a sense of loss or a nostalgia for earlier, seemingly less complicated eras when the constant questioning of religious beliefs and practices was not so apparent. This is, no doubt, something of a reified reading of history. There is, however, a decidedly anxious tone to the questioning and soul-searching that appears to haunt many contemporary religious groups as they seek to find their particular role in the midst of rapid technological change and dominant secular values.

One of the greatest challenges, however, to contemporary religions remains how to respond to the environmental crisis, which many believe has been perpetuated because of the enormous inroads made by unrestrained materialism, secularization, and industrialization in contemporary societies, especially those societies arising in or influenced by the modern West. Indeed, some suggest that the very division of religion from secular life may be a major cause of the crisis.

Others, such as the medieval historian Lynn White, have cited religion's negative role in the crisis. White has suggested that the emphasis in Judaism and Christianity on the transcendence of God above nature and the dominion of humans over nature has led to a devaluing of the natural world and a subsequent destruction of its resources for utilitarian ends.[12] While the particulars of this argument have been vehemently debated, it is increasingly clear that the environmental crisis and its perpetuation due to industrialization, secularization, and ethical indifference present a serious challenge to the world's religions. This is especially true because many of these religions have traditionally been concerned with the path of personal salvation, which frequently emphasized otherworldly goals and rejected this world as corrupting. Thus, as we have noted, how to adapt religious teachings to this task of revaluing nature so as to prevent its destruction marks a significant new phase in religious thought. Indeed, as Thomas Berry has so aptly pointed out, what is necessary is a comprehensive reevaluation of human-earth relations if the human is to continue as a viable species on an increasingly degraded planet. This will require, in addition to major economic and political changes, examining worldviews and ethics among the world's religions that differ from those that have captured the imagination of contemporary industrialized societies which regard nature primarily as a commodity to be utilized. It should be noted that when we are searching for effective resources for formulating environmental ethics, each of the religious traditions have both positive and negative features.

For the most part, the worldviews associated with the Western Abrahamic traditions of Judaism, Christianity, and Islam have created a dominantly human-focused morality. Because these worldviews are largely anthropocentric, nature is viewed as being of secondary importance. This is reinforced by a strong sense of the transcendence of God above nature. On the other hand, there are rich resources for rethinking views of nature in the covenantal tradition of the Hebrew Bible, in sacramental theology, in incarnational Christology, and in the vice-regency (*khalifa Allah*) concept of the Qur'an. The covenantal tradition draws on the legal agreements of biblical thought which are extended to all of creation. Sacramental theology in Christianity underscores the sacred dimension of material reality, especially for ritual purposes.[13] Incarnational Christology proposes that because God became flesh in the person of Christ, the entire natural order can be viewed as sacred. The concept of humans as vice-regents of Allah on earth suggests that humans have particular privileges, responsibilities, and obligations to creation.[14]

In Hinduism, although there is a significant emphasis on performing one's *dharma,* or duty, in the world, there is also a strong pull toward *mokśa,* or liberation, from the world of suffering, or *saṃsāra*. To heal this kind of suffering and alienation through spiritual discipline and meditation, one turns away from the world (*prakṛti*) to a timeless world of spirit (*puruṣa*). Yet at the same time there are numerous traditions in Hinduism which affirm particular rivers, mountains, or forests as sacred. Moreover, in the concept of *līlā,* the creative play of the gods, Hindu theology engages the world as a creative manifestation of the divine. This same tension between withdrawal from the world and affirmation of it is present in Buddhism. Certain Theravāda schools of Buddhism emphasize withdrawing in meditation from the transient world of suffering (*saṃsāra*) to seek release in *nirvāṇa*. On the other hand, later Mahāyāna schools of Buddhism, such as Hua-yen, underscore the remarkable interconnection of reality in such images as the jeweled net of Indra, where each jewel reflects all the others in the universe. Likewise, the Zen gardens in East Asia express the fullness of the Buddha-nature (*tathāgatagarbha*) in the natural world. In recent years, socially engaged Buddhism has been active in protecting the environment in both Asia and the United States.

The East Asian traditions of Confucianism and Taoism remain, in certain ways, some of the most life-affirming in the spectrum of world religions.[15] The seamless interconnection between the divine, human, and natural worlds that characterizes these traditions has been described as an anthropocosmic worldview.[16] There is no emphasis on radical transcendence as there is in the Western traditions. Rather, there is a cosmology of a continuity of creation stressing the dynamic movements of nature through the seasons and the agricultural cycles. This organic cosmology is grounded in the philosophy of *ch'i* (material force), which provides a basis for appreciating the profound interconnection of matter and spirit. To be in harmony with nature and with other humans while being attentive to the movements of the *Tao* (Way) is the aim of personal cultivation in both Confucianism and Taoism. It should be noted, however, that this positive worldview has not prevented environmental degradation (such as deforestation) in parts of East Asia in both the premodern and modern period.

In a similar vein, indigenous peoples, while having ecological cosmologies have, in some instances, caused damage to local environments through such practices as slash-and-burn agriculture. Nonetheless, most indigenous peoples have environmental ethics embedded in their worldviews. This is evident in the complex reciprocal obligations surrounding life-taking and resource-gathering which mark a community's relations with the local bioregion. The religious views at the basis of indigenous lifeways involve respect for the sources of food, clothing, and shelter that nature provides. Gratitude to the creator and to the spiritual forces in creation is at the heart of most indigenous traditions. The ritual calendars of many indigenous peoples are carefully coordinated with seasonal events such as the sound of returning birds, the blooming of certain plants, the movements of the sun, and the changes of the moon.

The difficulty at present is that for the most part we have developed in the world's religions certain ethical prohibitions regarding homicide and restraints concerning genocide and suicide, but none for biocide or geocide. We are clearly in need of exploring such comprehensive cosmological perspectives and communitarian environmental ethics as the most compelling context for motivating change regarding the destruction of the natural world.

Responses of Religions to the Environmental Crisis

How to chart possible paths toward mutually enhancing human-earth relations remains, thus, one of the greatest challenges to the world's religions. It is with some encouragement, however, that we note the growing calls for the world's religions to participate in these efforts toward a more sustainable planetary future. There have been various appeals from environmental groups and from scientists and parliamentarians for religious leaders to respond to the environmental crisis. For example, in 1990 the Joint Appeal in Religion and Science was released highlighting the urgency of collaboration around the issue of the destruction of the environment. In 1992 the Union of Concerned Scientists issued the statement "Warning to Humanity," signed by over 1,000 scientists from 70 countries, including 105 Nobel laureates, regarding the gravity of the environmental crisis. They specifically cited the need for a new ethic toward the earth.

Numerous national and international conferences have also been held on this subject and collaborative efforts have been established. Environmental groups such as World Wildlife Fund have sponsored interreligious meetings such as the one in Assisi in 1986. The Center for Respect of Life and Environment of the Humane Society of the United States has also held a series of conferences in Assisi on

Spirituality and Sustainability and has helped to organize one at the World Bank. The United Nations Environmental Programme in North America has established an Environmental Sabbath, each year distributing thousands of packets of materials for use in congregations throughout North America. Similarly, the National Religious Partnership on the Environment at the Cathedral of St. John the Divine in New York City has promoted dialogue, distributed materials, and created a remarkable alliance of the various Jewish and Christian denominations in the United States around the issue of the environment. The Parliament of World Religions held in 1993 in Chicago and attended by some 8,000 people from all over the globe issued a statement of Global Ethics of Cooperation of Religions on Human and Environmental Issues. International meetings on the environment have been organized. One example of these, the Global Forum of Spiritual and Parliamentary Leaders held in Oxford in 1988, Moscow in 1990, Rio in 1992, and Kyoto in 1993, included world religious leaders, such as the Dalai Lama, and diplomats and heads of state, such as Mikhail Gorbachev. Indeed, Gorbachev hosted the Moscow conference and attended the Kyoto conference to set up a Green Cross International for environmental emergencies.

Since the United Nations Conference on Environment and Development (the Earth Summit) held in Rio in 1992, there have been concerted efforts intended to lead toward the adoption of an *Earth Charter* by the year 2000. This *Earth Charter* initiative is under way with the leadership of the Earth Council and Green Cross International, with support from the government of the Netherlands. Maurice Strong, Mikhail Gorbachev, Steven Rockefeller, and other members of the Earth Charter Project have been instrumental in this process. At the March 1997 Rio + 5 Conference a benchmark draft of the *Earth Charter* was issued. The time is thus propitious for further investigation of the potential contributions of particular religions toward mitigating the environmental crisis, especially by developing more comprehensive environmental ethics for the earth community.

Expanding the Dialogue of Religion and Ecology

More than two decades ago Thomas Berry anticipated such an exploration when he called for "creating a new consciousness of the multiform religious traditions of humankind" as a means toward renewal of the human spirit in addressing the urgent problems of contemporary society.[17] Tu Weiming has written of the need to go "Beyond the Enlightenment Mentality" in exploring the spiritual resources of the global community to meet the challenge of the ecological crisis.[18] While this exploration has also been the intention of both the conferences and these volumes, other significant efforts have preceded our current endeavor.[19] Our discussion here highlights only the last decade.

In 1986 Eugene Hargrove edited a volume titled *Religion and Environmental Crisis*.[20] In 1991 Charlene Spretnak explored this topic in her book *States of Grace: The Recovery of Meaning in the Post-Modern Age*.[21] Her subtitle states her constructivist project clearly: "Reclaiming the Core Teachings and Practices of the Great Wisdom Traditions for the Well-Being of the Earth Community." In 1992 Steven Rockefeller and John Elder edited a book based on a conference at Middlebury College titled *Spirit and Nature: Why the Environment Is a Religious Issue*.[22] In the same year Peter Marshall published *Nature's Web: Rethinking Our Place on Earth,*[23] drawing on the resources of the world's traditions. An edited volume titled *Worldviews and Ecology,* compiled in 1993, contains articles reflecting on views of nature from the world's religions and from contemporary philosophies, such as process thought and deep ecology.[24] In this same vein, in 1994 J. Baird Callicott published *Earth's Insights,* which examines the intellectual resources of the world's religions for a more comprehensive global environmental ethics.[25] This expands on his 1989 volumes, *Nature in Asian Traditions of Thought* and *In Defense of the Land Ethic*.[26] In 1995 David Kinsley issued a book titled *Ecology and Religion: Ecological Spirituality in a Cross-Cultural Perspective,*[27] which draws on traditional religions and contemporary movements, such as deep ecology and ecospirituality. Seyyed Hossein Nasr wrote his comprehensive study *Religion and the Order of Nature* in 1996.[28] Several volumes of religious responses to a particular topic or theme have also been published. For example, J. Ronald Engel and Joan Gibb Engel compiled a monograph in 1990 titled *Ethics of Environment and Development: Global Challenge, International Response*[29] and in 1995 Harold Coward edited the volume *Population, Consumption and the Environment: Religious and Secular Responses*.[30] Roger Gottlieb edited a useful source book, *This Sacred Earth: Religion, Nature, Environment*.[31] Single volumes on the world's religions and ecology were published by the Worldwide Fund for Nature.[32]

The series Religions of the World and Ecology is thus intended to expand the discussion already under way in certain circles and to invite further collaboration on a topic of common concern—the fate of the earth as a religious responsibility. To broaden and deepen the reflective basis for mutual collaboration was an underlying aim of the conferences themselves. While some might see this as a diversion from pressing scientific or policy issues, it was with a sense of humility and yet conviction that we entered into the arena of reflection and debate on this issue. In the field of the study of world religions, we have seen this as a timely challenge for scholars of religion to respond as engaged intellectuals with deepening creative reflection. We hope that these volumes will be simply a beginning of further study of conceptual and symbolic resources, methodological concerns, and practical directions for meeting this environmental crisis.

Notes

1. He goes on to say, "And that is qualitatively and epochally true. If religion does not speak to [this], it is an obsolete distraction." Daniel Maguire, *The Moral Core of Judaism and Christianity: Reclaiming the Revolution* (Philadelphia: Fortress Press, 1993), 13.

2. Gerald Barney, *Global 2000 Report to the President of the United States* (Washington, D.C.: Supt. of Docs. U.S. Government Printing Office, 1980–1981), 40.

3. Lynn White, Jr., "The Historical Roots of Our Ecologic Crisis," *Science* 155 (March 1967):1204.

4. Thomas Berry, *The Dream of the Earth* (San Francisco: Sierra Club Books, 1988).

5. Brian Swimme and Thomas Berry, *The Universe Story* (San Francisco: Harper San Francisco, 1992).

6. At the same time we recognize the limits to such a project, especially because ideas and action, theory and practice do not always occur in conjunction.

7. E. N. Anderson, Ecologies of the Heart: Emotion, Belief, and the Environment (New York and Oxford: Oxford University Press, 1996), 166. He qualifies this statement by saying, "The key point is not religion per se, but the use of emotionally powerful symbols to sell particular moral codes and management systems" (166). He notes, however, in various case studies how ecological wisdom is embedded in myths, symbols, and cosmologies of traditional societies.

8. *Is It Too Late?* is also the title of a book by John Cobb, first published in 1972 by Bruce and reissued in 1995 by Environmental Ethics Books.

9. Because we cannot identify here all of the methodological issues that need to be addressed, we invite further discussion by other engaged scholars.

10. See J. Baird Callicott, *Earth's Insights: A Survey of Ecological Ethics from the Mediterranean Basin to the Australian Outback* (Berkeley: University of California Press, 1994).

11. See, for example, The Quality of Life, ed. Martha C. Nussbaum and Amartya Sen, WIDER Studies in Development Economics (Oxford: Oxford University Press, 1993).

12. White, "The Historical Roots of Our Ecologic Crisis," 1203–7.

13. Process theology, creation-centered spirituality, and ecotheology have done much to promote these kinds of holistic perspectives within Christianity.

14. These are resources already being explored by theologians and biblical scholars.

15. While this is true theoretically, it should be noted that, like all ideologies, these traditions have at times been used for purposes of political power and social control. Moreover, they have not been able to prevent certain kinds of environmental destruction, such as deforestation in China.

16. The term "anthropocosmic" has been used by Tu Weiming in *Centrality and Commonality* (Albany: State University of New York Press, 1989).

17. Thomas Berry, "Religious Studies and the Global Human Community," unpublished manuscript.

18. Tu Weiming, "Beyond the Enlightenment Mentality," in *Worldviews and Ecology,* ed. Mary Evelyn Tucker and John Grim (Lewisburg, Pa.: Bucknell University Press, 1993; reissued, Maryknoll, N.Y.: Orbis Books, 1994).

19. This history has been described more fully by Roderick Nash in his chapter entitled "The Greening of Religion," in The Rights of Nature: A History of Environmental Ethics (Madison: University of Wisconsin Press, 1989).

20. *Religion and Environmental Crisis,* ed. Eugene Hargrove (Athens: University of Georgia Press, 1986).

21. Charlene Spretnak, *States of Grace: The Recovery of Meaning in the Post-Modern Age* (San Francisco: Harper San Francisco, 1991).

22. *Spirit and Nature: Why the Environment Is a Religious Issue,* ed. Steven Rockefeller and John Elder (Boston: Beacon Press, 1992).

23. Peter Marshall, *Nature's Web: Rethinking Our Place on Earth* (Armonk, N.Y.: M. E. Sharpe, 1992).

24. *Worldviews and Ecology,* ed. Mary Evelyn Tucker and John Grim (Lewisburg, Pa.: Bucknell University Press, 1993; reissued, Maryknoll, N.Y.: Orbis Books, 1994).

25. Callicott, *Earth's Insights.*

26. Both are State University of New York Press publications.

27. David Kinsley, *Ecology and Religion: Ecological Spirituality in a Cross-Cultural Perspective* (Englewood Cliffs, N.J.: Prentice Hall, 1995).

28. Seyyed Hossein Nasr, *Religion and the Order of Nature* (Oxford: Oxford University Press, 1996).

29. *Ethics of Environment and Development: Global Challenge, International Response,* ed. J. Ronald Engel and Joan Gibb Engel (Tucson: University of Arizona Press, 1990).

30. *Population, Consumption, and the Environment: Religious and Secular Responses,* ed. Harold Coward (Albany: State University of New York Press, 1995).

31. This Sacred Earth: Religion, Nature, Environment, ed. Roger S. Gottlieb (New York and London: Routledge, 1996).

32. These include volumes on Hinduism, Buddhism, Judaism, Christianity, and Islam.

Preface to *Islam and Ecology*

ADNAN Z. AMIN

In this new century characterized by sweeping and fundamental change, posing new opportunities and risks, a major new challenge facing us all is the security and sustainability of the earth.

As issues of sustainable development become ever more critical to the future of our planet, the world's religions are emerging as key advocates of long-term environmental ethics. The world's religions have traditionally been supporters of justice and equity among humans and have had important implications for society, politics, and economics. While the human community is still striving to attain the goals of justice, it is clear that environmental justice is becoming part of these broad aspirations. The rights to pure air, clean water and fertile soil are being seen as fundamental human rights.

The conference on Islam and ecology held at the Center for the Study of World Religions, Harvard Divinity School, in May 1998 marked a watershed moment in bringing together for the first time Islamic scholars and practitioners from Africa, South and Southeast Asia, the Middle East, Europe, and North America. Islam has a particular contribution to make to these discussions as is evident in this volume.

The traditional concern of Islam for social justice and care for the poor, the orphaned, and the widowed has a broader relevance that embraces concern for the natural environment as well. Protection of land and proper treatment of biodiversity are now being advocated by Islamic scholars and teachers. In addition, the unity of all reality (*tawḥīd*) and the balance of nature (*mīzān*) as recognized by Islam constitutes an important basis for religious ecology and environmental ethics. Islamic teachings on land management hold great promise for protection of fragile ecosystems, namely, valuing sacred precincts (*ḥarām*) and setting aside land for the common good (*ḥimā*). Similarly, Islamic reflections on the metaphor of the garden and on images of water provide fertile resources to rethink human relationships with the natural world. The vital role in Islam of humans as trustees of creation is highlighted in these papers and in conferences on this topic in the Middle East and beyond.

The United Nations Environment Programme (UNEP) established some two decades ago, through its Interfaith Partnership for the Environment, a long-standing dialogue among religious and faith communities. It grew from the realization that although a wide gap is perceived between religions, all faiths share a common ethic based on harmony with nature and care for creation. This Partnership has most recently produced a book titled *Earth and Faith: A Book of Reflection for Action* for use in congregations around the world, with more than thirty thousand copies distributed. The members of the Partnership share the conviction that it is through such a dialogue between scientific, political, and faith communities that a greater understanding of the complexity of the environmental challenges facing us will emerge and that a stronger commitment to take responsible action for our common good will prevail.

In this spirit, UNEP, together with the Islamic Republic of Iran, sponsored the International Seminar on Environment, Religion and Culture in Tehran in June 2001. Leaders of the Iranian Government, President Mohammad Khatami, and Vice President and Minister for the Environment Massoumeh Ebtekar, as well as UNEP Executive Director Klaus Toepfer addressed the conference. Dr. Toepfer has highlighted at numerous international conferences the importance of religions as agents of environmental change, including at the Earth Dialogues conference in Lyon, France, in February 2002 entitled "Globalization: Is Ethics the Missing Link?"

At the 2002 World Summit on Sustainable Development held in Johannesburg, South Africa, UNEP, in cooperation with UNESCO, organized a high-level round table, entitled "Cultural Diversity and Biodiversity for Sustainable Development," in order to bring due attention, at the highest political level, to the need to integrate ethical and spiritual value considerations into sustainable development policies. This high-level event was an opportunity to recognize that problems of weakening cultural diversity and loss of biological diversity are intrinsically linked and that a comprehensive approach for action at all levels is required to address them adequately. It also highlighted the need to promote a new ethic of conservation and environmental stewardship based on a common understanding and moral responsibility for all human beings in our commitment to make sustainable development a reality.

Coming from the world's fastest growing religion, with more than one billion adherents, Islamic voices will carry particular weight in the discussions on religion, environmental stewardship, and diversity, as they become woven into the strands of varied cultural contexts in nations as diverse as Indonesia, Pakistan, Kenya, Jordan, Morocco, and Senegal. This volume assembles voices from across the Islamic world who are speaking with depth, breadth, and urgency on the emerging alliance of Islam and ecology. We applaud the efforts of the conference organizers and volume editors to bring these voices to the attention of a wider public in the Islamic world and beyond.

Introduction

RICHARD C. FOLTZ

Islam is the religion of over one billion people—roughly one-sixth of humanity. One of the major "universal" faiths, it is practiced in virtually every country on earth. Though popular stereotypes often equate Islam with the Middle East and with the Arab world, it is important to note that some 75 percent of the world's Muslims live further east, in Asia, with the largest concentration (over 350 million, about one-third of the total) in the countries of South Asia. Bangladesh, Pakistan, and India rank second, third and fourth in the world in terms of their total Muslim populations, while the world's most populous Muslim nation, Indonesia, lies even further east. Muslim minority communities exist in locations as diverse as Finland, Ecuador, and New Zealand. Most "Western" nations now have significant Muslim populations, and in the United States Islam is considered by many to be the fastest growing religion.

Islam, like Christianity and Judaism, is a monotheistic faith based on a sacred scripture. While Muslims accept the other two "Abrahamic" religions as divinely inspired and authentic, they consider the revealed message of the Qur'an to supersede the Bible and the Torah. The Prophet of Islam, an Arab merchant of Mecca by the name of Muhammad (ca. 570–632 C.E.), is revered and honored by Muslims, but they do not consider him to be divine. Muhammad's example, however, makes him a natural role model for Muslims; indeed, the Qur'an itself notes that "in the Messenger of God you have a beautiful example (*uswa ḥasana*)" (Qur'an 33:21). As such, the records of the Prophet's words and deeds, which are preserved in a vast body of literature known as *ḥadīth*s, supplement the Qur'an as a basis for helping Muslims understand the Islamic way of life (*sharī'a*).

Although the overwhelming majority of Muslims today are not Arabs and do not live in the Middle East, the influence of Arab culture on the cosmopolitan tradition of Islam is undeniable. As a desert dweller Muhammad must have been sensitive to the delicate natural balance within which his people were able to survive. The Qur'an is replete with references to the precious resources of water, air, and land, and proscribes wastefulness. The *ḥadīth*s likewise report Muhammad's concern for the protection of natural resources and their equitable availability to all. Clearly, from its very origins fourteen centuries ago Islam offers a basis for ecological understanding and stewardship.

Yet the articulation of an Islamic environmental ethic in contemporary terms—recognizing the urgency of the global crisis now facing us all—is quite new. The first Muslim intellectual to do so was the American-trained Iranian Shi'ite philosopher Seyyed Hossein Nasr, a proponent of the *philosophia perennis* associated with Frithjof Schuon, Titus Burckhardt, and Rene Guenon, in which timeless truths are seen as being expressed in a variety of historical cultural and philosophical traditions. Nasr's environmentalist critique of Western modernity began with a series of lectures at the University of Chicago in 1966, which were published the following year as *Man and Nature: The Spiritual Crisis in Modern Man.*[1] Nasr has continued to explore the spiritual dimension of the environmental crisis over the past four decades through further articles, lectures, and his 1996 book *Religion and the Order of Nature.*[2]

The conference on Islam and ecology organized by John Grim, Fazlun Khalid, and Mary Evelyn Tucker and held at the Center for the Study of World Religions, Harvard Divinity School, 7–10 May 1998, was, so far as we know, the first of its kind. Subsequent conferences on Islam and the environment, organized not privately but by national governments, were held in Tehran, Iran, in 1999 and in Jeddah, Saudi Arabia, in 2000. Jeddah was also the site of the first Islamic Conference of Environment Ministers in June 2002. More such international gatherings will surely follow.

The present volume includes a number of papers presented at the Harvard conference on Islam and ecology, along with several that were not. Three previous books on the topic—*Islam and the Environmental Crisis*, by Akhtaruddin Ahmed (1997), *Islam and the Environment*, edited by Harfiyah Abdel Haleem (1998), and *The Environmental Dimensions of Islam*, by Mawil Izzi Dien (2000)—were directed mainly at a readership of practicing Muslims. A short, earlier collection (featuring several of the authors represented here) also entitled *Islam and Ecology*, edited by Fazlun Khalid and Joanne O'Brien (1992), was published as part of a series sponsored by the Worldwide Fund for Nature (WWF). The present work seeks a broader audience, both non-Muslim and Muslim, scholars and lay readers.

Indian sociologist Ramachandra Guha, in a 1989 essay, argued against a one-size-fits-all solution to the problem of global environmental degradation.[3] Speaking from the vantage point of a postcolonial, Guha eloquently pointed out that the approach to conservation seen in the West—and which tends to characterize international organizations such as the Worldwide Fund for Nature (WWF) and the International Union for the Conservation of Nature and Natural Resources (IUCN)—is the product of a particular culture (mainly White North American) with its own historical processes, and it cannot therefore simply be exported and imposed on other societies with their very different historical experiences and cultural norms. The attempt to do so, Guha argued, more often than not results in "a direct transfer of resources from the poor to the rich."[4]

No concern could better shed light on the very "un-Western" perspective of the Muslim contributors to this volume. It is a tragic reality that the poor suffer far more directly from environmental degradation than do the rich, who are better able to insulate themselves from its effects. And on a global scale, a disproportionate percentage of the world's poor happen to be Muslim.

It is no accident, therefore, that for the most part our writers are more immediately concerned with issues of social justice and the human relationship with the Divine than they are with the state of the environment per se. Environmental problems exist, to be sure, but in the perspective of many Muslim thinkers, environmental degradation is merely a symptom of the broader (and, to a Muslim concerned not just with this world but also the next, more alarming) calamity that human societies are not living in accordance with God's will. A just society, one in which humans relate to each other and to God as they should, will be one in which environmental problems simply will not exist.

The essays in the first section, "God, Humans, and Nature," outline the Islamic view of the cosmic order. İbrahim Özdemir's essay, focusing as it does on the Qur'an, is an appropriate introduction to the Islamic view of where humans belong in the hierarchy of being. Drawing on the approaches of commentaries both medieval and modern, Özdemir contends that a Muslim who correctly understands the relationship between the Creator, humans, and the rest of creation as stipulated in the Qur'an will see in it an environmental ethic. L. Clarke explores the cosmology found in the mystical poetry of Jalal al-Din Rumi (1207–1273), one of the most influential and beloved of all the Sufi poets. In Rumi's vision, the entire universe is alive; humans are but one part of the Divine Creation, all of which worships Allah. Saadia Khawar Khan Chishti's essay offers an ecological commentary on the notion of *fiṭra*, understood as the primordial nature of things. Islam is described as the religion that expresses this fundamental reality. Chishti goes on to posit that the original nature of humans is to live in accordance with their environment; thus, environmental consciousness is something that needs not to be taught, but merely awakened.

The next section, "The Challenge of (Re)Interpretation," brings the preceding overview of traditional paradigms into a contemporary context. The essays invite us to look at how the established Islamic worldview can be applied to the environmental problems of the present day. Seyyed Hossein Nasr discusses the many obstacles to practicing Islamic environmental ethics in the modern world, and goes on to suggest ways in which these obstacles might be overcome. Mawil Izzi Dien, who, following Nasr, has been one of the first Muslim intellectuals to make the environment a central concern, mentions the real-life crises of pollution, water scarcity, and other environmental issues facing Muslims today. Izzi Dien then shows how Islamic values can be directly applied to addressing these problems. S. Nomanul Haq examines the normative sources of Islam—the Qur'an, the *ḥadīth*s, and classical Islamic law—in an attempt to "recover" how traditional Islam can guide contemporary Muslims in dealing with the environmental crisis. Haq suggests, however (subtly corroborating, perhaps, my comments above), that "a much wider net" will have to be cast if one is to explore the full range of Islam's contribution to this problem. Abdul Aziz Said and Nathan C. Funk bring an ecological reading to the traditional Islamic concepts of unity (*tawḥīd*) and peace (*salām*), suggesting that environmental problems represent a lack of the latter resulting from a failure to acknowledge the former. Othman Abd-ar-Rahman Llewellyn provides a comprehensive overview of how traditional Islamic law addressed environmental management, then, noting that such laws are no longer practiced in much of the Muslim world, makes detailed suggestions as to how they might be reinterpreted and applied today. Next, in my own essay, I point the way from theory to practice, showing how Islamic principles are beginning to be applied to environmental protection at both the government and grassroots level in the Islamic Republic of Iran. I further suggest that since religious traditions are constantly being reinterpreted to meet present-day needs, it may matter less what Islam has said about the environment in the past than what it might say now. Kaveh L. Afrasiabi takes this notion a step further, arguing that while Islam does possess important resources for valuing the environment, Muslim thinkers will need to go further and reassess some basic assumptions if the tradition is to respond effectively to the current crisis.

The essays in the third section, "Environment and Social Justice," focus on a theme that is seen by many as one of the central priorities of Islam. Fazlun M. Khalid finds the roots of the environmental crisis in Western modernity, which has been imposed on Muslim societies for the past several centuries. Yasin Dutton elaborates on certain features of the modern world—in particular, the interest-based global banking system—that he argues are un-Islamic. Dutton sees environmental problems as arising largely from illegitimate profit-seeking at the expense of human communities. Hashim Ismail Dockrat expands on Dutton's critique by providing an outline for how a hypothetical modern Islamic system would differ from the model that currently exists. Nawal Ammar combines an ecofeminist critique with one based on Islamic social justice, arguing that environmental issues must be addressed within a broader context that includes women's rights of equal access to both natural and social resources.

The fourth section, "Toward a Sustainable Society," looks at real-life issues of development facing Muslims today, many of which have environmental implications. Mohammad Aslam Parvaiz begins with a short essay focusing on the Qur'anic conept of balance (*mīzān*). He cites several contemporary examples to show how current models of development are violating this principle. Safei-Eldin A. Hamed looks at development in contemporary Muslim societies within the wider scope of existing development paradigms. Finding the idealism of some of the preceding writers "overly optimistic," Hamed asks to what extent purely Islamic models can be put into actual practice. Nancy W. Jabbra and Joseph G. Jabbra present contrasting examples of family planning in Muslim societies, citing case studies from Egypt and Iran. Mohammad Yusuf Siddiq draws on the experience of Bangladesh, one of the world's most populous Muslim countries and also one of the poorest, to argue that environmental protection cannot be separated from efforts to alleviate human poverty. Abu Bakar Abdul Majeed presents an overview of Malaysia's current development platform, called Vision 2020. Although Malaysia is a multiethnic country with a number of recognized religions, Abdul Majeed sees the principles underlying Malaysia's development program as being compatible with Islamic definitions of a just society. In the final essay, Tazim R. Kassam writes of the many development projects in Muslim communities supported by the Aga Khan Foundation.

The fifth and concluding section focuses on the Islamic garden as a metaphor for Paradise, a notion which features prominently in the Qur'an. Attilio Petruccioli discusses ways in which traditional Muslim societies have manifested their place within the natural order through architecture and the building of gardens. Using case studies from Algeria and from India, Petruccioli contrasts the Muslim view of human participation in natural space transformations with the modern Western notion of preserving "virgin" nature. James L. Wescoat, Jr., highlights the specific example of the royal gardens built under the Mughal emperors in Lahore (now Pakistan) during the seventeenth century. Finally, Farzaneh Milani looks at the garden metaphor in the modern feminist poetry of Forugh Farrokhzad.

The attempt by Muslims (and those who study them) to discover what the tradition has to say about the global environmental crisis today has only recently begun, and this volume is fortunate to include many of the voices which have been prominent in this endeavor. We will surely hear many more such voices in the years to come.

Notes

1. Seyyed Hossein Nasr, *Man and Nature: The Spiritual Crisis of Modern Man*, rev. ed. (1967; Chicago: Kazi Publishers, 1997).

2. Seyyed Hossein Nasr, *Religion and the Order of Nature* (New York: Oxford University Press, 1996). See also idem, "Islam and the Environmental Crisis," in *Spirit and Nature*, ed. Steven C. Rockefeller and John C. Elder (Boston: Beacon Press, 1992), 83–108; "The Ecological Problem in Light of Sufism: The Conquest of Nature and the Teachings of Eastern Science," in *Sufi Essays*, 2d ed. (Albany: State University of New York Press, 1991), 152–63; "Islam and the Environmental Crisis," *Islamic Quarterly* 34, no. 4 (1991): 217–34; Islam and the Environmental Crisis," *MAAS Journal of Islamic Science* 6, no. 2 (1990): 31–51.

3. Ramachandra Guha, "Radical Environmentalism: A Third World Critique," *Environmental Ethics* 11, no. 1 (1989): 71–83.

4. Ibid., 75. One of Guha's more striking examples is of Indian peasants being removed from their ancestral lands to create park preserves for tigers and other such "charismatic megafauna" that attract wealthy tourists.

God, Humans, and Nature

Toward an Understanding of Environmental Ethics from a Qur'anic Perspective

İBRAHIM ÖZDEMIR

> Do they not ponder over the Qur'an in order to understand its deep meaning, or is it that their minds are locked up from within? (Qur'an 47:24)

Introduction

The Qur'an, which Muslims consider to be the last of the chain of divine revelations, has been a source of inspiration, illumination, and guidance for Muslim philosophers, theologians, Sufi masters, scientists, jurists, and average Muslims who have accepted it as their sacred revelation, in addition to others of divergent ways and different paths of thought that may be found in the Islamic tradition, that is, heretical schools of thought. It could be said that the Qur'an has been regarded by Muslims as a book of law, prayer, wisdom, worship, invocation—in short, a unique and comprehensive sacred text that contains whatever pertains essentially to the human condition. For this reason, it is unanimously considered by insiders and outsiders alike to be the most fundamental basis both for the faith of the individual Muslim and for what is called Islamic civilization. Muslims naturally believe that the Qur'an can and should continue to play such a role today in our quest to conduct a meaningfully ethical life. As is clear from the records of history, the Qur'an has played this role in the life of Muslims from the very beginning of revelation, providing a comprehensive, integrated, and holistic worldview based on the unity of reality (*tawḥīd*).

It is an irony of history that during the second half of the nineteenth century and the first half of the twentieth, the predominant view held by the positivists and the scientifically minded philosophers was that science and technology could satisfy humanity and solve all its problems, without creating new problems. Further, such people tried to convince us that not only religions but also all metaphysical propositions and speculations were meaningless and should, therefore, be eliminated from that which concerns modern man.[1] As a result of this view, modern man lost his awareness of the sacred dimension of nature and alienated himself from it. Today, however, thanks to a growing ecological awakening, we can understand clearly that humans are not separate from or above nature, but rather are part of the web of life.

Since the appearance of the environmental crisis, modern humans have begun to perceive religions from a new standpoint, an ecological outlook in which everything is connected to everything else and nature is seen as an organic unity.[2] It is this type of reasoning that has motivated members of all faiths to study and reevaluate their traditions.

What is more surprising is that the global character of our environmental problems has encouraged the members of diverse world religions to cooperate with each other, to see the problems in a real context. To put it differently, this new understanding brings members of different faiths and traditions to a new frontier and paves the way for a dialogue between them that has never before been experienced in human history. With the commencement of a new millennium, it seems that humanity is once more turning its mind, heart, and face toward a transcendental Being, not only to study it for its own sake, but also for hope in a better future; and not only for humans, but for all creation as well. Since by its nature, ecological reasoning is holistic and interdependent, it urges us to reconsider and to rediscover our religious values at the threshold of a new millennium. There is now the immediate necessity to fill what Hans Jonas calls an "ethical vacuum at the core of the contemporary modern culture."[3] It is also necessary, therefore, to begin by outlining the main propositions underlying the modern worldview.

One of these is the notion that nature is a machine, that it has no value and expresses no sense of purpose. In a nutshell, this view robs nature of all its inherent qualities. John Locke's theory of primary and secondary qualities also should be remembered in this context. Locke argues that only primary qualities exist in nature; there is no place for secondary qualities. Rather, the latter are products of the human mind that are imposed on nature, which in itself is devoid of soul and intelligence and has no inherent or intrinsic value at all. In short, "*nature is a dull affair, soundless, scentless, colorless: merely the hurrying of material, endlessly, meaninglessly.*"[4] A tree, for example, has no intrinsic value of its own being as such. According to the modern materialistic concept of nature, a tree gains its value through human intervention, such as when it becomes a chair, a table, or whatever. The only value that nature can have is instrumental value. Such an understanding of nature has provided justification for the exploitative use of nature and natural resources.[5]

The instrumental view of nature which characterizes modern thought has been very severely criticized by environmentalists in recent decades. Environmentalists claim that there is a strong and direct relationship between environmental problems and our modern understanding of nature. To put it more concretely, the value systems that we hold and which, in turn, shape and mold our behavior and attitudes toward society and nature, are the result of our overall beliefs and metaphysical views concerning all reality. Consequently, any alternative theories of environmental ethics can be expected to challenge the basic propositions of the dominant modern understanding of nature.

Although it can be claimed that the modern scientific worldview is a Western phenomenon, its influence can be felt everywhere, and Islamic lands are not an exception to this.[6] This is due in large part to the followers of traditional value systems being educated in the West or in Western-style institutions; as a result, their hearts and minds have been dominated by modern, Western concepts and values. This observation leads us to seek to rediscover the meaning of the universe, which may be regarded as the missing dimension of modernity, or "the sacred dimension of reality," as some would name it. Our interest is in exploring a Qur'anic alternative, that is, discovering the meaning of nature and humankind's place within it from a Qur'anic perspective. If we address ourselves to these questions attentively, then we can develop a Qur'anic environmental ethic. At the same time, our position assumes that the members of other faiths also can propose their own ethic. Presumably religion, as a system defining cultures and guiding human behavior, can provide the metaphysical foundation necessary for an environmental ethic.[7]

Looking at the earliest revelations in the Qur'an, which were revealed during the Meccan period, we see that their main purpose is "to awaken in man the higher consciousness of his manifold relations with God and the universe."[8] The result will be, first, to change his overall worldview, then to construct his image of himself, and finally, his attitudes, feelings, sentiments and the patterns of his relationships with reality will begin to change accordingly. These important verses are a key to understanding the overall Qur'anic worldview. The great Muslim philosopher and Sufi, Muhammad al-Ghazali (d. 1111 C.E.), for example, in evaluating the meaning of the Qur'anic verses, argues that the early *sūra*s are "the essence of the Qur'an, its heart, its pith, and its secret."[9] For al-Ghazali, it is these verses that give us and show us the meaning of reality. They are about God and how we can understand and comprehend His existence and presence through the natural world. Therefore, al-Ghazali encourages us to make a serious effort to know the deep meaning hidden within the verses of the Qur'an.[10]

The Qur'an, with its emphasis on the metaphysical dimension of nature, replaced the pagan Arabs' conception of nature with a new and vivid understanding. It is surprising to see the striking similarity between the Arabs' view of nature as lifeless, meaningless and purposeless and the ideas put forward in the name of the so-called scientific worldview of modern times. Today, the Qur'an is as ready as ever to challenge the modern materialistic conception of nature and to provide a more comprehensive and holistic approach to developing an environmental ethical theory. The questions we face are as follows:

- Does nature have any objective and independent existence?
- What is the meaning of nature?
- What does nature stand for?
- How does the Qur'an look at nature as a whole?
- What is the place of human beings in the great chain of being?

It is my firm conviction that once the metaphysical foundation for an environmental ethic is discovered within the Qur'anic value system, it will not be difficult to develop an environmental ethic on this basis. Furthermore, understanding the metaphysical dimension of the Qur'anic message will give us the opportunity of understanding and appreciating the development of sensitive ideas and attitudes concerning the environment during the course of Islamic history.

Nature from the Qur'anic Perspective

The Metaphysical Dimension of Nature

Nature from the Qur'anic perspective can be seen best in the first revelations to the prophet Muhammad, which he received in the cave Hira on Mount Jabal al-Nur. We know that the first verse was a command from God, "Read! (or Recite!)," to which Muhammad immediately responded, "I do not know how." And the angel Gabriel, the bearer of revelation, insisted, "Read!" Then Gabriel repeated the command a third time, saying, "Read in the name of your Lord and Sustainer who created. . ." (Qur'an 96:1).

The point is that Muhammad was not literate, and there was not yet a text in any form to be read. So what was the meaning of this first holy command, "Read!"? One answer, I think, is that "reading" here means a completely new way of looking at the world. The key notion is that this reading should be in the name of our Sustainer. So, at the very beginning it is taught that God, as the Sustainer and Creator, gives existence and meaning to everything else. God, according to the Qur'an, is the real Creator, Owner, and Sustainer of all reality. Hence, all reality should be seen and read with this point of view in mind. It may be pointed out that all books written by Muslims begin with the sentence, "In the name of God Most Gracious, Most Merciful," a phrase which is also repeated by Muslims throughout their daily lives as an indication of this Qur'anic outlook.

A careful examination of the early verses of the Qur'an reveals an invitation to examine and investigate the heavens and the earth, and everything that can be seen in the environment: birds, sheep, clouds, seas, grapes, dates, olives, flies, the moon, the sun, fish, camels, bees, mountains, rain, wind—in short, all natural phenomena. In its oft-repeated insistence on the investigation of nature, the Qur'an was aiming at developing an active and dynamic individual. The basic characteristic of such an individual, as far as we can understand from these verses, is that his mind is open to new events and he is aware of what is occurring around him in the heavens and on the earth. He also seeks to understand these things from a Qur'anic perspective. He will then reach the conclusion: "Our Lord! not for nothing have You created (all) this! Glory to You!" (Qur'an 3:191). This is one of the basic conclusions that the Qur'an enjoins and helps us to reach: the quest for meaning.

On many occasions the Qur'an emphasizes and reemphasizes the ultimate principle that lies beyond nature—why nature exists and what it means. What the Qur'an is trying to explain is simple and clear: nature is not there just by accident, as a result of the process of evolution or chaotic configurations, without meaning or purpose; it has order and meaning. Therefore, if humans ponder and scrutinize the very structure of natural phenomena, we can deduce the existence of a Creator who is All-Powerful, All-Knowing, and All-Merciful.

The Qur'an challenged the polytheism of the pagan Arabs by referring to nature as an assembly of orderly, meaningful, and purposive phenomena and inviting them to study its order carefully so that they could deduce from it the existence of God, who reveals and manifests His power and mercy through the universe. According to the Qur'an, nature, "having a firm and well-knit structure with no gaps, no ruptures, and no dislocations is one of the grand handiworks of the Almighty."[11] Like a mirror,[12] it reflects the power, beauty, wisdom and mercy of its Creator. This is explained by Said Nursi, a contemporary Muslim scholar,[13] as follows:

> The world is also a collection of mirrors which continuously pass on one after the other; so know the One Who is manifest in them, see His light, understand the manifestations of the Names which appear in them, and love the One they signify.[14]

Again, the overall aim of the Qur'an comes to the fore through its insistence on the natural order, as was pointed out by one of the great students of the Qur'an, Muhammad Iqbal: "No doubt, the immediate purpose of the Quran in this reflective observation of nature is to awaken in man the consciousness of that of which nature is regarded a symbol," and then "to awaken in man the higher consciousness of his manifold relations with God and the universe."[15]

Another implicit result of this attitude and of the Qur'an's insistence on the order in nature is that both the author of the Qur'an and the creator of nature—and nature in the Islamic tradition is also regarded as a Book—are the same: God. This can be seen from the following verse:

> He who created the seven heavens one above another; no want of proportion will you see in the Creation of (God) Most Gracious. So turn your vision again: do you see any flaw?
>
> Again turn your vision a second time: (your) vision will come back to you dull and discomfited, in a state worn out. (Qur'an 67:3–4)

Nature has been regarded as "the prime miracle of God, cited untiringly in the Qur'an, due to its well-knit structure and regularity."[16] The Qur'an's insistence on the order, beauty, and harmony of nature implies that there is no demarcation between what the Qur'an reveals and what nature manifests. We can see this at once if we reflect in the way that the Qur'an invites us to, by using our intellect and freeing ourselves from the boundaries and limitations of culture and tradition, looking at everything with an observant eye in the name of God.[17]

One reason for the abundance of such verses in the early chapters of the Qur'an may have been to abolish the previous pagan outlook and to provide a fresh perspective and viewpoint, which was also explained by the previous scriptures but forgotten in the course of time. Another example is the following verse, which again points to the order of nature and the maker of this order:

> You see the mountains and think them firmly fixed: but they shall pass away as the clouds pass away: (such is) the artistry of God, who disposes of all things in perfect order: for He is well-acquainted with all that you do. (Qur'an 27:88)

The Qur'an employs the perfect order of the universe as the proof not only of God's existence, but also of His unity, which is known as the "cosmological evidence of God's existence" in the philosophy of Islamic theology (*kalām*).[18] God is the very meaning of reality; a meaning manifested, and clarified, and brought home by the universe, developed further by humans. God is the dimension that makes other dimensions possible: He gives meaning and life to everything. For example, the Qur'an sees in the humble bee a recipient of divine inspiration, and constantly calls upon the reader to observe the perpetual change of the winds, the alternation of day and night, the clouds, the starry heavens, and the planets swimming through infinite space.[19]

It is not difficult to grasp that the Qur'an is emphasizing nature in order to prove the existence of God and His majesty, on the one hand, and, on the other, the fact that it requests us to read and understand both of these attributes in their exact context. The Qur'an invited the pagan Arabs, who were illiterate, to ponder nature and the universe for at least two purposes: first, to have an idea about God's existence and His presence through whatever He creates; and second, to have a moral feeling of obligation toward a transcendental being, God. Parvez Manzoor's remarks support this argument: "Nature and ethics are, as a matter of fact, at the very core of the Qur'anic *weltanschauung*. To infuse the natural world with transcendent (revealed) ethics is the main purpose of man according to the Qur'an."[20]

When the meaning and language of the early verses are examined in this way, it is not difficult to grasp their basic idea. The Qur'an underlines the moral dimension very clearly: "Not without purpose did We create heaven and earth and all between! That were the thought of Unbelievers! . . ." (Qur'an 38:27). The Qur'an rejects the argument that nature is meaningless and purposeless, as well as the resulting conclusion that human life also is meaningless and purposeless. To the contrary, if there is meaning and purpose in nature, then there must be meaning and purpose in human life, too. The basic point seems to be that there is a relationship between the purposefulness and meaningfulness of the natural world and of humankind's conduct in life.[21]

An argument can be made, then, that the metaphysical and moral dimension of the Qur'an comes first and precedes other dimensions. The Qur'an's frequent statements about the meaningful and orderly aspects of nature and natural phenomena are there to point out that these things reflect the unlimited power and majesty of God, and that humankind should accept this as a metaphysical reality and, by submitting and surrendering to it, be grateful to Him.[22] The opposite argument is that if God does not exist and everything is absurd, existing by accident, then, in the words of Albert Camus, who provided the general outline for a philosophy of absurdity: "all is allowed since God does not exist and man dies."[23]

Another conclusion of the Qur'anic perspective that is important for environmental ethics is that God does not create as "frivolity, pastime, or sport, without a serious purpose. It is incompatible with the power of the Powerful and the mercy of the Merciful that He should produce toys for amusement or as sheer whim—a blind Fate can do this but God cannot."[24] To support this conclusion, the following verses are sufficient:

> Behold! In the creation of the heavens and the earth, and the alternation of night and day, there are indeed Signs for men of understanding,—
> Men who celebrate the praises of God, standing, sitting, and lying down on their sides, and contemplate the (wonders of) creation in the heavens and the earth (with the thought): "Our Lord! not for nothing have You created (all) this!" (Qur'an 3:190–91)

> Not for (idle) sport did We create the heavens and the earth and all that is between!
> If it had been Our wish to take (just) a pastime, We should surely have taken it from the things nearest to Us, if We would do (such a thing)! (Qur'an 21:16–17)

> Did you then think that We had created you in jest, and that you would not be brought back to Us (for account)? (Qur'an 23:115)

One immediate conclusion, from an environmentalist perspective, is that every individual creature or being has its own ontological existence as a sign of God, and by its very being manifests and reveals His majesty and mercy. Therefore, every creature deserves attention and consideration for its relation to the Divine. A sincere follower of the Qur'an is always aware of the fact that "Our Lord is He who gave to each (created) thing its form and nature, and further gave (it) guidance" (Qur'an 20:50). Still another example is this:

> Then let man look at his food, (and how We provide it):
> For that We pour forth water in abundance,
> And We split the earth into fragments,
> And We produce therein corn,
> And grapes and nutritious plants,
> And olives and dates,
> And enclosed gardens, dense with lofty trees,
> And fruits and fodder,—
> For use and convenience to you and your cattle. (Qur'an 80:24–32)

By mentioning miracles of divine power in a purposeful sequence, these verses bind causes to effects and point to a conclusive aim with the words, "For use and convenience to you. . . ." Nursi comments on this point as follows:

> This aim proves that within the sequence of all the causes and effects is a hidden disposer who sees and follows the aim, and that the causes are a veil to him. Indeed, with the phrase, "For use and convenience to you and your cattle," it dismisses all the causes from the ability to create. It is in effect saying: "Rain comes from the sky in order to produce food for you and your animals. Since water does not possess the ability to pity and feel compassion for you and produce food, it means that the rain does not come, [by itself but] it is sent. And the earth produces plants and your food comes from there. But lacking feelings and intelligence, it is far beyond the ability of the earth to think of your sustenance and feel compassion for you, so it does not produce it itself. Furthermore, since it is remote from plants and trees to consider your food and compassionately produce fruits and grains for you, the verse demonstrates that they are strings and ropes which One All-Wise and Compassionate extends from behind the veil, to which He attaches His bounties and holds out to animate creatures. And so from this explanation numerous Divine Names [a]rise, like All-Compassionate, Provider, Bestower, and All-Generous.[25]

A further conclusion is that, as God reveals and manifests Himself through His creation, it gives humans the impression that God is within us. If God reveals Himself—that is, His majesty, mercy, and all other sacred beautiful names and attributes through the esthetic dimension of nature as well as its orderly structure—then it is not difficult to get the idea that wherever humans look we can easily feel the presence of God all around and within us.

> To God belong the East and the West: whithersoever you turn there is the presence of God. For God is All-Pervading, All-Knowing. (Qur'an 2:115)

Seeing God everywhere and being fully aware of the divine environment that surrounds and permeates both the world of nature and the ambience of humanity[26] strengthens humankind's moral dimension and motivates us to act accordingly. It is in this sense that Fazlur Rahman considers the Qur'an "a document that primarily exhorts [humankind] to virtue and a strong sense of moral responsibility."[27]

Another point that we should consider in this context is that God is absolute and infinite, whereas every creature is finite. Modern humans have reached this understanding, thanks to recent developments in the field of ecology.[28] To quote Rahman:

> . . . what the Qur'an means when it says that everything except God is "measured out" (*qadar* or *qadr*, *taqdīr*, etc.), and hence dependent upon God. . . . When God creates anything, He places within it its powers or laws of behavior, called in the Qur'an "guidance," "command," or "measure" whereby it fits into the rest of the universe.[29]

The following verses underline the same point and once more emphasize the importance of balance in the Qur'anic discourse:

> The sun and the moon follow courses (exactly) computed;
> And the herbs and the trees—both (alike) bow in adoration.
> And the Firmament has He raised high, and He has set up the balance (of Justice),
> In order that you may not transgress (due) balance.
> So establish weight with justice and fall not short in the balance. (Qur'an 55:5–9)

The key term here is *balance*, which is repeated three times. In his comments on these verses, Yusuf Ali says:

> The "balance of justice" in this verse is connected with "the Balance" in the next two verses, that men may act justly to each other and observe due balance in all their actions, following the golden mean and not transgressing due bounds. But the Balance is also connected figuratively with the heavens above in three symbols: (1) Justice is a heavenly virtue; (2) the heavens themselves are sustained by mathematical balance; and (3) the constellation Libra (the Balance) is entered by the sun at the middle of zodiacal year.

For the second parts he argues that:

> A man should be honest and straight in every daily matter, such as weighting out things which he is selling: and he should be straight, just and honest, in all the highest dealings, not only with other people, but with himself and in his obedience to God's Law.[30]

It is evident from the above discussion that justice and balance are a universal law (of God), and that (as a result) humankind should conduct a just and balanced life. It might reasonably be argued that these verses alone would be enough for developing an environmental ethic from the Qur'an itself, for they establish, first, that justice and balance are universal, second, that this universal balance is created by God, and third, that humans must attempt both to comprehend this universal balance and to follow it in their social life as well as in their interactions with the environment. It could be concluded by any sincere follower of the Qur'an—philosopher, scientist, economist, engineer, technocrat, statesman, or ordinary human being—that he or she must respect and preserve this balance in all relations with nature.

The Qur'an's insistence on the absolute and infinite character of God, on the one hand, and the finitude of everything other than God, on the other, is very significant in terms of current discussions about economics and development. Any economical and developmental theory that claims to be Islamic should presuppose this fact from the start.[31]

In this connection, it might be important just to remember a prophetic attitude that reflects the Qur'anic spirit very clearly and powerfully. Muhammad attached great importance to the moderate use of water[32] and forbade the excessive use of it even when performing ablutions, saying that to do so was "detestable" (*makrūḥ*). He even prevented people from using too much water for ablutions when preparing to enter the Divine Presence for prayer. The following *ḥadīth* tells the story:

> "God's Messenger appeared while Sa'ad was performing the ablutions. When he saw that Sa'ad was using a lot of water, he intervened saying:
>
> 'What is this? You are wasting water."
>
> Sa'ad replied asking: "Can there be wastefulness while performing the ablutions?" To which God's Messenger replied:
>
> "Yes, even if you perform them on the bank of a rushing river."[33]

I believe this *ḥadīth*, and the attitude of the Prophet, refers not only to using less water while performing ablutions, but to a basic and ultimate principle that is to be followed by all Muslims. The following points should be emphasized in connection with it:

- God's Messenger is stating an important prohibition.
- The prohibition concerns something for which no effort was exerted to obtain it, nor was any money spent, as it is free: the water of a flowing river.
- Moreover, the excessive use of water in this instance causes no

deficiency to nature, nor does it cause pollution or spoil the ecological balance.

• It causes no harm to living beings.

• Furthermore, the matter in question, that is, performing ablutions, is not some trivial matter; it is a necessary condition for obligatory prayers.

If then, despite all the above, it is still "detestable" to use water from a river in excess while performing ablutions, and it was prohibited by the Prophet, how much stronger is the proscription on being wasteful and extravagant in those matters in which the above statements are not applicable? That is, if wastefulness

• is in something that requires the expending of effort, expense, or at least time;

• causes deficiency to or pollution of nature, thus spoiling the ecological balance;

• harms living beings;

• violates the rights of forthcoming generations to live in a healthy environment;

• is arbitrary and meaningless and merely for enjoyment, that is, for the satisfaction of the destructive side of humans;[34]

• is contrary to the basic aim—

then how much greater would be the degree of prohibition!

The Qur'an and the *sunna*, stipulating that water is the basic need of life, place a number of obligations and responsibilities upon Muslims: the conservation of existing water supplies in the best possible way; the prevention of any activity that might lead to the pollution of water resources or spoil the purity and characteristics of the water; and never adopting an extravagant or irresponsible attitude in the consumption of water.

This example, not to mention other related ones, illustrates very clearly that the Qur'anic emphasis that there is nothing useless in the balance of nature is exemplified in the life of the Prophet himself. As we are told by A'isha, the beloved wife of the Prophet, his personality and personal conduct was that of the Qur'an. Therefore, his attitudes toward nature may be regarded as concrete examples of the Qur'anic spirit.

The foregoing discussion makes clear that we must not and cannot live merely as we wish—which would be a meaningless and purposeless life—but rather, that we can and should lead a purposeful and meaningful life, that is, live as Muslims who surrender themselves to the law of God. This law is evident in nature and in the Qur'an. Alija Ali Izzetbegovic rightly underlines the fact that "a Muslim, due to the balance of physical and moral requirements, will be in better harmony with his surroundings than any other type of man,"[35] presupposing that he lives according to the Qur'anic principles.[36] The Qur'an goes further, and calls all nature *muslim* ("submissive"). The only difference between nature and humankind is that nature is *muslim* without free will, implying that only humankind can be Muslim through free choice.

Nature as Muslim

The very idea that nature is created by God and is an indication and sign of His existence leads to the Qur'anic idea just mentioned, that all nature is *muslim*.[37] For, as discussed above, the whole of nature works according to divine laws—the so-called natural laws—and according to the way God designed and created it. The Qur'an therefore applies the term *islām* ("submission") to the entire universe insofar as it (ineluctably) obeys God's law. Working according to God's laws, nature submits itself to God's will.[38] As a result of its position, nature does not and cannot disobey God's commands and cannot violate natural laws, as explained in the following verses:

> Don't you see that to God bow down in worship all things that are in the heavens and on earth,—the sun, the moon, the stars; the hills, the trees, the animals; and a great number among mankind? But a great number are (also) such as are fit for Punishment: and such as God shall disgrace,—none can raise to honor: for God carries out all that He wills. (Qur'an 22:18)

> The seven heavens and the earth, and all beings therein, declare His glory: there is not a thing but celebrates His praise; and yet you don't understand how they declare His glory! Verily He is Oft-Forbearing, Most Forgiving! (Qur'an 17:44)

> Nay, thunder repeats His praises, and so do the angels, with awe: He flings the loud-voiced thunder-bolts, and therewith He strikes whom-

soever He will. . . . Yet these (are the men) who (dare to) dispute about God, with the strength of His power (supreme)! (Qur'an 13:13)

Don't you see that it is God Whose praises all beings in the heavens and on earth do celebrate, and the birds (of the air) with wings outspread? Each one knows its own (mode of) prayer and praise. And God knows well all that they do. (Qur'an 24:41–42)

Since every thing in the universe behaves in accordance with laws enacted by God, the whole universe is therefore *muslim*, surrendering to the will of God. "Do they seek for other than the religion of God? While all creatures in the heavens and on earth have, willing or unwilling, bowed to His will (i.e., accepted Islam) and to Him shall they all be brought back" (Qur'an 3: 83). As the Qur'an emphasizes, humans are the only exception to this universal law, for they are the only beings endowed with the free choice of obeying or disobeying the command of God. The only difference is that while every other creature follows its nature automatically, humans *ought* to follow their natures; this transformation of the *is* into *ought* is both the unique privilege and unique risk of being human.[39]

Another important point related to nature as being *muslim* is that the Islamic way of prayer is a synthesis of the methods of prayer of all the beings in the universe. Muhammad Hamidullah relates that one day, as he was reciting verse 22:18, he began to think of the significance of the acts of Islamic prayers with regard to the prayer of nature as a whole:

The universe consists of three kingdoms, minerals, animals, and vegetables. Their particularities are respectively resting, erect, and motionless, remaining perpetually bent, and resting perpetually prostrate. I mean to say that since the roots constitute the mouths for the plants, they are perpetually posed on the ground. A Muslim purifies himself/herself like water, praises God aloud like thunder, remains erect like hills, bends himself like animals, and prostrates like plants. Service means obeying to the orders of the Lord. God has ordered mountains to rest immobile and (to Muslims the Qur'an 2:238 says) "and stand before Allāh devoutly"; to animals to remain perpetually bent and (to Muslims the Qur'an 2:43 commands) "and to trees to remain prostrate and (to Muslims the Qur'an 53:62 orders) "But you fall down in prostration to God and adore (Him)!"[40]

Thus, with his daily prayers, the Muslim is first participating in the call of all creation, on the one hand, and realizing the integration of his self with all reality, on the other. Then, he looks upon all creation as his brethren before God.[41] The Qur'an aims at the realization of an integrated and holistic selfhood.

Still another important point is that "there is not a thing but celebrates His praise; and yet you don't understand how they declare His glory!" (Qur'an 17:44). This has led many Muslim thinkers to consider nature as a whole as a living being. For example, al-Ghazali, when commenting on this and similar verses, regards it as the language of creation:

> . . . you suppose that in the universe there is only the language of statement. This is why you did not understand the meaning of the words of God (may He be exalted!) "There is not a thing but celebrates His praise." Nor do you understand the meaning of the words of God (may He be exalted!) "They [the heavens and the earth] submitted [to You] willingly (41:11)," unless you suppose that the earth has a language and life.[42]

Jalal al-Din Rumi, the great Sufi master and thinker of the thirteenth century, makes similar observations on the same subject, and offers a warning:

> Since God hath made Man from dust, it behooves thee to recognize the real nature of every particle of the universe,
>
> That while from this aspect they are dead, from that aspect they are living: silent here, but speaking Yonder.
>
> When He sends them down to our world, the rod of Moses becomes a dragon in regard to us;
>
> The mountains sing with David, iron becomes as wax in his hand;
>
> The wind becomes a carrier for Solomon, the sea understands what God said to Moses concerning it.
>
> The moon obeys the sign given by Muhammad, the fire (of Nimrod) becomes a garden of roses for Abraham.
>
> They all cry, "we are hearing and seeing and responsive, though to you, the uninitiated, we are mute."
>
> Ascend from materiality into the world of spirit, hearken to the loud voice of the universe;
>
> Then thou wilt know that God is glorified by all inanimate things: the doubts raised by false interpreters will not beguile thee.[43]

Said Nursi also reflects on this Qur'anic perspective as follows: "the All-Wise Qur'an speaks of the universe in order to make known the Divine Essence, Attributes, and Names. That is, it explains the meaning of the Book of the Universe to make known its Creator. That means it looks at beings, not for themselves, but for their Creator."[44] And Nursi provides many examples for his claim. The following will suffice to understand his reasoning, which also reflects the Qur'anic spirit:

> Now consider the springs, the streams, and the rivers! Their welling-up out of the ground and out of mountains is not by chance. For it is demonstrated by the testimony of their benefits and fruits, the works of Divine Mercy, and by the statement of their being stored up in mountains with the balance of wisdom in proportion to need, that they are subjugated and stored up by an All-Wise Sustainer, and that their flowing forth is their conforming exuberantly to His command.
>
> Now consider all the varieties of stones and jewels and minerals in the earth! Their decorations and beneficial properties, the wise benefits connected to them, and their being prepared in a manner appropriate to human and animal needs and vital necessities all show that they are made in that way through the decoration, arrangement, planning, and forming of an All-Wise Maker.
>
> Now consider the flowers and fruits! Their smiles, tastes, beauties, embroideries, and scents are each like an invitation to and menu for the table of a Most Munificent Maker, an All-Compassionate Bestower of Bounties; they are given as various menus and invitations to each species of beings through their different colors, scents, and tastes.[45]

In the forgoing discussion, as we have seen, a different view of nature—which is unique to the Qur'an—emerges. Muslims live in a world that is alive, meaningful, purposeful, and more importantly, *muslim* like themselves, even prostrating itself before God. The immediate result is the discovery of the wholeness of all creation and integration with it, physically and spiritually. When devout Muslims look at their environment, everything seems to be somehow familiar and friendly. Moreover, everything is a symbol and a sign, pointing to an all-wise and all-merciful Creator.

Nature as Signs of God

When the Qur'an invites people to believe in God, it bases its claim on some arguments. It does not invite people to believe in a God who is incomprehensible. The Qur'an begins its invitation by inviting people to ponder over their environment. The universe and everything in it, the Qur'an claims, are signs (*āyāt*) pointing to something "beyond" themselves, that is, something without which the universe, despite all its natural causes, would be nothing. Therefore, with the following and other similar verses the Qur'an invites people to read the universe as signs of God:

> We shall show them Our signs upon the horizons and within their own souls, until it is clear to them that He is the Real. (Qur'an 41:53)

> On the earth are Signs for those of assured Faith,
> As also in your own selves: will you not then see? (Qur'an 51:20–21)

So, a sign—the word is repeated in singular or plural form two hundred eighty-eight times in the Qur'an—is "any phenomenon that gives news of God. *It may be a prophet, a prophetic message, a prophetic miracle, or simply the things of the natural world. . . .* In short everything in the universe is a sign of God."[46] Rahman also underlines this point when dealing with the concept of nature from a Qur'anic perspective: "Nature with its incomprehensible vastness and regularity should serve as God's sign for humans, since none but an infinite and unique Being could have created it. This may be called a 'natural sign.' "[47] And thus, "this gigantic machine, the universe, with all its causal processes, is the prime 'sign' (*āya*) or proof of its Maker."[48]

When the pagan people of the time demanded proofs, "signs," or miracles for the existence of God, the Qur'an's usual response is to point to the complexity, the regularity, and the order in nature and to emphasize that the universe and all that is in it could not have come into existence alone. Within the Qur'anic discourse, nature is a living, holistic, orderly, and perfect world, populated by angels, jinn, human beings, and animals. Above all, the universe, with all its causal processes, is the prime sign and proof of its Maker.[49]

It should be obvious that every masterpiece of art deserves not only our attention, appreciation, and admiration, but also our protection. We are quick to recognize that a masterpiece of painting deserves every sort of care and appreciation. Nature, likewise, which is full of signs of God and is furthermore a masterpiece of His creative effort, deserves our watchfulness, gratefulness, and respect. In addition, nature, consisting of signs of God, somehow possesses intrinsic value beyond what human beings attribute to it instrumentally. In this context, the following verses deserve our attention:

> And verily in cattle [too] will you find an instructive Sign. For what is within their bodies, between excretions and blood, we produce, for your drink, milk, pure and agreeable to those who drink it. (Qur'an 16:66)

> Do they not look at the Camels, how they are made?
> And at the Sky, how it is raised high?
> And at the Mountains, how they are fixed firm?
> And at the Earth, how it is spread out? (Qur'an 88:17–20)

These verses invite us to think over the creation which surrounds us, which we can see in our everyday lives, and which is full of meaning, high design, and the goodness of God to humankind.[50] In Nasr's words, nature is "the theatre wherein are manifested His signs."[51] The overall influence of this understanding of nature as signs of God is very evident in the history of Islamic thought. Muslim thinkers regard nature as a sacred book, full of symbols and signs. For example, Nursi says about the universe:

> The cosmos [is] meaningful and well-ordered in that it took on the shape of a personified book of the Glorious One, an incarnate Dominical Qur'an, a finely-adorned city of the Compassionate One. All *sūra*s, verses and words of that book, even its very letters, chapters, divisions, pages, and lines, through their constant meaningful effacement and re-affirmation, their wise changes and alternations, gave unanimous expression to the existence and presence of One Knowledgeable of all things and Empowered over all things as the author of the book, of a Glorious Inscriber and Perfect Scribe seeing all things in all things and knowing the relationship of all things with all things.[52]

Nature might reasonably be considered a well-ordered and well-bounded book, and even called "the book of the universe." This implies that, just like the Qur'an, the universe reveals to us the existence of a Sustainer and Creator. As a result, it can be deduced that the book of the universe has been entrusted to us in order that we might preserve and protect it. Should those believers who hold the Qur'an in respect and awe—not touching it unless purified by ablutions—not also treat the book of the universe respectfully and lovingly? Our duty, therefore, as God's vicegerents and trustees on earth, is to show respect for the primal trust, and to preserve it carefully, and this means not wasting natural resources when making use of them. Sachiko Murata reaches a similar conclusion:

> When the Koran commands people to see all things as God's signs, it is encouraging them to make use of a particular type of mental process that is not oriented toward objects, things, or data. On the contrary, the Koran tells us that we must perceive things not so much for what they are in themselves but for what they tell us of something beyond themselves.[53]

Still another implication is the disappearance of any demarcation between human and nature as disconnected entities or objects. They are, as signs of God, interconnected with each other and interdependent; in environmentalist terms this implies a holistic, spiritual, and balanced view of all reality.

The Case of Animals

Another important question related to the environment is the proper treatment of the animals, the protection which is due to them—or, more correctly, extending and expressing our kindness and compassion to them. But, unfortunately, today many animal species are becoming extinct. Other animals stray abandoned and hungry in the streets of many parts of the world. On the whole, it cannot be said that we treat animals as well as we should, or carry out our responsibilities toward them. In my view, one of the most important causes for this is our unawareness of Qur'anic values, which regulate not only the believers' relations between human and human and between human and the environment, but also humankind's relations with other living species. A natural consequence of this is that humans are answerable to God for our attitudes and actions toward nature and animals.[54] Hence, questions regarding animal rights and humankind's attitude toward animals, as well as the subject of species extinction, have been discussed extensively by environmentalists all over the globe and constitute some of the major problems that environmentalists have been trying to solve. The Qur'anic view of animals therefore deserves further consideration here.

The first point to be made about animals in the Qur'an, which may surprise the environmentally sensitive reader, is the fact that numerous chapters (sūras) of the sacred scripture bear the names of animals—for example, *al-Baqara* (The Cow); *al-Naḥl* (The Bee), *al-'Anqabūt* (The Spider), and *al-Naml* (The Ant). Moreover, one of the striking expressions the Qur'an uses in referring to animals is that they constitute a "community" (*umma*), just like us. It is especially noteworthy that this concept, which is a highly significant theme in Islamic tradition and literature, should also be used for animals:

> There is not an animal [that lives] on the earth, nor a being that flies on its wings, but [forms part of] communities like you. Nothing have We omitted from the Book, and they [all] shall be gathered to their Sustainer in the end. (Qur'an 6:38)

In addition, there exists a very close relationship between God, as Lord and Sustainer of all worlds, and animals. Our attention is drawn to the animal world once again with the following verse:

> There is no moving creature on earth but its sustenance depends on God: He knows the time and place of its definite abode and its temporary deposit: all is in a clear record. (Qur'an 11:6)

Furthermore, the Qur'an emphasizes that the natural world has not been created just for humankind's use. Even if humankind is the vicegerent of God on earth,[55] it does not necessarily mean that the whole of nature and its resources are designed for humans' benefits only. This can be seen from the following verse:

> And the earth has He spread out for all living beings, with fruit thereon, and palm trees with sheathed clusters [of dates], and grain growing tall on its stalks, and sweet-smelling plants.[56]

Here, the meaning of *anām*, which signifies "all living beings," is crucial for our study. From this verse it can be deduced that the bounties of the earth and all other resources are not solely for humankind's use, but for all creatures of God that live on the same earth.

The Qur'an also draws our attention to another aspect regarding animals: that it is possible to communicate with them, although the extent and nature of this communication is not defined. For example, in narrating the story of the prophet Solomon, the Qur'an informs us that he had been taught the language of birds by God:

> And Solomon was David's heir. He said: "O you people! We have been taught the speech of birds, and on us has been bestowed (a little) of all things: this is indeed grace manifest (from God)."
>
> And before Solomon were marshalled his hosts—of Jinn [genies] and men and birds—and they were all kept in order and rank.
>
> At length when they came to a (lowly) valley of ants, one of the ants said: "O you ants, get into your habitations lest Solomon and his hosts crush you (under foot) without knowing it." (Qur'an 27:16–18)

The fact that, according to the Qur'an, Solomon could understand the languages of birds and ants suggests at least two points. First, communication with animals is possible, though the extent of this is not defined for the time being. This may also point to a transmission of meaning to other living beings.[57] Second, we must understand that animals are just like our fellow humans, at least in some respects. Contrary to prevailing modern views, there is no clear-cut distinction between humans and nonhumans; they are both creatures of the same Creator. Nursi, when commenting on the miracles of prophets as mentioned in the Qur'an in connection with Solomon's comprehension of the birds' language, argues that the Qur'an encourages humans to try to imitate the prophets' deeds and to attain the goals illustrated by these miracles.[58] The basic idea is that the Qur'an, by enumerating the prophets' miracles, is also hinting that human reason should develop and reach similar conclusions by means of scientific inquiries.

It is not difficult to see that animals are not mentioned here for their instrumental use as such, and that our relationship with them cannot be based only on the principle of utility. Of course, humanity will make use of them and benefit from them, but this is not the only legitimate relationship we have with them. It is expected from us that we should see nature and all its inhabitants in a broad and more holistic perspective, appreciating its metaphysical, aesthetic, and other aspects as well.[59]

Humankind's Responsibility: Master or Vicegerent?

By now the Qur'anic discourse about humans and their position in the overall scheme of beings and humankind's legitimate relationship with other beings should be clear. Since the publication of Lynn White's provocative article,[60] many have held the Judeo-Christian tradition responsible for environmental degradation.[61] Some critics have tried to include Islam in the same category. Indeed, a piecemeal and oversimplified approach to some verses of the Qur'an would seem to support the Christian view as summarized by Keith Thomas, "giving the impression that everything on earth is created for the sake of man and that man's authority over nature is unlimited. He is entitled to use it as he pleases, for profit or for pleasure. Vegetables obviously have no rights, for they are destitute of sense and therefore incapable of injury. Animals have no rights either."[62] The following Qur'anic verses, for example, could be construed to support such a position if taken out of the broader context:

> It is He Who has created for you all things that are on earth. (Qur'an 2:29)

> It is He Who has made the earth manageable for you, so you traverse through its tracts and enjoy of the Sustenance which He furnishes: but unto Him is the Resurrection. (Qur'an 67:15)[63]

> It is God Who has created the heavens and the earth and sends down rain from the skies, and with it brings out fruits wherewith to feed you; it is He Who has made the ships subject to you, that they may sail through the sea by His command; and the rivers (also) has He made subject to you.
>
> And He has made subject to you the sun and the moon both diligently pursuing their courses; and the Night and the Day has He (also) made subject you.
>
> And He gives you of all that you ask for. But if you count the favors of God, never will you be able to number them. Verily, man is given up to injustice and ingratitude. (Qur'an 14: 32–34)[64]

To be sure, human beings are at the top of the great chain of being, but they are not the owners of nature as such. In other words, the sole aim of nature is not only to serve human beings and their ends. When the Qur'an is taken and perceived as a whole—that is, in a comprehensive and integrated way—this impression disappears immediately.

When the history of Islam, especially the history of Qur'anic exegesis, is studied from such a perspective, it can be seen that Muslims deduced from these and other similar verses that "although the various components of the natural environment serve humanity as one of their functions, this does not imply that human use is the sole reason for their creation."[65] Both classical and contemporary Muslim scholars have interesting views on this matter. For example, al-Biruni, one of the most learned Muslim scholars and compilers of the tenth century, argues that "man does not have a right to exploit the other kingdoms for his own desires, which are insatiable, but may use them only in conformity with the law of God and in His way."[66] Further, Ibn Taymiyya, commenting on the above verses of the Qur'an, underlines his point with these words:

> In considering all these verses it must be remembered that God in His wisdom created these creatures for reasons other than serving man, because in these verses He explains only the benefits of these creatures [to man].[67]

Said Nursi draws a similar conclusion, arguing that "there are numerous purposes for the existence of everything, and numerous results flow from its being," and that "these are not restricted to this world and to the souls of men." On the contrary, the purposes for the existence of all things and their results relate to the following three categories:

> The first and the most exalted pertains to the Creator. It consists of presenting to the gaze of the Pre-Eternal Witness the bejewelled and miraculous wonders He has affixed to the object in question. . . . Thus the first purpose of all things is to proclaim, by means of their life and existence, the miracles of power and the traces of artistry of the Maker and display them to the gaze of the Glorious Monarch.
>
> The second purpose of all existence and the result of all being pertains to conscious creation. Everything is like a truth-displaying missive, an artistic poem, or a wise word of the Glorious Maker, offered to the gaze of angels and jinn, of men and animals, and desiring to be read by them. It is an object for the contemplation and instruction of every conscious being that looks upon it.
>
> The third purpose of all existence and result of all being pertains to the soul of the thing itself, and consists of such minor consequences as the experience of pleasure and joy, and living with some degree of permanence and comfort.[68]

It should be apparent that nature has been entrusted to us, as we are God's vicegerents on Earth. We are not the lords of nature and the world, however; the world is not our property, at our disposal to be used haphazardly and irresponsibly. On the contrary, nature was created by God, and it belongs to Him. What is important in the Qur'anic context is that we are responsible and accountable for our actions here on Earth. This means that we are answerable for all that we do, both the good and the evil. As God's vicegerents, at the Last Judgment we will be called to account for our actions in fulfilling this trust: "Whoever does an atom's weight of good shall see it, And whoever does an atom's weight of evil, shall see it" (Qur'an 99:7–8). And again: "So glory to Him in whose hands is the dominion of all things: And to Him will you be all brought back" (Qur'an 36:83). According to Yusuf Ali, the message conveyed in this verse is the core of revelation; it explains the hereafter. All things were created by God, are maintained by Him, and will go back to Him. But the point of special interest to humans is that humans will also be brought back to God and will be answerable to Him, and to Him alone.[69]

In short, although humankind has been given a special place and rank in the hierarchy of creation, and nature, with all its rich resources, has been given and entrusted to us, we should not forget that we are also servants of God and that the ultimate end of our creation is to serve God. Hence, "man is invited to use the opportunity for good and not to corrupt the earth (*fasād fi' l-arḍ*)."[70]

Conclusion

Our discussion of the Qur'anic view of the environment is based on the understanding that everything in the universe is created by God. It is God who adorns the skies with the sun, the moon, and the stars and the face of the earth with flowers, trees, gardens, orchards, and the various animal species. It is again God who causes the rivers and streams to flow on the earth, who upholds the skies (without support), causes the rain to fall, and places the boundary between night and day. The universe with all its richness and vitality is the work and art of God, that is, of the Creator. It is again God who creates all plants and animals as pairs, in this way causing their procreation. God created man and woman subsequent to all these.

Therefore, I conclude that an environmental ethic is the logical outcome of a Qur'anic understanding of nature and humankind. The Qur'anic value system has the necessary elements for developing and constructing an environmental ethic. The Qur'an's emphasis on the sacred and metaphysical dimension of the universe should lead to a change in Muslims' overall image of nature and themselves as well. This Qur'anic worldview is first observed and exemplified in the life of the prophet Muhammad, since his life is regarded by Muslims as the living Qur'an and has had a powerful exemplary effect on Muslims throughout the ages. Being imbued with the Prophet's attitude, Muslims have looked on nature compassionately and with tolerance. Today, all these principles are awaiting rediscovery and analysis, so that a Qur'anic environmental ethic appropriate to meeting the present crisis can be worked out.

The following principles, which are necessary for any environmental ethic, can be elicited and deduced from the Qur'an:

- The natural world has an ontological and objective existence as has been created by God and which reflects His Divine Names and Attributes.
- Nature as a whole, being created and sustained by God, has intrinsic and inherent value, independent of its usefulness for human beings.
- Human beings, though at the top of creation, are only members of the community of nature. They have responsibilities toward the whole environment, just as they have responsibilities toward their families.
- Human beings are the vicegerents of God on earth, and therefore they will be judged in the hereafter for their actions here. They will also be held accountable for their actions related with the environment.
- Biodiversity and the richness of the ecosystem is a result of God's creation and His will; therefore the ecosystem should be respected and maintained.
- Nature has been created in order and balance and with extraordinary esthetic beauty, and all these aspects of nature, while enhancing humankind's life here, should be honored, developed, and protected accordingly.
- All patterns of human production and consumption should be based on an overall order and balance of nature. The rights of human-

kind are not absolute and unlimited. We cannot consume and pollute nature as we wish, carelessly.

• To prevent the appearance and emergence of corruption in ecosystems, to prevent corruption on earth (*fasād fi' l-arḍ*), is one of the primary responsibilities of all believers.

The Qur'an changed the hearts and minds of its hearers when it dawned on the Arabian peninsula, enriching humankind and providing a vivid lens through which we could look at nature. Today, at the dawn of the twenty-first century and in a time of worldwide environmental crisis, the Qur'an can again play such a role and give us, who believe in its truth, a fresh perspective and consciousness of nature—if we are ready to open our hearts and minds to its teaching. The relationship that the Qur'an enjoins between humans and nonhumans is stated very eloquently and succinctly by Yunus Emre, a Sufi poet of the thirteenth century: "We love all creation for the sake of its Creator."

Notes

1. For a philosophical account of this position see, for example, Alfred Jules Ayer, *Language, Truth, and Logic* (New York: Dover, 1946).

2. See Eugene P. Odum, *Fundamentals of Ecology*, 3d ed. (Philadelphia: W. B. Saunders Co., 1971), 3.

3. Hans Jonas, *The Imperative of Responsibility* (Chicago: University of Chicago Press, 1984), 22.

4. Locke's theory of primary and secondary qualities is best summarized by A. N. Whitehead, who realized the full implications of this theory, as follows: "The primary qualities are the essential qualities of substances whose spatio-temporal relationships constitute nature. The orderliness of these relationships constitutes the order of nature. . . . But the mind in apprehending also experiences sensations which, properly speaking, are qualities of the mind alone. These sensations are projected by the mind so as to clothe appropriate bodies in external nature. Thus the bodies are perceived as with qualities which in reality do not belong to them, qualities which in fact are purely the offspring of the mind. Thus nature gets credit which should in truth be reserved for ourselves: the rose for its scent: the nightingale for his song: and the sun for his radiance. The poets are entirely mistaken. They should address their lyrics to themselves, and should turn them into odes of self-congratulation on the excellency of the human mind." See A. N. Whitehead, *Science and the Modern World* (New York: Macmillan Company, 1926), 79–80. For a recent exposition and critique of the theory of qualities, see David Ray Griffin, *God and Religion in the Postmodern World: Essays in Postmodern Theology* (Albany: State University of New York Press, 1989), 16–17.

5. According to this understanding, "extrahuman nature is indifferent to itself and also to human beings who are cast adrift in it. We may matter to ourselves, but there is no larger scheme of mattering to which we belong. Though human beings may be subjects who posit ends and act in light of purposes, nonhuman organisms are mere objects: matter in motion. And eventually humans, as part of nature, become objects of their own fabrications to be shaped according to the designs of biotechnology. If nature presents us with no ethical norms, then no effort to change our own nature in the name of perfection, convenience, of experimentation could count as a transgression of essential limits or a violation of a natural standard of goodness." Lawrence Vogel, "Does Environmental Ethics Need a Metaphysical Grounding?" *The Hastings Center Report* 25 (1995): 30–39.

6. Seyyed Hossein Nasr argues that the Islamic world is not totally Islamic today, and much that is Islamic lies hidden behind the cover of Western cultural, scientific, and technological ideas and practices emulated and aped to various degrees of perfection—or rather, one should say of imperfection—by Muslims during the past century and a half. See Seyyed Hossein Nasr, "Islam and the Environmental Crisis," in *Spirit and Nature*, ed. Steven C. Rockefeller and John C. Elder (Boston: Beacon Press, 1992), 87.

7. For our present purpose, I take George Lindbeck's definition of religion, which is in essence a sociolinguistic perspective. Lindbeck argues that "A religion can be viewed as a kind of cultural and/or linguistic framework or medium that shapes the

entirety of life and thought. . . . It is similar to an idiom that makes possible the description of realities, the formulation of beliefs, and the experiencing of inner attitudes, feelings, and sentiments." Quoted in Max Oelschlaeger, *Caring for Creation: An Ecumenical Approach to the Environmental Crisis* (New Haven: Yale University Press, 1994), 28.

8. Sir Muhammad Iqbal, *The Reconstruction of Religious Thought in Islam* (Lahore: The Ashraf Press, 1958), 8–9.

9. Abu Hamid Al-Ghazali, *The Jewels of the Qur'an*, trans. M. Abul Quasem (London: Kegan Paul, 1983), 25.

10. Ibid., 19–20. According to him, "the Qur'an is like an ocean. As at the bottom of the ocean, pearls remain hidden, so also are hidden the wonderful meanings behind the Qur'anic verses." Al-Ghazali therefore argues that it is the duty of a Muslim to understand these meanings.

11. Fazlur Rahman, *Major Themes of the Qur'an* (Minneapolis: Bibliotheca Islamica, 1980), 3, 79.

12. The mirror is used in Sufi literature as a symbol that reflects what is not part of something's own essence. For example, al-Ghazali explains this point very clearly, while keeping in mind the verse "God is the Light of the heavens and the earth" (Qur'an 24:35): ". . . the seeker and the Sought are comparable to a picture present in a mirror: The picture is not revealed in it because of rust on its surface; when, however, you polish the mirror the picture is revealed in it, neither by the movement of the picture towards it nor by its movement towards the picture, but by removal of the veil. God (may He be exalted!) is revealed by His essence and not concealed, for concealment of light is impossible, and by light everything which is concealed becomes obvious, and God is the Light of the heavens and the earth." See *Jewels of the Qur'an*, 26–27. See also Parviz Morewedge, "Mystical Icons in Rumi's Metaphysical Poetry: Light, the Mediator and the Way," in *Essays in Islamic Philosophy, Theology, and Mysticism* (Oneonta, N.Y.: State University of New York, 1995), 193.

13. See Sükran Vahide, *Bediüzzaman Said Nursi* (Istanbul: Sozler, 1995); Serif Mardin, *Religion and Social Change in Modern Turkey: The Case of Bediüzzaman Said Nursi* (Albany: State University of New York Press, 1989); Hamid Algar, "Said Nursi and the Risala-i Nur: An Aspect of Islam in Contemporary Turkey," in K. Ahmad and Z. Ishaq Ansary, eds., *Islamic Perspectives* (Leicester: Islamic Foundation, 1979), 313–33.

14. Bediüzzaman Said Nursi, *The Words*, trans. Sükran Vahide (Istanbul: Sözler, 1992), 221.

15. Iqbal, *Reconstruction*, 14, 8–9.

16. Rahman, *Major Themes*, 68.

17. Iqbal, *Reconstruction*, 14. Nasr, when pointing out the same fact, that "Nature is a book which is the macrocosmic counterpart of the Qur'an itself and which must be read and understood before it can be put away," gives us the following example of Aziz al-Nasafi, a fifteenth-century Sufi, who compares nature to the Qur'an in such a way that a genus in nature corresponds to a *sūra*, each species to a verse, and each particular being to a letter. Concerning this book of nature, al-Nasafi writes: "Each day destiny and the passage of time set this book before you, *sūra* for *sūra*, verse for verse, letter for letter, that you may learn the content of these lines and letters. . . ."

See Seyyed Hossein Nasr, *An Introduction to Islamic Cosmological Doctrines*, rev. ed. (London: Thames and Hudson, 1978), 2. See also Nasr, *Man and Nature* (1967; Chicago: Kazi Publications, 1997), and *Religion and the Order of Nature* (New York: Oxford University Press, 1996).

18. See Qur'an 21:22; 27:60–64; also Harvey Austryn Wolfson, *The Philosophy of the Kalām* (Cambridge: Harvard University Press, 1976).

19. Iqbal, *Reconstruction*, 3–4.

20. S. Parvez Manzoor, "Environment and Values: The Islamic Perspective," in *The Touch of Midas: Science, Values and Environment in Islam and the West*, ed. Ziauddin Sardar (Manchester: Manchester University Press, 1984), 154. Muhammad Iqbal also remarks on the differences between two faiths: "The great point in Christianity is the search for an independent content for spiritual life which, according to the insight of its founder, could be elevated, not by the forces of a world external to the soul of man, but by the revelation of a new world within the soul. Islam fully agrees with this insight and supplements it by the further insight that *the illumination of the new world thus revealed is not something foreign to the world of matter but permeates it through and through*"; Iqbal, *Reconstruction*, 9 (italics mine).

21. Hans Jonas, when dealing with some conclusions of Heideggerian existentialism, underlines this point: "That nature does not care, one way or another, is the true abyss. That only man cares, in his finitude facing nothing but death, alone with his contingency and the objective meaninglessness of his projecting meanings, is a truly unprecedented situation. . . . And the product of the indifferent, his being, too, must be indifferent. Then, the facing of his mortality would simply warrant the reaction: Let us eat and drink. For tomorrow we must die. There is no point in caring for what has sanction behind it in any creative intention." Quoted in Vogel, "Does Environmental Ethics Need a Metaphysical Grounding?"

22. Isma'il R. Faruqi also points out this aspect of the Qur'an as "the *raison d'être* or 'ground of being' of man and cosmos," and "that man may do the good works that is the reason and purpose of the creation of man, of all creation." See "On the Raison d'être of The Ummah," *Islamic Studies* 2, no. 2 (1963): 159.

23. David Ray Griffin also emphasizes this point very eloquently when criticizing the ideas that lie at the heart of modernity. He argues that the meaninglessness and absurdity of the universe was a peculiar characteristic of existential philosophy, and asks this crucial question: if the universe—as the leading philosophers of existential thought, such as Martin Heidegger, Jean-Paul Sartre, Albert Camus, and even Franz Kafka, believed—has no sense of importance, and moreover everything in it is absurd, then "How could sensitive human beings make a go of human life in this context?" That is, a universe in which there is "No natural law, no divine purpose, no objective importance, no hierarchy of values . . . inherent in the nature of things, to which we should conform." As a result of this understanding, Griffin concludes, "many people have not made a go of it, becoming alcoholics, drug addicts, war addicts, mental patients, or suicides." See David Ray Griffin, *God and Religion in the Postmodern World: Essays in Postmodern Theology* (Albany: State University of New York Press, 1989), 17.

24. Rahman, *Major Themes*, 7–8.

25. Nursi, *The Words*, 435–36.

26. Nasr, "Islam and the Environmental Crisis," 92. See also William Chittick, "God Surrounds All Things: An Islamic Perspective on the Environment," *The World and I* 1, no. 6, (1986): 671–78.

27. Rahman, *Major Themes*, 46. In fact, this transformative character of the Qur'an exists in other religions as well. Iqbal, while emphasizing this aspect of religion, argues that "the transformation and guidance of man's inner and outer life is the essential aim of religion." To support this point, he quotes Whitehead as saying that religion is "a system of general truths which have the effect of transforming character when they are sincerely held and vividly apprehended." See Iqbal, *Reconstruction*, 2.

28. As we know, "the materialistic as well as the anthropocentric understanding of nature, which regards nature as an unchangeable, indubitable and abundant machine, has been changed for more than two decades. Now, as a result, *a new perception of nature and a new way of looking at nature begin to emerge from the recent discussion of the nature of [the] man-nature relationship*. For example, the fact that the supply of coal and copper, oil and tin, and the other resources on or in the earth are limited has shown the dominant belief in linear and limitless progress to be inaccurate. We have recognized that it is impossible to continue progress with the speed and in the manner we have been pursuing for not more than two centuries. The idea of a sustainable development is a result of this thought, and it is based upon an understanding of the limits of natural resources as well as of human dependency on this world." See my *The Ethical Dimension of Human Attitude[s] Towards Nature* (Ankara: Ministry of Environment, 1997), 95. Also, Garrett Hardin argues that "progress was born in 1795 with the publication of the Marquis de Condercet's *Sketch for a Historical Picture of the Progress of the Human Mind*. It died on Wednesday, March 24, 1970 when the United States Senate, treading closely on the heels of the House, denied any funds for the SST (supersonic transport plane) by a vote of fifty-one to forty-six." Garrett Hardin, *Exploring New Ethics for Survival* (New York: Viking Press, 1971), 141.

29. Rahman, *Major Themes*, 67. Cf. Qur'an 54:49: "Verily We have created all things in proportion and measure"; also 15:21 and 20:50.

30. See *The Holy Qur'an*, trans. Yusuf Ali (Beltsville, Md.: Amana Corp., 1983), 1472–73 nn. 5177–78.

31. Mohammad I. Ansari argues that "development is a value-laden issue and is now being recognized more than ever before" and quotes these words from Denis Goulet: "Development is above all a question of values. It involves human attitudes and preferences, self-defined goals, and criteria for determining what are tolerable costs to be borne in the course of change. These are far more important than better resource allocation, upgraded skills, or the rationalization of administrative procedures"; "Islamic Perspective of Sustainable Development," *American Journal of Islamic Social Sciences* 11, no. 3 (1994): 394–401.

32. As we know, the Qur'an regards water as the source of life and gives great importance to water as an essential and primary element of the ecosystem. With this emphasis it also draws our attention toward water: "And God has created every animal from water: of them there are some that creep on their bellies; some that walk on two legs; and some that walk on four. God creates what He wills: for verily God has power over all things." Qur'an 24:45; see also 25:54.

33. *Musnād*, ii, 22; *Ibn Majā*, "Ṭahāra," 48, no. 425; i, 147 (translation mine).

34. It might reasonably be argued that there are very good reasons for Islam prohibiting wastefulness and prodigality so forcefully. We may put it this way: there are over six billion people living in the world today. Just think of each individual person cutting down a tree or killing an animal just for the fun of it. Six billion trees or animals would perish. Or think of the water they would waste, or the bread or other foodstuffs they would throw away. The serious consequences of those apparently insignificant actions are clear. Moreover, for the most part it is not possible to reclaim the resources we have polluted, destroyed, or annihilated. It is in this light that we may understand how meaningful was the point God's Messenger was emphasizing when he said, "Even if you take the ablutions in a flowing river, do not waste the water," and how important this is for the preservation of the ecological balance.

35. Alija Ali Izzetbegovic, *Islam between East and West* (Ankara, 1994), 226.

36. I consider having meaning in life to be crucial not only for a better attitude toward the environment, but also for the well-being of human life. Goulet emphasizes this point as follows: "high indices of suicide in 'developed' countries have often blinded observers to the [fact that] material sufficiency, or abundance, may be less essential—even for survival—than is the presence of meaning. In order to survive one must want to survive, but how can one want to survive unless life has a meaning? Accordingly, *having a meaningful existence may well be the most basic of human needs*." Denis Goulet, "Development Experts: The One-Eyed Giants," *World Development* 8 (1980): 481–89 (italics mine).

37. The term *muslim* comes from the word *islām,* and the latter is derived from the root s.l.m., which means "to be safe," "to be whole and integral," "not to be disintegrated." The basic idea is that by accepting the law of God and "surrendering" to it, one avoids disintegration. See Fazlur Rahman, "Some Key Ethical Concepts of the Qur'an," *Journal of Religious Ethics* 2 (1983): 183.

38. According to the Qur'an, people can and ought to avoid moral and physical peril by obeying and surrendering to the law of God. The basic idea is that, *peace, safety, and integrity are not possible without having a firm belief in God, trusting in Him and surrendering to Him and His law, and then avoiding all kinds of perils, for His sake*. See Rahman, "Some Key Ethical Concepts."

39. Rahman, *Major Themes*, 23–24.

40. Muhammad Hamidullah, "Religious Symbolism," *Hamdard Islamicus* 2, no. 4 (1978): 7.

41. There are many examples of Muslim Sufis who call other creatures "my brother" and treat them with respect. See, for example, Annemarie Schimmel, *Deciphering the Signs of God: A Phenomenological Approach to Islam* (Edinburgh: Edinburgh University Press, 1994).

42. Al-Ghazali, *The Jewels of the Qur'an*, 57.

43. Reynold A. Nicholson, *Rumi, Poet and Mystic (1207–1273)* (London: George Allen and Unwin, 1950), 119. The above notes belong to Nicholson. This once again underlines our main argument that the Qur'an has a profound role in the making of the Muslim conception of oneself and the natural environment. Rumi's verses refers to the following verses of the Qur'an: 7:104–7; 21:79; 34:10; the wind was subject to Solomon (21:81) and transported his throne from one country to another. God said to Moses "Smite the sea with thy rod" (26:63, whereupon it opened a way for the Israel-

ites, but engulfed Pharaoh and his hosts; 54:1; 21:69). According to the Qur'an (17:46), "there is not a thing in heaven or earth but glorifies Him."

44. Nursi, *Words*, 251. On another occasion he expresses the same point with these words: "The world is a book of the Eternally Besought One. Its letters and words point not to themselves but to the essence, attributes, and Names of another [i.e., God]." Ibid., 221.

45. Nursi, *The Words,* 701–2.

46. Sachiko Murata, *The Tao of Islam: A Sourcebook on Gender Relationships in Islamic Thought* (Albany: State University of New York Press, 1992), 24 (italics mine).

47. Rahman, *Major Themes,* 68.

48. Ibid., 69.

49. Ibid., 68–69.

50. As we know, the camel is a "domesticated animal, which for Arab countries is *par excellence* the Camel. What a wonderful structure has this Ship of the Desert? He can store water in his stomach for days. He can live on dry and thorny desert shrubs. His limb are adapted to his life. . . . And withal, he is so gentle! Who can sing his praises enough?" (*The Holy Qur'an*, trans. Yusuf Ali, 1728 n. 6103).

51. Seyyed Hossein Nasr, "Man and Nature: Beyond Current Alternatives" (paper delivered at the International Seminar on Islamic Philosophy and Science, Kuala Lumpur, Malaysia, 30 May–2 June 1989), 3.

52. Bediüzzaman Said Nursi, *The Supreme Sign*, trans. Hamid Algar (Istanbul: Sözler, 1985), 78. Many Muslim cosmologists studied the outside world in order to extract what we can learn about God from the qualities in the visible universe. Also, many commentators have similar views on interpreting the above-mentioned verses, that is 41:53 and 51:20–21. Murata gives us a good example of this tradition in the Islamic history of thought in Rashid al-Din Mayubi's *Kashf al-asrār*, a commentary on the Qur'an written in 520/1126. See Murato, *The Tao of Islam*, 25–27; and S. Waqar Ahmed Hussaini, *Islamic Environmental Systems Engineering* (London: Macmillan, 1980), 3, 6.

53. Murata, *The Tao of Islam*, 24.

54. A *ḥadīth* of the Prophet says that: "If without good reason anyone kills a sparrow, or a creature lesser than that even, the living creature will put his complaint to God on the Day of Judgement, saying: 'So-and-so killed me for no purpose.' " Nasai, *Sayd*, 34.

55. Qur'an 33:72: "We did indeed offer the Trust to the Heavens and the Earth and the Mountains; but they refused to undertake it, being afraid thereof; but man undertook it; he was indeed unjust and foolish."

56. Qur'an 55:10–12. This translation is taken from Muhammad Asad, *The Message of the Qur'an* (Gibraltar: Dar al Andalus, 1980).

57. Said Nursi makes an interesting interpretation about this point and argues that even minor events the All-Wise Qur'an mentions and considers conceal a universal principal, and he points to a hint of a general law. When interpreting the verse "Nor anything fresh or dry, but is in a record clear," he argues that "this verse states that everything, fresh or dry, is found within it, is that so? Yes, everything is found in it, but everyone cannot see everything in it, for they are found at different levels. Sometimes the seeds, sometimes the nuclei, sometimes the summaries. Sometimes the

principles, sometimes the signs, are found either explicitly, or implicitly, or allusively, or vaguely, or as a reminder" (Nursi, *The Words*, 260).

58. Ibid., 261.

59. Reynold A. Nicholson, in his book *The Mystics of Islam*, narrates for us an interesting story that reflects Muslims' appreciation of animals and their intrinsic values: "Bayazid [the ninth-century Muslim mystic] purchased some cardamom seed at Hamadan, and before departing put into his gabardine a small quantity which was left over. On reaching Bistam and recollecting what he had done, he took out the seed and found out that it contained a number of ants. Saying, 'I have carried the poor creatures away from their home,' he immediately set off and journeyed back to Hamadan—a distance of several hundred miles" (108–9).

60. Lynn White, Jr., "The Historical Roots of Our Ecologic Crisis," *Science* 155 (1967): 1203–7.

61. It is not within the scope of this paper to indulge in a discussion of White's argument. However, it should be pointed out that his article resulted in a fierce debate and produced very fruitful literature on the subject. It can be said that, with this critique, White contributed greatly to a reevaluation by Christians of their tradition, eliciting new interpretations. See, for example, Sydney E. Ahlstrom, "Reflections on Religion, Nature, and the Exploitative Mentality," in *Growth in America* (Westport, Ct.: Greenwood Press, 1976); Robin Attfield, "Christian Attitudes to Nature," *Journal of the History of Ideas* 44, no. 3, (1983): 369–86; John B. Bennett, "On Responding to Lynn White: Ecology and Christianity," *Ohio Journal of Religious Studies* 5 (1977): 71–77; Thomas Berry, "The Earth Community: We Must Be Clear about What Happens When We Destroy the Living Forms of This Planet," *Christian Social Action* 1 (1988): 11–13; J. Baird Callicott, "Genesis and John Muir," in *Covenant for a New Creation* (Maryknoll, N.Y.: Orbis Books, 1991); John B. Cobb, Jr., "Biblical Responsibility for the Ecological Crisis [L. White, Jr., on Gen. 1]," *Second Opinion* 18 (1992): 11–21.

62. Keith Thomas, *Man and the Natural World: Changing Attitudes in England,1500–1899* (London: Allen Lane, 1983), 21.

63. See also 14:32; 16:12–14; 22:65; 29:61; 31:29; 35:13; 39:5; 43:12–14; 45:12–13.

64. Nasr also underlines that the modernist and fundamentalist interpretation of the Qur'anic concept *taskhir* as meaning the total subjugation of nature is very different from the traditional Islamic perspective. See Nasr, "Man and Nature: Beyond Current Alternatives," 2.

65. Mawil Y. Izzi Dien (Samarrai), "Islamic Environmental Ethics, Law, and Society," in *Ethics of Environment and Development. Global Challenge, International Response*, ed. J. Ronald Engel and Joan Gibb Engel (London: Belhaver Press, 1990), 189.

66. Nasr, *Introduction to Islamic Cosmological Doctrines*, 148 n. 43. Nasr also provides valuable information about al-Biruni: "Al-Biruni represents the point of view of the scholar and compiler as well as that of the mathematician and astronomer. As a very competent scientist, historian, and general observer and commentator on the civilizations of mankind, *he approaches the study of Nature as a devout Muslim*

who sees the world as the handiwork of God and considers the observation and study of Nature as a religious duty" (275–76, italics added).

67. Quoted in Izzi Dien, "Islamic Environmental Ethics, Law, and Society," 190.

68. Nursi, *The Words*, 86–87. See also Bediüzzaman Said Nursi, *The Flashes Collection*, trans. Sükran Vahide (Istanbul: Sözler, 1995), 446.

69. *The Holy Qur'an*, trans. Yusuf Ali, 1188 n. 4029.

70. Rahman, *Major Themes*, 79. Qur'an 30:41: "Mischief [corruption] has appeared on land and sea because of (the meed) that the hands of men have earned," and the very idea of corruption is repeated in the Qur'an on many occasions.

The Universe Alive: Nature in the *Masnavī* of Jalal al-Din Rumi

L. CLARKE

Jalal al-Din Rumi, the poet and mystic of the title, was born in Balkh, in ancient Bactria (now Afghanistan), at the beginning of the thirteenth century. The greater part of his life, however, was spent in Anatolia, chiefly in the town of Konya, where he died in 1273. Thus he lived in the midst of that epoch from the twelfth through the fourteenth centuries which, not only in Islam but also in Christendom and among the Jewish peoples, saw an unparalleled efflorescence of mystical thought.[1]

Rumi inspired the foundation of the Mevleviyya order of Sufis, famous in the West as the "Whirling Dervishes." But more important, he composed a very large quantity of mystical poetry. His lyrics are collected under the name *Dīvān-i Shams,* or "The Poetical Works of Shams," after a mysterious dervish who, before he suddenly disappeared without a trace, was Rumi's first saintly "mystical beloved." The *Dīvān-i Shams* is an outpouring of the ecstasy of mystical experience. Rumi's theosophy, on the other hand, is expounded in the twenty-six thousand–line *Masnavī* (literally, "poem in rhymed couplets"). The *Masnavī* is a didactic work filled with colorful parables and allegory, and most of this essay depends upon it.

The essay begins by reconstructing Rumi's vision of nature. This part of my discussion is divided into three sections: first, the universe in general; second, the animal world; and third, the workings of Eros (*'ishq*). My liberal use of quotations here and throughout the discussion is intended to illustrate not only the substance but also the tenor of Rumi's teaching. In the fourth section I go on to describe the metaphysical context of these views and to locate Rumi's vision of nature at a particular juncture—between the antimaterialist, Idealist impulses of mysticism and Gnosticism, on the one hand, and the positive, natural realism of the "orthodox" Islam of the revelation, on the other. Finally, I attempt to evaluate Rumi's ecological message. What can we learn from this master of theosophic Sufism for the purposes of our modern thinking about the environment? I find that, while the poet's primary purpose is, without doubt, to make a statement about God and Man and not about nature, he does, nevertheless, suggest an intuitive, ecstatic mode of *experiencing* nature that may have something to teach us. This essay is also intended as a contribution to debate about the ecological potentials of monotheism and mysticism. Monotheism, since it implies anthropocentrism, has been accused of desacralizing nature, while mysticism, since it appears to be world denying, has sometimes been seen as rejecting the value of a natural world thought to be illusory. The *Masnavī*, I think, challenges both these propositions.

Reconstructing Rumi's Vision of Nature

The Universe

We are able to speak of Rumi's "ecology" because his mystical worldview is, above all, holistic. His theosophy embraces, as systematically as mystical inspiration allows, the whole universe; there is no more appropriate translation of the title of his poem *Masnavī-ye ma'navī* than "The Meaning of All Things." This includes the totality of interrelations of organisms—although it should be understood that, as with the Greeks and Romans, nature for Rumi implies everything around us, not just organic, natural, or tangible things. The universe, moreover, when seen as the mystic possessed of insight sees it—as a totality (*kull*) rather than in this or that part (*juz'*)[2]—is ordered, harmonious, purposive, and good. This view is partly an inheritance from the Greeks, driven as they were by the search for intelligibility and order in the cosmos. The order the Greeks imagined, however, was mechanistic, to the point of being mathematically calculable, whereas the order of Rumi's cosmos, since it directly depends on the Grace and Mercy of a Living God, is moral and beyond calculation.

Rumi's mystical worldview is shaped by the belief, on which he so often insists—even commenting at one point that it is this with which "the whole of the Qur'an is concerned" (*Masnavī* 3.2520)—that there are no secondary causes (pl. *asbāb*). Secondary causes are an illusion. This view derives from Islamic occasionalism—a metaphysics expounded by the orthodox, Asharite Islamic theology to which Rumi was attached, but turned by him to mystical purposes. Thus nature is not subject to any necessary mechanical law. Rather, every thing is created anew and sustained by God at every moment; "all the atoms of earth and heaven are God's army" (4.783), and "in all the earth and heavens not an atom moves a wing, not a straw turns, / Save by His eternal and effectual command . . ." (3.1902–3). Rumi recites in book one of the *Masnavī*:

> What is the meaning of this Arabic word "cause"? Say rather, "cord." This cord came into the well of this world by Divine artifice.
> The revolution of the waterwheel causes the cord to move, but not to see the mover of the waterwheel is an error.
> Beware imagining that these cords are moved by the giddy wheel of heaven. . . . (1.847–49)

That is to say, one should not imagine anything like a set of "laws of nature" that functions by itself. God may, if and when He chooses, make the "waterwheel" (or "the wheel of heaven," that is causation) turn in a certain way; but it is nevertheless still He and He alone who turns the wheel that moves the rope (or the "cause," the Arabic word *sabab* having both meanings). If nature is constant, it is only because God, by His Mercy, lets it be so; the course of nature could equally be inverted:

> Know that the subtlety of water is not derived from the water; it is only the gift of the Bounteous Originator.
> If He makes air and fire low in place, and if He lets the thorn surpass the rose,
> He is the Ruler—God does as He wills. . . . (2.1617–19)

The universe is, moreover, *alive*. This recalls Plato's idea, expounded in the *Timaeus*, of the universe as a living being regulated by the World Soul. Rumi's occasionalism, however, gives rise to significant differences between himself and Plato. For while the *Timaeus* deems the world a "visible living being"[3] merely by analogy between its functioning and the functioning of organisms, the *Masnavī* tells us that the world is alive because it is given life directly by God, He being the real and direct cause of every thing. Moreover, while according to Plato the world as a "living being" is also "single,"[4] with one part set in motion by another, for Rumi, *each separate part* is animated by God's continual and separate creative acts.

Rumi's verses on the living universe can be appreciated only if we keep in mind that all this is for him literal truth. "Earth and water and fire are His slaves," says the *Masnavī*, "with you and me they are dead, but with God they are alive" (1.838). This is not to say that their "aliveness" is metaphoric—that most grave error of interpretation committed by the rationalist Mu'tazilites.[5] It is not merely that they are subordinate to God to a degree best expressed through metaphor. Rather they are alive actually, in as real a sense as any reality of this contingent world. But this evident truth is hidden from those without mystical insight, and the poet often reproaches the philosopher and the skeptic who depend upon intellect rather than heart, and thus fail to see. For if one is not misled by the senses and the illusion of secondary causes, that nature is alive, and even percipient, will not seem more amazing than that humans should be so, since we also are alive only through God's intervention at each moment.

Because God arranges it so, nature is also articulate. Again, the literal truth of this reality is not to be doubted, even though it is veiled from the skeptic:

> The speech of water, the speech of earth, and the speech of mud are apprehended by the sense of them that have hearts [that is the mystics].
> The philosopher who disbelieves in the moaning pillar[6] is a stranger to the sense of the saints;
> He says that melancholia brings many phantasies into people's minds.
> Nay, but the reflexion of his wickedness and infidelity cast this idle fancy of skepticism upon him! (1.3279–82)

The speech of nature is continual and multidirectional; Rumi describes it as "an uproar" (*ghulghulī*). Some of these conversations are carried on between the natural things themselves, suggesting that the processes of nature, far from being mechanical, are intelligent, intimate, and affective:

> You yourself [the reader] know [instinctively] what words the sun, in the sign of Aries, speaks to the plants and the date palms;[7]
>
> You yourself, too, know what the limpid water is saying to the sweet herbs and the sapling. (6.1068–69)

But most such conversation, or the ultimate conversation, is speech between nature and God:

> The doing of God toward all the particles of the world is like spells breathed by enchanters.
>
> The Divine attraction holds a hundred discourses with the effects and the secondary causes, without uttering a word or moving a lip.
>
> Not that the production of effects by the Divine decree is not actual; but His production of effects thereby is inconceivable to reason. (6.1070–72)

The import of the "hundred discourses" of God with nature becomes clear when we remember the place in Islam of the Word of God as revelation. Thus, we might think, each thing receives revelation in its own mode; to each thing is delivered its own Truth. And indeed, nature does have its own and particular wisdom. To one gifted with sense, as was Solomon, nature does speak and communicates those truths. Rumi tells how Solomon used to come each morning into the Furthest Place in Jerusalem (*al-Aqsa*, here meaning Solomon's Temple) and question the herbs growing there:

> He saw that a new plant had grown there; then he would say, "Tell your name and use—
>
> What medicine are you? What are you? What is your name?
>
> To whom are you hateful and to whom are you useful?"
>
> Then every plant would tell its effect and name, saying, "I am life to that one, and death to this one.
>
> I am poison to this one, and sugar to that one: this is my name inscribed on the Tablet by the Pen of the divine Decree."

And this, according to the *Masnavī*, led to Solomon teaching the physicians, who then compiled their pharmacopoeia (4.1287ff.). Nature yields its wisdom to those who understand and care to enquire; and this wisdom may perchance be heard by those whose focus is on practical use.

There are, however, morally instructive differences between nature and humankind. For instance, unlike Man, nature constantly uses its speech to praise God. "All particles of phenomenal being," declares the *Masnavī*, "whether in movement or at rest, are speakers, and declare: 'Verily, to Him we are returning' / The praises and glorifications of the hidden particles have filled heaven with an uproar" (3.465–66). Nature, in fact, is in close conversation with the Divine: "Stone and earth and mountain have their invisible recourse to Him" (6.2420). Although humankind may doubt and is unaware of it, everything on earth glorifies God:

> Inasmuch as Thou has made everything a glorifier of Thee—both the discerning and undiscerning entity—
> Each glorifies Thee in a different fashion, and that one is unaware of the state of this one.
> Man disbelieves in the glorification uttered by inanimate things, but those inanimate things are masters in performing worship. (3.1495–97)

The Qur'anic inspiration for this passage, and likely for the idea of an articulate world in general, is found in the chapter "Ascension at Night": "The seven heavens and the earth and their inhabitants," says the Qur'an, "praise Him. There is nothing that does not praise Him—but you do not understand their praise" (17:44).

Nature is exemplary above all because it submits wholly to the Divine Will. So also should we give up our own will, in order to become like fire, "standing ready to do God's behest, writhing continually day and night, like a lover" (1.839). But Man repeatedly fails to reach the standard of the natural world (even though his potential is far greater). Thus Rumi likens the "universals" (*kulliyāt*) to a ball that prostrates itself before God's polo mallet, and then he poses the question: "How should you, O heart, you who are but one of these hundred thousand particulars, not [also] be in restless movement at His decree?" (6.926–27).[8] The consciousness of the elements, unlike human consciousness, is never diverted from their Lord.

The elements, Rumi says, are unacquainted with us, but acquainted with God, while we are aware of things other than God, but heedless of God and the many prophets He has sent us (2.2371). In fact, it was because the elements did not wish to disturb this perfect relationship that they were reluctant to accept the trust that humankind accepted: "They said, 'We are averse to this life—that one should be living in relation to created beings and dead in relation to God'" (2.2373). On the other hand, the elements and heavenly bodies will not be rewarded by God for this obedience, since it does not involve choice:

> . . . This celestial sphere revolves involuntarily
> Hence its revolution has neither reward nor punishment, for free-will is (accounted) a merit at the time of Reckoning.
> All created beings indeed are glorifiers of God, but that compulsory glorification is not wage-earning. (3.3287–89)

Nature does, nevertheless, have a moral sense. Its activity in this world is not automatic; it is purposive and meaningful. In order for nature to have this quality, it must, of course, be able to relate to the moral drama here on earth. And to relate, it must be percipient; it must literally see and hear. And so it does, by the command of God—in exactly the same way and no less so than we do. From the mountains to the wind to the stones, all nature declares: "We have hearing and sight, and are happy" (3.1019). Only an unenlightened mind that imagined the eye to be the necessary organ of sight would think nature to be unseeing. The eye is not, in fact, the organ of sight at all. Rather, it is God alone who enables sight, as the poet explains:

> Deem not the fat [the white of the eye] to be the cause of sight, O son; otherwise none would see [visible] forms in dream. . . .
> The genie and the demon see the like, and there is no fat in the sight-organ of either.
> In fact, there was [originally] no relationship between light and the fat [of the eye]: the loving Creator gave them relationship (4.2403ff.).[9]

Thus nature, through the direct intervention of God, sees and witnesses and is a moral actor. Nature's moral action is evident most strikingly in its interventions in favor of the prophets. "If I relate the help," says Rumi, "given rationally [*'āqilāna*, that is with conscious intent and understanding] to the prophets by the inanimate things of the world, the *Masnavī* will become of such extent that if forty camels carry it, they will be unable to bear the full load" (4.789–90). The poet reproaches those who fail to appreciate this truth and thus deny nature's real moral sense as it works in concert with God:

> If God did not give the wind vision without eye, how did it make a distinction among the people of 'Ad?[10]
> How did it know the true believer from the unbeliever? . . .

> If the fire of Nimrod has no eye, how can it be explained that it takes care to show respect to Abraham?
> If the Nile had not possessed that light and sight, how should it have picked out the Egyptians from the Israelites? (4.2411–15)[11]

Nature also observes and remembers the deeds of humankind, in order to act, as it is said in the Qur'an itself, as witness on the Day of Judgment:

> At the Resurrection, how should this earth give testimonies concerning good and evil without having seen?
> For [it is said in the Qur'an] that "she [that is, the earth] will relate her experiences and informations" (94:1): the earth will reveal her secrets to us (4.2421–22)

In a charming etiology, Rumi attributes his ritual prostrations in prayer to a desire to make the earth his witness:

> For that reason I am laying my head [humbly] on the earth, so that she [the earth] may be my witness on the Day of Judgment.
> On the Day of Judgment, when "she shall be made to quake mightily" (98:1) this earth will bear witness to all that passed [in and from us];
> For "she will plainly declare what she knows" (99:4): earth and rocks will begin to speak.
> The philosopher, in his [vain] thought and opinion, becomes disbelieving; let him go and dash his head against this wall! (1.3275ff.)

Here we see that the natural world is not only obedient and good in itself, but also capable of distinguishing—and thus, in a measure, judging—the qualities of our acts.

The Animal World

Animals are a natural target of symbolic discourse about human behavior because they are animate and in close contact with us, which prompts us to attribute to them personalities as a way of speaking about ourselves—while at the same time, since we approach them as species rather than individuals, we are able to fasten to them certain characteristics, which they then exemplify. Rumi does use animals and animal fables in this way as an ordinary didactic device. His stories are populated by timorous, foolish mice, cunning foxes, brave lions, wise elephants—and, most famously, the stubborn, gluttonous donkey, representing the appetitive soul. On the level of hidden reality, however, animals in the *Masnavī* are more than simply ciphers used by the poet to construct allegories. They have their own metaphysical truth *qua* animals, from which the aspiring mystic may learn. They are, for instance, content. Their trust and reliance on God is implicit:

> In this world thousands of animals are living happily, without anxiety.
> The dove on the tree is uttering thanks to God, though her food is not yet ready.
> The nightingale is singing glory to God, saying, "I rely on Thee for my daily bread, O Thou who answerest prayer."
> . . . .
> You may take every animal from the gnat to the elephant: they all have become God's dependents . . .
> [While] these griefs within our breasts arise from the vapor and dust of our existence and vain desire. (1.2291–96)[12]

Most important, the natural, God-given instinct of animals is not obscured, as is ours, by intellect and false imaginings:

> Sheep know the smell of the harmful wolf and creep away in every direction.
> The brain of animals knows the smell of the lion and bids farewell to grazing.
> You have smelled the wrath of God. Turn back! Consort with prayer and dread! (2.387–89)

Instead, the animals follow, intuitively and without confusion, the basic instinct and motive force of the universe—Love (though the unenlightened may deny that this is so):

> Wolf and bear and lion know what love is: he that is blind to love is inferior to a dog!
> If the dog had not a vein of love, how should the dog of the Cave have sought to win the heart of the Seven Sleepers?[13]
> . . . .
> You have not smelt the heart in your own kind: how should you smell the heart in wolf and sheep? (5.2008–11)[14]

Because animals in myth often take on the role of mediator between human and divine, their mysterious "speech" is thought to contain divine wisdom. This is the impulse behind the story in Jewish and Islamic lore of King Solomon, who understood the speech of the birds and beasts. Rumi relates the tale of a man who demanded of Moses that he teach him the language of the birds and beasts "that perchance I may get a lesson concerning my religion" (3.3267). The man reasonably proposed: "Since the languages of the sons of Adam are entirely for the sake of acquiring water and bread and renown / It may be that the animals have a different care, namely that of taking thought for the hour of passing away from this world" (3.3268–69).

Moses taught him what he asked, and the speech of the animals did reveal to him the future. But this knowledge, which is suited only to the enlightened saints, brought him nothing but grief, as what he finally heard was the animals' conversation about his own imminent death. In this story, nature is invested with an elemental occult power. Nature, or aspects of it, has become taboo, has become sacred. And the sacred yields its power only to those who have the wisdom and insight to properly deal with it—while those who overstep the bounds (even, it is implied here, if their intentions are good) are destroyed.

The Workings of Eros

For Rumi, as for Plato and Aristotle, the activity of all mortal things stems from Eros (*'ishq*). Eros is life; Eros is at once the Mover and the Cause:

> Know that the wheeling heavens are turned by waves of Love: were it not for Love, the world would be frozen, inanimate.
>
> How would an inorganic thing disappear by changing into a plant? How would vegetative things sacrifice themselves to become endowed with spirit?
>
> . . . .
>
> Each one of them would be as stiff and immovable as ice; how should they be seeking and flying like locusts? (5.3854–56)[15]

The dynamic power of Eros, or Love, is manifested in a web of mutual attraction. The skies, for example, yearn for the earth and the earth for the skies; "unless these two sweethearts are tasting delight from one another," says the poet, "then why are they creeping together, like mates?" (3.4412). Humankind is equally caught in this system of mutual attraction, not only in relation to its own fellows, but to all that it needs and desires:

> No sound of clapping comes forth from one hand of thine without the other hand.
>
> The thirsty man is moaning: "O delicious water!" The water moans too, saying, "Where is the water-drinker?"
>
> The thirst in our souls is the attraction exerted by the Water: we are Its and It is ours.
>
> The Wisdom of God in destiny and in decree made us lovers of one another.
>
> Because of that fore-ordainment, all the particles of the world are paired as mates and each is in love with its own mate.
>
> And every particle of the universe is desiring its mate, just like amber and the blade of straw. (3.4397–402)

Mutual attraction animates the whole universe as the meeting of causes continually produces effects—for instance, sound, or nourishment through drinking. The attraction of Eros also results, of course, in the effect of generation; God, says Rumi, "implants the desire of every part for another part [so that] from the union of both an act of generation results" (3.4416). The ultimate end of generation, in turn, is to perpetuate the great cycle of life; as Aristotle says, since "being is better than nonbeing, and living than nonliving" and an organism cannot be eternal in itself, it is "eternal in the way that is possible for it,"[16] that is, through attempting to perpetuate its kind. Thus, the process of the universe animated by Love is that of a continually recurring cycle. And Man is an integral part of this great cycle of life, of the "caravan of spirits incessantly arriving from heaven, that they may traffic on the earth and go back again. . . ." (3.4191):

> The grace of God bestows a throat on the earth, to the end that it may drink water and make a hundred herbs to grow.
>
> Again, He bestows on the animals a throat and a lip, in order that they may eat the earth's herbage and desire.
>
> When the animal has eaten its herbage, it becomes fat: the animal becomes a mouthful for Man and disappears.
>
> In turn it becomes earth and becomes a devourer of Man when the spirit and the sight are separated from him.

> I beheld the atoms (of created existence) with their mouths all open: if I should tell of their food, the tale would become long.
>
> . . . .
>
> Know that all the world is eating and eaten. . . . (3.22–30)

But within this cycle, there is a linear, upward-moving process in which material is made to ascend toward spirit. Through this process, all being, including natural things, proceeds heavenward. In Platonic terms, we might say that such motion results from the defects of matter as it seeks to fulfill itself by moving closer to perfection, only the Perfect being fully at rest—the principle of plenitude. The *Masnavī*, however, vigorously communicates a sense that the movement of natural things is driven by emotion—that it is even, in some way, voluntary. All nature, Rumi says, is impelled upward by its own aspiration for a higher state of being, which it achieves by gladly—even rapturously—sacrificing its life so as to join with that which stands above it. Thus, for every "mineral that aspires toward the vegetable"—that is, the vegetative state—"life grows from the tree of its fortune / Every plant that turns its face toward the [animal] spirit drinks . . . from the Fountain of Life" (6.126–27). "Every mote," says the *Masnavī*, "is in love with that Perfection and hastening upward like a sapling / Their haste is saying implicitly "Glory to God!" They are purifying the body for the sake of the spirit" (5.3858–59). Nature's strenuous, purposeful ascent is exemplary for humankind. Man must try, just as nature eagerly does, to "die" to himself and then to welcome Death itself in order to attain to a higher state of being: "You have seen this life," says the *Masnavī*, "to be implicit in previous deaths; how, then, are you so attached to the life of the body?" (5.807).

Rumi's scheme at the same time integrates humankind into nature. Constituted as he is from the natural world, Man continues to be unconsciously tied to it even as he turns away to reach toward formlessness and spirit. The craving of the animal soul for animal things—for stinking dung and "fodder"—is repeatedly condemned by the *Masnavī*. But the longing for vegetable origins is portrayed in a most positive way—apparently because it is not directed, avariciously, at any particular object of desire, but represents the stirrings of a wholly natural affinity:

> First he came into the clime of inorganic things, and from the state of inorganic things he passed into the vegetable state.

> Many years he lived in the vegetable state and did not remember the inorganic state because of the opposition between them.
>
> And when he passed from the vegetable into the animal state, the vegetable state was remembered by him not at all,
>
> Save only the inclination that he has toward that state, especially in the season of spring and sweet herbs—
>
> Like the inclination of babes toward their mothers: the babe does not know the secret of its desire for being suckled. (4.3637ff.)

This instinctive affinity of the human to the green world is, in fact, parallel to that of the soul for its original sustenance: "The desire of the body for green herbs and running water is because of its origin from those . . . / The desire of the soul is for wisdom and the sciences; the desire of the body is for orchards and vines" (3.4436–38).

The enlightened mystic, however, *consciously* remembers his secret origins in nature and understands their significance. This insight allows him to accept his own death as the glad culmination of plenitude and so to contemplate his destiny after:

> I died to the organic state and became endowed with growth, and [then] I died to [vegetable] growth and attained to the animal.
>
> I died from animality and became Adam [man]: why, then should I fear? When Have I become less for dying?
>
> At the next remove I shall die to man, that I may soar and lift my head above the angels;
>
> And I must escape even from [that state of] the angel: "everything is perishing except His Face" (Qur'an 55:26).
>
> Once more shall I be sacrificed and die to the angel;
>
> I shall become that which enters not into the imagination.
>
> Then I shall become non-existence; non-existence saith to me, (in tones loud) as an organ: "Verily, unto Him shall we return." (Qur'an 2:156) (3.3901–6)[17]

Like Sufism in general, the *Masnavī* has antimaterialist overtones. This antimaterialism is centered on the body. The lesson most repeated by Rumi, through a variety of figures and allegories, is that the aspirant must begin by conquering the fleshly appetites of the lower, animal soul (*nafs*) that fix it to the material world. We are, says Rumi, trapped in a "disgraceful body" (5.2279; *nang-i tan*, recalling Plotinus's "shame at being in a body" famously reported by Porphyry). Inhabiting the body is like nothing so much as being trapped in a cage with loathsome companions;[18] our ambition should be to escape this trap to become instead "simple and all one substance . . . knotless and pure like water" (1.686–87). The death of the body is "a welcome gift to the adepts of the mystery: what damage is done by the scissors to pure gold?" (4.1681). One should determinedly demolish the house of the body in order to discover the spiritual treasure beneath it; if it simply falls into ruin itself, that is, if natural death intervenes without ascetic exercise, "the treasure will not be yours, since the spirit receives that Divine gift as wages for destroying the house" (4.2450–54).

Rumi derides the material world somewhat less. Still, it is described as a "dark and narrow pit," while we within it are embryos, gladly drinking blood and disbelieving in the real world outside (3.53–68).[19] The mystics know that this world, while it might seem spacious to others, is uncomfortably cramped, narrow, and hot, like a bathhouse; Spirit needs a wider space to soar (3.3535 ff.). The world is a "rotten walnut," the walnut symbolizing a worthless plaything (6.3471); it is a phantom (3.314 ff.; 4.1367–69); it is a deceitful ghoul (3.216–226). The world is a loathsome old woman who imprisons the falcon of the soul (4.2628 ff.); it is an old witch with a stinking vulva who manages to enthrall the young prince, the Spirit of Man (4.3085 ff.).

Nevertheless, it is very clear from the *Masnavī* that it is not nature *qua* nature that is at fault. The problem is not nature, but our incorrect relations with it. For the enlightened soul who experiences the whole of nature as it really is rather than grasping at this or that part, it is a foretaste, replete with blessing, of Paradise to come. In fact, God has diverted trickles of the rivers of that Garden into this world, which, though defiled here by "the poison of mortality and indigestion," can lead us toward their paradisial source:

> God has given milk and nourishment for babes: He has made the breast of every wife a fountain.
>
> He has given wine to drive away grief and care: He has made of the grape a fountain to inspire courage.
>
> He has given honey as a remedy for the sick body: He has given the inward part of the bee a fountain of honey.
>
> He gave water universally to high and low for cleanliness and for drinking.
>
> The object is that you should follow the track of these derivatives towards the origins; but you are content with this offshoot. . . . (1.1630–38)

Thus, consistent with the emanationist worldview of Neoplatonic Sufism, the world is seen as an effulgence, an overflow of Reality. And while the overflow as the poet describes it is not the main stream, it is fulsome and delightful in its own way. The bountiful earth, Rumi says, contains "a hundred thousand impressions of the Unseen World . . . waiting graciously and kindly to spring forth from non-existence" (5.4214).[20] "The four elements of this world obtain a hundred supplies from a City beyond space," and "the water and seeds" we find in our cage have appeared "from that Garden and Expanse" (3.3971–72). The whole world is the form of Universal Reason, and if one is in harmony with that Reason, it will show itself to be Paradise, filled with water and greenery and constantly revealing new forms and beauties (4.3259–70). To him who is able to perceive nature as a manifestation of the Unseen, it is ever fresh, always changing, dynamic, "moving swiftly" so that it "appears anew and anew . . . like a fleeting picture" (4.2382):

> One by one, the atoms of the universe momently open their doors to him, like tents, in a hundred diverse ways.
>
> The door becomes now the window, now the sunbeams; the earth becomes now the wheat, now the bushel.
>
> In men's eyes the heavens are very old and threadbare; in the eye [of such a one] there is a new creation at every moment. (6.4641–43)[21]

Even the human body, when properly perceived and employed, is a positive part of the universe and divine plan. To begin, the body is from a practical point of view a necessary instrument for the working out of salvation. The purpose God has in mind for history, that being the manifestation of faith and unfaith, can be carried out only by marriage of the body and spirit. Neither can function without the other, and even a revered saint such as Bayazid is undeniably both spirit *and* body (5.3419–28). The bodily appetites, for example, exist as a test of temperance, for "there can be no restraint when you have no desire; when there is no adversary, what need for your strength?" (5.576). But more than this, the body when properly understood will be seen to be intimately linked to the Divine, just as the spirit is. The body is the microcosm, created in the image of God; it is, according to the *Masnavī*, an "astrolabe" which, when read by the saint, points to the meanings in the heavens (6.3138–43). Body and spirit have a close connection with and action on each other: "Though the spirit cannot be seen [while the body is tangible and can be seen], body is not veiled from soul, nor soul from body" (1.8). Thus, repairing the spirit also repairs and transfigures the body:

> The spiritual way ruins the body and, after having ruined it, restores it to prosperity:
> Ruined the house for the sake of golden treasure [buried within it], and with that same treasure builds it better [than before];
> Cut off the water and cleansed the river-bed, then caused drinking-water to flow in the river-bed;
> Cleft the skin and drew out the iron point [of the arrow or spear]—then fresh skin grew over it [the wound]. (1.306–9)

The proximity of body to spirit is most evident in the saints. Their bodies are literally luminous with divine light; they are made of a special material to contain that light, which would blind if one were to look directly upon it.[22] Since the spirit of the saint "fares to the Kaba at every moment," since "in a single moment, the caravan is going from Heaven and coming here," his body "assumes the nature of the heart"—that is it is "transmuted" (n. *tabdīl*) so that time and place are no longer material to it (4.521 ff.).

The key to achieving such productive, transformative harmony with nature, body, and world is holistic understanding—a vision of what Rumi calls the Whole (*kull*) or Unity (*tawḥīd*). Nature should be understood as a system and process, with an overall meaning and end in which all parts have their place, without exception—whether they might be considered from a more limited point of view beneficial or deleterious, good or evil. The vision desired is, in a word, *ecological*—an ecology that includes not only biology and physics, but also metaphysics.

The Metaphysical Context of Rumi's Vision of Nature

The metaphysical process of the universe according to Rumi is similar to that described by Heraklitus and perhaps Anaximander before him. For both Milesians and for Rumi, nature is a product of the opposing forces of strife and harmony, its matter endlessly changing; just as Heraklitus says that "the sun is new each day," for Rumi, nature is constantly fresh and new. The universe, Heraklitus says, is always igniting and extinguishing, death turning over into life and life into death. Just so, Rumi says:

> If [a drop of water] enters into non-existence or a hundred non-existences, it will return in headlong haste when You call it.
>
> Hundreds of thousands of opposites are killing their opposites: Thy decree is calling them forth again [from non-existence].
>
> There is caravan on caravan, O Lord, [speeding] continually from non-existence toward existence.
>
> . . . .
>
> In autumn the myriads of boughs and leaves go in rout into the sea of Death,
>
> [While] in the garden the crow clothed in black like a mourner makes lament over the [withered] greenery.
>
> Again from the Lord of the land comes the edict [saying] to Non-existence, "Give back what you have devoured!
>
> Give up, O black Death, what you have devoured of plants and healing herbs and leaves and grass!" (1.1887–95)

Heraklitus considers day and night, winter and summer, war and peace, satiety and hunger to be all different aspects of the same One, out of which all things come. And this is in fact the same dialectic described by Rumi, who names in various places in the *Masnavī* the very same sets of opposites. The waves of the sea of this phenomenal world, he says, continually "dash one against the other," the collision being due to the "mingling of the spirits in peace and war" as they are confined to bodies:

> The waves of peace dash against each other and root up hatreds from [men's] breasts.
>
> In other form do the waves of war turn [men's] loves upside down.
>
> Love is drawing the bitter ones to the sweet, because the foundation of [all] loves is righteousness.
>
> Wrath is carrying away the sweet one to bitterness: how should the bitter sort be suited to the sweet?
>
> The bitter and the sweet are not visible to this [ocular] sight, [but] they can be seen through the window of the latter end. (1.2576–83)

There is, however, a crucial difference between the Heraklitian dialectic and Rumi's worldview. Heraklitus's scheme is cyclical; "beginning and end are common." Thus, his universe exists in a state of "dynamic permanence."[23] But Rumi's universe moves, on balance, forward toward the Good. According to Rumi and other Sufi theosophists, the world came into being as the manifestation of God's Attributes; and this included Attributes both at the pole of Mercy and at the pole of Wrath, so that He might be fully manifested. Existence is sustained by tension between the two: "By means of these two wings the world is [kept up like a bird] in the air . . . to the end that it may be [always] trembling like a leaf in the north-wind and simoom of resurrection and death" (6.1853–54). Mercy and Good, however, are necessarily predominant. For, as God is reported to have said[24] and as is so often repeated and illustrated in the *Masnavī*, "My Mercy preceded my Wrath."

> Although the filthy commit foulnesses, (yet) the (pure) waters are intent on purification.
>
> Though the snakes are scattering venom . . .
>
> (Yet) in mountain and hive and tree the bees are depositing a sugar-store of honey.
>
> However much the venoms show venomousness, the antidotes quickly root them out. (6.32–35)

The true mystic, who sees through to the process of the Whole and is at the same time confident of and trustful in God's Infinite Mercy, shall be like the Sufi who fell into ecstasy at seeing the empty food wallet (3.3013 ff.); evil and penury can only remind him of the good and bounty that is sure to follow. For the work of God in the sensible world is nothing but "the transmutation of essences," a "continual alchemy" in which countless states of existence are incessantly exchanged for better (5.780 ff.). Thus, while Rumi's worldview is certainly closer to Idealism than Materialism, here is an Idealism that does not lament the state of the world or reject matter, but carries them instead entirely upward.

As for anthropocentrism, it is certainly true that in the Islamic tradition, including Sufism, the universe is created for and around *Anthropos*. The natural world functions as the setting for human salvation-history. Nature points to God's existence and displays His provident Mercy;[25] but in the end, when it has served its purpose, it shall be completely overturned.[26] Added to this, Sufi cosmology is constructed around the personalities of those exemplary human beings, the prophets and saints, in order to place them as exalted intermediaries between this world and the Divine. The whole world, it is said by Rumi and other Sufi theosophers, is a display of the Attributes of God through the Logos-like figure of the chief saint, the Perfect Man. Any value of nature and natural things, it would seem, must derive from Humanity.

We have already seen how the impact of anthropocentrism is blunted in the *Masnavī* by the suggestion that the things of nature are also alive, that they have their own special relation to God, and that they teach humankind by their example. But how to reconcile living nature with the imperative that Man, in order to free his soul, must ultimately leave the world behind? Is nature, with the Soul it contains, to be abandoned while Man is saved? Or if it must, as by the rule of Mercy, also move toward perfection, how is that achieved? One possible answer, consistent with the linear scheme of Islamic salvation-history, is that nature shall continue to exist in Paradise, but more fully. There is a faint suggestion of this idea in the *Masnavī*. In comparison, says Rumi, to the "gates and walls and pitchers and fruits" of Paradise in the Next World, this living world would seem a "dead carcass" (5.3591). "*Every* atom of that World," says Rumi, "is living, able to understand discourse, and eloquent . . ." (5.3591):

> God says that the wall of Paradise is not lifeless and ugly like (other) walls;
> Like the door and wall of the body, it is (endowed) with intelligence; the house (Paradise) is living since it belongs to the King of Kings.
> Both tree and fruit and limpid water (take part) with the inhabitant of Paradise in conversation and discourse. (4.472–74)

Here is also a suggestion that, in the next world, the disjunction between human beings and nature bridged in this world only by the mystic shall disappear altogether. Intimacy with nature, it seems, is one of the realized conditions of Paradise.

This is not, however, the answer on which Rumi ultimately settles. Instead, he turns to the emanationist aspect of his system to offer a solution for nature and for Man's relation to nature in the present time and through human endeavor. This he does by making humankind the gate to salvation for matter. According to the *Masnavī*, it is ultimately Man, the being on the earth most endowed with Spirit, toward whom all matter strives. Then, through assimilation to him, it is finally released upward toward the spirit world:

> Water goes from above to below; then from below it goes up above.
> The wheat went beneath the earth from above; afterwards it became ears of corn and sprang up quickly.
>
> . . . .
>
> The source of all blessings descended from Heaven to the earth and became the nutrient of the vital spirit.
> Forasmuch as it came down from Heaven on account of humility, it became part of the living and valiant man.
> Hence that inanimate matter—rain and sunlight—was turned into human qualities and soared joyously in the skies,
> Saying, "We came at first from the living world, and have now gone back from below to above." (3.457 ff.)[27]

The same idea is expressed by Rumi in the homely story of the housewife who admonishes the chickpeas, beating them down with her ladle as they try to raise themselves up out of her boiling pot: "I boil you," she says, "not because you are hateful to me," but so that "you may become nutriment and mingle with the vital spirit."

> "If you have been parted from the garden of water and earth, (yet) you have become food in the mouth and [thus] have entered into the living.
>
> . . . .
>
> By God, you grew from God's attributes in the beginning: go back nimbly and fleetly into His attributes.
>
> . . . .
>
> You were a part of the sun and the cloud and the stars: you became soul and action and speech and thoughts."
> The existence of the animal arose from the death of the plant. . . .
> And when that morsel became the food of Man, it mounted from the (state of) inanimateness and became possessed of Soul. (3.4159 ff.)

Thus, though certainly still above nature, humankind does the work, in effect, of freeing the soul entrapped in it. This doctrine resembles in some ways the thought of the Manichaeans, who believed that the Elect among them had the capacity to purify the Soul imprisoned in vegetables and grains—the same foods that figure most prominently in Rumi's narrations—so as to release it upward.[28] A direct influence is, in fact, quite possible, as Rumi's birthplace was located in Khorasan at the gates of Central Asia, where Manichaeism had some success and may have held out until his time in the thirteenth century.

It is the differences between the two worldviews, however, that are most instructive for us here. To begin, the Manichaeans held that Soul indwelt only in certain kinds of foods—vegetables and grains—while other foods and matter, such as meat and decayed organisms, were dead and hence not to be consumed. Rumi, in contrast, takes care to emphasize that *all* nature is living. Everything has Soul; everything is salvable—and, of course, in accord with Islamic norms, everything is consumable. The Manichaeans also considered the ensouled world to be sensitive to suffering, so that trampling, reaping, and digging were viewed as harmful activities (unless, that is, the produce was redeemed by being offered to the Elect).[29]

According to Rumi, however, the earth, vegetables, and animals, far from being harmed, sacrifice themselves gladly to Eros in order to ascend the ladder of Being. Just as the eater loves the food, so does the food love the eater: "Just as you are pitiably enamored of the daily bread, so the daily bread is enamored of the consumer,"[30] through whom it gains life:

> If there had not been Love . . . how should bread have attached itself to you and become (assimilated) to you?
>
> The bread became you: through what? Through (your) love and appetite; otherwise, how should the bread have had any access to the (vital) spirit?
>
> Love makes the dead bread into spirit: it makes the spirit that was perishable everlasting. (5.2012–14)

The Manichaean discipline intended to separate its practicants from matter also included a prohibition against sex, at least for the Elect. There is no trace of such a negative attitude toward sex in Rumi's work[31]—and indeed, this is foreign to the Islamic tradition in general.

Thus, placed against the worldview of the Manichaeans, the following characteristic of Rumi's world is thrown into relief: While for Manichaeans Soul is strained out of matter and the dark remnants left to damnation—along with, even, very weak vestiges of soul—for Rumi, *all* of nature, without exception, is to be transformed, redeemed, and saved. *Every* living and apparently nonliving thing has its necessary and useful place in the great cycle that is God's plan for universal salvation, in which it participates knowingly, actively, and fully. Nothing is without use, and nothing is lost.

This view is surely facilitated by the positive, natural realism of the Qur'an. The Qur'an is cited and expounded throughout the *Masnavī* and, along with the sayings (*ḥadīth*) of the Prophet, is the source of much of the poet's inspiration. In the Qur'an, nature is Real in itself. It is not merely the overflowing of a greater reality. Rather, it is the place we are, in our bodies, experienced not in a time that is eternal or reoccurring but in the Now. Nature is also inherently good. Just as, according to the revelation, Man is naturally noble and good, unstained by sin and exalted even above the angels,[32] so is nature a sign of God's Providence and Mercy, a blessing from Him to be fully enjoyed and utilized, as the Qur'an testifies in the following verse and in many other places:

> In the creation of the heavens and earth, in the alternation of Night and Day, in the sailing of ships through the Ocean for the profit of Mankind, in the rain which God sends down from the skies, and the life He gives thereby to the earth that was dead; in the beasts of all kinds distributed in the earth, in the shifting of the winds and the clouds they trail like their slaves between heaven and earth—here indeed are signs for those who are wise.[33]

Of course, our relation to nature, as good and fulsome as nature is, must be correct. The "adornments" (*zīna*) of this world are to be enjoyed as they are (for example, Qur'an 10:87, 18:7), not coveted and hoarded as an end in themselves (28:66, 33:28). This is also one of Rumi's central lessons.

Other Sufis before Jalal al-Din Rumi had declared the universe to be alive. The noted twelfth-century mystic and systematizer of practical mysticism Abu Hamid al-Ghazali states, consistent with the verse of the Qur'an (17:44) quoted above, that all the atoms of heaven and earth praise God. According to al-Ghazali, however, only the mystics are able to hear that praise.[34] Ibn 'Arabi, the first great theosopher of Islam, who died in Damascus in 1240 while Rumi was still flourishing in Konya, taught that minerals, plants, and animals all naturally know and worship God—while Man, being most bound by consciousness and intellect, often fails to do so.[35] Rumi's father and teacher, the mystic theologian Baha' al-Din Walad (also known as Baha'-i Walad), expounded a system in which all existents (*mawjūdāt*) are percipient (*bi-'aql'and*)[36] servants and knowers (*'ārif*) of God.[37] "The inanimate things (*jamādāt*)," says Baha'-i Walad, "the trees, rivers, and fruits of this world, are under God's command and act according to His command";[38] "water and fire are His slaves."[39] These ideas are recorded in his magnum opus, the *Ma'ārif*, or "Gnostic Perceptions." The text of the *Ma'ārif* in general indicates that a significant part of Rumi's thought was formed around the kernel of his father's ideas. Rumi's important contribution is to amplify and systematize these insights of his predecessors.

Rumi's Ecological Message

What meaningful understanding can be extracted from Rumi for the ecology movement today? We are no longer in a position to adopt thirteenth-century metaphysics; but a metaphysics, however developed, is initially inspired by and then built upon an unmediated perception of Truth. The significance of the *Masnavī* for ecology thus lies, I believe, in what it has to say about our experience and perception of the world around us. This is communicated not entirely explicitly, but rather within the poetic expression itself, the better to be received by intuition—for the first principle of mysticism is that true knowledge is acquired through intuition awakened by experience, and not through rational enquiry.[40]

What shines through the *Masnavī* is an exuberant optimism in relation to nature—an optimism crushed, perhaps, by our present anxieties. Several more precise inferences, however, can be drawn from the text that give us further hints of how to experience and understand nature. We are told, first, to maintain a direct—or, as Ralph Waldo Emerson would say, "original"—relation with nature. If each thing is animated directly by the Divine (a proposition we can accept at least metaphorically), then that thing demands our immediate attention as an individual. We are also told that we need not consider ourselves alone in the world. Nature is our companion. For all its parts are living exactly as we are; and if we are properly attuned to them, they speak to and instruct us—and may, indeed, speak more truthfully than our own kind.

Rumi re-mythologizes nature so that we regain the sense of a world full of personalities who have their own particular, even affective, relations with each other and with us. Nature, in fact, is entwined with our world even to the point of possessing morality and judging over us. These are things, I believe, that we feel instinctively even today when we stand alone with nature. But those feelings are obscured by the notion that our relation to nature must be scientific and efficient. It is as if we have become shy of speaking our relationship to nature. Rumi's work is a call to listen to our instincts and take them seriously—to reject the veil of *'aql*, or false rationality.

Further, Rumi acknowledges that we have a spiritual (today we would say "psychological") affinity with and yearning for our origins in nature, as in several passages cited above and the following:

> The heart is eating a [particular] food from every single companion . . .
>
> . . . .
>
> You eat [receive] something from meeting with any one, and you carry away something from conjunction with any associate.
>
> . . . .
>
> As from the conjunction of earth and rains [there are produced] fruits and greenery and sweet herbs;
>
> And [as] from the conjunction of green things with man [there is produced] joy of heart and carelessness and happiness. (2.1089–95)

The phenomenon Rumi is speaking of here is exactly that which E. O. Wilson terms "biophilia."[41]

We are told by the *Masnavī* also to regard nature as full of hidden potential, and to know that discovery of this potential is part of the process of our own enlightenment. We cannot make spiritual progress without understanding nature and our place within it—even if we are inclined to consider that place to be exceptional, as the Islamic tradition clearly does. Ultimately, we will understand that we should behave instinctively, as nature does, unencumbered by false rationality and the anxiety that produces. At the same time, we are to know that nature is—again as Emerson says—"a continuous creation." Nature is necessarily dynamic. Far from dead, inert, or mechanical, it is always surprising and new, a series of epiphanies for those who know to expect them. This also means, of course, that nature cannot be efficiently predicted or controlled (even though false rationality may tell us otherwise). We should not, however, perceive it to be capricious or without purpose and end—even when it appears, in particular moments, to be maleficent. The laws and action of nature have their own moral sense, even if that is hidden from us. For the most essential intuition of all is that, when viewed as a Whole, the universe reveals itself to be constantly evolving, moving always toward the necessarily dominant good.

Notes

This chapter was originally published as "The Universe Alive," in *Thinking about the Environment*, ed. Thomas M. Robinson and Laura Westra (Lanham, Md.: Lexington Books, 2002). Reprinted by permission of Rowman & Littlefield Publishers, Inc.

I am indebted to Ms. R. Ftaya, graduate student of the Department of Religion, Concordia University, for reading drafts of the paper and contributing numerous valuable suggestions and emendations; the paper was presented in a colloquium of the same department, and the remarks of my colleagues also helped to clarify my thoughts. The clue that led to investigation of a Manichaean connection was provided by Professor Madonna Adams, one of the participants in the conference at which this paper was first presented; comments by graduate student Mr. Hosseinali Houshmand prompted me to focus on the problem of extracting ecological thought from Rumi independent of his particular metaphysics.

1. Though the three mysticisms display apparently similar characteristics, beginning with dependence on emanation and soul-psychology, there has been no extensive work of comparison. This remains a major task in the study of Western religion.

2. "Leave the part," says Rumi, "and fix your eye upon the Whole . . . smell all the way from the part to the Whole, smell all the way from opposite to opposite." Thus shall you realize that "the angers of Mankind are for the sake of Peace; restlessness is ever a snare for Rest." The whole is perceived through Universal Reason (*'aql-i kull*), the part through Partial Reason (*'aql-i juz*). Citations from the *Masnavī* follow the numbering of R. A. Nicholson, as well as his translation, with minor emendations; original edition, *The Mathnawi of Jalalu'ddin Rumi* (London: E. J. W. Gibb Memorial Trust, 1926), reprinted in various editions and places several times since. The quotation above is from volume 3, lines 988 and on, thus: 3.988 ff.

3. Plato *Timaeus* 30D.

4. Ibid.

5. See *Masnavī* 3.1020 ff., where the metaphorical interpretation of living nature (the poet likely refers to exegesis of Qur'an 17:44, cited further on in the text) is condemned as being of the rationalism of the Mu'tazilites.

6. Referring to the pillar against which the Prophet used to lean while speaking, which moaned out of longing for him after he abandoned it in favor of a pulpit.

7. When the sun, it is said, enters the sign of Aries, the earth warms and the plants stir and grow.

8. The soil, similarly, is "faithful to its trust," having "derived this faithfulness from that [Divine] faithfulness, inasmuch as the sun of Justice has shone upon it." Yet "His wrath makes blind the men of understanding"; that is, humankind, who was given understanding, fails to do as much as even the earth does (1.509–13).

9. See also 4.2818–32 and 3532–35.

10. The tribe of 'Ad, according to the Qur'an (e.g., 5:95) was destroyed by the windstorm for their obstinate unbelief.

11. Cf. 3.1009 ff.

12. Cf. Matt. 6:25 ff. and Luke 12:25 ff.—the "fowls of the air" who "neither sow nor reap," and the "lilies of the field" who "neither toil nor spin."

13. Referring to the legend of the Seven Sleepers of Ephesus, which also has a place in Islamic lore (see Qur'an 18:17–21).

14. Because they were able to recognize unmistakably that Majnun, the famous lover of Layla who took to the desert, was filled with Love, the animals did not devour him (5.2721–25; see also ibid., 2005–7). Majnun was reproached for kissing and stroking a dog—dogs being unclean according to Islamic law. He explained that a being is to be measured by its "heart, soul, and knowledge," that is, by its love and devotion, rather than by its apparent form. The dog, who frequented the lane by the house of Majnun's beloved, was perfect in both (3.567 ff.).

15. Cf. the lines of one of Rumi's *ghazal*s (lyric poems) from the *Dīvān-i Shams*:

> Since straw moves not save by a wind, how shall the world move without desire [*havā*, also meaning wind]?"
>
> All the parts of the world are lovers, and every part of the universe is drunk with encounter;
>
> Only they do not tell you their secrets—it is not proper to tell a secret save to one worthy. (*Dīvān-i Shams*, Furuzanfar edition, no. 2674).

The ideas explained in the *Masnavī* emerge everywhere in Rumi's lyrics; this example is cited because a complete translation is available to the reader: *Mystical Poems of Rumi: Second Selection, Poems 201–400*, trans. A. J. Arberry (Chicago: University of Chicago Press, 1979), no. 342.

16. Aristotle *De Generatione Animalium* 3.1.731b30-33.

17. Cf. 5.800–803:

> From inanimateness did you move unconsciously towards vegetal growth, and from vegetal growth towards animal life and tribulation;
>
> And again towards reason and goodly discernment; again toward what lies outside these five senses and six directions.
>
> These footprints extend as far as the Ocean [that is, of Gnosis or Divine Being]; then the footprints disappear.

18. 5.833–43. For another extended comment on the body, see 1.1735–45.

19. See also 3.3964–70 and 1.791–93.

20. See also 3.3405.

21. See the comments following on Heraklitus.

22. 6.3008–13; it is for this reason that blessing may be gotten from physical contact with the graves of saints. See also 6.3059 ff.

23. Hans Regnéll, *Ancient Views on the Nature of Life* (Lund: CWK Gleerup, 1967), 87 ff. and passim.

24. Pronounced in a famous *ḥadīth qudsī*. Certain reported sayings (*ḥadīth*) of the Prophet—even though they are not considered part of the revelation—are called "Holy" (*qudsī*) because they were communicated to him by God. Many *ḥadīth*s *qudsī* are favorite texts of the Sufis.

25. E.g., Qur'an 3:164, 6:99, 2:164 (quoted in the text below), and in many other places in the Qur'an.

26. E.g., Qur'an, chapters 99 and 101.

27. This section of the *Masnavī* is headed "The diverse modes and stages of the creation (*khilqat*) of Man from the beginning."

28. Note also a similarity to the *Masnavī*'s view of body: The Manichaeans believed Soul and Body to be intertwined, and that perfected souls resulted in perfected bodies, "not differing from each other . . . [luminous] like similar lamps" (al-Biruni,

Alberuni's India, trans. Eduard Sachau [London: K. Paul, Trench, Trubner, 1888], cited with further discussion in Jason David BeDuhn, *The Manichaean Body in Discipline and Ritual* [Baltimore: Johns Hopkins University Press, 2000], 223). Not only does Rumi describe the perfected body of the saint as luminous; he also uses the image of lamps, all the same and lit from the same light (4.1842; 6.3069 ff.).

29. The story of the "fool" who cried out against a man overturning the soil (4.2341 ff.) may refer to this Manichaean stricture. The fool was unable, comments the *Masnavī*, to recognize the difference between cultivation and devastation and that the soil could not become "crops and leaves and fruit" until it was "turned upside down."

30. 5.2400.

31. See for instance 5.574 ff., a passage expounding the Prophet's famous saying, "There is no monkery in Islam."

32. So that the angels were commanded to bow down to Adam, the father of humankind: Qur'an 2:34 ff.

33. Qur'an 2:164. The heightened realism of the Qur'an results in this difference between it and Rumi's thought: for Rumi, the meaning of nature is apparent only to those with mystical insight (although, as always with mystical truths, it is "obvious but not perceived"); whereas, according to the Qur'an, the evidence of God contained in the "signs" (*āyāt*) of this world are readily perceived by any who simply "reflect," "remember," "listen," or use "reason" or "common sense" (*'aql*). These processes are linked with the *āyāt* in many places in the Qur'an; see, for example 16:11–69, where they appear together.

34. *Ihyā' 'ulūm al-dīn*, book 5 of the *Munjiyāt*, *Kitāb al-tawḥīd wa-al-tawakkul* ("the speech of the atoms is without word and without end"); for translation and commentary, see Richard Gramlich, *Muhammad al-Gazzalis Lehre von den Stufen zur Gottesliebe* (Wiesbaden: F. Steiner, 1984), 526–27.

35. *Fuṣūṣ al-ḥikām*, translated as *Bezels of Wisdom* by R. J. W. Austin (Mahwah, N.J.: Paulist Press, 1980), 103 ff.

36. Cf. *Masnavī* 4.2821–22: "Out of kindness, God created intelligence (*'aql*) in lifeless things (*jamādāt*) . . . by His grace an intelligence appeared in lifeless matter."

37. *Ma'ārif*, ed. Badi' al-Zaman Furuzanfar, 2 vols. (Tehran: Tahuri, 1333 H.Sh.), 1:293.

38. Ibid.

39. Ibid., 37. For a discussion of Baha'-i Walad's living universe, see Fritz Meier, *Baha'-i Walad: Grundzüge seines Lebens und seiner Mystik* (Leiden: E. J. Brill, 1989), 201 ff. (the chapter "Die Religiosität der Dinge und Atome").

40. Rumi lays out this didactic strategy many times in his writings, as in this line near the beginning of the *Masnavī*: "In expounding love, intellect lay down helplessly like an ass in the mire: it was love alone that uttered the explanation of love and loverhood" (1.115).

41. Baha'-i Walad also proposes that the *mazzah*, or "sensation of enjoyment," we experience in this world from various phenomena, including natural things, is a reflection of our attraction to God and the bliss we shall experience in heaven. See Meier, *Baha'-i Walad*, 222 ff. ("Das Lustgefühl [Maza]").

Fiṭra: An Islamic Model for Humans and the Environment

SAADIA KHAWAR KHAN CHISHTI

Introduction

Environmental compromise generally results from some combination of a lack of knowledge[1] and a free-rider problem.[2] From the Qur'anic[3] perspective, both lack of knowledge and the inability to internalize the holistic consequences of individual actions are symptoms of humankind's dissociation from Allah.[4] The *Sharī'a*, or Divine Law revealed by Allah through al-Qur'ān[5] and the *Sunna*[6] (the example of Muhammad [s]),[7] provides a path for reversing this disassociation. A reversal of this disassociation through the practice of the *Sharī'a* offers a strong framework within which to address the causes and symptoms of environmental compromise.

Al-Qur'ān and *Ḥadīth* refer to Islam as "*dīn al-fiṭra*," or a religion true to the primordial nature of humankind. As a consequence, the environmental messages explored and developed in this paper are, from the Islamic view, a part of the instinctive nature of humankind and need not be instilled, but rather awakened. In this paper I will describe some aspects of the *fiṭra* (or instinctive) model of life encouraged by the *Sharī'a*, and how these aspects tie into the development of environmental consciousness. I will close by offering some suggestions for future action based on some of the conclusions offered.

Environmental Compromise

The symptoms of a general environmental compromise are markedly in evidence. Global warming is a strong indicator of the rise of greenhouse gas levels due to human environmental intervention. Chlorofluorocarbons (CFCs) have degraded the ozone layer, resulting in an increase in skin cancer rates. Rapid, unchecked depletion of forest cover continues to press the earth's ability to maintain ecosystem equilibrium. An accelerating reduction in biodiversity further threatens this equilibrium. Perhaps most prominently, rapid global population growth has brought the earth's natural resource base under considerable pressure; in localized areas, population pressures are resulting in the decimation of the ecological balance. The inability of many countries to provide adequate nutrition to their populations is becoming an increasingly pressing concern.

The untempered global economic paradigm of an increase in consumer demand, translating into a perceived but illusory improvement in global standards of living, continues to drive this process. In this context, the exploitation of natural resources and the intensification of individual self-interest are considered to be the driving forces of long-term growth and development of global benefit. Pure market forces have not correctly internalized the long-term consequences of such growth. Short-term economic growth has continued apace at the expense of long-term environmental integrity.

Enlightened efforts to address this trend have met with only moderate success. Several industrially developed nations have managed to limit, and in some instances even reverse, domestic air, water, and other pollution. Nevertheless, the industrial countries remain the largest source of global pollution and represent the largest source of global demand for primary resources. Global efforts to establish a monitoring and control system that is equitable and enforceable, despite many good intentions, have been undermined by regional and political self-interest. Attempts by developed nations to encourage global environmental moderation and to alleviate the environmental degradation in developing countries have, on balance, met with at best mild success.

The Relationship between Humankind and Allah

I will argue here that the current environmental crisis is a consequence of the loss of a relationship between humans, the natural realm, and Allah. Such a relationship provides for a much-heightened sense of self-discipline both individually and, if correctly implemented, on a national level that allows for an environmental conscience to take firm root. Further, such a relationship allows a personal progression that ultimately drives the individual to a personal relationship between himself and his environment that results in an intuitively sensitive approach to environmental considerations.

The reversal of this disassociation takes effect on two levels. The first level is that of the day-to-day conduct of humans, as regulated by the practice of the *Sharīʿa*. I explore the pervasive nature of this regulation in this paper; I will assert that this pervasiveness allows for an achievable implementation of environmental ethics in daily affairs.

The second level is that of the spiritual development of humankind, as encouraged by an ardent devotion to the practice of the *Sharīʿa*. The spiritual development of the devout Muslim is also explored in this paper, together with the consequent effects of such development on the believer's worldview.

The *Sharīʿa*'s regulation of daily conduct and the subsequent spiritual development are further amplified in their environmental impact by a number of messages implicit and explicit in the Divine Law. I devote a substantial portion of this paper to deriving and describing some of these messages.

The Sharīʿa

The *Sharīʿa* refers to the philosophy and law of Islam both in its exoteric and esoteric[8] aspects as enunciated in the Book of Allah and the *Sunna* (example) of the Prophet of Islam. A believer seeking to follow the Islamic tradition would seek to implement the *Sharīʿa* in his life.

The *Sharīʿa* constitutes an absolute standard[9] of performance for a Muslim. A fundamental exposition of al-Qur'ān and *Ḥadīth* is needed to fully describe the *Sharīʿa*; such a comprehensive study is much beyond the scope of this paper. A description of the relationship among al-Qur'ān, the *Sunna*, human, and the natural realm is, however, in order and is sufficient to establish a framework for addressing specific environmental concerns, such as environmental preservation and sustainable development.

For a Muslim, the supreme source of guidance is al-Qur'ān. By implication, then, al-Qur'ān is also the foundation of the *Sharīʿa* and is accorded the highest level of reverence as the Book of Allah containing Divine wisdom and sacred knowledge. From the mainstream Muslim perspective,[10] al-Qur'ān is coeternal with Allah, as He has expressed His will in it. Each word is a direct transmission from Allah to the angel Gabriel and, in turn, to the last of the prophets, the prophet Muhammad (s). As such, a sincere believer holds this "Divine Writ" in supreme reverence and regards it as the "Mother of All Books." The 6,666 *āyāt*[11] of al-Qur'ān are intended for universal application, across any geography or time.

For the believer, a sign of Allah's blessing is that He has not only sent an authoritative "Divine Writ" in which the principles of faith and practice are established, He has also sent a living example to show the perfect expression of these principles in human life. Al-Qur'ān is the written message of Allah, and the Blessed Prophet of Islam is the human message, the projection of the written message into the sphere of human behavior and purposeful activity. The *Sharī'a* as a code of life incorporates political, educational, economic, social, familial, environmental, and other aspects of life. The Divine Laws enunciated in the Book of Allah are by His Divine will projected in the life of the Messenger of Allah and shaped as clear rulings, tenets, and values to be practiced by humans in their daily lives.

The *Sunna* emphasizes the active participation of humans in the environment. Celibacy, detachment, austerity, and other ascetic practices are not encouraged. Instead, the examples of the Prophet of Islam, his family, and his close companions set a clear imperative for individual initiative in productive work, healthy and happy family life, social and welfare considerations, and statecraft. This engagement becomes an imperative for the Muslim to learn about and understand the functioning of his environment. "Go even unto China to seek knowledge,"[12] advised the prophet Muhammad (s), a dictate that triggered centuries of enlightened Islamic scientific research.

This does not, however, raise the scientific quest to a level of arrogance and misuse like that of modern scientific outlook. For a believer, al-Qur'ān establishes a mode of scientific inquiry and a quest for knowledge that is enveloped in a reverence for and humility toward the Divine. Al-Qur'ān reveals that without such humility and reverence, "Nay, but man does transgress all bounds, in that he looks upon himself as self-sufficient."[13] This transgression is a source of the environmental decline brought about by humankind.

Al-Qur'ān and the *Sunna* describe Islam as *dīn al-fiṭra*, a way of life based on the nature of humankind, and *dīn al-sahl*, a religion fostering a way of ease. By reconciling the outward practices of humankind with humankind's inward nature, al-Qur'ān provides the *ṣirāṭ al-mustaqīm*, or the straight path leading toward wellness and a wholesome lifestyle, culminating in fulfillment both in this life and in the hereafter.

The *Sharī'a*, then, is a well-defined code of conduct for human life. In the physical world, the *Sharī'a* guides the Muslim across the spectrum of human affairs. There is no concept of separation of the affairs of religion from the affairs of state; in the *Sharī'a* they are one. Further, the tone of the *Sharī'a* is one of a strong sense of engagement between humankind and the physical world, not one of detachment. The combination allows for a strong management of the interface between humans and the environment within a Qur'anic social and ethical framework.

This is the critical point: the comprehensive, pervasive nature of Islam as a *dīn*, or way of life, as experienced by a practicing Muslim, allows the regulation of his affairs to a high degree. An implementation of environmental sensitivity is simply a special case of a broader set of imperatives embraced by a Muslim under the *Sharī'a*—the Divine Law.

Proximity to Allah

Devoted practice of the *Sharī'a* in both its exoteric and esoteric forms establishes an increasingly strong bond between humankind and Allah and triggers increasingly greater levels of spiritual awareness in the practicing believer. In the spiritual development of a believer, at a point in time when the believer exhibits sincere faith and sincere devotion to Allah, the *baraka*[14] of Allah descends on and transforms the believer. The believer then enters into a state known as *'abūdiyyat*, or servanthood.

The servant, or *'abd,*[15] begins to feel the presence of Allah and His infinite attributes. This servitude is not born just of obligation, but is one of intoxication with Divine love. As the object of this intoxication, Allah is *al-rabūbiyya*, or "the Divine Beloved." As the lover, the servant enters into a state of selfless service, or "*al-'ubūdiyya*." This service, performed with an immeasurable depth of adoration for the Divine Master keeps the *'abd* ready to lay down his life to earn the pleasure of his Master and develops in him an intense longing for the supreme moment when he would hear the Master's voice saying, "O Soul! Thou art at rest, return to thy Master well pleased and well pleasing, so enter amongst my servants and enter my garden" (Qur'an 89:27–30). The *'abd*'s inner experience of Allah's various attributes in turn transforms him, leading the *'abd* toward greater ultimate realization of his Divine Beloved.

Al-Qur'ān and *Ḥadīth* describe the spiritual journey of the *'abd* as one of increasing perception of *nūr-un 'ala-nūr*, or the "light" of Allah. Abdullah Yusuf Ali, in his translation of al-Qur'ān, describes *nūr-un 'ala-nūr* as "Glorious, inimitable light, grades and grades of it passing transcendently into regions of spiritual height which man's imagination can scarcely conceive."

The development of the faculty to perceive this light is a function of the spiritual development of the *'abd*. The development of this faculty in turn allows an individual to begin the perception of the true interrelationships between himself, the Divine, and all creation.

With this perception, the *'abd* recognizes the depth of his commitment to the communities of creation around him—all living and inanimate creations are perceived as part of a unified whole. The balance of life, death, and survival of all species enters into the consciousness of the *'abd*.

This brings up a critical point. The transcendent awareness of the interrelationships between humankind, Allah, and creation is ultimately defining of conduct commensurate with environmental integrity. The use of no more than what is necessary, a respect for the privileges of other species, and a desire to preserve and protect creation in all its various forms are simply derivatives of the fundamental perception of the core unity of creation.

This is an awareness decidedly different (although perhaps similar in consequence) from a modern scientific advocacy of a paradigm for sustainable development or tolerant resource use. This is awareness based on a fundamental understanding of the commonalities between all elements of creation and the Creator, and on an understanding of the role of humankind within this context.

The spiritual journey of the *'abd* is a continuous process; there is an unending spectrum of spiritual development. Many *Aḥādīth* describe the full journey as one of sequential penetration of seventy thousand "veils of light." Progress on the journey corresponds to increasing levels of awareness. Accordingly, most can perceive at least some degree of the interrelationship between humankind, the Divine, and creation. Such awareness can come in the form of beauty perceived in natural surroundings, a kinship felt for other living species, or perhaps even a simple awareness of the community of humankind taking precedence over the individual. The progressive stages of *'abūdiyyat* allow for the increasing realization of this reality.

The Divine Names of Allah

Al-Qur'ān declares, "Allah! There is no God but He. To Him belong the Most Beautiful Names" (al-Qur'ān 20:8), and "Say: Call upon Allah or call upon *Raḥmān*:[16] by whatever name you call upon Him, it is well: for to Him belong the Most Beautiful Names."[17] Allah's Divine Essence (*ẓāt*) is beyond description and described as such in al-Qur'ān; the name "Allah" is held to embrace His infinite attributes. However, Islamic tradition holds that Allah has selectively revealed many of His attributes to humankind; to each such attribute Islamic tradition relates a particular name. Allah's names provide an indication of His interaction with both the physical world and the spiritual development of an *'abd.*

Of particular interest is the Divine Name "*al-Muḥīṭ*." Translated alternatively as "the All-Encompasing Being" or "the Divine Environment," the name *al-Muḥīṭ* reflects the pervasive presence of Allah. In the Qur'anic perspective, the Divine Environment is present on both physical and spiritual planes. On the physical plane the Divine Environment manifests itself in an underlying sacredness of all creation; Allah's permeation of His attributes in His creation in all His forms dictates a reverence of and respect for the believer's physical environment. On the spiritual plane, the Divine Environment connects the *'abd* to all kinds of life and species on this planet.

A believer's reverence and respect for the environment does not directly translate into an environmentally friendly message, however. *Al-Muḥīṭ* is as present in a polluted urban environment as in virgin nature; there is no explicit duty to cherish one over the other. For the believer, however, the knowledge of *al-Muḥīṭ*'s presence in the believer's surroundings dictates a need for understanding and appreciation of one's environment in order to better the believer's awareness of *al-Muḥīṭ*. In this view, the quest to seek the Divine can be met, at least in part, by an imperative to learn, understand, and appreciate the context of life.

Allah also reveals Himself as *al-Ḥasīb*, or the "One Who Takes Perfect Account." Again, this Divine Attribute manifests itself on both the spiritual and the physical planes. On the spiritual plane, *al-Ḥasīb* accounts for the fervency of devotion of the believer. On the physical plane, *al-Ḥasīb* accounts for the earthly actions of humans. The perfection of accountability in *al-Ḥasīb* is a powerful driver of thought and action for a believer. For the believer, the knowledge of *al-Ḥasīb* drives a desire to seek out an understanding of the holistic consequences of individual actions; a believer seeks a fine understanding of the effects one's actions generate in order to best prepare for the ultimate accounting. This is the basis for the believer's taking the long-term view of the consequences of personal actions.

Between the attributes of Allah as *al-Muḥīṭ* and *al-Ḥasīb*, the believer has a framework for seeking out and understanding the physical environmental context, as well as taking action within it that reflects an accounting of the long-term consequences of such action. In short, this worldview is not dissimilar to those championed under modern paradigms of sustainable development[18] and environmental consciousness. The critical difference is that of motivation: for the *'abd*, the motivation is a consequence of the pursuit of proximity to the Divine.

This motivation at once addresses both the drivers of environmental compromise: ignorance and a short-term, self-interested view.

Signs of the Creator

Al-Qur'ān states explicitly and repeatedly that the natural world is a vast fabric into which the "signs" of the Creator are woven. Al-Qur'ān and the phenomena of nature are twin manifestations of Allah as the Sender of Qur'anic revelation and the Creator of its expression in the realm of nature. As suggested earlier, it is significant that the Qur'anic word for "sign" is *āya*, the same word used to describe a phrase-unit of al-Qur'ān. Earth and its mountains, snow-covered peaks, waterfalls, oceans, forests and the species they contain, and the sky and other heavenly bodies are signs of Allah, in the same way that each phrase-unit of al-Qur'ān witnesses the Creator. Al-Qur'ān reveals: "Soon will We show them Our Signs in the (furthest) regions (of the earth), and in their own souls, until it becomes manifest to them that this is the Truth. Is it not that Thy Rabb doth witness All things?"[19]

Both the signs of natural phenomena and the *āyāt* of al-Qur'ān are means of communication from the Creator to His creatures. Muslim sages emphasizing the significance of the natural world have considered it a complement to the Qur'anic Revelation; the observation of natural surroundings causes a reverberation in the heart of the faithful observer that facilitates the understanding of the message of al-Qur'ān.

One consistent conclusion is that of a duty to preserve nature. To the believer, the value of the signs of Allah should substantially outweigh the benefits of purely economic development that obscure the presence of such signs. The equation of the physical signs of Allah with the signs of Allah in al-Qur'ān renders them worthy of preservation and respect derived from that accorded to the ultimate sign of Allah—al-Qur'ān itself. Stated differently, the believer should respect and seek to preserve pristine nature because of the value of such nature in its communication of the presence of Allah.

Several *Aḥādīth* draw on this insight copiously. The Prophet of Islam declared, "The whole of the earth is a mosque that is a place of worship." The notion of creation as an indication of the presence of Allah, and, as a derivative, a method for reaching Him, is vivid in this context. Attending this notion of sacrality are duties of care, preservation, and upkeep consistent with that a believer would accord any humanly constructed place of worship.

Vicegerency

Al-Qur'ān establishes humankind's position in the physical world as one of vicegerent, or steward, of creation: "It is He Who has made you his vicegerents of the earth; He has raised you in ranks, some above others that He may try you in the gifts He has given you; for He is quick in punishment yet He is indeed oft-forgiving and most merciful" (al-Qur'ān 6:165). The earth is presented to the vicegerent in the *Sharī'a* as a "usufruct," with attendant duties of maintenance and, where possible, improvement for the benefit of the coming descendant generations. In this role, humankind is responsible for the survival and good condition of the various communities within the physical sphere.

Al-Qur'ān, for example, highlights the need for human sensitivity to its co-inhabitants of the earth: "There is not an animal on Earth, nor a bird that flies on its wings, but they are communities like you; nothing have we omitted from the Book and they all shall be gathered before their Rabb in the end" (al-Qur'ān 6:38). Similarly, certain *Aḥādīth* record the Prophet of Islam as saying: "All in the community are equal partners in three things: water, fire, and pasture. Each individual and each species is a part of life as a whole."

Al-Qur'ān even cites Allah's interaction with other species: "And thy Rabb revealed to the Bee: make your honeycomb in the mountains and in the trees and in the hives which men build and eat all the flowers and fruits and do it in the way of thy Rabb, submissively. There comes forth from their bellies a liquid of many hues in which there is healing for man, therein is surely a sign for men who reflect" (al-Qur'ān 16:68).

The notion of interdependence of living communities stewarded by humankind is prominent in al-Qur'ān. This gives rise to what is possibly the most direct imperative for environmental ethics in Islam. As vicegerents or stewards, individuals are personally responsible for the care and preservation of their brethren communities, be they human, plant, or animal. In this context, every life-form possesses intrinsic value independent of its resource worth to humanity.

As vicegerents, humans are obligated to balance their needs with the needs of the other communities and species that come under their care. The responsibility is, of course, bounded by individual knowledge and by individual capacity. Ignorance of the consequences of one's actions, as discussed earlier, hampers the individual in his capacity as vicegerent. Similarly, spiritual development allows an increased understanding of the subtle connection between individuals and communities, thus facilitating stewardship.

The *Fiṭra* Model of Living: Islam as *Dīn al-Fitra*

Islam claims to be in accord with human nature, and the religious dispensation that al-Qur'ān calls "*al-dīn al-qāyyim*," or "the right religion," does not allow altering that nature. Al-Qur'ān reveals: "So set your face towards religion uprightly; it is the original nature according to which Allah fashioned mankind; there is no altering Allah's creation; that is the true religion; but most men do not know" (al-Qur'ān 30:30).

The root of the Arabic word *fiṭra* is the three-consonant combination f-ṭ-r. The f-t-r root communicates a sense of original or life-giving nature. The Arabic word *fiṭrī*, for example, means natural or instinctive. Similarly, *faṭīra* means unleavened bread—fresh and life-giving. In the same vein, *fiṭra* refers to the primordial nature of things.

Al-Qur'ān and *Ḥadith* refer to Islam as *dīn al-fiṭra*, or, literally, "the religion of the primordial nature." An adherent of Islam, according to this definition, is acting according to the primeval instinct already present in him. It is helpful, then, to explore some of the practices of Islam, which, when examined in this context, describe the Qur'anic view of the primordial nature of humankind.

The overriding characteristic of the Islamic economic system as developed in the *Sharī'a* is that of an institutional system of taxation on behalf of the needy. This is formalized in the *zakāt*, a mandatory tax distributed to the poor and consisting of 2.5 percent of the total annual assets of a Muslim. In addition, the *Sharī'a* calls upon believers to participate in *ṣadaqa*, or voluntary alms to the poor, if the believer can do so. Al-Qur'ān describes the alms-giving process as, "For those who give in charity, men and women, and loan to Allah a Beautiful Loan, it shall be increased manifold (to their credit), and they shall have (besides) a liberal reward" (al-Qur'ān 57:7).

The overriding of an intuitive concern for humankind's peer creation is a function, in the Islamic view, of the distancing of humans from their true nature. However, the reassuring implication of Islam's inclusion of charity as part of the *fiṭra*, or primordial nature, of humans is that they, at the core, are altruistic beings.

Similarly, the *Sharī'a* describes an Islamic judicial system based on a straightforward cost-benefit analysis of individual action. For a given action, the Islamic judicial system asks the following question: "Does the good outweigh the harm?" If the action results in a balance between the two, or if it favors harm, then it is to be avoided. If a decision needs to be made between the needs of the poor and the needs of the rich, the judicial system favors the needs of the poor. In short, the judicial system presumes that the nature of humankind is one that allows for the comprehensive judgment of consequences and one that favors the success of those most in need.

Islam also ascribes an essential conservationist bias in the nature of humankind. The Prophet (s) was recorded as forbidding the waste of water during ritual cleansing in preparation for prayer on the bank of a river.[20] Several *Aḥādīth* corroborate a dictate of lean resource use, including the use of food resources, animal energy, and forest resources. According to this view, humans are, in *fiṭra*, lean consumers of natural resources.

It is important to highlight the Qur'anic message that, while the human soul is genderless and common to both sexes, aspects of the *fiṭra* of men differ from those of women. The *Sharī'a* recognizes the constitutional differences between men and women and ascribes varying *fiṭra*s accordingly in certain aspects of the natures of the male and the female. In the Qur'anic view, men, for example, have a first instinct to provide upkeep and sustenance for the family unit. Women, in partnership, have a first instinct to provide for the immediate care of offspring. The view of "equal but different" that characterizes this outlook opens the door for the possibly varying assignments of environmentally relevant natures to each gender. This issue calls for substantial exploration and is only touched upon in this paper as a possibility.

The *fiṭra* of humankind, then, encompasses an altruistic spirit, thoughtfulness in action, and a conservationist bias. As a consequence, in developing a model of interaction between humans and the environment derived from the *Sharī'a* (a "*fiṭra* model"), it is important to reserve scope for these primal traits. In accordance with the *Sharī'a*, a *fiṭra* model advocates regulation that encourages the altruistic behavior of humans toward their fellow humans, other living co-communities, and the nonliving environment.

Further, a *fiṭra* model encourages societal organization designed to further thoughtfulness in action, be it through education, a system of justice designed to amplify the relationships between cause and effect, or other means. In the Muslim view, the *fiṭra* of humankind encourages a *Sharī'a*-derived development of regulation that formalizes a conservationist ethic.

Conclusions

From my viewpoint, it is the dissociation of humankind from Allah, and the attendant dissociation of humans from their own natures, that is the source of individual ignorance and apathy toward a holistic worldview. Through a recovery of the relationship between humankind and Allah as established in the Qur'anic message, the altruistic instinct and the search for understanding and knowledge that underpins environmental conscience can be reestablished. At first, this reestablishment is felt on a physical level, with the dictates of the *Sharī'a* guiding the actions of the believer. In time, this reestablishment moves to a spiritual plane, with a desire for proximity to the Divine and a corresponding growing understanding of the Divine translating into environmental action on a much more fundamental, enlightened level.

Further, Islam views itself as in accordance with the *fiṭra*, or primeval nature, of humankind. An examination of the *Sharī'a* allows for a glimpse into this nature. Such a glimpse, in turn, reveals an optimistic view of humankind's innate potentialities, particularly in regard to the interrelationship between humans and the environment. A conservation ethic, within this view, is part of human natural instinct and is easy to follow once awakened. Within a model of life derived from an understanding of the *fiṭra* of humankind, the *Sharī'a* provides strong guidance for establishing codes of conduct and a regulation of life that encourages the expression of the core nature of humankind.

Without the framework that a religious solution offers, secular attempts to establish economic systems for policing environmental policy are hamstrung. Current trends pay witness to the ineffectiveness of purely political policy in addressing fundamental environmental concerns: agreement on goals is hard to come by, and what few goals are established are even harder to police. A purely secular approach to establishing a paradigm of sustainable development has not and will not cure the root cause of the illness: the absence of an individual desire to learn and understand and the absence of an individual sense of responsibility for the holistic consequences of one's actions. A secular indoctrination of these principles is, at best, temporary in effect.

This analysis allows for a broad appeal. Those who follow other religious traditions can bring similar reasoning to bear; indeed, the three Abrahamic religions have much of the same framework in common. The Qur'anic view serves as one particularly amenable to environmental analysis. Those of a more secular perspective can, at a minimum, appreciate the opportunity for such an analysis to encourage appropriate behavior among their more religious peers.

Next Steps

This paper has advanced the view that a life in accordance with the *Sharīʻa* translates into a life in accordance with the *fiṭra*, or true nature, of humankind. In turn, such a life allows for a regulation of one's actions in harmony with environmental considerations. Further, such a life offers a path of spiritual development for the follower that results in instinctual activity of environmental benefit.

The most immediate next step is to build awareness of this path to environmental integrity among the body most likely to receive it: the Islamic world. Modern methods of communication and dissemination of thought allow for a substantial advantage in such a process. For Muslims, the understanding and appreciation of such a view is simply one of understanding their own heritage.

In parallel, the general global dissemination of this point of view is of benefit to broader populations. Again, the Abrahamic religions share much of this same framework and have the opportunity to use it to global environmental benefit. It is a matter of allowing the kind of awareness that will encourage appropriate behavior.

Without the personal connection with environmental considerations and sustainable development that religion allows, a purely secular approach to assuring ecological stability is bereft of a valuable ally. Encouragement of this view on an intrastate level will offer a key to the maintenance of environmental integrity that is in the interest of both our lives and the lives of our co-communities on Earth—our planet.

The hope is that these steps, suffused with a reawakening of the spiritually defined potentialities of humankind, will over time encourage a paradigm shift from the status quo of consumerism to one of enlightened interaction between humans and the environment.

In the words of al-Qur'ān (20:47): "Peace to all who follow guidance."

Notes

The author wishes to use al-Qur'ān, in place of the practice followed in the rest of this volume of using the English article, "the Qur'an." *Ed.*

1. An example of an environmental concern resulting from a lack of knowledge is that of the overuse of fertilizer. Fertilizer use increases crop yields—but only up to a point. An uneducated farmer, noticing the correlation between an initial use of fertilizer and an increase in crop yields, might expect the relationship to persist much beyond the most practical level of fertilizer application. In such a case, however, a farmer may simply be wasting fertilizer, with no corresponding increase in crop production, while damaging the local water table with excess nitrates.

2. A free-rider problem is one in which the negative consequences of an action are widely distributed but the positive consequences of the action accrue heavily to the actor. A good example is that of a steadily sinking, overloaded lifeboat that no passenger wishes to abandon: each passenger stands to live by being on board and so elects to stay on board—yet this course of action will result in the death of all. Each passenger hopes that "someone else" will be self-sacrificing. Many environmental problems are similar: a factory polluting the atmosphere stands to gain tremendously by staying in operation—as do all other factories so polluting. In time, such a trend will result in the destruction of all, but each individual factory owner hopes that it will be some other owner who decides to cease polluting and thereby avoid disaster.

3. This paper frequently uses the term "Qur'anic" in preference to the term "Islamic," since the latter is often associated (however mistakenly) with non-Islamic practices commonplace in the Muslim world today. Most of the un-Islamic practices undertaken by Muslims today are reflective of misinterpretations or misrepresentations of the pristine intent of al-Qur'ān. That there are Muslims today who practice Islam in its intended form is without doubt; it is the association of Islam with some of the prevalent non-Islamic practices and beliefs today that I seek to avoid. As such, the term "Islamic" is used sparingly.

4. Allah is the One God of Muslims.

5. Al-Qur'ān constitutes the sum of divine revelation received by the Prophet Muhammad (s) from the angel Gabriel over the course of twenty-three years for the guidance of humankind.

6. *Ḥadīth* incorporate the collected sayings of the prophet Muhammad (s) and the *Sunna*, or example, consisting of the deeds of the prophet Muhammad (s).

7. The (s) term abbreviates the Arabic term *Sallallahu alaihi wa's-salām*, or "peace and blessings of Allah be upon him." For a Muslim, adding such an invocation is traditional.

8. According to the prophet Muhammad (s) there is no *āya* in al-Qur'ān which does not have an inner (esoteric) as well as an outer (exoteric) aspect, together with a number of different meanings. Every definition is potentially a source of enlightenment. The literal or exoteric meaning is like a transparent veil covering the *jalāl* (majesty, glory, grandeur), the *jamāl* (indescribable beauty), and the *kamāl* (precise perfection) of the esoteric meaning of the *āyāt*. The exoteric and esoteric aspects do not split: they are two sides of the same coin and they reinforce each other.

9. In practice, many Muslims today fail to meet this standard in its purity and

perfection. Accordingly, the practices of individuals who refer to themselves as Muslims are not definitive of the *Sharī'a*. Between a common failure to comply with the *Sharī'a* and its flexibility in allowing local cultural variance within its basic framework, an observation of the life of a casually selected Muslim would prove an inadequate benchmark for establishing the core of the *Sharī'a*.

10. "From the mainstream Muslim perspective" is, for the rest of the paper, the standpoint of analysis, unless explicitly stated otherwise.

11. The term *āya(t)* (pl. *āyāt*) is usually translated as "verse," which is incorrect. An *āya* is not a poetical expression; syntactically, the construction of the Qur'anic sentence is very different from that of a verse. Accordingly, the Qur'anic term *āya* is retained in this paper. Shaikh Abdul Qadir al-Sufi ad-Darqawi writes (*Qur'anic Tawḥīd*, Diwan Press, 64): "Ayat indicates a phrase structure of al-Qur'ān and also means a sign, both in the linguistic and semiotic sense."

12. China, at the time of the prophet Muhammad (s), constituted the most distant area of the known world. The reference is from *Ḥadīth* collections.

13. Al-Qur'ān 96:6–7.

14. *Baraka* is a Qur'anic word that stands for "Allah's blessings," which manifest themselves and contain the power of sanctity. It is more comprehensive in meaning than the term "grace."

15. One of the titles of the Prophet of Islam is *'abd-allah*, or "servant of Allah."

16. "Raḥmān" is one of the Divine Names of Allah, reflecting His attributes of graciousness toward His creation.

17. Al-Qur'ān 17:110.

18. In the context of this paper, the term "sustainable development" is "development that meets the needs of the present without compromising the ability of future generations to meet their own needs"; the Brundtland Report, in *Our Common Future* (New York: Oxford University Press, 1987).

19. Al-Qur'ān 41:53.

20. Fazlun M. Khalid and Joanne O'Brien, eds., *Islam and Ecology* (London and New York: Cassell, 1992).

The Challenge of (Re)Interpretation

Islam, the Contemporary Islamic World, and the Environmental Crisis

SEYYED HOSSEIN NASR

The Significance of the Issue

Both people and governments in the Islamic world, as elsewhere, are naturally paying attention to sundry problems, but outside the purely spiritual and religious dimensions of life, nothing is more important and worthy of consideration today than the environmental crisis. This crisis encompasses the natural ecological system of the globe as well as the human ambience, the air we breathe, the food we consume, the water we drink, and even the inner workings of our bodies. The crisis also endangers the harmony of the whole fabric of life on Earth and the system that makes human life possible. And yet, most Muslims, much like other fellow human beings, are walking through this unprecedented crisis like sleepwalkers, little aware of what goes on about them or of the deeper causes of a crisis that threatens human existence itself here on Earth. And this sleepwalking by the majority is taking place despite the powerful and persuasive spiritual teachings of Islam about the natural world and the relation of human beings to it.

My own concern with issues of the environmental crisis goes back to the early 1950s and my student days at the Massachusetts Institute of Technology and Harvard University. Always sensitive to the beauty of nature, I used to walk alone, like Thoreau, around Walden Pond when the natural scenery of the area was still well preserved. It was the construction of Route 128 around Boston and the consequent separation, ecologically speaking, of the area inside the beltway from the relatively unhindered countryside beyond that brought home to me the fact that something was basically wrong in our relationship to nature. As a result of this human experience and of years of study not only of modern but also of traditional science along with religious perspectives concerning the natural world, I was led to foresee a major environmental crisis, whose real causes were spiritual, looming on the horizon. I saw the blind development of modern industry as a cancer in the body of nature, a cancerous substance which would finally lead to the destruction of the harmony and balance of the natural world and to its "death" in the form that we knew it.

Upon returning to Iran in 1958, I took every opportunity to speak about the subject of the environmental crisis, and in 1966 I delivered the Rockefeller Series Lectures at the Divinity School of the University of Chicago on the theme of the encounter of human beings and nature and the spiritual crisis of the modern world, which predicted the environmental crisis and pointed to its spiritual roots. Although my book *Man and Nature*[1] containing the text of these lectures appeared in 1968 and was translated into several European languages, it was not translated into Persian until a couple of years ago and has never appeared in Arabic. Despite my efforts and those of a small number of Islamic scholars who turned to the subject from the 1970s onward, general indifference to the environmental crisis and apathy in seeking to find solutions to it based on Islamic principles continued until the 1980s and 1990s when, gradually, voices began to be heard concerning this issue among both members of the general public and various governmental agencies. Yet, even now those voices are often drowned out by those of others in many situations crucial to the preservation of the environment. Furthermore, among religious scholars in the Islamic world, who wield so much influence among ordinary people, only a few have risen to defend with a strong voice the Islamic teachings about the natural environment and to criticize in depth actions taken by both governmental and nongovernmental agencies which are detrimental to the health of the environment.

One can say, therefore, that despite a gradual rise in recognition of the seriousness of the environmental crisis in many Islamic countries and the reformulation in a contemporary language of both legal and philosophico-theological teachings of Islam about the natural environmental, there is still a general lack of awareness of this crucial matter and of the will necessary to prevent further deterioration of the environment through actions carried out usually in the name of human welfare, but with the result of the destruction of the health of the natural world without which human welfare, and in fact human existence itself, would not be possible. We must ask, therefore, why it is that the Islamic view of nature and concrete directives for human action in the natural world are not being emphasized by governmental authorities or even by the majority of *'ulamā'*, who are the traditional guardians of Islamic knowledge in its various dimensions.

Obstacles to Realizing and Implementing the Islamic View of the Natural Environment

When one studies the Islamic view of nature and humankind's relation to the natural environment, as well as the way classical Islamic civilization created a society and especially an urban setting in harmony with nature, and when one compares these realities with the situation in the Islamic world today, it becomes obvious that neither governments nor most people in Muslim countries are following Islamic principles in their treatment of the natural environment. Nor are most of the *'ulamā'* teaching and preaching the Islamic view of this subject to the public. Furthermore, many Muslims, especially those uprooted from their villages and the countryside and residing often in squalid conditions in larger towns and cities, are not even continuing the practices of their parents and grandparents back in their villages as far as matters pertaining to the natural environment are concerned. One must therefore ask what the obstacles are to knowing and then implementing Islamic teachings concerning the natural environment. This question becomes particularly pertinent if one remembers that throughout nearly the whole Islamic world, the religion of Islam is still strong. The mosques are full, and on Fridays thousands upon thousands listen to preachers discussing various issues. Books and media programs dealing with Islam have a vast readership and audience. To answer this question, we must turn to deeper causes that concern, not the religion of Islam, which places so much responsibility on human beings in their relation to nature, but the external obstacles that prevent these teachings (to which we shall turn later in this essay) from being propagated and implemented in a society in which the voice of religion is still very strong and where all ethics, whether they be personal, social, or environmental, have a religious foundation.

Let us then turn to a number of the major obstacles:

1. The present environmental crisis is directly related to the use of modern technology and the various applications of modern science. One can see this in problems as far apart as the rise in population due to the practice of modern medicine and global warming caused by a set of complex industrial factors. But modern science and technology also provide those who possess them with power and are in fact the main reason the West can exercise domination over other societies, including the Islamic countries. Consequently, both Muslim governments and many Muslim individuals want to gain access to the very technology which has had devastating environmental consequences. Seeking to gain power for themselves in the intricate political and economic situation of today's world, they are, at best, always at the receiving end of a technology that is ever changing and needs to be constantly borrowed anew from the West and, to some extent, Japan. There is no pause in the development of ever newer forms of technology, a pause that might allow Islamic societies to create some form of equilibrium with the technology that is borrowed, to "humanize" certain aspects of it to the degree possible, and to minimize its negative environmental impact.[2] The governing classes in the Islamic world have their eyes only on emulating the West when it comes to the question of science and technology, but they are emulating an ever-changing model. They therefore remain constantly on the receiving end in a situation in which it is difficult, although not impossible, to apply Islamic principles to the economic and environmental fields while still being part of what is euphemistically called the global economic order. They seem to have neither the insight nor the courage and will to create an Islamic economic order in which the Islamic view of the relation of human beings to the natural environment would be central. And, being at the receiving end, they are even less prepared than the highly industrialized countries to ameliorate, to some extent at least, the negative effects of modern technology.

2. In the present period of human history, the agenda for major social and economic matters, including the applications of science and technology, is set by the West, while the rest of the world tries its best to provide answers on the basis of its own cultures. Rarely do non-Western cultures and societies have the power to set the agenda them-

selves. This includes newer factors contributing to the environmental crisis itself and proposals for its solution. For example, recently the West has developed biotechnologies that are already having a global impact not only in medicine but also in agriculture. Muslims did not invent the problems arising from genetically altered crops. That agenda was set by the West. But they must now grapple with them, as they must grapple with the ethical consequences of cloning. Muslims, like nearly all other non-Westerners except perhaps the Japanese, have to accept the fact that in so many crucial issues the technologically more powerful West chooses both the playing field and the rules of the game. Obviously, this constitutes a formidable challenge to Islamic governments and societies if they wish both to implement the Islamic principles involved and to play the game. If they choose not to do so, external pressures become so great as to force them to enter the playing field. Only smaller units can in some cases remain separate and not have to participate in the game of the day, whose rules are set beyond one's borders.

3. Such rapid transformations are made possible by those who constitute the vanguard of what one could call "Faustian Science," to use the language of Goethe. There are only a few Muslims in that vanguard group, but they are for the most part different from others only in that they have Muslim names. Otherwise, they usually accept completely the modern scientistic worldview and are champions of "Faustian Science." They also usually look upon Islamic science as simply a prelude to modern science, not as a science based on a sacralized and not secularized view of nature. Although the number of such advanced scientists in the Islamic world is small, scientism has a fairly substantial following, especially among the ruling classes in various Islamic societies. In fact, modernists as well as so-called fundamentalists are all in favor of the propagation of modern science and technology, to the extent possible, and of increasing Muslim participation in furthering the growth of "Faustian Science." Needless to say, such an attitude constitutes a major obstacle to the propagation of the Islamic view of nature and the cultivation of sciences based on Islamic principles.[3]

4. On a more practical level there is the major obstacle of the migration of the vast number of people from the countryside to urban areas. Typically, such people lived in ecological harmony with their environment back home in their villages. They cared for animals and

plants and were careful not to pollute their water resources. But once cut off from their traditional surrounding, they become uprooted people, dislocated not only on the human plane but also in their relation to the natural world. In urban settings usually impoverished and full of all kinds of pollution, their task becomes solely the survival of themselves and their families, with little interest in anything else. Even if the municipality plants trees before their houses, they usually care little for them and are often instrumental in their destruction. In contrast to the earlier population, which occupied the centers of the older Islamic cities and lived with an awareness of its responsibilities toward its environment, the new occupants, although from the countryside, wreak havoc not only upon shanty towns but also upon the old urban centers they now occupy. One need only to look at the old city in Fez or the heart of Cairo to realize the problem and to see how difficult it is to reeducate the more recent migrated groups in environmental concerns and make them regain the same respect for their new environment that they displayed back home in the countryside where they felt that the tree outside was *their* tree to be protected and the stream flowing by their house was *their* stream, not to be polluted. The mass migration of people from the countryside to the cities, which is a global phenomenon and one of the results of modern industrialization, is as fully evident in the Islamic world as elsewhere. Its effect on both the cities and the countryside has been devastating as far as the natural environment is concerned.

5. Governments in the Islamic world are, needless to say, confronted with these and many other social and economic difficulties not all of their own making. But solutions offered even by relatively benign governments interested in the welfare of their people have been and remain to a large extent based on Western models. Nearly always they seek to apply attempted Western solutions to problems of Islamic society. Although there have been a few changes here and there in recent years, blind imitation of the West in this domain remains the norm in most places. Now, these governments wield power over their societies and use their power to oppose by force any movement which would challenge them. Since they base their solution to the environmental crisis on various Western models, they remain, naturally, opposed to any voice which seeks Islamic solutions, unless there is a situation in which such a solution would be favorable to the government in question.

6. The autocratic, and in some cases dictatorial, nature of regimes in many Islamic countries makes an environmental movement based on Islamic principles a threatening undertaking if it challenges government policies and plans—many of which are dangerous from the environmental point of view. One needs only to recall the opposition of the Ministry of Housing in Egypt two generations ago to the remarkable village built by the great Egyptian architect Hasan Fathy, because his philosophy of architecture—based on the use of local materials with full awareness of the necessity of the integration of architecture and the natural environment—was opposed to the views of the Ministry, which were based completely on prevalent Western ideas of the day. Considering how volatile opposition to state planning can be in such instances, in many Islamic countries open criticism of environmentally dangerous programs supported by the government can be politically dangerous. It is true that there are now "green groups" in certain Islamic countries, such as Iran, and that these groups assemble here and there to resist the destruction of the environment. And it is true that some governments have ministries and bureaus in charge of environmental matters. Nevertheless, in much of the Islamic world, open opposition to governmental policies which are environmentally dangerous can be politically risky, as it is also in India, China, and many other countries. This lack of freedom to oppose openly government policies which endanger the environment is a major obstacle in many countries from Bangladesh to Malaysia. This is one of the tragic conditions of our times, just when we so need to have heard those voices which speak for the health of the whole planet, and do not only claim to address the need for self-gratification of only one species, that is, human beings.

7. Strangely enough, movements in the Islamic world which have sought to revive Islamic teachings, often in opposition to existing political orders, have been for the most part blind to Islamic teachings about the natural environmental. When such groups have opposed modernists and secularists on many issues, they have for the most part agreed completely with the latter group in their blind imitation of Western technology, servitude toward modern science and its application, and indifference to the consequences of the adoption of modern technology for the natural environment, as well as for the souls and minds of Muslims. They always speak of justice, but not of justice for all forms of life; although they espouse the causes of Islamic revival,

they do not contribute to the revival of the Islamic understanding of the natural environment and of our responsibilities toward God's creation beyond the human world. It is interesting to note that Saudi Arabia, which is dominated by Wahhabism and which is usually called "fundamentalist," was the theater in the 1970s and 1980s for the largest transfer of Western technology in history. Yet, very few voices were raised concerning the consequences of this technology on the environment. Such concerns are only now being expressed in that country and some action is being taken. Also, when the Islamic Revolution of 1979 in Iran occurred, there was at first strong opposition to the national park system created during the royal regime and many protected animals were killed. It was years before the government realized the importance of environmental issues and created the position of a vice president to deal with the subject. Altogether, the political revival of Islam has not meant an automatic revival of Islamic teachings concerning nature. The revival of the latter has come through individuals and small groups who have made governments, whether modernist or "fundamentalist," gradually realize the crucial significance of the environmental crisis and the role that Islamic teachings can play in solving that crisis.

8. Finally, in enumerating the obstacles in Islamic societies confronting the task of reformulating Islamic teachings about the environment and implementing them in society at large, one must mention the lack of awareness and preparation of the traditional scholars (*'ulamā'*) who are the custodians of Islam and who have the ear of the vast majority of Muslims in all matters, including those pertaining to the environmental crisis. There are several reasons for this state of affairs. First, human beings traditionally were not a danger to the environment and lived more or less in equilibrium with it. Preachers in mosques, when addressing the relation between human beings and nature, usually spoke about ethical matters, including kindness to animals and the virtue of planting trees as the Prophet had commanded. They did not have to address the dangers of the destruction of biodiversity and global warming. Second, during the past two centuries Islam was attacked by intrusive colonialists and aggressively proselytized by either Christian or secularist missionaries from the West. Much of the energy of Muslim religious scholars was spent defending Islam from those attacks and preserving the people's religious identity. Third, as modernism spread within Islamic society itself, the

'ulamā' saw their duty primarily as one of guiding people to the right path amid the chaos created within sectors of Islamic society itself, and they did not spend their energies studying in depth what was going on in the West.

As far as the environment is concerned, even in the West itself Christian and Jewish theologians and thinkers did not turn to the "theology" of nature until the 1980s and 1990s; in the Islamic world the same trend is now gradually being seen. There are now a few eminent Muslim *'ulamā'*, such as the grand mufti of Syria Shaykh Aḥmad Kiftaru, who speak often of the Islamic teachings about the environment. But the majority are still unaware of the urgency of this matter. When they do speak about it, it is often at the instigation of governments which want people to clean up the stream near their home or not to litter the park next door—but nothing more basic that could threaten various government projects. Governments know full well the power of the *'ulamā'* to influence the public at large. The problem, as far as the environment is concerned, is that most *'ulamā'* still remain unaware of the centrality of environmental issues. Nor do they realize how important their contributions can be to the physical, psychological, and social health of their communities. These traditional scholars need to become fully aware of Islamic teachings about the environment and be willing to speak about and act on them with courage in the face of immediate political considerations and contingencies.

Islamic Sources and Their Teachings on the Environment

As in the case of everything else Islamic, the primary source of Islamic teachings about the natural environment is the Qur'an, in which the foundation of the relation between human beings and the world of nature is clearly stated. Then there are the collections of *ḥadīth*, in which one can find numerous sayings of the Prophet concerning the treatment of nature by human beings. After these twin sources of Islam, one must point to the injunctions of Islamic Law, or *al-Sharī'a*. Although environmental law is not considered a distinct and separate part of the *Sharī'a* in the same way that it has developed as a distinct domain of law in the West, recently there have been numerous *sharī'ite* injunctions dealing specifically with the environment, with such matters as water, soil, animal, and plants—issues that have a distinct bearing on the natural world and, in fact, constitute the natural environment. Likewise, texts of Islamic ethics are of significance, in their concern both with such human passions as greed, which have such a devastating effect on the environment in the modern context, and with animals and even plants.

On another level, one must mention texts of Islamic philosophy dealing with nature. The main schools of Islamic theology, or *kalām*, did not pay much attention to a "theology of nature" which would be of significance in the present-day environmental crisis. By contrast, numerous works of Islamic philosophy provide not only an Islamic philosophy of nature, but what in the West would be called a "theology of nature." This is also true of Sufism, which contains the most profound expressions of an Islamic "metaphysics and theology of nature." Certain Sufi texts bring out the most inward meaning of the Qur'anic doctrine concerning the cosmos and human beings' relation to the world of nature.

Over the centuries Islam produced a major scientific tradition which dealt with the world of nature and at the same time functioned within an Islamic universe of discourse. This scientific tradition has much to offer in the process of formulating a contemporary language expressing Islamic views of the relation of human beings and the natural environment. This contemporary Islamic view, in conjunction with various forms of technology developed in Islamic civilization, could help find a way out of the impasse created by the current environmental crisis.

Islamic art complements Islamic science and its expressions, especially in architecture, landscaping, and urban design. These are visible applications and embodiments of the Islamic sciences of nature and cosmology. A careful study of the traditional Islamic arts, especially those just mentioned, could be an important source of both knowledge and inspiration for creating human living spaces in harmony, rather than discord, with the natural environment.

One of the Islamic arts is literature, which, in the form of poetry especially, has been able to propagate the most profound teachings about the spiritual significance of nature among intellectual elite and ordinary people. Numerous Arabic-speaking peoples recall the verse of the Arab poet Abu Nuwas:

Wa li-kulli shay' in lahu āyatun,
Tadullu 'alā annahu wāḥidun.

In everything there resides a sign of Him,
Providing proof that He is one.

And, is there a Persian speaker who has not heard the verse of Sa'di in his *Gulistān*?

Bi jahān khurram az ānam ki jahān khurram az ūst,
'Āshiqam bar hama 'ālam ki hama 'ālam az ūst.

I am joyous in the world of nature for the world of nature is joyous through Him,
I am in love with the whole cosmos for the whole cosmos comes from Him.

Various literatures of the Islamic people, ranging from Arabic and Persian to Bengali and Swahili, contain a vast wealth of material on the Islamic view of the relationships between human beings and the natural environment. Literature is also an excellent means for the propagation of that view among contemporaries, not only through recourse to classical works, but also through the help of present-day writers and poets, some of whom could surely turn their attention to this subject if they were to be made aware of its crucial importance.

If we were to examine these sources, what would we learn about Islamic teachings concerning the environment? Some work has already been done in this domain, and here one can only summarize some of its most relevant and salient features.[4] The Qur'an in a sense addresses the cosmos as well as human beings, and the world of nature participates in the Qur'anic revelation. The cosmos itself is in fact God's first revelation, and upon the leaves of trees, the faces of mountains, the features of animals, as well as in the sounds of the winds and gently flowing brooks, are to be found the signs of God. These are the messages of that primordial revelation. That is why classical Islamic thought refers to both the recorded Qur'an (*al-qur' ān al-takwīnī*) and the cosmic Qur'an (*al-qur' ān al-takwīnī*). Furthermore, the verses of the Qur'an, the phenomena in the world of nature, and events within the souls of human beings are all referred to as portents or signs (*āyāt*) of God by the Qur'an itself, as in the verse, "We shall show them our portents (*āyāt*) upon the horizons and within themselves, until it becomes manifest unto them that it is the truth" (41:53, Pickthall translation). Likewise, all the creatures in the natural world sing the praise of God. In destroying a species, we are in reality silencing a whole class of God's worshipers.

In the Qur'anic view creation is sacred but not divine, for divinity belongs to God alone. Nature is sacred because it is the effect of the Divine Creative Act to which the Qur'an refers in the verse, "But, His command, when He intendeth a thing, is only that He saith unto it: Be! and it is (*kun fa-yakūn*)" (36:81). What issues directly from the Will of the One who is also called the All-Sacred (*al-Quddūs*) in Islam and what reflects His Wisdom cannot but be sacred. Nature reflects the Wisdom (*hikma*) of God and His Will (*irāda*), as also the Qur'an repeats in different places that it was created in truth and not falsehood. Nature is not there only for our use. It is there to reflect the creative Power of God, and grace, or *baraka*, also flows in the arteries and veins of the universe. Human beings are created to be a channel of grace for the cosmic ambience around them. Creatures in the world of nature not only have a relation with human beings and through them with God, they also have a direct relation with God and possess an eschatological significance. The Islamic paradise is full of animals and plants and is not only crystalline. Creatures will speak directly to God on the Day of Judgment. As Rumi says, "they are silent here but eloquent there." He adds in another poem:

> If only creatures had tongues (here below),
> They could lift the veil from the Divine mysteries.

In fact, like the Qur'an whose verses have levels of meaning, the phenomena of nature possess inward levels of meaning and significance. The reality of nature is not exhausted by its outward appearance. Each phenomenon is precisely "an appearance" of a noumenal reality. The phenomena of nature are not only facts but primarily symbols related to the states of being above. Nature is not only the domain of quantity, the source of power and resource. It is above all the abode of spiritual presence and source for the understanding and contemplation of divine wisdom. Our need for nature is not only to feed and shelter our physical bodies, but also and above all to nurture our souls. As the complement to the Qur'an as revelation, nature responds to our spiritual needs.

A central concept of Islam cited often in the Qur'an is *ḥaqq* (pl. *ḥuqūq*), which means at once truth, reality, right, law, and due. The term *al-Ḥaqq* is also a Name of God as well as of the Qur'an.[5] It is also of the utmost importance for understanding the Islamic view of human beings in relation to the natural environment when it is used in the case of creatures. According to Islam, each being exists by virtue of the truth (*ḥaqq*) and is also owed its due (*ḥaqq*) according to its nature. The trees have their due, as do animals or even rivers and mountains. In dealing with nature, human beings must respect and pay what is due to each creature, and each creature has its rights accordingly. Islam stands totally against the idea that we human beings have all the rights and other creatures have none except what we decide to give them. The rights of creatures were given by God and not by us, to be taken away when we decide to do so.

The Qur'an speaks of human beings as both servants of God (*'abd Allāh*) and vicegerents of God (*khalīfat Allāh*). We have the right to practice our vicegerency on Earth only on the condition that we remain God's servants and obey His Will and His Laws. Even the permission to dominate (*taskhīr*) the earth is given to us on the condition that we remain in a state of submission to and servanthood of God. God dominates over His creation, but He also cares for it. In contrast to the interpretation of certain Muslim modernists and so-called fundamentalists, the Qur'an does not under any condition give human beings the right to dominate nature without protecting it and acting as its steward. We cannot take away the *ḥaqq* of various creatures given to them by God, but must pay each being its due (*ḥaqq*) in accordance with the nature of that creature. As for our rights (*ḥuqūq*) over nature, like other rights, they must follow our responsibilities toward God and the world of nature. In Islam there are no human rights without human responsibilities. Rights follow and do not precede responsibilities.[6]

The Prophet of Islam, who was the first and surest guide for the understanding of the Qur'an and whose sayings (*aḥādīth*) and actions and deeds (*sunna*) complement the Qur'anic teachings about the natural world, reflected the Qur'anic teachings about the treatment of the natural world in his daily life. He encouraged the planting of trees, banned destroying vegetation even during war, loved animals and displayed great kindness to them, and encouraged other Muslims to do likewise. He even established protected areas for natural life, which may be considered Islamic prototypes for contemporary natural parks and nature conservancies. The books of *ḥadīth* are replete with sayings pertaining to the world of nature and the attitude of human beings to it, including strong opposition to wastefulness and the needless destruction of nature based only on greed and avarice. The *aḥādīth* emphasize cleanliness and disapprove of the pollution of water and other substances that support life. It is the Prophet who said that it was a blessed act to plant a tree, even if it were the day before the end of the world.

There is a traditional account which displays the Prophet's attitude toward the natural environmental and which should serve as a powerful lesson for contemporary Muslims. It has to do with the famous reclining palm tree of Seville, which the celebrated Andalusian Sufi Ibn 'Arabi mentioned in his account of the life of the Prophet and considered the Prophet's dealing with the tree to be one of his miracles. The account given by Ibn 'Arabi is as follows:

> In the vicinity of the Cemetery of Mushka [in Seville] . . . there was a palm tree which, as one could see, was leaning over a great deal. The people in the neighboring houses, fearing that it might fall on their homes and damage them, complained to the local ruler who, in response to their concern, ordered it to be cut down. Those who were going to cut it down arrived at the place after the evening prayer and said: "It will soon be dark. Let us cut it down tomorrow, if God wills". . . .
>
> Now, it so happened that one of our companions [had a vision in which] he saw the Envoy of God—may God bless him and give him peace—sitting in a mosque situated in the middle of the Cemetery of Mushka. [And he saw how] the palm tree in question was ploughing through the ground with its roots until it arrived at his side. It then complained to him that the people wanted to cut it down on account of its curvature, for fear that it might harm their houses, and it said to him, "O Envoy of God, pray for me!"
>
> The person who had the vision related that the Envoy of God then placed his hand on the palm tree, which immediately straightened, remaining upright and erect, and returned to its place.
>
> In the morning, when the people got up, I went with a group of individuals to establish the veracity of that vision and we all saw that it had straightened up and become erect, without any curvature.[7]

Would that present-day Muslims remember this account when they next try to cut trees only for the sake of convenience or greed!

As for the Divine Law, or *al-Sharī'a*, it contains numerous injunctions pertaining to the natural environment. These include insistence on making natural resources that are used by the community as a whole, such as water and forests, public and not private property and guarding and protecting them. They also include the just treatment of animals and plants and the prohibition of killing living beings for wasteful or needless purposes. The ritual sacrifice of animals that can be eaten and whose flesh then becomes *ḥalāl*, or permissible, is itself of the greatest importance in creating a spiritual relation between human beings and the animal world. Also, *Sharī'ite* teachings about economic matters, including opposition to usury, to wasteful consumerism, and to the excessive amassing of wealth, are of the greatest direct and indirect import for human beings' relation to the natural environment. Altogether the *Sharī'a* contains both concrete laws and principles for the regulations needed to help the Islamic community confront the critical environmental situation today and to find solutions that would be much easier to implement than secular laws and regulations, because Muslims would be more willing to accept and implement them. They would see them as God's Laws, rather than simply governmental regulations to be circumvented whenever possible.

What Is to Be Done?

Facing the environmental crisis, which threatens human life itself, is of the utmost urgency precisely because of the rapidity with which the natural environment is being destroyed. The solution to this crisis requires the most urgent action, a turning to a sacralized vision of nature, as well as performing concrete actions on the earthly plane. In light of the Islamic teachings about the natural environment and the present situation, a number of actions can be taken in the Islamic world to ameliorate the severe crisis caused by the human treatment of the natural world today. Some of these actions are briefly outlined below:

1. Since the nineteenth century, scientism and the blind adulation of modern technology have spread gradually within the Islamic world so that today, among those who rule over various Muslim societies, as well as among most modernized Muslims and even a number of religious scholars there exists a prevalent scientism outwardly not very different from that existing in the West. Whether there is a modernist

or a so-called fundamentalist government ruling over a Muslim society, there is a blind acceptance of modern Western science, and Western technology is adopted as rapidly as possible, with little interest in the environmental consequences of such actions. Where the Islamic world differs from the West is that the Western scientistic worldview—with its reduction of both human beings and nature to a set of complicated molecular structures bereft of any sacred significance, except in a sentimental sense—has a less tenuous hold upon the Muslim mind than it has in the West, which has had several centuries of confrontation with the materialistic and quantitative view of nature. The first step in the Islamic world must be to criticize this stifling scientistic view of reality and to demonstrate why it is opposed to the authentic Islamic and more generally religious point of view as such. There is no way to reconstruct the edifice of the Islamic view of human beings and nature without clearing the ground of all the decrepit ideological ruins posing as imposing monuments and cleansing the mental space of the Islamic world of all of the errors resulting from scientism, reductionism, and materialism—just as the Prophet cleared the Ka'ba of idols in the Age of Ignorance.

2. Having cleared the mental space and removed the obstacles which exist in the minds of so many Muslims and which prevent them from comprehending their own traditional universe, the Islamic understanding of the natural environment and humanity's relation to it must then be formulated and expressed in the clearest language possible, one that is comprehensible to contemporary Muslims.[8] The formulation of these Islamic teachings, drawing from the sources already mentioned, must be made on several levels. These formulations must be able to address the philosopher as well as the cobbler, the religious scholar as well as the peasant. There must exist the deepest metaphysical exposition comprehensible to those few rooted in the Islamic intellectual tradition and/or well aware of Western philosophy, as well as poetic expressions to attract the large numbers drawn to literature and to sermons preached to the multitudes in mosques. There is no reason why, if there is the will, in a few years the Islamic teachings about humanity's relationship to the environment cannot be made known to all levels of Islamic society using contemporary language. Much has been done, but has not as yet been widely disseminated.

3. Those who run the affairs of Islamic society are men and women who, obviously, have been trained in various schools and disciplines.

It is essential to introduce courses on the environment at all levels of education and to emphasize themes and subjects pertaining to the environmental dimensions of other disciplines within those disciplines. For example, it is almost criminally negligent to teach various fields of engineering without acquainting the students with the environmental impact of this or that engineering project. Likewise, economic planning should never be taught without consideration of the environmental costs involved. The West has been more successful in this matter in recent years than the Islamic world, because modern educational institutions in the Islamic world simply emulate the West and are therefore usually a step behind. In many places educational systems are still following older, obsolete curricula of their Western models.

Courses on the environment, and emphasis upon subjects pertaining to the environment in other courses, should not, however, be limited to modern educational institutions, but most definitely should include the traditional schools, or *madāris*, in which the future religious leaders of the community are trained. These leaders are much more effective than governmental officials in turning the attention of the populace to a particular issue, and their role is crucial in creating awareness of the environmental crisis and of Islam's answers to it. But the religious teachers and scholars must first become aware of these issues themselves through appropriate education. They must be educated to realize that the environmental crisis is not going to be solved by condoning outlandish industrial projects which do irreparable harm to the environment, but which are supported by the government, while preaching against the urban poor who pollute streams with garbage. In order for this educational effort to succeed, there is the need to teach these matters from the Islamic point of view, not just from the Western one, and for governments to gain the approval of religious authorities in charge of the *madāris* rather than trying to force the issue through some governmental decree which will only backfire. Fortunately, as already mentioned, there are a number of leading religious authorities throughout the Islamic world who are aware of the great danger of the environmental crisis, but there has not, as yet, been a concerted effort to make this issue central to the curricula of religious schools throughout the Islamic world.

4. While such religious scholars are being trained, those who are already aware of the various dimensions of the environmental crisis

must be encouraged by governments which control the media in the Islamic world to spend as much effort as possible in their weekly sermons in mosques and in daily contact with ordinary people, radio and television talks, and writings to increase awareness of environmental issues. As matters stand today, in most Islamic countries what the religious scholars say and preach is controlled by the government. And when the government does not want a hotly contested political or economic issue to be discussed, it usually orders the preachers in mosques to speak about bodily cleanliness, keeping the water pure, and not molesting cats and dogs in the street. These admonitions are fine, but they are not sufficient, especially when the government itself is the primary agent causing the deterioration of the environment. In such cases, little freedom to criticize the government is given to either religious scholars or civil leaders or teachers. Hence, the lack of political freedom becomes a factor in weakening efforts to solve the environmental crisis.

Nevertheless, there is still much that can be done in the educational field, so that a few years from now both government leaders and those outside of government will see the stark reality of the problem. For this to be realized, it would be much easier to have the efforts of the two sides be complementary, and to have religious scholars, preachers, and *imāms* who have the ear of the people, spearhead efforts to save the environment with governmental approval, rather than having ordinary people blame the government and the government ordinary people. Because faith in Islam is still strong, joint efforts by religious scholars and political and social leaders would have much more success in combating the increasing deterioration of the natural environment we see in so many parts of the Islamic world today.

5. Only recently have nongovernmental institutions begun to have some impact in the Islamic world, despite opposition in many cases by local governments. Now that such institutions are taking root, it is important to create some institutions which deal primarily with the environment, rather than with economic and social issues independent of the environment, as we see so often today. Such environmentally aware institutions have sprung up in the West during the past few decades, and a few have been instrumental in realizing laudable goals in the preservation of the environment through the purchase of pristine land and the protection of forests. There is no reason why such institutions cannot expand in the Islamic world if they are created

more in keeping with Islamic teachings and norms, including the institutions of religious endowments (*awqāf*), rather then simply imitating Western models. There are many religious endowments for the creation of mosques, schools, and hospitals. There is no reason why endowments could not be created for the preservation of water, soil, trees, and animals. Of course, the degree of freedom of nongovernmental organizations in the Islamic world is restricted by government regulations, but here again, there is a wide margin within which such institutions could function and flourish.

6. Both blindness to the dangers of many forms of modern technology and external and internal economic and political pressures have caused nearly all governments in the Islamic world to disregard their indigenous technologies, ranging from irrigation to medical drugs, in favor of Western substitutes. There must be a major campaign by those aware of the significance of many of the traditional technologies to preserve such technologies and to use, whenever possible, alternative technologies that usually need less energy and have much less negative impact upon the natural environment. One sees such an awareness growing here and there, but much more work needs to be done. The implementation of alternative technologies can have a major impact, reducing the destructive effects of modern technology upon the environment.

7. In the contemporary Islamic world various forms of encouragement are used to further the cause of what the governments or various private or religious organizations consider to be important. There are national and international awards given within the Islamic world for the best book, artistic creation, and service to the cause of Islam, but there is little encouragement when it comes to the question of the environment. It would not be difficult to attract the attention of the gifted to this field through various forms of encouragement, such as are also beginning to appear in the West.

There are, of course, many other steps that could be taken, but the few enumerated here are among the most important and most feasible.

Concluding Comments

In conclusion, one must ask who is going to carry out the program thus outlined, and what force can confront the powerful international economic and technological engine that is wreaking havoc upon the earth in nearly every continent? The answer for the Islamic world cannot be only governments, because although they wield great power, they are more a part of the problem than the solution. The solution, at the present moment, lies for the most part with individuals and small groups which can perhaps expand in the future. What is certain is that, first of all, the environmental crisis must be recognized in its spiritual and religious depth as well as its outward effects. Second, the authentic Islamic view must be resuscitated with rigor and clarity and without compromise. Those who can be awakened must be made to open their eyes and to realize that the modern world is walking on the edge of a precipice and needs only to take another "forward step" to face its own perdition. Awareness leads to further awareness. The Islamic teachings about God, human beings, nature, and the relation between them all constitute a clarion call for this awakening from the dangerous dream of scientism and humanity's selfish conquest of nature. They can set Muslims again on the correct path to a harmonious modus vivendi with nature, and they can also help the Western world to regain and recollect its own forgotten tradition concerning the role of human beings in God's creation. Let us hope that this awakening takes place through proactive human efforts and not as a consequence of the rude awakening resulting from ecological disasters that threaten the very possibility of human life on earth. In discussing such momentous matters, it is appropriate to remember the Islamic teaching that the future is in God's hands. Ultimately, God is, as one of His Sacred Names, *al-Muḥīṭ*, tells us, literally, our "environment."

Notes

1. Seyyed Hossein Nasr, *Man and Nature: The Spiritual Crisis of Modern Man* (1967; Chicago: ABC International, 2000).

2. The analyses of Ivan Illich made a generation ago still hold true. See his *Tools for Conviviality* (New York: Harper, 1980). Also, although Jacques Ellul holds a rather anti-Islamic stand, his works have been well received in certain circles in the Islamic world precisely because he deals with the issue of the negative impact of modern technology upon human society in such a way that his words speak eloquently to those Muslims aware of the deeper issues involved in the introduction of modern technology into their own societies.

3. During the past two decades a number of both religious philosophers and scientists in the Islamic world have become aware of this question and of the necessity for reviving Islamic science along lines that I suggested several decades ago in *Science and Civilization in Islam* (1968; Chicago: ABC International, 2001) and several other works. Today, there are a number of centers in Malaysia, India, Pakistan, Iran, Turkey, and elsewhere concerned with the Islamic meaning of Islamic science and the danger of imitating modern science as if it were simply a continuation of the Islamic scientific tradition.

4. See Seyyed Hossein Nasr, *The Need for a Sacred Science* (Albany: State University of New York Press, 1993), 129 ff.

5. See Seyyed Hossein Nasr, *The Heart of Islam: Enduring Values for Humanity* (San Francisco: HarperSanFrancisco, 2002), 281–82.

6. Ibid., 273 ff.

7. See Pablo Beneito Arias, "Life of the Prophet and Miracles of the Palm Tree," *Journal of Muhayiddin Ibn 'Arabi Society* 30 (2001): 88–91. This vision was made famous throughout the Islamic world through al-Qazwini's mention of it in his *Āthār al-bilād*.

8. This task has already begun and, besides my own works, a number of books and essays from different perspectives have appeared on this subject. See, for example, Richard C. Foltz, ed., *Worldviews, Religion, and the Environment* (Belmont, Calif.: Wadsworth, 2002), 357–91; Akhtaruddin Ahmad, *Islam and the Environmental Crisis* (London: Ta-Ha Publishers, 1997); and Fazlun M. Khalid and Joanne O'Brien, eds., *Islam and Ecology* (New York: Cassell, 1992). See also the *Journal of Islamic Science* 16, no. 1-2 (2000), where several essays are devoted to the issue of Islamic teachings on the environment.

Islam and the Environment: Theory and Practice

MAWIL IZZI DIEN

In searching for the real reasons that have led to current, worldwide, environmental problems, many modern scholars put the blame on the philosophical foundation of modern thinking. For example, S. R. Sterling maintains that the world problem started because of the eclipse of the earlier worldview of medieval Christendom. This eclipse took place when the church was no longer seen to offer a parallel intellectual view for scholars like Galileo, Bacon, Descartes, and Newton. The new secular worldview became inherently materialistic, with no recognition for concepts such as value, spirit, feeling, emotions, intuition, and intrinsic goals. Most importantly, Cartesian duality (which separated mind from body) set human beings apart from and over nature, thus opening the way for a relationship that is primarily exploitative and manipulative.[1]

The Theory

In Islam the problem did not arise, at least, during what Sir Hamilton Gibb called the "Golden age of Islamic culture when literature and science widened out in every direction, and economical prosperity reached its climax."[2] During that time all researches and discoveries were revolving around the profoundly dominating concept of *tawḥīd*, which states that the only god is Allah. This basic principle is described to mean that there is no reality outside the Absolute Reality.[3] Accordingly, all scientific and intellectual effort was seen to have been kindled from the same light of God and lit to offer further "lights" for humanity. The calculations of mathematicians were for religious or Islamic objectives; the same applied to the chemist, the engineer, and all other technical innovators.

In a speech delivered at Wilton Park on 13 December 1996, the Prince of Wales referred to the Islamic "sense of the sacred" as having an important role in the rediscovery of our human responsibilities, of which the environment is but one. The Qur'anic verse "whithersoever you turn, there is the face of God" was apparently understood by the prince as a manifestation of a "profound sense of the sacred and the spiritual." This verse was originally revealed to assist those who were unable to ascertain the direction for prayer *qibla*. The Qur'an replied that "whithersoever you turn, there is the face of God." This indicates that reverence for God is not only for what is sacred but is also a part of the reason for the existence of creatures upon the earth. The Islamic attitude toward the environment that surrounds humanity is not merely restricted to the presence of God everywhere, but also to the following dimensions.

By submitting to God, Islam establishes the bedrock of the relationship between finite, mortal human beings and the infinite Divine, the secular and the sacred. This relationship cannot be understood without first realizing the meaning of the "submission" that the "created" should concede in his relationship with the creator. Humans have to accept that they are created beings who act as the "agents" of God on Earth. These agents are creative in their own way, but they are not God. Humans, however will become closer to the sacred by operating according to God's instructions. Muhammad is reported to have narrated that God said,

> When a worshipper moves closer to me by good virtues and worship, I will be his hearing by which he can hear, I will be his eyes by which he can see, I will be his hand by which he can act, and his feet by which he can walk. If he asks Me I will give him what he wants, and if he asks for protection I will protect him.[4]

Islam, as a way of life, expects human beings to conserve the environment for several reasons, which may be summarized as follows: The environment is God's creation. The creation of this earth and all its natural resources is a sign of His wisdom, mercy, power, and His other attributes and therefore serves to develop human awareness and understanding of the Creator.[5] Muslims should seek to protect and preserve the environment, because by so doing they protect God's creatures, which pray to Him and praise Him. Humankind might not be able to understand how these creatures praise God, but this does not mean that they do not do so:

> The seven heavens and the earth,
> And all beings therein,
> Declare His glory:
> There is not a thing
> But celebrates His praise:
> And yet ye understand not
> How they declare His Glory! (Qur'an 17:44)

Third, the environment contains God's creatures, which the *'ulamā'*, or Muslim scholars, consider to also deserve protection (*ḥurma*). A fourth reason why Islam seeks to protect and preserve the environment is that, as a way of life, it is established on the concept of good (*khayr*). Therefore it is expected that Islam will protect the environment once it is understood that such protection is good by itself. The Qur'an states that:

> He whoso doeth good
> An atom's weight
> Will see it.
> And whoso do ill
> An atom's weight
> Will see it. (Qur'an 99:7–8)

Fifth, all human relationships in Islam have to be based on the concept of justice (*'adl*) and kindness (*ishn*), and not on material or economical gain. The Qur'an strongly emphasizes this concept in the following verse: "God enjoins justice and kindness" (16:90).

In Islam, humans are expected to protect the environment since no other creature is able to perform this task. Humans are the only beings that God has "entrusted" with the responsibility of looking after the earth. This trusteeship is seen by Islam to be so onerous and burdensome that no other creature would "accept" it. The Qur'an says:

> Lo! We offered the trust
> Unto the heavens and the
> Earth and the hills,
> But they shrank from bearing it
> And were afraid of it
> And man assumed it
> Lo! he is a tyrant and fool. (33:72)

Accordingly, not every human can claim this appointment. Only those who are aware of this caring pact of respect for life can claim it.

The Practice

It must be admitted that Islamic culture and society has not been free from a historical transition similar to that which took place to produce a twentieth-century West with different moral standards than those prevalent in the fourteenth century. In Islam, to use Professor Gibb's statement:

> The course of moral and religious integration and the progress of the Community toward deepening self-consciousness and universality call for an entirely different standard of measurement than those by which the intellectual breadth or economical property of the Islamic civilization in its "Golden Age" is judged.[6]

However, the traditional consciousness of its "divine" calling has remained within the community. Was this because of the comparatively young age of the faith compared to other similar divinely based linear faiths? Or could such a consciousness be attributed to the concept of divine grace and divine guidance, or *baraka*, that lies beyond human understanding?[7] Perhaps Islam remained as an effective social and political force in the Muslim world because it paid the organic element (the human) an attention equal to that it paid to the organization (the establishment). Despite the historical decadence of the political establishment and existing religious legal system, Islam was "cultured" into the human in such a way that it continued even after the establishment had died. Thus, all discussions about right and wrong were still considered in Islam as part of the decision-making process that took place collectively between the roots and uppermost branches of the tree. This is in contrast to modern politics that denies such a feature to the process of political decision making.[8]

The schism between the spiritual and the "scientific" was imported into the Muslim mind and land when the material, industrial culture was introduced, effectively separating the political system from the traditions of the community. This had a devastating effect on the indigenous culture and the environment and its biota.

Saudi Arabia represents a self-professed, pioneering model of a modern Islamic state that adopts the "Islamic solution," which was established in August 1932 by the sword and wisdom of the late king 'Abd al-'Aziz bin Sa'ud.[9] The country had started to import the materialistic culture by the late 1970s, when increasing oil revenues were being utilized to improve living conditions. By the late 1980s the huge jump from a nomadic desert society to a society that has all the facilities of an industrial world at its disposal had been all but completed. The fully fledged features of industrial façade were achieved when large cities like Riyadh and Jeddah were constructed. The style of living which accompanied multistory housing and office work meant a further drift away from the earth and what it can provide.

The tools which were provided by a keen and rich government budget had, in many ways, a negative effect on the human element of the environment and resulted in massive degradation of the natural ecosystem. Expensive water was provided to the consumer in a subsidized price close to nothing, causing people to waste it with no consideration of the cost of its production. Comparing the city of Riyadh's water consumption (four hundred twelve liters per person per day) with that of the small villages and countryside (Hafr al-Batin and other small villages consume twenty-nine liters per person per day), the great difference in the pressure that each culture places on the environment can be appreciated.[10] The impressive road network, which was meant to facilitate life, had a catastrophic effect on both traditional village and agricultural life. The young were encouraged to migrate to the town to take the place of the many foreign workers. The farmers stopped planting their lands either because the imported crops were cheaper, although not better, or because they found the task demeaning and only suitable for employed workers whose pay was unrelated to yield. The easy availability of funds led many people to feel too proud to practice manual or agricultural work, as their fathers and grandfathers had before them. In other words, humans were forced to cope with the new pattern of life, alien to them. The Islamic holistic concept of one society like one body living on God's gift to His creatures, the earth, began to crumble. The earth became only an object which is measured by meters and valued by dollars. Mother Earth became building plots, and high-rise towers climbed to take the virginity of nature.

The environment lost out when remote rural agricultural land was abandoned because many species of fauna and flora, which had come to depend on centuries-old agricultural practices, lost their habitat. In contrast to this, many of those who planted the land misused it and drained all its reserves, often solely because they could afford the technology to recover fossil water.

The scenario has been repeated in Middle Eastern countries; the threats to the environment started when the "modern" material philosophy was brought in. A new culture was imported with the modern, fast, petrol-thirsty cars which were driven by the same individuals who had driven camels or donkeys only a few years before. The language of the Middle East provides strong evidence of a human whose body has a Western appearance but whose mind was still evolving toward that different high-speed culture. One example can be cited here from the local Gulf dialect, in which the word "shepherd"—*ra'i*—is still used when referring to the owner of a car. The human-animal relationship represented in this word exists to indicate care and attention, although the animal has been replaced with colored metal. Until the early 1980s scrap cars used to be disposed of at the desert roadside in a long metallic line. Many were only two or three years old, discarded because the rich owners wanted newer models or because they were too troublesome to repair.

Despite the fact that Islam's attitude in the theoretical environmental debate is both straightforward and well respected, many parts of the Muslim world are currently witnessing a cultural environmental rupture which can be ascribed to two causes. The sudden, almost shocking introduction of the industrial age to these countries was not supported by a value system compatible with the prevalent Islamic values. The outcome has been a sad alteration of "satisfaction" with the little that can be acquired from the environment to a "dissatisfaction" that can only be appeased by ever-increasing consumption. Human values were and still are witnessing a dangerous level of deformation that cannot be controlled without going back to the bottle that once contained the genie. Both Islamic values and industrial values need to be reexamined to extract from them a new value system that fits modern human beings, without rejecting the bedrock of Islam and the environmental elements that it supports.

The Middle East started to experience environmental problems after the Second World War, when large cities were built to serve the world's huge machine of industry.[11] The first impact of this urbanization was the fracturing of traditional social bonds that led to a self-centered relationship within the fabric of society.

The environment was the first to suffer the impact of such a cultural and economical transfusion. Humans started replacing huts with mansions, and their date-palm diet with date expiry food with all its disposable packaging. This was done with no consideration for water supply, sewage disposal, or any environmental hazard. Peter Beaumont, Gerald Blake, and J. Malcolm Wagstaff reported the following situation that resulted from building new cities in the Middle East:

> The serious effects of such rapid growth on the environment have not always been appreciated. Large areas of cultivated or potentially cultivatable land have been swallowed up by the expansion of many cities. . . . In many places, especially where industrial development has become important, new pollutants are beginning to cause ecological damage. Petrochemical and other chemical waste products present the greatest dangers to what is [sic] often very fragile ecosystems. Pollution by solid waste from urban centers is another growing problem throughout the region. Waste disposal methods are generally primitive. The usual practice is either to throw domestic and industrial refuse into the nearest water course, whether dry or flowing with water, or to tip it indiscriminately just outside the city boundaries.
>
> Regrettably, atmospheric pollution is already characteristic of the Middle Eastern urban environment. Exhaust fumes from automobiles are probably the greatest single cause of this nuisance, but domestic and industrial consumption of hydrocarbons is also an important contributory factor. In winter, Ankara is frequently blanketed by a thick brown smog which collects in its enclosed basin as a result of temperature inversion and the use of lignite in central heating systems. Photochemical smog is now apparent in the larger cities during the hot summer months, and is likely to grow worse because of the lax regulations governing automobile exhaust emission. Closely associated with the automobile and air pollution is the growing amount of urban noise and its deleterious effect on the inhabitants. From this point of view, cities

> such as Cairo, Teheran, Tel Aviv, Beirut and Istanbul are now as unpleasant to visit or work in as London or New York. The tranquility and charm which recently characterized Jerusalem and Esfahan, for example, have been lost, possibly for ever.[12]

The new industrial culture did not pay attention to the fact that some of the resources are only there for a short time and that inappropriate use will harm not only one nation but all the nations in the region. Water shortage is one example of the resource problems that need a solution.

The Water Problem

According to former United Nations Secretary General Boutros Boutros Ghali, "the next war in the Middle East will be fought over water not politics," a statement made when he was Egypt's minister of foreign affairs in 1985. The region's spiraling population growth, expanding agriculture, and rising standard of living demand ever more water and other environmental resources. Joyce Starr, of the Washington, D.C.–based Global Water Summit Initiative, stated: "Nations like Israel and Jordan have only ten to fifteen years left before their agriculture and ultimately their food security is threatened."[13]

Water seems to be replacing oil as the region's most contentious commodity and, in Saudi Arabia, water is, for obvious reasons, more expensive than oil. A country in which rain is considered a great novelty has to resort to expensive measures to survive the hot climate of the desert. Desalination plants represent a major synthetic "river" available not merely to Saudi Arabia but to the entire world. Saudi Arabia's twenty-two desalination plants produce about 30 percent of the world's desalinated water. The sharp increase in population that accompanied the economical leap that the country witnessed with the oil boom during the 1970s and 1980s resulted in doubling the population figure from 7,012,642 in 1980 to 16,929,000 in 1994.[14] This led to an increased demand for water. Saudi Arabia today is opening itself to internal analysis and is searching for the means of repairing the large gaps in its internal environmental needs. Saudi academics now are monitoring the potential environmental problems that the country will have to resolve during the next two decades resulting from the further increases in the population, which will demand more water, and improved sewer systems and treatment plants for waste water.[15]

Many reports indicate that water wells are sometimes being dug as deep as two thousand meters for the purpose of irrigation. There are also some "rumors" that farmers who dig that deep are not getting fresh water but water contaminated with sulfur.[16] The agricultural water consumption increased during the year 1994 to reach twenty-two billion cubic meters, which has resulted in the dramatic depletion and contamination of the irreplaceable underground water.[17]

However, with the catastrophic effect that the Iranian and Gulf Wars have had on the Saudi budget, there have had to be many cuts and a reconsideration of future plans. In a country where taxes are still seen as not appropriate, there is an apparent undercurrent calling for big investors to put their hands in their pockets to help. A recent article by a leading academic in Saudi Arabia suggested that some contribution should be provided by "those who are making hundreds of billions" to help maintain the country's infrastructure, including the great road network.[18] The argument seems to be justified, bearing in mind that the same people (mainly bankers for the time being) who were asked to make a contribution were only there because of the presence of such expensive facilities.

Another country in the region which is a key regional player in today's, and any future, environmental dilemma is Turkey. This is a country that seems to express serious interest in Islam. Islam appears to be the important historical political platform upon which the ruling Welfare Party stands. This fits very well with my argument that Islam as a common factor between the regional states is one of the main keys, if not *the* key, to the resolution of the region's environmental problems. Turkey, as a main player in the region, considers water distribution vital in solving many of its economical problems resulting from the paucity of alternative natural resources. It is this consideration that led Turkey to build the giant Ataturk Dam in the late 1980s. The dam contains the Euphrates River and fills a reservoir ten times the size of the Sea of Galilee. It is part of the Anatolia Project, which also created twenty-two dams and nineteen power stations on the Tigris.[19]

The Ataturk Dam limits the Euphrates downstream flow to five hundred cubic meters a second until the reservoir behind the dam reaches its full operational level.[20] Both Syria and Iraq are anxious about the reduced annual flow, which in actual fact amounts to approximately half that which flowed previously.[21] Both complained about the shortage of water and power when Turkey held back the river to begin filling up the Ataturk reservoir. Many rivers that once teemed with life are dead now, one example being the Quwaya River. At the present time the main dispute between Turkey, Syria, and Iraq is about how best to use the waters of the Tigris and Euphrates.

Egypt is another area of regional concern. It is expected that Egypt will have to feed a projected twenty-five million additional people by the year 2010, which will necessitate the removal of a large number of people who have depended on the river Nile for generations. These populations will have to be uprooted and replanted in the desert. They will also have to accustom themselves to making better use of Nile water, adjusting to multiple use.

The Nile drains eight other nations: Ethiopia, Sudan, Tanzania, Uganda, Kenya, Zaïre, Burundi, and, Rwanda. The water is currently divided by quota. Farmers in the delta have been accused of wasting water by flood irrigation, letting water run into the fields until they are soaked. However, recent studies seem to have vindicated these practices, for thorough soaking avoids the buildup of salts. The long-term goal, however, must be to intercept drainage water and reuse it just before it goes into the sea. Twelve billion cubic meters used to drain into the Mediterranean Sea. Egypt is already recycling about two billion cubic meters of that water. Further reclamation can be made by lining irrigation canals with plastic and by capturing water underground with drainage systems.[22]

The Islamic Paradigm

Islam today is a recognized power in Turkey, Syria, and Iraq. Although this recognition might appear at times only superficial, the value to the masses should not be underestimated. The mass of people in the Muslim world is experiencing the worldwide phenomenon of "searching for religious roots" that can be utilized to solve rather than to create problems.

I maintain here that Islam may offer valid grounds to resolve not only the environmental problem but also the water distribution problem, which is strongly associated with it. The proposal does not preclude other non-Islamic regional states from fair access to water, nor does it deny international law its role as the main arbitrator to resolve disputes. However, I suggest that Islam is an important potential ground for settling disputes, from which the international law may proceed. Islamic law has a considerable amount of legislation that can provide a possible basis for international arbitration when disagreements and disputes take place.

In Islam the relationship between humankind and the environment is part of social existence, an existence based on the fact that everything on Earth worships the same God. This worship is not merely ritual practice, since rituals are simply the symbolic human manifestation of submission to God. The actual devotions are actions which can be practiced by all the creatures of Earth sharing the planet with the human race. Moreover, humans are responsible for the welfare and sustenance of the other citizens of this global environment. The Qur'an contains many verses that can be referred to for guidance in this respect. The following verse is one example:

> O people! Worship your Lord, Who hath created you and those before you, so that you may ward off (evil); Who hath appointed the earth a resting-place for you, and the sky a canopy; and causeth water to pour down from the sky, thereby producing fruits as food for you. And do not set up rivals to Allah when ye know (better). (Qur'an 2:21)

The word in this verse which is translated as "may ward off evil" is, in Arabic, *tatūqun*. It enjoins piety and awareness, which is accompanied by an appreciation of the surrounding environment. In this verse the Qur'an speaks directly to all groups of people, whether believers, or not. It attempts to mobilize people to the importance of "worshiping God" as a symbol and a way of life that enjoins justice and equity in handling the system created by Him.

This system has been placed under human responsibility, to be cared for and not misused, as can be concluded by returning to Qur'an 2:22. The word *lakum* (for you) in the phrase "created for you" contains the message that the earth is not for one generation, but for every generation, past, present, and future, and that would include humans as well as other creatures on this earth. Accordingly, rivers and minerals are the property of all. These should be distributed fairly and justly, especially when they happen to be owned collectively, like the rivers Tigris and Euphrates.

Water distribution has very clear-cut legislation in Islam. In general terms its rules are based on the principle of benefiting all those who share its watercourse. Water rules are laid down according to the origin of the water source. These are divided according to the size of the source, the kind of water, and its usage. Accordingly, water sources are divided into rivers, water springs, wells, and rain water. Rivers are divided into natural rivers, large and small, and human-dug canals and irrigation channels.

The rivers Tigris, Euphrates, and Nile are often referred to in the standard text books of Islamic law (*fiqh*) as examples of large public rivers (*anhūr 'amma*). These rivers belong to all the community, and everyone can benefit from them providing that no harm is caused to others. These rights vary from the right of watering (*ḥaqq al-shiffa*) to the right of drinking (*ḥaqq al-shurb*). The main condition to be borne in mind for all users is that no harm should to be caused to other partners.[23] The right of flowing (*ḥaqq al-majra*) is recognized in Islam and is protected according to the saying of the Prophet, who addressed an obstinate landowner, saying, "by God, the water will be passed to others even over your belly."[24] The partnership between people and water is indicated as part of the general human partnership in all the sources of life. The Prophet of Islam states that "people are partners in three, water, vegetation, and fire."

According to the rules of legal interpretation (*tafsīr*), this statement is an unrestricted text (*nas mutlāq*), which should be extended to cover all other elements of the environment that may be associated with the three mentioned. Accordingly, water would include all kinds of water and access to it. This also includes other protection and conservation rights. Vegetation is considered to indicate all kinds of plants, while fire includes all minerals and mined fuels. It is interesting that the *ḥadīth* did not include animals, although the term vegetation implicitly includes pasturing and grazing land.

The main environmental problems in the Middle East are caused by a disturbance of the prevalent value system. Industrial concepts, which have not recognized spiritual or ethical values as commercially significant, have led to a severe cultural rupture that has taken the human inhabitants away from the earth that supports them. The proposed solution is to go back to the traditional Islamic relationship between humans and the earth, and between humans and the other elements of the ecosystem, and perhaps most essentially, between humans themselves.

Finally, it must be stated that Islam does not constitute a magic word that can be uttered to solve all problems. Islam as a religion has many difficulties when it comes to practice, not to mention those that have developed over the last fourteen centuries due to misunderstanding, misinterpretation, and misappropriation. Islam can only make sense if it is taken as a system and utilized in such a way that makes it applicable within the notion of "submission" to the paradigm of *tawḥīd* that governs the whole.

Notes

This article was first published in *Journal of Beliefs and Values* 18, no. 1 (1997): 47–58, and is reprinted here by permission of Taylor and Francis Ltd; http://www.tandf.co.uk/journals.

1. S. R. Sterling, "Towards an Ecological World View," in *Ethics of Environment and Development*, ed. J. Ronald Engel and Joan Gibb Engel (London: Belhaven, 1990), 78.

2. Cited in Seyyed Hossein Nasr, *Islamic Cosmological Doctrines* (London: Thames and Hudson, 1978), xiii.

3. Ibid., 5.

4. I. H. al-'Askalani, *Fat al-Bārī bisharha al-Bukhari* (Saudi Arabia: Al-makātaba al-salāfiyya, 1959), 11, 341.

5. See Qur'an 13:2–4; 21:79.

6. Cited in Nasr, *Islamic Cosmological Doctrines*, xv.

7. Ibid.

8. Sterling, "Towards an Ecological World View," 78.

9. Muhammad Jalal Kishk, *Al-Sa'ūdiyyun wa al-hall al-islāmī* (Quincy, Mass.: Halliday Lithograph Corporation, 1981), 77, 91.

10. U. S. Abu Rizayza, *Yamama* (1996/1409).

11. Peter Beaumont, Gerald H. Blake, and J. Malcolm Wagstaff, *The Middle East: A Geographical Study* (London: Wiley, 1978).

12. Ibid.

13. P. J. Vesilind, "The Middle East's Water," *National Geographic* 183, no. 5 (1993): 38–71.

14. Abu Rizayza, *Yamama.*

15. Ibid.

16. M. Humayd, *Yamama* (1996/1427), 98.

17. Abu Rizayza, *Yamama.*

18. F. 'Urayfi, *Yamama*, (1996/1426), 12.

19. Vesilind, "The Middle East's Water."

20. Beaumont et al., *The Middle East.*

21. Ibid.

22. Vesilind, "The Middle East's Water."

23. W. Zuayli, *Al-fiqh al-Islamī wa-addillātuh* (Beirut: Dar al-fikir, 1985), 5, 597.

24. Ibid., 5, 605.

Islam and Ecology: Toward Retrieval and Reconstruction

S. NOMANUL HAQ

A consideration of the question of Islam and ecology ought to begin with one fundamental observation of a historical kind: in the construction of what we call the modern world, Islam has had only an indirect role to play. To be sure, one cannot possibly imagine, nor meaningfully speak of, the phenomenon generally known as the scientific revolution, or that which we refer to as the Renaissance, without keeping in view the formidable intellectual influence of Islam on Latin Christendom. But this legacy was appropriated—and here we see the complexities and ironies of the historical process—in ways that often were alien to the world of Islam itself. The reception in both the Islamic and Christian worlds of the work of the towering giant Alhazen (Ibn al-Haytham, d. 1038), or that of the great Avicenna (Ibn Sina, d. 1037), constitutes a case in point. Alhazen, who revolutionized the field of optics, was ignored in the Islamic world even as he became a central scientific figure in the West. Avicenna, an outstanding philosopher and physician, was *the* medical authority in Europe well into the early seventeenth century; but his system was developed on highly abstract mystical-spiritual lines in Islam, where he was often seen more as a "Visionary Reciter"[1] than a Hellenized rational thinker. Indeed, it is the Latin career of these figures that endured in the modern world, not the elaboration of their thought by latter-day Muslims.

I use the term "modern world" in its standard sense—signifying both the world-system and the worldview that began their joint career in Western culture after the passage of the European Dark Ages, and which, after going through a highly complex process of development, came to full maturity during what we call the Enlightenment. This modern world is marked not only by a set of spectacular scientific and technological achievements, all of which were cultivated and produced in the Western milieu; it is marked also by a set of attitudes, a *Weltbild*, that has become in our era the dominant global framework of our collective life, the only framework we recognize as defining the terms of our contemporary discourse. This *Weltbild* has given us its views of human nature, its economic theories, its governmental system, its lifestyles, and its secular ideology.

At the same time, there always lurk on the horizon of the modern worldview politically charged questions of power and control: this *Weltbild*, it has been feverishly argued, was coercively imposed upon the larger part of the globe we call the developing world. Here, operating in a strictly historical rather than moral perspective, one phenomenon ought to be thrown into sharp relief: we do see disappearing from the developing world practically all indigenous systems and institutions—a disappearance brought about in the recent past largely by direct European colonization, effected as a matter of deliberate colonial policy, and sometimes attended by fierce local resistance. These days, the destruction of indigenous systems is largely a result of Western market forces whose reach has now acquired staggering global dimensions. The developing world's military apparatus and technique, the dress and lifestyle of its majority, its industries, economy, banking and finance, system of education, public-health practices, bureaucratic agencies and organs of government, and, above all, its print and electronic media—all these entities and institutions have, in general, been taken from the Western world or have been constructed in emulation of Western models.

The dependence of the developing societies on the Western world inevitably raises the overwhelming question of sheer survival. Take, for example, the issue of public health. We note not only that indigenous institutions of health and healing have either died or been irrevocably marginalized; we note as well that modern life has brought with it illnesses, epidemics, and injuries that could not possibly be handled by these institutions as they stood, or as they stand on the periphery today. This means that the developing world desperately depends on Western pharmaceutical industries and medical establishments; and this in turn means a need for hard currency to buy drugs and equipment and to train doctors and health professionals; and this then weaves an intricate web of need, dependence, frustration, fatalities, and political machinations.

All these issues rap at our doors when we take up the question of Islam and ecology. In the Islamic world a whole range of attitudes has developed in response to what is generally referred to as Western hegemony, a highly loaded term. In the social spectrum of the contemporary world of Islam—whose rulers and high officials typically belong to a small Western-educated elite—one finds crude apologetic attitudes on the one extreme, bitter resentment against whatever is perceived as Western on the other, and all manner of Islamic revivalist and reformist tendencies lying somewhere in the middle.[2] Thus, much literature is found among contemporary Muslims claiming that all intellectual achievements of modernity, all successful present-day scientific theories and technological ideas, in their *most minute detail* are to be found in the Qur'ān, if only Muslims were to search. Considering Islamic and Western societies to be incommensurable, this literature teaches that the environmental problems of today's world result from the hegemony of the West—the control of the world fell into the wrong hands. At the same time, other Muslim writers place the blame of the ecological crisis squarely upon Western science and technology, entities conceived to be *distinct* from Islamic science and technology, distinct both in substance and in morphology. This second line of argument, compared to the first, is relatively moderate; but it happens to be intractably problematic nonetheless.

Here lies a profound irony. Some seventy years ago, Sir Hamilton Gibb articulated a fundamental historical fact: Islam in its foundations belongs to and is an integral part of the larger Western society. He put it strongly: "Islam cannot deny its foundations and live."[3] In other words, a conscious recognition of the fundamental fact of Islam's community with the West is essential to its very survival. Like al-Biruni in the twelfth century, and reflecting the spirit of the Islamic modernist movement of the nineteenth and twentieth centuries, Gibb argued that Islam stands side by side with the Western world, in contrast to what he called the "true" oriental societies, those of India and East Asia.[4] This was because Islam had found itself—and had creatively and consciously made itself—heir to Classical Civilization. Moreover, in many ways that are nontrivial, Islamic culture can indeed be characterized legitimately as embodying Hellenism. Sir Hamilton had expressed it more picturesquely—the two civilizations of Islam and Europe, he wrote, were "nourished at the same springs, breathing the same air . . . , [only] artificially sundered at the Renaissance."[5]

Notwithstanding the specific details of Hamilton Gibb's thesis, we have here an outline of a constructive methodology; in fact, it is a methodology that flows from the ideas of many a modern Muslim thinker. So we note that even though Islam's role in the construction of the modern world is indirect, in its historical foundations this world descends directly from an Islamic intellectual milieu. It is more obscuring than illuminating to suppose that there is an inherent incompatibility between Islam and the Christian West, or a total historical break between them. But once the intellectual community between Islam and the modern world is acknowledged, we may recognize the Islamic roots of contemporary ideas, preoccupations, and institutions. At the same time—and this speaks to a more urgent need—we may see that the intellectual resources for understanding some of today's pressing global concerns can be found in the Islamic tradition itself. Indeed, given the durability of the classical Islamic civilization that Gibb's thesis brings into focus, one may legitimately seek ideas from Islam to guide the struggle against the environmental problems that threaten our globe today.[6]

We face an enormous task. It requires, *inter alia*, a grasp of both the complexities of the contemporary world and the substance and the historical context of the Islamic legacy; and it involves much reconstruction, adjustment, and revision. In the case at hand, the task becomes all the more daunting due to its real as compared to purely theoretical nature.[7] The issue cannot be handled meaningfully if its real dimensions are glossed over in the glow of a sophisticated theoretical discourse. The questions of power and control, distributive justice, economics and finance, the currents of market forces, policymaking and tactical politics, lifestyles and social values—these are all directly relevant here. And this means that the issue belongs in a complex manner to several disciplinary domains at once: social sciences, ethics, and religion among them.

Still, it ought to be noted that this essay is essentially concerned with theoretical matters; and even in this domain, it is concerned narrowly with the normative sources of the Islamic religious tradition.

Indeed, its scope is narrower still: it undertakes only to reconstruct doctrinally certain Qur'ānic concepts, to expound certain imperatives of what is known as the Prophetic Tradition, and to articulate briefly certain Islamic legal categories—a reconstruction, exposition, and articulation carried out with a view to recovering Islamic religious material that might serve to illuminate how Islamic culture regards our current global environmental concerns and guide Islamic thinking about them. But what is most interesting, in the internal context of traditional Islam, is that this enterprise, *by its nature,* would be considered not a partial but a comprehensive task, since religion is claimed, literally, to be all-embracing. For traditional Islam, examining religious sources means examining the universal canopy under which fall *all* aspects of life—since all aspects are religious aspects.

The Nature of the Normative Sources

It should be understood at the very outset that the Qur'ān, believed to be the actual speech of God revealed through an angel, is not a book of laws, or a manual of procedures, or a collection of tales; nor is it a systematic treatise meant to convey ethical doctrines or principles. As the experts say, the Qur'ān has to be received on its own terms—that is, as a genre unto itself.[8] A striking feature of this sacred Islamic text is its highly stylized cadence, its rhetorical structure, its literary diction, and its elegant use of language with "semantic depth, where one meaning leads to another by a fertile fusion of associated ideas."[9] Thus, scholars have characterized the Qur'ān not so much as a doctrinal textbook but "more valuably as a rich and subtle stimulus to religious *imagination*."[10] If this text is to yield a concrete system, it requires an imaginative reconstruction on the part of the reader; in principle, this reconstruction cannot claim epistemological finality, even though it may stand firm on grounds of overwhelming community consensus. This is precisely the position of classical Islam.

With regard to the question of the cosmos and its relationship to human beings, one notes that the Qur'ān moves at three levels simultaneously—metaphysical, naturalistic, and human. But when one examines these levels in the totality of the Qur'ān, they turn out to interdigitate: on the one hand, the Qur'ānic notion of the natural world and the natural environment is semantically and logically bound up with the very concept of God; on the other hand, this notion is linked with the general principle of the very creation of humanity. The three levels of Qur'ānic discourse, therefore, do not manifest any independent conceptual self-sufficiency of, or a conceptual discontinuity between, the three realms of the divine, of nature, and of humanity. Indeed, this linkage is of fundamental importance to our concerns, for in our reconstruction of the cosmology of the Qur'ān, we can see that the historical-naturalistic is linked to the transcendental-eternal, and this means that there is no ontological separation between the divine and natural environments. At the human, psychological level, all this generates a particular attitude to the world as a whole.

As we shall see, the Qur'ān emphasizes the transcendental significance of nature. Because nature cannot explain its own being, it stands as a sign (*āya*, plural *āyāt*) of something beyond itself, pointing to some transcendental entity that bestows the principle of being upon the world and its objects. Nature, then, is an emblem of God; it is a means through which God communicates with humanity. One may legitimately say that insofar as the Islamic tradition allows for God's entry into the flow of history at all—that is, in the realm bounded by space and time—nature embodies one of the two modes of this entry, the other mode being God's Word, namely, the Qur'ān itself. Most significantly, the verses of the Qur'ān are also called *āyāt*, signs, and in the same emblematic vein—and this means that the objects of the natural world and the Qur'ānic verses are metaphysically on a par with each other.

On the naturalistic plane, the Qur'ān speaks of the cosmos as an integral system governed by a set of immutable laws that embody God's command (*amr*, plural *awāmir*). The phenomena of nature in the general run of things follow a strict system marked by regularity and uniformity, since nature cannot violate its *amr*, that is, its immutable laws. In this naturalistic vein, we find the Qur'ān teaching that the cosmos exists to nourish, support, and sustain the process of life—all of life, and in particular human life. Though human life does have centrality in the Qur'ānic system, it is a centrality mediated and reined in by a set of moral and metaphysical controls; this we shall examine in more detail as we proceed.

A remarkable fact about the genesis story in the Qur'ān is that it speaks of God announcing to the angels that he is about to create a *khalīfa* (vicegerent) *on the earth*—in other words, Adam and his "equal half" (*zauj*)[11] were bound for Earth even *before* they committed the transgression. Life on Earth is here an integral part of the very concept of the human being, not a punitive fall from glory; the human being does not exist in a state of disgrace in the world of nature, nor is nature in any sense unredeemed.[12] To expound the Qur'ānic position summarily, the very principle of the vicegerency of God (*khilāfa*) made human beings his servants (*'abd*, plural *'ibād*), custodians of the entire natural world. Human beings exist by virtue of a primordial covenant (*mīthāq*) whereby they have testified to their own theomorphic nature, and by virtue of a trust that they have taken upon themselves in pre-eternity. There is a due measure (*qadr*) to things, and a balance (*mīzān*) in the cosmos, and humanity is transcendentally committed not to disturb or violate this *qadr* and *mīzān*; indeed, the fulfillment of this commitment is the fundamental moral imperative of humanity.

The three dimensions of the Qur'ānic discourse—metaphysical, naturalistic, and human—are thus mutually related in a complex manner, and any one of them cannot be understood in isolation from the others. Nature in its Qur'ānic conception is *anchored in* the divine, both metaphysically and morally. The expression is strong: "But to God belongs all things in the heavens and on the earth; And He it is who encompasseth (*Muḥīṭ*) all things" (4:126); note that the word *Muḥīṭ* can also be translated legitimately as "environment."[13] So we see that when the Qur'ān's notion of nature is reconstructed in the larger framework of this supreme Islamic source, it appears inherently connected with its notions of God and humanity—and all these notions, as we have seen, have their roots in the transcendental realm and then issue forth in the moral-historical field.

When we come to the Ḥadīth literature, the corpus often referred to as Prophetic Traditions, we are in a different atmosphere altogether. Here we have a vast body of collections of formally authenticated reports about the words and actions of the Prophet of Islam, and sometimes of his companions who enjoy a derivative authority. The collection and authentication of Ḥadīth was an enormous undertaking aimed at articulating Islam *as a function*, and for this purpose God's Way (*sharī'a*) had to be translated into a viable body of concrete codes of action and laws. Indeed, one material source for the understanding (*fiqh*) of *sharī'a* was the established tradition of the prophetic way (*sunna*). An authenticated Ḥadīth was legally binding.

But the impressive discipline called the Science of Ḥadīth *('Ilm al-Ḥadīth)* did not develop until more than two hundred years after the death of the Prophet, and in the meantime a whole corpus of fabricated Ḥadīth had come into being. It was only in the middle of the ninth century that the first Correct (*Ṣaḥīḥ*) collection of Ḥadīth appeared; this was established after much sifting, systematizing, and a rigorous process of authentication. Five more massive *Ṣaḥīḥ* collections were compiled during the following hundred years. But given the very size of the corpus of these transmitted reports and the inherent complications in the very nature of the chain of transmitters (*isnād*), even the six Correct collections vary widely in authenticity and content. Note that in Ḥadīth authentication, as a general rule, practically all attention was paid to the *isnād* rather than to the actual content (*matn*) of what was transmitted.

It is for reasons such as these that the use of Ḥadīth material in reconstructing the Islamic position on the environment and ecology is not a straightforward task. Ḥadīth collections are manuals of what one may in a qualified sense describe as a body of case law. An *isolated* and independent ecological concern is not to be found here—this is a present-day development—but spread all over the body of Ḥadīth, one does find reports concerning the general status and meaning of nature, and concerning land cultivation and agriculture, construction of buildings, livestock, water resources, animals, birds, plants, and so on. In addition, one notes the remarkable fact that the Ḥadīth corpus also contains the two fateful doctrines of *ḥimā* and *ḥarām*, land distribution and consecration. These two related notions were indeed developed by Muslim legists who articulated them particularly in their environmental dimensions, designating some places as protected sanctuaries. *Ḥimā* and *ḥarām* developed into legislative principles of land equity on the one hand, and of environmental ethics on the other, and were subsequently incorporated into the larger body of the Islamic legal code. Note that ethical questions and environmental questions are here moving hand in hand; they are interconnected.

The most systematic source of codified Islamic religious norms is that of *fiqh*-law, developed on the foundations of the Qur'ān and Ḥadīth. One may legitimately say that *fiqh*-law is the comprehensive blueprint for the whole of Muslim life, covering the minutest detail of external human conduct, both public and private. Within this enormous body of legal regulations—which have now acquired a dogmatic character since the *fiqh* discipline is now practically dormant—the principle of *ḥimā* is particularly well developed in the Mālikī school, one of the four legal schools followed by the vast majority of Muslims. But we note in the formally articulated and generally codified Islamic legal writings several other environmental concepts derived directly from the two primary material sources (*uṣūl*), the Qur'ān and Ḥadīth.

One such concept is that of *mawāt*, literally "wasteland." Some *fiqh*-legists have worked on *mawāt* in great detail; the concept typically appears in the extensive discussions on rivers, canals, and other water resources, their distribution and maintenance, rights and control. Similarly, for example, arising directly out of the moral and conceptual ethos of the two *uṣūl* are *fiqh* rules governing the hunting, treatment, welfare, and use of animals, including birds. Once again, note how Islamic law is meant to implement Islamic ethics—legal and moral concerns belong to one and the same functional framework.

Human Nature and the Natural World: Qur'ānic Excursus

Moving on the transcendental plane, the Qur'ān presents in its seventh *sūra* that famous sonorous verse known to embody the primordial covenant between humanity and its creator: "And when your Lord extracted from the children of Adam, from their spinal cord, their entire progeny and made them witness upon themselves, saying, Am I not your Lord? And they replied, No doubt You are, we bear witness!"[14] So powerful is the narrative here, and so deeply entrenched in the Muslim consciousness is the expression *alastu bi-rabbikum* (Am I not your Lord?), that the interrogative *alastu* has reverberated in the mystical and poetic chambers of Islam until this day. We see here that humanity in the very *principle of its being* has testified to the lordship of God. In other words, human nature is essentially theomorphic. To recognize God is to be in a natural state. Indeed, God had made human beings in the *best* of forms;[15] and, furthermore, to this supreme creature, to human beings, he subjected (*sakhkhara lakum*, "He subjected to you") *all* that is in the heavens and the earth.[16]

But, then, in the next breath the Qur'ān links this metaphysical exaltation to a weighty moral burden. Humankind's superiority lies not in its enjoying any higher power or control or authority among created beings; it lies rather in the fact that it is accountable before God, such as no other creature is. This accountability arises out of the trust (*al-amāna*) that human beings accepted at their transcendental origin. It should be observed at once that this *amāna* entails a kind of global trusteeship, and this reading does no offense to the Qur'ānic concept of trust: "We did indeed offer the Trust to the Heavens and the Earth and the mountains—but they refused to carry it, being afraid of it. But the human being carried it: Ho! humankind is unfair to itself and foolhardy."[17]

Note here the cosmological ethos of a transcendental narrative. And note also the last sentence—so enormous was the burden that the Qur'ān recognizes it by way of what Rahman called a "tender rebuke," calling human beings unfair to themselves and foolhardy.

We see here the moral-naturalistic dimension of human theomorphism. Humanity cannot arrogate to itself absolute power or unbridled control over nature: in the *very principle* of its being, humanity was committed to following God's *sharī'a*, his Way. Furthermore, this *sharī'a* was not given to humanity as a fully articulated body of laws; rather, it was spread all over God's signs (*āyāt*) in the form of indicators with probative value (*adilla*). Recall that the term *āyāt* designates both the verses of the Qur'ān as well as the phenomena and the objects of the natural world. Thus the natural world is a bona fide source for the understanding (*fiqh*) of *sharī'a*, and therefore cannot be considered subservient to human whims. Indeed, as we have noted, for human beings to be on the earth is part of the divine plan; to be human is by definition to be in the flow of history. There is, then, no justification in the Qur'ānic context to consider human existence in historical time a curse, or to deem nature as something opposed to grace, or to consider salvation as a process of the humbling of the natural by the supernatural. Echoing Mircea Eliade, one may say that all nature, indeed, is capable of revealing itself as cosmic sacrality.

Quite evident too is the ethical thrust of the frequent Qur'ānic declaration that God has made the natural world "subject to" human beings. This clearly does not mean that nature is subject to man's unbridled, exploitative powers—for it is God's command (*amr*), not that of the human being, that nature obeys (see below). We note that the expression *sakhkhara lakum* ("he made subject to you . . .") appears *always* with its attending moral dimension. So: "It is all from Him. . . . And He hath made subject to you whatsoever is in the heavens and whatsoever is in the earth—It is all from Him. Lo! herein indeed are portents for those who reflect."[18] The point is made frequently and with overwhelming rhetorical force:

> He has made subject to you the night and the day, the sun and the moon, and the stars—they are in subjection by His command (*amr*): Surely, in this are signs for those who reflect! And the things on this earth which He has multiplied in colors diverse—indeed, in this is a sign for those who recollect! It is He Who had made the sea subject [to His law], that ye may eat thereof flesh, tender and fresh, and that ye may extract therefrom ornaments to wear—See, how the ships plough the waves! So ye seek of the bounty of God: Perhaps ye shall be grateful![19]

Nature's intelligibility to the human intellect, on the one hand, and its quality of yielding itself to human works and sustaining human life, on the other, both flow from the same principle of *amr:*

> Seest thou not that by His command (*amr*) God has made subject to you all that is on the earth? And that by His command He has made subject to you the ships that sail through the sea? He withholds the sky from falling on the earth—but for His leave. For God is Most Compassionate and Most Merciful to humankind. It is He Who gave you life, and then He will cause you to die, and then He will bring you back to life again: Ah, humankind is most ungrateful![20]

In this natural-transcendental linkage, the moral question is fundamental. The Qur'ān promulgates what one may call a cosmology of justice, a cosmology that takes into its fold two realms at once, the human and the cosmic—or, rather, the human *within* the cosmic. As for the human realm, a concern for social justice runs throughout the Qur'ānic text, even in its chronologically earlier verses whose focus is on metaphysical issues such as the oneness of God, the Beginning and the End, and the finitude of the world. The dignity of the disabled,[21] the rights of the indigent and particularly of orphans,[22] honesty in trade dealings,[23] feeding of the poor,[24] condemnation of greed, and admonishment against hoarding wealth[25]—all these concerns are to be found from the earliest of the Qur'ānic verses, which are, by general scholarly consensus, the most powerful and the most sublime in their stylistic embellishment.

But these concerns operate within the universal field of cosmic justice; human relations thus acquire their meaning by virtue of their location at the very core of natural law. This effectively forges a conceptual link between natural law and moral law—natural law *is* never violated as things run their customary course; moral law *ought not* to be violated. The Qur'ān speaks of the existence of a cosmic balance (*mīzān*) and declares that everything except God is "measured out" (*qadar, qadr, taqdīr*)—that is, everything is given its natural principle of being and its place in the larger cosmic whole—and this is precisely the meaning of the *amr* (command) of an entity, a concept I shall take up again a little later. The same message is expressed in a moral language: "God intends no injustice to any of His creatures. To Him belongs all that is in the heavens and the earth."[26]

The dread of humankind "corrupting the earth" (*fasād fi' l-arḍ*), the catastrophe such transgression will unleash, and exhortations against it loom so large that they hang like a backdrop in the Qur'ānic cosmology of justice. The creation of the world was not a frivolous or trivial act: "And We have not created the heavens and the earth and what is therein purposelessly—that is the view of those who reject [the truth] or who are ungrateful."[27] Created with divine deliberation, nature is so coherently interconnected and integrated, and works with such regularity and order, that it is God's prime miracle: if good is done to it or in it, good will return; if evil is wrought to it or in it, what accrues is sheer terror:

> And you see mountains and think them solid [and stationary] but they are fleeting like clouds—such is the artistry of God Who has well-completed [the creation] of everything. He is well acquainted with all that you do.
>
> If any do good, good will accrue to them therefrom; and they will be secure from the terror of the Doom. And if any do evil, their faces will be thrown headlong into the Fire.[28]

It ought to be recognized that the Qur'ān does contain verses that *prima facie* give the impression that the natural world and all its creatures exist for the sake of human beings, but it would be a gross oversimplification to view such declarations in a moral vacuum. "In considering all these verses," wrote the outstanding jurist of medieval Islam Ibn Taymiyya (d. 1328), "it must be remembered that God in his wisdom brought into being these creatures for reasons *other than serving human beings.* In these verses God only explains the [human] benefits of these."[29] It is interesting to note in this context that among the three grand monotheistic faiths, Islam does not have to carry the burden of any scriptural imperative to "subdue" the earth and seek to establish "dominion" over the natural world. There is a clear and explicit answer to the question as to where and to whom belongs the dominion over the natural world, an answer so obvious in the overall drift of the Qur'ān that it is expressed rhetorically: "Knowest thou not that to God belongeth the dominion of the heavens and the earth!?"[30] And again: "Yea, to God belongs the dominion of the heavens and the earth. And to God is the final goal [of all]."[31]

Ironic though it may seem, human superiority—humans being created in the best of forms (*fī aḥsānī taqwīm*), and humans being considered in the Islamic tradition the noblest of creatures (*ashraf al-makhlūqāt*)—turns out to be a supremely humbling quality. And the Qur'ān does humble humanity by saying that the creation of the rest of the cosmos is a matter *greater than* the creation of people: "Assuredly the creation of the heavens and the earth is [a matter] greater than the creation of human beings: Yet most people understand not!"[32] We do not have exclusive claim to the earth, for "the earth He has assigned to all living creatures."[33] And all living creatures are natural communities, with their own habitat, their own laws, and their inviolable natural rights: "And there is no animal in the earth nor bird that flies with its two wings but that they are communities like yourselves."[34]

One is here reminded of a medieval Arabic fable found in the famous *Rasā'il* (Epistles) collectively written in the tenth century by the fraternity that called itself *Ikhwān al-Ṣafā'* (Brethren of Purity). This colorful and dramatically constructed fable is about a company of animals who present their case before the king of the *jinn* (genies), raising the question of whether human beings are superior to animals, and if so in what respect. The verdict is "natural and inevitable":[35] human beings are superior to the animals—but not because they enjoy any higher moral or functional status. They are superior because of their heavy moral burden, of being the custodians of the earth. As God's regents on the earth (*Khalīfat Allāh fi' l-arḍ*), they are accountable for their acts; nonhuman animals are not. The verdict, handed down by a nonhuman creature, reads further:

> Let man not imagine . . . that just because he is superior to the animals they are his slaves. Rather it is that we are all slaves of the Almighty

> and must obey His commands . . . Let man not forget that he is accountable to his Maker for the way in which he treats all animals, just as he is accountable for his behavior towards his fellow human beings. Man bears a heavy responsibility. . . .[36]

Qur'ānic Naturalism and the Nature-Prophecy Parallel

If one makes an analytical excursion into the Qur'ānic discourse on the created world, three defining characteristics of nature fall into sharp perspective: first, that natural phenomena have regularity, internal coherence, and elegance, and that they are self-sustaining; second, that nature as a whole has, within its own being, no logical or metaphysical warrant to exist; and, finally, that nature is an embodiment of God's mercy, or, more fully, that God's mercy is expressed through the creation of nature. These defining characteristics, one notes, do not appear in the Qur'ānic narrative in a doctrinal or even textual isolation from one another—they are frequently spoken of in the same breath, in the same passages, and in the same vein; together, they make a conceptual whole.

The principle of autonomy of nature—that it is regulated by its own laws—manifests itself forcefully in the fact that whenever the Qur'ān speaks of the *actual cosmological processes* of natural phenomena—and it does so quite often—it speaks in naturalistic terms. Thus, the human being was a natural creation: Adam was fashioned out of baked clay (*ṣalṣāl*), from mud molded into shape (*ḥamā' masnūn*);[37] from dust (*turāb*);[38] from a blood clot (*'alāq*);[39] from earth (*ṭīn*)[40] that produced through a confluence of natural processes an extract, *sulāla*, that functions as reproductive semen.[41] In fact, there exists a fully biological account:

> Humankind We did create from a reproductive extract of clay. Then We placed it as a drop of sperm in a receptacle, secure. Then we made the sperm into a clot of congealed blood. Then of that clot We made a fetus lump. Then We made out of that lump bones and clothed the bones with flesh . . . So blessed be God, the Best of Creators![42]

References to nature, natural forces, natural phenomena, and natural beings abound in the Qur'ān; out of its 114 *sūra*s some 31 are named after these. In all cases, the physical world in its *real* operation is described in a naturalistic framework, in the framework of physical forces and processes that occur uniformly and with regularity. Thus, we see here the contours of a theistic naturalism:

> Why! do they not look at the sky above them? How We have built it and adorned it and there are no gaps in it?
>
> And the earth—We have spread it out, and set thereon mountains, standing firm, and produced therein all manner of beautiful growth. This, for the observation and commemoration of every created being who reflects.
>
> And We send down from the sky rain, charged with blessings. And We produce therewith gardens and grains for harvests. And tall and stately palm trees with shoots of fruit stalks, piled over one another—as provision for God's servants. And We give new life therewith to the land dead. . . .[43]

In an even more robust expression of naturalism, the refrain re-emerges:

> And the earth—We have spread it out, set thereon mountains firm and immovable, and produced therein all kinds of things in due balance (*mauzūn*). And We have provided therein livelihood (*ma'āyish*)—for you and for those whose sustenance (*rizq*) does not depend on you. And there is not a thing but its bountiful sources are with Us; and nought do We send down unless it be in due and knowable measure (*bi-qadrim ma'lūm*).
>
> And We send down winds to fertilize vegetation in abundance, then cause the rain to descend from the sky, therewith providing you with water in plenty—though you are not the guardians of its sources. . . .[44]
>
> We fashioned humankind out of baked clay, from mud molded into shape. And, in the time preceding, We had fashioned the *jinn* from the fire of scorching winds.[45]

The Qur'ān, then, admits the principle of natural causation, avowing the sum total of natural processes as the proximate, autonomous, efficient causative forces operating in the world. It is the fertility of the earth, we see, and the natural qualities of water, and favorable winds—in other words, certain natural phenomena themselves—that causally but proximately explain all vegetation; it was rain that revived dead and uncultivable land, and it was clay that constituted the substratum for the human animal as a natural entity. Besides, in what is to be legitimately considered an anthropological vein, all this in its turn is causally related to human livelihood *ma'āyish*) and actual subsistence of the human community—the narrative here brings into clear view activities and processes such as land cultivation, harvest, fertility, production of gardens, yielding of fruits and grains; it speaks of real, as distinct from metaphysical, human provision (*rizq*), with its attending economic and social ramifications.

It is the dual principle of cosmic justice, which we have examined earlier, and this thoroughgoing naturalism that explains a central doctrine of Qur'ānic ethics—that of *ẓulm al-nafs* (self-injury).[46] Indeed, this doctrine embodies a moral tenet that seems to carry the seeds of a comprehensive ecological philosophy. As I have said elsewhere,[47] in the actual world as it exists in the immediate palpable reality, human beings are *part* of nature; they are a *natural* entity, subject fully to the laws of nature just like any other entity, participating as an integral element in the overall ecological balance (*mīzān*) that exists in the larger cosmic whole. And this means that to damage, offend, or destroy the balance of the natural environment is to damage, offend, or destroy *oneself.* Any injury inflicted upon "the other" is *self*-injury, *ẓulm al-nafs*—and this is a prime doctrinal element in the foundations of Qur'ānic ethics: "Whoever transgresses the bounds of God has done wrong but to himself";[48] and again: "God wronged them not, but themselves they wronged."[49] The rule is that wrongdoing ultimately recoils back upon the perpetrator—for when the balance is willfully disturbed, this disturbance takes the culprit too into its fold.[50]

On the other hand, the naturalistic posture of the Qur'ān is attended by an epistemological posture that has fundamental heuristic and methodological consequences for the human search for natural knowledge. There is nothing in the cosmos that does not possess a due balance (*mauzūn*), and nothing that is not fully differentiated and measured out in a way that it is beyond the comprehension of the human intellect; everything, we read, exists in a *knowable* measure (*bi-qadrim ma'lūm*), and the cosmos is thus, in principle, intelligible. The epistemological point is compelling: there exist immutable laws to regulate nature, these laws are both uniform and subject to systematic cognition, and they are captured when human reason casts its net. Indeed, in the Qur'ānic narrative we find virtually countless exhortations for the use of reason, appearing often in the pathos of the subjunctive: "Perhaps you may exert your mind!" or "They might perchance reflect!" or "May you not see?" or "Would you not exercise your intellect?" or

"What! Would you not reason out?" So, heuristically, we have here a Qur'ānic anchorage for a scientific exploration of the cosmos, an exploration with which humanity has been squarely charged.

This links our discourse with both the second defining characteristic of nature as it appears in the Qur'ān and the methodological implications of its epistemological stance, which we just examined. Throughout, I have been pointing out a fundamental feature of the Qur'ānic narrative—namely, that it identifies the *locus* and *ground* of the real and the temporal in the transcendental and the eternal, constantly forging a link. And so the second defining element of nature we already noted: nature is nonultimate, for within its own being it has no logical or metaphysical warrant to exist. Nature exists only because God had bestowed existence upon its being. A plant did not bring about its own existence; it *received* existence and thus became a sign (*āya*) of something beyond itself. And again, it was through an act of divine mercy (*raḥma*) that humankind *found itself* in existence, for within itself lay no inherent principle to cause this existence. The ontological point is that the existence of nature in historical time is a flowing process of a cosmic observance of God's *amr.*

Let me take up the Qur'ānic notion of *amr* again. Recall that the word literally means "command." At the mechanistic level, one may consider *amr* to be a denotation of a universal operative principle whereby every created natural entity plays its assigned role and takes its assigned place as an integral element in the larger cosmic whole. Thus, *amr* is the specific principle of being of each thing in *relation to that of all other things*, inhering in it according to the command it uniquely receives from God. This can be put in another way: laws of nature express God's commands, commands that nature cannot possibly violate—and this explains why the entire world of phenomena is declared *muslim* by the Qur'ān : "Do they, then, seek an obedience other than that to God, while it is to Him that everyone [and everything] in the heavens and the earth submits (*aslama*)?"[51] So once again, we have here an integral conceptual system in which the transcendental is coherently linked to the naturalistic, the temporal. Nature originates in and ultimately recoils back into the transcendental.

But at the operational level—and here is the methodological point—*amr* can be viewed legitimately to be a system of independent, self-governing, and self-sustaining laws of nature. Thus it was the *amr* of a mango seed to grow into a mango tree; and that of an egg to hatch into a bird; and that of sperm to develop into an embryo; and that of the oceans to sustain a multiplicity of life in their bosom; and that of the sun to rise from the far horizon. In the scientific investigation of the physical world, then, in this process of the human intellect's discovery of natural laws as such, no nonnaturalistic, no nonrational principle need be invoked. But there is a caveat: such investigation is without reference, and therefore meaningless, if it remains suspended without being anchored ultimately in the transcendental from which issues forth moral imperatives—that is, moral law, God's *sharī'a.*

And this leads us finally to the third defining characteristic of nature given by the Qur'ān: nature is an embodiment of God's mercy. Indeed, given that God's will is not bound by any other will, and given further that God is omnipotent, he could well have chosen the chasm of utter nothingness as opposed to the creation of a full plenitude of being. That he chose the latter is a manifestation of his mercy (*raḥma*). Louis Gardet once observed that in the totality of the Qur'ānic teaching God's mercy and his omnipotence are inseparable: "These two perfections," he wrote, "are the two poles of divine action, at the same time contrasted and complementary."[52] God's creative action is a special expression of his mercy—for not only did he bestow being upon his creation; he also provided sustenance for that creation, and sent guidance for that creation; and made himself the very end (*al-Ākhir*)[53] to which the entire created world was commanded by him to return finally.

Plentiful in the Qur'ān are references to the bounty of nature as an unfalsifiable expression of God's mercy. Indeed, this is the very refrain of the chapter *al-Raḥmān*, The Merciful, a collection of verses unique in the codex for its stylistic beauty, its rhythm and rhyme and cadence, and its lush imagery. Speaking eloquently of nature's bounty and the naturalistic cosmic order as constituting divine favors and blessings, and asking rhetorically how they can possibly be denied, the Qur'ān says:

> The sun and the moon follow courses exactly computed. And the stars and the trees, both alike bow in adoration. And the Firmament—God has raised it high, and set the Balance . . . It is He Who has spread out the earth for His creatures: Therein is fruit and date palms, with their clusters sheathed. Also corn, with its leaves and stalk for fodder, and sweet-smelling plants. . . .

From this arises the resounding question that serves here as the refrain: "So, which of the favors of your Lord will you deny?" Again, turning back to the world in a naturalistic vein: "He created human beings from sounding clay, like the potter's . . . He let free the two seas that meet together, between them is a barrier that they do not transgress . . . Out of them come pearls and coral. . . ." Then comes the finale: "Of God seeks [its sustenance] every creature in the heavens and on the earth. Every day in a new splendor does He shine!" The undercurrent of the intervening refrain flows on: "So which of the favors of your Lord will you deny?"[54]

But this vast plenitude of being we call the cosmos was also an embodiment of God's *tanzīl* (sending down) of guidance (*hidāya*) to humanity. The *sharī'a*, we have already noted, is not given ready-made in the form of a systematic, fixed, and fully spelled-out corpus of divine instructions for the creation of a moral order. Rather, it is up to humankind to exercise its moral and intellectual faculties, its *amr*, and perpetually construct and reconstruct God's *sharī'a* through an understanding (*fiqh*) of the guiding signs (*adilla*) that are provided in two modes—one of them the *āyāt* constituting the natural world. Thus, by virtue of what I would refer to as the Qur'ānic dynamics of *tanzīl*, nature is accorded the status of a legitimate source for the very knowledge of *sharī'a*—a status that is divinely sanctioned. And a dynamic process of ever-new *sharī'a* constructions it is, since human knowledge could never claim, nor is it capable of acquiring, epistemological certainty or finality.

But then God's guidance also came in a direct *tanzīl* in a clear and articulate language (*bayān*); this second mode of sending down *adilla* was the Qur'ān, that is, the Speech (*Kalām*) of God himself. Given this, we have here a remarkable metaphysical equivalence between natural entities and revelation, and thereby between nature and prophecy. Indeed, in numerous Qur'ānic passages the creation of nature is coupled with the revelation of the verses of the Qur'ān, and this has led many medieval Muslim sages to speak of an intimate connection and ontological parallel between the two; they spoke even of the identity of the two.[55] So just as nature represents the inexhaustible *logoi* of God,[56] so does the Qur'ān , but even more so—since, in fact, while the former is referred to as *āyāt*, the latter is the clarification (*tabyīn*)[57] of these *āyāt*, the bringing home of these *āyāt* (*nuṣarrifu'l-āyāt*),[58] and the detailing of these *āyāt* (*faṣṣalna' l-āyāt*).[59] The verses of the Qur'ān are often said to be clear *āyāt* (*āyāt bayyināt*), or, simply, clarifications or manifestations (*bayyināt*). Note that this last expression is never applied to nature, and this creates a hierarchy of God's signs—a hierarchy in which the Qur'ān remains epistemologically prior.

Just as natural entities exist in the form of real-historical objects, so God's revelation is delivered by a real-historical Prophet, a human apostle who is no god and no supernatural being but is "from amongst yourselves."[60] And just as nature is a guide, so is the Prophet a guide (*hādī*)[61] *par excellence.* Just as nature receives and follows God's *amr*, so does the Prophet receive "a spirit from (God's) *amr*"[62] that the Prophet himself and the rest of humanity *ought to* follow. And just as natural entities, God's *āyāt*, express and manifest God's mercy, so was Prophet Muhammad , the one chosen to receive God's speech, his *āyāt*, "nothing but a mercy (*raḥma*) to all beings."[63]

Given the uncompromising and radical monotheism of Islam, nature can never acquire divine status. Any idea of nature worship would crack the very core of Islam. But with this in view, one notes a further and delicate parallelism between nature and prophecy. The Qur'ān does speak of obeying the Prophet, his authority deriving from God. In juxtaposition to this, we place an interpretation of the great fourteenth-century Qur'ān commentator Ibn Kathir : When the Qur'ān calls God "the Lord of the worlds (*Rabb al-'Ālamīn*),"[64] it means the Lord of *different kinds of creatures*, says Ibn Kathīr. Muslims affirm, he points out, that they submit to the Creator who made them and who made all other worlds. But, then, the commentator adds: "Muslims also submit themselves to the *signs* of the existence of the Creator and his unity. This secondary meaning exists because the word *'ālamīn* (worlds) comes from the same root [out of which stems the word *'alam*, which means 'sign']." Note that Ibn Kathīr is not alone in looking at the matter in this way.[65] So one may say that while the Qur'ān teaches obedience to the Prophet as God's delegated commander, it also teaches obedience to the laws of nature. This generates an attitude of tremendous respect for the cosmos, and also implies, *inter alia*, a divine stricture prohibiting the destruction or injury of the natural environment.

Practical Issues: Models of Conduct and Islamic Law

In the famous Correct *(Ṣaḥīḥ)* Ḥadīth collection of al-Bukhārī (d. 870), we read the elegant saying of the Prophet: "The earth has been created for me as a mosque (*masjid*) and as a means of purification."[66] Indeed, to declare the whole earth not only pure in itself, but also purifying of that which it touches, is to elevate it both materially and symbolically. The word *masjid* literally means a place of prostration, and prostration involves *touching* the ground. Thus, by virtue of this Ḥadīth, the earth in its entirety acquires and manifests sacrality. And here we have a standard situation: an elaboration and extension of a Qur'ānic principle, which in this particular case appears in 5:6. It is, in effect, a bringing of a Qur'ānic rule into the human fold of action and conduct.

In one important sense, Ḥadīth, as a discipline, can of course be described simply as a practical enterprise: it is a phenomenon of translating broad and general principles of the Qur'ān into detailed rules for the actual practice of the community. One may say that Ḥadīth brings metaphysics into the domain of history. But more than that, it has an independent status too, for Ḥadīth adds new practical issues to those found in the Qur'ān, sometimes even amending them or choosing between differing Qur'ānic positions on the same question. But it remains a practical enterprise nonetheless—the life of the Prophet, his established tradition (*sunna*), is a perfect model for all Muslims to follow; indeed, emulation (*ittibā'*) of this model is a *requirement* for the Muslim.

As a standard feature, Ḥadīth collections are corpora of authenticated reports of prophetic traditions, thematically classified; the body of reports under a single broad theme constitutes a Book (*Kitāb*), and these books strung together constitute the whole collection. In the Sunni Islamic world—and to this belong the vast majority of Muslims—the most authoritative of Ḥadīth collections are held to be the "Six Corrects" (*Ṣaḥīḥ Sitta*),[67] among which the cited "Correct of al-Bukhārī" enjoys primacy; the Bukhārī corpus has eighty-eight books. The range of subjects covered in these collections is enormously wide, since Ḥadīth is aimed at comprehending universally all aspects of private and public, individual and collective life. Diffused throughout the body of a single Ḥadīth collection one finds concerns, expressed with a degree of urgency, pertaining to the natural environment, its status, its relation to human life, and what we may call environmental ethics. These concerns do not appear as isolated issues in their own right, to be sure; rather, they are fully integrated into a host of naturalistic, moral, and practical principles that form the core of righteous conduct.

Typically, among its many parts the Bukhārī collection includes separate books on animal sacrifice, agriculture and land cultivation, medicine, hunting, and water and irrigation. The "Book of Agriculture" is rich in material concerning the environment, speaking of the nobility of *sustainable* cultivation of land and encouraging it with moral force. Issues of land irrigation and the strict law of equal sharing of water are found in the "Book of Distribution of Water," of course, but also in the "Book of Ablution"; the report I cited at the beginning of this section comes from the "Book of *Tayammum*" (ritual ablution performed with earth). Also, spread all over one finds a very large number of reports concerning the treatment of animals and pastures, as well as what one may call animal rights. And in the "Book of Generalities" *(al-Jāmi')* of the famous collection *al-Muwaṭṭā'* of Mālik ibn Anas (d. 795), the Master of the Mālikī school of law, one finds a reference to the important principle of *ḥimā*—land protection and consecration—which is there linked, in its very essence, to the question of social and economic justice. So we see that much relevant material exists in Ḥadīth collections, but this material exists as such, without having received any theoretical treatment in the framework of a system of environmental or ecological ethics. All we have is a body of classified reports, like case law collections, and this is what Ḥadīth is.

But in the Islamic legal writings the principles contained in Ḥadīth reports are identified and subjected to a highly sophisticated processing into a rigorous body of legal theory. These legal writings, often considered the *summum bonum* of the literary output of the Islamic intellectual culture, embody the discipline of *fiqh*, a word that literally means "understanding," as we have already noted. *Fiqh*, or the Islamic science of jurisprudence, is a systematic and fully structured theoretical search for God's *sharī'a*, or Way, that had to be gleaned from and constructed out of the myriad *adilla* (here, legal indicators) provided for reflection throughout God's *āyāt*. In concrete disciplinary terms, *fiqh* is the determination of the legal status (*ḥukm*) of an act, a determination arrived at through the application of *correct*, though not epistemologically certain, procedural rules (*uṣūl*). These rules of correct procedure had been established by the middle of the ninth century, with the formal structure of logical inferences from the sources of law (*uṣūl al-fiqh)* fully articulated. The supreme material source of *fiqh*-law was, of course, the Qur'ān—but next to that, and sometimes parallel to and in addition to it, was the *sunna* (custom) of the Prophet, which was by then available in authenticated Ḥadīth collections. Again, true to Islam's claim that it is a complete way of life, *fiqh*-laws are as a whole meant to be universal in scope—that is, comprehending all conceivable human acts. One may say, then, that *fiqh* is the structured articulation of the totality of Islam in its external functional manifestation.

The case of *ḥimā* constitutes a pertinent example. As I have already indicated, this principle appears in the *Muwaṭṭā'*; it is reported as a Ḥadīth of the Prophet's rather well-known companion and the second Rightly Guided (*Rashīd*) caliph 'Umar ibn al-Khaṭṭāb, his word having derivative prophetic authority:

> 'Umar ibn al-Khaṭṭāb said to his freedman . . . whom he had placed in charge of *ḥimā*, "Beware of the cry of the oppressed for it is answered. Do admit to *ḥimā* the owners of small herds of camel and sheep . . . By God! this is their land for which they fought in pre-Islamic times and which was included in their terms when they became Muslims. They would certainly feel that I am an adversary [for having declared their land *ḥimā*]— but, indeed, had it not been for the cattle to be used in the cause of God, I would never make a part of people's land *ḥimā*."[68]

It is clear from this report that the principle of *ḥimā*, which I shall explicate further, is at once an ecological issue as well as one of distributive justice and fairness. This twin significance of the principle is amply illustrated by the fact that it is explicitly invoked in the "Book of Business Transactions" of the highly respected *Mishkāt al-Maṣābīḥ* (Niche for Lamps), a manual of Ḥadīth deriving from a work of one al-Baghawī (d. ca. 1116);[69] the book in question is concerned with the ethics of trade and commercial dealings. In the *Ṣaḥīḥ* of Bukhārī too it is found in a chapter with the same title,[70] as well as in the "Book of [Equitable and Fair] Distribution of Water."[71] All this further reinforces the point: *ḥimā* is both an environmental concern and an ethical issue of fair public policy.

But it remained up to the *fiqh* legists to develop the *ḥimā* principle systematically into a legal entity amenable to legislation, and this process is carried out, by definition, in the framework of practical ethics. In fact, *ḥimā* had a long history of abuse. The word, literally meaning "protected, forbidden place," names a pre-Islamic institution whereby some powerful individual or a ruling chief declared a piece of fertile land forbidden to the public or out of bounds. This was generally an exploitative act of dispossession and land confiscation. By virtue of *ḥimā*, those in power arrogated to themselves exclusive grazing, watering, and cultivation rights within the area the ground covered. Islam abrogated this practice and transformed the institution. Thus we read in the Qur'ān, "O my people, this is the camel of God, which is for you a sign (*āya*). Leave it to graze on the land of God."[72] And in the Bukhārī we have the Ḥadīth : "Nobody has the right to declare a place *ḥimā* except God and His Messenger."[73] In this way, *ḥimā* became a symbol of redress and restoration of justice and gradually acquired a status close to that of *ḥarām* (see below), in that it denoted a sanctuary, with its flora and fauna receiving special protection.[74]

But the environmental dimensions of the institution of *ḥimā* are readily apparent, and the Maliki school of law, in particular, has developed these dimensions, preserving their intimate connection with social and ethical balance. Thus, four conditions were to be met for a piece of land to qualify as a possible *ḥimā*: First was the condition of need and fairness. *Ḥimā* was to be governed not by the whim or greed of some powerful individual or group, but by people's generally felt need to maintain a restricted area; that is, it had to be an act *pro bono*. Second, under the condition of what we may call ecological proportion, the area to be declared as *ḥimā* could not be too large, for this would be disproportionate. Third was the condition of environmental protection—the area under the *ḥimā* protection was not to be built upon or commercialized, nor was it to be cultivated for financial gain. Fourth was the condition of social welfare; the overriding aim of *ḥimā* was the economic and environmental benefit of the people.[75] This provides the outline of a concrete environmental policy concerning protected areas.

A similar institution articulated by the legists is that of *ḥarām* (or *ḥarīm*)—sacred territory, inviolable zone, sanctuary. Mecca was a *ḥarām* by the decree of God Himself.[76] Here, for example, no animal of the game species is ever put to death. By extension *ḥarām* became an environmental institution; it is often discussed in the section devoted to wasteland in legal works. Izzi Deen writes, "The *ḥarām* is usually found in association with wells, natural springs, underground water channels, rivers and trees planted on barren lands or *mawāt* [wasteland]. There is [in some parts of the Islamic world] a careful administration of the *ḥarām* zones based on the practice of the Prophet Muḥammad and the precedent of his companions as recorded in the sources of Islamic law."[77]

It is quite striking that there exists in the Ḥadīth corpora an abundance of reports concerning plants and trees, land cultivation and irrigation, crops, livestock, grazing, water distribution, water sources and their maintenance, wells and rivers, water rights—all this is most promising material for our contemporary environmental concerns. Thus, in a report in Bukhārī's *Ṣaḥīḥ*, the Prophet is quoted as saying, "There is none amongst the believers who plants a tree, or sows a seed, and then a bird, or a person, or an animal eats thereof, but is regarded as having given a charitable gift [for which there is great recompense]."[78] So praiseworthy and noble is the task of a *sustainable* cultivation of land that even in Paradise (*al-Janna*, which significantly means "the Garden"), existing beyond the physical world, it does not come to an end. So we read the Prophet telling his companions:

> One of the inhabitants of Paradise will beseech God to allow him land cultivation. God will ask him, "But are you not in your desired state of being?" "Yes," he will say, "but I would still like to cultivate land" . . . When the man will be granted God's leave for this task, he will sow seeds, and plants will soon grow out of them, becoming ripe and mature, ready for reaping. They will become colossal as mountains. God will then say: "O Son of Adam, gather!"[79]

In another place, the Prophet is reported to have said: "When doomsday comes, and someone has a palm shoot in his hand, he should plant it."[80] This saying accords a Prophetic sacrality to all life: the bounty of nature is a good *in itself*, even at Doom—a good beyond any immediate or conceivable benefits that one may draw from it.

In Bukhari's section on issues concerning the use, ownership, management, and distribution of water, one finds a meaningful play on the word *faḍl*, which means both "excess" and "grace": "[Among the] . . . three types of people with whom God on the Day of Resurrection will exchange no words, nor will He look at them," the Prophet is said to have declared, ". . . [is] the one who possesses an excess of water but withholds it from others. To him God will say, 'Today I shall withhold from you my grace (*faḍlī*) as you withheld from others the superfluity (*faḍl*) of what you had not created yourself.' "[81]

Note the moral principle here linking the real to the transcendental: it was not humankind that created water; God is the creator. Indeed, while in its legal developments the question of the ownership of wells, rivers, and other natural drinking and irrigation sources became a complex one, one thing remained abundantly clear on the moral plane: water must be shared *equally*, as the Prophet is consistently and insistently reported to have taught. This egalitarian ethical principle yields far-reaching ecological consequences: by virtue of this principle, no living individual, and this includes animals, can be deprived of water if it is available; likewise no piece of cultivable land, irrespective of its ownership, can be left without irrigation if water resources have the capacity. Again, and even more strongly, the "Book of Business Transactions" of the *Mishkāt* quotes the Prophet's solemn declaration of a fundamental rule: "Muslims share alike in three things—water, herbage, and fire."[82]

One is astounded to see how a large number of these Ḥadīth principles were developed in their most minute detail, layer after layer, point by point, in the writings of *fiqh*-jurists, and woven into the vast legal fabric of normative ethics. A monumental example of such work is the *Hidāya* of the twelfth-century jurist al-Marghinānī, held to be the most authoritative single work of the Ḥanafī school of law, followed by the majority of Muslims. In this grand manual, already translated into English in the eighteenth century,[83] one finds detailed discourses on wasteland (*mawāt*) and, in this connection, systematic discussions of water rights and resources and their maintenance.

The *Hidāya* contains an extensive "Book on the Cultivation of Waste Lands" with sections on the definition of *mawāt*, the rights of cultivating it, the treatment of adjacent territories, the status of adjacent territories, water courses in *mawāt*, matters related to aqueducts running through the *mawāt*, and so on. There is a large section here on waters, including issues of control and direction of flow, a large section on digging canals, on rivers, their kinds and cleaning, and rules with respect to drains and water courses. There is, furthermore, a whole section on water rights, which discusses the right to alter or obstruct water courses, dams, the digging of trenches, the construction of water engines or bridges, water vents—the minutiae here are daunting.[84]

Even more striking than the abundance of Prophetic reports on vegetation and irrigation is the existence in the Ḥadīth corpora of a large body of traditions, admonitions, rules, and stories concerning animals, their treatment, rights, natural dignity, and even their unique individual identities. Contained in the "Book of Striving" (*Jiḥād*) of the *Muwaṭṭā'* is the resounding tradition about horses: "In the forehead of horses," the Prophet is quoted as saying, "are tied up welfare and bliss until the Day of Resurrection."[85] Such compassion and care for animals is reflected in the same book in an account of the Prophet wiping the mouth of his horse with his personal cloth. Asked why, he replied: "Last night I was rebuked [by God] for not looking after my horse."[86] Again, in Bukhārī's "Book of Water," we have this report:

> The one to whom his horse is a source of reward is the one who keeps it in the path of God, and ties it by a long rope in a pasture or a garden. Such a person will get a reward equal to what the horse's long rope allows it to eat in the pasture or the garden. And if the horse breaks its rope and crosses one or two hills, then all marks of its hoofs and its dung will be counted as good deeds for its owner. And if it passes by a river and drinks from it, then that will also be regarded as a good deed on the part of its owner. . . .[87]

Appearing in the "Book of Jihād" in the *Mishkāt* is a set of rules that the Prophet pronounced concerning the treatment of camels. "When you travel in fertile country," he said, "give the camels their due from the ground, and when you travel in time of drought make them go quickly. When you encamp at night keep away from the roads, for they are where beasts pass and are the resort of insects at night."[88] It is remarkable that a sensitive concern for animals does not disappear from the horizon even during military engagements. In the same book, there exists a particularly stern admonishment against animal abuse—"Do not treat the back of your animals as pulpits, for God the most high has made them subject to you only to convey you to a place which you could not otherwise reach without much difficulty."[89]

Likewise we have a fable from the Prophet in Bukhari's "Book of Agriculture": "While a man was riding a cow, it turned toward him and said, 'I have not been created for this purpose [of riding]; I have been created for plowing.'"[90] Here we have the Qur'ānic principles of *amr* and *qadr*, effectively the principles of natural and moral law and ecological balance, translated into practical ethics. And again, in the "Book of Jihād" of another *Ṣaḥīḥ* (Correct) Ḥadīth collection, the *Sunan* of Abū Dā'ūd (d. 888), one tradition clearly implies—and note that this implication is recognized by Muslim commentators—that each animal is to be considered *as an individual*, since the tradition speaks of animals being given proper names ("a donkey called 'Afīr").[91] Quite remarkably, this individuation effectively admits a *unique* identity on the part of each and every member of a given animal species. One wonders, then, if Islam constitutes an exception to the "speciesism" of the classical world—as I have said elsewhere, this would indeed be a highly fruitful question to pursue.[92]

Rather well-known in the Islamic world is the Ḥadīth story of a woman who was condemned to hellfire "because of a cat which she had imprisoned, and it died of starvation. . . . God told her, 'You are condemned because you did not feed the cat, and did not give it water to drink, nor did you set it free so that it could eat of the creatures of the earth.'"[93] This Ḥadīth story forms the basis of the *fiqh*-legislation that the owner of an animal is legally responsible for its well-being. If such owners are unable to provide for their animals, jurists further stipulate, then they should sell them, or let them go free in such a way that they can find food and shelter, or slaughter them if eating their flesh is permissible. Given the requirement that animals should be allowed as far as possible to live out their lives in a natural manner, keeping birds in cages is deemed unlawful.[94]

Large sections, or books, devoted exclusively to the hunting of animals and game, and animal sacrifice, are a standard feature of the Ḥadīth corpora. All of this is treated with an ethical focus, underlying which is a particular conception of the natural environment that ultimately derives from the Qur'ān. At the same time, this ethical treatment of the issue generates both a philosophical and a moral attitude to the physical world that is uniquely Islamic, an attitude that manifests itself as an actual fact of the practices of Islamic societies. It is most instructive to recall E. W. Lane noting in his famous nineteenth-century work *Manners and Customs of the Modern Egyptians*: "I was much pleased at observing their humanity to dumb animals." But Lane found that the Egyptians had subsequently lost some of their traditional sensitivity to animals, and he explains: "I am inclined to think that the conduct of Europeans has greatly conduced to produce this effect, for I do not remember to have seen acts of cruelty to dumb animals except in places where Franks either reside or are frequent visitors."[95]

The Egyptians' "humanity to animals" appears to be the moral harvest of Prophetic teachings with its numerous ecological ramifications. In fact, there is in the *Mishkāt* the saying of the Prophet, "If anyone wrongfully kills [even] a sparrow, [let alone] anything greater, he will face God's interrogation."[96] We read in the same collection how vehemently the Prophet condemned the practice of branding animals; the story is narrated that he saw a donkey branded on the face, and it upset him so much that he invoked God's curse: "God curse the one who branded it!" In fact, it is explicitly stated here that "God's messenger forbade striking the face of an animal or branding on its face." Similarly, he is reported to have forbidden all forms of blood sports, including inciting living creatures to fight with one another, or using them as targets—"The Prophet cursed those who used a living creature as targets."[97] The unusual intensity of this condemnation is to be gauged by the fact that these accounts speak of the Prophet cursing, and this is an exceptional feature of his character as it is portrayed in the tradition. In the same vein and with clear ecological dimensions, we have a story in Abū Dā'ūd's *Sunan*: "Once a companion of the Prophet was seen crumbling up bread for some ants with the words, 'They are our neighbors and have rights over us.'"[98]

Islam does not prescribe vegetarianism and, of course, killing of certain kinds of animals for food is permitted, but only if the animal is killed in a specified manner *and*—in order to prevent cruel and arrogant tendencies from developing—God's name is pronounced over it. Islamic tradition has it that it is precisely the prevention of human arrogance and the inculcation of an ecological sensitivity in which lies the wisdom (*ḥikma*) of the whole idea of *dhabḥ* (lawful killing of animals for food). Thus, there exist in Ḥadīth collections exceedingly detailed instructions concerning animal slaughtering. A report in the *Mishkāt* has the Prophet saying, "God who is blessed and exalted has decreed that everything should be done in a good way, so when you kill [an animal] use a good method, and when you cut an animal's throat you should use a good method, for each of you should sharpen his knife and give the animal as little pain as possible."[99] It is declared reprehensible by the Prophet to let one animal witness the slaughtering of another, or to keep animals waiting to be slaughtered, or sharpening the knife in their presence—"Do you wish to slaughter the animal twice: once by sharpening your blade in front of it and another time by cutting its throat?"[100]

The jurist Marginānī, whom we have already met, has a whole chapter on *dhabḥ* in his *Hidāya*; elaborating the matter in the finest of its details, as it was his manner, he writes:

> It is abominable first to throw the animal down on its side, and then to sharpen the knife; for it is related that the Prophet once observing a man who had done so, said to him, "How many deaths do you intend that this animal should die? Why did you not sharpen your knife before you threw it down?" IT is abominable to let the knife reach the spinal marrow, or to cut off the head of the animal. The reasons . . . are, FIRST, because the Prophet has forbidden this; and, SECONDLY, because it unnecessarily augments the pain of the animal, which is prohibited in our LAW.—In short, everything which unnecessarily augments the pain of the animal is abominable . . . IT is abominable to seize an animal destined for slaughter by the feet, and drag it . . . IT is abominable to break the neck of the animal whilst it is in the struggle of death. . . .[101]

We have already noted the rule of equal sharing of water, and this rule makes no distinction between human beings and animals. Thus, for example, in the "Book of Ablution" of the Bukhārī corpus, as well as in other corpora, there is the account of a man who was walking along a road and felt thirsty. Finding a well, he lowered himself into it and drank. When he came out he found a dog panting from thirst and licking at the earth. He therefore went down again into the well and filled his shoe with water and gave it to the dog. For this act God Almighty forgave him his sins. The Prophet was then asked whether man had a reward through animals, and he replied: "In everything that lives there is a reward."[102] "In everything that lives there is a reward" may be considered a broad central principle of Islam's environmental ethics.

So we see the richness of Islamic material relevant to the question of the environment and ecology, and we also note the sophistication of treatment this material received in the Islamic culture, but the question is complex and larger. To capture a fuller sweep of the question of Islam and ecology, we will have to cast a much wider net—this essay does not even claim to contribute a smaller net; if anything, it offers some of its twine.

Notes

This essay is reprinted here by permission of *Dædalus*, Journal of the American Academy of Arts and Sciences, from the issue entitled "Religion and Ecology: Can the Climate Change?" 130, no. 4 (fall 2001).

1. See Henry Corbin, *Avicenna and the Visionary Recital* (New York: Pantheon Books, 1960).

2. Some samples of the first attitude are to be found in Ziauddin Sardar, ed., *The Touch of Midas* (Manchester: Manchester University Press, 1984); on resentment toward all things Western, see the discussion of "Westoxification" in John Esposito, *Islam and Politics* (Syracuse, N.Y.: Syracuse University Press, 1984). In the third view one would place the ideas of some of those called Modernists; see Esposito, *Islam and Politics*; also Fazlur Rahman, *Islam* (Chicago: The University of Chicago Press, 1979).

3. Hamilton Gibb, *Whither Islam?* (London: Victor Gollancz Ltd., 1932), 376.

4. Ibid., 377–78.

5. Ibid., 376.

6. See ibid., 377.

7. Seyyed Hossein Nasr is one of the pioneers who has undertaken this exercising task. See Nasr, "Islam and the Environmental Crisis," *Islamic Quarterly* 34, no. 4 (1991): 217–34; and Nasr, *The Encounter of Man and Nature* (London: Allen and Unwin, 1978).

8. Cf. Hanna E. Kassis, *A Concordance of the Qur'ān* (Berkeley: University of California Press, 1983).

9. George F. Hourani, *Reason and Tradition in Islamic Ethics* (Cambridge: Cambridge University Press, 1985), 86.

10. Ibid., 86; my emphasis.

11. The literal meaning of *zauj* is, indeed, "equal half"; in the creation story in the second chapter (verse 35) of the Qur'ān, this is the word used for the human being recognized by the tradition as Eve (*Ḥawwā*).

12. For Thomas Aquinas, nature was unredeemed.

13. This is pointed out by Nasr, "Islam and the Environmental Crisis," 219.

14. 7:72. Translations of the Qur'ān used for this essay are *The Holy Qur'ān*, trans. Abdullah Y. Ali (Brentwood, Md.: Amana Corporation, 1989); and *The Qur'ān Interpreted,* trans. Arthur J. Arberry (New York: Macmillan, 1955). Commentaries include Ibn Kathīr, *Tafsīr*, in Muhammad A. al-Sabuni, ed., *Mukhtaṣar Tafsīr ibn Kathīr* (Beirut: Dar al-Qur'ān al-Karīm, 1981).

15. 15:1–4.

16. 2:22; 13:17; 14:32–33; 16:5–16; 16:80–81; 17:70; 21:31–32; 23:18–22; 43:10–12; 45:12–13; 55:1–78; 78:6–16.

17. 33:72.

18. 45:13.

19. 16:12–14.

20. 22:65–66.

21. 80:1–9.

22. 93 (entire); 89:17–18.

23. 83:1–13.
24. 89:17–23.
25. 89:19; 100:6–11.
26. 3:108–9.
27. 38:27; cf. 3:191.
28. 27:88–90.
29. *Majmū' Fatāwā*, quoted in Mawil Yousuf Izzi Deen (Samarrai), "Islamic Environmental Ethics," in *Ethics of Environment and Development*, ed. J. Ronald Engel and Joan Gibb Engel (Tucson: University of Arizona Press, 1990), 190; my emphasis.
30. 2:107.
31. 24:42.
32. 40:57.
33. 55:10.
34. 6:38.
35. Denys Johnson-Davies, *The Island of Animals, Adapted from an Arabic Fable* (Austin: University of Texas Press, 1994), viii.
36. Ibid., 75.
37. 15:26, 28, 33.
38. 22:5.
39. 96:1.
40. 6:2; 7:12, etc.
41. Fazlur Rahman, *Major Themes of the Qur'ān* (Minneapolis: Bibliotheca Islamica, 1989), 17. This work is a highly learned excursus on Qur'ānic themes by one of the finest modern scholars of our times.
42. 23:13–14.
43. 50:6–11.
44. 15:19–22.
45. 15:26–27.
46. On *ẓulm al-nafs*, see Hourani, *Reason and Tradition in Islamic Ethics.*
47. See my chapter "Islam" in *A Companion to Environmental Philosophy*, Blackwell Companions to Philosophy series, ed. Dale Jamieson (Oxford: Blackwell, 2001). It ought to be noted here that this was the first articulation of my ideas on the question of Islam and ecology, and readers will note some parallels in the present essay; this is inevitable since the core of the primary normative sources remains constant.
48. 65:1.
49. 16:33.
50. The Qur'ān is replete with the verbal form of the root word *ẓalama* (to do wrong), along with several other verbal and nominal forms that morphologically arise out of it. But for *ẓulm al-nafs*, see particularly 2:231; 3:135; 7:23; 11:101; 27:44; 28:16; 34:19; 43:76.
51. 3:83.
52. L. Gardet, "God in Islam," *Encyclopedia of Religion*, ed. Mircea Eliade (New York: Macmillan, 1987), 30.
53. 57:3.

54. 55:5–29.
55. Rahman, *Major Themes*, 71.
56. See 18:109–10.
57. See 2:118, 219, 266; 3:118; 5:75.
58. 6:65. I draw upon Rahman's *Major Themes* here.
59. 6:97–98.
60. 9:128.
61. 13:7.
62. 45:52.
63. 21:107.
64. 1:1.
65. See Izzi Deen (Samarrai), "Islamic Environmental Ethics," 95.
66. *Ṣaḥīḥ al-Bukhārī*, ed. and trans. M. Muhsin Khan (Chicago: Kazi Publications, 1976–1979), 1:331.
67. These are named after the masters who compiled them, thus: al-Bukhārī, Muslim (d. 875), Abū Dā'ūd (d. 888), al-Tirmidhī (d. 892), al-Nasā'ī (d. 916), and Ibn Māja (d. 886).
68. *Muwaṭṭā'* of Mālik ibn Anas, trans. Muhammad Rahimuddin (Lahore: Sh. Muhammad Ashraf, 1985), no. 1830.
69. *Mishkāt al-Maṣābīḥ*, trans. James Robson (Lahore: Sh. Muhammad Ashraf, 1990), 592.
70. *Ṣaḥīḥ al-Bukhārī,* ed. and trans. Khan, 3:267.
71. Ibid., 3:558.
72. 11:64.
73. *Ṣaḥīḥ al-Bukhārī,* ed. and trans. Khan, 3:558.
74. See J. Chelhold, "Ḥimā," in *Encyclopaedia of Islam,* new ed., vol. 3, ed. H. A. R. Gibb et al. (Leiden: E. J. Brill, 1971), 393.
75. Wahba al-Zuhailī, *al-Fiqh al-Islamī wa Adillatuhu*, vol. 5 (Islamic Law and Its Material Foundations) (Damascus: Dar al-Fikr, 1984), 23–24; 571–575; quoted in Izzi Deen (Samarrai), "Islamic Environmental Ethics," 196.
76. 17:91.
77. Izzi Deen (Samarrai), "Islamic Environmental Ethics," 190.
78. *Ṣaḥīḥ al-Bukhārī,* ed. and trans. Khan, 3:513.
79. Ibid., 3:538.
80. *Sunan al-Baihaqī al-Kubrā*, quoted in Izzi Deen (Samarrai), "Islamic Environmental Ethics," 194.
81. *Ṣaḥīḥ al-Bukhārī,* ed. and trans. Khan, 3:557.
82. *Mishkāt al-Maṣābīḥ*, trans. Robson, 640.
83. *Hidāya of al-Marghnānī*, trans. Charles Hamilton (London: T. Bensley, 1791); cited here is the reprint from the 2d ed. of 1870 (Lahore: Premier Book House, 1957).
84. Ibid., 4:609–18.
85. *Muwaṭṭā'* of Mālik ibn Anas, trans. Rahimuddin, no. 990.
86. Ibid., no. 993.
87. *Ṣaḥīḥ al-Bukhārī,* ed. and trans. Khan, 3:559.
88. *Mishkāt al-Maṣābīḥ*, trans. Robson, 826.
89. Ibid., 829; translation slightly amended.

90. *Ṣaḥīḥ al-Bukhārī,* ed. and trans. Khan, 3:517.
91. *Sunan Abū Dā' ūd*, trans. Wahid al-Zamân (Urdu) (Lahore: Islamic Academy, 1983), 308–312.
92. Haq, "Islam," 123.
93. *Ṣaḥīḥ al-Bukhārī,* ed. and trans. Khan, 3:553.
94. Johnson-Davies, *The Island of Animals*, xii.
95. Quoted in ibid., xv, from the 1836 publication.
96. *Mishkāt al-Maṣābīḥ*, trans. Robson, 874.
97. Ibid., 872.
98. Quoted in Johnson-Davies, *The Island of Animals*, xvii.
99. *Mishkāt al-Maṣābīḥ*, trans. Robson, 872.
100. Quoted in Johnson-Davies, *The Island of Animals*, ix.
101. *Hidāya,* trans. Hamilton, 4:558.
102. Johnson-Davies, *The Island of Animals*, ix.

Peace in Islam: An Ecology of the Spirit

ABDUL AZIZ SAID AND NATHAN C. FUNK

The Islamic understanding of peace is rooted in *tawḥīd*, the principle of unity that provides a fertile soil for Islamic faith and spirituality. Unity is essential to Islam. Islam underscores the unity of God, the unity of the many streams of revelation, the unity of humanity, and, ultimately, the unity of existence. Unity embraces and sustains diversity; the Whole is reflected in the parts. As the Qur'an affirms, "To Allah belong the East and the West: whithersoever ye turn, there is Allah's face. For Allah is All-Embracing, All-Knowing" (2:115). The transcendent and the immanent are One, for God is both the Hidden (*bāṭin*) and the Manifest (*ẓāhir*), the Inward and the Outward.[1]

If unity is the truth (*ḥaqq*) or essence (*ẓāt*) of Islam, humans and other creatures approach this truth through harmony. The strength of Islam is its capacity to reconcile seeming opposites and harmonize diversity until the underlying unity is perceived and disharmony returns to peace. When proper relationships are established within and among created things, justice (*'adl*) is established and peace becomes manifest.

The Islamic understanding of peace suggests an ecology of the spirit, an ecology predicated on *tawḥīd*, the fundamental unity of God and of all existence. Humans and nature are one and are at peace in the consciousness of *tawḥīd*. When *tawḥīd* is forgotten, the relationship becomes unpeaceful. Through exploring the nature of peace in Islam, we gain a special approach to the Islamic understanding of ecology in light of this principle of unity.

In this essay, we shall first examine in greater depth the principle of *tawḥīd* and its relation to peace. We will then examine the ways in which Islamic principles of unity and peace apply in Islamic teachings regarding ecology. After clarifying essential precepts, we will turn to four paradigms of Islamic thought and practice and identify their ecological implications. We hope to reveal both underlying consistencies in the Islamic outlook and significant differences in interpretation and action. We will conclude with a diagnosis of the contemporary global situation, and an attempt to identify modalities of faith needed in the present time.

Tawḥīd: An Affirmation of Wholeness

Islam is, at its core, a message of unity, peace, and reconciliation.[2] This message applies to the inner person, to society, and to the cosmos. Islam is the process of submission to God, through which the part—the human microcosm—becomes reconciled to the Whole, to the universe or the macrocosm. The recognition of *tawḥīd* begins with belief and culminates in faith (*īmān*) and existential surrender. Surrender is not only a goal of Islamic ethics and law, but also a source of knowledge and activity and effort. The ideal of Islam is that the creature should come to know the Creator, and through the Creator, the unity of being, *waḥdat al-wujūd*. Through this knowledge, the knower is transformed, becoming peaceful.

Tawḥīd is a conception whose reality enters into human life at many levels, shaping both Islamic thought and Islamic practice. Interpretations of the implications of *tawḥīd* distinguish not only jurisprudence and theology but also philosophy, social and political thought, science, and theosophy. Beyond the doctrinal and ideological planes where the oneness of humanity is stressed, *tawḥīd* mediates the direct personal relation to the Absolute, and the maintenance of harmony with the universe.

Tawḥīd expresses the Islamic ideal of the fundamental unity of all humankind and of all life and rejects a vision of reality rooted in exclusiveness. The universalism, tolerance, and inclusiveness of Islam is beautifully evoked in the Qur'an (49:13), with the words: "Oh mankind! We created you from a single (pair) of a male and a female, and made you peoples (or 'nations') and tribes that you may know one another." At the heart of the message of universalistic Islam is a respect for cultural pluralism that is inextricably linked to a recognition of the fundamental solidarity and connectedness of all human beings. The unity of humankind is not premised on uniformity; rather, unity embraces myriad cultural and communal differences. From the standpoint of Islamic universalism, particularly as it has been articulated by those who have contemplated the Qur'anic passage "To every people (was sent) a Messenger" (10:47),[3] humankind is ultimately one community; comparative evaluation of prophets is discouraged, for all are deemed messengers of God.[4] Islam affirms pluralism, prescribes respect in interreligious relations,[5] and condemns racial and ethnic discrimination.[6]

From a Qur'anic perspective, particularity and universality are not inherently contradictory principles. Particularity inheres in outward form and historical experience, and does not preclude universality of spirit. The distinctions and differences among individuals, as well as among cultures and communities of faith, fade in comparison to the majesty of God. It is significant that the word Islam derives not from the name of a particular prophet or people, but from the same root as *salām—silm. Silm* suggests a condition of peace, security, wholeness, and safety from harm which is attained through surrender (*taslīm*) to the Divine.[7] The term *muslim*, at its most inclusive level of meaning, includes all human beings and all of creation, for all creatures necessarily submit to the will of the Creator. The more particular sense of the term, which receives capitalized form in English transliteration, refers to those who derive their religious orientation from the prophethood of Muhammad.

Human beings and all other created things share in the existential condition of submission to the Divine. All things are necessarily *muslim* because, consciously or unconsciously, they perform the will of Allah; Muslims are those who consciously follow the revelation given through Muhammad. Likewise, *islām* is the natural religion of all creatures and the religion revealed by all prophets; Islam is the religion perfected in the Qur'an.[8]

The search for unity is a powerful impetus in Islam. Unity is to be sought within each human being, within the *umma* (community) of Muslims, within the broader community of all peoples who have faith in God, and within the context of the earth as a whole. From the standpoint of the individual believer, unity is both an essential premise about the deep nature of reality and a modality of faith which integrates task and experience. As the Qur'an repeatedly underscores, spiritual inspiration for sustaining the work of faith is available through keen observation of nature, which manifests the signs (*āyāt*) of God:

> Behold! If the creation of the heavens and the earth; in the alternation of the Night and the Day; in the sailing of the ships through the Ocean for the profit of mankind; in the rain which Allah sends down from the skies, and the life which He gives therewith to an earth that is dead; in the beasts of all kinds that He scatters through the earth; in the change of the winds, and the clouds which they trail like their slaves between the sky and the earth; (Here) indeed are Signs for a people that are wise. (2:164)

Human spirituality is informed by the wisdom, harmony, and beauty manifest in the diversity and wholeness of nature. Contemplation of these qualities brings a sense of stability, tranquillity, and peace.

The Priority of Peace in Islamic Faith

As Seyyed Hossein Nasr has emphasized, the Islamic understanding of peace differs from the modern Western conception.[9] While in the modern world peace is generally understood as an absence of war or tension, peace in Islam is a presence. Peace in Islam begins with God; God is peace, for peace (*al-salām*) is one of the "ninety-nine most beautiful names" of God. Peace in the world descends from the Origin of peace and reflects higher realities.[10] As the Qur'an states, peace is the greeting, language, and condition of Paradise.[11] God calls believers unto the "abode of peace" (*dār al-salām*),[12] and the yearning for peace derives from the innermost nature, or *fiṭra*, of humankind.[13] Peace in Islam suggests an equilibrium of parts or a pattern of harmony, the internalization and upholding of which is the responsibility of every Muslim. The term *jihād*, often translated superficially as "holy war," actually means "striving," and the "greater jihad" (*jihād al-akbar*) in the Islamic tradition has always been the inner struggle to purify the self and behave in a manner which furthers rather than disrupts the divine harmony.

Islam adopts a positive view of human nature, insisting that the original human constitution (*fiṭra*) is good and "*muslim*" in character. There is no conception of "original sin," but rather a hopeful conception of human potential that is integrally related to a vision of existential freedom—freedom to be—which is not predicated upon the more Western notion of freedom from constraint—freedom to do. In the Islamic understanding, human privilege and human responsibility are intertwined—it is a privilege to fulfill human responsibility, and responsibility to actualize human privilege. Human actions are outwardly constrained insofar as is necessary to preserve the freedom of the community—human as well as nonhuman—and live in accordance with divine law. True freedom is found in service, in "doing what is beautiful" (*iḥsān*).[14] Human consciousness is not constrained and, through proper cultivation and divine grace, opens into the Infinite.

A striking feature of Qur'anic discourse is the emphasis on people's use of their innate intelligence in comprehending the revealed guidance, which is accessible both in the Holy Book and in the Book of Nature. Time and again the Qur'an exhorts its hearers to ponder, reflect, think, and understand. Religion is armed with arguments designed to persuade through force of logic, emotional appeal, appeals to universal cosmic order and divine providential purpose, and, failing these, promises of eschatological rewards or punishments.

Above all, it is recognized that people cannot be dissuaded from pursuing the wrong course in this life through force or violence: "There is no compulsion in faith!" asserts the Qur'an (2:256). While it is true that certain political movements which associate themselves with Islam have renounced prohibitions against the misuse of force, both the spirit in which these groups apply force and the methods by which it has been used contradict essential Islamic precepts which afford respect to those who differ and protect noncombatants and nonaggressors.

Compassion and mercy are integral and oft-repeated attributes of God, whom the Qur'an refers to as al-Raḥmān, al-Raḥīm, the Merciful and the Compassionate. Although Islam does not limit God to any particular quality, attributes such as *raḥmān* and *raḥīm* suggest the nearness as well as the forbearance of God. God forgives and transforms those who turn toward Him (*tawba*) with infinite mercy and graciousness. And God's mercy extends to all worlds; the Qur'an describes the prophethood of Muhammad by stating, "We sent thee not, but as a Mercy for all creatures" (21:107).

Islam is a religion not only of divine majesty (*jalāl*), but also of divine beauty (*jamāl*) and love.[15] Islam directs attention both to the incomparability, omnipotence, and transcendence of God and to the omnipresence of God.[16] God is both far (*tanzīl*) and near (*tashbīḥ*). The nearness of God is affirmed in the Qur'anic affirmation, "And He is with you wheresoever ye may be" (57:4). The transcendence of God puts the trials and preoccupations of life in their proper perspective; the vision of the immanence of God alludes to the source and purpose of all creation. As is stated in the *ḥadīth*s, "God has inscribed beauty upon all things." The unveiling of the beauty of creation provides inspiration for *iḥsān*, "doing what is beautiful"—the fulfillment of religion.

The Practice of Peace in Islam

While political expediency has often affected interpretations and applications of the Qur'an and *sunna*, the essential theme of the Qur'anic revelation is surrender to and integration in God, suggesting a worldview premised on universalism, tolerance, inclusiveness, and coexistence.[17] Likewise, while intoxication with modern technology and the received imperatives of the nation-state system have overridden traditional safeguards for environmental integrity, Islamic ecological traditions remain vital and accessible.

The principal concern of the *sharī'a*, or law of Islam, is the maintenance of proper, harmonious relationships on and across all levels—between the individual and God, within the individual, within the family and community, among Muslims, between religions, and with all of humanity and creation. As has been the case with Christianity, Judaism, and other religious traditions, Islamic practices have not always reflected Islamic precepts, but the historical record of Muslim communities on matters of cultural and religious pluralism excelled that of premodern Europe.[18] Religious tolerance is built into Islamic precepts, which designate the "People of the Book" as protected peoples.

There is a clearly articulated preference in Islam for nonviolence over violence, and for forgiveness (*'afū*) over retribution. The principle of unity is reflected in the Qur'anic concern to regulate the commonplace, retributive responses of people to conflict and violence. Forgiveness is consistently held out as the preferred option for humanity in matters of requiting clear injustice or crime: "The recompense of an injury is an injury the like thereof; but whoever forgives and thereby brings about a reestablishment of harmony, his reward is with God; and God loves not the wrongdoers" (Qur'an 42:40). Neither naive pardon nor a mechanical retribution is urged; what is sought is a reformation or moral good accomplished by sincere forgiveness. Many communities in the Islamic culture area continue to make use of traditional rituals of forgiveness and reconciliation (*maṣlaha*), the goal of which is to restore wholeness and harmony through a truce, or *ṣulh*.[19]

In Islam, actions that are disproportionate and improper deviate from truth (*ḥaqq*) and are ultimately self-destructive: they turn on themselves, incur God's disfavor, and obscure unity and interconnectedness. The Qur'an frequently cautions people against going to excess when attempting to pursue rights or correct injustice. Of course, this attitude itself is only an extension of the Islamic precept of adopting the middle way in all activities, of moderation and evenhandedness. The Qur'an heaps utter condemnation on those who, by selfishly pursuing their own limited goals, seek infinite satisfaction from a finite world and bring destruction, oppression, and violence (*fitna*) down upon the rest of their fellows, "committing excesses on earth" (Qur'an 5:33). Islam also holds that greater harm is done to the world by indifference and unconcern—by the failure of good persons to rally in support of true causes—than by active deliberate mischief.

The real basis of peace in Islam is the transformative knowledge of unity. Islam does not exist to impose an idealized pattern upon the world, but rather to establish *tawḥīd*, and to promote harmony and justice through right relationships, moderation, and holistic integration. Islamic precepts therefore do not apply only to relations among human beings, but also to relations among humans and nonhuman creations. Injustice can be done not only to human beings, but also to nature. Islam underscores responsibility and the importance of respecting limits, as well as a positive, internalized sense of care and stewardship.

Ecological Harmony: Upholding the Pattern of Existence

The Islamic perspective on ecology mirrors the Islamic perspective on peace. The ecological sensibility in Islam is not predicated upon anthropocentrism or biocentrism, but rather on *tawḥīd*. There is a divine claim over human actions, and a sacred purpose in creation. Ultimately, human beings are one with nature through surrender to the presence of the Divine.

Islam does not oppose nature to spirit or heaven to earth, because all created things are by definition *muslim*, in the sense that they live in submission to God.[20] Likewise, the original sources of Islam do not postulate an intractable opposition between passion and reason,[21] but rather appeal to the innate human disposition, *fiṭra*, the purity which remains accessible, despite forgetfulness and ignorance. The vision of Islam is integral rather than dualistic. Even Satan, portrayed in the Qur'an as the one who misleads, cannot work contrary to the will of God.[22] Notions of taming a "godless wilderness" are foreign to Islam. The Qur'an repeatedly points to the blessings conferred upon and through creation to inspire an attitude of gratitude and responsibility:

> The Most Gracious! It is He Who has taught the Qur'an. He has created man: He has taught him an intelligent speech. The sun and the moon follow courses (exactly) computed; and the herbs and the trees—both (alike) bow in adoration. And the Firmament has He raised high, and He has set up the Balance (of Justice), in order that ye may not transgress (due) balance. So establish weight with justice and fall not short in the balance. It is He Who has spread out the earth for (His) creatures: therein is fruit and date-palms, producing spathes (enclosing dates); also corn, with (its) leaves and stalk for fodder, and sweet-smelling plants. Then which of the favors of your Lord will ye deny? (Qur'an 55:1–13)

Both human beings and other creatures partake in the blessings of existence; both are part of a single harmonious order.

While human beings share with nonhuman creations in the common condition of submission, they are also endowed with special privileges and responsibilities which reflect their actual capacities. The human being is challenged to perform the role of *khalīfa*, or vicegerent. The vicegerent of God fulfills *amāna*, the covenant, the primordial bond of trust and recognition with the Creator. The earth and its resources are placed in the care of human beings as custodians for their preservation, development, and enhancement.

The human being possesses a special stature in Islam, but the potential fulfillment of human dignity depends upon acceptance of increased responsibility, continual self-effacement, and active pursuit of knowledge. The freedom of the human being is actualized through recognition of the Divine, which encompasses and embraces all creatures, and through performance of the divine will. Ignorance of the Divine and failure to live in a way that activates the higher faculties of the human being results in an actual loss of existential freedom and stature. Human beings must use the faculties that have been given to them, respecting the vital energies within a context of discernment and self-transcendence. As Karim Douglas Crow has suggested, the "Islamic anthropology" is reflected in the saying, "the person whose 'intelligence' overcomes their 'cravings' is superior to the angels and the person whose 'cravings' overcomes their 'intelligence' is inferior to the beasts."[23] A person who fails to subdue, refine, and efface his or her ego can do far more harm to creation than a predatory animal. The animal fulfills its ecological function; the human does not.

In calling attention to human faculties and capabilities which transcend those of animals, the Islamic tradition warns that human beings can fall to a position lower than the animals through failure to fulfill the covenant and the duties of a servant of God. Unlike animals, trees, and mountains, human beings must consciously uphold God's trust. Humans are entitled to feel privileged,[24] but arrogance is a great folly and, indeed, a form of idolatry. Animals, which act upon their instincts, incur no blame, but human beings who fail to respond to the grace of their Creator with gratitude and service risk great loss to themselves and others.

Islam recognizes and accentuates the interdependence of humankind and creation, and their mutual dependence upon God.[25] These relationships of interdependence and dependence have moral corollaries, requiring on the part of humans due regard for the rights of nature, understood in light of the rights and purposes of God.[26] To adapt a phrase used by environmental lawyer Christopher Stone,[27] "trees have standing" in Islam independent of their value to human beings. Animals, like human beings, form communities. They have their own forms of prayer, and they, too, will return to their Lord.

> There is not an animal (that lives) on the earth, nor a being that flies on its wings, but (forms part of) communities like you. Nothing have We omitted from the Book, and they (all) shall be gathered to their Lord in the end. (Qur'an 6:38)

> Seest thou not that it is Allah Whose praises all beings in the heavens and on earth do celebrate, and the birds (of the air) with wings outspread? Each one knows its own (mode of) prayer and praise. And Allah knows well all that they do. (Qur'an 24:41)

Nature provides positive lessons for human beings, demonstrating the proper relationship between creature and Creator. All of creation forms a harmonious pattern which, when viewed with eyes of faith, affirms the beauty, compassion, and power of the divine reality. As is said in the *ḥadīth*, "God is beautiful and He loves beauty."[28]

Nature satisfies genuine needs of humanity—physical as well as aesthetic and spiritual—but not the greed or caprice of humanity. Islam reminds human beings of their ecological function—that is, of their place within a greater, spiritual context which transcends and embraces all things. Humans realize freedom by surrendering to the divine will and participating in the divine creativity, which renews creation in each instant. They purify themselves inwardly to become receptive, free of external conditions which constrain this creativity. Internally, humans are absolutely free; externally, they are limited in their powers and rights in relation to God, nature, and fellow humans.

The Qur'anic ethos challenges human beings to attain to a sense of proportion rooted in *tawḥīd*, the all-inclusive environment of the Divine.[29] The root meanings of wrong-doing and right-doing in Islam are not judgmental in a stereotypical sense; they indicate whether or not things have been put in their proper places.[30] Individual beings and relationships among created things both veil and reveal the Divine; the most proper, virtuous actions and conditions are those which mirror the Divine in the most perfect and complete way. Humans are entitled to provide for their own sustenance and flourishing from nature, and, in turn, to develop nature in ways that are beautiful and contribute to the remembrance and glorification of God. It is in this way that the human performs the role of *khalīfa*. The capabilities entrusted to human beings require commensurate humility and sensitivity, predicated upon respect and reverence for the divine purpose in every created thing.

The Sacred Dimension of Nature

While it is not difficult to derive an ethic of environmental stewardship from the Qur'an, the ultimate significance of nature in Islam is spiritual. The harmony of nature is a source of spiritual inspiration and edification. As the Qur'an repeatedly emphasizes, nature is filled with the signs of God. "The seven heavens and the earth, and all beings therein, declare His glory: There is not a thing but celebrates His praise" (Qur'an 17:46). Nature is both a medium and a receptacle of revelation. All reflect and partake in the divine *sakīna*, the harmony and peace of God.

In the final analysis, the soundest basis of environmental ethics and responsibility in Islam is the experience of human integration through connectedness with the Divine and with nature. This theme is integral to the Qur'an and is affirmed in Islamic literature and poetry. An Islamic attitude of love and respect for nature is exemplified in the following verse by Assad Ali, Professor of Arabic Literature at the University of Damascus:

> God,
> I love you and whoever and whatever loves You.
> I've recognized that every creature loves You in a certain way,
> so, I thought of loving every creature, too,
> for each is your creation.[31]

In Assad Ali's poem, created things are not oblivious to the divine presence; through love, nature partakes in and reflects the Divine. In other poems, Ali follows the Qur'anic pattern of meditating on the spiritual significance of natural processes, evoking images of desert sands, rain, running water, and growth. In his imagery, he experiences identification with the desert, and he portrays nature as a process associated with the sacred—that is, as a process within which human beings experience connection to the Divine. Nature is a mirror, a sign of God, a medium of remembrance (*dhikr*). Ali's poetry suggests that remembrance of God, and concomitant recognition of the presence of the Divine in the ecological harmonies of nature, is the surest guarantee of peace between human beings and nonhuman creations. Faith is not a distraction from the world of time and place, but an all-encompassing awareness.[32] Nature can be preserved when love for the divine wisdom and beauty reflected in living things is awakened.

At best, recourse to fear in calls to protect the earth's environment will only prevent people from engaging in certain forms of behavior; it is unlikely to prompt truly creative and sustainable responses to ecological crises. A feeling of connectedness to nature that touches the very core of the human being, on the other hand, generates spontaneous loyalty and constructive actions. In this respect, it is worthwhile noting the complementarity between the global renewal of interest in ecology and the outlook encouraged by integral spirituality as represented, in this case, by Islam. Ecology has been defined as "the totality or pattern of relations between organisms and their environment";[33] Islam encourages appreciation of an ecology of the spirit. Contemplation of this ecology brings peace through the unveiling of the sacred, which could aptly be described as the "pattern that connects."[34]

The Maintenance of Harmony in Islamic Life and Spirituality

Rapid change has increased the tension between precept and practice in the Islamic world. The patterns and rhythms of life have changed; localized, traditional approaches to symbiosis have been greatly altered by modernization, technification, the monetization of economic life, and consumerism. Traditions of art and architecture, which reflected a natural aesthetics and a spirit of harmony, have suffered from neglect.

Failure to protect the natural environment does not represent a shortcoming in essential Islamic precepts. The Islamic outlook does not condone the exploitation of nature. Disregard for nature follows both from preoccupation with imported models of state, economy, and society and from an incongruity between long-established assumptions about the potential impact of human activities upon nature and the unprecedented power of modern technology. Traditional Islamic humanism, which was profoundly ecological in spirit, has been reinterpreted to support the human exercise of power over nature, without regard for ecological balance or the spiritual welfare of the human being.[35]

While ecology was rarely an issue debated in the same manner as the political and religious legitimacy of various regimes and movements, the classical Islamic tradition nonetheless provided a context for discussing such unconventional subjects as the rights of animals, as the Pure Brethren of Basra (*Ikhwān al-Safā*) discovered when writing their remarkable tenth-century tale, *The Case of the Animals versus Man before the King of the Jinn.*[36] In this story, a group of humans lands on a remote island inhabited by a great variety of animals. Acting on the premise that human beings are masters and animals slaves, the humans begin to exploit the animals. Unwilling to endure such treatment, the animals bring their dispute with the humans before the king of the jinn, whose folk also inhabit the island.

The assembled animals testify to their plight at the hands of humans; representatives of a great variety of creatures—including domestic animals, birds, aquatic animals, insects, and crawling creatures—unite to challenge human presumptions of superiority and entitlement. The humans, among whom are representatives of a great diversity of cultures and races, largely fail to defend their claimed rights to lord it over animals, enduring sustained and harsh criticisms, not only for inhumane and presumptuous conduct toward animals, but also for the pervasive iniquities of human societies. Human beings manage to assert special privileges in relation to animals only by remembering the human capacity for sainthood and its heavenly rewards—about which the assembled men can say but little. The king of the jinn upholds the human right to control and benefit from animals, but affirms that God is the protector of the animals.

Surprising as it may be in its intellectual and historical context, this story reflects important aspects of the Islamic understanding of ecology and demonstrates that Muslims have in their possession the intellectual and spiritual resources necessary for reconciling human capabilities with ecological realities and ethical challenges. In particular, the position staked out by the Ikhwān illuminates the Islamic premise that, while nature satisfies human needs, it is not merely a "resource." The Qur'an points to the usefulness of nature to humans as a sign of the mercy and wisdom of God, but Islam is not strictly "utilitarian," because all created things have value independent of the values that humans ascribe to them. There is no utility in Islam without reference to divine purpose, which can never be fully comprehended by human beings. An attitude of respect and an appreciation of natural harmonies mediate the relationship of humans to the rest of creation.

Variations in Islamic Thought and Practice: Four Paradigms

The Power Political Paradigm of Islam

While Islamic precepts provide Muslims with a repertoire that is highly responsive to ecological concerns, the translation of precept into practice has become increasingly difficult as human capabilities to disturb the balance of nature have expanded. Moreover, the Islamic repertoire for peace and ecology has been translated in different ways by people of different social groups and dispositions in their attempts to meet various challenges facing Islamic communities. Different constituencies of Muslims have interpreted their faith in response to different issues, foregrounding particular values while downplaying or de-emphasizing others. As a result, commitments to peace and ecology have often suffered.

In what we shall call the "power political" paradigm of peace, *tawḥīd* has been understood as the transcendence and remoteness of the Absolute. In this approach to peace, the unity of existence is downplayed; the reflection of divine attributes in human beings and nature is understood to be ephemeral, insignificant, and untrustworthy. Intimations of the Divine in nature are as likely to be mirages as reflections and are considered a source of temptation and misdirection. Natural events are perceived atomistically; interconnectedness and interdependence are downplayed. Love and nearness in the relationship between creation and the Divine are largely ignored. The vulnerability of human nature to degradation is accentuated. Human cravings exceed the satisfiers for them, resulting in scarcity, competition, and armed conflict.

In this paradigm, peace is understood as the absence of war and *fitna* (subversion or civil discord). In domestic politics, the "just ruler" is the focal point of the ideal social order, but believers are often encouraged to accept the stability provided by unjust rule. Respect for specific human authority figures is cultivated; the extravagance of elites is tolerated as an inevitability. The learned classes of Muslims are enlisted to support the political or military leadership, because security is to be preferred to anarchy and vulnerability. Religion legitimizes political power, military expenditures, and decisions justified more by "necessity" and public interest than by religious norms, in effect providing Islamic garb for a largely secular state. Religion does duty for nationalism; divine will is invoked while human responsibility is reduced to acting in defense of the status quo.

In international politics, peace is pursued through the threat and use of coercion. In this domain, underlying assumptions are remarkably similar to the assumptions underlying the dominant Western paradigm of "political realism," which stipulates that a people who wish for peace should prepare for war. Like Western exponents of power politics, Muslims who perceive the world through a power political lens emphasize scarcity, a need for controlling authority, preeminence of the state, inoperability or absence of universal values, and the necessity of accentuating national interests, national security, and indices of power based on military strength and economic productivity. This outlook has evolved historically from the triumphalism of the early Islamic empires—which adapted Byzantine and Sassanian attitudes, organizational techniques, and literary genres of statecraft—and from the practices of the sultanates which emerged after the eclipse of the caliphate. The power political paradigm persists in modern times in association with a variety of regimes.

The constellation of ideas and assumptions making up this paradigm makes it susceptible to cooptation by a "reason of state" mentality, in which a great deal can be sacrificed for the security of the political order—including harmony with nature, human rights, and rules protecting innocents in the limited wars accepted by Muslim jurists. Nature becomes a means for the pursuit of political, military, and economic power. Traditional safeguards against the abuse of nature and human beings are overrun in the competitive pursuit of technological progress and security. Juristic rules for the conduct of statecraft (*siyār*) are largely ignored in practice, even as Muslim rulers selectively appropriate historical precedents, symbols, and ideological formulas.

The Reformist Paradigm: Islāḥ

While the preservation of order, the maintenance of stability, and the exercise of coercive power have been important ways in which peace has been pursued by Muslim states, many Muslims have also pursued peace through reform, or *islāḥ*. As a framework for the pursuit of peace, *islāḥ* implies a twofold process of returning to essential precepts and reforming belief systems and social practices in order to bring them into accord with the spirit of Islam.

In centuries past, *islāḥ* was a means of differentiating salutary traditions from non-Islamic accretions in Islamic thought and practice; more recently, *islāḥ* has been a means of selective innovation. Hence, *islāḥ* has implied not only the reevaluation of received ideas, opinions, and practices, but also the evaluation, adaptation, and application of new influences in light of enduring values and existing circumstances.

Whereas the weight of the power political approach to peace is centered in the judgment of a political elite and supported by habits of accommodation among the learned classes, the fulcrum of *islāḥ* is the *ijtihād* (exertion, interpretation) of conscientious proponents of social reform. Protagonists of *islāḥ* pursue peace by advancing Islamic values. They believe that peace should be sought through intentional preparation for peace, not war. In this respect they resemble Western advocates of a just world order, although they underscore the importance of explicitly religious sources of inspiration and are aware of limitations inherent in over-reliance on structures and institutions. In addition to rationality, planning, and law, internal reform of the human person is also required for peace.

Islāḥ has tended toward cosmopolitanism in outlook. At its best, Islamic reform blends reason, philosophical reflection, and sensitivity to history with a vital faith. Reform must provide continuity based on religious precepts; creativity is encouraged, but community and cultural tradition are respected and valued. Careful evaluation is required to differentiate what is good from other civilizations from that which runs contrary to the spirit of Islam.

As an approach to peace, Islamic reform favors tolerance, peaceful reconciliation of cultural conflicts, broader and more effective application of principles and policies, and full utilization of the faculties endowed to human beings by their creator. Contemporary advocates of the *islāḥ* position are frequently inclined to value ecumenism, democratization, social justice, solidarity, human rights, gender equity, activism, and responses to material conditions and systemic pressures which are both principled and practical. Stress is placed upon education and constructive social thought; reform is to be accomplished within the present historical context on the basis of the essential principles of faith.

Islāḥ-based movements have sought to differentiate that which is eternal in Islam from practices which represent the efforts of human beings to embody Islamic principles within particular cultural, social, and historical contexts.[37] While advocates of *islāḥ* have sometimes been too uncritical of imported development and modernization models which are harmful both to important Islamic values and to the environment, the wisest reformers have been able to bring new vitality, flexibility, and a global outlook to enduring as well as emergent problems facing Muslim communities. Double standards and inconsistencies of powerful states on such issues as nuclear proliferation and human rights are rejected as a basis for valid decision-making among Muslims.

The Renewalist Paradigm: Tajdīd

Over-reliance on both the power political approach to peace and the superficial application of reformist principles has provided considerable impetus to another approach defined by *tajdīd*, or renewalism. Whereas the power political approach focuses on the priorities of the holder of political and military power, and the *islāḥ* approach emphasizes the importance of cosmopolitan reformers and educators, the renewalist approach is characterized by an outlook that is at once communitarian and popularizing. The advocate of *tajdīd* seeks to renew or revive community and social justice; peace is to be attained through a renewal of religious identity, a revival of religious rituals or spiritual practices, and the formation of broad-based social movements.

From a renewalist perspective, the decline and corruption of Islamic societies is attributed to a slackening of adherence to Islamic precepts—not only with regard to prayer, *ilāhī* relationships (relationships within families), and communal responsibility, but also with regard to the entire social and cultural system. An integral dimension of Islamic revivalism, historical as well as modern, is the pursuit of peace through the restoration of justice and authentic values and the reestablishment of continuity with the formative moments of religious history.

Tajdīd in contemporary Islamic societies manifests a dissatisfaction with what the materialist, consumer-oriented society offers and an effort to defend a culture and way of life which has been dislocated and undervalued in the midst of Westernization and modernization. Islamic revivalism differs from what has been called Islamic "fundamentalism," however, in that the former seeks to renew the community (*umma*) from within, while the latter manifests more militant reaction to external threats. Historical movements of revival in Islam have expressed such themes as authentic religious identity, social cohesion and justice, nonviolent actualization of Islamic values, and mutual encouragement of Muslims in cooperative endeavors. Peace has been understood in terms of moral reintegration, purification, revitalization, and a process of deepening and internalizing motivation. Emphasis is placed on differentiation between essential practices and practices which represent historical accretions or external influences. There is an ambivalent, mixed attitude toward received traditions and a focus on grassroots efforts; while traditional attitudes toward the role of authority or leadership in human relationships are often preserved, established institutions are scrutinized by advocates of *tajdīd*.

While it is true that some revivalist movements are more concerned with cultural identity and defensive reaction to Western assertiveness than with creative solutions to changing circumstances, many social movements manifest creative imagination, patience, and tolerance of diversity. Important social movements of renewal and reform, such as Abdul Ghaffar Khan's Khudai Kitmagar movement[38] and Mahmoud Taha's Sudanese movement,[39] have creatively upheld the idea that peace and justice must be sought through peaceful means, and that peace requires the activation of the power of human will in service to the Divine. While ecology has not been a leading issue of such renewalist movements, potential for action supportive of environmental stability is inherent in the renewalists' sensitivity to grassroots realities and preference for countering anomie with Islamic principles. Traditional Sufi approaches to revival (*ihyā*) offer an essential complement to contemporary renewalist programs; God is understood to renew creation in each instant.

Mystical Islam: Taṣawwuf

While the power political understanding of peace underscores the integrity and defensibility of a state and the programs of reformists and renewalists accentuate the role of social and cultural institutions, *taṣawwuf*, or Islamic mysticism, foregrounds the need for harmony in the relationship of the individual to the Divine, which manifests in and through created things. Also known as Sufism, *taṣawwuf* approaches peace through the internal renewal, reform, and empowerment of the human being. Power political approaches to peace aim to preserve order and stability through coercive measures, reformist approaches underscore a process of reinterpretation and application, and renewalists complement reason with emotion and community. Sufis recognize the merits and limitations of all these approaches and faculties, while highlighting the importance of creative imagination and the need for divine unveiling, spiritual maturity, vision, truth, beauty, and love.

Taṣawwuf encourages believers to seek freedom through harmonizing themselves with the Divine. There is a definite humanistic chord in Sufism. Emphasis is placed on inner freedom, the spiritual elevation of the individual, and integration of religious ideals with everyday life. Spirituality is understood as the way to peace, through which the individual undertakes the challenge of applied spirituality, testing received doctrines and ideals in the light of experience. Islam is understood as an internal state as well as an institutionalized religion; seemingly contradictory principles and realities, such as divine will and human responsibility, are reconciled within each practitioner of faith.[40]

The Sufi orders (*ṭarīqa*s) of Islam have traditionally emphasized the internalization of the message of the Qur'an and the integration of precept, realization, and practice. Sufis have attempted to embody the Qur'anic injunction for Muslims to be a "Middle People" (2:143)—universalist in outlook and tolerant of the great diversity of humankind. From a Sufi perspective, cultural diversity is a manifestation of divine blessing that can be affirmed and not merely tolerated.

Sufis are careful not to project their own shortcomings and fears onto others, and they perceive that human behavior often reflects expectations. While they do not necessarily criticize efforts to deter antisocial or anti-ecological behavior through fear of worldly or divine punishment, they prefer to appeal to the creative capacity of human beings to do what is beautiful. Sufi teaching is in accord with the conception of *fiṭra*. From a Sufi perspective, works of evil derive from alienation from the Source; people do not become misguided and wicked because of their innermost nature, but rather because their inner nature has become veiled or even deadened by the vicissitudes and distractions of life. Yet every human being is in principle redeemable through the mercy of God, capable of reawakening to *fiṭra* through the trials of experience and an inward opening to the Divine.

Taṣawwuf underscores the need for harmony and equilibrium in all relationships. Sufi Islam is endowed with a strong ecological sensitivity, understanding spirituality in a way compatible with a definition offered by the Scottish Council of Churches: "Spirituality is an attempt to grow in sensitivity to self, to others, to non-human creations and to God who is within and beyond this totality."[41] Spiritual growth requires a sensitivity to the environment. As the individual purifies herself or himself, nature becomes more transparent to the Divine. Sufis therefore look for the signs of God in humans and in nature, and contemplate the divine beauty in creation. *Ḥadīth*s on kindness to animals are not lost on them; some individuals engaged in *taṣawwuf* have advocated harmlessness as a principle of faith and engaged in vegetarianism. The Sufis have also been particularly resistant to all closed systems of thought—including modern ideologies and "-isms" and dogmatic formulations of traditional creeds—and have therefore been hesitant to sacrifice peace and ecological balance for meretricious ends.[42] Feeling peaceful (full of peace) requires being empty of other things so that peace has a place to enter and be. This means, first and foremost, removing the idols, the delusive belief systems, which separate a person from the Divine. Inner purification becomes joined to the consecration of life, and to the perception that God's unity embraces all of creation.

Like contemporary renewalism, *taṣawwuf* is concerned with identity, but on the most fundamental, spiritual level more than on the collective level. The cultural community is not an end in itself, but rather a context within which human realization takes place. According to the Sufi teaching, knowledge of one's own authentic individuality is the precondition for recognition of the authentic individuality of other beings. Knowledge of authentic identity comes about through surrendering the illusion of separation for the truth of Unity, resulting in connectedness and spontaneous loyalty.[43]

Peace, Ecology, and the Pursuit of Unity

Diagnosing the Contemporary Ecological Challenge

The four approaches to peace and ecology outlined above—power politics, Islamic reform, renewalism, and Sufism—do not exhaust the diversity within Islam. They do, however, characterize broad patterns of historical interpretation and practice which remain vital to this day. While power politics is dominant and the less harmonious offshoots of renewalist movements provide material for the unflattering image of Islam presented by the global news media, ongoing traditions of reform, renewal, and mysticism offer means of access to the breadth and depth of the Islamic heritage.

Unfortunately, traditional safeguards for the environment are now honored more in the breach than in the observance, and the means of exploiting the natural environment have been augmented in ways that the Ikhwān al-Safā could never have conceived. The driving force behind contemporary ecological predicaments, though, is a deficient conception of development.

Global processes of change have blurred the distinctions between modernization and development. The developmental process is the way in which society and its members seek to reach their potential within the context of their environment. Development is a process with a goal, even if this goal is perceived as an ever-receding one. True, there is always a utopia by which this process is measured, one that is extracted from the experience of people and generalized into a vision of the desired society and its relationship with nature. However, since experience is constantly enlarged, it is natural that the utopian ideal changes. How we manage the tension between theory and practice, between reflection and experience—our praxeological style—determines how well we keep the dream alive. If we fail, the dream becomes a nightmare.

Modernization is the adoption of modern technologies for the uses of society. It attempts to make society more rational, efficient, and predictable, especially through the use of comprehensive planning, rational administration, and scientific evolution. Modernization also carries the connotation of a more productive society, at least in economic terms. Like development, modernization is always at least a partially conscious effort on the part of individuals who have a vision of what modern society should look like. In the Islamic world, however, important societal values are excluded from emerging patterns of development.

Modernization is not a substitute for development but, in much of the Islamic world, development is simply identified with modernization imposed from above without construction of a popular base of support. Ecology, social justice, and political participation in the Islamic world are sacrificed for modernization. The opiate of consumerism preoccupies the upper strata of society.

The vitality of the vision of development can be derived only from cultural realities of Muslim societies. It cannot grow from either

Western liberalism or from some variety of socialism. Some Muslims will no doubt draw considerable inspiration from the Earth Charter, but they will need to relate this to their precepts, to the historical development of Islamic cultures, and to their own felt needs. Regardless of time and place, individuals and cultures must sweat out their own development to ensure the greater expansion of their identity and dignity.

There is a tremendous amount of thinking to be done about development and Islam, precisely because Muslims are forced by today's conditions to make the connection between two worlds. The Islamic economic doctrine included in the *sharī'a* is compromised by traditionalist-capitalist and secularist-socialist states alike. Present-day Islamic countries do not practice Islamic precepts patterned after the *sharī'a*. The socialists and secularists deny that religious law has strategic utility for modern materialism. The capitalists and traditionalists have bent *sharī'a* values out of their original shape. This perceived irrelevance of Islamic precepts to present conditions, whether implicit or explicit, has not been accompanied by indigenous intellectual development.

Prescriptions

Islamic teachings suggest that peace with nature begins with the harmonization of the human being. Nature offers a warning—a reminder—that modernization and technification are no substitutes for the sustainable and balanced development of human societies and personalities. Reformed conceptions of development could be premised on sufficiency, moderation, and spiritual values rather than on scarcity and consumerism. Islam does not demand the sacrifice of the material needs of humanity for higher, transcendent aims, nor does it sanctify the worship of the means of earthly subsistence. Islam does not oppose the spiritual to the material, but rather underscores the spiritual as the context of the material.

The ecological impasse demands a response through love and identification, not fear; the most excellent "use" of nature is for spiritual development and the consecration of life, through contemplation of the divine presence. Islam upholds a sense of proportion and discernment and issues a call to imbue even the most mundane of human activities with a holistic, spiritual sensibility. Worshiping the idol of linear, technological process demands the sacrifice of natural harmony and the atrophy of the spirit; appreciation for the divine blessing in creation generates spontaneous loyalty to the integrity of the natural order and puts human innovations in a context of respect and symbiosis.

Islam, development, and ecology can be reconciled by freeing development from the linear, rationalistic idea of progress canonized by the Western mind. What is needed is an Islamic alternative that is neither a superficial compromise nor a schizophrenic reaction. What is needed is a response based on Islamic values that reflects the historical development of Islam and responds to the challenges of contemporary life. Islam can make important contributions to an integrated world order—one that affirms the unique value of all cultural traditions. In particular, Islam prescribes a strong sense of community and solidarity of people; it postulates a collaborative concept of freedom; and it demystifies the Western myth of triumphant material progress.

Much good could come through the rearticulation of traditional *sharī'a* teachings on the preservation of nature and a revitalization of education through experiential learning. Children must not only be taught the precepts of Islam as they apply to ecology; they must also be encouraged to appreciate their connection to nature as they interact with it on a daily basis. Education must not only inform and prescribe, but also elicit the enthusiasm and commitment of the young.

Reconciliation between Islam and democracy will also be necessary. There is a great and pressing need for a revitalization of participation in public life and decision making in Islamic countries. Without democracy, the innovative thinking of reformists will be muffled or suppressed, and the energy of renewalism will be forced into narrower channels marked by extremism and violence. The exclusion of the people of the Muslim world from active participation in political life undermines global stability and stymies the cooperation within and between societies that will be necessary for a return to ecological balance.

Islam and democracy are not incompatible. The practice of democracy is always less tidy than its definition, but its practice is more dynamic than its formal description and prescription. There are democratic precepts in Islam, just as there are in other religions. There are also Islamic traditions which, like traditions in other religions, result in transgressions against democratic ideals. The claim of incompatibility between Islam and democracy equates Western (liberal) institutional forms of democracy with the substance of democracy. The substance of democracy is a human society that has a sense of common goals, a sense of community, wide participation in making decisions, and protective safeguards for dissenters. The form of democracy, on the other hand, is cast in the mold of the culture of a people.

There is nothing in Islam that precludes common goals, community participation, and protective safeguards. It is true that Western liberal forms of democracy with their provisions for political parties, interest groups, and an electoral system are alien to Islamic tradition. But democracy is not built upon institutions; it is built upon participation. The absence of democracy in Islamic countries is more the result of lack of preparation for it and less because of lack of religious and cultural foundations. Democratic traditions in Islam, however, have been more commonly abused than used.

Presently, the door is open for a new thinking and reconceptualization regarding democracy. Muslims should factor into this new thinking of democracy consideration of the roles of the community, the individual, the state, and religion, so that they can develop their own viable model for cooperative, participatory politics.

Steps could be taken to formulate and encourage Islamic approaches to micro-lending as a means of broad-based, ecologically sustainable, and culture-enhancing development. In many countries, small sums of money have enabled the poor to start small businesses and make agricultural improvements. This development strategy has the added advantage of minimizing opportunities for graft and corruption and keeping the bureaucracy of implementation small. Muslims in resource-rich but population-poor countries could also begin to plan for the future by making use of oil wealth to promote the development of renewable sources of energy. Gulf states, for example, could take the lead in the development of the solar technology that will be needed for a global transition from fossil fuels to non-greenhouse energy sources.

Lastly and most fundamentally, there is a need to revive the Islamic understanding of the spiritual significance of nature. *Tawḥīd* may be approached as an ecology of the spirit that reconciles the apparent multiplicity of created things within the Unity of Existence. This reconciliation is what the "Greatest Shaykh" (*shaykh al-akbar*, the equivalent of the Latin doctor maximus) Ibn al-'Arabi referred to as the "Breath of the Merciful," *nafs al-raḥmān*. Ibn al-'Arabi depicted the manifestation of created multiplicity and its reabsorption into Primordial Singularity to be the Divine Being's drawing a breath. Viewed from the perspective of the microcosm, God comes to self-realization in us.

Islamic teaching affirms that a person must cultivate in the self the character traits of God (*takhālluq bi-akhlāq Allāh*). In the daily life of the veritable practitioners of Islam, there is a practical demonstration of how to cherish social, ethical, and ecological values leading men and women to the good life. Islam offers the stimulus and strength for performing deeds which are distinctively human in the deepest sense, to bring the human being nearer to God and to have respect for the sanctity of human and ecological relationships, in which must be mirrored a glimmer of divine attributes. The impassioned mind and the informed heart can together call upon the grace to move the planet, awakening humanity to the ecology of the spirit and embrace of universal peace.

Notes

1. "He is the First and the Last, the Evident and the Hidden" (Qur'an 57:3).

2. "In most of their secret talks there is no good: but if one exhorts to a deed of charity or goodness or conciliation between people (secrecy is permissible): To him who does this, seeking the good pleasure of Allah, We shall soon give a reward of the highest (value)" (Qur'an 4:114).

3. "To every people (was sent) a Messenger: when their Messenger comes (before them), the matter will be judged between them with justice, and they will not be wronged" (Qur'an 10:47).

4. "Say ye: 'We believe in Allah, and the revelation given to us, and to Abraham, Isma'il, Isaac, Jacob, and the Tribes, and that given to Moses and Jesus, and that given to (all) Prophets from their Lord: We make no difference between one and another of them: And we submit to Allah" (Qur'an 2:136).

5. "To each among you have We prescribed a Law and an Open Way. If Allah had so willed, He would have made you a single People, but (His Plan is) to test you in what He hath given you: so strive as in a race in all virtues. The goal of you all is to Allah; It is He that will show you the truth of the matters in which ye dispute" (Qur'an 5:48).

6. "There is no special merit of an Arab over a non-Arab, nor a non-Arab over an Arab, nor a white man over a black man, nor a black man over a white, except by righteousness and piety." Cited in Muhammad Abu Laila, "Islam and Peace," *Islamic Quarterly* 35, no. 1 (1991): 63.

7. "Nay, whoever submits His whole self to Allah and is a doer of good—he will get his reward with his Lord; On such shall be no fear, nor shall they grieve" (Qur'an 2:112).

8. Sachiko Murata and William C. Chittick discuss the levels of meaning associated with the words M(m)uslim and I(i)slam in their accessible work, *The Vision of Islam* (New York: Paragon House, 1994).

9. Seyyed Hossein Nasr, "What Is Peace? The Islamic Perspective" (speech delivered 6 February 1998 at the conference "Islam and Peace," the American University).

10. "Allah is He, than Whom there is no other god; the Sovereign, the Holy One, the Source of Peace (and Perfection), the Guardian of Faith, the Preserver of Safety, the Exalted in Might, the Irresistible, the justly Proud. Glory to Allah! (High is He) above the partners they attribute to Him. He is Allah, the Creator, the Originator, the Fashioner. To Him belong the Most Beautiful Names: Whatever is in the heavens and on earth, doth declare His Praises and Glory: And He is Exalted in Might, the Wise" (Qur'an 59:23–24).

11. "Gardens of Eternity, those which (Allah) Most Gracious has promised to His servants in the Unseen: for His promise Must (necessarily) come to pass. They will not there hear any vain discourse, but only salutations of Peace: and they will have therein their sustenance, morning and evening. Such is the Garden which We give as an inheritance to those of Our Servants who guard against evil" (Qur'an 19:61–63). See also 10:9–10, 14:23, and 36:58.

12. "But Allah doth call to the Home of Peace: He doth guide whom He pleaseth to a Way that is straight" (10:25).

13. "There hath come to you from Allah a (new) light and a perspicuous book—Wherewith Allah guideth all who seek His good pleasure to ways of peace and safety, and leadeth them out of darkness, by His Will, unto the light, guideth them to a Path that is Straight" (Qur'an 5:15–16).

14. For an introduction to *iḥsān*, see Murata and Chittick, *The Vision of Islam.*

15. "Say: 'If ye do love Allah, follow me: Allah will love you and forgive you your sins: for Allah is Oft-Forgiving, Most Merciful' " (Qur'an 3:31).

16. "For the pious Muslim, islam shows itself everywhere in the universe—in the blood circulation, the movement of the stars in their orbits, in the growth of plants—everything is bound by islam. . . ." Annemarie Schimmel, *Deciphering the Signs of God: A Phenomenological Approach to Islam* (Albany: State University of New York Press, 1994), 255.

17. "It may be that Allah will establish friendship between you and those whom ye (now) hold as enemies. For Allah has power (over all things); and Allah is Oft-forgiving, Most Merciful" (Qur'an 60:7).

18. Ali A. Mazrui, "Islamic and Western Values," *Foreign Affairs* 76, no. 5 (1997): 118–32.

19. George E. Irani and Nathan C. Funk, "Rituals of Reconciliation: Arab-Islamic Perspectives," *Arab Studies Quarterly* 20, no. 20 (fall 1998): 53–73.

20. Murata and Chittick, *The Vision of Islam*, 135.

21. The tendency to elevate reason and denigrate passion was particularly characteristic of Greek thought. In contrast, the Qur'an emphasizes spiritual purification. Abraham, the one whom God "rendered pure in this world" (Qur'an 2:130), prayed for his descendants: " 'Our Lord! send amongst them a Messenger of their own, who shall rehearse Thy Signs to them and instruct them in Scripture and Wisdom, and purify them: For Thou art the Exalted in Might, the Wise' " (Qur'an 2:129).

22. Evil has no essential existence in Islam; it is distance from the Source, a lack of essence which brings destructiveness and loss.

23. Karim Douglas Crow, "Islamic Ethics and Values: Relevance for Conflict Resolution," unpublished manuscript.

24. The greatest human privilege is the capability to grasp the unity of existence. The human capability for knowledge of the most profound variety is compatible with the idea of a *tawḥīdī* episteme, as articulated by Dr. Mona Abul-Fadl. Abul-Fadl suggests that the greatest gift Islam can offer to the world is a truly integral perspective which renders the truths of direct experience (including mysticism and theosophy), philosophy, and science complementary rather than contradictory. See Mona Abul-Fadl, "Islamization as a Force of Global Cultural Renewal or: The Relevance of the Tawhidi Episteme to Modernity," *American Journal of Islamic Social Sciences* 5, no. 2 (1988): 163–79.

25. There is a symbiotic relationship between humans and their natural environment; the blessings of existence are a sign of God's grace, for "His are all things in the heavens and on earth" (Qur'an 2:255).

26. Seyyed Hossein Nasr has suggested that the fear which angels express in the Qur'an—that the human will become "corrupter of the earth" (*al-mufsid fi' l-arḍ*)—applies not only to failure to uphold the divine law in one's personal life and in social relations, but also in relation to nature. The idea of "corrupting the earth" possesses a

natural and cosmic dimension and can be easily applied to the corruption of the earth from the point of view of the destruction of the environment today"; Nasr, *Religion and the Order of Nature*, 1994 Cadbury Lectures at the University of Birmingham (New York: Oxford University Press, 1996), 290–91 n. 13.

27. Christopher D. Stone, *Should Trees Have Standing? Toward Legal Rights for Natural Objects* (Los Altos, Calif.: William Kaufman, Inc., 1973).

28. Muslim al-Ṣaḥīh, *Īmān* (Cairo: Maṭba'a Muḥammad 'Alī Ṣabīḥ, 1334/1915–16), 147.

29. William C. Chittick, "God Surrounds All Things," *The World and I* 1, no. 6 (1986): 671–78.

30. The Qur'an contrasts justice (*'adl*) with wrongdoing (*zulm*), "usually defined as putting a thing in the wrong place. . . . [P]eople can and do wrong themselves every time they put something in the wrong place. They distort their own natures, and they lead themselves astray." Murata and Chittick, *The Vision of Islam*, 113.

31. Assad Ali, *Happiness Without Death* (Putney, Vt.: Threshold Books, 1991), 70.

32. "So delicious is the juice of faithfulness to You throughout the ages, that it grants physical soundness and intellectual health; it restores the environment by conscious living; it opens the soul with truth." Ali, *Happiness Without Death*, 37–38.

33. *Merriam-Webster's Collegiate Dictionary*, 10th ed., s.v. "ecology."

34. Gregory Bateson and Mary Catherine Bateson, *Angels Fear: Towards an Epistemology of the Sacred* (New York: Macmillan, 1987).

35. On this subject, we agree with K. L. Afrasiabi's contention that modern interpretations of *khilāfa* have negative ecological implications; "Toward an Islamic Ecotheology," *Hamdard Islamicus* 18 (1995): 33–49; reprinted in this volume. We differ with Afrasiabi, however, in that we do not attribute these interpretations to "Islamic humanism," and would like to suggest that traditional Sufi understandings of *khilāfa* represent a profound resource for the pursuit of ecological values. It is not "Islamic humanism," per se, that is implicated in contemporary ecological crises, but rather the secularization of Islamic humanism in accord with dominant models of development and modernization. Traditional Islamic humanism underscores recognition of the divine presence in all creation and in the human heart, which becomes the seat of knowledge of the unity of existence, *waḥdat al-wujūd*.

36. Ikhwān al-Safā, *The Case of the Animals versus Man before the King of the Jinn: A Tenth-Century Ecological Fable of the Pure Brethren of Basra*, trans. Lenn Evan Goodman (Boston: Twayne, 1978).

37. See, for example, the scholarly work of Fazlur Rahman.

38. Abdul Ghaffar Khan's leadership among the Muslim Pathans of the Northwest Frontier province of British India played a critical role in bringing about the end of British colonial rule in South Asia. Firmly committed to Islamic precepts and peaceful change, Khan organized a nonviolent army of Khudai Khidmatgars, or "Servants of God," who worked both to resist imperialism and promote general social uplift. For his life story, see Eknath Easwaran, *A Man to Match His Mountains: Badshah Khan, Nonviolent Soldier of Islam* (Petaluma, Calif.: Nilgiri Press, 1984).

39. Discussion of Mahmoud Taha's Islamic discourse has, unfortunately, become quite politicized, shaped more by the dramatic title of his manifesto, *The Second Message of Islam* (trans. Abdullahi Ahmed An-Na'im [Syracuse University Press:

Syracuse University Press, 1987]), than by the general tendency of his thought and practice, which underscored the need to renew attention to the most universal, inclusive, and egalitarian dimensions of the Islamic message, particularly as reflected in the early, Meccan *sūra*s of the Qur'an, which address all mankind.

40. The practice of Sufism is inspired by the faith that God guides unto Himself those who turn to Him—"Those who believe, and whose hearts find satisfaction in the remembrance of Allah: for without doubt in the remembrance of Allah do hearts find satisfaction" (Qur'an 13:28). Peace in the world is a reflection of peace in the inner worlds of human beings, and is founded on spiritual principles.

41. Cited in Abdul Aziz Said, Charles O. Lerche, Jr., and Charles O. Lerche, III, *Concepts of International Politics in Global Perspective,* 4th ed. (Englewood Cliffs, N.J.: Prentice Hall, 1995), 291.

42. The breadth of heart represented by the Sufi traditions of Islam is suggested by Ibn al-'Arabi's verses: "My heart has become capable of every form: it is a pasture for gazelles and a convent for Christian monks, And a temple for idols and the pilgrim's Ka'ba and the tables of the Tora and the book of the Koran. I follow the religion of Love: whatever way Love's camels take, that is my religion and my faith"; *The Tarjuman al-Ashwaq: A Collection of Mystical Odes by Muhyi'ddin Ibn al-'Arabi*, trans. Reynold A. Nicholson (Wheaton, Ill.: Theosophical Publishing House, 1978).

43. This sense of spontaneous loyalty is aptly expressed by the Persian poet Sa'di: "I am joyous with the cosmos, for the cosmos receives its joy from Him; I love the world, for the world belongs to Him." Cited in Charles Le Gai Eaton, "Islam and the Environment," *Islamica: The Journal of the London School of Economics and Political Science* 1, no. 2 (1993): 18–21.

The Basis for a Discipline of Islamic Environmental Law

OTHMAN ABD-AR-RAHMAN LLEWELLYN

Introduction: Why a Discipline of Islamic Environmental Law?

Imagine the planet Earth as a ship, an ark of Noah sailing round the sun with its precious cargo, the species of life, all interlinked and united in destiny. The prophet Muhammad, upon him be peace and the blessing of God, used the parable of a ship to illustrate interdependence. The passengers in their various positions on deck and below required each other's services, as in the distribution of drinking water. In his impatience to obtain water, one of the passengers below deck began to chop a hole in the hull with an ax, claiming the right to use his position as he pleased. "Now, if they were to hold back his hand," said the Prophet, "both he and they would be saved. But if they were to leave him alone, both he and they would be doomed."[1] The passenger's attitude and behavior is that of modern humans, who have significantly diminished the capacity of the earth to support life. Environmental law is the means by which human hands may be restrained.

In recent decades, environmental crises of unprecedented magnitude have spurred the development of the new and growing discipline of environmental law. Although the profession of environmental law as such is only a few decades old, it is now firmly established, and a substantial body of literature has already been written.

Like all the countries of the earth, the Islamic lands are afflicted by intensifying environmental problems: desertification, extinction of species and varieties, destruction of the forests, contamination of the water, soil, and air, depletion of atmospheric ozone, climate change, and the degradation of farmlands, rangelands, and fisheries. Yet even though Islamic law is one of the most widespread legal and ethical systems on earth, adhered to by nearly a fifth of humankind, in modern times Muslim jurists have lagged far behind in contributing solutions.

Virtually all environmental legislation in Muslim countries is borrowed from the industrialized West, in spite of the many principles, policies, and precedents of Islamic law governing the protection and conservation of the environment and the use of natural resources. Much of this legislation remains inadequate and unenforced. One reason is that many people in the Muslim world have little sympathy with laws that are derived from alien beliefs and values and have no legitimacy in their eyes. A number of *sharīʻa* practices do continue to govern or influence the ways in which people use their natural resources, particularly in rural areas. In most Muslim countries, however, these practices do not receive official recognition, and even where Islamic legislation is constitutionally recognized, it is seldom applied effectively or creatively. The exceedingly rich contributions that Islamic law and ethics have to offer remain largely unarticulated and unrealized.

Although environmental law is not yet recognized as an independent discipline within Islamic law, ample bases do exist for its development. Much as the discipline of Islamic economics has been formulated and developed in recent decades, that of environmental law can be derived from the objectives, principles, precepts, and instruments of Islamic jurisprudence, as well as the myriad substantive rulings of the *sharīʻa* that pertain to the environment. The purpose of this paper is to consider some of the essential elements and issues that should be addressed in the course of formulating the discipline of Islamic environmental law, including issues which pertain to environmental policy and planning in Islamic society, and practicalities involved in establishment of the discipline.

Legal and Ethical Philosophy

Law and Ethics: Their Fundamental Unity in Islam

Islam, it is often said, is in its essence a religion of law. In the context of Western civilization, however, the very term "Islamic law" may be misleading. At worst, the idea of religious law may conjure an image of unreasonable restrictions and harsh punishments. At best, law in the West is considered rather dry and somewhat distasteful, even if it is essential for the functioning of civilized society and the defense of individual freedoms. It is viewed almost as a necessary evil. After all, why does a person seek a lawyer? In order to press a lawsuit, perhaps, or to defend oneself against one; to find out how to pay the lowest possible amount in taxes; or to secure the most advantageous terms in a business contract, a divorce, or the like. How far from the spiritual and ethical values of religion! Despite the history of canon law in the West, the idea of religious law seems almost self-contradictory.

In the context of Islamic civilization, however, the Law or *sharīʻa*, is perceived altogether differently. The *sharīʻa* is, literally, the Way, the path to water, the source of life. *Fiqh*, the science of law, means understanding; understanding how to do the will of the Merciful, Compassionate Lord of all beings; to live life—individually and collectively—in the most moral and ethical way. Indeed, the science of ethics and that of law are essentially one and the same. The most common reason that one seeks out a mufti, or expert in Islamic law, is to ask what is the most ethical, moral course of action in a given situation, the act most pleasing to the Lord of all beings, and leading most surely to eternal spiritual bliss.

The *sharīʻa* embraces in its scope every human act, including religious devotions and purely ethical issues, as well as the various fields of law known to the modern world, such as constitutional and international law, family law, penal law, law of contracts, property law, and indeed, environmental law. Each act is examined to determine how much good and harm it may lead to, not only in the material realm of the present world, but also in the spiritual realm of the hereafter.

Acts are evaluated according to a five-tiered scale; an act may be obligatory, recommended, permitted, reprehended, or prohibited. The law is thus not only prohibitive and injunctive, but also prescriptive, charting the ethical course of what "ought" to be, setting forth ideal standards of behavior which can only be enforced by individual and social conscience, in addition to the essential imperatives enforced by the jurisdiction of the courts. Even when the courts fail, or where Islamic courts do not exist, the *sharīʻa* remains the eternal norm incumbent on all believers.

Tawḥīd*: The Unity of God, and the Unity of His Creation*

Among the essential aspects of *tawḥīd*, the affirmation of God's oneness, is to recognize that God is the one and only Lord of every created being. Therefore every single creature must be treated with *taqwa*, or reverence toward its Creator, and, to serve the Lord of all being, one must do the greatest good one can to His entire creation.

Every obligatory prayer begins with the praise of God as *rabb al-'ālamīn*, which may be translated as "Lord of the worlds" or "Lord of all beings." The word *rabb* denotes, on the one hand, the Lord and Master to be served and, on the other, the Sustainer who brings a being into existence, then nurtures and develops it until its destiny is fulfilled. In explaining the word *'ālamīn*, Qur'anic commentators have said that every species of God's creatures is a world unto itself, and likewise every generation.[2] God is thus the Lord of every species, every generation, and every individual created being.

God—be He exalted—has not made any of His creatures worthless: the very fact that He has created a thing gives it value. Moreover, He has created each thing *bi'l-ḥaqq*, in truth and for right. "Not for sport have we created the heavens and the earth and all that is between them. We have not created them but for truth" (Qur'an 44:38–39). "Those . . . who reflect on the creation of the heavens and the earth: Our Lord, Thou hast not made this in vain—Glory to Thee!" (Qur'an 3:191).

Every single form of life is the product of a special and divine creation and warrants special respect. Each species and variety is unique and irreplaceable. Moreover, each created being, however minute, is a miracle, a wondrous sign that points beyond itself to its Maker, His wisdom, and His mercy; each creature is a portent filled with meaning and lessons to be learned. Furthermore, each creature glorifies its Creator, even if we do not understand its glorification. "The seven heavens and the earth and all the beings therein proclaim His glory: There is not a thing but celebrates His praise, but you understand not how they declare His glory" (Qur'an 17:44).

Beyond its intrinsic value, each thing has practical or instrumental value as a component of the ecosystems that support life on earth. An observation of 'Izz al-Din ibn 'Abd al-Salam's regarding human society pertains equally to the creation as a whole: "Know that God has created His creatures and made them to depend upon each other, so that each group would support the welfare of the others."[3] Through its divinely ordained roles, each being contributes to the welfare of the whole. This leads to a cosmic symbiosis (*takaful*) by which God sustains all living things. The prophet Muhammad, upon him be blessings and peace, is reported to have declared, "Created beings are the dependents of God, and the creatures dearest unto God are they who do most good to His dependents."[4] The universal common good is a principle that pervades creation, and an important implication of God's unity, for one cannot truly serve the Lord of all beings except by working for the common good of all.[5]

Taqwa*: The Attitude of Reverence*

God is the Lord of every thing, and He will try us with regard to His creatures: so we are to revere Him in every thing. "Most noble of you in the sight of God is he who is most reverent" (Qur'an 49:13).

We must revere Him in our treatment of every man, every woman, every child. We must revere Him in our treatment of every beast, every bird, every insect, every plant. Each creature, though it be almost nothing in itself, is a creature of Him who is Tremendous beyond everything; a sign of Him who has created it; and a world that will never be repeated, and by its being glorifies its Maker.[6] Nothing is insignificant. None has been created in vain; all are created for right. We must therefore treat none wantonly, and take no life except for right.[7]

Raḥmat *and* Iḥsān*: Compassion and Beneficial Works*

The attitude of reverence must find its completion in compassion and beneficial works. Good works are the very purpose of life and death. "Blessed is He in Whose Hand is dominion—and He has power over every thing: He Who has created death and life to try you, which of you work the most good" (Qur'an 67:1–2).

The prophet Muhammad, upon him be peace and the blessing of God, said that God has prescribed goodness with regard to every thing, and that in goodness to every living creature is a reward.[8] He also said, "The compassionate are shown compassion by the All-Compassionate. Show compassion to those on earth, and He Who is in heaven will show compassion to you."[9]

Khilāfa*: Stewardship*

> He it is Who has made you stewards on the earth, and raised some of you by degrees above others, so that He might try you by means of what He has bestowed upon you. (Qur'an 6:165)

> Thus We have made you to succeed one another as stewards on the earth, that We might behold how you acquit yourselves. (Qur'an 10:14)

The Prophet, upon him be blessings and peace, declared, "The world is beautiful and verdant, and verily God, be He exalted, has made you His stewards in it, and He sees how you acquit yourselves."[10]

The position of each human being as a *khalīfa* on the earth has received considerable attention by Muslim writers during the past century. Much of the discussion has misrepresented the concept, however, by overemphasizing the privilege and honor implied by the term. Perhaps, under the influence of European Humanism, and in response to allegations that Islam gives too little value to the human being, Muslim writers have felt the need to prove that man has exalted status. As enthusiasm for "progress" and "development" swept the poorer countries of the world, some reformist thinkers even interpreted the concept of *khilāfa* as a mandate to exploit and develop the earth on behalf of God.[11]

But is *khilāfa* essentially a privilege? It is an honor, yes, for humans are created "in the best of forms," that is, with the greatest potential for good. But if we do not realize this potential, we are rejected as "lower than the low."[12] *Khilāfa* is not a privilege, but a trust, a responsibility, and a trial, for God has created death and life to try us, which of us work the most good. Not for himself does a *khalīfa* act, but for his Lord, and according to his Lord's purposes. On the Day of Judgment, this *khilāfa* will be a source of shame and torment to the one who does not fulfill it. To be a *khalīfa* is not to receive, it is to serve. A *khalīfa* is a shepherd and will be asked about his flock. Each human being is a shepherd over all the lives on Earth that he may touch for good or ill, and shall be asked regarding every atom's weight of good that he or she has caused, and every atom's weight of harm.[13]

Humankind has been given enormous ability to do both good and evil; with ability comes responsibility. As the prophet Muhammad, upon him be peace and the blessing of God, declared, with each day's dawning one rises to bargain with one's soul as a stake, and either ransoms it or ruins it.[14] Each day between rising in the dawn and settling into sleep, we build and destroy uncounted lives. Whatever we do, we will not leave this world unchanged. We must take heed, then, that we leave it for the better.[15]

Humankind bears a trust that the heavens and the earth and the mountains shrank from bearing. In managing the earth, we have proven ourselves thoroughly unjust and foolish.[16] We cannot fulfill this trust unless the horizons of our care extend through space and time to embrace all the species, individuals, and generations of God's creatures from today until the Day of Resurrection, in the world of the living and the world of the return. Then, and only then, will we be *khalīfa*s on the earth.[17]

Uṣūl al-Fiqh: Islamic Jurisprudence

At least as important to the discipline of environmental law as substantive legislation is the legal methodology or jurisprudence of Islam, *uṣūl al-fiqh*, literally the roots or sources of *fiqh*. Rulings found in the basic texts of Islamic law and in the books of *fiqh* pertain in many cases to particular technologies and practices that are no longer widely used, while new practices and technologies are emerging daily. Knowledge of *uṣūl al-fiqh* is indispensable to discover the objectives and principles embodied in particular rulings or precedents and to apply them to new practices and technologies.

Sources and Methods of Islamic Jurisprudence

Although grossly oversimplified, the following discussion of the sources and methods of Islamic jurisprudence may serve to summarize the basic elements of *uṣūl al-fiqh*. Each of the schools (*madhāhib*) of Islamic law represents a broad methodological approach, in which the various sources and methods are given different degrees of authority. Rules for applying these sources and methods also tend to differ both among the *madhāhib* and within them.

The basic sources—The two primary sources in all schools of Islamic law are the legal texts of the Qur'an and the Prophetic *sunna*, or example. The text of the Qur'an is universally agreed upon; its legal rulings pertaining to environmental law are relatively few and general, and there is little divergence in their interpretation. *Aḥādīth* constitute the main textual source of the *sunna* and are graded according to their degree of authenticity; *aḥādīth* of weaker authenticity give way to those which are stronger if contradicted by them, but provide valuable details and insights where they are complementary.

Sources for understanding the Prophetic *sunna* that are supplementary to the *aḥādīth* include the legal opinions (*fatāwā*) of the companions of the Prophet, upon whom be blessings and peace; reports of their deeds and sayings (*athār*); the established practice (*'amāl*) of Medina, the early Islamic capital where most of the Prophet's companions and their successors lived; and rulings on which there was universal or near universal consensus (*ijma'*) by the early generations. Of these sources, *ijma'* is authoritative in every school of Islamic law, while the others have varying degrees of authority in the different schools. Interpretation of these sources, as of the *aḥādīth*, requires knowledge of the context and significance of each case and the principles that pertain to it.

Methods of reasoning: ijtiḥād—A jurist's exertion of his reason to formulate the principles of the revealed law and apply them to new problems or new situations is known as *ijtiḥād.* On one hand, *ijtiḥād* is a source of Islamic law when one draws upon the opinions of previous jurists; on the other, it is the methodology of reasoning to make independent judgments. The primary method of *ijtiḥād* is deductive reasoning by juristic analogy (*qiyās*). Analogical rulings, however, may give way to considerations deriving from stronger or more fundamental values, which are given preference (*istiḥsān*) over them; where no suitable precedent is to be found, judgments may be made on the basis of public welfare (*al-masāliḥ al-mursāla*), those unrestricted benefits which are neither bound directly to texts of the Qur'an and *sunna*, nor can be deduced from them by analogical reasoning. Other methods of *ijtiḥād* include *sadd al-dharā'ī*, by which outwardly legitimate means may be prevented from being used as pretexts for illegitimate ends, and *al-'urf al-sāliḥ*, by which customary practices and definitions (*'āda* and *'urf*) may acquire legal force when they accord with the aims of the *sharī'a.*

These methods involve much inductive reasoning and are enormously important in clarifying the objectives (*maqāsid*) of the *sharī'a.* Drawing on the totality of Islamic texts rather than isolated texts, they provide the broad perspective to ensure that one does not miss seeing the forest for the trees. At the same time, because these methods are less precise than *qiyās*, they rely heavily upon sound judgment.

In our enthusiasm to bring about the welfare of society, and our certainty that we know what that welfare is, we are liable to perceive "benefits" that are not derived from the values of the *sharī'a*, or even contradict those values. Hence the need to exercise caution in wielding the "sword" of *al-masāliḥ al-mursāla.* Indeed, every tyrant in the Muslim world who enacts an unjust law is sure to seek a religious justification, and if he cannot find a text by which to justify himself, he will usually resort to *al-masāliḥ al-mursāla* or *sadd al-dharā'ī.*

*The Ultimate Objectives (*Maqāsid*) of Islamic Law*

Maqāsid al-sharī'a is a distinctive branch of knowledge within, or some might say above, *uṣūl al-fiqh*; the importance of the *maqāsid* is receiving ever greater attention by contemporary Muslim jurists.

Masālih al-khalq*: the universal common good*—The ultimate objective of the *sharī'a* is defined as the welfare of God's creatures (*masāliḥ al-khalq* or *masāliḥ al-'ibād*), encompassing both our immediate welfare in the present and our ultimate welfare in the hereafter. The ultimate purpose of the *sharī'a* is the universal common good, the welfare of the entire *creation* (*masāliḥ al-khalqī kaffātan*). This objective of the universal common good is a distinctive characteristic of Islamic law. It means, first, that both material and nonmaterial dimensions must be taken into account, and second, that the welfare of humans and of nonhuman sentient beings must be considered in the course of planning and administration. No species or generation may be excluded from consideration, for every atom's weight of good and every atom's weight of harm that has resulted from our actions will be weighed on the Day of Judgment.[18]

The five fundamentals: dīn, *life, posterity, reason, and property*—Muslim jurists have generally agreed that there are at least five essential prerequisites that must be safeguarded for human society to function and prosper. The first is *dīn*, or religion, the foundation of beliefs, moral values, and ethics upon which Islamic society is built. Life (*nafs*) is the second prerequisite; without safeguarding the lives of its members, no society can function. Third, a society's posterity (*nasl*) must be safeguarded through ensuring that its progeny are born and raised within secure family relationships. Fourth, reason (*'aql*) must be safeguarded to ensure rational behavior, both individually and collectively. Finally, rights to private property (*māl*) are necessary to enable individuals to secure their livelihoods. Among the many rulings pertaining to these fundamentals, the *hadd* penalties for apostasy, murder, adultery, use and sale of intoxicants, and theft are cited as examples of the means by which they are safeguarded.

What are the implications for environmental law? It is now well recognized that meeting the basic needs of society through development is a prerequisite for effective environmental conservation. Furthermore, these fundamentals clearly apply to the welfare both of present and future generations, explicitly in the case of posterity and implicitly with regard to religion, life, reason, and property.

It would be interesting to consider to what extent these fundamentals could be said to apply to species other than human beings. In the Qur'an, God declares that "There is no animal on the earth, nor any bird that wings its flight, but it is an *umma* (community, society) like yourselves" (Qur'an 6:38). The *sharī'a* safeguards the lives of individual animals from wanton destruction. The posterity of animals is protected by the ruling that captive animals should be allowed to breed in season and the positions of many *fuqahā'* against surgical sterilization. The sanity and psychological well-being of animals is regarded in the prohibition on imprisoning animals in unsuitably cramped conditions and the view of many *fuqahā'* that it is morally wrong and illegal to keep wild animals in captivity as pets, as well as in the prohibition on slaughtering a young animal within view of its parents, and the prohibition of holding fights between animals. While animals do not have rights to property, their rights to adequate maintenance are safeguarded.

Masāliḥ *and* mafāsid*: benefits and detriments*—In Islamic jurisprudence all acts are evaluated in terms of their consequences as social goods and benefits (*masāliḥ*) and social detriments and evils (*mafāsid*).

A major challenge of contemporary planning methodology is the search for reliable, comprehensive and efficient means to measure and weigh costs and benefits. Muslim jurists will likewise have to face this challenge. The objectives of Islamic law demand that total benefits or *masāliḥ* be maximized and that total costs, or *mafāsid*, be minimized. The concepts of *maṣāliḥ* and *mafāsid* are not identical to Western ideas of benefits and costs, although there is much common ground.

How does one measure total benefits and costs, material and nonmaterial, for humans and other creatures? Quantitative measures are far easier to compare and weigh than qualitative measures; if convertible to monetary values, they can also be entered into economic equations, such as national accounts. On the other hand, nonmaterial values are hard to quantify and to express in monetary terms; however, a more complete and accurate means of assessing effects on all creatures than the language of finance is yet to be discovered. Might the methods of Islamic jurisprudence hold promise in this regard?

Principles for Weighing Benefits and Detriments

Through the comparative study of similar rulings, jurists such as as-Subki, as-Suyuti, and Ibn Nujaym formulated general legislative principles (*qawā'id fiqhīya*), which serve as guidelines in solving particular legal problems.[19] Several of these legislative principles are central to *'ilm al-muwazanat*, the science of measuring benefits and detriments, and *'ilm al-awlawiyat*, the science of establishing priorities.

Muslim legislators, planners, and administrators should always aim at the universal common good of all created beings. This means that they must strive to harmonize and fulfill all interests. However, when it is impossible to satisfy all immediate interests, the universal common good requires prioritization by weighing the welfare of the greatest number, the importance and urgency of the various interests involved, the certainty or probability of benefit or injury, and the ability of those affected to secure their interests without assistance. The basic principle has been articulated thus:

> What is required is to safeguard all benefits and bring them to completion, and to eliminate all detriments or at least minimize them. And if they prove irreconcilable, it is to safeguard the greater good by the exclusion of the lesser, and to remove the greater harm by acceptance of the lesser. This is the mandate of the Law.[20]

Universal welfare and individual welfare—The interests of society as a whole take priority over the interests of individuals and particular groups when they cannot be reconciled. Among the principles of Islamic law are: "Priority is given to preserving the universal interest over particular interests," and "The general welfare takes priority over individual welfare." From this basis is derived the principle that "A private injury is accepted to avert a general injury to the public."[21] Sacrificing a private interest for the purpose of achieving and protecting the common interest of the public is surely accepted in one way or another by every society and legal system. The problem lies in working out the details and defining the limits so that individual rights are not obliterated in the name of the public interest.

A particular question that needs to be addressed is, at what point does the welfare of the majority become universal? To be sure, Islamic law does not countenance the tyranny of the majority over minorities. The interest of a 60 percent majority is certainly not universal. What about a 96 percent majority, or a 99.6 percent majority? How small must the number of individuals be for their interests to be regarded as private or particular, and how large must a majority be for its interests to be considered public or universal?

Greater needs and lesser needs—Social goods or interests are to be assessed according to their importance and urgency. There are necessities (*darūrīyyat*), which are absolutely indispensable to preserve religion, life, posterity, reason, and property; then needs (*ḥājjīyyat*), which if unfulfilled will lead to real hardship and distress; and finally supplementary benefits (*taḥsīnīyyat*), which involve the refinement and perfection of ethics and the enhancement of life. Priority is given to fundamental necessities if these conflict with less acute needs or supplementary benefits, and to the lesser needs if these conflict with supplementary benefits. Pertinent juristic principles are: "The lesser of two evils shall be chosen," "Severe damage shall be removed by means of lighter damage," and "If one of two opposing detriments is unavoidable, the more injurious is averted by the commission of the less injurious."

The interests of the powerful and the powerless—Consideration is to be given to the abilities of various groups to secure their welfare without the government's intervention. The governing authorities are obliged to protect the disadvantaged and less influential groups in accordance with the juristic principles that "The averting of harm from the poor takes priority over the averting of harm from the wealthy," and "The welfare of the poor takes priority over the welfare of the wealthy."[22]

Averting of detriments—The governing authorities have the obligation to take all necessary measures and actions to avoid, prevent, or minimize damage before it occurs in application of the principles "There shall be no damage and no infliction of damage," "Damage shall be removed," and when it cannot be removed entirely, "Damage shall be removed to the extent that is possible."

When benefits bring about unavoidable detriments of similar or greater magnitude, the juristic principle to be applied is, "The averting of harm takes precedence over the acquisition of benefits." On the basis of this principle, a factory may be closed down, mineral extraction permits may be denied, or housing may be prevented in environmentally sensitive locations.[23] Herein is a strong justification for adoption of the precautionary principle, namely, that activities which involve a risk of irreversible or serious harm should be prevented. On the other hand, this could in some cases be seen to conflict with another principle of Islamic law, namely, that priority is to be given to actual or known interests in case of conflict with conjectural or probable interests of similar importance; certain costs and benefits are to be given greater weight than uncertain costs and benefits. Both of these principles are valid; but could the latter be used to approve a project of which the economic benefits are known, while scientific information regarding harmful impacts to human health and ecosystems is incomplete or inconclusive? Among the questions that jurists should examine are: how are these two principles to be reconciled, and how should the precautionary principle be articulated in Islamic law?

Fiqh: Substantive Law

The substantive rulings of the *sharīʻa* which pertain to environmental law are found in the books of *fiqh*, mainly in the branch *of muʻāmalāt*, or transactions, under topics such as revival of vacant lands (*iḥyā al-mawāt*), protected areas (*ḥimā*) the use of water for irrigation and livestock (*shirb*), land grants (*iqtāʼ*), leases (*ijāra*), maintenance (*nafāqa*), laws of hunting and slaughter (*sayd* and *dhabāʼiḥ*), property (*milk* and *māl*), economic transactions (*buyuʼ*), reconciliation (*sulḥ*), endowments (*awqāf*); and alms and taxes (*zakāt*, *ṣadaqa*, *ʻushr*, and *kharāj*), which are discussed in both *muʻāmalāt* and ritual devotions (*ibādat*). Principles related to land use are also found in the branch of law dealing with public policy and administration (*siyāsa*), and in the branch covering crimes and penal law (*jināyat* and *uqūbat*), under usurpation (*ghasb*) and damages (*talāf*).[24]

Precepts from the Laws of Property

The precepts that pertain to the laws of property are of fundamental importance to environmental law. Ultimately, God alone is the owner of the heavens and the earth and all that they contain. "People do not in fact own things, for the only real owner of things is their Creator, be He glorified and exalted. Indeed, people do not own anything but their usufruct in the manner permitted by the revealed Law."[25] All properties and resources are held in trust by human beings, to be used only in accordance with their divinely ordained purposes. Therefore, while the right to *hold* private property is rigorously safeguarded, there are important restrictions on its *use.* Among the most important of these restrictions are those which pertain to the abuse of rights.[26]

The prophet Muhammad, upon him be peace and the blessing of God, declared that "There shall be no infliction of damage and no retaliation through damage."[27] Accordingly, Muslim jurists have ruled that a person invalidates his right if by exercising it he intends to cause damage to another; or if its exercise results in damage to another without corresponding benefit to its possessor; or if in spite of bringing benefit to himself, its exercise results in either excessive damage to other individuals or general damage to society.[28]

The ethic governing the use and development of the earth's resources was put thus by 'Ali ibn Abi Talib to a man who had developed and reclaimed abandoned land: "Partake of it gladly, so long as you are a benefactor, not a despoiler; a cultivator, not a destroyer."[29]

Prohibition of Waste and Corruption on the Earth

> Do not spread corruption in the earth after it has been so well ordered. And call unto Him with fear and hope: verily, God's mercy is ever near to the doers of good. (Qur'an 7:56)

> Do not waste: verily He loves not the wasteful! (Qur'an 6:141 and 7:31)

Corruption of the earth (*al-fasād fī' l-arḍ*), including destruction of the environment, is forbidden in the Qur'an, as are wasteful overconsumption and extravagance (*isrāf* and *tabdhīr*).[30] That the prohibition of extravagance applies in small matters as well as large, and in times of abundance as well as scarcity, was emphasized by the prophet Muhammad, upon him be peace and the blessing of God, when he forbade that a person waste water even in washing for prayer beside a flowing river.[31]

This clearly demands that all natural resources be used frugally and efficiently, and that pollution be prevented, reduced, and cleaned up. Muslim jurists will have to translate these general precepts into specific policies and regulations governing the modern technologies by which the earth's resources are extracted, processed, used, and returned to the environment as waste.

Jurists will need to translate the general prohibition of corruption of the earth into environmental impact regulations, with environmental standards designed to safeguard human health and the environment. Environmental impact assessment procedures can ensure that environmental, social, and economic considerations are taken into account before a development project, program, or policy is approved, and before investments are committed.

Effective environmental impact regulations require that the precautionary principle be adopted with regard to development activities, such as the discharge of substances that have not been proven to cause damage but are likely to be harmful. Effective monitoring procedures are necessary to detect infringements and also to evaluate regulations and adjust them in cases where they prove too lax to be effective or too stringent to be enforced. It is important that the regulations contain provisions to guarantee rapid restoration of damaged ecosystems and prompt treatment of injury to human health, at the polluter's expense—and that they provide for adequate compensation where restoration is not possible. Finally, public access to environmental impact assessments, environmental audits, and monitoring results is essential to ensure that these do not become a meaningless routine or, worse, a smokescreen.

Muslim jurists will have to work together with environmental specialists to develop integrated schemes of waste management that promote the reuse of products, recycling of parts and materials, and use of nontoxic materials derived from renewable resources. Integrated schemes of pest management, which use cultural controls—such as crop diversification and rotation, timing of planting and harvesting dates to avoid peak pest periods, use of resistant or tolerant cultivars, appropriate biological controls, and selective and nonpersistent chemical controls—are surely mandated by Islamic ethics, which prohibit unnecessary killing.

Environmental Planning

Islamic law defines the role of the governing authorities by the principle, "The management of subjects' affairs by the ruler shall be in accordance with their welfare."[32] While the governing authorities of Islamic states have sometimes taken an active role in planning, until this century most development has taken place in a decentralized manner, as communities implemented the rules of the well-known *sharīʿa.* This is still true to a large extent, despite the fact that the *sharīʿa* is presently not the only regulatory system operating in Muslim countries.

The *sharīʿa*'s firm and constant basis, applied flexibly to changing circumstances in different times and places, provides a set of ground rules aimed at ensuring cooperation and responsible behavior. It does not require imposition through strong central government; it requires only that people believe in it and are prepared to accept arbitration by those with learning to interpret the rules. With its distillation of expertise gained over more than a millennium and "through an emphasis on open and fair dealing the *sharīʿa* has provided a 'true way' by which any Islamic community may find a solution to its . . . problems. It is for this reason that isolated societies inhabiting a wide range of . . . environments from the Sahara to central Asia (and the Indonesian archipelago) recognize and apply a code which regulates the very basis of their economic life without any central government intervention."[33]

The inherent tensions between the interests of individual cultivators and planning authorities are illustrated in *iḥyā al-mawāt*, or land reclamation. Virgin land (*mawāt*) may normally be acquired by anyone who "brings it to life" in the language of Islamic law. The prophet Muhammad, upon him be peace and the blessing of God, declared that "Whoever revives dead land, it shall be his."[34] Ownership gives people a strong incentive to invest in the sustainable use of the land to provide for themselves, their families, and their posterity.

A person may stake a claim to virgin land by fencing or otherwise delimiting it. Whatever he then reclaims through his labor or capital, by planting, building, excavating a well, or irrigating, becomes his property. Only those actions which "bring new life" to the land lead to ownership; in the view of most jurists, mere exploitation—by grazing, for example—does not constitute *iḥyā*. The developer loses his claim to whatever land he has not revived within a reasonable time ('Umar ibn al-Khattab set a limit of three years; the limit is five years in contemporary Saudi Arabian law), for it is beneficial utilization and not merely acquisition that establishes the right of ownership. Once the right of ownership is established, it can be transferred by sale, inheritance, gift, or lease.

However, lands in which development would be injurious to the public interest may not be acquired through *iḥyā* because "the general welfare takes priority over individual welfare" and "the averting of harm takes priority over the acquisition of benefits." Such lands include sources of water and surface minerals, and the inviolate zones (*ḥarīm*) pertaining to water sources, settlements, roads, and squares, as well as protected areas (*ḥimā*).[35]

What is the role of the governing authorities in regulating *iḥyā*? Muslim jurists have taken various positions. The Hanafi school has maintained that developers may not acquire virgin lands without first securing permission from the governing authorities. Shafi'i jurists have held that such permission is not necessary, while Maliki jurists have said that prior permission is required only for sites about which there is a question of whether development may be detrimental to the public welfare.[36]

With increasing human impact, there is an ever-increasing need to plan with foresight based on a sound understanding of natural processes and the intrinsic suitabilities of different places for different uses. In accordance with the precedent established in the prohibition of building and settlement in flood-prone areas, unsuitable land use practices and activities should not be permitted in areas that are inherently or potentially hazardous to human life, nor should they be permitted in areas that are vulnerable to disruption of natural processes. Planning for development should in every case include assessment of environmental impacts, to minimize damage to the natural environment and depletion of natural resources.[37]

Although the governing authorities have a mandate to plan, they have a corresponding obligation to do so in consultation (*shūra*) with the people who are affected by such plans. This may best be realized through participatory planning and collaborative management in which key stakeholders or their representatives take part.

Allocation and Accountability in the Use of Natural Resources

Essential environmental elements and resources, such as water, rangeland, fire (including fuelwood and other sources of energy), forests and woodlands, fish and wildlife, cannot be owned in their natural state; they are held in common by all members of society. Each individual is entitled to benefit from these common resources to the extent of his need, so long as he does not infringe or violate the rights of other members. In return for profiting from the resource, he is obliged, as far as possible, to maintain its original value; if he causes its destruction, impairment, or degradation, he is held liable to the extent of repairing the damage, because he has violated the rights of every other member of society.[38]

Rights of usufruct are linked to accountability for the proper use and maintenance or conservation of the resource, in accordance with the fundamental legal principle established by the prophet Muhammad, upon him be peace and the blessing of God, "The benefit of a thing is in return for the liability attaching to it,"[39] and its converse, "Liability for a thing is an obligation accompanying the benefit thereof." In decreeing that farmers who develop irrigation facilities are exempt half of the tithe due on rain-fed agriculture, he recognized the effort invested in developing natural resources and established a precedent for economic incentives for their beneficial use.[40]

People in competitive open access rangelands or fisheries have no incentive to limit their harvests, nor do those whose rights are limited to a few years, whereas people who have exclusive rights to graze or fish a certain area, and whose rights extend far into the future have the incentive to limit their harvests to conserve their resources and manage them for continued productivity.[41] "Local communities that depend on a resource take a longer view of management requirements than outside commercial interests that come and go."[42]

People's rights to harvest and extract the natural resources on which society depends should be allocated according to the effort people invest in the beneficial use and conservation of these resources and should be linked to accountability for the way people use these common assets of society. The right to use a resource sustainably for profit provides an incentive to reinvest in its conservation and enhancement. Similarly, the economic benefits of the conservation of a resource should return to those people who have borne the burden of its conservation.[43]

Renewable and Nonrenewable Resources

The principles described above require that all natural resources be used efficiently and frugally. The soil, surface waters and wetlands, fisheries, forests and woodlands, rangelands and farmlands, as well as wild and domesticated species and the ecosystems to which they belong are renewable. This means that they can be used sustainably, provided that they are harvested at rates that do not exceed their capacity for regeneration. The processes by which most minerals, including fossil fuels and fossil groundwater, are produced, stored, and cycled in the earth occur over spans of time so vast that they are effectively nonrenewable as far as human beings are concerned. Hence, it is not possible to use them sustainably. The lives of these resources can be extended, however, by recycling, using less, and using renewable substitutes.[44]

Muslim jurists will have to translate the general principles which prohibit excessive and wasteful use of resources into detailed regulations pertaining to the entire range of technologies and practices used today in order to ensure that the use of renewable resources is sustainable and to minimize the depletion of nonrenewable resources.

Water Law

The expertise of Muslim jurists in the allocation of water rights represents the distillation of experience that civilizations in the arid and semi-arid Middle East have gained over millennia in managing a scarce resource, and then bringing its management within the ethical parameters of Islam. This most vital resource, of which every living thing is made and upon which each depends, may serve as an analogical basis for the allocation of rights to other resources that were formerly abundant but are now becoming progressively more scarce. "Water is to some extent a fugitive resource and therefore a particularly appropriate precedent for other resources such as wildlife and even grazing, with their fugitive properties in arid lands. Conceptually there are striking parallels between the benefits to be derived from the best possible allocation and use of a flow of water and those that can be harvested from the flow of energy in natural ecosystems."[45]

Water cannot be privately owned in its natural state; at its source it is publicly owned as common property and it remains so where it is sufficiently plentiful, as in a major river. All people may use it in moderation, but they may not waste it by excessive consumption, or impair its quality by pollution. Restrictions on common use increase with growing scarcity of the supply, but possessors of usufructuary rights may not withhold from others that which is surplus to their own needs. Uses of water are prioritized according to need and the amount of water consumed. Highest priority is given to the "right of thirst"; access to water for drinking cannot be denied because a person's life may depend upon it. Second, everyone is normally entitled to a sufficient quantity of water for washing, cooking, and similar domestic needs. The right to water livestock is next in priority, and finally, the most consumptive use, irrigation of crops. Hence, irrigation water may not be withheld from livestock unless damage to irrigation facilities or failure of crops is likely to result, in which case the owner of the irrigation rights is required to give only that water which is surplus to his needs. This prioritization among uses favors those whose needs are most acute. It also favors the uses that are least consumptive, or have least impact on the resource.

Farmers who develop land for irrigated agriculture have a right to a fair share of the available water. How, then, are irrigation rights allocated? On a naturally occurring water source that is not sufficiently plentiful to allow unrestricted use, as in an ephemeral stream or a small perennial stream, riparian landowners have senior rights of usufruct but may not withhold from others any water that is surplus to their needs. Normally, the upstream riparian user may take the amount of water allocated to his crops and releases the surplus water to the next user downstream, who in turn releases his surplus to the next, and so on until the needs of all farms are satisfied or the flow is exhausted. This system ensures that in times of drought there will be sufficient water for some farms to flourish, with the sacrifice of farms that are marginal. It is more efficient than systems based on proportional allocation, which can result in a general failure of crops when water is scarce. In effect, this helps to discourage overextension of agriculture by restricting it to the extent that is economically viable in accordance with the availability of water at any given time.

If a new farm or plot is cultivated upstream from one or more existing farms, however, the farms that were first established take priority and the new plot receives a share only after the previously established farms have been irrigated. Riparian rights are thus subordinate to rights of prior claim. This ensures that future users will not prejudice a farmer's investment in the resource.

Similar principles govern the use of groundwater. The owner of a well enjoys senior rights of usufruct, but he may not withhold surplus water beyond his needs so long as there is no degradation of the resource. Nor may he pollute the aquifer or, in the view of many jurists, deplete it to the extent that he causes previously established wells to fail.

The excavation of a well or canal gives rise to rights of ownership of the property. If a group of farmers constructs such a facility, they own it jointly in accordance with the shares of labor and capital they have invested in it. The owners of these facilities enjoy senior rights of usufruct, but the water itself remains a public resource, because it flows to—and from—the land. Only when water is appropriated and separated from its source, as in a vessel or a cistern, does it become the possessor's private property, which can be sold, gifted, and otherwise disposed of.[46]

Other Renewable Natural Resources

It has been said that "The sheer pragmatic logic and versatility of the Islamic water law suggests that . . . it could readily be expanded into an Islamic law for the conservation of renewable resources."[47]

At the time that Muslim jurists developed the *fiqh* pertaining to grazing, forestry, hunting, and fishing, these were generally not scarce resources. Wildlife populations were sufficiently large for many peoples in Muslim countries to subsist largely by hunting until into the twentieth century. The ability of pastoralists to exploit the range was limited by the availability of water; to withhold surplus water from livestock was to deny the use of the pasture.[48] In times of drought, starvation ensured that livestock numbers did not greatly exceed the carrying capacity of the range.

Now, however, the technologies of resource use have changed, as have the social and environmental circumstances that made many traditional resource uses sustainable. Many of the rangelands in Muslim countries have been devastated by overgrazing, and forests and woodlands have been deforested by the timber, firewood, and charcoal industries. Wildlife habitats have been destroyed through overgrazing of rangelands and clearance of forests for settlement and agriculture, and the populations of many species of wildlife have plummeted. Some species are extinct, and others are threatened with extinction. Resources that once were abundant have become as scarce as water, or scarcer still.

Since the rates of natural regeneration of these resources have been exceeded, there is hardly any question of a surplus, which it would be wrong to withhold. On the contrary, harvests must be greatly reduced if pastoralism, forestry, hunting, and fishing are to be economically viable. As currently practiced, they are simply not sustainable. General and excessive damage has occurred and the public welfare has been seriously affected.

Inevitably, some of the people who presently use these resources will have to find other means of livelihood when present uses are no longer sustainable or economically viable. "The general welfare takes priority over individual welfare"; "a private injury is accepted to avert a general injury to the public"; and "the averting of harm takes priority over the acquisition of benefits."[49]

How, then, might rights to these common natural resources be allocated when they cannot sustain unrestricted use? The restrictions on common use increase with the consumptiveness of the use and the scarcity of the supply. Drawing an analogy from water law, the uses that are most vital to human welfare should take priority, as well as the uses that are least consumptive. With growing scarcity, there must also be greater protection for those with usufructuary rights: the people who live in closest proximity to these resources and particularly the graziers, woodsmen, hunters, and fishermen who have prior traditional claims of usufruct would have priority. In Islamic law, a person who constructs a birdhouse, beehive, or otherwise provides habitat for wildlife holds prior rights to the animals he attracts.[50] "The securing of prior rights to water through the construction of irrigation facilities could readily be equated with a demonstration of responsibility in conserving and developing grazing and wildlife resources over a period of time. Both require effort and sacrifice on the part of the individuals, as an investment for future favorable treatment."[51] Accordingly, people who invest their capital and labor in the conservation and rehabilitation of the resource by way of wildlife conservation and habitat enhancement, range improvement, or agroforestry would earn senior rights of usufruct in return for their investment, and all the improvements that they have made would belong to them.

Wildlife resources have potential economic advantages over domestic livestock, since they are better adapted to the ecological conditions of their native habitats and produce not only meat and hides, as do domestic animals, but also can be "sold" several times over for game viewing and hunting opportunities. Under conditions of good management, the use of wildlife can be less consumptive and have lower impact on rangelands. Since domestic livestock will necessarily have to be displaced from certain ranges in order to allow development of wildlife resources, the graziers who have been affected should have prior rights to the wildlife, in compensation for their loss of grazing rights.[52]

Legal Instruments

Effective legal instruments for environmental protection and conservation of natural resources are essential elements of environmental legislation. What institutions of the *sharīʿa* have served as legal instruments for conservation, providing regulations, models, and incentives for responsible stewardship of the earth and its resources? Jurists should consider ways in which these instruments may be extended and applied creatively to solve new problems and offer new opportunities. In cases where they are in decline but are potentially effective, jurists should investigate the reasons for their decline and consider ways in which they might be restored.

These institutions of the *sharīʿa* survive mainly as traditional or customary conservation practices. The fundamental needs are, first, to adapt these institutions of the *sharīʿa* to new technologies and socioeconomic realities and thus enable them to survive, and second and perhaps most importantly, to learn their basic lessons and principles, and then apply these principles to conservation of our renewable natural resources.

The customary practices that have embodied these principles may at times provide solutions that are well adapted to the problems we face in managing the resource, while at times they themselves must be adapted to new technologies and economic realities. The heart of tradition is often in its details—the specific practices and prohibitions in using a *ḥimā*; the dimensions of the *ḥarīm*s of water sources; the actual stones of the terraces—and these details should not be dismissed lightly. Yet, important as the details of these traditional conservation practices are, many of them will need to be amended and adapted to new technologies and economic realities, if they are to survive. Hence, still more important than preservation of the details of these conservation practices is preservation of the principles that underlie them, and the creative application of these principles to the conservation of natural resources.

In the endeavor to revitalize these traditional conservation practices, it should be borne in mind that the success of traditional practices and technologies comes from—and depends on—the presence of arrangements that enable the local communities that are the repositories and practitioners of these traditions to participate equitably in the management of their natural resources.

Al-Ḥarāmayn*: The Two Inviolable Sanctuaries*

Islamic law defines each of the sacred territories surrounding Mecca and Medina as an inviolable sanctuary (*ḥarām*) for human beings, wildlife, and native vegetation. Within them the injury—even disturbance—of wildlife is forbidden. On the day that the population of Mecca entered into Islam, the prophet Muhammad, upon him be peace and the blessing of God, proclaimed with regard to its sacred precincts: "It is sacred by virtue of the sanctity conferred on it by God until the day of resurrection. Its thorn trees shall not be cut down, its game shall not be disturbed . . . and its fresh herbage shall not be cut."[53]

He established a similar sanctuary between the mountains and lava flows surrounding Medina, saying, "Verily Abraham declared Makkah a sanctuary and I declare Al-Madinah, that which lies between its two lava flows, to be a sanctuary; its trees shall not be cut and its game shall not be hunted."[54] His companion Abu Hurayra stated, "Were I to find gazelles in the land between its two lava flows, I would not disturb them; and he (the Prophet) also made the environs of al-Madinah for twelve miles a reserve (*ḥimā*)."[55]

These two inviolable sanctuaries are the primordial protected areas in Islam. The *ḥarām* of Mecca extends roughly thirty-five kilometers east to west, and twenty kilometers north to south. In addition to the city of Mecca with its population of approximately one million, it includes some rural wadis, plains, sand dunes, and mountain peaks containing a fair diversity of native wildlife. The predominant vegetation is *Acacia-Commiphora* scrub; sand partridge, sandgrouse, doves, swifts, martins, and various raptors inhabit the *ḥarām*, as well as a wide variety of snakes and lizards. Gazelle and ibex occurred until recent times, and in addition to smaller mammals, wolf, hyena, caracal, ratel, and wildcat are still found.[56] The small *ḥarām* occupying the area between the two lava flows of Medina is now almost entirely urbanized. However, it contains some productive groves of date palms, which are habitat for a diverse array of resident and migratory birds.

Hunting does not take place within the two inviolable sanctuaries, but otherwise the *sharī'a*'s strict environmental rulings pertaining to them are largely suspended in practice. It has been argued that these rulings are incompatible with development, that development is a necessity and, according to a principle of Islamic law, "Dire necessity makes the prohibited permissible." In fact, however, there are many sacred and cultural sites in the world, including cities, which set environmental standards approaching the strictness of those standards which, in theory, apply to Mecca and Medina.

What does it mean to say that the *ḥarāmayn* are inviolable? If these stringent environmental regulations were meant to be put aside, why were they laid down in the first place? Jurists should consider the possibility that they are meant to be implemented literally. Of course, strict avoidance of injury to native vegetation and wildlife is possible only through minimization of negative impacts on their habitats. All planning, design, and construction within the sacred precincts of Mecca and Medina would therefore have to be carried out with extraordinary sensitivity and care.[57]

If these rulings were to be implemented literally, the two inviolable sanctuaries would become models of environmental protection and sustainable development, demonstrations of best practice in integrated urban and rural planning. Surely the primordial protected areas of Islam merit no less than this—and is it unreasonable to suppose that they are meant to serve as models? These two sites are visited each year by millions of pilgrims for *ḥājj* and *'umra*. By demonstrating the highest standards of environmental excellence, as embodiments of harmony between humanity and nature and as expressions of human stewardship (*khilāfa*), they have great potential to spread environmental consciousness throughout the Muslim world. Conversely, if the most sacred sites on the face of the earth are degraded and abused, the message will be broadcast throughout the Muslim countries that to despoil the planet is not wrong!

Ḥarīm *Zones: Greenbelts and Easements*

Their roles in traditional socioeconomic systems—Islamic law designates various inviolable zones, called *ḥarīm*, within which developments are prohibited or restricted to prevent the impairment of utilities and natural resources. "Whatever is near developed land and affects its welfare, such as its roads and watercourses, its rubbish dump, and the place where its soil and tools are stored, its development is not permitted. Likewise that which pertains to the welfare of a village, such as its square, the pasture of its livestock, its woodlands, its roads, and its water channels, is not acquired individually by *iḥyā*. Likewise with regard to the *ḥarīm* of a well or stream or any other property, *iḥyā* is not permitted in sites that affect its welfare."[58]

According to Islamic law, every settlement (*'amir*) should have a surrounding *ḥarīm* resembling a greenbelt within which the right to acquire vacant land by developing it is restricted. These municipal common lands are to be managed by the people of the settlement to provide for their needs, such as forage, firewood, and the like, and to facilitate the use and development of these lands in the manner most conducive to the inhabitants' welfare.

Natural sources of water, such as seas and lakes, rivers, streams and springs, and developed sources such as wells, cisterns, and canals, and utilities, such as roads and squares, should also have inviolable zones resembling easements to prevent their impairment, to facilitate their management, and to prevent nuisances and hazards. The standard measurements of such *ḥarīms* are: a radius of five hundred cubits for a natural spring; twenty-five cubits for a well; and for a watercourse, an area of adjacent land that is equal to the distance from the center of the channel to the bank. In the view of many legal scholars, however, these distances are to be modified in accordance with the characteristics of the site and the requirements of the resource.[59]

Unfortunately, the municipal commons of settlements are presently overexploited and not managed; the inviolable zones of water sources are largely ignored.

Potential applications of ḥarīm *zones*—The municipal lands of settlements have immense potential as a means for local communities to secure their own sustainable development. Jurists need to work with socioeconomists, planners, and local communities to enable these lands to fulfill their potential. How may they best be managed to provide for the inhabitants' needs on a sustainable basis, and to reduce pressure on the surrounding range and woodlands? How may the inhabitants be encouraged to invest in the restoration of these lands and be held accountable for their maintenance?

The inviolable zones of water sources have great potential for watershed conservation and management, for the sustainable use of wetlands and the conservation of their biological diversity. Jurists must work with hydrologists, biologists, environmental planners, and local communities to investigate the potential uses of these zones and the management prescriptions necessary to realize their benefits. How best may they be protected and their provisions enforced? How may the inhabitants be encouraged to invest in the restoration of these *ḥarīms* and how best may they be held accountable for their maintenance? Perhaps the standard measurements of *ḥarīm* zones should represent their minimum areas, which could be extended as necessary to protect water resources. What *ḥarīm* regulations are applicable to sea, reservoir, and lake shores? To marshes, ephemeral wetlands, and playas? How are prohibitions on settlement and inappropriate development activities in flood-prone areas best enforced? How should the individual, group, or agency to which the benefits of the water are allocated be made accountable for maintenance of the *ḥarīm*, and for whatever conservation measures, such as bank stabilization, erosion control, aquifer recharge, and habitat enhancement, are required?

The Ḥimā*: Protected Areas*

The role of the ḥimā *in traditional socioeconomic systems*—In Islamic law, all unowned lands that are reserved for purposes pertaining to the public good are known as *ḥimā*, meaning a "protected area." It may be, as suggested by some land managers, that the *ḥimā* was used as an instrument of conservation in pre-Islamic times.[60] Certainly, the term *ḥimā* was in use by the time of the prophet Muhammad, upon whom be peace and the blessing of God, for he is recorded to have mentioned that "every ruler has a *ḥimā*."[61] It is difficult to ascertain what were the purposes of these pre-Islamic *ḥimā*s, the ways in which they were managed, and to what extent they were used for the conservation of natural resources. Al-Shafi'i (founder of one of the four recognized schools of Sunni law) reported that when a nomadic tribe came into a new area, it was customary for the tribal leader to ascend an eminence and shout or make his dog bark, and that all the land as far as the sound could be heard would be reserved for his exclusive use, as his *ḥimā*. A good ruler or tribal chieftain would presumably have used his *ḥimā* for purposes pertaining to the welfare of his people; however, according to Al-Shafi'i, the pre-Islamic institution of the *ḥimā* was widely regarded by the common people as an instrument of oppression.[62]

In any event, the prophet Muhammad, upon him be peace and the blessing of God, transformed the *ḥimā*, laying down the rules by which it became one of the essential instruments of conservation in Islamic law. He abolished the pre-Islamic practice of making private reserves for the exclusive use of powerful individuals, and ruled that a *ḥimā* could be established only in the way of God and His Prophet—in other words, for the public welfare.[63] He established the *ḥimā* of an-Naqi' for the cavalry, and made a *ḥimā* surrounding the *ḥarām* (inviolable) of Medina, forbidding hunting within a radius of four miles and the destruction of trees and shrubs within twelve.[64] The caliphs who succeeded him established additional *ḥimā*s for the cavalry, the camels allocated for charity, and the livestock of the poor.

*Ḥimā*s are to be managed in a manner that is not injurious to the local people. Rulers "may make reserves only to an extent that does not oppress or injure the Islamic community—for it is allowed only for the benefit that is realized through its reservation, and it is no benefit to bring about an injury to the majority of the people."[65] The caliph 'Umar ibn al-Khattab instructed the manager of Hima ar-Rabadhah, "Take care, O Hunayy! Lift your wing from the people! Heed the complaint of the oppressed for it will be heard by God. Let enter those who are dependent on their camels and sheep, and turn away the livestock of Ibn 'Awf and Ibn 'Affan, for they, if their livestock should perish, will fall back on their palms and fields; whereas the needy one, if his livestock perish, will come to me crying 'O Commander of the Faithful! . . .' It is easier for me to provide them with pasture than to spend on them gold or silver. Indeed it is their land, for which they fought in the time of ignorance and upon which they embraced Islam." He also said, "All property belongs to God and all creatures are but servants of God. By God! if it did not bear upon the cause of God, I would not have reserved a hand's span of the land."[66]

The *ḥimā* tradition is characterized by great flexibility. To be valid in Islamic law, according to Al-Suyuti and other jurists, a *ḥimā* must meet four conditions, which they derived from the practices of the Prophet and the early caliphs.[67]

1) It must be constituted by the legitimate Islamic governing authority;

2) It must be established in the way of God—that is, for purposes pertaining to the public welfare;

3) It must avoid causing undue hardship to the local people—that is, it should not deprive them of indispensable resources; and

4) It must realize greater actual benefits to society than detriments.

No other conditions need be met.

Historically, *ḥimā*s have varied in size from a few hectares to hundreds of square kilometers. Ḥima al-Rabadha, which was established by the caliph 'Umar ibn al-Khattab and was expanded by the caliph 'Uthman ibn 'Affan, was one of the largest, extending from the site of ar-Rabadhah in western Najd to near the village of Dariyah. Among the traditional *ḥimā*s are the best managed rangelands in the Arabian Peninsula; some have been grazed correctly since early Islamic times and are among the most long-standing examples of rangeland conservation known. Indeed, few established systems of protected areas are known that have a history comparable in length with traditional *ḥimā*s. It was estimated that in 1965 there were about three thousand *ḥimā*s in Saudi Arabia, comprising a vast area of land under conservation and sustainable management. Nearly every village in the southwestern mountains of the country was associated with one or more *ḥimā*s, either alone or in cooperation with an adjacent settlement. The *ḥimā*s varied from 10 to over 1,000 hectares and averaged about 250 hectares.

Customary management of *ḥimā*s has been highly adaptive to the particular needs of the local people and the characteristics of the site. Each *ḥimā* is managed in accordance with the specific purposes for which it has been established and the specific characteristics of the site. In some *ḥimā*s, grazing is prohibited, although grass is harvested by hand at designated times and places during years of drought. Others are protected woodlands within which the cutting of trees is either prohibited or regulated. Still others are protected rangelands in which grazing or the cutting of grass is permitted on a seasonal basis, after the grasses and other plants have grown out and flowered, or in which grazing is restricted to specified kinds and numbers of livestock, such as milk cattle, or within which a limited number of livestock may be grazed for a specified time during periods of drought. There are reserves for the production of honey, within which grazing is prohibited seasonally or is excluded altogether. One site has been managed as a reserve for the conservation of ibex for nearly two hundred years. Most *ḥimā*s are managed by and for a particular village, clan, or tribe.[68]

Because a *ḥimā* may be established for any purpose that pertains to the common good, it may be managed for either conservation or sustainable production, although historically most *ḥimā*s have combined both aims. The institution was ecologically sustainable; it was socially acceptable and was desired by the people who carried the cost of implementing it, and it was economically viable because of the benefits it yielded and the social security it provided. By allocating tangible benefits to particular people who benefit directly from conservation, it has provided the necessary incentive for local communities to invest in the maintenance of their natural resources and to protect them from abuse.

As most *ḥimā*s were managed locally, management was subject to community consensus and individuals in the community were able to influence this consensus and thus have had a meaningful voice in management decisions. The pragmatic flexibility of the system has provided an important cultural precedent for protecting and managing public resources over which individuals enjoy usufructuary rights, including rights to grazing. This is especially significant in countries where most of the land is given over to communal grazing and where there are few designated landholdings.

The use of *ḥimā*s has undergone considerable change in recent decades, as tribal lands have been nationalized, a growing population has demanded more land for housing, farms, and pasture, and the needs of village farmers have changed. Traditional *ḥimā*s had their management grounded in tribal loyalties and were sometimes a source of conflict. Most of them were managed by and for a specific village or tribe, and the governing authorities have tended to see them as contradicting the common good. Most *ḥimā*s have now been abandoned, and their number has plummeted to a few dozen. The remaining *ḥimā*s are now often used to graze sheep and goats, rather than cattle and horses, as with the mechanization of terrace agriculture the need for pasture for draft animals has declined. *Ḥimā*s are still regarded as an essential source of fodder and are especially important in years of drought. Some are retained as an insurance against poor seasons, when designated portions may be cut on a rotational basis under the supervision of the village shaykh, with each stockowner cutting fodder according to the needs of his livestock. Among the most successful *ḥimā*s are those used for honey production, as high quality wildflower honeys fetch a high price in the market and are economically competitive against livestock.[69]

Potential applications of the ḥimā—The value of *ḥimā*s for the rehabilitation of rangeland, the stabilization and control of nomadic grazing, as indicators of range potential and better animal husbandry practices, and for the proper management of water catchment areas has been identified by a succession of researchers. Many *ḥimā*s are also located in areas of high species diversity or support woodlands and other key biological habitats and are thus important in preserving biological diversity. Their great potential for ecological and socioeconomic research and development has received less attention.

The importance to ecological research of areas that have been protected under a more or less defined management regime for a substantial period of time cannot be stressed too strongly. Reclamation of the grazing resources and their level of use during and after rehabilitation will be difficult to plan in the absence of base-line information on which to judge recovery and the capacity of the range to support wild or domestic herbivores at different stages during recovery. Such information is difficult to obtain in the absence of trial range sites protected from overgrazing. Well-protected *ḥimā*s provide a measure of potential plant species diversity and standing plant biomass under particular climatic conditions and management treatments.[70]

As the accelerating loss of species and ecosystems diminishes the fertility and productivity of the earth, the *ḥimā* has emerged as potentially, perhaps, the most important legal instrument in the *sharīʻa* for conservation of biological diversity. For this potential to be realized, however, each Muslim country needs to establish a comprehensive system of *ḥimā*s—protected areas—based on accurate inventory and analysis of its biological resources. Such a system should conserve (and restore) an adequate representation of each physiographic region and biotope. It should conserve (and restore) sites of outstanding biological productivity and ecological significance, such as freshwater wetlands, mountain refugia, forests and woodlands, islands, coral reefs, seagrass beds, mangrove thickets, and salt marshes. And it should conserve viable populations of rare and endangered species, endemics, and species of special ecological importance or economic value.

The conservation of biological diversity is inevitably interwoven with sustainable use of natural resources, and the *ḥimā* has shown considerable value as an instrument for sustainable development. The most enduring *ḥimā*s have been those that were planned and managed, not by central governments, but by the local communities of stakeholders who are dependent upon them for their livelihood. To enable *ḥimā*s to achieve their potential value for sustainable development, it is necessary to ensure community participation in their management, and to manage them to generate tangible benefits that are shared equitably among stakeholders, who in turn are held accountable for maintaining the resources.

Traditional *ḥimā*s must adapt to the new and socioeconomic realities to fulfill the changing needs of the local communities. In particular, the management of traditional *ḥimā*s needs to be shifted from tribal objectives, which inherently carry the potential for conflict, to geographical objectives, which tend toward the common good. Provisions will still be needed to ensure that allocation of the rights to use natural resources and accountability for maintaining them in good condition are invested in identified individuals so as to avert the "tragedy of the commons," but on a more equitable basis than tribal lineage.

Most important, perhaps, is the need to reorient the management of modern protected area systems to embody the principles articulated in the juristic discussions of the *ḥimā* and realized in their actual traditional management. This can only be done through close collaboration with the local people. The traditional management of *ḥimā*s was close to the people who used them. Now the authorities who manage the protected areas are usually remote, in their centralized offices in the capital cities. We need to develop arrangements that will enable local communities to participate meaningfully in the management of protected areas.

Within the framework of the *sharī'a*, Muslim jurists will have to draw upon the full spectrum of local and international experience in protected area management to revitalize the institution of the *ḥimā*. They will have to work out its application to marine and coastal areas, and to answer a host of practical questions pertaining to the rights of local people. What limitations may the managing authority impose on the use of private enclaves within a *ḥimā* or private properties adjacent to it? What are the rules governing the acquisition of private property adjacent to a *ḥimā* or surrounded by it, if such property is needed for the *ḥimā*'s management? What are the conditions pertaining to voluntary purchase? To compulsory purchase? Can the managing authority exercise rights of option and preemption (*shuf'ā*)? What mechanisms, such as grants and lease-back, exist in Islamic law to provide compensation for land that is taken for a *ḥimā* or for pasture and other resources to which access is denied?

The Waqf*: Charitable Foundations and Endowments*

The role of the waqf *in traditional socioeconomic systems*—The most important institution of Islamic law by which individual Muslims may contribute to the public good is the charitable endowment (*waqf*), dedicated in perpetuity to the cause of God. It is related that when 'Umar ibn al-Khattab acquired land in Khaybar, he consulted the prophet Muhammad, upon him be peace and the blessing of God, and said, "O Messenger of God, I have acquired land in Khaybar; never have I received property dearer to me than this, so what do you direct me to do with it? The Prophet, upon him be peace and the blessing of God, replied, "If you wish you may make it an endowment and give its produce as charity." So 'Umar gave it in charity, declaring that it should not be sold or gifted or inherited, and that its yield should be devoted to the poor, to kinsfolk, to the freeing of slaves, for the cause of God, and to provide for guests and travelers.[71]

A *waqf* may be established for any charitable purpose. It becomes inalienable public property, administered in accordance with the stipulations specified by the donor, under the supervision of the religious courts. Historically, the role of charitable gifts has been enormous; the *waqf* has been the primary source of funding for mosques, schools, hospitals, and other public works in the Muslim world. Among the most common endowments in rural areas are wells and cisterns donated for the public good, following the example of 'Uthman ibn 'Affan who bought the well of Rawma and dedicated it to the public.[72]

Even now, after governments have assumed the primary responsibility of financing public welfare, charitable contributions are underestimated, including, notably, the contributions of women, whose financial assets may be less bound up in family maintenance. But although there have long been endowments for the feeding of birds and the maintenance of domestic animals, the *waqf* remains virtually untapped as an instrument for conservation.

Potential applications of the waqf—In many countries of the world, charitable contributions are major sources of material and financial support for conservation. Governments cannot bear the full costs of conservation, especially in the poorer countries. Nor should they. Through private contributions, people exercise their role as *khulafā'* on Earth, and support the projects which they believe are most beneficial.

Muslim jurists should investigate the contemporary uses to which endowments, trusts, funds, gifts, and other private contributions of land and money have been put as instruments of conservation worldwide, in order to find appropriate uses of the *waqf*. For example, a *waqf* might take the form of a land trust for charitable purposes, such as ecological and range research, wildlife propagation, habitat development, village woodlots and pastures, or areas for recreation and ecological education. Alternatively, it might take the form of a fund for the finance of such research and breeding, of acquisition of land for purposes of conservation, or of habitat development within or outside protected areas. New endowments should be encouraged within protected areas to complement the purposes of the *ḥimā*.[73]

Jurists should investigate ways to manage a *waqf* as an accumulating fund that solicits the contribution of further endowments, or as a cumulative land trust that solicits the endowment of additional wildlife habitats. They should look into the conditions under which both private organizations and public agencies might initiate, sponsor, and manage such funds and land trusts, allowing for stipulations by both the managing organization and contributors. They should also consider what guidelines are appropriate to ensure efficient and effective management of endowments for conservation.

Other Legal Instruments: Iqtā', Iqtā' Istighlāl, Ijāra, *and* Ihtikār

The governing authorities may make grants (*iqtā'*) of unowned land for purposes of agriculture and other kinds of development. Such grants may be used to channel such developments to environmentally suitable locations and away from areas that are unsuitable. Land grants may also serve as means of compensation to people whose lands are appropriated for a public good, or in whose lands development is restricted in the public interest. Land grants are subject to the principles that govern *iḥyā*: They may not contain resources upon which the public welfare depends. A grant does not in itself confer ownership; only that land which the recipient actually revives becomes his property. Whatever land the recipient fails to develop within a reasonable time returns to its previous unowned state, so that others may benefit from it.[74]

The governing authorities may institute the *lease* (*ijāra*) of state-owned lands or grant their usufruct (*iqtā' manfa'āt al-arḍ* or *iqtā' al-istighlāl*) for agricultural and other purposes, and to specify the kinds of improvements to be undertaken or the crops to be grown, and the management practices and techniques to be employed. Long-term leases and grants of usufruct give the recipients an incentive to invest in the sustainable use of the land while making them directly accountable to the authorities who continue to supervise its utilization. Both leases and grants of usufruct are well suited for environmentally vulnerable lands that require special management practices.[75]

Sites can also be designated for special purposes through *ihtikār*. Prime agricultural soils, for example, are of enormous importance for food production, yet they are rapidly succumbing to urban settlement because agriculture cannot complete economically with urban uses. Through *ihtikār*, suitable sites may be reserved for agricultural use.

Muslim jurists should investigate the ways in which these and other legal instruments have been used historically, and their potential environmental applications.

Legal Sanctions

The Ḥisba

> Let there be of you a society that calls to goodness, establishes right and eradicates wrong. Such are they who shall prosper. (Qur'an 3:104)

The obligation to establish good and eradicate evil is known in Islamic law as the *ḥisba.* The prophet Muhammad, upon him be peace and the blessing of God, declared that "If one witnesses a wrong, he should change it with his hand; if he cannot do so, he should change it with his tongue; and if he cannot do that, he should change it in his heart—but that is the weakest degree of faith."[76]

The role of individual and social conscience—This obligation is both individual and collective. On the individual level, each man and woman is responsible for his or her own behavior and obliged to influence family, neighbors, and the society at large in accordance with an enlightened conscience. On the collective level also, social conscience can be immensely powerful, and when functioning effectively, obviates much of the need for coercion by the governing authorities.

The conservation of the natural environment is a moral and ethical imperative. Environmental problems cannot be solved through knowledge and technology alone. While incentives such as equitable allocation of rights to benefit from natural resources in return for their conservation are essential to motivate people to use them wisely, enlightened self-interest does not motivate people to do more than is convenient and profitable for themselves. Only moral conviction and ethical consciousness—on both individual and social levels—can motivate people to forgo some of the short-range profits of this life, and to make personal sacrifices for the common good.[77]

The role of the governing authorities—At the same time, ethical teachings must be backed with sanctions. Appeals to conscience without positive inducement and enforcement put those who respond to their nobler ethical instincts with self-restraint at a disadvantage with respect to those who fail to rise above their most petty and selfish desires, exceed the bounds of fairness, and infringe upon the rights of others as they please. Even conscientious people know their own needs and interests and their associates' needs and interests far better than they can know the competing needs and interests of other people and other social groups; thus, even moral impulses can work against the common good. The force of law and political authority are therefore indispensable to bring about justice and equity.[78] The caliph 'Uthman ibn 'Affan declared that "God establishes through the *sulṭān* (political power) what He does not establish through the *furqān* (the Qur'an, the criterion that distinguishes right from wrong.)[79] Ibn Taymiyya declared that government is one of the most important requirements of Islam, for the fundamental obligation to command the right and forbid the wrong cannot be discharged without power and authority.[80]

The Office of the Muḥtāsib

Historically, one of the most important institutions with coercive power to safeguard the rights of society when individual conscience and social conscience fail has been the office of the *muḥtāsib*. The *muḥtāsib* was a jurist who had to be thoroughly familiar with the rulings of Islamic law that pertained to his position. He was assisted by a staff of experts in pertinent fields. Many of the responsibilities of environmental protection and conservation have come under his jurisdiction. He was responsible for the inspection of markets, roads, buildings, watercourses, *ḥimā*s, and so forth. Among his duties were the supervision and enforcement of regulations and standards pertaining to safety, hygiene, and cleanliness; the removal and disposal of wastes and pollutants; the prevention and elimination of hazards and nuisances; the protection of *ḥimā*s from violation and trespass; and the prevention of abuse and ill treatment of animals. He was responsible for assessing damages and imposing fines and other penalties. In addition, he had wide discretionary authority to take what measures he deemed necessary to ensure the public welfare.[81]

This institution has all but disappeared. The regulatory functions of the *muḥtāsib* have been inherited by such agencies as municipalities, environmental protection agencies, wildlife conservation agencies, and humane societies. The essential difference, of course, is that the *muḥtāsib* was an expert in the application of Islamic law, whereas the agencies that have replaced his office and the regulations by which they operate are secular in origin. Muslim jurists should consider whether it is feasible and desirable to revive this institution, extend it, and update it to discharge the responsibilities of its contemporary successors. Or is it more efficient and effective—or possible—to reform these contemporary agencies in a manner that would enable them to interpret and implement Islamic law?

Al-Siyāsat al-Sharī'a: *Sharī'a*-based Policies

Muslim jurists will have to address a number of issues that are fundamental to environmental policy and legislation. Among them are individual responsibilities and rights, valuing of natural resources, development and lifestyle, population control, genetic resources, animal rights, and international cooperation and conflict.

Individual Responsibilities and Rights

The prophet Muḥammad, upon him be peace and the blessing of God, declared that "the believer who is strong is better, and better loved by God, than the believer who is weak."[82] Each individual man and woman is a *khalīfa* on the earth and will be judged alone on the Day of Judgment for what he or she did with his or her life. This enormous responsibility requires freedom to participate effectively in planning and decision-making processes.

The individual is responsible before God to protect himself and his community, regardless of what the governing authorities may or may not require of him. Accurate information is indispensable to enable people to make enlightened decisions for the conservation of the natural environment, to avoid acts that lead to its degradation, and to rectify damage that already has occurred.

A fundamental right of people is consultation (*shūra*) in all matters that affect their welfare. It is essential that people of all social and ethnic groups be consulted without discrimination, and that the weakest citizens be held as strongest until their rights are fully established, and the strongest held as weakest until they comply fully with the law.[83] Women as well as men took oaths of allegiance to the Prophet, upon him be peace and the blessing of God. Upon the death of the second caliph, 'Umar ibn al-Khattab, the committee whom he appointed to select his successor hastened to consult not only the people of knowledge and the leaders of the tribes, but also the ordinary people, including the women in their homes.[84]

The reality today is that the citizens of Muslim countries are among the least empowered people on the planet. The average citizen is not a man—or woman—but a mouse! How can he or she be a *khalīfa*? Perhaps the worst thing about authoritarian rule is that it causes human beings to abdicate their role as *khalīfa*s on the earth: it reduces them to something less than fully human.

Muslim jurists must consider what measures and mechanisms are needed to empower the powerless of the Muslim world—women as well as men, rural as well as urban, unlettered as well as literate. How can we ensure that people are enabled to make full use of their intelligence and experience? How may effective consultation of people whose interests are at stake be ensured in decision-making processes? How may racial, ethnic, sexual, religious, and other forms of discrimination be prevented? How may standing in judicial and administrative processes be secured for individuals and citizens' groups, so that they may contribute to enforcement of environmental law and seek remedy for environmental damage? How may public access to information be ensured, so that people may make enlightened decisions? How may openness and truthfulness be ensured in governance and administration? How may the agencies responsible for implementation and enforcement of environmental legislation be made accountable for their actions and inactions? And how may local stakeholders be enabled to manage the resources on which their livelihoods depend?

Valuing of Natural Resources

Undervaluing of resources—When the real economic values of natural resources are ignored by underpricing, they tend to be undervalued in a moral as well as an economic sense, and their survival may be put at risk. Elephants, for example, have high potential economic value for their ivory, meat, and leather, as well as the considerable revenues that they can bring through hunting licenses and tourism. They also cause considerable social and economic costs in view of their destruction of fields, homes, and danger to human life. In countries where the hunting of elephants and the sale of their products is prohibited—or where the proceeds return to the central treasury rather then to the rural people who bear the costs of their conservation—elephants have little perceived value to offset these costs, and the people have no incentive to conserve them. As a result, wildlife officers are engaged in a costly, brutal war with poachers to save elephants from extinction. And the poachers are winning.

On the other hand, in countries of southern Africa where local communities receive significant financial returns from the hunting, culling, and viewing of elephants, they are enthusiastically conserved, and their populations are stable. If rural communities are prevented from turning the potential economic advantages of wildlife resources into financial profit, they will sacrifice wildlife in favor of domestic livestock. Likewise, if forage is undervalued, it may be overgrazed almost to the point of extinction.[85]

Economic instruments—Economic instruments help to correct biases caused by underpricing of life-support systems and natural resources. They provide incentives for industries and consumers to meet environmental standards, while allowing them to choose which measures they adopt. Among the most important principles for valuing resources and pricing goods are "the polluter pays" and "the user pays." A factory, for example, should pay the costs of ensuring that its emissions and effluents do not affect human health or damage fisheries. Consequently, market prices reflect the full costs of preventing environmental damage that may result from pollution. A timber industry should pay the costs of soil loss, flooding, and loss of biological diversity that its activities cause, in addition to the cost of extracting timber. Again, market prices will then reflect the full social cost of uses or depletion of the resource, including any damage to ecosystems and any future resource benefits foregone because they have been reduced by current use.[86]

These principles appear to accord with the principles of the *sharī'a* that "The benefit of a thing is in return for the liability attaching to it," and "Liability for a thing is an obligation accompanying the benefit thereof." Muslim jurists should examine the application of economic instruments, such as charges, resource taxes, subsidies, deposit and refund schemes, performance bonds, and tradable permits, to ascertain their relative appropriateness for Islamic societies and any variants, modifications, or alternative economic instruments that might be derived from the *sharī'a.*

Economic indicators—The standard measures of national income and economic performance, the gross national product and net national product, fail to take account of the depletion or depreciation of natural assets or the social costs of environmental damage. In reality, deforestation, desertification, the loss of fertile topsoil, and the depletion of mineral resources lead to lower yields and raise the costs of production. But because expenditures to counteract environmental damage and to give medical care add to the income of suppliers, they are counted as income rather than expenses. These measures are dangerously misleading. They may give an illusion of economic health when a country is heading for bankruptcy by destroying its forests and rangelands, polluting its air and waters, and depleting its topsoil and mineral resources.[87] Muslim jurists and socioeconomists must work together to develop new economic indicators and methods of environmental and resource accounting that will enable governments to understand the effects of their policies and to calculate the true economic condition of their countries.

Development and Lifestyle

> Our Lord, grant us good in the present world, and good in the hereafter, and save us from the torment of the fire. (Qur'an 2:201)

Conservation divorced from sustainable development is neither socially acceptable nor economically viable. "People whose very survival is precarious and whose prospects of even temporary prosperity are bleak cannot be expected to respond sympathetically to calls to subordinate their acute short term needs to the possibility of long term returns. Conservation must therefore be combined with measures to meet short-term economic needs. The vicious circle by which poverty causes ecological degradation, which in turn leads to more poverty can be broken only by development. But if it is not to be self-defeating, it must be development that is sustainable—and conservation helps to make it so."[88]

Taken as a whole, the Muslim countries are presently among the most impoverished and least developed on the earth. Life expectancy, maternal and infant mortality, literacy, and income are low in most Muslim countries, appallingly low in some. Development—the modification of the earth and its resources to satisfy human needs and improve the quality of life—is high on the list of priorities in the Muslim world. But what exactly does development mean in an Islamic context, and what are its environmental costs? This is a fundamental question that Muslim jurists must consider.

We like to describe Islam as a balanced way, neither extravagant nor ascetic, seeking the good of the present material world together with the ultimate spiritual good of the hereafter. What does this imply with regard to the lifestyles to which we aspire?

At the present time, an individual living in most countries of the Muslim world consumes a small fraction of the energy and materials consumed by his counterpart in the industrialized North, and his environmental impacts are in consequence much less severe. One of the most useful indicators of environmental impact is commercial energy consumption per person. A person in a high consumption country consumes, on average, eighteen times the commercial energy used by a person in a low consumption country, as well as causing much more pollution. The low consumption countries contain three-quarters of the earth's human population and nearly all of the world's Muslims, yet they account for only some 20 percent of commercial energy consumption.[89]

It is equally true, however, that the Muslim peoples aspire to lifestyles more like those of the industrialized nations and that in the wealthiest Muslim countries, per capita rates of consumption and pollution may well exceed those of Western Europe and North America. The industrialized nations manage to maintain their lifestyles by drawing on the resources of the entire globe. If the burgeoning populations of Indonesia, Nigeria, Pakistan, Bangladesh, and the other countries of the Muslim world are to enjoy a similar material standard of living, from where will the resources come?

Economic growth cannot go on forever. We must consider the possibility that contemporary capitalism, based on continual economic growth fuelled by interest (*ribā*), is by nature insatiably consumptive, unsustainable, and antithetical to the principles of Islam.

Apart from whether it is possible for the Muslim world to enjoy the lifestyle of the modern industrialized nations, it must be questioned whether, in light of the *sharī'a*, it is permissible. While the prophet Muhammad and his companions took great joy in the things of this world—their spouses and children, a drink of cold water, a verdant glen, a fine riding animal, and the rain falling on their shoulders—by today's standards their lives were decidedly ascetic.

The object of development is surely not to consume as much as possible, but to enable people to lead healthy, fulfilling, and ennobling lives. It is indeed possible to live a healthy and joyous life without excessive consumption of the earth's resources. This is easy to proclaim, but more difficult to practice, especially on a national or global scale. Muslim jurists must work together with specialists in the social and technical sciences to prescribe measures to stabilize and, where possible, reduce our consumption of resources while enhancing the real quality of life. They must work to ensure that development in the Muslim world is sustainable: that it meets the needs of the present without compromising the ability of future generations to meet their own needs, and that it does not threaten the integrity of nature or the survival of other species.

In seeking the good of the present, ephemeral world, we must not lose sight of the fact that the everlasting good of the hereafter must take precedence. We must not allow our quest for material welfare to be achieved at the expense of our spiritual welfare; it must be subject to ethical constraints.

Population Control

Population control is a particularly thorny issue, affecting people's most cherished individual rights and personal freedoms in addition to its political and economic ramifications.

Contraception has been widely discussed in *fiqh* literature from the outset, with almost universal consensus that it is permissible, based on the fact that the prophet Muhammad, upon him be peace and the blessing of God, did not prohibit *'azl* (*coitus interruptus*). Different views were expressed by the various *fuqahā'* concerning the stipulations and conditions pertaining to birth control (e.g., whether it is permissible without the consent of the husband, or the wife) but, with the exception of Ibn Hazm, the jurists did not dispute its basic permissibility.[90]

With the advent of concerns about overpopulation in the latter half of the present century, Muslims, like other peoples in the less developed countries, understandably felt threatened by calls for population control issuing from wealthy industrial countries, obviously keen to preserve their own standard of living and with a history of hostility toward Islamic civilizations. After their initial anxieties regarding population control, however, Muslim scholars and leaders have increasingly endorsed it as they have gained experience in dealing with the socioeconomic realities of development. Vigorous population control programs have now been adopted in a number of Muslim countries, with the blessing of the religious establishment.

The limits to population growth—What population the earth, or any one of its countries, can sustain depends both on how many people there are and on how much energy and other resources each person consumes and wastes. Muslims and non-Muslims of the "South" have been quick to point out that through excessive and wasteful use of resources, the smaller populations of the industrialized countries cause at least as much environmental damage as the larger populations of the nonindustrialized world. It was estimated in 1974 that one person in Switzerland consumed as much as forty Somalis.[91]

Many Muslims—and others—have called for the redistribution of resources as an alternative to population control. But with or without more equitable distribution of resources, we must face the fact that the rates at which we procreate will have a direct bearing on the way of life to which we and our descendants can realistically aspire. The question is not simply what number of human beings the earth can sustain, but what number it can sustain in health and happiness. Greater, perhaps, than the danger that we humans are headed for a catastrophic Malthusian denouement, is the danger that we will eventually control our population and adjust to the limits of our natural resources—but at a level that will deprive our posterity of so many of the blessings that make life worth living.

Personal freedoms—The right to enjoy the blessing of children is fundamental in Islam, and it is difficult to limit an individual's freedom to procreate by force of law. Offspring are described in the Qur'an as an adornment of this world, and as mentioned earlier, jurists have held that safeguarding of *nasl*, progeny or posterity, is one of the essential aims of Islamic law. The prophet Muhammad, upon him be peace and the blessing of God, encouraged Muslim men to "marry loving and fertile women, for I would outnumber the peoples by you."[92] Indeed, within the coming decades, Islam will have a larger number of adherents than any other faith, if population projections are to be believed; and this is due more than anything else to our birth rate. But should this *ḥadīth* be construed as a commandment or a license to multiply ad infinitum? Like everyone else on earth, Muslims are faced with a trade-off between the blessings of raising a large quantity of children and providing a high quality of upbringing, education, and health care. Policymakers will have to provide the conditions and information to enable individuals—and nations—to make rational, ethical choices in light of the relevant principles of Islamic law. If two good things prove mutually exclusive, "the greater good is to be secured by exclusion of the lesser good." "If two obligations come into conflict, that which is more fundamental is to be fulfilled." If a benefit unavoidably brings with it a detriment, "the averting of harm takes precedence over the securing of benefits."

Numerous policy issues are related to population control, and each must be assessed in light of the *sharī'a.* Universal access to maternal and child health care is essential to preserve the fundamental values of life and posterity. It has been estimated that by enabling couples to space their children and avoid high-risk pregnancies, family planning alone could save the lives of two hundred thousand women and five million children annually.[93] Improving the education of women and girls is fully consonant with the *sharī'a*, as is basic economic security. On the other hand, policies such as making contraceptives available to unmarried adolescents and adults, and the unrestricted use of abortion as an alternative to contraception have social implications that contradict basic *sharī'a* values. Delaying the legal age of marriage beyond sexual maturity is conducive to premarital sexual relations. But if early marriage is to be encouraged it must be joined with family-planning services and measures to facilitate women's education after marriage.

Genetic Resources

Biological diversity encompasses the total variety of life on Earth—all species of plants, animals, and microorganisms, the range of genetic varieties within each species, and the ecosystems of which they are components. As a living genetic resource, each species and variety is unique and irreplaceable. On the conservation of biological diversity depends the functioning of the ecological processes and life-support systems that we need for our survival. On it depend our agricultural breeding programs for protection and improvement of cultivated plants and domestic animals, many of our scientific and medical advances and technological innovations, as well as the security of our forests, rangelands, fisheries . . . and all the industries that are based on living resources.[94]

According to Islamic ethics, human beings have no right to extirpate any species of God's creatures from the face of the earth. The governing authorities have the obligation to take all measures necessary to safeguard rare and endangered species of animals and plants and the habitats or biotopes needed for the survival of viable populations.[95] By far the most efficient and effective way to safeguard biological diversity is to conserve each species within its native habitat. The need for a comprehensive network of marine and terrestrial protected areas, or *ḥimās*, has already been discussed. So have the need for comprehensive environmental planning, rehabilitation and restoration of degraded ecosystems, measures to safeguard vulnerable species and promote the recovery of species threatened with extinction, and regulations governing hunting, fishing, forestry, and other harvesting of biological resources as well as trade in wildlife and wildlife products. Here, other issues relating to the conservation of biological diversity, both philosophical and practical, will be considered.

God has made His creatures to be of service to one another, and all things are of service to humankind. We can never number the favors of our Lord. But we must not walk exultantly on the earth: "verily the creation of heaven and earth is greater than the creation of man" (Qur'an 40:57). Nowhere has God indicated that other creatures are created only—or even primarily—to serve human beings. It would be preposterous to imagine that these things were created merely for our enjoyment, and the height of arrogance to suppose that we have the right to stamp out any species in which we see no benefit! Taqi ad-Din Ahmad ibn Taymiyya remarked with regard to those Qur'anic verses in which God declares that He created His creatures for the children of Adam, "It is well known that in these creatures God has exalted purposes other than the service of man, *and greater than the service of man*; He only explains to the children of Adam what benefits there are in them and what bounty He has bestowed upon mankind."[96]

But vitally important as genetic resources are to our survival, their utilitarian value cannot be the primary legal reason for conserving them. It is not possible for us to measure the utilitarian value of any creature because we do not even know what direct benefits to ourselves may be hidden within it, much less the ramifications of its ecological role in the biosphere. The primary legal basis, therefore, for conserving each and every species must be its intrinsic value as a creation of God, a sign and wonder, and a unique and irreplaceable manifestation of His glory.[97] The prophet Muhammad, upon him be peace and the blessing of God, told of a prophet who, having been stung by

an ant, caused the entire anthill to be burned; God rebuked him, saying, "Because an ant stung you, you have destroyed a whole nation
that celebrates God's glory."[98]

Ants feature in a number of illustrations of Islamic ethics, perhaps
because they are among the smallest living creatures perceived by human eyes. When the prophet Muhammad, upon him be peace and the
blessing of God, came upon a man who had lit a fire on an anthill, he
commanded, "Put it out, put it out!"[99] But what of deadly viruses and
other pathogens? Is the absolute destruction of a deadly virus justified, or should it be preserved as a creature of God—and a potential
medicinal resource?

Another issue that Muslim jurists must address is the regulation of
predator and pest control. Killing of animals and plants is legitimate
in defense of human life, health, and property. But what are the limits? Once, when the prophet Muhammad, upon him be peace and the
blessing of God, was with some of his companions in a cave at Mina,
a viper fell among them. He ordered them to kill it; but as it fled out of
the cave, he said, "It has escaped from your evil just as you have escaped from its evil."[100] Jurists must translate this principle of restraint
into regulations to ensure that defense of our lives, our livestock, and
our crops does not lead to unnecessary killing, much less the utter
extermination of any species of God's creatures.

A major threat to biological diversity is the introduction of alien
species. Of course, ecosystems are not static, and every species anywhere was at one time not there—but introductions normally occur
gradually over long periods of time, so that ecosystems are able to
adapt. Introductions caused by humans have resulted in a significant
reduction of the earth's biological diversity. It is neither possible nor
desirable to prevent every introduction— introduced crops and domestic livestock are essential to human survival. However, it is necessary to prevent the introduction of alien species that are likely to
threaten ecosystems or native species and to control or eradicate such
species where damage has occurred.

Genetic engineering brings with it a host of ethical and practical
problems which Muslim jurists will be unable to avoid addressing. Is
genetic manipulation to be prohibited absolutely as the satanic "changing of God's creation,"[101] which may lead to environmental catastrophe? Or does it offer legitimate means to cure genetic illnesses or to
stave off starvation by enhancing the drought resistance or disease

resistance of our crops? Jurists might bear in mind Seyyed Hossein Nasr's observation that justifications are offered for most evils on the basis of the benefits they bring, whereas if, like intoxicants and gambling, the harm in them is greater them the good, the *sharī'a* requires their prohibition.[102] If, on the other hand, genetic engineering is permissible within limits, how are these limits to be defined? What safeguards are necessary? And what are the territorial rights of the country—and local community—from which the genetic material has been obtained, to a fair share of ensuing profits, as well as the intellectual rights of individuals and laboratories to patent genetically engineered products?

Animal Rights

Animals are distinguished from other natural resources in that, as sentient beings, they have certain legal rights in Islamic law. Not only is abuse of the resource prohibited, but also the abuse of individuals. The rights or legal claims of animals are less comprehensive than those of humans. Islamic law explicitly permits hunting, fishing, and the raising of bees and livestock for honey, work, milk and meat, wool, hair, and leather. But it forbids that God's creatures be used cruelly or wastefully. There is no prohibition on eating meat in Islam, provided that animals are given the conditions for good and healthy lives and that they are slaughtered or hunted as mercifully as possible.[103]

When all the losses of sentient life associated with farming and ranching are taken into account, including not only animals that are slaughtered, but also their parasites, and all the insect, bird, and mammal pests that must be killed to raise a viable crop, all the microscopic creatures in the soil that are crushed by ploughing or trampling, and all the lives affected by the biological controls and chemicals we use, we cannot escape the fact that our lives involve the death of an appalling amount of sentient life. Of course we are morally bound to minimize this suffering and destruction. But we must recognize that agriculture is at least as costly in terms of life and suffering—and environmental impact—as is the raising and harvesting of livestock.

To live in this world we must take from it, for life must feed on life to live. The daily bread and meat from which we draw our strength and build our flesh is at the cost of a myriad lives. How shall we redeem their killing? If we do not use this strength to give back more than we have taken, then what are we ourselves but parasites? But if, in slaughtering and eating, we take God's name in gratitude and render thanks by building beauty, teaching truth, bringing new life to the land, or striving in His cause, we may transmute their lives into yet more life, and give meaning to their deaths, and sanctify them. Then the selfsame act of slaughter will no more be an act of desecration, but an offering of sacrifice.[104]

Many conservationists would exclude the subject of animal rights from discussions of conservation, because it has tended to confuse the conservation of species with purely ethical concerns relating to the treatment of individuals. This is partly a reaction to the positions of some animal rights activists against hunting, the raising of livestock, and the eating of meat, and stems partly from the fact that in contemporary Western legal theory animals do not have legal rights. Among the difficulties with the concept of animal rights are the absence of any universal criterion to determine what those rights are and the fact that animals do not have "standing" or representation in court.

In Islamic law, however, it is hardly possible to avoid discussion of the rights of animals in the context of conservation. The rights of animals, *ḥuqūq al-bahā'im wa 'l-hayawān*, are enshrined as one of the categories of *ḥuqūq al-'ibād*, the rights of God's servants, that is, human beings and animals.[105] These rights are detailed in numerous *aḥādīth* and are summarized in the following passage by 'Izz al-Din ibn 'Abd al-Salam:

> The rights of livestock and animals with regard to their treatment by man: These are that he spend on them the provision that their kinds require, even if they have aged or sickened such that no benefit comes from them; that he not burden them beyond what they can bear; that he not put them together with anything by which they would be injured, whether of their own kind or other species, and whether by breaking their bones or butting or wounding; that he slaughter them with kindness if he slaughters them, and neither flay their skins nor break their bones until their bodies have become cold and their lives have passed away; that he not slaughter their young within their sight; that he set them apart individually; that he make comfortable their resting places and watering places; that he put their males and females together during their mating seasons; that he not discard those which he takes in hunting; and neither shoot them with anything that breaks their bones nor bring about their destruction by any means that renders their meat unlawful to eat.[106]

With the exception of the two last clauses, which pertain to the hunting of wild animals, these rights apply to domestic animals and captive individuals of wild species. Our ethical obligations naturally apply primarily to those creatures whose welfare is most dependent on our actions. In the past, most wild populations were little affected by the acts of human beings. Now, their welfare and survival are increasingly, sometimes utterly, dependent on acts of humanity.

Although the rights of animals are limited, they are definitely meant to be safeguarded by the force of the law—not only through the office of the *muḥtāsib*, but also, in the view of the majority of jurists, by the courts. The governing authorities are obliged to intervene for the protection of animals whenever they are abused; to prohibit their killing by illicit methods or for illicit purposes, and to protect them from cruelty and wanton destruction. If an animal's owner mistreats it or fails to provide it adequate maintenance with food, water, shelter, and the like, the governing authorities are to compel him to provide for its needs.[107] The question of standing has been addressed as follows.

Whereas the predominant position in the Hanafi school of law, much like contemporary Western law, held that it is not possible for animals to be represented in court because they are analogous to crops, Muwaffaq al-Din Ibn Qudama argued for the majority of Sunni schools that animals are in reality analogous to slaves, and that their rights are to be safeguarded by the courts.[108] In 1972 Christopher D. Stone argued that, like various inanimate objects such as corporations, ships at sea, and municipalities, natural objects should have the right to legal representation in United States law.[109]

If these rights of animals are secured, this will have a revolutionary impact on modern industrial farming and fishing practices. It will require major changes in the ways that biological and medical research and trade in wildlife are conducted, and in the design and management of abattoirs, livestock markets, zoos, and pet shops. Muslim jurists will have to look closely at the implications of the *sharīʻa* with regard to the use and abuse of living beings, and take bold stands to rectify the wrongs. They will also have to work together with specialists in veterinary medicine, wildlife biology, and related fields to translate the general precepts of the *sharīʻa* into detailed and specific regulations to secure the well-being of each species in light of its nutritional, thermal, spatial, psychological, and other needs.

Under what conditions should people be permitted to keep wildlife in captivity? What regulations should govern trade in wildlife and wildlife products? Predator and pest control? Hunting, trapping, and fishing? According to a principle of Islamic law, "hunting is permissible, except for sport, because killing for sport is *sarf* and *badhakh* and destruction of the favors God has bestowed upon His servants."[110] What measures are appropriate to prevent killing for sport? This is largely a matter of the hunter's intent, and it is not easy to regulate. At what point does the hunter's pleasure in his tracking and stalking skills, or the excitement of the chase, become blameworthy killing for sport? Should huntable species be narrowly defined as those which are customarily taken for food? Should penalties be imposed for wastage of game and fish? Should trophy hunting be prohibited as conducive to frivolous killing, or used as a means to enhance the value of wildlife resources and generate funds for wildlife conservation? These are questions that jurists in every Muslim country must examine carefully and strive to answer.

International Cooperation and Conflict

The natural elements and processes that support life on Earth do not recognize the political boundaries imposed by man. This is particularly clear in the case of migratory species, international river basins, marine resources, and air pollution, including global warming, ozone depletion, and acid rain. Regional and international treaties and agreements have been drawn up to conserve shared resources and avert environmental disasters. Recognizing that, in line with basic principles which forbid oppression and aggression, no nation has the right to deprive another of the means of subsistence. Muslim jurists should participate actively in the framing of such agreements.

They should apply the precedents and the general principles of *siyār* to international environmental issues, to help ensure that development undertaken in one country does not lead to damage or degradation in the natural environment or resources of another country.

Second, there is the need for creative approaches to conflict resolution, to settle international disputes over environmental impacts and the use of shared natural resources. Jurists must fight the tendency of nations and their rulers to retaliate in kind when wronged. The prophet Muhammad, upon him be peace and the blessing of God, said, "Do not be a people who say, 'if others do good to us, we will do good to them, and if they wrong us, we will wrong them.' Rather, make up your minds to do good to those who do you good, and do not wrong those who do you evil."[111]

Third, there is the need to secure the natural environment and the earth's resources from severe or irreparable damage caused by military actions. Muslim legal scholars have ruled that God's creatures possess inviolability (*ḥurma*) which pertains even in war: "The Prophet, upon him be peace and the blessing of God, forbade the killing of bees and any captured livestock, for killing them is a form of corruption included in what God has prohibited in His saying, 'And when he turns away, he hastens through the land to cause corruption therein and to destroy the tilth and herds: And God loves not corruption' (Qur'an 2:205). For they are animals with the spirit of life, so it is not lawful to kill them. . . . They are animals possessing inviolability just as do women and children."[112]

Muslim jurists need to issue unequivocal condemnation of scorched-earth tactics and the use of nuclear and other weapons of mass destruction, to strive to ensure that their governments abjure them, and to work together with other countries for their elimination.

Establishment of the Discipline

The Gap between the Professions of Islamic Law and Conservation

The greatest single obstacle to establishing the discipline of Islamic environmental law is the wide gulf that separates the conservation professions from those of Islamic law. The origin of this gap is the progressive marginalization of the *fuqahā'* that has taken place throughout the Muslim world over the past century or so. As the business of administration, policy, planning, management, and legislation has been taken over by legislators, technicians, and politicians with secular training, the *fuqahā'* have been isolated as professors in the universities and colleges, as scholars and writers. In most countries even the judges in the *sharī'a* courts have no jurisdiction over cases pertaining to environmental problems.

This is not to say that the *fuqahā'* are unconcerned about environmental issues. Indeed, a number of jurists are not only concerned, but also have wide knowledge of the relevant *aḥādīth* and *aḥkam.* Nor is there a lack of environmental specialists—planners, administrators, engineers, resource managers, lawyers, and others—who are passionately committed to implementing the *sharī'a.*

The problem is that environmental law requires not only legal rulings and precedents from centuries gone by or ideal statements of general principle, but creative, practical, detailed application of these precedents and principles to specific environmental, socioeconomic, and technological problems. In other words, it requires *ijtiḥād*. One cannot be a *mujtāhid* without being thoroughly grounded in both the substantive law, *fiqh*, and legal methodology, *uṣūl al-fiqh*, as well as having a thorough knowledge of the issues and problems at hand. No matter how sincere and well intentioned, attempts at *ijtiḥād* by environmental specialists without qualifications in Islamic jurisprudence are invalid, and attempts at *ijtiḥād* by jurists without practical experience in environmental issues are irrelevant.

Bridging the Gap

Among the first steps that must be taken is to build a network of people concerned about environmental law in Islam, including *fuqahā'* and *'ulamā'* as well as members of the conservation and environmental protection professions, planners, lawyers, economists, social scientists, educators, and others. Such a network may exchange information both formally and informally. A web site on the internet would be a most useful vehicle of communication for those who have access to it, and periodic workshops and conferences as well as a professional journal would serve as catalysts for research and discussion.

Together with the building of a network of people, a compilation of sources and references on Islamic environmental law should be initiated. To begin with, books, articles, masters' theses, and doctoral dissertations pertaining to the subject should be compiled, together with all the references listed in their bibliographies. People in the network could then be invited to submit annotated bibliographies and reviews. The entire list should be posted on the web site referred to above, and periodically updated. It would also be advisable to have all source materials collected physically in a library of Islamic environmental law.

Training materials and courses in environmental issues should be designed for *fuqahā'* and made available to them in different Muslim countries. These materials and courses could be designed by people selected from the network, perhaps with the assistance of international groups of experts such as the World Conservation Union's Commission on Environmental Law and its Commission on Environmental Education and Social Policy. At the same time, training materials and courses in Islamic jurisprudence should be made available to the conservation and environmental protection agencies, planners, and administrators in Muslim countries. These courses and training materials would also serve as the basis for incorporating basic principles of environmental policy in *fiqh* curricula and incorporation of Islamic legal principles in environmental studies curricula in countries of the Muslim world.

Among the most important steps that need to be taken to bridge the gap between the professions of environmental conservation and Islamic law is for Muslim jurists to participate in tackling and resolving environmental issues. This requires employment of *fuqahā'* in agencies charged with developing and implementing environmental legislation, at least in those countries which recognize the *sharī'a* as a source of legislation. *Ijtihād* cannot occur through hypothetical discussion; it requires real problems for which solutions are proposed, tested, and, as they succeed or fail, progressively refined.

Development of a Curriculum for the Profession

The profession of Islamic environmental law will require academic degree programs to prepare the professionals to fill its posts. To begin with, one or more universities should be approached to initiate a course of study. The initial curriculum would be drawn largely from the compilation of sources and references and the training materials already discussed, and would have much in common with the curriculum of Islamic economics. It would have to be multidisciplinary, as the profession requires equally strong grounding in the religious, social, natural, and technical sciences.

Among the religious sciences, both *fiqh* and *uṣūl al-fiqh* will be essential. *Fiqh* would provide the substantive material, with emphasis on the *mu'āmalāt* or transactions. *Uṣūl al-fiqh* must be taught in such a manner as to provide a methodology for the application of legal principles to new problems, not as theoretical justification for juristic rulings. Taught properly, *uṣūl al-fiqh* would not only enable scholars to apply legal principles with integrity, versatility, and creativity; it would also help them to appreciate and respect the reasoning behind other opinions and approaches with which they may not necessarily agree. Proficiency in the Arabic language is a prerequisite to reading Islamic texts and references, and Arabic would be integral to the curriculum.

The social sciences must provide a sound understanding of the relationship between people and their environment. Human ecology and resource economics are essential subjects. Both qualitative and quantitative methods of sociological research and analysis should be taught. Related skills include communication and law enforcement.

Of the natural and applied sciences, a basic understanding of biology and geomorphology is essential, with emphasis on the practical applications to environmental planning, environmental impact assessment, management of wildlife, soils, rangelands, forests, watersheds and wetlands, and marine and coastal resources. Knowledge of comparative environmental legislation is required to keep abreast of developments around the world.

It is important that the curriculum focus on live issues in the real world rather than idealized arcadian or utopian visions, and that teaching methods equip students with problem-solving skills.

One of the practical difficulties in initiating a new profession is finding the professors. Until there is a large enough number of graduates to fill both managerial posts and university chairs, there will be a lack of teaching personnel who have received integrated education in Islamic environmental law. Interim solutions should include team teaching, in which *fuqahā'* and environmental professionals teach courses together, and multidisciplinary courses in which students learn from a wide variety of experts in different fields. Another useful approach, used with considerable success at the International Islamic University in Malaysia, is to require students to take double majors or a major and minor subject in which they combine *sharī'a* studies with the applied or social sciences.

Prospects for the Profession of Islamic Environmental Law

In view of the rapid increase in environmental awareness and the strong environmental concerns of many Muslim thinkers, there is little doubt that the discipline of Islamic environmental law will soon be recognized. We would be well advised, however, to anticipate its needs so as to avoid repetition of ideals and generalities or reacting to sectoral needs and emergencies in a piecemeal and haphazard manner. We should act promptly and with foresight, to plan for the education and training of professionals and professors, prepare balanced and comprehensive curricula, and ensure that a practical, equitable, and implementable system of environmental legislation is derived from the noble principles of the *sharīʿa.*

Notes

1. Rigorously authenticated *ḥadīth* related by Muhammad ibn Isma'il Al-Bukhari (194–256 H.) from An-Nu'man ibn Bashir.

2. See Abu Ja'far Muhammad ibn Jarir At-Tabari (d. 310 H. / 922 C.E.) and Isma'il ibn 'Amr Ibn Kathir (d. 774 H. / 1372 C.E.), in their respective *tafsīrs* of the words *rabb al-'ālamīn* in *Sūrat al-Fatiha*. Also see Mawil Izzidien Samarrai, "Environmental Protection and Islam," *Journal of the Faculty of Arts and Humanities* (Jeddah) 5 (1985): 37.

3. 'Izz al-Din ibn 'Abd al-Salam (d. 660 H. / 1263 C.E.), *Qawā'id al-Aḥkām fi Masāliḥ al-Anām, (fasl fī bayān masāliḥ al-mu'āmalāt wa't-tasarrufāt.)* See also Hamd Al-Khattabi's commentary in *Ma'ālim al-Sunān* on the prophet Muhammad's command to cease killing black dogs, "The black dog was one of the *ummas* (communities, societies). Thus it was not created but for some good purpose, so the obliteration of its kind must create some deficiency (*khalāl*) in nature."

4. *Ḥadīth* of unsubstantiated authenticity related by Abu Bakr Ahmad ibn Husayn Al-Bayhaqi (d. 458 H. / 1066 C.E.), in *Shu'ab al-Imān*, chapter 49 *(bāb fī ta'ātu lī 'l-amr) fasl fī nasihat al-wilāt wa wa'zihim*, and by Wali ad-Din Muhammad ibn 'Abd-Allah Al-Khatib at-Tabrizi, in *Mishkat al-Masābiḥ*, compiled in 737 H. / 1337 C.E., *kitāb al-adāb, bāb al-shafāqa wa 'r-rahmat 'ala 'l-khalq, ḥadīths* nos. 4998, 4999, from Anas ibn Malik and 'Abd-Allah ibn Mas'ud.

5. Abubakr A. Bagader, Abdullatif T. E. El-Sabbagh, Mohamed A. Al-Glayand, and Mawil Y. I. Samarrai, in collaboration with Othman A. Llewellyn, *Environmental Protection in Islam*, 2d rev. ed., IUCN Environmental Policy and Law paper no. 20, World Conservation Union / Meteorology and Environmental Protection Administration of the Kingdom of Saudi Arabia (Gland, Switzerland, and Cambridge: IUCN, 1994), 1–2. Also see Othman A. Llewellyn, "Islamic Jurisprudence and Environmental Planning," *Journal of Research in Islamic Economics* (Jeddah) 1, 2 (1984): 29; Othman Llewellyn, "Desert Reclamation and Islamic Law," *The Muslim Scientist* (Plainfield, Ind.) 11, no. 1 (1982): 10; and Othman Llewellyn, "Shari'ah Values Pertaining to Landscape Planning and Design," in *Islamic Architecture and Urbanism* (Dammam, Saudi Arabia: King Faisal University, 1983), 32.

6. O. Llewellyn, unpublished letter; Samarrai, "Environmental Protection and Islam"; Bagader et al., *Environmental Protection in Islam*, 5–6, 9–10.

7. O. Llewellyn, unpublished letter; Qur'an, *Sūrat al-Dukhān, āyāt* 38–39, *Sūrat al-Anbiyā'*, *āyāt* 16–18, *Sūrat Ṣād, āyāt* 26–28, *Sūrat Al 'Imrān, āyāt* 190–91, *Sūrat Ibrahim, āya* 19, *Sūrat al-Naḥl, āya* 3, *Sūrat al-'Ankabūt, āya* 44, *Sūrat al-Jāthiya, āya* 22, *Sūrat al-Taghābun, āya* 3, etc.

8. Rigorously authenticated *ḥadīth* related by Muslim and Abu Dawud from Shaddad ibn Aws; and rigorously authenticated *ḥadīth* related by Al-Bukhari and Muslim from Abu Hurayra.

9. *Ḥadīth* related by Abu Dawud and At-Tirmidhi from 'Abd-Allah ibn 'Amr.

10. Rigorously authenticated *ḥadīth* related by Muslim from Abu Sa'id al-Khudri.

11. Abdal Hamid Fitzwilliam-Hall, "Exploring the Islamic Environmental Ethic." This paper, not yet published, eloquently discusses the concept of *khilāfa* and its interpretation by modern scholars, with specific reference to Sayyid Qutb, *Fī Zilāl al-*

Qur'an, commentary on *Sūrat al-Māīda*, *āyāt* 55–56, *Sūrat al-Baqara*, *āya* 30, etc.

12. Qur'an, *Sūrat al-Tīn*, *āyāt* 4–8.

13. O. Llewellyn, unpublished letter; Qur'an, *Sūrat al-Zalzala*, *āyāt* 7–8; rigorously authenticated *ḥadīth* related by Al-Bukhari and Muslim from Abdullah ibn 'Umar.

14. Rigorously authenticated *ḥadīth* related by Muslim from Abu Malik Al-Ash'ari.

15. O. Llewellyn, unpublished letter, cf. Abu Yusuf Ya'qub ibn Ibrahim (d. 182 H. / 798 C.E.), *Kitab al-Kharaj*, opening exhortation.

16. Qur'an, *Sūrat al-Ahzab*, *āyāt* 72.

17. O. Llewellyn, unpublished letter; Bagader et al., *Environmental Protection in Islam*, 30.

18. Qur'an, *Sūrat al-Zalzala*, *āyāt* 7–8; also see *Sūrat al-Jāthiya*, *āya* 15, *Sūrat al-Najm*, *āya* 31, etc.; Llewellyn, "Islamic Jurisprudence and Environmental Planning," 28; Llewellyn, "Desert Reclamation and Islamic Law," 10; Llewellyn, "Shari'ah Values Pertaining to Landscape Planning and Design," 32; Bagader et al., *Environmental Protection in Islam*, 17, 20,30.

19. See Taj ad-Din 'Abd al-Wahhab ibn 'Ali As-Subki (d. 771 H.), *Al-Ashba wa 'n-Nazā'ir*; Jalal al-Din 'Abd al-Rahman Al-Suyuti (d. 911 H.), *Al-Ashba wa 'n-Nazā'ir*; Zayn al-'Abidin ibn al-Nujaym (d. 970 H.), *Al-Ashba wa 'n-Nazā'ir*; *Majallat al-Aḥkām al-'Adliyah* (the Ottoman *Corpus of Judicial Rules*, compiled on the basis of major Hanafi legal works and enacted in 1293 H. / 1876 C.E.).

20. Taqi ad-Din Ahmad ibn 'Abd al-Halim ibn Taymiyah (d. 728 H. / 1328 C.E.), *Al-Siyāsat al-Shar'īa, al-bāb al-thānī: al-amwāl, al-fasl al-khāmis: al-zulm al-wāqi' min al-wilat wa-'ra'iya*; Llewellyn, "Desert Reclamation in Islamic Law," 13; Bagader et al., *Environmental Protection in Islam*, 20.

21. As-Suyuti, quoted in 'Uthman ibn Fudi, *Bayān Wujūb al-hijra 'ala 'l-'ibad*, ed. and trans. F. H. El-Masri (Khartoum: Khartoum University Press; New York: Oxford University Press, 1978), Arabic text, p. 82, English translation, p. 104; Bagader et al., *Environmental Protection in Islam*, 20; Llewellyn, "Desert Reclamation in Islamic Law," 13–14.

22. 'Izz al-Din ibn 'Abd al-Salam, *Qawā'id al-Aḥkām fi Masāliḥ al-Anām: fasl fī tanfidh tasarrufat al-bugha wa a'immat al-jur lima wafaq al-ḥaqq li-darūrat al-'amma.* Also see Bagader et al., *Environmental Protection in Islam*, 21; Llewellyn, "Desert Reclamation in Islamic Law," 14.

23. Bagader et al., *Environmental Protection in Islam*, 21; S. Waqar Ahmad Husaini, *Islamic Environmental Systems Engineering* (London: MacMillan, 1980), 80–81, reference to *Majallah*, article 30.

24. Llewellyn, "Islamic Jurisprudence and Environmental Planning," 30.

25. Abu 'l-Faraj 'Abd al-Rahman ibn Rajab (d. 795 H. / 1393 C.E.), *Al-Qawa'id: qa'idah* no. 86.

26. Bagader et al., *Environmental Protection in Islam*, 18; Llewellyn, "Desert Reclamation and Islamic Law," 11.

27. *Ḥadīth* related by the Imam Malik in the *Muwatta'* with an incomplete (*mursal*) chain of transmission, and by Al-Hakim in the *Mustadrak* with a complete chain, which he described as rigorously authenticated according to the criteria of Muslim.

28. Llewellyn, "Islamic Jurisprudence and Environmental Planning," 39; Bagader

et al., *Environmental Protection in Islam*, 18; Llewellyn, "Desert Reclamation and Islamic Law," 11; Llewellyn, "Shari'ah-Values Pertaining to Landscape Planning and Design," p. 34.

29. *Athar* related by Yahya ibn Adam al-Qurashi in *Kitab al-Kharaj*, from Sa'id ad-Dabbi. Also see Bagader et al., *Environmental Protection in Islam*, 3; Llewellyn, "Desert Reclamation in Islamic Law," 11; Llewellyn, "Islamic Jurisprudence and Environmental Planning,"36.

30. In addition to the *āyāt* quoted above, see the Qur'an, *Sūrat al-Qaṣaṣ*, *āya* 77, *Sūrat al-Shu'arā'*, *āyāt* 151–52, *Sūrat al-Baqara*, *āya* 205, *Surat al-Isra'*, *āyāt* 26–27. Also see Bagader et al., *Environmental Protection in Islam*, 17; Llewellyn, "Desert Reclamation and Islamic Law," 13.

31. *Ḥadīth* of unsubstantiated authenticity related by the Imam Ahmad in the *Musnad* and by ibn Majah from 'Abd-Allah ibn 'Amr, *Mishkat al-Masabih*, *ḥadīth* no. 427. Also see Bagader et al., *Environmental Protection in Islam*, 7; Llewellyn, "Desert Reclamation and Islamic Law," 13.

32. *Majallat al-Aḥkām al-'Adliyah*, article no. 58; Bagader et al., *Environmental Protection in Islam*, 19.

33. J. C. Wilkinson, "Islamic Water Law with special Reference to Oasis Settlement," *Journal of Arid Environments* (London), 1978, 95.

34. *Ḥadīth*s related by the Imam Ahmad, At-Tirmidhi and Abu Dawud from Sa'id ibn Zayd, with a sound (*jayyid*) chain of transmission, by Al-Bukhari from Aishah, and by Al-Shafi'i from Tawus (*mursal*). *Mishkat al-Masabih*, *ahādith* nos. 2944, 2991, 3003.

35. See Muwaffaq ad-Din Abdullah ibn Qudamah, Al-Mughni, *Kitāb iḥyā' al-mawāt*; Ibn Rushd, *Bidāyat al-Mujtāhid* / Al-Qarafi; Othman A. Llewellyn, "Conservation in Islamic Law," in *National Legal Strategies for Protected Areas Conservation and Management*, Fourth World Congress on National Parks and Protected Areas, Caracas, Venezuela, 1992, 45–46; Bagader et al., *Environmental Protection in Islam*, 24–25.

36. Al-Mughnī, *Kitāb iḥyā' al-mawāt: fasl wa ma qaruba min al-'amir wa ta'allaqa bimasaliḥihi* . . . , Ibn Rushd or Al-Qarafi.

37. Al-Mughnī, *Kitāb iḥyā' al-mawāt: fasl wa ma nadiba 'anhu al-ma' min al-jazā'ir* . . . ; Bagader et al., *Environmental Protection in Islam*, 24, 31; Llewellyn, "Islamic Jurisprudence and Environmental Planning," 44–46.

38. Bagader et al., *Environmental Protection in Islam*, 19; Llewellyn, "Islamic Jurisprudence and Environmental Planning," 42.

39. *Ḥadīth* related by Abu Dawud, Al-Tirmidhi and Al-Nasa'i from 'Aisha; Also see *Majallat al-Aḥkām al-'Adliyah*, articles nos. 85, 87, and 88; Bagader et al., *Environmental Protection in Islam*, 19.

40. Graham Child and John Grainger, *A System Plan for Protected Areas for Wildlife Conservation and Sustainable Rural Development in Saudi Arabia* (Gland, Switerzerland: National Commission for Wildlife Conservation and Development and IUCN, The World Conservation Union, 1990), 109.

41. *Caring for the Earth: A Strategy for Sustainable Living* (Gland, Switzerland: Published in partnership by IUCN, UNEP, and WWF, 1991), 42.

42. Ibid., 58; also see *Global Biodiversity Strategy*, 82.

43. Bagader et al., *Environmental Protection in Islam*, 30–31.

44. *Caring for the Earth*, 9–10.

45. Child and Grainger, *A System Plan for Protected Areas*, 107. A fugitive resource is not fixed in time or space; it may move from place to place and be fleeting, transient or ephemeral.

46. On Islamic water law, see Michael E. Norvelle, "Water Use and Ownership According to Texts of Hanbali Fiqh" (Master's ThesisMcGill University, 1974); Michael E. Norvelle, "The Development of Water Law in the Arid Lands of the Middle East and the United States: A Comparative Study," in *Arid Lands Today and Tomorrow, Proceedings, International Resource and Development Conference*, Tucson, Arizona, 1985 (Boulder, Colo.: Westview Press, 1988); Wilkinson, "Islamic Water Law with special Reference to Oasis Settlement," 87–96; Child and Grainger, *A System Plan for Protected Areas*, 107–10; Bagader et al., *Environmental Protection in Islam*, 6–7.

47. Child and Grainger, *A System Plan for Protected Areas*, 110.

48. Rigorously authenticated *ḥadīth* related by Al-Bukhari and Muslim from Abu Hurayra, *Mishkat al-Masābiḥ*, *ḥadīth* no. 2994; Al-Mughnī, *Kitāb iḥyā' al-mawāt: fasl fī aḥkām al-miya*; Llewellyn, "Conservation in Islamic Law," 46–47.

49. Llewellyn, "Conservation in Islamic Law," 47.

50. Ibid., 43–48; Bagader et al., *Environmental Protection in Islam*, 19.

51. Child and Grainger, *A System Plan for Protected Areas*, 110

52. Child and Grainger, *A System Plan for Protected Areas*, 143–59, 169–72; Llewellyn, "Conservation in Islamic Law," 46–48; Bagader et al., *Environmental Protection in Islam*, 30–31.

53. Rigorously authenticated *ḥadīth* related by Al-Bukhari and Muslim from 'Abd-Allah ibn 'Abbas; Bagader et al., *Environmental Protection in Islam*, 26.

54. Rigorously authenticated *ḥadīth* related by Muslim from Jabir ibn 'Abd-Allah; Bagader et al., *Environmental Protection in Islam*, 26.

55. Rigorously authenticated *ḥadīth* related by Muslim from Abu Hurayra; Bagader et al., *Environmental Protection in Islam*, 26.

56. Patricia R. Gasperetti, "Natural History Survey of the Makkah By-Pass—Preliminary Report," *Journal of the Saudi Arabian Natural History Society* 2, no. 6 (July 1986): 7–27.

57. Bagader et al., *Environmental Protection in Islam*, 26.

58. Al-Mughnī, *Kitāb iḥyā' al-mawāt: fasl wa ma qaruba min al-'amir wa ta'allaqa bimasalihihi. . . .*

59. Bagader et al., *Environmental Protection in Islam*, 26–27; Llewellyn, "Conservation in Islamic Law," 51–52; 'Uthman ibn Fudi, *Bayān Wujūb al-hijra 'ala 'l-'ibad.*

60. Omar Draz, *Rangeland Development in Saudi Arabia* (Riyadh University, 1965); Omar Draz, *The Hima System of Range Reserves in the Arabian Peninsula: Its Possibilities in Range Improvement and Conservation Projects in the Middle East*, FAO/PL:PFC/13.11,FAO (Rome, 1969); Child and Grainger, *A System Plan for Protected Areas*, 94.

61. Rigorously authenticated *ḥadīth* related by Al-Bukhari and Muslim from Nu'man ibn Bashir.

62. Muhammad ibn Idris al-Shafi'i (150–204 H. / 767–820 C.E.), *Kitab al-Umm*; Al-Mughnī, *Kitāb iḥyā' al-mawāt: fasl fi 'l-ḥimā.*

63. Rigorously authenticated *ḥadīth* related by Al-Bukhari from 'Abd-Allah ibn 'Abbas (*Mishkat al-Masābiḥ*, *ḥadīth* no. 2992); Al-Mughnī, *kitāb iḥyā' al-mawāt: fasl fi 'l-ḥimā*; John Grainger and Othman Llewellyn, "Sustainable Use: Lessons from a Cultural Tradition in Saudi Arabia," *Parks: The International Journal for Protected Area Managers* (Gland) 4, no. 3 (1994): 8–9.

64. Rigorously authenticated *ḥadīth* related by Muslim from Abu Hurayra; Abu Yusuf, *Kitāb al-Kharāj, fasl fi 'l-kala' wa 'l-murūj*; Al-Mughnī, *Kitāb iḥyā' al-mawāt: fasl fi 'l-ḥimā*; Bagader et al., *Environmental Protection in Islam*, 25–26.

65. Al-Mughnī, *Kitāb iḥyā' al-mawāt: fasl fi 'l-ḥimā.*

66. Abu Yusuf, *Kitab al-Kharaj: fasl fi 'l-kala' wa 'l-muruj*; Al-Mughnī, *Kitāb iḥyā' al-mawāt: fasl fi 'l-ḥimā.*

67. 'Uthman ibn Fudi, *Bayān Wujūb al-hijrah 'ala 'l-'ibad.*

68. On customary *ḥimā*s in Saudi Arabia, see Draz, *The Hima System of Range Reserves in the Arabian Peninsula*, and Grainger and Llewellyn, "Sustainable Use," 8–11.

69. Grainger and Llewellyn, "Sustainable Use," 11–12.

70. Ibid., 12–15; Llewellyn, "Conservation in Islamic Law," 49–50.

71. Rigorously authenticated *ḥadīth* related by Al-Bukhari and Muslim from 'Abd-Allah ibn 'Umar.

72. Bagader et al., *Environmental Protection in Islam*, 27; Llewellyn, "Desert Reclamation and Islamic Law," 19; Llewellyn, "Conservation in Islamic Law," 52–53.

73. Llewellyn, "Conservation in Islamic Law," 53; Bagader et al., *Environmental Protection in Islam*, 27.

74. Bagader et al., *Environmental Protection in Islam*, 25; Llewellyn, "Desert Reclamation and Islamic Law," 15; Llewellyn, "Conservation in Islamic Law," 50.

75. Bagader et al., *Environmental Protection in Islam*, 25; Llewellyn, "Desert Reclamation and Islamic Law," 15–16; Llewellyn, "Conservation in Islamic Law," 51.

76. Rigorously authenticated *ḥadīth* related by Muslim from Abu Sa'id al-Khudri.

77. Bagader et al., *Environmental Protection in Islam*, 30.

78. Ibid.

79. See *Al-Kawākib al-Durriyah*; 'Uthman ibn Fudi, *Bayān Wujūb al-hijra 'ala 'l-'ibad.*

80. See E. I. J. Rosenthal, *Political Thought in Medieval Islam* (Cambridge: Cambridge University Press, 1958); Husaini, *Islamic Environmental Systems Engineering*, 92, reference to Taqi ad-Din Ahmad ibn Taymiyya.

81. Bagader et al., *Environmental Protection in Islam*, 21; Llewellyn, "Desert Reclamation and Islamic Law," 19–20. On the *ḥisba* and the *muhtasib*, see Taj ad-Din As-Subki, *Mu'id al-Ni'ām wa Mabda' al-Niqām*, and Muhammad ibn Muhammad ibn al-Ukhuwah, *Ma'alim al-Qurbah fi Ahkam al-Ḥisba.*

82. Rigorously authenticated *ḥadīth* related by Muslim from Abu Hurayra.

83. Abu 'Ubayd Al-Qasim ibn Sallam (d. 224 H.), *Kitāb al-Amwāl*; Llewellyn, "Islamic Jurisprudence and Environmental Planning," 45.

84. Ali al-Sammani Muhammad 'Umar.

85. Child, and Grainger, *A System Plan for Protected Areas.*

86. *Caring for the Earth*, 69–72.

87. Ibid.

88. *World Conservation Strategy: Living Resource Conservation for Sustainable Development* (Gland, Switzerland: IUCN, 1980), article 1:11.

89. *Caring for the Earth*, 45 (box 8) and 194–97 (annex 5).

90. Basim F. Musallam, "The Islamic Sanction of Contraception," in *Population and Its Problems: A Plain Man's Guide*, ed. H. B. Parry (Oxford: Clarendon Press, 1974), 300–310.

91. *World Conservation Strategy*, 1, introduction (box: "Why a World Conservation Strategy Is Needed").

92. Rigorously authenticated *ḥadīth* related by Abu Dawud and An-Nasa'i from Ma'qil ibn Yasar (*Mishkat* no. 3091).

93. *Caring for the Earth*, 51.

94. *World Conservation Strategy*, executive summary 1b, article 1:7.

95. Bagader et al., *Environmental Protection in Islam*, 6, 10, 23–24, 29.

96. Taqi ad-Din Ahmad ibn Taymiyya, *Majmu' al-Fatawa*, 2:96–97, quoted in Samarrai, "Environmental Protection and Islam," 37–38; Bagader et al., *Environmental Protection in Islam*, 5.

97. Samarrai, "Environmental Protection and Islam," 37; Bagader et al., *Environmental Protection in Islam*, 5–6.

98. Rigorously authenticated *ḥadīth*, related by Al-Bukhari and Muslim and others from Abu Hurayra.

99. *Ḥadīth*; M. Al-Khidr Husayn p. 85, English supplement p. 29; Llewellyn, O., "Islamic Jurisprudence and Environmental Planning", p. 35

100. *Ḥadīth*; see M. Anas az-Zarqa.

101. Qur'an, *Sūrat al-Nisā'*, *āya* 119.

102. Seyyed Hossein Nasr, personal communication (at the conference on Islam and ecology), re. Qur'an, *Sūrat al-Baqara*, *āya* 219.

103. *Aḥādīth*; 'Izz al-Din ibn 'Abd al-Salam, *Qawā'id al-Aḥkām fi Masāliḥ al-Anām: al-qism al-thalith min aqsām al-darb al-thānī min jalb al-masāliḥ wa dar' al-mafāsid.*

104. Llewellyn, unpublished letter.

105. 'Izz al-Din ibn 'Abd al-Salam, *Qawā'id al-Aḥkām fi Masāliḥ al-Anām*, ed. Mahmud ibn at-Talamid Ash-Shinqiti (Beirut: Dar al-Kutub al-'Ilmiyah, Beirut), 1:141; Llewellyn, "Desert Reclamation and Islamic Law," 12; Othman A. Llewellyn, rejoinder in *Journal of Research in Islamic Economics* (Jeddah) 3, no. 1 (1985): 90; Bagader et al., *Environmental Protection in Islam*, 11, 35.

106. 'Izz al-Din ibn 'Abd al-Salam, *Qawā'id al-Aḥkām fi Masāliḥ al-Anām*, 1:141.

107. Bagader et al., *Environmental Protection in Islam*, 23.

108. Al-Mughnī, *Kitāb al-nafāqa, fasl wa man malaka bahima. . . .*

109. Christopher D. Stone, *Should Trees Have Standing? Toward Legal Rights for Natural Objects* (New York: Avon Books, 1975).

110. Ibn Nujaym, *Al-Ashba wa 'n-Nazā'ir*, ed. Abdul Aziz Muhammad Al-Wakil (Egypt: Mu'assasat Al-Habbi wa Shuraka'uhu li 'n-Nashr wa 't-Tawzi'), 286.

111. *Ḥadīth* of unsubstantiated authenticity related by Al-Tirmidhi from Hudhayfah (*Mishkat* no. 5129); a rigorously authenticated *isnad* goes back to ʻAbd-Allah ibn Mas'ud (*mawqūf*).

112. Al-Mughnī, *kitāb al-jihād, mas'ala: qāla wa la yaghriqu al-naḥl*; Bagader et al., *Environmental Protection in Islam*, 11; Samarrai, "Environmental Protection and Islam," 39. In the Qur'anic verse quoted, the words *al-harth wa 'n-nasl* might be understood to cover not only tilth and herds, but flora and fauna in general.

Islamic Environmentalism: A Matter of Interpretation

RICHARD C. FOLTZ

One of the continuing concerns facing those of us working on religion and nature issues and trying to help define this as an emerging field of inquiry is that ever since Lynn White's critique more than three decades ago, practitioners of all the world's religions seem to have dominated the discussion with claims that the "true" interpretation of their own tradition is eco-friendly, if only it would be practiced right, or if others would stop interfering with their traditional systems, and so on. Among those taking such an approach, Muslim apologists have been prominent.

While I personally see some validity in the "outside interference" argument, it should be confessed that even traditional societies have now modernized to such an extent—and not *entirely* under duress, even if perhaps largely so—that going back to some imagined past seems impossible, and its unfulfillable promise misleading, if not dangerous. As for the pursuit of "true" interpretations, I see that as a bit of a dead end as well, since "correctness," like beauty, is perhaps in the eye of the beholder. As I have stated in my earlier writings on the subject, my own opinion is that we need not be overly concerned with *which* of the many existing interpretations (e.g., eco-friendly or not, patriarchal or not, etc.) of Islam or any other religion is historically or originally "the correct one," but rather, we should acknowledge that among all possible interpretations available to us, it is the eco-friendly, nonhierarchical ones that we desperately need to articulate and put into practice today.

In order to do this, however, we need to acknowledge and engage the kinds of other interpretations that have been used throughout history (and, in many cases, continue in the present) to justify the poor environmental choices that human societies have made up to now. While some of the more sensitive of a religion's practitioners occasionally react defensively to such an analysis, seeing it as an attack on their faith, I do not believe that critical appraisals need necessarily constitute "religion-bashing"—it is merely a case of being honest.

Nature in the Premodern Islamic Worldview

The Arabic term *ṭabīʿa*, typically rendered in English as "nature," was used by medieval Muslim philosophers in the sense of the Greek *physis*. Avicenna (Ibn Sina) wrote that "*ṭabīʿa* is an essential first principle for the essential movement of that in which it is present"—a visibly Aristotelian definition. Another medieval Muslim philosopher, pseudo-Majriti, gives the definition of the physicians: "They apply the term *ṭabīʿa* to humor, natural heat, aspects of the bodily organs, movements, and the vegetative soul." The definition given in the *Treatise* of the Pure Brethren, on the other hand, reflects Neoplatonic notions of emanation: ". . . *ṭabīʿa* is only one of the potentialities of the Universal Soul, a potentiality spreading through all sublunar bodies, flowing through each of their parts." Within the Neoplatonic hierarchy of creation as appropriated by many Muslim philosophers, only humans possessed all three attributes of *ṭabīʿa*, intellect, and desire.[1]

Yet, for Muslims an important qualification is found in the divine revelation of the Qur'an, where one reads, "In whose hand is the dominion of all things" (23:88). In the words of the contemporary philosopher Seyyed Hossein Nasr, this makes clear that the natural order "is not an independent domain of reality, but that its principle resides in another realm of reality, which is Divine."[2] The medieval Andalusian Muslim Ibn ʿArabi (1165–1240) writes that "There is no property in the cosmos without a divine support and lordly attribute."[3] Ibn ʿArabi found support for his concept of *waḥdat al-wujūd*, or "unity of being," in the Qur'anic verse (2:115) which states that "Whithersoever you turn, there is the Face of God." Although Ibn ʿArabi's monist metaphysics have been enormously influential on the thought of Sufi mystics in particular, especially in South Asia even to the present day, orthodox Islam has tended to reject the doctrine of *waḥdat al-wujūd* as verging dangerously close to pantheism. In the seventeenth century Ibn 'Arabi's popularity in India gave rise to a response by the conservative Sufi teacher Shah Waliullah, in which the latter attempted to substitute a concept he called *waḥdat al-shuḥūd*, or "unity of witness," through which the boundary lines between the Creator and creation could be firmly maintained.

The ecological aspects embedded in the treatise entitled *The Case of the Animals versus Man*, by a group of tenth-century Muslim philosophers who called themselves the *Ikhwān al-safā*, or "Pure Brethren" of Basra, were explored by Lenn Evan Goodman over twenty years ago in a study which remains little noticed but ought to be of considerable interest to environmental philosophers. Goodman points out that this treatise introduces into medieval Islamic philosophy

> two of the central notions of the science of ecology, that of the eco-niche and that of succession. Species are adapted each to a particular sector of the environment not by natural selection but by the adjustment of their specific organs and behaviors to the resources and hazards of the environments they inhabit . . . these adjustments are accomplished in the organisms' behalf by divine design. Moreover, the organisms, species by species and kind by kind, form a system in which no organism exists solely for its own sake. . . . There is not merely a food chain but a food circle or food circles. The interconnectedness of all the links in this system of cycles creates an ecosystem—a third central concept of ecology.[4]

The Brethren's view of the natural world is all the more striking for its exceptionality in the context of tenth-century Muslim society. They were a radical group, as indicated by their choice to remain anonymous; in subsequent centuries, only the heterodox Sevener-Shi'i, or Isma'ili sect, identified today with the Aga Khan, adopted their writings as authoritative.

Contemporary Islamic Environmental Ethics

Yet in recent years a number of Muslim writers, mainly living in the West, have published essays to the effect that, based on the scriptural sources of the tradition, Islam is an ecologically oriented religion.[5]

Whereas the medieval philosophers, when they addressed issues of the natural world, were concerned primarily with constructing theoretical arguments about justice, Islamic environmental ethics as articulated by contemporary writers tend to be rooted in more practical terms, often by way of response to Lynn White's 1967 critique of Western Christianity. Iqtidar Zaidi, for example, is clearly paraphrasing White when he states that the ecological crisis is "a crisis rooted in moral deprivation."[6] Seyyed Hossein Nasr actually anticipated White's critique in his own lectures given at the University of Chicago earlier in the same year as White's address.[7]

It may be useful to restrict use of the term "Islamic" to that which can be derived from the canonical sources of Islam, as opposed to the activities or attitudes of Muslims, which may or may not be directly motivated by those sources. In other words, one may distinguish between *Islamic* environmentalism—that is, an environmentalism that can be demonstrably enjoined by the textual sources of Islam—and *Muslim* environmentalism, which may draw its inspiration from a variety of sources, possibly including but not limited to religion.[8] Around the world today one can find increasing examples of both.

Muslims have always been culturally diverse, and never more so than today when they number a billion or more and inhabit every corner of the globe. Historically, the one indisputable source of authority which all Muslims have agreed upon is the will of Allah as expressed in the revealed scripture of the Qur'an. In addition, the Sunni majority (perhaps 80 percent of all Muslims) accepts six collections of reports about the deeds and words of the prophet Muhammad, called *ḥadīth*s, as supplementary sources of authority. (Shi'ites agree with some, but not all, of these reports and have compiled collections of their own.)

Islamic environmentalists today have therefore attempted to derive an environmental ethic based on the Qur'an and *ḥadīth*, generally giving little attention to possible cultural contributions from the various societies in which Muslims live. This is because local or regional attitudes cannot form a basis for any kind of universal Islamic ethic, since they are almost invariably perceived by Islamists as "accretions," and therefore un-Islamic. For example, in a paper presented at the Harvard conference on Islam and Ecology (but regrettably not included in this volume), a Muslim anthropologist's presentation depicting the survival of an age-old river festival in Bangladesh as a positive sign of the rural Bengali Muslims' continuing sense of connectedness with the river, elicited angry accusations from Muslims in the audience of polytheism (*shirk*)—the worst sin in Islam.[9]

The politics of environmental activism among Muslims, where present, have tended to be region-specific. For example, when Palestinians seek to assert territorial claims by planting olive groves,[10] one cannot say that this is an "Islamic" issue, since many Palestinians are not Muslim. From an Islamist perspective, the mere involvement of Muslims does not make an activity or ideology "Islamic"; only a basis in the Qur'an and the *ḥadīth* does. This is not to suggest that broader cultural contributions by Muslims living in diverse societies around the world will not be significant in addressing the environmental crisis.

The Scriptural Basis for Islamic Environmentalism

For an idea to achieve anything approaching universal acceptance by Muslims as "Islamic," it must be convincingly demonstrated that it derives from the Qur'an or, failing that, from the example of the prophet Muhammad. Recognizing this, contemporary Islamic environmentalists have defined environmentalism as a facet of the Qur'anic concept of stewardship, expressed by the Arabic term *khilāfa*. The following verses are cited: "I am setting on the earth a vicegerent (*khalīfa*)" (2:30); and "It is He who has made you his vicegerent on earth" (6:165). Citing a *ḥadīth* which states that "Verily, this world is sweet and appealing, and Allah placed you as vicegerents therein; He will see what you do," one contemporary scholar has gone so far as to suggest that "vicegerency forms a test which includes how human beings relate to the environment."[11]

The Qur'anic concept of *tawḥīd* (unity) has historically been interpreted by Muslim writers mainly in terms of the oneness of God (in contradistinction to polytheism), but some contemporary Islamic environmentalists have preferred to see *tawḥīd* as meaning "all-inclusive." It has been suggested that the idea of *waḥdat al-wujūd*, or "unity of being," associated with the medieval philosopher Ibn 'Arabi, can be understood in environmentalist terms. Ibn 'Arabi, however, has always been a highly controversial figure for Muslims, since many have accused him of holding pantheist or monist views incompatible with Islam's radical monotheism.

In support of the more inclusive interpretation of *tawḥīd,* a Qur'anic verse (17:44) is often cited which states that all creation praises God, even if this praise is not expressed in human language. Another verse (6:38) states that "There is not an animal in the earth, nor a flying creature on two wings, but they are peoples like unto you." There would seem to be here a basis for tempering the hierarchical notion of stewardship implied in the concept of *khilāfa*. The Qur'an also describes Islam as the religion of *fiṭra*, "the very nature of things." By extension, some contemporary thinkers have reasoned that a genuinely Islamic lifestyle will "naturally" be environmentally sensitive.[12]

Traditional accounts of the deeds and sayings of Muhammad, which together with the Qur'an have formed the basis for Islamic law, emphasize compassion toward animals. The Prophet is believed to have said, "If you kill, kill well, and if you slaughter, slaughter well. Let each of you sharpen his blade and let him spare suffering to the animal he slaughters"; also, "For [charity shown to] each creature which has a wet heart (i.e., is alive), there is a reward." Muslims are urged to respect plant life as well, as in the Prophetic saying, "Some trees are as blessed as the Muslim himself, especially the palm."

The Qur'an contains judgment against those who despoil the earth (2:205): "And when he turns away [from thee] his effort in the land is to make mischief therein and to destroy the crops and the cattle; and Allah loveth not mischief"; and (7:85) "Do no mischief on the earth after it has been set in order." Wastefulness and excess consumption are likewise condemned (7:31): "O Children of Adam! Look to your adornment at every place of worship, and eat and drink, but be not wasteful. Lo! He [Allah] loveth not the wasteful." The Qur'an repeatedly calls for maintaining balance in all things (13:8, 15:21, 25:2, and elsewhere). Certain sayings of the Prophet seem particularly relevant to contemporary issues of sustainability: "Live in this world as if you will live in it forever, and live for the next world as if you will die tomorrow"; and, "When doomsday comes if someone has a palm shoot in his hand, then he should plant it."[13]

Direct application of these injunctions to contemporary environmental problems is a matter for interpretation by analogy (*qiyās*). Mustafa Abu-Sway has argued that *ḥadīth* reports which enjoin Muslims from relieving themselves on public pathways or into water sources can be understood "to prevent pollution in the language of today." Since we now know that discharging toxic chemicals and waste into the water supply is harmful to human health, Abu-Sway reasons that, "by analogy, from the perspective of the *sharī'a*, this is prohibited."[14]

From Theory to Reality

Are the ecological applications of these sources by Islamic environmentalists, the most prominent of whom live in the West and write for Western audiences, in any way representative of the attitudes of most Muslims worldwide, or even of a significant number of them? Strong environmentalist interpretations have recently been derived from traditions such as Buddhism and Hinduism, as well as from indigenous local traditions. A growing number of Jewish and Christian theologians and laypersons have been actively seeking to reinterpret the sources of their faiths in environmentally sensitive ways. By contrast, Islam has not figured prominently in discussions on religion and the environment; rather, the same articles and faces keep appearing in anthologies and at meetings, little more than tokens of Islamic representation.

For the most part contemporary Muslim writers on the environment have characterized environmental degradation as merely a symptom of social injustice. The problem is not, it is argued, that humans as a species are destroying the balance of nature, but rather that *some* humans are taking more than their share. If, in accordance with the Qur'anic prohibition of interest-taking (*ribā*), the interest-based global banking system is eliminated, then there will be no more environmentally destructive development projects, and there will be plenty of resources for all. Overpopulation is usually dismissed as a nonissue. The problem is stated to be the restriction of movement; if visa restrictions are eliminated, then people will simply migrate from overpopulated areas to "underpopulated" ones.

In recent times global initiatives on birth control and women's reproductive rights have been most strongly opposed in Muslim countries. Such efforts are frequently met with accusations that "the West is trying to limit the number of Muslims." Warnings of starvation and deprivation from overpopulation generally elicit the response that "God will provide," which draws its support from the Qur'anic verse , "There is no beast upon the earth for which Allah does not provide" (11:6).

Yet, unlike Roman Catholicism, in Islam there are no inherent barriers to practicing contraception. The medieval theologian Abu Hamid Muhammad al-Ghazali (1058–1111), who has been called "the second greatest Muslim after Muhammad" and whose writings remain highly influential throughout the Muslim world today, argues in his book *The Proper Conduct of Marriage* (*Kitāb adāb al-nikāh*) that birth control in the form of coitus interruptus (*'azl*) is permitted in Islam. He suggests, furthermore, that "The fear of great hardship as a result of having too many children . . . is also not forbidden, since freedom from hardship is an aid to religious devotion." In response to the "God will provide" argument, al-Ghazali comments that "to examine consequences . . . while perhaps at odds with the attitude of trust in Providence, cannot be called forbidden."[15]

In fact, the founder of the Family Planning Society of Kenya, Dr. Yusuf Ali Eraj, is a Muslim. "Using birth control does not mean following the West," he says. "Muslims can practice family planning, following Islamic principles. It is a *myth* that Islamic doctrine opposes it! All methods are approved, even sterilization."[16]

Despite these arguments, many Muslims still see arguments against having more children than one can afford as being symptomatic of unbelief (*kufr*), which to Muslims is quite a serious charge. Today, Iran appears to be the only Muslim country where an official policy of birth control and birthrate reduction is backed up with Islamic rhetoric.

The traditional Muslim response to doomsday scenarios is that of *tawākkul*, or trust in God (Qur'an 5:23, 14:11–12, 65:3, 25:58, 26:217–18). This tendency, which is often perceived by Westerners as fatalism, reminds one of the *ḥadīth* in which a companion of Muhammad neglected to tie up his camel, and the camel wandered off and was lost. The owner complained of his loss to the Prophet, saying, "I trusted in God, but my camel is gone." Muhammad replied, "First tie up your camel, then trust in God." There is ample evidence today that human growth—reproductive as well as economic—is creating a dangerous imbalance within the biosphere. One wonders, are Muslims who refuse to acknowledge this perhaps leaving their camels untied? In counterbalance to the familiar refrain of *tawākkul*, some Islamic environmentalists have, in the spirit of al-Ghazali, posited the concept of *'aql*, or rational intelligence, which according to Islam is a gift from God, given for a purpose (Qur'an 39:9).[17] There would appear to be nothing un-Islamic about suggesting that the gift of *'aql* has applications in recognizing a crisis and finding ways to avert impending disaster.

Nevertheless, among Muslim ethicists today there is far greater interest in human-centered issues of justice than in the biosphere as an integral whole. This would seem to bear some similarity to attitudes in the West, which is not surprising given Islam's common heritage with Judaism and Christianity. Islam holds that the world is a passing phenomenon, created to serve God's purpose, which will cease to be once that purpose has been fulfilled. Islam likewise emphasizes the relationship between humans and God above all else and has, by comparison, little to say about the importance of our myriad fellow creatures. Whether the "true essence" of Islam is pro-environment or not, in practice throughout most of its history, Muslim theologians, philosophers, and laypersons have been focused almost exclusively on the relationship between Allah and humanity. Islam, like Christianity and Judaism, has for the most part been manifestly "theanthropocentric," to use Karl Barth's somewhat unwieldy term. Iqtidar Zaidi implicitly confirms this when he states that "we are seeking a religious matrix which maintains man's position as an ecologically dominant being. . . ."[18] Indeed, one Muslim writer has recently concluded that "Islamic anthropocentrism negates the claims of Islamic ecology."[19]

Keith Thomas has remarked that whether or not Christianity is inherently environmentally destructive, the reality is that its proponents often *have* been.[20] The same observation may apply to Muslims as well. Given the importance of the petroleum industry and the widespread pursuit of materialistic, consumption-oriented lifestyles in numerous Muslim-majority countries, it would appear that Muslims must now share with Christians and others some of the blame for the present and rapidly deteriorating state of the environment.

Some of the most severe environmental problems in the world today are found in countries where the majority of inhabitants are Muslim. Even accepting a degree of outside responsibility, these problems would clearly be less pronounced if large numbers of Muslims were shaping their lifestyles according to an interpretation of Islam which strongly emphasized *khilāfa* as applied to the natural environment. The reality is that most are not, and this includes governments for whom development and economic growth are the top priority.

Islamic Environmentalism in Practice

If Islamic sources do offer models for increased environmental responsibility among Muslims, the urgency of the environmental crisis implies a need to assess whether and to what degree the latent potential for Islamic models of stewardship (*khilāfa*) is currently being realized anywhere in the Muslim world today.

A possible starting point for this inquiry would be to analyze current environmental policy in countries where Islam is claimed as a basis for legislation by the government in power. The Kingdom of Saudi Arabia, the Islamic Republic of Pakistan, and the Islamic Republic of Iran are three countries that currently make this claim.[21]

In 1983 the government of Saudi Arabia commissioned a group of Islamic scholars at the University of Jeddah to formulate an Islamic policy on the environment. A short paper was prepared and published in English, French, and Arabic by the International Union for Conservation of Nature and Natural Resources (IUCN) in Switzerland, but unfortunately this paper has not been widely circulated.[22] Nevertheless, according to two non-Saudi Muslims who have worked for the Saudi government, Mawil Izzi Dien (an Iraqi) and Othman Abd-ar Rahman Llewellyn (an American), the ideological basis for the Meteorology and Environmental Protection Administration of Saudi Arabia is one of Islamic environmentalism.[23]

The government of Pakistan, which began to adopt an Islamist platform in 1978, created a National Conservation Strategy Unit (NCS) in 1992 within the Ministry of Environment, Local Government and Rural Development. There are also several environmentalist NGOs active in Pakistan that have been striving to influence government policy toward the environment. These include the Sustainable Development Policy Institute (SDPI) and a national branch of the IUCN, which together formulated the Pakistan Environment Programme (PEP) in 1994.[24]

These organizations have achieved some successes in bringing about environmental legislation in Pakistan, such as the Environmental Protection Act of 1997. However, specifically Islamic rhetoric has not thus far been part of their approach. Only as recently as 1998 did the government of the Northwest Frontier province begin to envision an "ulema project" as part of the Sarhad Provincial Conservation Strategy (SPCS). According to reports, this initiative, in which religious scholars were urged to seek out and implement environmental teaching in Islamic sources, did not meet with a large degree of success as most of the scholars involved did not see the environment as a primary concern.[25]

Environmentalism in the Islamic Republic of Iran

Developments in the Islamic Republic of Iran may offer the strongest evidence of an applied Islamic environmental ethic in the world today.[26] Since the country's revolution of 1978–1979, which ousted the repressive, U.S.-backed Pahlavi monarchy, Iran has been led by an avowedly Islamist government whose legitimacy depends on its claims to be working toward an Islamic state. As such, Iran's government has had to face the hard realities of reconciling Islamic principles with the exigencies of contemporary statecraft.

Among the most pressing problems that have vexed Iran's revolutionary government—subsequent, of course, to its eight-year war with Iraq in the 1980s—are pollution, environmental degradation, and overpopulation. In attempting to address these issues through Islamic discourse, Iranian Islamists have perhaps gone further than any of the world's Muslims today in deriving and articulating an Islamic environmental ethic that does not merely revert to premodern models, but rather expresses itself in terms of modern realities.

Iran possesses the greatest degree of biodiversity in Southwestern Asia.[27] The country contains many of the world's major ecosystem types, from high mountains and deserts to semitropical forests and marine environments. Yet, as a recent writer concludes, "with rapid overpopulation, desertification, and the endangerment of virtually all species in the country . . . Iran's environmental problem is among the most critical in the world."[28]

Iran's capital, Tehran, has been classified as one of the ten most polluted cities in the world. About one and a half million tons of airborne pollutants are produced annually in Tehran.[29] The main cause is the two million cars that spew out emissions every day, including some seven hundred thousand that are over twenty years old. According to Iranian government officials, the amount of sulfur in Iranian diesel fuel is fifteen to twenty times higher than European standards. Overall carbon emissions have risen by 240 percent since 1980. Other sources of toxic emissions include factories, power plants, and oil refineries, many of which have been shown to exceed world pollution standards by as much as 70 percent. According to a recent report, four thousand people die of air pollution–related lung cancer and almost as many again from other lung diseases every year in Iran. Proposed solutions have ranged from slicing off nearby mountaintops to facilitate air circulation to simply moving the capital to another location.[30]

A severe drought from 1999 to 2001 led to a nationwide water crisis, which came to rival air quality as a source of immediate concern. The livestock population plummeted, and twenty-five of the country's twenty-eight provinces faced shortages of drinking water. Water tables were lowered to dangerous levels, and some lakes and wetlands disappeared entirely, including Lake Hamoun near the Afghan border, which had been the largest freshwater body in the country. As much as 60 percent of the rural population was threatened with displacement. In August 2000 the Zayandeh River in Esfahan ran dry. The effects of the crisis so overwhelmed the government's resources that in May 2000 it began accepting foreign aid donations for only the second time since the 1979 revolution.[31]

Iran's wildlife species, meanwhile, are facing worsening strains due to habitat depletion. A number of unique species (such as the Caspian tiger and Persian lion) are believed extinct. In 2000 the extinction of the Moghan deer was officially declared.[32]

Official Responses

Iran's reformist president, Mohammad Khatami, has acknowledged the seriousness of his country's environmental crisis on numerous occasions. In February 1998 he suggested before a meeting of environmental ministers from neighboring Persian Gulf countries that pollution poses an even greater threat than war, and that the fight to preserve the environment could be the most positive issue for bringing the Gulf nations together.[33]

Whether despite or because of the severity of Iran's environmental crisis, official statements on a range of issues connected with the environment sound strikingly progressive, especially when compared with other parts of the Muslim world. Iran's population policy, for example, stands in marked contrast to the sentiments most loudly voiced at the 1994 Women's conference in Cairo, where an unholy

Muslim-Vatican alliance hampered efforts to hold meaningful discussions on women's reproductive rights. Iran's Department of the Environment (DOE) has set the remarkably ambitious goal of reducing the country's rate of population growth, which was nearly 4 percent in the 1980s, from 2.82 percent in 1993 to 1 percent by 2010. A government report on population control concludes with the observation that

> Although these changes will not happen overnight, the economic pressures of contemporary life along with education provided by political, religious and scientific leaders should convince the people that family planning and population control is not mere propaganda, but [rather] it is to their own benefit to have fewer children, *ensha'llah*![34]

Iran now has what has been acknowledged as "one of the most extensive birth control programs anywhere."[35] Couples wishing to be married must first pass a family-planning course, and various forms of birth control are distributed for free. The Iranian government's willingness to give an Islamic color to population control seems unique in the contemporary Muslim world.

Iran is probably the only country at present where Islam is claimed as a basis for environmental ethics at the official level.[36] In 1996 the DOE stated in a published paper that "the religious leaders in Iran have found the principles of environmental conservation compatible with the general guidelines of the holy religion of Islam. It is now the duty of environmentalists to encourage the Friday Prayer speakers to convey environmental messages to the public."[37] The revolutionary government went so far as to assert its ideological commitment to environmental protection by including it in thc 1979 constitution. Article 50 reads:

> In the Islamic Republic protection of the natural environment, in which the present and future generations must lead an ever-improving community life, is a public obligation. Therefore all activities, economic or otherwise, which may cause irreversible damage to the environment are forbidden.

Such a dramatic policy is, of course, unenforceable in a modern country; even so, it would be difficult to imagine any of the industrialized nations employing such bold language on the environmental crisis. For the sake of contrast, one may cite former U.S. President George

Bush's statement on the occasion of the Rio Earth Summit in 1992, that "the American way of life is not up for negotiation," or the reasoning by which his son, current President George W. Bush, has justified rejecting the 1997 Kyoto Agreement and reneged on campaign promises to reduce carbon emissions. While Iran's pro-environment rhetoric may in some cases be just that—rhetoric—at least it is a step in the right direction.

Iran's Department of the Environment (DOE), originally established in 1972, was reorganized under the new government in 1986. The DOE has a Provincial Directorate for each of Iran's twenty-eight provinces. Its mission includes research on appropriate technology, a national biological survey, public education, and national regulation of air, water, urban development, biodiversity, waste disposal, noise pollution, and agricultural toxics. The principle of sustainable development as outlined at the Rio Earth Summit (Agenda 21) is stated to be the framework for Iranian legislation, and environmental impact statements are supposed to be a major consideration in all projects.[38] Recently, increased priority has been given to family planning, bringing women into conservation, and encouraging grassroots movements.[39]

The DOE is also responsible for administering Iran's seven national parks, four national nature monuments, twenty-four wildlife refuges, and forty-two protected areas. In a national strategy paper published in conjunction with the United Nations Development Program and the World Bank in 1994, the DOE called for 1) a land-use planning strategy based on integrated ecological and socioeconomic issues rather than solely socioeconomic ones, 2) promotion of NGOs and community participation, 3) provisions for the preparation of management plans for protected areas, 4) provisions for the formation of a "Green Corps" to reinforce the manpower needed for fulfillment of national strategies, and 5) a nine-point plan of action, incorporating details about the degree of sensitivity, sizes, and relative cover of the country's protected areas as well as the types of destructive activities threatening those areas, and including a program to finance the proposed strategies.[40] The DOE has produced educational programs on the environment for television and radio, and it publishes a scholarly journal, *Mohīt-e zīst* (*The Environment*), four times a year. In 1996 plans were announced for an Environmental University, at which "all aspects of the environmental sciences" will be taught and "the expertise needed in the field of the environment will be trained according to the needs of the country."[41]

The Iranian delegation to the Kyoto Conference on Climate Change in December 1997 was led by vice president and director of the DOE and the Environmental Protection Organization (EPO), former revolutionary spokeswoman Massumeh Ebtekar. Though the vice president cited in her address Iran's successes in reforestation, control of desertification, and emissions regulations, she sided with other developing countries in arguing that "Before the actual materialization of promises made by industrialized countries, including technology transfer and financial assistance, it seems unfair that developing countries should undertake considerations that could seriously hinder their pace of development and damage their fragile economies."[42]

Nevertheless, following the Montreal Protocol of 1987, Iran currently has the world's second-largest program (after China) for the phasing out of ozone-depleting chlorofluorocarbons (CFCs). Though Iran does not produce CFCs, it imports them, and the figure of five and a quarter billion tons imported in 1993 is to be reduced to zero by 2005.[43]

Also in 1997, the DOE introduced a National Environment Plan of Action (NEPA), which was submitted to the cabinet. A workshop at Tehran University in May 1999 brought members of the DOE together with academics and representatives from environmental NGOs, for the purpose of incorporating environmental policies into Iran's Third Development Plan.

The DOE has also sought to treat the environment as a component of President Khatami's "dialogue of civilizations" initiatives. In June 2001 it convened an international seminar entitled "Environment, Religion, and Culture" in Tehran, in an effort to bring together scholars from around the world working on the spiritual and cultural dimensions of the environmental crisis.

Unfortunately, government initiatives have so far been hampered by unenforceability, as well as by lack of sufficient public response. Since 1998, January 19 has been officially declared "National Clean Air Day," with citizens encouraged to turn off their car engines for a symbolic three minutes. Even this small gesture has gone unobserved by most Iranians, however.[44]

Nongovernmental Organizations

Yet, slowly, public awareness of Iran's environmental crisis seems to be on the rise, due in part no doubt to the increasing visibility of new environmental nongovernmental organizations (ENGOs). As of late 2000 there were 149 registered and unregistered ENGOs in Iran.

For the most part NGOs are a recent phenomenon in Iran, and they are desperately attempting to establish contacts with similar organizations worldwide. Like many such organizations, they are chronically underfunded. While some have received contributions from foreign donors, most of their funding comes from private donations within Iran. Since they are dependent upon ongoing government authorization to function as independent entities, they tend to abstain from direct political involvement, such as lobbying for environmental legislation. There are no Sierra Clubs or Natural Resource Defense Councils in Iran at present. Instead, most of Iran's environmentalist NGOs concentrate on raising public awareness of environmental issues, often through direct contact, such as volunteers going door-to-door or taking inner-city children on field trips to the countryside.

The first registered environmental NGO in Iran was BoomIran, founded in 1980. In 1983 BoomIran's director, Farrokh Mostofi, traveled to Switzerland to muster support for opposition to draining the Anzali lagoon near Rasht on the Caspian coast. The World Wide Fund for Nature (WWF) pressured the Iranian government, and the project was abandoned. Mostofi himself was featured in a 1999 issue of *National Geographic*.[45]

BoomIran, which currently counts some 250 members, publishes a monthly magazine, *Shekār o Tabī'at* (*Wildlife and Nature*), as well as a children's magazine and an encyclopedia of Iran's fauna. The organization maintains a library, provides lecturers, and produces an educational television program. It has initiated a Pathfinders Program, which seeks to identify road and trail networks for use by hikers and travelers with regard to preserving the environment, and a program called "Save Our Rivers," which seeks to identify and protect polluted rivers and determine sources of pollution.[46] The organization recently established links with E-Law in the United States, which aims to provide information and support on issues of international conservation law, liability for environmental damage, biodiversity legislation, and the effects on the environment of trade.

BoomIran is currently working to organize opposition to the proposed Tehran-Shomal freeway project, which would link the capital with the Caspian coast, and to put together an environmental impact statement, since the government has failed to do so. With six chapters now located around the country, BoomIran also has a birdwatching club, which is currently monitoring eight endangered bird species in Iran, including the Siberian crane.

The Green Front of Iran (*Jabheh-ye Sabz-e Īrān*), founded in 1989, is another environmental NGO that has become increasingly visible in recent years, with over two thousand members nationwide. Avowedly apolitical, the Green Front aims to increase public awareness of environmental concerns and to foster public participation in clean-up projects. The most extensive such project involved thirty-three sites over eight hundred kilometers along the Caspian seacoast on 27 and 28 August 1999, when over ten tons of garbage was picked up on beaches from Astara near the border of Azerbaijan in the west to the southeast Caspian port of Bandar-e Torkaman. An earlier afforestation trip organized by the Green Front in March 1998 was attended by President Khatami. More recently, on 20 April 2001, the GFI organized an environmental education workshop retreat in a nature preserve in the Alborz Mountains, attended by two hundred participants from Tehran and Babol. In preparation for Earth Day 2001, the GFI organized a seminar in conjunction with the Youth Earth Conservation Association in Tehran and a lecture sponsored by the Tehran municipality and campaigned for a "Car-Free Day" in the capital.

Siamak Moattari, a medical doctor who is the Green Front's founder and director, offers his own perspective on the oft-proposed tension between the environment and development. "We do not feel that tending to ecological issues is a luxury," he says; "it is a necessity." He points out that environmental degradation and poverty constitute a cycle. "Economic, social justice, and environmental issues must be viewed together. While it may be unrealistic to expect a forest-dweller with an empty stomach not to cut down a tree, we must realize that in the following years there will be no tree for his children to cut down." Yet, "In Gilan we met individuals willing to lie in front of trucks carrying away lumber and even risk their lives in defense of those trees. . . . These are people living in poverty." In Moattari's view, "individuals bring about environmental degradation not as a result of poverty, but as a result of ignorance or misinformation."[47] Despite its social justice agenda, the Green Front is not explicitly Islamic; it has, however, established a committee that seeks out references to environmental stewardship in the Qur'an and *ḥadīth*s, which it sends to religious leaders and organizations.[48]

The Iranian Society of Environmentalists (IRSEN) is an organization founded by academics and scientists. It is part of the multinational Caspian Environment Program (CEP) and studies, among other things, pollution point sources, wildlife, and aquatic systems in the Caspian region, with an aim to advising the government on environmental policy issues. More recently a related organization, the Iranian Association of Environmental Health, was established with a specific focus on health concerns. Both organizations have carried out various projects to monitor water, soil, and air pollution throughout Iran.

The major Iranian NGO concerned with wildlife is the Wildlife and Nature Conservancy Foundation. The WNCF has undertaken an array of studies, ranging from wetlands assessments, to drops in riverine fish populations, to problems of park management and the impacts of human population growth. It is also seeking to determine whether the Caspian tiger and the Iranian cheetah are indeed extinct.

A group of mountaineers formed the Mountain Environment Protection Committee (*Hefāzat-e mohīt-e kuhestān*) in 1993. In Tehran especially, weekend family outings to the mountains, whether to Darband above Tehran or to 18,400-foot Mt. Damavand a short drive to the east, are extremely popular. Unfortunately, one hundred thousand or more visitors per week are loving the Alborz to death, leaving enormous amounts of garbage behind them and disrupting the mountain ecology. The MEPC has been attempting to educate Iranians about the fragility of mountain environments, the need to pack out garbage and to stay on trails to minimize erosion. According to the director, Abdollah Astari, the government has failed to enforce existing laws which could protect the mountains from overuse.[49]

All of the aforementioned NGOs are based in Tehran. One organization active outside the capital is Esfahan Green Message (*Payām-e sabz*). Originally founded by faculty at the Esfahan University of Technology in 1994, EGM now counts five hundred members. Like the Tehran-based NGOs, EGM seeks to increase public awareness and participation in environmental issues through educational initiatives, formulate policies through consultation with specialists, and influence decision makers through meetings and letter-writing campaigns.

Other organizations spread throughout Iran's twenty-eight provinces include the Kerman Earth Lovers, Zagros Friends of Nature, Fars Friends of the Environment, Khorasan Green Thought Group, the Green Defence Society of Mazandaran, the West Azerbaijan Association for Reconciliation with Nature, the Green Artists Association, and many others.[50]

One exception to the hitherto largely apolitical approach of Iran's ENGOs is that of the somewhat mysterious Green Party of Iran. According to its website,

> The Green Party of Iran is a political party founded to defend Iran's environment, particularly its forests, soil, air and water resources. We believe that the Iranian population has the right to a safe and clean environment, and to political, economical, social and cultural freedom. Furthermore, the Green Party of Iran intends to expose and oppose the current Iranian regime's nuclear, chemical, and biological mass production of weapons. In view of the increasing environmental destruction in Iran, we believe that a Green Party is required on the Iranian political stage. In addition to proposing environmental policies, the Green Party of Iran advocates a democratic political and economic system for Iran.[51]

The Green Party, which has close ties to green parties in other countries, is thus not only avowedly political, but actively opposes many of the policies of the current Iranian government. Its party platform calls for such radical measures as the separation of religion from politics, "the repeal of anti-women laws," and the elimination of the military draft. It openly calls for "the removal of the present regime of the Islamic Republic of Iran."[52] Not surprisingly, it is not among the NGOs officially registered with the Iranian government. In fact, in 1999 a rival green party was formed with government backing, "having as its main objects, the improvement of the youth's Islamic identity, the creation of an Islamic utopia based on Islamic ideals, and lastly, the protection of environment."[53]

In the United States, the Washington, D.C.–based organization Search for Common Ground has been working with ENGOs in Iran. SFCG brought ten leaders of Iranian ENGOs on a visit to the United States in the fall of 1999, where they met with representatives of American environmental organizations and delivered papers at a conference.[54] In February 2001 an American delegation traveled to Iran, principally to advise their Iranian counterparts on issues of international environmental law.

Women's Involvement

Public interest in environmental issues received a boost in the wake of the 1995 United Nations Conference on Women in Beijing, which was attended by some Iranian delegations. Mansoureh Shodjai, a self-described ecofeminist formerly of Iran's National Library, credits the Beijing conference with dramatically raising Iran's level of public awareness on both women's and environmental issues.[55]

Environmental action in Iran considerably predates 1995, however, as does women's involvement. As long ago as 1970, a group of rural women in the arid southern province of Yazd embarked on an anti-desertification planting project for which they received support from the Office of Natural Resources. That project continues today as part of a microcredit scheme underwritten by the Ministry of Construction Jihad and the ONR, and inspired the United Nations Development Program to film a documentary called "The Green Desert," which took first prize at the first Iranian International Environmental Film Festival held in Tehran in 1999. The Iran office of the UNDP, which has been functioning since 1965, devotes about half of its $25 million annual budget to environmental projects.[56]

At least three Tehran-based NGOs currently combine women's issues with environmental work. One is the Society of Women against Environmental Pollution (*Jami'at-e zanān mobārezeh bā alūdegī-ye mohīt-e zīst*), whose aim is to raise awareness of environmental problems among Iranian women. Among their activities are the gathering of statistics on urban pollution, the publishing of informational articles and brochures for the general public, organizing seminars, and preparing educational materials for public schools. They have scored a number of notable successes, including getting the Ministry of Education to include the environment as a part of the public school curriculum.

A second organization, the Struggle for Survival Society (*Jami'at-e talāshgarān-e baqā*), focuses on the poor, especially refugees, who suffer disproportionately from the effects of environmental degradation. A third group, the Children's Book Council of Iran, produces educational materials on the environment for children.

Mansoureh Shodjai, who has been active in children's environmental education programs, describes one technique she has found effective for engaging children with the natural environment, a technique she calls "nature concerts." This involves having children sit down in a natural area and simply listen for a half hour or so to whatever they hear going on around them. Afterwards they are asked their impressions. "For example, if a child mentions having heard a running stream," says Shodjai, "we understand that this particular child has an attraction to water, and we work with that, teaching the child about water pollution and what causes it and how it can be remedied. And so on for birds, wind, or whatever."[57]

ENGOs and the Iranian Government

The Khatami regime has maintained a policy of encouraging the development of civil society, recognizing the important role of NGOs. The involvement of women and youth has been especially encouraged.

In 1998 representatives from several ENGOs met with the DOE and established the Environmental NGO Network. This has provided obvious advantages, including government recognition. On the other hand, the government's relationship with ENGOs is still "guided by suspicion and a control mentality and agenda enacted through stifling administrative, regulatory procedures." The concept of NGOs is still unfamiliar to the Iranian public, and the NGOs themselves have been limited by short-term planning strategies.[58]

Shi'ite Clerics on the Environment

Unfortunately, despite official government urging, there has thus far been little overt interest on the part of Iran's religious scholars to take a leadership role in educating Muslims about environmental values.[59] According to Baqer Talebi, a young seminarian at the prestigious Fayzieh College in the holy shrine city of Qom, most Iranians fail to see environmental problems as a religious issue. "If I were to go back to my home village and, wearing my mullah's gown, personally open up the channels so that people could get water, it would be seen by the public as a religious act. But I'm not doing that, and neither are any other mullahs, and we're not going to because our professional culture has been that we have 'more pressing' concerns."[60] Talebi expressed his own personal dismay in making this assessment. Yet, while he asserted that environmental issues ought indeed to be a significant component of religious teaching, he doubted that this could actually occur in the extremely tradition-minded world of formal Shi'ite scholarship.

Ayatollah Musavi Ardebili, one of Qom's most prominent elder clerics, is more optimistic. Speaking privately with me in August 2001, he conceded that environmental degradation had not been addressed in any meaningful way by Iran's religious scholars, but he affirmed that this was a vital issue facing Muslims in today's world and one that clerics were duty-bound to better inform themselves about.

Ayatollah Hasan Emami of Esfahan, who, unlike the majority of Iran's leading religious figures, chooses not to live in Qom and has criticized Iran's present form of government, takes an even stronger position. He rejects the assessment that Iran's religious leaders have been lax in promoting Islamic environmental values. "I have personally been teaching my students about environmental responsibility every day for over twenty years," he told me.[61] To further prove his point, Ayatollah Emami presented me with a newly published book on environmental jurisprudence, *Al-fiqh al-bī'ah*, written by contemporary Shi'ite scholar Ayatollah Muhammad Husayni Shirazi.

Given Iranians' current attitudes toward their government, however, any attention to such matters on the part of leading Islamic figures may be a double-edged sword. Many feel that any kind of Islamic discourse in Iran today has been discredited by a government widely seen as corrupt and ineffective. Mostafa Qaderian, a public relations officer for the Esfahan office of the Department of Environment, doubts that with the present political climate ordinary Iranians will be swayed by Islamic arguments regarding environmental practices. Himself a devout Muslim, Qaderian admits that "Since people have become a little alienated from Islam under the present regime, it is perhaps better to have such discussions only with those genuinely interested in Islamic studies."[62]

Is Iran's Case Unique?

In Iran, official as well as public attitudes toward the natural environment appear to be unique in the Muslim world. The fact that Iran's official voice is expressing some unusually progressive perspectives vis-à-vis other Muslim countries may be related to the fact that, there, Islamists are in power and must therefore face certain hard realities that accompany the responsibility for directing their country's future policies.

Of course, it may be pointed out that Iran's environmental problems, on the whole, are worsening rather than improving, and that government policies on environmental protection are often not carried out. Development and the welfare of the industrial economy still tend to override concerns about the health of the general population. Still, what is most unique about Iran's Islamic environmentalism is that it is essentially entirely homegrown. As such, in the long term at least, it may well prove to be a more workable and influential form of environmentalism than models imported from the West or elsewhere.

Islamic Vegetarianism?

Even among the small minority of contemporary Muslim intellectuals who consider the environment to be a central concern, there has been surprisingly little discussion of animal welfare.[63] Yet, in a world of proportionately diminishing food resources—and Muslims account for a disproportionately high share of the world's poor and hungry—there are economic and social justice arguments to be made, in addition to ethical ones, in favor of vegetarianism.

A meat-based diet is a remarkably inefficient use of food resources; it takes roughly ten pounds of vegetable matter (fed into an animal) to produce one pound of meat. An image commonly used by vegetarians is that of one meat-eater sitting down to a large slab of steak while nine others sit around the table staring at empty plates. Another aspect of this issue is that around the world tropical rain forests are being cleared for the sake of grazing livestock to be sold as meat, mainly destined for Northern markets. Some ethicists have therefore argued that there is little excuse for freely *choosing* to eat meat in a world where so many are starving, and where the lungs of the earth are being hacked and burned on a daily basis merely to satisfy the tastes of wealthy meat-eaters.

In many parts of the world, however, especially among pastoral societies, Muslims are constrained to a meat-based diet.[64] In light of this fact, it would be difficult for Islam to proscribe the eating of meat and, of course, in reality it permits it. But in many other places where Muslims live today, it is possible to thrive on a varied and healthy vegetarian diet, and under such conditions abstaining from meat poses neither danger nor hardship.

Another issue connected with meat-eating is the customary sacrifice performed once a year on the occasion of *'Īd al-qurbān*. During the 1990s, however, King Hassan of Morocco on two occasions banned this slaughter for economic reasons, citing the well-being of Muslims. As an additional item for speculation, it may be noted in passing that, historically, several other religious traditions, including Judaism and Vedism, developed metaphorical substitutions for blood sacrifice; it is therefore not inconceivable that such a development could occur in the future within Islam. In any event, ritual slaughter in Islam is a customary practice, not one prescribed by law.[65]

The Qur'an and *sunna* have been shown to enjoin Muslims to treat animals with compassion. This is clearly reflected in the established procedure for *ḥalāl* slaughter. It seems obvious, however, that not slaughtering the animal at all would be even more compassionate.

It is often remarked, especially by hunters, that since the natural predators of so many animals have been suffering dramatically declining numbers, prey species are in many places proliferating beyond control, and should therefore be hunted by humans. One recent case in India concerned the nilgai, or "blue cow." With the disappearance of tigers the nilgai population has exploded, but Hindus will not allow the species to be hunted because of its name. In desperation, some have resorted to the cry, "For God's sake, let's not call it a blue cow. Let's call it a blue bull, and kill it!"[66]

What this sort of argument overlooks is that such population imbalances have been brought on by gross human alterations of habitats, such as those of predators like the tiger. The reasoning then is one of punishing the victims. Is that, one may ask, the act of a conscientious *khalīfa*?

A more sympathetic example can be found in a story about the eighth-century female Muslim mystic Rabi'a of Basra. According to the medieval Sufi poet Farid al-din 'Attar,

> It is related that one day Rabi'a had gone up on a mountain. Wild goats and gazelles gathered around, gazing upon her. Suddenly, Hasan Basri [another well-known early Muslim mystic] appeared. All the animals shied away. When Hasan saw that, he was perplexed and said, "Rabi'a, why do they shy away from me when they were so intimate with you?" Rabi'a said, "What did you eat today?" "Soup." "You ate their lard. How would they not shy away from you?"[67]

Though Muslims now inhabit every corner of the globe and live in societies as diverse as those of West Africa, Central Asia, the Philippines, and the United States, one social factor that they all seem to share is the eating of meat. Ethical questions surrounding the use of animals for food are not raised in the legal literature of classical Islam, and even today any serious discourse on the viability of an "Islamic" vegetarianism is difficult to find. Contemporary Islamic scholar Mawil Izzi Dien, in his recent book *The Environmental Dimensions of Islam*, even goes so far as to assert that "According to Islamic Law there are no grounds upon which one can argue that animals should not be killed for food."[68]

Yet today, a growing number of Muslims throughout the world are practicing vegetarian lifestyles, not only in the West but in traditional Islamic environments as well. The animal rights organization People for the Ethical Treatment of Animals (PETA) has launched, at the suggestion of its Muslim members, a website on Islam and vegetarianism (www.islamicconcern.com), which includes pro-vegetarian arguments based on the principles of classical jurisprudence, examples of Muslim mystics, and other sources.

Though this is clearly a discussion in its infant stages, it is beginning to be argued that from the standpoints of human health, social justice, ecological stewardship, and compassion toward nonhuman creation, a vegetarian lifestyle may in fact be preferable for Muslims. Some Muslims are beginning to feel that such a lifestyle is not incompatible with the teachings of the Islamic tradition, which can actually be read in ways that fully support vegetarianism.

Conclusion

For many Muslims and non-Muslims alike, the practical and active relationship between religion and the environmental crisis is often not immediately obvious. Even so, some Muslims, believing with Lynn White that the environmental crisis is at root a spiritual crisis, have been attempting to illuminate that connection through writing, activism, and policymaking.

Muslim reformers throughout history have claimed that the problems facing society result from the fact that an Islamic lifestyle based on the Qur'an and *sunna* was absent in the present age. Islamic reform movements have thus typically aimed to encourage Muslims to rediscover how the sources of the faith instruct one to live. This process of rediscovery is referred to as *islāḥ*, a cleansing of the tradition in order to return Islam to the "original" pristine state these sources are believed to evoke. There are indications that Islamic environmentalism will increasingly be expressed in these terms. One may cite the example of Turkey, where soon after taking power in 1994 the new Islamist mayor of Istanbul had the cobblestones surrounding city hall painted green, declaring that this symbolized the environmentalist aspect of his party's policy.[69]

There has been a tendency in recent years, especially among scholars of religion, to study the sources of various cultural traditions in order to find support for claims that this or that tradition is originally "eco-friendly"; a corollary argument is often made that the environmental crisis can be remedied through a "rediscovery" of ecological principles which have supposedly been lost. These arguments may be somewhat misguided. Assertions about what constitutes the "original" or "proper" interpretation of a tradition, or that "true" Christianity, Buddhism, Islam, or whatever, is eco-friendly, beg the counterargument that the proponent has falsely construed the pristine form of the worldview in question.

It might be more productive instead to adopt the "correlational method" proposed by Paul Tillich, that it is precisely through a tradition's success in drawing upon its own internal resources to confront an ever-changing array of historical crises and concerns that a tradition reinvigorates itself and demonstrates its ongoing vitality and relevance.[70] According to this approach it matters little whether the original essence of Islam (or any other religion) is eco-friendly or not;

the point is that an eco-friendly Islam is urgently needed in the world today, and as more and more Muslims come to realize this and to work toward its articulation and practice, Islamic environmental thought in its contemporary form is likely to play a major role in reshaping and revitalizing Islam as a guiding force and principle in Muslim communities around the globe.

Notes

Earlier versions of this essay appeared as "Islamic Environmentalism in Theory and Practice," in *Worldviews, Religion and the Environment: A Global Anthology*, ed. Richard C. Foltz (Belmont, Calif.: Wadsworth Thomson, 2002), 358–65; and "Is There an Islamic Environmentalism?" *Environmental Ethics* 22, no. 1 (2000): 63–72.

1. S. Nomanul Haq, "*Ṭabīʻa*," *Encyclopedia of Islam*, 2d ed. (Leiden: E. J. Brill, 1998), 8:25–28.
2. Seyyed Hossein Nasr, *Religion and the Order of Nature* (New York: Oxford University Press, 1996), 61.
3. William Chittick, *The Sufi Path of Knowledge* (Albany: State University of New York Press, 1989), 38.
4. Ikhwān al-Safā, *The Case of the Animals versus Man before the King of the Jinn: A Tenth-Century Ecological Fable of the Pure Brethren of Basra*, trans. Lenn Evan Goodman (Boston: Twayne, 1978), 5–6.
5. See, for example, Mawil Izzi Dien, *The Environmental Dimensions of Islam* (Cambridge: Lutterworth, 2000); Akhtaruddin Ahmad, *Islam and the Environmental Crisis* (London: Ta-ha Publishers, 1997); Abou Bakr Ahmed Ba Kader et al., eds., *Islamic Principles for the Conservation of the Natural Environment* (Gland, Switzerland: IUCN, 1983); Seyyed Hossein Nasr, *Man and Nature: The Spiritual Crisis of Modern Man* (1967; Chicago: Kazi, 2000); Iqtidar H. Zaidi, "On the Ethics of Man's Interaction with the Environment: An Islamic Approach," *Environmental Ethics* 3, no. 1 (1981), 35–47; and the essays in Harfiya Abdel Haleem, ed., *Islam and the Environment* (London: Ta-ha Publishers, 1998), and Fazlun Khalid and Joanne O'Brien, eds., *Islam and Ecology* (New York: Cassell, 1992).
6. Zaidi, "On the Ethics of Man's Interaction with the Environment," 35.
7. Nasr, *Religion and the Order of Nature*, 225 n. 12.
8. Safei El-Deen Hamed, "Seeing the Environment through Islamic Eyes: Application of Shariah to Natural Resources Planning and Management," *Journal of Agricultural and Environmental Ethics* 6, no. 2 (1993): 146.
9. Shakeel Hossain," Between Sinful Innovation and the Ethos of the Land: Sacred Traditions and Ritual Art of the Indian Muslims" (paper presented at the conference on Islam and Ecology, Center for the Study of World Religions, Harvard Divinity School, 7–10 May 1998).
10. I am grateful to Jeanne Kay for suggesting this example.
11. Mustafa Abu-Sway, "Towards an Islamic Jurisprudence of the Environment (*Fiqh al-Bī'ah f'il-Islām*) (lecture given at Belfast mosque, February 1998); <http://homepages.iol.ie/~afifi/Articles/environment.htm>.
12. See the paper by Saadia Khawar Khan Chishti in this volume.
13. A nearly identical saying exists in Jewish Mishnah: "Rabbi Yochanan ben Zakkai used to say, 'If you happen to be standing with a sapling in your hand and someone says to you, "Behold, the Messiah has come!" first plant the tree and then go out to greet the Messiah' " (*Avot de Rabbi Natan*, Nossel et al., 12).
14. Abu Sway, "Towards an Islamic Jurisprudence."
15. Abu Hamid Muhammad al-Ghazali, *The Proper Conduct of Marriage in Islam* (*Adāb an-Nikāh*), trans. Muhtar Holland (Hollywood, Fl.: Al-Baz Publishing, 1998), 79.

16. Marjorie Hope and James Young, *Voices of Hope in the Struggle to Save the Planet* (New York: Apex Press, 2000), 173.

17. See Zaidi, "On the Ethics of Man's Interaction with the Environment," 41. For a fuller discussion of the Islamic terms *tawākkul* and *'aql*, see the relevant articles in *Encyclopedia of Islam*, 2d ed.

18. Zaidi, "On the Ethics of Man's Interaction with the Environment," 36.

19. Oguz Erdur, "Reappropriating the 'Green': Islamist Environmentalism," *New Perspectives on Turkey* 17 (fall 1997): 160.

20. Keith Thomas, *Man and the Natural World* (New York: Oxford University Press, 1984), 24.

21. The Green Party of Egypt was granted official status in 1990, but Islamic rhetoric plays only a small part in its activities.

22. Ba Kader et al., *Islamic Principles.* A revised version, however, is available online: <http://www.islamset.com/env/contenv.html >.

23. Izzi Dien, *Environmental Dimensions of Islam.*

24. Aban Kabraji, IUCN Pakistan office, Karachi, personal communication.

25. See the report by Ali Raza Rizvi, "Pakistan," in *Environmental Education in the Asia and Pacific Region: Status, Issues and Practices*, ed. Bishnu B. Bhandari and Osamu Abe (Hayama, Japan: Institute for Global Environmental Strategies, 2001), 171–91.

26. This section is drawn from my earlier article, "Environmental Initiatives in Contemporary Iran," *Central Asian Survey* 20, no. 2 (2001): 155–65.

27. A recent U.N. report lists 160 species of mammals, 300 of birds, 1,000 of fishes, 9,000 of plants, and 60,000 of insects. Baquer Namazi, "Environmental NGOs," *Situational Analysis of NGOs in Iran* (Tehran: United Nations Development Programme, 2000).

28. N. Patrick Peritore, "Iran: From Revolution to Ecological Collapse," in *Third World Environmentalism: Case Studies from the Global South* (Gainesville: University Press of Florida, 1999), 209.

29. United States Energy Information Administration, "Iran: Environmental Issues," <www.eia.doe.gov/emeu/cabs/iranenv.htm>, 1.

30. "Air Pollution in Tehran: A Worsening Scenario," <www.persian.com/air_pollution/index.html>.

31. "UN Warns Drought on Verge of Becoming "Full-fledged Disaster,'" Agence France-Presse, 3 August 2000.

32. "Iran Has No More Moghan Deer," *Tehran Times*, 12 June 2000.

33. "Pollution More Fatal than War," *Iran Times*, 27 Esfand 1376 (17 March 1998).

34. *Islamic Republic of Iran Country Paper, Third Session of the Committee on Environment and Sustainable Development, Bangkok, 7–11 October 1996* (Tehran: Department of the Environment, 1996), 27.

35. Robin Wright, "We Invite the Hostages to Return to Iran," *New Yorker*, 8 November 1999, 42–43. See also the paper by Nancy W. Jabbra and Joseph G. Jabbra in this volume.

36. See Richard Foltz, "Is There an Islamic Environmentalism?" *Environmental Ethics* 22, no. 1 (2000): 63–72.

37. *Iran Country Paper*, 36.

38. *National Report to the United Nations Conference on Environment and Development (Rio, 1–12 June 1992, The Earth Summit)* (Tehran: Department of the Environment, 1992).

39. Peritore, "Iran: From Revolution to Ecological Collapse," 212.

40. Majid Makhdoum et al., *Biodiversity Conservation and Management of Protected Areas* (background paper commissioned for the National Strategy for Environment and Sustainable Development) (Tehran: Department of the Environment, 1994).

41. *Iran Country Paper*, 27.

42. Massumeh Ebtekar, address to Kyoto International Conference on Climate Change, 1–10 December 1997.

43. Reshma Prakash, "Atmosphere: Dealing with Ozone," *Earth Times*, 1–15 April 1999, 10.

44. USEIA, "Iran: Environmental Issues," 2.

45. Fen Montaigne, "Iran: Testing the Waters of Reform," *National Geographic*, July 1999, 13.

46. Farrokh Mostofi, "[The] Role of NGOs in Protecting Wildlife in Iran," in *Persian Lion, Caspian Tiger: The Role of Iranian Environmental NGOs in Environmental Protection in Iran*, ed. Jonathan Winder and Haleh Esfandiari (Washington, D.C.: Search for Common Ground, 2000), 21.

47. Shadi Mokhtari, "The Green Front of Iran," *Iran News*, 17 May 1998, 2.

48. Ibid., 3.

49. Reshma Prakash, "Mountain: Cleaning It Up," *Earth Times*, 1–15 April 1999, 11.

50. For a complete list, including contact addresses, see Baquer Namazi, "Iranian Environmental Non-Government Organizations (ENGOs)," in *Persian Lion, Caspian Tiger*, ed. Winder and Esfandiari.

51. <www.iran-e-sabz.org/eindex.html>. It is unclear to me where the GPI is based, or who its leaders are. Though their website "welcomes" e-mails, they did not respond to my inquiries regarding the details of their organization.

52. <www.iran-e-sabz.org/program/program.htm>.

53. Islamic Republic News Agency release, 12 October 1999.

54. See *Persian Lion, Caspian Tiger*, ed. Winder and Esfandiari.

55. Mansoureh Shodjai, classroom visit, Columbia University, 1 May 2000.

56. Reshma Prakash, "Technology, Tradition and Environment Projects in Iran," *Earth Times*, 1–15 April 1999, 8, 10.

57. Mansoureh Shodjai, classroom visit, Columbia University, 1 May 2000.

58. Namazi, "Iranian Environmental Non-Government Organizations (ENGOs)," 11.

59. This section is excerpted from my "Iran's Water Crisis: Cultural, Political and Ethical Dimensions," *Journal of Agricultural and Environmental Ethics* 15, no. 4 (2002).

60. Private conversation, 3 August 2001.

61. Private conversation, 6 August 2001.

62. Private conversation, 1 August 2001.

63. An extended version of this discussion is found in my "Is Vegetarianism Un-Islamic?" *Studies in Contemporary Islam* 3, no. 1 (2001): 39–54.

64. Seyyed Hossein Nasr, in pointing out this fact during his keynote address at the Harvard conference on Islam and ecology, used it to dismiss any possibility of an Islamic vegetarianism.

65. Philip J. Stewart, "Islamic Law as a Factor in Grazing Management: The Pilgrimage Sacrifice," in *Proceedings of the First International Rangeland Congress* (Denver, Colo.: Society for Range Management, 1978): 119–20.

66. Related by Muhammad Aslam Parvaiz at the Islam and ecology conference, Center for the Study of World Religions, Harvard Divinity School, 8 May 1998.

67. Farid al-din 'Attar, *Tazkirāt al-Awliyā*, trans. Paul Losensky and Michael Sells, in Michael Sells, *Early Islamic Mysticism* (Mahwah, N.J.: Paulist Press, 1996), 160.

68. Izzi Dien, *The Environmental Dimensions of Islam*, 146.

69. Erdur, "Reappropriating the 'Green'," 151. Green is traditionally the color associated with the prophet Muhammad; hence its prominence in the flags of Saudi Arabia and Pakistan.

70. Paul Tillich, *Systematic Theology*, vol. 1 (Chicago: University of Chicago Press, 1951), 59–66.

Toward an Islamic Ecotheology

KAVEH L. AFRASIABI

Introduction

The awakening of ecological consciousness since the 1960s has had an immediate effect on Islamic theology: the basic tenets of Islam have come under the heavy fire of ecologists, and it is perhaps not an overstatement to describe these criticisms as devastating. The criticism begins from the argument that Islam, much like other monotheistic religions, is anthropocentric, and concludes that the pursuit of an ecologically minded theology must necessarily transcend these religions in search of alternative traditions and belief systems.[1] According to this line of criticism, Islam is anthropocentric because it takes human value and importance as its starting point: man is given dominion over nature and its other creatures and these have value only in their use to human beings who are bestowed with stewardship (*khalīfat*) by the Almighty.[2] What is criticized here are the Qur'anic ideas of nature as a tool, resource, favor, or even a trust (*amānat*), and its doctrine of creation which mandates the human subduing of the earth.[3] Deemed as entirely utilitarianist, these ideas are traced to the theological dualism of man and nature, and to the corollary axiom that nature as God's artifact has no purpose save to serve man.

These criticisms raise many difficulties. For one thing, they point to an Islamic basis for what ecologists and philosophers have come to deplore about the so-called technical rationality. The nub of technical rationality is a means-ends view of man's relations with nature that permits the objectification and exploitation of outer nature on an unlimited basis often in the name of human progress.[4] Closely identified with the productivist paradigm of modern capitalism, technical rationality is sometimes considered to be the real evil behind the plethora of ecological problems facing us today. The pertinent question is, of course, if there is an Islamic foundation for the evolution of technical rationality that has led to the wanton exploitation of nature in the name of human progress.

Islamic Responses to Ecological Criticism

The Islamic response to ecological criticism(s) has taken two forms: a) a defense of Islam based on an alternate reading of Islam and Islamic history; and b) moves toward the construction of a viable Islamic conception of nature.[5] Although somewhat different in scope and focus from the parallel attempts in Christianity and other religions, the volume and quality of Islamic literature devoted to the nature-and-religion problematic has begun to increase recently.

For the most part, this growing literature reflects strong objections to the ecological criticisms aforementioned. A number of authors, including Nasr, Sardar, Manzoor, and others have sought to dispel the criticism—that Islam lacks an ecological dimension—by appealing to the Qur'an, *ḥadīth,* as well as to the history of Islamic theological, philosophical, and scientific thought. Disputing the ecological criticism as a tissue of erroneous interpretation of Islam, these authors have presented an alternative view of Islam as a comprehensive religion that contains all the essential ingredients of "environmentalism." Essential to their argument arc the notions of *amr bi al-ma'arūf wa nahī al-munkir* (practicing good and prohibiting evil), ethical responsibility of "vicegerent" man toward his earthly environment, and the tradition of nature-conscious science in Muslim civilization.[6]

Concerning the latter, Nasr has cogently argued that medieval Muslim scientists, unlike their counterparts in the West, were keenly aware of the potential hazard of their work with respect to nature.[7] For Nasr in particular, the charge of technical rationality laid at the door of Islam represents an unfounded criticism that overlooks the difference of Islam and, say Christianity, vis-à-vis their respective views of the relation of man and nature. Behind Nasr's and other like-minded authors' call on Muslims to rediscover their authentic faith is a confident assertion that Islam proper is a self-contained religion that roughly corresponds with the ecological perspective which forms the core of these erroneous interpretations of Islam as unecological; their argument that there is no need to redress the wrongful neglect of nature has led these authors to question the key implication of the ecological criticism, namely, that there is a need to rethink the Islamic theology in radically new ways. But does this response really stand the weight of critical scrutiny? Have these authors satisfactorily addressed the question of ecology from their Islamic perspective?

Interestingly, Nasr himself reinforces the anthropocentric image of Islam when writing that within Islam's doctrine of creation "the causes for animals are the same [as man—KLA] except that their final cause is their use by man."[8] Likewise, Izutsu has written, "Man, his nature, conduct, psychology, duties, and destiny are, in fact, as much a central preoccupation of the Qur'anic thought as the problem of God himself."[9] This interpretation follows closely the interpretation of Islam offered by Qutb, Rahman, and others.[10] The common thread running through their work is an anthropocentric portrayal of life and, in some cases, of afterlife; the tendency to present an anthropocentric image of afterlife is rooted in the Qur'anic conception of heaven.[11]

The anthropocentric interpretation may, arguably, be based on a faithful reading of aspects of the Qur'an and *ḥadīth,* but it hardly confirms the nonutilitarian, ecological wisdom of Islam alluded to by Nasr and others mentioned above. This interpretation corresponds roughly with what we may define as Islamic humanism, that is, as an expression of a religious perspective which places man at the center of history and makes him the privileged creator on earth. Various authors have traced the genesis of Islamic humanism to the metaphysical notion of man as God-like, which has held sway among Muslim thinkers for generations.[12]

A central feature of the contemporary debate on Islam and ecology is whether or not the religious humanism of Islam can be reconciled with the ethical concerns of ecology. On a broader level, one might ask if this "Eastern" humanism can withstand the pressure of recent antihumanist, antihistoricist attacks on various anthropocentric philosophies. Both Foucault and Derrida have given us ample ammunition to deconstruct Islamic humanism, by virtue of the fact that this humanism and the secular humanism of the West have the anthropocentric core in common. Consequently, Foucault's denunciation, in the *Archaeology of Knowledge,* of the "sovereignty of the subject and the twin figures of anthropology and humanism" in Western thought applies, *mutatis mutandis,* to the humanist tradition in Islam.[13]

Following Derrida, we can, hypothetically, extend the provenance of Foucault's critique by arguing that the Islamic tendency to construe the anthropocentric view of man in terms of origins (that is, Adamic man) is the inevitable counterpart of the teleological concept of the highest man as a perfect and divine presence (*insān al-kāmil*). This criticism particularly applies to the modernist thinkers such as Shariati and Muttahari. Between the two, Shariati has been more explicitly forthcoming with his elaboration of *insān al-kāmil*: "This is an ideal human being (who) passes through nature and understands God and reaches God. . . . In nature he is God's successor . . . is a God-like in the exile of earth . . . (who) reaches the end of history and the borders of nature."[14]

It can be shown that the embrace of the idea of *insān al-kāmil* has definite anthropocentric implications. Even though Shariati and others have enveloped this idea in modernist language, in essence they have reinforced the traditional Islamic denial of the nonreductionist role of nature and the resultant lack of progress toward a theological doctrine of nature in contemporary Islam.

Furthermore, the question of whether such views of perfect man inadvertently carry atheistic connotations can be posed from a Fuerbach-Blochian angle which maintains that since the aim of all religion is the attainment of human perfection, it is in the final analysis based on an implicit elimination of God: "The utopia of Kingdom destroys the fictions of God the creator and the hypothesis of God in heaven."[15] This is not to necessarily endorse this point of view, rather to emphasize that the recent theorization(s) of *insān al-kāmil* have lent it an air of validity. As in the case of Shariati, in the custody of many modernist Muslims, "nature" has been denatured and interpreted deterministically and mechanically, bereft of its ethical value and autonomy. We may take this point one step further and make a sweeping claim: That the deconstruction of the Islamic humanism as it stands today is the essential prerequisite for the objective of arriving at the door of an alternative Islamic theology that would be capable of integrating within its horizon the fundamental ecological precepts. Amplifying a thesis recently debated in the ecological, religious, and philosophical literature, the force of this claim makes the culpability of the Islamic humanism in the neglect of nature a central issue; it shows that from an ecological critique of Islam to a critique of the Islamic humanism is but a small step, that the two types of critique are in fact highly intertwined; it also calls for an integral theology that meets the conditions for focusing on viable themes of nature and ecology. Contrary to Manzoor, Sardar, Agwan and others, it is not enough to show that pro-ecology insights can be found in Islam. Before the ecological criticism can be dismissed what is needed is a convincing presentation of ecological parameters *sui generis* to Islam, if there is any. There remains, at the outset of our work, an inconclusive if and but about the discovery of ecologically relevant facets of Islam, first of all, due to the broad deconstructionist implications of the ecological criticism: Will there be any thing retrievable for a viable Islamic theology once we apply the (hermeneutic and) deconstructionist method? Or will this lead us to give up on this project altogether?

Indeed, the jury is still out on this question and the related question of the nature of relationship between Islam and ecology; short of lapsing into dogmatic and emotional defense of Islam, I am afraid the intellectual debate over Islam and ecology is yet to be won in principle. What we know for sure is that the ecological perspective has unleashed a serious challenge to the Islamic thought and values, and that the attempts to deny any trace of anthropocentrism and technical rationality in Islam have often ended in the snares of their own contradictions. Given the force of ecological criticisms and the various shortcomings of the Islamic responses, such as evading the core criticisms as in the case of Sardar,[16] Islam has become resignative; its concept of "corruption on earth" *(mufsid fi' l-arḍ)* can at most unmask the unreason at the heart of what has passed for reason, without account of its own, in a word, has reached a dead end.

This unhappy situation is basically the product of a double, concurrent crisis, that is, on the one hand, the crisis of Islamic humanism and, on the other hand, the crisis of theoretical attempts to rethink the viability of Islam along ecological lines, the fact that these attempts have had to defend Islam against the ecological criticism in vain. These (largely modernist) attempts have suffered from a conspicuous absence of a past tradition to build upon; their crisis stems partially from the relative void of "ecological parameter" in the contemporary, twentieth-century discourses on Islam: From Abduh to Iqbal to Shariati, and so on, a common thread of the various so-called reconstructive projects in Islam has been a near complete obliviousness to the need to infuse a credible ecological dimension.[17] Thus, whereas Iqbal's pioneering "reconstruction of Islamic thought" was for the most part, except at the most abstract theological level, closed to ecological insights, Shariati on the other hand invoked the anti-ecological view of nature as the "objectified other" by describing nature as a "prison."[18] This deplorable lacuna in the reconstructive project has had vast ecological and even cultural implications; unintentionally, at least, it skewed the course of the modernistic Islamic thought in the direction of humanism and anthropocentrism, without achieving any major progress in Islamic theology of nature, and, consequently, without addressing the limitations of the pre-existing views of nature—as a prison or as the metaphoric "place of forgetfulness" (Ibn al-'Arabi) or as "dream of a sleeper" (Rumi).[19] Besides the absence of critical reflection on pre-modern Islamic interpretations of nature where nature was often downgraded as the antithesis of spirit, the reconstructive project has increasingly focused on sociological and cultural issues at the cost of neglecting the cosmological and theological implications. The "modernist" Islam in its main manifestation has lost credibility by its explicit and willful choice of priorities that has bracketed the large vision of the place of humanity in the cosmos; many of its pundits have stressed harmony with religion, but their flirtation with nature has rarely, if ever, led them in the direction of a new theology.

For the past couple of decades, the development of Islamic thought in the Muslim World has been dominated by the so-called fundamentalism and/or "revivalism," a phenomenon of such magnitude and force that has set the tone and agenda for many Muslim theologians, some of whom are self-styled "liberation theologians" not unlike their Christian counterparts. The vast vagaries and differentiated attitudes of this movement notwithstanding, it is not far-fetched to charge its proponents with a relative neglect of nature as a result of their prioritization of politico-economic and cultural issues. A survey of the recent revivalist works shows that concern for nature and the related ecological issues has never been a top priority. Even among the more academically inclined advocates of "Islamization of knowledge," we have yet to see attempts to address this deficiency and to propose a new theological approach that reintegrates the theme of nature.[20]

The very idea of Islamization of ecological knowledge, though it sounds appealing, nonetheless has the fault of carrying the seeds of an inseparable romanticism that romanticizes Islam's capability to address the various ecological themes and issues. Prompted in large measure by a catching-up new agenda to address ecological concerns from an authentic Islamic perspective, the proponents of this idea have assumed, a priori, both the self-contained quality of the Islamic view of nature and the unproblematic process of application of the Islamic insights to contemporary ecological issues. But in hindsight, both these positions may prove to be unwarranted, for neither the adequacy of Islamic theology of nature can be taken for granted, nor can we presume that the problematic of Islam and ecology is a simple one of drawing from the arsenal of Islamic insights to tackle the thematic and practical issues of ecology.

Furthermore, a related criticism of the "Islamization of knowledge" and "revivalist" projects is that, regardless of their points of dissimilarities, they evince a latent (and at times manifest) common tendency toward dogmatic self-enclosure vis-à-vis relevant insights from other cultures and traditions. Coupled with this tendency is another tendency, namely, the tendency to exaggerate the dashing views and interests between Islam and the West and, thereby, lose sight of the global issues and the globalization of ecological concerns in today's "globalized context."[21]

The phenomenon of global interdependence has created the drive to a new uniformity of concerns over such issues as global warming, air and water pollution, population explosion, depletion of natural resources on a planetary scale, and the like, and this runs against the temptation (among some Muslim thinkers and activists) to shun any meaningful dialogue with the non-Muslim West, which they regard from their prism of "hermeneutic of suspicion" as a dangerous prelude for a new "mental colonization," whose goals would be to obliterate the autonomy of their culture and impose conformity to the Western standards. Seeking to nullify these dangers, these Muslims have adopted a strategy of resistance that often invokes the crusade-type image of "fortress Islam," as if by excommunicating the radically other (that is, the West) at the discursive and knowledge levels, it is possible to rehabilitate the *umma.* Still, it must be recognized that this is to some extent a defensive strategy imposed from without, that is, by the Western cultural and ideological impositions that have recently taken on new guises such as the "end of ideology" and world historical "triumph of liberalism" that carry totalitarian connotations and either directly or indirectly question the validity of cultural polycentrism on a world scale.[22] In other words, the prejudices, the overt signs of hostility, the economically superior position of the West and its cultural "invasion" have directly dictated the defensive Islamic strategy (of survival) which has manufactured its own shields of protection laden with meanings and prejudices.[23] Acknowledging the merits of this strategy and its emancipatory potential is at the same time an acknowledgment of the difficulty of establishing the possibility of an undistorted communicative interaction, to borrow a term from Habermas, in a situation of asymmetry and conflict of interests.[24] What has so far blocked this possibility is a variety of factors emerging from the hermeneutical (mutual) lack of recognition of the other, ranging from ignorance of the other's tradition, to intolerance to outright repugnance. Thus, while the fear of "green threat" runs rampant in the West, the Islamic revivalists and populists often succumb to the image of the West as a hostile other that embodies only the evil.[25] For these Muslims, entering into a conversation with the West becomes like entering into a zero-sum game where the validity claims of each side are at stake; their strategy of self-insulating from the Western influences has, as stated above, a rational basis connected to the striving of Muslims for cultural autonomy and emancipation in the light of onslaught of Western values and norms.

But the difficulty with the rational side is that it coexists, and one might say is even buried, under an irrational side that comes from the dogmatic religious belief that places an antimodern emphasis on the autonomy of the *umma*, as if Islamic civilization is landlocked in a closed horizon. Inadequately cognizant of the common global problems that bind the human inhabitants of the planet together in an unprecedented way, the Muslim revivalists have, conceivably, overemphasized sociopolitical and cultural issues and underemphasized theological and ecological issues; the two types of issues are of course interrelated and cannot be divorced from each other, except through the fiat of pragmatic revivalist movements guided by a burning desire to change the Muslim society from various forms and manifestations of corruption on Earth, without fully addressing the ecological aspect of this corruption and its doctrinal roots in Islam itself: As a result, the recently surfaced ideas of the environmental *jihād,* an Islamic green movement, and the like, have yet to take hold of the imagination of worthy Muslim theologians and jurisprudents, most of whom appear to have confined themselves to rhetorical recycling of premodern norms and are hitherto unaffected by the ecologically imposed needs for rethinking their conceptions of nature, man, and the cosmos. Thus, for instance, there is a conspicuous absence of a credible Islamic notion of limit, one that could, theologically speaking, define and elaborate upon limits in the Islamically sanctioned usage and exploitation of nature. Sadly lacking is even a minimal theological discourse that would exhibit a keen awareness of the inadequacy of Islamic theology when it comes to human self-limitation vis-à-vis nature and animals.

To substantiate this latter criticism, we may glance at the Shi'ite jurisprudence (*fiqh*) in this century and the previous centuries. Such a scrutiny shows a remarkable uniformity of views in terms of a common obliviousness, on the part of the leading Shi'ite jurisprudents, to ecological insights.

Concretely, various ayatollahs (*āyāt Allāh*; literally, "signs of God") such as Golpayegani, Khoi, Brujerdi, Montazeri, and Khomeini, each has explicated as precisely as possible the meanings and limits of the vast issue of *dakhl va taṣṣarruf dar ṭabī'at* (drawing from and possession of nature), yet, not only has the attention placed one-sidedly on *taṣṣarruf* and *dakhl* been relatively neglected, an added problem with the exegesis of the *sharī'a* by these ayatollahs is their shared inability to go beyond vague references to Islamic limits of human *dakhl* in nature and to include ecologically relevant conditions. More specifically, all these ayatollahs have spelled out in great detail the Islamic law pertaining to animal hunting, yet none has grappled with the issue of endangered species. To give an example, Ayatollah Montazeri writes in his *Tawḍīḥ al-Masā'il* about the categories of birds whose meat is forbidden to Muslims, for example, vultures and eagles, since they are "rapacious and have claws."[26] However, no mention is made of the endangered birds and the role of the *sharī'a* in protecting them. Far from representing an exception, Montazeri's serious omissions are in fact shared by all the other leading ayatollahs aforementioned; the ecological shortcomings of their *Tawḍīḥ al-Masā'il* point at a major lacuna in the Shi'ite jurisprudence, which is unfortunately not limited to Shi'ism but engulfs other Muslim sects and denominations as well. This lacuna points at what is urgently needed at the present time: an up-to-date, ecologically conscious *Tawḍīḥ al-Masā'il.* From within Shi'ism, this would imply anew articulation of the issue of *dakhl va taṣṣarruf dar ṭabī'at* which, with the help of more refined concepts and understandings of limits, would be able to present moral and ethical solutions for the growing ecological problems. Yet, a satisfactory articulation of this issue cannot possibly be realized without occurring as part and parcel of a wider theological agenda and, perhaps, a theological detour.

The reason a theological detour may be necessary has to do with the need to remove the fundamental theological roadblocks that have obliterated the space for a new articulation of the Islamic *sharī'a*; in a word what is needed is an alternative Islamic theology which has Qur'an and *ḥadīth* on its side, that seeks to telescope this theology to the need for spiritual deepening and a renewed sense of hope among the Muslims, the young generation especially.

Indeed, the young Muslims everywhere are in dire need of a new religious "manifesto," a dynamic, genuinely Islamic perspective that is thoroughly contemporary and dynamic, theoretically appealing and action-oriented, idealistic and yet nonutopian, and nondogmatic, a perspective based on a systematic theology that would be deemed satisfactory by what Iqbal has identified to be a criterion of the modern Islamic mind, that is, "a concrete living experience of God."[27]

Integrating Ecology and Islamic Theology: The Tasks Ahead

The challenge to the Muslims of articulating and developing a sound ecological theology, which we may call ecotheology for purely heuristic purposes, are quite enormous. First of all, this is the challenge of establishing that, contra Tillich, a theology of the inorganic is potentially present in Islam.[28] Second, this is the challenge of proving that within Islam, utilitarianism does not reign supreme; and that creation outside human beings has more than just utilitarian values and, third, that the earth as a whole is thought of as a living, even an intelligent being. Fourth, the challenge is that of spelling out in a coherent fashion the fundamentals of an Islamic theology of "reverence for life" directed to man, nature, and animals as a whole, and, fifth, applying the parameters of this theology to such practical ecological issues such as clashing interests between human beings and animals. Given that the presentation of endangered species often involves some cost to human interests, the question of how Islamic ecotheology views this issue and what solutions it presents is of special importance. This is so because the theological concerns with the mundane global issues and their various moral and ethical questions form a central preoccupation of Islamic ecotheology; of course, this interpretation runs contrary to a popular misunderstanding of what theology is all about, that is, the notion that theology belongs exclusively to the realm of higher grounds, that is, metaphysics and eschatology. This points, sixth, to another challenge of ecotheology, that of establishing a series of mediating concepts to bridge the gap between theology and ecology.

Seventh, in the process of developing these mediating concepts, Islamic theology can and should translate itself into a fashionable language attractive to the modern mind of the present and future generations. As a responsible service to the *bildung* of Muslims, ecotheology's main task is to self-present as the repository of a future-oriented practical theology that is centered on hope in close proximity to preexisting values and interpretations. Certain discontinuities of language are nested in this project which must remain in a healthy state of hybridity vis-à-vis the elements of continuity. Surely, the Islamic ecotheology will rise or fall by its ability to provide a delicate balance between continuity and discontinuity. Relatedly, eighth, the Islamic ecotheology must walk the tight rope of, simultaneously, satisfying the requirement of addressing the concerns of (the Muslim and non-Muslim) ecological critics of Islam and, on the other hand, quieting the concerns of the Islamic conservatives and traditionalists, who may question it as heretical. Thus, unless the double tests of authenticity and innovation are passed successfully, which is no mean task by any measure of imagination, the Islamic theology will inevitably start down the road of identity crisis where the wolves of history prowl. Put in other words, the challenge before the self-declared Islamic ecotheologians is that, besides avoiding the ethnocentric temptation of self-imprisoning within the confines of the primordial tradition as perfect and complete, they must also prove that they can constructively and critically appropriate the wisdom of the non-Muslim world on ecology without succumbing to either unprincipled eclecticism or "Westoxication."[29] Following Ibn Khaldun's footsteps, it can be safely assumed that without an open mind capable of absorbing the wisdom of others, Islamic thought will inevitably ghettoize itself on ruinous grounds.[30] To prevent this unwanted outcome, and to lift the heavy chain of dogmatism that shuns the rest of the world as unessential to the development of its thought (perhaps except as negative points of reference), the Islamic ecotheology draws its inspiration—to borrow foreign ideas and infuse them into its repository—based on the inviolability of its communicative theological ethics that touches on universal human progress across visible and invisible frontiers; undoubtedly, such a progress means in today's shrinking world a process of forging partnership and collective action on the part of different peoples around the world.

Launched by a new sense of realism about the shared global problems and the welter of interdependencies that characterize today's world society, this communicative theology is bound to jailbreak from the twin hazards of Western and Eastern self-centrism. Responding to the enthusiasm generated by the impact of greater and greater intrafaith communication, this "school" of theology is potentially readied for substantial learning from without. And at the same time, its openness to interfaith communication implies that the Islamic ecotheology's requirement is not necessarily an epistemological *courpure* pure and simple, that in fact the parameters of this theology can perhaps be best described as neoconservative. The neo aspect of its conservatism comes from its particular view of what it takes to have an Islamic renaissance in the late twentieth century.

If we start from the view that the aim of the Islamic ecotheology is to present an authentic interpretation of Islam intimately in tune with the need for renewal in the historically changed circumstances, then it is easier to proceed with confidence toward the stated project of Islamic renaissance. Though this means taking Islam in a new direction, the course of Islamic ecotheology still retains the threads of continuity in many respects: it concurs with the prevalent view among the Muslim scholars that the refinement of theological method is the *sine qua non* of Islamic knowledge, that without theological beliefs the harmony of man and nature is difficult if not impossible to achieve, and that any attempt to rethink the unity of man and nature must by necessity travel through metaphysics as a viable, and not a self-defeating, solution.[31]

Henceforth, Islamic ecotheology has cut for itself a huge job. It must articulate a defensible non-anthropocentric conception of Islam; it must provide a nonobjectifying view of nature, and a dialectical view of man that is not overlaid with the stereotypical monarchical connotation of vicegerency; it must be an integrated theology which views all life as sacred and deals with man's relation with his Deity, man's relation with man, and man's relation with nature; it would open new inquiries about all these relations. Concerning the latter, it would seek deeper views than the conventional one according to which living beings are at the disposal of man; it would favor a more complex theological discourse to cast in new lights the religious interpretation of man-nature dualism; it would seek all these by and through a critical self-reflection that would amount to (a) a reconstruction of the meanings of key Islamic terms and their interrelationships, for example, *tawḥīd* (divine unity), *khalqiyat* (creation), *ahd* (covenant), *amānat* (trust), *qiyāmat* (apocalypse), and *umma* (community), and (b) a deconstruction of those Islamic cosmological, theological, and ethical perspectives deemed untenable either wholly or in part. In pursuing these objectives, Islamic ecotheology would contribute to the ongoing debates on ecology and ethics, showing the exalted place of Islam in the planetary struggle for survival and evolution. Should Islamic ecotheology succeed in rising to the occasion of challenges aforementioned, in that case its proponents will have very little difficulty proving that Islam and care for the earth and its creatures are one and the same, that where there is an Islamic theological vision there is no scarcity of ethics of responsibility toward the environment, and that Islamic attempts to conceive of nature as a moral category potentially give rise to a human species capable of self-limiting from undue exploitation, and which communicates with nature as part of a moral order. The shift to an Islamic ecotheology might well have consequences for the Muslims' sense of obligation to nature and for the norms governing their interaction with nature that they regard as justifiable. A final introductory note and that is, Islamic ecotheology is less concerned about the newness of its approach, as a new "paradigm," and more with the self-prescribed criterion of consistency vis-à-vis its theological route. This route is paved to a considerable degree with extractions from *kalām* and *falsafa* backgrounds. Transgressing the time-honored distinctions, the Islamic ecotheology's newness derives from its novel combination of manifestly hostile subviews within Islam, and from the addition of elements of novelty inspired by advances in human knowledge.

In bringing this introductory essay to a close, if we were to ask instead, whether or not the Islamic ecotheology promises more than it delivers, and whether its potential to distort surpasses its potential to illuminate, then we have a legitimate excuse to pause for a healthy moment of self-doubt, followed by a conscientious effort to delineate the specifics of Islamic ecotheology.

Notes

This article was originally published in *Hamdard Islamicus* 18, no. 1 (1998): 33–49 and is here reprinted with permission from the Hamdard Foundation Pakistan.

1. See Lynn White, Jr., "The Historical Roots of Our Ecologic Crisis," *Science* 155 (March 1967): 1203–7. Prior to White, Arnold Toynbee articulated the ecological attack on monotheistic religions. See, "The Religious Background of the Present Environmental Crisis," in *Ecology and Religion in History*, ed. David and Eileen Spring (New York: Harper and Row, 1974).

2. Qur'an 10:14: "Then We made you heirs in the land after them, to see how ye would behave." See also 27:62, 35:39 and 67:14.

3. "Seest thou not that God has made subject to you (men) all that is on the earth?" (Qur'an 22:65). "It is He Who hath made you (His) agents, inheritors of earth: He hath raised you in ranks, some above others: that He may try you in the gifts He hath given you." (Qur'an 6:165).

4. For a critique of technical rationality see, Jurgen Habermas, *The Theory of Communicative Action, I: Reason and Rationalization of Society* (Boston: Beacon Press, 1984); *Zur Rekonstruktion des Historischen Materialismus* (Frankfurt: Suhrkamp, 1976). Also Max Weber, *The Methodology of the Social Sciences* (New York: Free Press, 1949).

5. See Seyyed Hossein Nasr, *Man and Nature* (1967; Chicago: Kazi, 1997); Ziauddin Sardar, *The Future of Muslim Civilisation* (London: Croom Helm, 1979); S. Parvez Manzoor, "Environment and Values: The Islamic Perspective," in *The Touch of Midas: Science, Values and Environment in Islam and the West,* ed. Ziauddin Sardar (Manchester: Manchester University Press, 1984), 150–70; and A. R. Agwan, *The Environmental Concern of Islam* (New Delhi: Institute of Objective Studies, 1992).

6. See Fazlun Khalid and Joanne O'Brien, eds., *Islam and Ecology* (London: Cassel, 1992).

7. Seyyed Hossein Nasr, *Science and Civilization in Islam* (Cambridge: Cambridge University Press, 1987).

8. Seyyed Hossein Nasr, *Islamic Life and Thought* (Albany: State University of New York Press, 1981).

9. Toshihiko Izutsu, *God and Man in the Koran* (Tokyo: Keio Institute of Cultural and Linguistics Studies, 1964), 75.

10. Fazlur Rahman, *Major Themes of the Qur'an* (Chicago: University of Chicago Press, 1980); Sayyid Qutb, *This Religion of Islam* (1967; Salimiah, Kuwait: International Islamic Federation of Student Organizations, 1980); also Wan Mohd Nor Wan Daud, "God in the Quran: An Objective and Functional Existent," in *Islam and the Modern Age* 19, no. 3 (1988): 155–65.

11. "But those who believe and work deeds of righteousness—to them We shall give a Home in Heaven, —lofty mansions, beneath which flow rivers,—to dwell therein for aye;—an excellent reward for those who do (good)! (Qur'an 29:58). For more on this issue, see Colleen McDonnel and Bernard Lang, *Heaven: A History* (New Haven: Yale University Press, 1988). Also Juan Eduardo Campo, *The Other Sides of Paradise* (Columbia: University of South Carolina Press, 1991).

12. For example, see Murteza Muttahari, *Fundamentals of Islamic Thought: God, Man and the Universe,* trans. Hamid Algar (Berkeley: Mizan Press, 1985).

13. Michel Foucault, *The Archaeology of Knowledge* (New York: Pantheon Books, 1972). For a greater elaboration on postmodern antihumanism see Kate Soper, *Humanism and Anti-Humanism* (La Salle, Ill.: Open Court, 1986). Derrida's view can be found in his book *Margins of Philosophy* (Chicago: University of Chicago Press, 1983).

14. Ali Shariati, *Islamology* (Tehran, 1981), 100. (In Persian.)

15. Ernst Bloch, *Danz Prinzip Hoffnung* (Frankfurt: Suhrkamp, 1969), 1412.

16. One problem with Sardar's defense of Islam is that he does not grapple with those passages in the Qur'an and *ḥadīth* which, according to the ecological critics, are anthropocentric. See Sardar's introduction in the *Touch of Midas*, 8.

17. See Muhammad Abduh, *al-Islam wa'l-Nasraniyya* (Cairo, 1954); Muhammad Iqbal, *The Reconstruction of Religious Thought in Islam* (Lahore: Muhammad Ashraf, 1982); and Ali Shariati, *On the Sociology of Islam* (Berkeley: Mizan Press, 1979).

18. Shariati, *On the Sociology of Islam.*

19. Ibn 'Arabi writes about "the confines of nature. . . the place of forgetfulness." See William Chittick, *The Sufi Path of Knowledge* (Albany: State University of New York Press, 1989), 165. For Rumi's view, see *Discourses of Rumi,* trans. A. J. Arbery, (London, 1961), 60. Similar views can be found in the 'Ashari school. See Richard J. McCarthy, *The Theology of al-'Ashari* (Beirut, 1953).

20. *Towards Islamization of Disciplines* (Washington, 1989) and *Islamization of Knowledge* (Washington, 1991); also Seyyed Hossein Nasr, "Islam and the Environmental Crisis," *MAAS Journal of Islamic Science* 6, no. 2 (1990): 31–51.

21. See Max L. Stackhouse, *Apologia: Contextualization, Globalization and Mission in Theological Education* (Grand Rapids: Eerdman's, 1988). Also Hans Kung, *Global Responsibility: In Search of a World Ethic* (New York: Crossroad, 1991).

22. For example, see Francis Fukuyama, *The End of History and the Last Man* (New York: Free Press, 1992). In this book, Fukuyama portrays Islam as an "illiberal ideology" that is "very hard to reconcile with liberalism and the recognition of universal rights, particularly freedom of conscience or religion" (p. 217).

23. See Mona Abul-Fadl, *Where East Meets West: The West on the Agenda of the Islamic Revival* (Herndon, Va.: International Institute of Islamic Thought, 1992). Also John L. Esposito, *The Islamic Threat: Myth or Reality?* (New York: Oxford University Press, 1992).

24. Jurgen Habermas, *The Theory of Communicative Action.* For critical evaluations of Habermas, see Axel Honneth and Hans Joas, eds., *Communicative Action* (Cambridge: Polity Press, 1991).

25. David E. Gordon, *Images of the West* (Lanham, Md., 1989).

26. Hossein Ali Montazeri, *Tawzih al-Masa'il,*(Tehran, 1984), 516.

27. Iqbal, *Reconstruction of Religious Thought*, 183.

28. Paul Tillich, *Systematic Theology,* vol. 3 (Chicago: University of Chicago Press, 1963), 18. Similarly, Albert Schweitzer has written, "The greatest fault of ethics hitherto has been to deal only with man's relation with man" (*Ethics and Civilization* [London, 1929], 133). In this book, Schweitzer writes that no man is truly ethical unless all of life is sacred to him; "that of plants and animals as that of his fellowman" (p. 216). For contemporary attempts in Christianity and other religions to address the

ecological issues see, among others, John B. Cobb, Jr., *Sustainability,* (Maryknoll, N.Y.: Orbis, 1992); Jay B. McDaniel, *Of God and Pelicans: A Theology of Reverence for Life* (Louisville, Ky: Westminster/John Knox Press, 1989); Conrad Cherry, *Nature and Religious Imagination* (Philadelphia: Fortress Press, 1980); Dieter T. Hessel, *For Creation's Sake: Preaching, Ecology, and Justice* (Philadelphia: Geneva Press, 1985); Warwick Fox, *Toward a Transpersonal Ecology: Developing New Foundations for Environmentalism* (Boston: Shambhala, 1990); Judith Plant, ed., *Healing the Wounds: The Promise of Ecofeminism* (Philadelphia: New Society Publishers, 1989); Robert Disch, *The Ecological Conscience* (Englewood Cliffs: Prentice-Hall, 1971); and M. Sethna, "Zoroastrianism and the Protection of Nature," in *Religion, Nature and Survival* (New Delhi, 1992).

29. On the concept of Westoxication see, Jalal Al-e Ahmad, *Gharbzadegi* (Tehran, 1981).

30. In the beginning of his book, Ibn Khaldun admonishes his contemporary Muslims for their failure to imitate the Western visitors who learned what they could from the East. See *Muqaddimah,* trans. Franz Rosenthal (New York, 1958).

31. Habermas has argued that attempts to re-establish the unity of reason "would have to lead back to metaphysics, and thus behind the levels of learning reached in the modern age into a re-enchanted world." Jurgen Habermas, "Reply to My Critics," in John B. Thompson and David Held, eds., *Habermas: Critical Debates* (Cambridge, Mass.: MIT Press, 1982), 245. The question left unanswered by Habermas is how his own theory of communication can restore the autonomy of nature against the assault of technical rationality short of, at a minimum, falling back on the "quasi-transcendental" notion of human interests (which Habermas has bracketed since taking the linguistic turn in his philosophy).

Environment and Social Justice

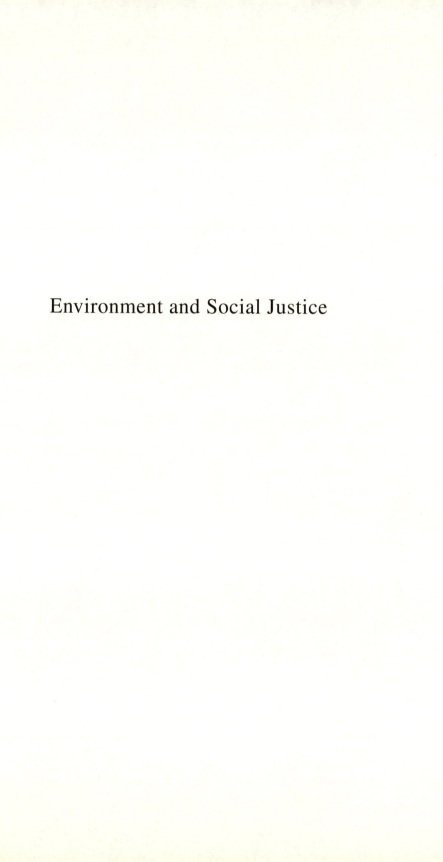

Islam, Ecology, and Modernity: An Islamic Critique of the Root Causes of Environmental Degradation

FAZLUN M. KHALID

Introduction

There are two things that can be said with some degree of certainty about the environmental crisis, which is without historical precedent. First, the entire human community is affected by it, and second, every single human being can play his or her part in working within their own capacities and traditions to do something to ameliorate the problem. Unfortunately, our species seems to be pulling in the opposite direction. The idea of a global village, with all the finiteness that it implies, is now common currency, on the one hand, yet, on the other, humankind continues to believe in its infinite capacity to provide for its continuously increasing desires. As Seyyed Hossein Nasr observes, "There is near total disequilibrium between modern man and nature as attested by nearly every expression of modern civilization which seeks to offer a challenge to nature rather than to co-operate with it."[1]

We are sufficiently distant from the genesis of this particular phase of human history to be able to discern the specific people, ideas, and events that have brought us to this point. The drive for the great events of the past five hundred or so years has come mainly from the bosom of Europe. This has been a period of intellectual brilliance and unsurpassed technological innovation, and the political dominance Europe has exercised over the rest of the people on this planet is unprecedented. What began as Christian Europe—or, to use the term loosely, Christendom—has transformed itself into a group of secular nation-states which has also succeeded in persuading or coercing the rest of the human community to organize their lives in a like manner. Along with this phenomenon, importantly, came schools and universities based on the European model run by Christian missionaries or local educationists who were impressed by this model. These institutions replaced (to everybody's detriment, it would now seem) tried and tested traditional systems of knowledge.

At the same time, this "modernizing" movement succeeded in producing an elite, including a Muslim elite, that wanted for themselves what the West wanted. In an aptly named book, *Monocultures of the Mind*, Vandana Shiva says, "Emerging from a dominating and colonizing culture, modern knowledge systems are themselves colonizing."[2] Thus, colonial education, which eventually became universal education, is seen now to be the fount of modernity. It played a major role in helping to lay the foundations for the establishment of a global system of nation-states. This system was based on an institutional model run according to secular principles subscribing to a philosophy of endless economic growth. It now functions within a political system that relies heavily on consumerism to hold it together. This paradigm is at the root of today's environmental crisis.

Colonialism has been replaced (though this needs to be reconsidered in light of the U.S.-led invasion of Iraq) by modernity as the force underpinning the economic dominance of the West over the rest of the world. China, for example, may not have been directly politically colonized, but it expresses itself as an evolving synthesis of a Marxist capitalist model in search of industrial expansion and consumerism. It desires to replicate the modern Western experience within the framework of secular scientism and consumer communism. The rejection of the Confucian-Daoist paradigm by the Chinese has been a loss, not just to China but to the rest of the world. Similarly, when the Ottoman caliphate was weakened by the West, it signalled the end of a milieu where another worldview prevailed. As Harvard political scientist Samuel Huntington notes: "The rise of the West undermined both the Ottoman and Mogul empires, and the end of the Ottoman Empire left Islam without a core state. Its territories were in considerable measure divided among Western powers which when they retreated left behind fragile nations formed on a Western model alien to the traditions of Islam."[3]

Huntington also points out that Kemalist Turkey set out deliberately to both Westernize and modernize.[4] Modernity manifests itself in different forms, as we can see in the cases of China and Turkey, but this does not detract from its homogenizing qualities, as this essay seeks to show. The West changed—modernized—rapidly, and as it changed, it changed the rest of the world with it.

What emerged in Europe that was radically different was a scientific worldview, which is seen as having provided a new impetus to history. Huntington claims that what Europe went through was "a revolutionary process comparable only to the shift from primitive to civilized societies . . . which began . . . about 5000 BC." These events took place when European states were conjunctively and collectively a power in the world. Modernity evolved as these countries attempted to consolidate themselves into new-style nation-states, through the period now known to us as "the Enlightenment" and the subsequent traumas of the industrial revolution. The Americas, not far behind, participated in this process once their own colonial wars were settled. The agricultural revolution that transformed human society nearly seven thousand years ago went through a slow and diffuse process. By contrast, the changes that have taken place in the past four to five hundred years have been rapid, violent, and devastating in their impact upon nature.

The hypothesis presented in this essay is that prior to the advent of modernity, the natural order functioned within its own limits and that the seeds of the ecological crisis that breached these limits were sown during the period that followed the Renaissance. This occurred from the sixteenth century onwards, when what we now know as "modernity" began to evolve.

Two fundamental causes altered the course of civilization that has now brought us to this point. The first of these is the shift in humankind's perception of itself in relation to the natural order. This is encoded in what has now come to be known as the secular scientific worldview, which emerged in the period under consideration. Having resided in nature's bosom for aeons, humans suddenly became its predator. The second cause has to do with wealth—more precisely, money, and how we now create it with gay abandon. John Kenneth Galbraith said in this regard, "The process by which we create money is so simple that the mind is repelled."[5] Frederic Benham, a writer of standard economic textbooks, has observed that "it seems like a gigantic confidence trick."[6]

Conveniently, the predator has now discovered a magical way of creating endless credit with which to devastate the earth. This makes much of our progress illusory and the basis of modernity highly questionable.

This essay is an attempt to identify and focus on these two causes that are seen to be at the root of the environmental crisis and that are an anathema to Islam. I first examine how the secular scientific ethic came to be preeminent in Europe at the expense of traditional worldviews. In the second section I explore modernity in this light and its evolution up to the present time in relation to the ecological crisis. This is followed by a discussion of how the ethic of human dominance crystallized alongside a new form of financial intermediation, and how they both go against the Islamic norm. I attempt to demonstrate how they have jointly contributed to the present crisis. The final part of my essay identifies principles which may form the foundation of an Islamic model for a sustainable lifestyle, based on a system of Islamic law (*sharī'a*) and governance.

The Ascendency of Science

The Qur'an, in one of its commentaries on existence, asserts that "We have not created the heavens and the earth, and what is between them, save with the truth and a stated term."[7] Every species, including the human, has a limited time on this planet, and the planet Earth itself will one day be turned to cinder by an expanding Sun. The knowledge of our own extinction, however distant it may seem to be, has yet to enter our consciousness. The Last Day, expressed in the Qur'an as "*al-yawm al-akhīr*" (2:7), is an article of faith in Islam. But there is the distinct possibility that we could be shortening the time that has been allocated to our species by a very large margin, in the way we have been conducting our affairs. Richard Leakey says in his recent book *The Sixth Extinction* that our "reason and insight have not prevented us from collectively exploiting Earth's resources—biologically and physically—in unprecedented ways."[8]

Leakey, to further his point, quotes Harvard biologist Edward Wilson, who, in addition to arguing that the human species is an environmental abnormality, suggests that intelligence has a tendency to extinguish itself.[9] What other species would consciously destroy its habitat deliberately within a *rational framework* that justifies such actions? There now appears to be agreement that "biological diversity is in the midst of its sixth great crisis (the previous five having occurred naturally in the pre-human history of the Earth) this time precipitated entirely by man."[10] Leakey concludes that "we homo sapiens may also be among the living dead."[11]

The human species, having broken loose from the imperatives that confined it to the natural order, now seeks to dominate it, much to the detriment both to itself and the biosphere. Many see science as being culpable in this respect. Thomas Berry explains that Francis Bacon (1561–1626) introduced a new historical vision of a better order in earthly affairs through "scientific control" over the functioning of the natural world, with its fulfillment in the industrial age of the nineteenth and twentieth centuries. Berry further asserts that both liberal capitalism and Marxist socialism committed themselves totally to this vision of industrial progress, which more than any other single cause has brought about the disintegration that is taking place throughout the entire planet.

By a supreme irony, this closing down of the basic life systems of the earth has resulted from a commitment to the betterment of the human condition, to "progress."[12] Seyyed Hossein Nasr, writing in 1968, suggests that Francis Bacon was part of a wider process that was "the gradual de-sacralization of the cosmos which took place in the West and especially the rationalism and humanism of the Renaissance which made possible the scientific revolution."[13]

Bacon advocated a new method of looking at natural phenomena and developed the inductive method of inquiry to reduce uncertainty in scientific experimentation. He was not a scientist per se, and in the view of Brian L. Silver "he left a legacy of belief in the evidence of the senses and in experimentation, and a vision of the role of science as the means of improving the material condition of man."[14] As Nasr points out, Francis Bacon was part of a process that was exclusively that of the West, which led in the seventeenth and eighteenth centuries to the period now known to us as the Enlightenment.

The rationalist movement which gained ascendancy in this period was ostensibly given its impetus by Descartes (1596–1650) and further epitomized by thinkers such as Locke (1632–1704), Voltaire (1694–1778) and Kant (1724–1804); Bentham (1748–1832) and Mill (1806–1832) advocated a form of hedonism in what is now known to us as utilitarianism; Smith (1723–1790) and Ricardo (1772–1823) gave us new insights into the taming of market forces by inaugurating the "science" of economics; Newton (1642–1727) is reputed to have reduced the universe to a "clockwork machine." Adventurers and politicians, bankers and capitalists, entrepreneurs and inventors, centers of learning and scientists found ample encouragement and justification to inaugurate the industrial revolution, establish the nation-state, and devise a political model that now panders to human hedonistic tendencies. This has brought us to the point where the human species has taken control of the biosphere in no uncertain terms. Seeing this as a linear movement which originated in the Renaissance, Nasr observes that "the absolutization of the human state is a heritage of the European Renaissance whose deadly consequences are being manifested only today. . . ."[15]

Science is now associated with technology and the industrial revolution. Silver asserts in its defense that science is not synonymous with technology, that "the stereotypical scientist is interested in how nature works and that the stereotypical technologist is interested in making more profitable soap powders."[16] But Silver does not distinguish between pure and applied science, or between science and scientists who may also be technologists, whose very work and survival would be at risk if their research was not financed by commerce and industry whose profits derive from making and selling "profitable soap powders."

Pure science tends to explore phenomena in minutia, which has caused it to be labeled reductionist, although there is nothing wrong with this. However, it has led the way to reductionist applications that ignore the wider ecological imperatives. The geneticist Mae-Wan Ho argues that reductionist science has been shown not to work in many cases—for example, the green revolution, eugenics, and nuclear energy.[17] Pure research has contributed much to our understanding of how the physical world and the life-forms it contains work. But this information can be misused for power or profit.

DNA was discovered in 1869. Modern molecular biology was initiated with the discovery of the double helix in 1953 by Crick and Watson. Dolly the sheep was cloned using the techniques of DNA manipulation, now conveniently known as genetic engineering, in 1997. Scientists have now become engineers; Ian Wilmut, the scientist who successfully cloned Dolly, is an embryologist.[18] Ho observes that "what makes Genetic Engineering Biotechnology (the formal name of this specialization) dangerous, in the first instance, is that it is an unprecedented close alliance between two great powers that can make or break the world: science and commerce."[19] These may be manifestations of the dark sides of scientists and business people, who, like the rest of us, are susceptible to the dark sides of our natures, which hang like a shadow over the whole of our species.

What religion and science have in common is that they both, each in their own ways, attempt to describe the natural world. The former does so with broad strokes of the brush that fill the canvas, while the latter attempts to fill in the colors, which, in spite of centuries of inquiry and research, still only occupy minute parts of the picture.

What similarities there are end there, however. Religion moves on to show us how to live within the fold of nature and harmonize our lives with the forces that hold it together. It teaches us to take from it what we need, and to give back to it by respecting it so that it will give us more. Science has no pretensions in this direction, and it is therefore amoral. The religion/science dichotomy is a false one which leads us to a false dialectic. Is there a dichotomy between a chicken and a bicycle? Science is a tool, a method, which helps us unlock the secrets of creation.

Scientists have now passed the frontiers of the gene and the galaxies in their understanding of them, and quantum physics has opened us to the mysteries of creation in ways that are both sudden and profound. As Thomas Berry puts it, there has been a shift in the "mode of consciousness" as scientists became aware that matter was not what it was thought to be: "Science was ultimately not the objective grasping of some reality extrinsic to ourselves. It was rather a moment of subjective communion in which the human was seen as the being in whom the universe in its evolutionary dimension became conscious of itself."[20]

The knowledge derived from scientific inquiry, however, is neutral. It tells us how things are, and whether we are moved by it or not is another matter. If science is amoral, does that allow scientists to be so too? Do they make decisions about the ultimate use of their discoveries? Or is this done by the research foundation, the university, or the large corporation they work for? Scientists are small cogs in the engine of modernity, just like the engineer who designs the technology, the factory worker who makes the end product, and the bookkeeper who produces the balance sheet.

The investigation of natural phenomena is an ancient occupation. Euclid studied the elements in 300 B.C.; Archimedes studied the functions of levers in 250 B.C.; Copernicus discovered that the earth moved around the sun and not vice versa in 1543, and there was Galileo in Bacon's own lifetime making telescopes[21] and seeing things he was supposed not to.

Muslims, too, had their scientists and methods, as indeed did the Chinese, the Indians, the Mayans, and the Egyptians. The terminology used by Muslim scientists is interesting. *Istidlāl* implied experimentation, measurement and observation; *istiqrā* is identical to the empirical, inductive method which was used five hundred years before Bacon; *istinbāl* could be described as the analytical method.[22] Muslim scientists contributed much to the advancement of the sciences which was then absorbed into the European tradition. Ibn Sina's (Avicenna; d. 1037) textbook on medicine was a standard work in Europe until the nineteenth century; al-Haytham (d. 1039) founded the science of optics; in the twelfth century al-Khazini recorded the specific gravity of fifty substances, which compares remarkably well with today's results.[23] There was no interest in this subject in Europe until Robert Boyle conducted his experiments five hundred years later.

Science, although not known as such and in fact described in many other ways, developed as a system of knowledge since antiquity to help human beings know and understand the natural world. Astronomy may have started as an exercise in curiosity, but travelers have known how to set a course by the stars for millennia. Similarly, medicine evolved from simple folk cures into a major scientific pharmaceutical endeavor, and hydrology from the need to understand simple irrigation systems by the ancient agriculturists to the complex scientific specialization it is today.

Many other specializations emerged as civilizations evolved, and the forces that drove them had nothing to do with economic or industrial "progress." The great Muslim advances in astronomy had more to do with discovering the times and directions of obligatory prayer. It was not until the seventeenth century, when attitudes changed sharply and seminal changes began to take place in post-Renaissance Europe, that science emerged with a new status for itself. It was one of the major elements in a confluence of a roaring torrent of ideas. If not for the rest of the intellectual movement, science could still be wending its staid way through history.

An Exploration of Modernity

It is posited here that modernity grew out of the predatory tendencies of the human species, which now had the means of unlocking the secrets of nature and sophisticated tools for extracting its wealth. The word "modern," according to Zygmunt Bauman, began to adopt a new meaning in the seventeenth century. It meant, among other things, an irreverence toward tradition, a readiness to innovate, and a recasting of the old as antiquated, obsolete, and something that needed to be replaced. "Modernity" is best described, says Bauman, as an age essentially of human accomplishment marked by constant change and progress. It has been a period where reason is deployed to the task of making the world a better place to serve human needs, where nature has been deemed meaningless, except in the sense that it can give meaning to the uses humans put it to, and where the creation of an artificial, rational order of human existence was not just an arbitrary choice but a necessity.

The satisfaction of human needs comes through resorting to science and technology, both the expression and vehicle of human ascendancy of nature, as the principal sources and instruments of political, cultural, and moral progress. Thus having identified the ideological foundation of modernity, Bauman then describes how modern Europe regarded itself as superior and the rest of the world as in a state of arrested development. It considered itself the carrier of a historical destiny, having a duty to spread the gospel of scientific rationality and to convert the world to its own orthodoxy and lifestyle. Thus, the period of modern European history became an age of proselytization, colonization of the non-European world, and repeated cultural crusades within its own boundaries.

This movement also ushered in the age of the nation-states, deployed nationalism in the service of state authority, and promoted national interests as the criteria of state policy. The stage was thus set for it to become the first global civilization in history, described as the ultimate form of human development capable of continuous creativity.[24] Eisenstadt writes that "modernization" was a term that was frequently used after the Second World War to describe a movement oriented toward modernity, as applied to underdeveloped countries of the Third World.

Modernization in its first institutional and cultural aspects developed in Western Europe and the Americas. These became crystallized during the sixteenth century in the form of a capitalist economy and a civilization characterized by the bureaucratization of social life and a secular worldview oriented toward modernity. The achievement of modernity was measured in terms of industrialization, urbanization, literacy, and education, as well as openness to modern modes of communication. Modernization expanded by economic, military, political, and ideological means throughout the world, creating a series of continually changing world systems.[25]

One of the greatest successes of the Trojan horse of modernity was to produce in less than two hundred years a Mercator map of the world, with lines on it that had never existed in previous history. The nation-state has replaced all other forms of managing human affairs. It has been recognized that the institution of the state became necessary as the human community settled into agricultural pursuits, which required irrigation, and also that some of the earliest states were established in temples. Due to the seminal changes that took place in post-Renaissance Europe, seen as being equal in import to those changes that took place during the agricultural revolution seven thousand years ago, a new model of governance evolved. The idea of the nation-state took hold in Europe to deal with the complexities of the new order. Additionally, its "rise to world hegemony was due to a dynamic which was broadly capitalist in spirit."[26]

In 1920 the League of Nations resolved that the only internationally legitimate form of governance was the nation-state. This resulted in the overthrow of two longstanding axioms of human history, the first of which was that all societies were ordered as hierarchies, and the second that human beings were vast religious collectives whose ultimate mission was to encompass the entire planet.[27]

The effect of this modern form of statism, for which much of the world was not ready, was profound, far-reaching, and rapid. Among these effects are cultural and ideological homogenization, centralization of the role of the state, emergence of the state as the secular arbiter and repository of cultural values, the disparagement and displacement of other notions of state, and a succumbing to the reductionist political sociology of Max Weber.[28]

There were further complications. A particular method of governance, which had evolved alongside a flowering intellectual tradition and aggressive industrialization in Europe, was forced onto the rest of the world, which was far from ready for it. Decolonization in the aftermath of the Second World War saw the accelerated growth of the United Nations, with increasing numbers of fledgling states taking their places in the Assembly. What they were measured by was a complex set of features that many of them had difficulty in coming to terms with. These features were: industrial capitalism geared to a postwar development model; a society driven by science and technology; economic growth, mass markets and demand management as a means of creating a consumer society; standardized and centralized institutions like a police force and conscription; education and central banks; bureaucratization of the administrative processes; expansion of literacy accompanied by the homogenization of the printed language.[29]

Ernst Gellner observes that education in modern society is standardized and minutely stratified. Unlike classical education, it is functionally geared to meet economic workforce needs.[30] Serge Latouche observes that the driving force of modernity is its obsession with success; its aspiration to create a grand society is illusory and is totalitarian in outlook in that it sees all other societies as irrational. Latouche describes modernity as the rape of traditional ancestral values, and sees a titanic struggle between it and tradition. The technological society it espouses has dehumanizing tendencies.[31]

An institution that is now integral to and seen as being essential to the stability of the nation-state is the central bank, the prototype of which was the Bank of England, created in 1694. It was set up to raise a "perpetual loan" on behalf of the state, the interest for which would be met by taxing the people.[32] Central banks are now an essential feature of the nation-state, and when new nations were created in the postwar decolonization process with central banks of their own, they were essentially born into a debt that had to be continually serviced by taxation, and now, it would seem, by the IMF as well.

Modernity, with its indissoluble link to the state and the market, leaves no individual free from the influence of the market.[33] The market today is no longer of the local community, where participants have a commonality of purpose and interests. Rather, the modern economy, which is now global in extent, devalues and destroys a whole range of human activities, human networks, solidarity, cooperation, and reciprocity.[34] What emerges from this is a selfish form of consumer individualism, which is destroying communal cohesion and solidarity. This individualism is illusory, as it denies true choice, individuals having been "functionalized" and transformed into "cogs and machines."[35]

In the view of Georg Simmel, today's individuals face the awesome task of patching together meaningful lives and making choices that neglect qualitative differences between objects of their choice. In an interesting reflection, Simmel says that intellect and money are simultaneously inevitable products and indispensable instruments of modern life. Both refer to the quantitative aspects of experienced phenomena and devalue their qualitative characteristics.[36] The global village is now a homogenized global culture defined largely in economic terms. It has been achieved through the progressive dilution and destruction of traditional cultures and the marginalization of the great religions by what has come to be known as the secular scientific order.

The Acceleration of History

The world we live in today is one that is dominated by a secular way of seeing and being. This is usually described as the triumph of science over religion. Richard Tarnas asserts that the psychological constitution of the modern character (influenced by secularism) has been developing since the Middle Ages, conspicuously emerged in the Renaissance, was sharply clarified and empowered in the scientific revolution, then extended and solidified in the course of the Enlightenment. By the nineteenth century, in the wake of the democratic and industrial revolutions, it achieved maturity, finally resulting in a radical shift of psychological allegiance from God to man.

Tarnas observes that Bacon and Descartes, the prophets of the scientific civilization, proclaimed the twin epistemological foundations of the modern mind: empiricism and rationalism. Descartes finally breached the floodgates of the old order by splitting mind from body and proclaiming a dualistic world in his well-known statement, "I think, therefore I am" (*cogito ergo sum*). The fruit of the dualism between rational subject and material world was science, including science's capacity for rendering certain knowledge of that world, and for making man (in Descartes' own words) "Master and possessor of Nature."[37]

This brings us to the point where it is possible to recognize that the basis of the secular order is opposite to the position that Islam takes on the two fronts identified in the hypothesis stated in the introduction. The first of these is Descartes' *cogito* argument, coupled with his statement on lordship. Having established the existence of the "I," Descartes then attempts a rationalistic proof of the existence of God. Failing in this, he ends up by creating what is now known as the "Cartesian circle."[38]

While the Qur'an itself uses reason, its foundation is revelation—knowledge through the divine unveiling of reality. The beginning of the "I" in Islam is in the act of submission, emerging from the seminal declaration of witnessing (*shahāda*): "There is no God but God." This delivers the human and his condition in submission (*islām*) to the Creator. The submissive "i" of the human primal condition is opposite to that of the predatory Cartesian "I."

The very first line of the first chapter of the Qur'an declares, "Praise belongs to God, Lord of all the worlds" (Qur'an 1:1). And the first line of the final chapter counsels, "Say: I take refuge with the Lord of men" (114:1). There is only one Lord, and the very act of submission denies the human any pretensions to this position. Within this paradigm, he does not possess anything except by the grace of the Creator. Creation exists as an act of His will and it holds together in its submission to Him. Thus, we are all slaves of the Creator (*'abd Allāh*) and cannot in any sense be masters and possessors of something we are intrinsically a part. Our problems emerge from our trying to be.

There is much misunderstanding, if not outright misrepresentation, of the position that Islam takes in this area. The anthropocentrism of the Western manifestation of the Christian approach to the understanding of God is unthinkingly attributed also to Islam, when both Muslim and non-Muslim writers refer sweepingly to "the Abrahamic tradition."

It has been argued that the two older doctrines in this tradition (the Jewish and the Christian) relegate nature to the status of a resource. Lynn White, in writing about this states, ". . . no item in the physical creation had any purpose save to serve man's purposes."[39] This is usually referred to as the Genesis position, that is, the dominion of human over nature. By contrast, Ismail and Lois Faruqi explain Muslims' relation to nature as moral in character: nature is a vehicle to perform good deeds; nature is a blessed gift (*ni'ma*) of God's bounty; it is not humankind's to possess or destroy; the Muslim is expected to treat nature with respect and deep gratitude to its Creator; and any transformation of it must have a purpose and benefit to all.[40] By extension, any transformation of nature which has a negative impact on itself and others is forbidden. Muslims hold that this caring and protective attitude to the natural order is one of the manifestations of the reforming role of Islam.

The second fundamental point of variance between Islam and the secular order is the issue relating to interest on money or, to use its classical term, "usury." The Bible prohibited usury except in favor of the Jew against the non-Jew (Deuteronomy 27:20). Calvin legalized usury in 1535 for the Christians.

There are strict prohibitions in the Qur'an against the practice of usury, but the vast majority of Muslims now ignore its injunctions. The Qur'an commands in no uncertain terms, "give up the usury that is outstanding if you are believers, if you do not, then take notice that God and His Messenger will war with you" (2:278–79). "The profit of usury is like a parasite in a market . . . as the market grows the parasite grows . . . usury produces an imbalance in natural trading and this has now penetrated everything . . . it has been defined as asking something for nothing . . . (and) . . . it is the opposite of a just or equivalent transaction."[41]

Usury, which is broadly defined as making money out of nothing, contains two elements, both of which are now integral parts of modern banking practice. The first is the institution of interest itself, and the second is the fractional reserve device which banks use to create endless money. This has been briefly dealt with in the introduction to this paper, but interest itself also creates money out of nothing. Margrit Kennedy of the Permaculture Institute in Germany has done some work on interest debt, and her model of taking out a loan of one penny at the birth of Jesus Christ produces the following figures:

Fig. 1. Interest Produces Balls of Gold by the Weight of the Earth

Interest	Number of Balls of Gold by Weight of the Earth	By the Year
At 4%	1	1750
	8190	1990
At 5%	1	1403
	2200 billion	1990

The mathematical term for this phenomenon is "exponential growth."[42] This explosion of artificial wealth, which includes created credit from the fractional reserve system and interest, is used to create new industries, exploit resources, and improve standards of living. Every facet of human life, including scientific inquiry and technological innovation, is now growing exponentially, fuelled by ephemeral credit. The intangible swallows up the tangible exponentially. This is how we finance ecological collapse.

The founder of the Club of Rome, Aurelio Peccei, says that there has been a large-scale overshoot in the way

> . . . the human population and economy extract resources from the earth and emit pollution and wastes to the environment. Many of these rates of extraction and emission have grown to be unsupportable. The environment cannot sustain them. Human society has overshot its limits, for the same reason that other overshoots occur. Changes are too fast. Signals are late, incomplete, distorted, ignored or denied. Momentum is great, responses are slow.[43]

There is no longer any doubt that exponential growth is the driving force causing the global economy to breach the physical limits of the earth.[44]

But these ideas are not new and, interestingly, were first postulated nearly a century ago. The scientist and historian Henry Adams propounded a theory in the early twentieth century which suggested that the acceleration of technological change was forcing the acceleration of history.[45] It will suffice to say that Adams constructed a graph on a logarithmic time base to show that there was a relationship between the rate of consumption and utilization of energy and what is described as technological progress.

The result was an exponential curve. Adams observed that the acceleration of the sixteenth and seventeenth centuries was rapid and startling, adding, "the world did not double or treble its movement between 1800 and 1900, but measured by any standard known to science the so-called progression of society was fully a thousand times greater in 1900 than in 1800. . . ."[46] What is interesting about Henry Adams's graph is that it ran parallel to the base line for a time (see fig. 2) and then suddenly began a steep incline. Now, at the beginning of the twenty-first century, this curve is close to and almost parallel to the vertical axis. Adams predicted in 1905 that ". . . at the accelerated rate of progression since 1600 it will not need another century to turn thought upside down. Law in that case would disappear . . . and give place to force. Morality would become police. Explosives would reach cosmic violence. Disintegration would overcome integration."[47]

Fig. 2. Henry Adams's Law of Acceleration

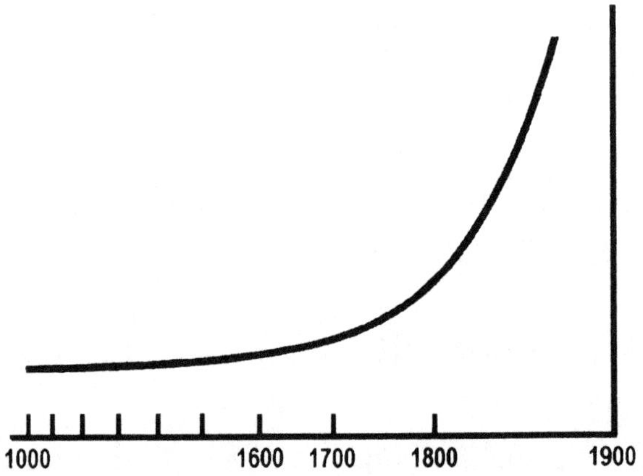

All these forecasts have either already unfolded or are in the process of doing so, but the point of crucial interest in this analysis is the time at which the graph began to rise. Examination shows that this abrupt, upward trajectory coincides exactly with the period covered by the sixteenth and seventeenth centuries. It is during this time that we can begin to discern the appearance of the historical factors, such as Calvin's edict in favor of lifting the biblical ban on usury early in the sixteenth century, the Enlightenment, the scientific revolution followed by the industrial revolution, and the growth of technology.

Henry Adams, within his own historical cultural context, was only aware of what we now see as secondary and tertiary causes. What was important to him was technological change allied to energy consumption, and his work nearly one hundred years ago produced the first alarming exponential growth curve. A closer examination will reveal the primary causes, which are uniquely visible from an Islamic perspective. These are the exponential creation of credit allied with the predatory tendencies of the human being, rationalized in the present dominant secular ethic.[48]

Guardians of the Natural Order

The biosphere is finite and delicate, and the natural domain works within its own limiting principles to stay in balance. Islamic teaching offers an opportunity to understand this and to define human responsibility within this paradigm. It could be said that the limits of the human condition are set within four principles: *tawḥīd*—the unity principle, *fiṭra*—the creation principle, *mīzān*—he balance principle, and *khilāfa*—the responsibility principle.

Tawḥīd is the fundamental statement of the oneness of the Creator, from which everything else follows. It is the primordial testimony to the unity of all creation and to the interlocking grid of the natural order, of which humanity is an intrinsic part. The Qur'an says of God:

> Say; He is God, One God,
> The Everlasting Refuge. (112:1–2)

The Qur'an also declares that God

> . . . Created everything
> Then He ordained it
> very exactly. (25:2)

The whole of creation—being the work of one Originator—works within one stable pattern, however complex it may be. Another verse in the Qur'an (2:255) refers to the heavens and the earth as comprising God's throne, thus conveying the idea that creation was designed to function as a whole. Each of its complementary parts, including humankind, plays its own self-preserving role, and in so doing supports the rest.

Fiṭra describes the primordial nature of creation itself and locates humankind within it. The Qur'an says:

> So set thy face to the religion, one of pure faith—
> God's original upon which He originated humankind.
> There is no changing God's creation.
> That is the right religion;
> But most men know it not. (30:29)

God originates humankind within His creation, which He also originated. Humanity is then inescapably subject to God's immutable laws, as is the rest of creation. Creation cannot be changed and if we attempt to do this we will destroy ourselves. We are now like a split atom in disintegrating matter. Having caused the chain reaction ourselves, we do not know how and when to stop.

The *mīzān* is the principle of the middle path. In one of its most eloquent passages, the Qur'an describes creation thus:

> The All-Merciful has taught the Qur'an
> He created man
> And He taught him the explanation
> The sun and moon to a reckoning
> And the stars and trees bow themselves
> And heaven—He raised it up and set the balance
> Transgress not in the balance
> And weigh with justice, and skimp not in the balance
> And earth—He set it down for all beings
> Therein fruits and palm trees with sheaths
> And grain in the blade, and fragrant herbs
> And which of your Lord's bounties will you and you deny? (55:1–12)

God has singled out humans and taught them reason—the capacity to understand. All creation has an order and a purpose. If the sun, the moon, the stars, the trees, and the rest of creation did not conform to the natural laws—"bow themselves"—it would be impossible for life to function on Earth. All of creation is in submission, and humankind is the only part of it, through the gift of reasoning that the Creator has endowed it with, that can choose to act otherwise. Submission is the natural law and it holds humanity's predatorial instincts in check. So there is a responsibility not to deny the "Lord's bounties" and actively to recognize the order that surrounds them for their own sake, as much as for the rest of creation.

Khilāfa—or the role of stewardship—is the sacred duty God has ascribed to the human race. There are many verses in the Qur'an that describe human duties and responsibilities, such as the following which aptly summarizes humanity's role:

> It is He Who has appointed
> You viceroys in the earth. (6:165)

Humankind has a special place in God's scheme, that of viceroy (*khalīfa*), bearing in mind that we are first and foremost submitters, slaves of God (*'abd Allāh*). This is our relationship to the Creator: that of guardian in the role of the slave. Although we are partners with everything else in the natural world, we have added responsibilities and we are also accountable for our actions. We are decidedly not its lords and masters.

We can deduce from these four principles that creation, although quite complex and yet finite, only works because each of its component parts does what is expected of it—in the language of the Qur'an, it "submits" to the Creator. Humanity is inextricably part of this pattern. The role of humans—who uniquely have wills of their own and are thus capable of interfering with the pattern of creation—is that of guardianship. This added responsibility imposes limits on their behavior, showing the way to a conscious recognition of their own fragility. They achieve this by submitting themselves to the divine law, *sharī'a*.

Modernity has brought obvious great advances in many fields of human endeavor, but has the price been worth paying? Many of these advances are also beyond the reach of the mass of humanity. The minority that has benefited to the full holds out promises for the rest, but the wealth gap between the two classes continues to widen. It is also this very same minority that, having fabricated the engine of modernity, continues to use it to improve its own position to further develop and grow at unsustainable rates.

The push comes from a political model that has economic growth as its main foundation. As the system is based on competitive market forces, those in front stay in front, getting stronger all the time. As the nations that enjoy high standards of living deplete their own resources, they can only maintain their lifestyles by depleting the resources of other nations. But, as all nations are in a race for growth, this becomes a sustained assault by one species, albeit represented by a small minority, against all other living beings and the rest of nature.

The carrying capacity of the earth is already severely tested, and if Russia or China or India achieves standards of consumption like anything approaching that of the West, substantial parts of the planet will look like the surface of Mars. It can be seen from Margrit Kennedy's analysis that even a modest growth rate of 1 percent is untenable, and it would now seem that the idea of "negative growth" is one that should be taken seriously by those who live in the global village. We have already devoured the earth many times over, and that it continues to take a battering is a telling commentary on its resilience.

As in the past, today's rulers survive by providing people with a decent life. Once this just meant food in the stomach, but now this has changed into "standard of living," with competing politicians in the democratic model promising to increase this year by year by manipulating growth rates, interest rates, exchange rates, and tax rates at the expense of a finite biosphere.

There is now an urgent need for a radical reappraisal of this model. What caused the problem in the first place cannot be expected to produce the solutions for it. In addition to a reevaluation of values, the human community needs to discover how to conduct its affairs in a way that will make it possible both to satisfy its needs and to survive in a finite planet.

Thomas Berry, in his reflections on the secular-religious dichotomy, suggests that "the remedy for this is to establish a deeper understanding of the spiritual dynamics of the universe as revealed through our own empirical insight into the mysteries of its functioning."[49] In other words, there could be a coming together of the secular and religious worldviews as science gives us insights into the deeper mysteries of creation. But a sensitive exploration of alternatives based on faith and deep spiritual insights, in the absence of a complementary political framework to bring these ideas to fruition, may not lead us to the changes we are seeking. The Islamic approach would be to reexamine a return to the holistic model of the *sharī'a* and the reestablishment of the caliphate.

The four principles discussed above could be seen as forming a sound basis on which to build an Islamic model, one which could help human beings to function within the natural pattern of creation, to lead satisfying lives, and at the same time to protect the earth from further degradation. For this to succeed, however, there will be a need for a political model and a system of financial intermediation different from that of the present banking system. Such a model, within the Islamic paradigm, is governance based on the caliphate, which existed from the early seventh to the early twentieth century, when the Ottoman caliphate was abolished.

The caliphate functioned without banks or massive bureaucracies, under the ethos of what is known as the millet system, that is, autonomous regions, similar to the ideas on bioregionalism which are now being propagated. In his work on the caliphate, Shaykh Abdul-qadir al-Sufi says:

> the congress (of March 1925, of Muslim countries, which was held in Cairo to discuss the fall of the Ottoman caliphate) noted that the instrument of division among the Muslims which had permitted this disaster was the European doctrine of nationalism. What it failed to grasp, for it was too early in its evolution, was that banking and not just frontiers delineated the national state as a debt receptor to a private and dynastic banking elite. . . .[50]

The important question now is: Will modernity tolerate pluralistic political and economic expressions as a means to seeking viable alternatives to the resolution of our global ecological crisis, or does it see progress as a linear movement defined entirely by itself?

Notes

1. Seyyed Hossein Nasr, *Man and Nature* (1967; London: Unwin Paperback, 1990), 20.

2. Vandana Shiva, *Monocultures of the Mind* (Penang, Malaysia: Third World Network, 1993), 8.

3. Samuel P. Huntington, *The Clash of Civilizations* (London: Touchstone, 1997), 177.

4. Ibid. Huntington distinguishes between Westernization and modernization and argues that they are two separate processes. See pp. 68–72.

5. In Anthony Sampson, *The Money Lenders* (London: Coronet Books, 1988). Galbraith is quoted on p. 29.

6. Frederic Benham, *Economics*, 6th ed. (London: Pitman, 1960), 426.

7. Qur'an 46:2. The translations used in this essay are from A. J. Arberry, *The Koran* (Oxford: Oxford University Press, 1983).

8. Richard Leakey and Roger Lewin, *The Sixth Extinction: Biodiversity and Its Survival* (London: Phoenix, 1996), 233, 234.

9. Ibid., 261.

10. Ibid., 235

11. Ibid., 245

12. Thomas Berry, *The Dream of the Earth* (San Francisco: Sierra Club Books, 1990), xii.

13. Nasr, *Man and Nature*, 6.

14. Brian L. Silver, *The Ascent of Science* (Oxford: Oxford University Press, 1998), 17.

15. Nasr, *Man and Nature*, 6.

16. Silver, *The Ascent of Science*, 481.

17. Mae-Wan Ho, *Genetic Engineering: Dream or Nightmare* (Bath, U.K.: Gateway Books, 1998), 41.

18. Ibid., 169.

19. Ibid., 8, 9.

20. Berry, *The Dream of the Earth*, 128

21. Peter Walker, ed., *Dictionary of Science and Technology* (Edinburgh: Larousse, 1995), 1234.

22. Ismail Faruqi and Lois Faruqi, *The Cultural Atlas of Islam* (New York: Macmillan, 1986); see the chapter "The Natural World," esp. p. 322.

23. Donald R. Hill, *Islamic Science and Engineering* (Edinburgh: Edinburgh University Press, 1993), 66.

24. Joel Krieger, ed., *The Oxford Companion to the Politics of the World* (Oxford: Oxford University Press, 1993), q.v. Zygmunt Bauman, "Modernity."

25. Ibid., q.v. S. N. Eisenstadt, "Modernization."

26. Ibid., q.v. John A. Hall, "State."

27. Ibid., q.v. Benedict R. O'Gorman Anderson, "Nationalism."

28. Wolfgang Sachs, ed., *The Development Dictionary* (London: Zed Books, 1992), q.v. Ashis Nandy, "State."

29. Krieger, ed., *The Oxford Companion to the Politics of the World*, q.v. Anderson, "Nationalism."

30. Ibid. See also Ernst Gelner, *Nations and Nationalism* (Oxford: Oxford University Press, 1986).

31. Serge Latouche, *In the Wake of the Affluent Society* (London: Zed Books, 1993).

32. Glyn Davies, *A History of Money from Ancient Times to the Present Day* (Cardiff: University of Wales Press, 1996), 257.

33. Sachs, ed., *The Development Dictionary*, q.v. Gerald Berthoud, "Market."

34. Ibid., q.v. Majid Rahnema, "Poverty."

35. Krieger, ed., *The Oxford Companion to the Politics of the World*, q.v. Bauman, "Modernity."

36. Ibid., q.v. Bauman, "Modernity."

37. Richard Tarnas, *The Passion of the Western Mind* (London: Pimlico, 1996), 275–81.

38. Ted Honderich, ed., *The Oxford Companion to Philosophy* (Oxford: Oxford University Press, 1995), 190.

39. Lynn White, Jr., "The Historic Roots of our Ecologic Crisis," *Science* 155 (1967): 1203–7.

40. Faruqi and Faruqi, *The Cultural Atlas of Islam.*

41. Fazlun Khalid and Joanne O'Brien, eds., *Islam and Ecology* (London: Cassell, 1992). In that volume, see especially Umar Vadillo and Fazlun Khalid, "Trade and Commerce in Islam."

42. Margrit Kennedy, *Interest and Inflation Free Money* (Steyerberg, Germany: Permaculture Institute, 1988).

43. Donella H. Meadows, Dennis L. Meadows, and Jørgen Randers, *Beyond the Limits: Confronting Global Collapse, Envisioning a Sustainable Future* (London: Earthscan, 1992); see the chapter "Overshoot."

44. Ibid.; see the chapter "The Driving Force: Exponential Growth."

45. *Future of a Troubled World*, gen. ed. Hussein Amirsadeghi, ed. Ritchie Calder (London: Heineman, London, 1983); see the chapter "The Acceleration of History."

46. Ibid.

47. Ibid.

48. This is a précis of a section of my paper, "Science, Technology and the Ecological Crisis: an Islamic Perspective" (presented at the International Conference on Values and Attitudes in Science and Technology, International Islamic University, Kuala Lumpur, Malaysia, 3–6 September 1996).

49. Berry, *The Dream of the Earth*, 131.

50. Shaykh Abdul-Qadir al-Sufi, *The Return of the Khalifate* (Cape Town: Madinah Press, 1996), 102.

The Environmental Crisis of Our Time: A Muslim Response

YASIN DUTTON

"He saw all ecological issues . . . as subsumed under the workings out of the usury economy."[1]

Finding a Solution to the Problem

It should be said at the outset that this article assumes that there *is* a problem, and not just a minor one. As Michael Northcott notes in his *Environment and Christian Ethics* (to take but one recent example): "as we survey the range of impacts which human activities in less than a century have had on the planet, it should become apparent that there is indeed a crisis, and a crisis of momentous proportions."[2]

A problem demands a solution, but it is important that this solution be the right solution, that is, an effective solution. Muslims are called by the Qur'an to enjoin the right and forbid the wrong (3:104 and other verses), first with the hand, and, if that is not possible, with the tongue, and, if that is not possible, with the heart.[3] That is, Muslims are called to activism—to actively establish justice and combat injustice wherever and whenever possible. There is a famous *ḥadīth* on this topic recorded from the Prophet (may Allah bless him and grant him peace), in which he said:

> The likeness of those who uphold the limits laid down by Allah and those who transgress them is like that of a group of people who draw lots on a boat [as to who will go where] and some of them get the upper

> deck and some of them get the lower. When the people on the lower deck want to get water, they have to pass by those who are above them, so they say, "Let's make a hole in our part of the boat and then we won't be inconveniencing those above us." If the others let them do this, they will all perish; but if they stop them, they will not only save themselves, but save everyone.[4]

This is effectively our situation today, when, whether the problem has been created intentionally or unintentionally, it is necessary to act as soon and as effectively as possible in order to remedy it.

It may be that we cannot solve this problem all at once because of its sheer size and complexity, but we should at least try to understand it and help others to understand it so that we can rule out ineffective solutions and concentrate our energies where there are most likely to be results. We do not want to go round putting more holes in the boat when we are trying to fill up the already existing ones. Rather, we must learn to recognize hole-making activities when we see them and, where possible, prevent them from taking place.

Part of finding a solution to the problem must also be to understand how we arrived at the problem. This again has been well studied, although there are conflicting views as to the real cause of what we see today.[5] Thus you could say we have a second problem: of how to arrive at an understanding of the origins of the problem.

Different worldviews will result in different approaches to this, and, indeed, any problem. In Qur'anic terms, there are two basic worldviews: that of the believers, known as *īmān* ("belief," "trust," "acceptance") and that of the nonbelievers, known as *kufr* ("unbelief," "ingratitude"; lit., "covering-up"). That is, there are those who accept reality-as-it-is, and those who in some way cover up reality-as-it-is and claim that something else is going on. This positing of some other energy in existence alongside the one source of all energy is also referred to as *shirk*, "association," that is, the associating of other powers alongside the One, All-Powerful Cause and Originator of everything in existence.

This is an important distinction, because on it depends the rest of our analysis. This is because the person of *īmān*, the *mu'min* ("believer")—or we could say "the person of Islam," the Muslim (lit., "submitter," one who submits to God), as he or she becomes in the realm of outward action—is the one who accepts reality-as-it-is and who looks to this reality for an understanding not only of the problem but also of its solution. This is possible because the nature of this reality has been expressed in humanly comprehensible terms—that is, in human language—on the tongues of those that are referred to as "prophets" and "messengers." It is this communication that forms the basis of scripture, the "books" revealed to these prophets and messengers.

For Muslims, the prophet Muhammad was the last of these prophets and messengers, and the book revealed to him, the Qur'an, was the last of these books. It is therefore to the Qur'an, on the one hand, and the more general teachings and practice of the prophet Muhammad—known collectively as the *sunna*—on the other, that Muslims look for authoritative answers to the questions that constantly arise in human life, including those of an environmental nature.

However, resorting to the Qur'an and the *sunna* is clearly not the practice of the majority of people on Earth at the present time. Most people nowadays, and certainly most policymakers, would probably assume that answers are to be looked for and found in a scientific rather than a scriptural context. That is, it is assumed that there is in some way a "scientific" solution to these problems (just as it is assumed that it is for "scientific" reasons that they came about in the first place).

Scriptural versus Scientific Authority?

We have thus, in effect, two worldviews: one that, in putting scriptural authority uppermost, declares its allegiance to a God-centered view of the world; and one that, in putting the human authority of scientific discovery uppermost, declares its allegiance to a human-centered view of the world.

This is not to say that the two may not and do not overlap. There is a well-known *ḥadīth* where we are told that the Prophet, may Allah bless him and grant him peace, was once passing by some people who were pollinating their palm trees (a practice which is necessary to ensure effective pollination of the palms). As he saw them doing this, he expressed surprise at this being of any benefit and suggested that perhaps it might be better if they didn't do it. So the people stopped doing it that year, but, as a result, the palms produced very substandard fruit. When they complained about this to the Prophet, he told them, "I am just a human being. Do what is of benefit to yourselves." In another version of the report, the Prophet said, "It was merely a thought that I had and thoughts can be right and wrong [or, "so do not take me to task for such thoughts"]. But if I tell you something about Allah, accept it from me, because I will never say what is untrue about Allah."[6]

It is clear from this that there is no intrinsic conflict in Islam between what we might call "religious" and "scientific" knowledge; rather, the two are seen as complementary. Indeed, traditional Muslim scholars have always been aware of different ways of acquiring knowledge. Commenting on the above-mentioned *ḥadīth*, Ibn Rushd the Grandfather (the grandfather of the famous philosopher of the same name who was known in the West as Averroës) says:

> Allah is the one who causes harm (*al-mufsid*) and the one who causes benefit (*al-muṣliḥ*) since He is the doer of everything. However, He—may He be exalted—has made it part of the way things are (*al-'āda*, "custom") that He causes harm and benefit by means of other things. This is known by people who have direct experience of this and have found this custom (*'āda*) to be constant, such as doctors, who know which drugs cause benefit and which cause harm because of their experience and the experience of others before them, whereas others who do not have this experience do not know what is safe in this respect. It is the same with pollinating date-palms. Those with long experience of date-palms know that this practice is useful, whereas the Prophet, may Allah bless him and grant him peace, did not know this because of his lack of experience of date-palms, which is why he said what he said, as mentioned in the various *ḥadīth* reports.
>
> When I say "such as doctors, who know which drugs cause benefit and which cause harm," I am allowing myself some liberty of expression, since in reality drugs neither cause benefit nor harm in themselves. Rather the causer of benefit and the causer of harm is Allah, the Lord of all the worlds.[7]

Indeed, we find this position systematized in classical Islam into the following three-way division of "facts" (*aḥkām*) (using this latter term in the sense of definitive statements and/or judgments about "the way things are"):

1) Facts which can only be known through the *sharī'a* (*aḥkām shar'īyya*), for example, that fasting the month of Ramadan (the fourth of the Five Pillars of Islam) is obligatory, or that fasting the Day of 'Ashura is not obligatory. These form the standard legal judgments of

Islamic law and are assumed to be the dominant category, since disobeying them means disobeying Allah and His Messenger, and obedience to Allah and His Messenger is the prime obligation.

2) Facts which are arrived at purely by means of the intellect (*aḥkām ʻaqliyya*), for example, that ten is an even number, or that seven is not an even number.

3) Facts which are arrived at by experience of the phenomenal world, for example, that fire burns, or that knives cut, or that certain foods are difficult to digest.[8] It is this category that includes "scientific" judgments, and is assumed by Muslims as well as non-Muslims to be valid, although traditional Muslims acknowledge that such laws, although experienced as constant, can be broken by "miracles."

It is thus apparent that, in response to the environmental crisis of our time, Muslims may indeed have recourse to "scientific" solutions arrived at by human intellectual activity, but judgments arrived at by such a means must never overrule judgments arrived at by the *sharīʻa*. Rather, it is understood that the *sharīʻa* will provide the parameters for the best use of the human intellect.

The Nature of Scriptural Authority

The judgments of the *sharīʻa* are based on scriptural authority, expressed in terms of scriptural commands. Scriptural commands have both an inner and an outer aspect. That is, there are commands that address themselves predominantly to individuals as individuals, such as asking Allah for guidance or not worrying about what the morrow will bring, while there are others that address themselves to individuals as members of society, such as not abusing other people's property. There is thus an inner domain of application, which is the individual, and an outer domain of application, which is the community, or society at large. For change to occur, it is essential that both these aspects are activated, for neither can be achieved without the other. As it says in the Qur'an, "Allah does not change the state of a people until they change what is in themselves" (13:11).

Indeed, what is inward necessarily has an outer aspect and what is outward necessarily has an inner aspect. Thus, for example, the spiritual activity of doing the prayer (the Second Pillar of Islam) has at the same time a clear outward form; it is also preceded by the very physical act of washing certain limbs of the body. Conversely, the communal activity of distributing the *zakāt*, or alms-tax (the Third Pillar of Islam), has the spiritual result of inwardly purifying those who give it, as indicated by the Qur'anic verse instituting the practice: "Take alms from their wealth to purify and cleanse them" (9:103).

Furthermore, taking scripture as an authority and guide implies a certain approach and attitude. As the Qur'an says:

> That is the Book: there is no doubt. In it is guidance for the God-fearing, those who believe in the Unseen and establish the prayer and spend out from what We have provided them with; those who believe in what has been sent down to you, and what was sent down before you, and who have certainty about the Next World. Those are guided by their Lord, and those are the prosperous. (2:1–4)

So it is only those who are God-fearing, who believe "in the Unseen" and thus their accountability after death and who exhibit the other characteristics mentioned, who will accept and respect these scriptural commands. For those who do not believe, there is necessarily only the humanly-arrived-at scientific solution.

Stewardship

Much has been said about the question of stewardship in modern environmental thinking.[9] From the Qur'anic point of view, the position is clear. Allah says about Adam: "I am going to put a caliph (*khalīfa*) on the earth" (2:30). Thus, all humankind, as the children of Adam, share this attribute of *khalīfa*-dom, of being like Allah's deputy or representative, the one left in charge in the (seeming) absence of the (ever-present) Lord to make sure that His commands are carried out.[10] There is a *ḥadīth* in which the Prophet, may Allah bless him and grant him peace, said: "The world is a green and pleasant thing. Allah has left you in charge of it (*mustakhlifukum fīhā*) and looks at how you behave."[11] Elsewhere, the Qur'an declares that "[He is] the one who created life and death to test you, which of you is best in action" (67:2).

This, then, is humankind's position on Earth. Allah has created everything that is on the earth for humans (2:29: "He created for you everything that is on the earth"), as He has also subjugated (*sakhkhara*) the sun and the moon, day and night, the rivers and the sea, and indeed everything, for humans;[12] at the same time, He looks at how humankind behaves with all these gifts. Thus, it is not humankind that subdues the earth, but Allah that subdues the earth for humankind. Nor do humans have complete freedom to do with the earth what they like. Humans are neither equal to all other living beings, nor are they masters of all creation. Rather, humans are in the middle of a two-way relationship: humankind is *khalīfa*, that is, in charge of, and therefore responsible for, what is below, but humankind is *'abd*, slave, to what is above; humans must look after what is below because of their answerability to what is above. Indeed, humans have to be *khalīfa* precisely because they are *'abd*: Allah has appointed humankind *khalīfa* and therefore it is part of this *'abd*-ness that they be *khalīfa*, since the chief characteristic of slavehood is obedience to the master. Thus, humans, in their *khalīfa*-dom, are free to use the good things of the earth, but, in their *'abd*-ness, are bound by the laws of Allah.

Islamic Law and the Environment

What, then, are the laws of Allah in this context? First and foremost, one should mention the laws relating to land, water, and other natural resources. These are indeed important, but have been dealt with in detail elsewhere.[13] Here we need only note that the prime concern in every case is to protect the rights of access to land and water and the benefits that accrue from them, and to ensure that these rights are exercised equitably. One might also note briefly the question of animal "rights" and the correct treatment of animals. Again, this has been dealt with in detail elsewhere,[14] and for our present purposes we need only note that, according to Islamic law, it is imperative that all animals, both domestic and wild, be treated with kindness and concern, even if they are being slaughtered (which is permitted, for food and certain other purposes, according to well-known conditions of correctness laid down in the legal manuals).

But we need to be able to prioritize. If we want to be able to succeed before it is too late, we need to be able to pitch our critique at the right level. Thus, for example, there was little point in blaming wildfowlers and anglers for lead pollution in the environment (as was the case in Britain in the late 1980s) when their activities accounted for only 1 percent and 4 percent, respectively, of this pollution, while cars and various industrial concerns were responsible for the other 95 percent. Similarly, if someone finds spots on the skin, it is not enough simply to put some cream or salve on the affected area: it is important to be able to identify, for example, the poisoned blood which is causing the spots, and thus work at purifying the blood.

In the same way the classical Muslim scholars point out that in a society where, for example, drinking is the chief wrong action, emphasis should be put on the application of the penalty against drinking; if adultery is the chief wrong action, emphasis should be put on the penalty against adultery; and so on with all the other wrong actions that humans are prone to. In other words, one should concentrate on eradicating the wrong action most relevant to the place and time: one should be able to prioritize.

One might then ask, what is the most serious wrong action in Islam? The first answer would have to be *shirk*, that is, associating anyone or anything else with Allah as Creator and Sole Power in the universe. As the Qur'an says: "Allah does not forgive anything being associated with Him, but He forgives whoever He wills for anything less than that" (4:48 and 116). In other words, to have the wrong inner picture of what existence is like and to deny Allah is the greatest wrong any human being can do.

But what is the next most serious judgment in Islamic law? One might think of apostasy, with its possible penalty of execution, or of *zinā* (illicit sexual intercourse), with its possible penalty of stoning to death, or of stealing, with its possible penalty of having the hand cut off. However, although these are obviously serious offences against God's law, there is one wrong action which is described as being thirty-six, or seventy, or even ninety-nine times worse than a man having intercourse with his mother.[15] This is the taking of *ribā*, or usury, which refers to the taking of money at interest—any amount of interest, however small—and various associated practices. We are therefore entitled to assume that the prohibition against *ribā* is an extremely important judgment. Indeed, the Qur'an tells us:

> Those who consume usury will not rise up [that is, out of their graves] except as one who has been made mad by Satan. This is because they say that trade is like usury, whereas Allah has permitted trade and forbidden usury. . . . Allah wipes out usury and makes charity grow, and

> Allah does not love every unbelieving wrong-doer. Those who believe and act correctly, who establish the prayer and pay the *zakāt*, will have their reward with their Lord. There will be no fear on them, nor will they grieve. O you who believe, have fear of Allah and leave what remains of *ribā* if you are truly believers; and if you do not, then be informed of a war from Allah and His Messenger. If you repent, you will have your capital, without you either wronging or being wronged. (2:275–79)

There is therefore the possibility of *war* from Allah and His Messenger, which must be taken as a very severe threat.

Usury and the Environment

Why, then, might this issue of *ribā* be so important to our subject matter of Islam and the environment?

The answer lies in the nature of the present-day economy, for, as we hear from many quarters, it is the economic activities of present-day humankind that are the main cause for the environmental destruction that we see happening around us.[16] What people have not been told is that it is usury that underpins this whole economy. Indeed, it is a usurious economy par excellence. And usury, as we have seen, is totally forbidden in Islam.

How then does it affect the environment? One immediate answer is that every permitted thing brings with it a blessing from the Divine, while every prohibited thing brings with it its opposite. Given, then, that the prohibition against usury is so severe, there is little wonder that, with so much usury in evidence, there is so much degradation around us. As it says in the Qur'an: "Corruption has appeared on the land and the sea because of what men's hands have done" (30:41). Corruption, then, in the outward form of environmental degradation, is the direct result of humankind's activities, and it is only by putting right humankind's activities that such corruption can be combatted. The taking of usury is one of the most serious of these corruptive activities.

However, the destructive nature of usury is more systematic than this simple assessment might suggest. In order to understand it, one needs to understand the nature of money in the modern economy.

The Nature of Money

The first point to understand about this question is that the vast majority of what goes for "money" on the face of this earth is not in the form of coins, or even paper representing coins ("I promise to pay the bearer on demand the sum of . . . ," as British banknotes optimistically put it), but rather in the form of bank deposits in the account books of the banks. Furthermore, the vast majority of these deposits do not represent any solid wealth—that is, they are not backed by gold or anything else—but have been created as purely fictitious loans issued in favor of the banking systems of the world. They are thus, as Frederick Soddy succinctly put it, simply "imagined to exist for the purpose of charging interest on [them]."[17]

But how, one might ask, is it possible to have effective transactions with something that is only "imagined to exist"? The answer lies in understanding how the providers of "money"—the banks—work, and, in particular, the process of credit and/or money creation. As H. D. McLeod notes: "A bank is not an office for borrowing and lending money, but it is a manufactory of credit."[18] Indeed, William Paterson, the founder of the (private) Bank of England, encouraged his prospective shareholders in 1694 by explaining to them that "The bank hath profit on the interest of all the moneys which it creates out of nothing."[19]

What, then, is this process by which money is created "out of nothing"? John Kenneth Galbraith, the famous economic historian, says quite candidly in his book on the history of money: "The process whereby credit is issued and money thereby created is so simple that the mind is repelled."[20] And it *is* simple. It is based on the fact that, when people deposit their money with a bank or other savings institution, they leave most of it untouched most of the time. But what you or I have left in the bank for safekeeping is not left untouched by the bank: rather, it is lent out by them at interest. This, after all, is their business. But this is not the end of the story: most of what is lent out to others also finds its way back into the system, since these new "owners" in turn find it convenient to use only a small amount in cash and to deposit most of it in a bank or other savings institution, with the result that most of it remains in the system and is available for further loans. In fact, by a simple application of this process, it is possible to create many times more money than what was originally deposited.

In order to illustrate this more concretely, let us consider the following description, taken from a standard economics textbook in use throughout schools today:

> *The banking system and the creation of money*
> The banking system has the power to create money. Its power to do this is rooted in the fact that all bank depositors are unlikely to want to withdraw all their money at the same time.
>
> Consider an economy with only one bank operating. Customers have deposited £100 million in the bank and it is going to make a profit by lending out that money to its customers. Not all of the £100 million will be lent out. From experience, the bank knows that its depositors will from time to time withdraw some of the deposits and expect cash. Over long years the bank in our economy has come to know just what proportion it needs to cope with even unexpected withdrawals. Let us assume that it needs to keep £1 in cash for every £10 of deposits. Hence, it can lend out £90 million of the £100 million originally deposited, keeping £10 million in cash. That £90 million in cash is unlikely to remain for long in the real economy. It will turn up as new deposits in the banking system, placed by customers who have received money from the original borrowers. Hence the bank can now lend out another 90% of £90 million, keeping £9 million in cash to cover possible cash withdrawals. That £81 million lent out will also reappear as new deposits in the banking system. Ninety per cent of that will be lent out, and this process carries on until the sums are too small to be worth mentioning. If all the money deposited is added up (£100 million + £90 million + £81 million + . . .) it will come to £1,000 million. The bank will have all of the original £100 million of cash (£10 million + £9 million + £8.1 million + . . .) but that will be supporting another £900 million of book entry money. It will owe £1,000 million to its customers who have deposited money. To balance that, it will have £100 million in cash and £900 million owing to it in the form of loans.[21]

Let us see what this means. If, for the sake of argument, we assume a (very conservative) annual interest rate of 5 percent on these loans, then, in the course of one year the bank will have made £45 million (that is, 5 percent of the total £900 million which it has "created" from the original £100 million deposited) out of other people's money, which was actually deposited with them for safekeeping! If we add to that the general banking charges that these customers may be paying for the privilege of having their money in this system, the simple truth emerges that whatever the original sum deposited, the bank can, from interest and other charges, make almost half as much again in just one year. If we further bear in mind that the cash ratio (or "reserve ratio," as it is sometimes called) assumed above of 1:10 is more likely to be in the order of 1:50 or 1:100 (that is, the banks only need to keep between 1 and 2 percent of their deposits in the form of cash)[22] and that interest rates on these loans are frequently much higher than 5 percent, so that the bank could easily be making many more times the amount originally deposited with it *every year*, then one can hardly be blamed for being surprised at both the simplicity and outrageousness of the whole operation, which, as we noted Galbraith as saying, is "so simple that the mind is repelled."

The implications of this system are made amply clear by Soddy (using the terminology of the 1920s):

> Let everyone with money that is his very own—borrowed from or lent by nobody—present himself at the bank at the same time and ask for it. As everyone knows, they would be lucky if they got 2*s*. in the £ (or ten cents on the dollar). Even if banks do keep 15 per cent. of their liability in cash, they would only get 3*s*. in the £.
>
> As the owners of it have not got the money they own, and as the banks have not got it, and as the people who borrowed it have not got it, where is it? Obviously nowhere. It is imagined to exist for the purpose of charging interest upon it.[23]

However, there is a further implication to this system which passes most people by. As Jeffrey Mark remarked in 1934:

> Of the absolute authority of Finance today there can be no question. To those who still cling to an illusion that politicians, bishops, military authorities, judges and educators, or some combination of any two, three, four or all five of them, have the fate of nations and the world in their hands, it should be unnecessary to submit evidence to the contrary. . . .
>
> Seeing that all things are produced through the agency of money, and that all money now comes into existence as a debt to the banking systems of the world, this simply means . . . that our now internationally organized moneylenders "are the actual or potential owners of everything produced in the world."[24]

That this is still very much the situation today was made clear on a recent British television program where Sir Fred Atkinson, a former government chief economic adviser (1977–1979) who had spent most of his life advising governments of both major political parties in Britain on economic policy, had this to say about who is in control of a nation's economic policy:

> A government has very little control, because it needs the approval, so to speak, of world financial centers, otherwise the money will be taken out and the exchange rate will fall. So it has to play the game according to the opinions of international banks, you might say, which means that it has to have its interest rates at what the world thinks is a correct level for a country in that position. It has to keep its budget within limits that people think are reasonable. So it is under a discipline not from an international authority, but from all the moneymen of the world, all the banks of the world.

The narrator went on to conclude:

> This is the reality of the forces of global integration. A national politician has about as much power in the world economy as a village has in a national economy. Nineteen ninety-four was the year in which one of President Clinton's advisers said that if he believed in reincarnation, he would come back not as the president or the pope, but as the world bond markets. As he said, "You can intimidate anybody."[25]

The point is that this created money gives power to those who create it. Not only can they dictate policies to their debtors, but, if those indebted to them cannot pay up, they can then help themselves to the collateral—real, tangible wealth such as land, houses, mineral resources, and so on. It is this single fact that has such devastating consequences for the environment, for the creation of credit—which means the creation of debt—is the prime cause of the destruction of the environment that we see around us. As Eugene Linden put it in an article reporting on the environment conference held in Boulder, Colorado, in 1988:

> Why are so many species and environments threatened? The main reason is that throughout the tropics, developing nations are struggling to feed their peoples and raise cash to make payments on international debts.[26]

Stated very simply, the problem is that whereas the bankers' money is always growing at whatever rate the banks dictate (limited only by whatever the current reserve ratio is), solid objects don't, and natural resources only at a very limited rate. (Whales, for instance, reproduce at a rate of about 2 percent per year, which is far lower than any standard interest rate.) Over the years, the amount of so-called "money" created in this way has snowballed to massive proportions, and so too has the size of the projects which this "money" is used to create. For it is not just big projects that demand big sums of money. It is also big sums of money that demand big projects, and this is where environmental destruction comes in. While the money is sitting "idle" in the banks' coffers, it is useless to them, but while it is being lent, it is gaining them their living, through interest. It is therefore imperative that the banks, with their large sums of money, find suitable projects for such large sums of money. And if they don't exist, then they have to be created. Hence the large number of totally unnecessary projects that we see being financed around the world (for example, ten dams in a South Indian province where one would be enough), regardless of their environmental impact.[27]

The point is, that while the money is sitting idle it is burning a hole in the banker's pocket. He must lend it out, no matter what the environmental cost, for interest is his business. But if it is lent to the whaling business, for example, or to a mining corporation, there is a problem: for whereas money might be lent at 10 percent, the whales only reproduce at 2 percent—and mineral resources run out! How then can a "sustainable development" of such resources keep up with the cost of money? The answer is, they cannot. The only "economic" answer is to exploit the resource as quickly as possible and then, when it has run out (or become "economically extinct," as in the case of the whales), to put the money into some other resource and exploit that before that too is exhausted in the same way. Given these concerns, environmental friendliness is a luxury few can afford. Despoliation is the inevitable, "natural" result.

The Way Ahead?

The Sufis note that the terrestrial is above the celestial and the outer is above the inner: if a baby is crying in the middle of a room where some highly intellectual discussion is taking place, it is the baby that will win out. Thus, although an inner change is of course part of the picture, there cannot just be an inner change: there must be an outer change as well. It is not just our thinking that must change, but also our actions.

We return to the Qur'anic quotation that we mentioned earlier: "Allah has permitted trade and forbidden usury." We live in a time when, as the Prophet predicted, even those who are not directly involved in taking usury will be "covered by its dust."[28] As part of enjoining the right and forbidding the wrong, Muslims are called to abolish usury and establish fair trade, so this must be their task. Their model in this task will be that of the Medina of the Prophet, may Allah bless him and grant him peace, where, after a mosque had been set up for worship of the One, a market was established in which usury was forbidden and all transactions were based on the just principles and precepts of the *sharī'a*.[29] This means that all transactions were based on a fair exchange of value, mediated by a measurable currency of pure gold and silver, which did not succumb to the vagaries of inflation (itself caused by usury) and which, unlike paper, was a true measure of value because it itself had value.

In the Qur'an Muslims are exhorted to establish just weights and measures and not to cheat in doing so (55:9: "Give just weight, and do not skimp in the balance"). In order to do this, Muslims must aim to follow the *sunna* of the Prophet, may Allah bless him and grant him peace. This means the reintroduction of gold and silver currency as the real measure of value, in accordance with his *sunna*; the reintroduction of free markets where no individual can permanently usurp space at the expense of others, in accordance with his *sunna*; and the reintroduction of production and distribution being in the hands of individuals rather than monopolies, in accordance with his *sunna*.

And, as will be apparent from other contributions to this volume, this is not simply a vision of the future. This is already happening.

Notes

1. Ian Dallas, *The Ten Symphonies of Gorka König* (London: Kegan Paul International, 1989), 84.

2. See Michael S. Northcott, *The Environment and Christian Ethics* (Cambridge: Cambridge University Press, 1996), 2. For a similar assessment, see, for example, Roger S. Gottlieb, ed., *This Sacred Earth* (New York and London: Routledge, 1996), 3–10, 14 n. 9; also the series foreword to the present volume by Mary Evelyn Tucker and John Grim.

3. See Muslim, *Ṣaḥīḥ Muslim bi-sharḥ al-Nawawī* (Beirut: Dār al-Kitāb al-ʻArabī, 1407/1987), 2:21–26; idem, *Ṣaḥīḥ Muslim*, trans. Abdul Hamid Siddiqi (Lahore: Sh. Muhammad Ashraf, 1976), 1:33.

4. al-Bukhārī, *Ṣaḥīḥ,* trans. Muhammad Muhsin Khan, Arabic-English parallel text, 2d rev. ed. (Ankara: Hilal Yayinlari, 1976), 3:406.

5. For a useful summary of the main views on this point, see Northcott, *The Environment and Christian Ethics*, chapter 2.

6. See Ibn Rushd al-Jadd, *al-Bayān wa-l-taḥṣīl wa-l-sharḥ wa-l-tawjīh wa-l-taʻlīl fī masāʼil al-Mustakhraja*, ed. Muḥammad Ḥajjī et al. (Beirut: Dār al-Gharb al-Islāmī, 1404–7/1984–87), 17:236; also Muslim, *Ṣaḥīḥ Muslim bi-sharḥ al-Nawawī*, 15:116–18; idem, *Ṣaḥīḥ Muslim*, trans. Abdul Hamid Siddiqi, 4:1259–60.

7. See Ibn Rushd al-Jadd, *Bayān*, 17:237.

8. See Muḥammad ibn Aḥmad Mayyāra, *al-Durr al-thamīn wa-l-mawrid al-maʻīn, sharḥ "al-Murshīd al-muʻīn"* (Beirut: Dār al-Fikr, n.d.), 15; Ibn Ḥamdūn, *Ḥāshiyat Ibn Ḥamdūn ʻalā sharḥ Mayyāra li-manẓūmat Ibn ʻĀshir al-musammāt bi-"al-Murshīd al-muʻīn,"* 2d ed. (Beirut: Dār al-Fikr, 1392/1972), 1:18.

9. For current views on this issue, see, for example, Northcott, *The Environment and Christian Ethics*, esp. 126 ff., 179–80; Roger S. Gottlieb, introduction to *This Sacred Earth*, 9 and 14 n. 9; David Kinsley, "Christianity as Ecologically Harmful" and "Christianity as Ecologically Responsible," in Gottlieb, ed., *This Sacred Earth*, 104–24.

10. This is the standard interpretation of major Qur'anic commentaries, such as the *Tafsīr al-Jalālayn* (see al-Ṣāwī, *Ḥāshiyat al-Ṣāwī ʻalā Tafsīr al-Jalālayn* [Beirut: Dār al-Fikr, n.d.],1:19–20) and *Tafsīr al-Bayḍāwī* (al-Bayḍāwī, *Anwār al-tanzīl wa-asrār al-taʼwīl* [Dār al-Kutub al-ʻArabiyya: Cairo, 1330 [1912], 1:135). The word can also be taken to mean "one who follows after" in a simple chronological sense, but this would not affect the basic argument, evident throughout the Qur'an, that humankind has been given "everything that is on the earth," but is at the same time responsible for what they do with it, as will become apparent in the following paragraphs.

11. Muslim, *Ṣaḥīḥ Muslim bi-sharḥ al-Nawawī*, 17:55; idem, *Ṣaḥīḥ Muslim*, trans. Abdul Hamid Siddiqi, 4:1432.

12. See, for example, Qur'an 14:33, 16:12, 29:61, 31:29, 35:13, 39:5 (the sun and the moon); 14:33, 16:12 (day and night); 14:32 (the rivers); 16:14 (the sea); 31:20, 45:13 (everything).

13. See, for example, Othman Llewellyn, "Desert Reclamation and Islamic Law," *The Muslim Scientist* 11 (1982): 9–29 (an edited version of this article appeared as "Desert Reclamation and Conservation in Islamic Law" in *Islam and Ecology*, ed.

Fazlun Khalid with Joanne O'Brien [London: Cassell, 1992], 87–97); Yasin Dutton, "Natural Resources in Islam," in Khalid and O'Brien, eds., *Islam and Ecology*, 51–67; idem, "Islam and the Environment: A Framework for Enquiry," in *Faith in Dialogue*, number one/1996, *Faiths and the Environment: Conference Papers*, ed. Christopher Lamb (Middlesex University: Centre for Inter-Faith Dialogue, 1996), 46–70 (an edited version was reprinted in *Islam and the Environment*, ed. Harfiyyah Abdel Haleem [London: Ta-Ha Publishers, 1998], 56–74, 138–43).

14. See preceding note for references.

15. See Ibn Mājah, *Sunan*, ed. Muḥammad Fu'ād 'Abd al-Bāqī (n.p.: Dār Iḥyā' al-Turāth al-'Arabī, n.d.), 2:1325 (seventy times); al-Qurṭubī, *Aḥkām al-Qur'ān* (Cairo: Maṭba'at Dār al-Kutub al-Miṣriyya, 1935–50), 3:364 (thirty-six and ninety-nine times).

16. See, for example, Northcott, *The Environment and Christian Ethics*, chapter 2, esp. 45–46.

17. Frederick Soddy, *Wealth, Virtual Wealth and Debt* (London: Allen and Unwin, 1926), 157; cited also in Jeffrey Mark, *The Modern Idolatry* (London: Chatto and Windus, 1934), 85.

18. Cited in Mark, *The Modern Idolatry*, 81.

19. Cited in Ezra Pound, *What Is Money For?* (London: Greater Britain Publications, 1939), 2; reprinted in Ezra Pound, *Selected Prose: 1909–1965*, ed. William Cookson (London: Faber and Faber, 1973), 260. Cf. Ezra Pound, *Impact* (Chicago: Henry Regnery, 1960), 46–47, 101, 108, 187.

20. John Kenneth Galbraith, *Money: Whence It Came, Where It Went* (London: Pelican, 1976), 29.

21. A. G. Anderton, *Economics: A New Approach*, new ed. (London: Unwin Hyman, 1990), 18. See also idem, *Economics* (Ormskirk: Causeway Press, 1991), 355–56. For non-economic textbook descriptions of the same process, see, for example: Mark, *The Modern Idolatry*, 64–68; idem, *Analysis of Usury* (London: J. M. Dent and Sons, 1935), 121–23; Soddy, *Wealth, Virtual Wealth and Debt*, 153–54; idem, *The Arch-Enemy of Economic Freedom* (Knapp, Enstone, Oxon: 1943), 2–7; C. H. Douglas, *The Monopoly of Credit*, 4th ed. (Sudbury: Bloomfield Books, 1979), 19–21, 158–60; C. P. Jacob, *Economic Salvation* (London: Thornton Butterworth, 1933), 123–24.

22. In the 1930s the percentages were in the order of 2 percent coins, 18 percent banknotes, and 80 percent bank deposits (see Mark, *The Modern Idolatry*, 55; idem, *Analysis of Usury*, 29). Now, with the advent of credit cards and other forms of "electronic money," the percentage of "cash," that is, coins and banknotes, in the economy is between 1 and 2 percent, with this figure likely to decrease further; see Anderton, *Economics*, 355.

23. For references, see n. 17 above.

24. Mark, *The Modern Idolatry*, 70.

25. "Undercurrents of 1994," broadcast on BBC2 TV, 31 December 1994.

26. Eugene Linden, "The Birth of Death," *Time*, 2 January 1989, 22; cited also in Umar Vadillo, *The End of Economics* (Granada: Madinah Press, 1991), 26.

27. For three other such examples, see the London *Financial Times*, 23 January 1989, 16 (the French nuclear program); Paul and Anne Ehrlich, *Extinction: The*

Causes and Consequences of the Disappearance of Species (London: Victor Gollancz, 1982), 106, 203–4 (the mining of molybdenum in Colorado, and the whaling industry); and Dutton, "Islam and the Environment," 60–61.

28. See Aḥmad ibn Ḥanbal, *Musnad* (Cairo: al-Maṭba'a al-Maymaniyya, 1313 [1895]), 2:494; also Ibn Mājah, *Sunan*, 2:765; al-Nasā'ī, *Sunan* (Cairo: al-Maṭba'a al-Maymaniyya, 1312 [1894]), 2:212.

29. For the establishment of this market and some of the conditions of its use, see, for example, Ibn Shabba, *Tārīkh al-Madīna al-Munawwara*, ed. Fahīm Muḥammad Shaltūt, 2d ed. (Jeddah: Dār al-Iṣfahānī li-l-Ṭibā'a, 1393 [1973]), 1:304; al-Samhūdī, *Wafā' al-wafā' bi-akhbār dār al-Muṣṭafā*, ed. Muḥammad Muḥyī al-Dīn 'Abd al-Ḥamīd (Beirut: Dār Iḥyā' al-Turāth al-'Arabī, 1374/1955), 2:747–49; M. J. Kister, "The Market of the Prophet," *Journal of the Economic and Social History of the Orient* 8 (1965): 273–75; Pedro Chalmeta, *El "Señor del Zoco" en España* (Madrid: Instituto Hispano-Árabe de Cultura, 1973), 62–64.

Islam, Muslim Society, and Environmental Concerns: A Development Model Based on Islam's Organic Society

HASHIM ISMAIL DOCKRAT

Introduction

In his fourteenth-century work the *Muqāddima* (Introduction to History), Ibn Khaldun arranges the essence of Aristotle's *Politics* into eight sentences:

> The world is a garden the fence of which is the dynasty. The dynasty is an authority through which life is given to proper behavior. Proper behavior is a policy directed by the ruler. The ruler is an institution supported by soldiers. The soldiers are helpers who are maintained by money. Money is sustenance brought together by the subjects. The subjects are servants who are protected by justice. Justice is something harmonious, and through it the world persists. The world is a garden. . . .[1]

With repetitive lyrical force, this rhythm permeates Aristotle's political philosophy. Each concept leads into the next, as a circle with no beginning or end.

This paper draws inspiration from the above lyrical exposition of a world in harmony. The symbolism of the circle is as true to Islam as it was for Aristotle and his times. It holds truths about the reality of politics and the economy of things in relation to a world dependent on the "just balance." It has relevance to our world today. Our world is a decaying garden, of which Fritjof Capra aptly remarked:

> We find ourselves in a state of profound, worldwide crisis. It is a complex, multi-dimensional crisis whose facets touch every aspect of our lives. It is a crisis of intellectual, moral, and spiritual dimensions; a crisis of a scale and urgency unprecedented in recorded human history. For the first time we have to face the very real threat of extinction of the human race and all life on this planet.[2]

Under the haze of scientific and technological progress and the boast of free market economics, all is not well. As Eugene Linden wrote for *Time*:

> Like Oscar Wilde's fictional creation Dorian Gray, who stayed forever young while a portrait of him in the attic aged horribly, the modern economy masks a disfigured planet. The engine of consumption has scarred the land and stained the seas, eating away at the foundations of nature and threatening to destroy humanity's only means of survival.[3]

Islam lays down clear parameters for humans in terms of their relationship with the environment. In the Qur'an, Allah indicates to humankind the perfection of His worldly creation: "Glorify the name of your Guardian Lord Most High, who created, and further given order and proportion; Who measured and granted guidance . . ." (Qur'an 87:1–5). He commands, "Do no mischief on the earth, after it has been set in order . . ." (7:56). He also honors humans with a high station: "Then we made you the heirs (*khulafā*) in the land after them, to see how you behave" (10:14). Islam offers to humankind both the honor of guardianship and the blessings of worship in our relationship with the environment.

Transvaluation of Values

Ecology, derived from the Greek words *oikos* (house) and *logos* (word, hence "study of"), is defined as the study of the relationships between living organisms and their environment. Human ecology is the study of the relationship between human organisms and their environment. Put together, these activities are termed *bionomics*. The word economy is also derived from the Greek *oikonomia*: *oikon* from *oikos*, and *nomia* from *namien*, meaning to manage. Hence, in its classical definition economics means the management of the household.[4] In terms of the unity of this conceptual arrangement—that is, between ecology and economy, using bionomics as its median—ecology can also mean, in an implicit sense, the management of the environment. This conceptual relationship is crucial to an understanding of the bionomic crisis of the twentieth century. It leads us to the assumption that bad economic management has resulted in bad environmental management. The overwhelming consensus among ecology specialists is that the unregulated use and development of technology and industrialization has promulgated the present environmental crisis.

Yet technology and industrial processes are inanimate, almost neutral elements; they depend upon a systemic order to give them functional meaning. In this sense technology and industry are processes determined by a system of economic management. Alvin Toffler commented that technological questions cannot be answered in technological terms alone, arguing that they are political questions.[5] Indeed, the political economic dimensions permeate the entire spectrum of ecological discourse. Economic management in this century has been defined by dual dominant systemic orders: capitalism and communism. Capra views these systems as paradigms that are beyond mere economic methods, but that extend to include the entire political and philosophical foundation of a society.[6]

Eric de Maré refers to capitalism and communism as opposite faces of the same coin, for both support the work ethic and both are subservient to money power.[7] In this sense all economists and economies subscribe to the "labor theory of value,"[8] thus reducing humans, and their labor, to a commodity among commodities. More devastating, however, is what de Maré calls the lie of economic democracy: "We live under an oligarchy that is all-powerful, permanent, responsible to no one and directly or indirectly, dominates and restricts every individual, every industry and every government in the world. Such is the power conferred by the monopoly of credit."[9] This is a strong assertion that questions the very nature of sovereignty: the sovereignty of individuals, entire societies, and governments to act independently, culturally, and organically in their own best interest.

We need to move away from the narrow compass of the economic calculus. E. F. Schumacher points to the narrow methodology of economics based on the maximizing of profit at any cost, in which "the entire God-given environment has a 'return on capital employed.' This means that an activity can be economic although it plays hell with the environment, and that a competing activity, if at some cost it protects and conserves the environment, will be uneconomic."[10] The challenge remains to create a model that represents a perfect symbiosis between traditional precedents that governed trade and commerce and the demanding and accelerating nature of our technological environment.

We have to find a suitable cure for the inequitable progress of modern economics. We need to reevaluate our current economic behavior. Islam offers a pattern of economic behavior that is centered in *fiṭra*,[11] is rational, and is sufficiently enduring to serve as a blueprint for a meaningful paradigm shift or transition from an almost nihilistic economic pattern of behavior to a holistic, life-saving, and life-confirming pattern. Christopher Flavin alludes to society's ability to achieve ecological harmony only if human demands are prepared to accommodate other values: "less-polluting . . . science and engineering alone will not suffice. New values could be just as crucial to our future prosperity, and perhaps to our very existence."[12] In this sense Islam not only offers new values; it offers a set of values that have withstood the test of time for thirteen and a half centuries.[13]

In order to establish a path between concern for the preservation of our ecological environment and the door of Islam, we must allow humans the space to manage themselves and their environment without interference from outside agencies, such as the state and supra-financial institutions. The great German composer Richard Wagner called the ideal social ethos a system of "government without state and commerce without usury."[14] In Nietzche's language, to achieve this will demand a complete transvaluation of all values.[15] Such transvaluation implies shutting the door on three centuries of usurious economic orthodoxy and unlocking the door of what Muslims call *mu'āmalāt*.[16]

As Shaykh 'Abd al-Qadir as-Sufi so eloquently put it, what is of relevant concern to Muslims today

> is to project a future Islam, viable for the electronic age, stripped of all its ritualism and anti-rational modes, stripped of its elitism, its reductionist thinking, its cultism and its sects. Restored to the social and personal reality of a *dīn* (true religion), it is possible for modern man to find in Islam the perfect way, combining as it does so elegantly and nobly, the science of inner knowledge and the science of outer action. The key to this new state is to avoid the bigoted thinking that has marred so many dialogues between Muslims in the past, precisely be-

cause they had taken on a religious, and therefore, not rational character. This situation entails that the truths of *ihsan* (virtue) remain and the Qur'anic injunctions of outwardness remain. The *sharīʻa* is nowhere denied, and gnosis is the promised gift of the *muḥsin* (practitioner of *iḥsān*) when he 'watches the night': We as Muslims are the only people who can offer an inner technology alongside the outer project of the modern society.[17]

The Foundation of Islamic Society

In Islam the complete existential social contract, which is binding on the individual within society, is contained within the idea of *jamāʻat* (congregation). This binding of the complete social contract is based on *ibāda* (ritual faith and worship), *muʻāmalāt* (private and public affairs, the zone of commercial and related transactions), and *imāra* (political governance). The opposite of this understanding of *jamāʻat* results in the helplessness of individualism, the dissipation of wealth, and the end of political sovereignty.

Conversely, the more subservient the *jamāʻat* is, in terms of this social contract, to Allah, the more powerful the *jamāʻat* will be. This is recognition that power belongs only to the divine presence and simultaneously confirms the helplessness of humans in all matters. Therefore, the social contract of the Muslim is really an essential divine contract. The divine contract of the *jamāʻat* is understood to be based on obedience, the assumption of responsibility, and accountability.

This three-dimensional set of relationships is orderly; it indicates "Supreme" design and at a temporal level allows for self-will. As an expression of this orderedness, we revert to the allegory of the circle in our opening paragraph. Of all geometric forms, only the circle alludes to the cosmic and unitary sense of space and time. It is symbolic of purity and perfection. Our diagram (see appendix A)[18] is an integrative, symbiotic, and existentially relevant interpretation of the organic Islamic society. It symbolizes the free movement of the functional (public) person and the contemplative (private) person. The outer (*ẓāhir*) nature and inner (*bātin*) nature of humans constantly merge and separate, yet they are contained within the limits of the circumference, in this sense within the limits of the *sharīʻa* (divine law). All three dimensions, that of command and adherence to being commanded, the social and commercial transactions, and the rituals of inner and public worship, are mutually dependent and function as a singular organism.

At the core or center of the *jamā'at* are the acts of *ibādat* (ritual worship). *Ibādat* encompass the Five Pillars of Islam: *shahāda* (testimony of faith), *salāt* (ritual daily prayer), *zakāt* (almsgiving), *sawm* (daylight fast during the month of Ramadan), and *ḥājj* (pilgrimage to Mecca). These are compulsory acts of worship which represent the inner (*bātin*) dimension of worship of Islamic society. It also manifests a strong outer physical and tangible form.

In its outer dimension (*ẓāhir*), we have the everyday *mu'āmalāt*. It is not my purpose in this paper to discuss the many laws that fall under the definition of *mu'āmalāt*. Rather, I will highlight the most significant institutions within which various aspects of the *mu'āmalāt* functioned in traditional Islamic society. More significantly, I emphasize those institutions that articulated the socioeconomic life of Muslim society through the ages. These institutions are all integrated. Among the most important of these institutions are:

1. Open markets/free market—The physical arena where trading takes place.

2. Guilds (professional societies)—The organizing bodies of traders, workers, craftsmen, and artisans. Old societies can also be referred to as guild-representative societies.

3. The *imārat* system—A complex that fulfills the spiritual, social, and economic needs of a community within towns and cities and which was most common during the Ottoman period.

4. Islamic currency—The bimetal currency consisting of gold dinars and silver dirhams.

5. Islamic business contracts—The nature of the various types of business and partnership contracts permitted in Islamic law.

6. Caravans—The networking of distance trading and international trade.

7. Muslim personal law—Emphasizes (in the context of this paper) the gender issue only.

8. *Waqf*s—The charitable real estate foundations common to Muslim societies.

9. *Zawīya*s—The homes of the Sufi orders to which all the guilds belong.

10. Architecture—The importance of architecture and urbanism in Islamic development.

Governing this nexus, which is the inner *(bāṭin)* and outer *(ẓāhir)* condition of the community, is *imāra*. *Imāra* is that form of divinely sanctioned governance embedded in the *sunna* (example) of the prophet Muhammed (PBUH) and the *'amal* of Medina. A functioning emirate includes the zone of delegation, the *wazirate* (ministry), and the establishment of the rule of law (the *sharī'a*) by way of the *fuqahā* (jurisprudents) or the court of the *qāḍī* (judge).

This model of the organic Islamic society highlights three primal categories of *fiqh* (Islamic jurisprudence), which are contractual and transactional in nature. They also embody the complete behavioral pattern of the Muslim, a model of social behavior centered in *fitra* (the natural state of things).

Whereas *ibāda* is an implicit condition of being Muslim, *mu'āmalāt,* containing as it does economic activities, demands the restoration of the above-mentioned institutions, giving it a functional reality. Only in this way will *mu'āmalāt* enable people to transact according to the prescriptions and limits of *tijāra* (Islamic trade and commerce).

The economic arena of traditional Islamic society offers precedents that best articulate Islam's organic and self-sustaining nature, its profound sense of justice, and the symbiosis between the rule of religious law and economic behavior. Implicit to its nature are the principles of equity, the absence of monopoly, the encouragement of trade through partnership, and the obvious absence of usury. The *mu'āmalāt* constitutes two thirds of the *fiqh* (jurisprudence). Its underlying rationale is based on equity rather than profit.[19] This concern with equity is what makes the economic behavior contained within Islam fundamentally different from the irrationality of the macroeconomic paradigm. In this paper I utilize traditional principles of trade and commerce as the foundation for constructing rational planning models for the future.

Open/Free Markets

The principal concern of the macroeconomic, and hence fiscal, worldview, has been, and remains, the deliberate reengineering of society on the basis of the divisions of labor, the division of resources, and, finally, of ownership itself. The aim of this social reengineering at an economic level has been the consolidation and concentration of national and global market shares in the hands of an elite. This process of monopoly at the primary (fiscal) and secondary (industrial) levels of the economic chain has effectively altered the nature of power control away from political entities to global financial entities.[20] This has prevented the rule of law from prevailing effectively over the use of global rcsourccs.

At a political level, therefore, the macroeconomic worldview has effectively replaced the sovereignty of man with the sovereignty of institutions. This transfer of sovereignty means that humanity has abdicated its right to be responsible in favor of obscure corporate bodies, such as financial institutions and the arms of institutionalized democracy. In financial institutions, power is maintained on the basis that the creditor always has the right-of-call over the debtor, while insitutionalized democracy presumes that it has power on the basis of popular support.

Today, governments, as the managers of fiscal states,[21] hold two things in common with the average citizenry: both are debtors, and, generally, both lack any meaningful ownership of wealth. This has given birth to a dual crisis: governments unable to function effectively, and societies rendered dysfunctional through debt and unemployment. The restoration of free trade is therefore the only rational prognosis for this age.

Trade has always been an essential ingredient in the process of creating equity. It has mitigated many of our important scientific and scholastic discoveries and has been one of the driving forces behind the spread of religions. Looked at in this way, no human endeavor has affected the freedom of people the way trading has when restricted (capitalism and the fiscal state) or banned (communism). The commercial exchange—if carried out in equity—is a social act granting immediate justice and mutual benefit to all involved parties. If restricted, it invariably creates social injustice.

The existence of free trade depended, however, on openly accessible markets. Every free city was built around an open market that could not be rented or owned. The market was the main attraction for foreign traders and thereby became the primary source of wealth for the city. For this reason, the freely accessible market as a physical reality should be the most important element in a city—it will be noticed by either its absence or its presence. In contrast to the medieval Christian and Islamic cities that were all built around a central marketplace, our modern cities are noted for the complete absence of any form of marketplace.

Deprived of the Islamic model, Europe, since the Renaissance, developed trading and markets in a way that served the purpose of world domination. Capitalist development created a new concept of the city. From the physical market, with physical merchants and real money, we have been pushed into abstract markets (the supermarket and the stock exchange), with invisible traders (the corporate entity and shareholder) and abstract money (plastic and electronic money). The orthodoxy of modern economic theories has effectively banned free trade from our system of exchange by replacing equity with the profit motive.[22]

Trading is an important part of the life of a Muslim community, and the most essential element of trading is the existence and regulation of the marketplace. This in Islamic law is commonly known as *ḥisba* (accounting) or *iḥtisāb* (taking into consideration).[23] *Ḥisba* regulations were aimed at the prevention of fraudulent transactions, profiteering, price fixing, and monopoly. It also controlled weights and measures, established fair prices, and inspected quality of merchandise.

The entire foundation of the *mu'āmalāt* is based on the very simple precedent laid down by the Prophet of Islam (PBUH).[24] Soon after his arrival in the city of Medina in 622, he built a mosque and set up a new market. He made it clear by his statements and explicit injunctions that the marketplace was a freely accessible space for everybody, with no delimitations (such as shops) and where no taxes, levies, or rent could be charged. The following principles were established:

1) The market is like a mosque (that is, freely accessible to all):

> The Prophet (PBUH) said: "Markets should follow the same *sunna* as the Mosques: whoever gets his place first has the right to it until he gets up and goes back to his house or finishes his selling."[25]

2) It is *ṣadaqa* (a charitable gift), with no private ownership:

> The Prophet (PBUH) said: "The Messenger of Allah (S.A.W), gave the Muslims their markets as a charitable gift."[26]

3) With no rent charged (to the trader):

> Ibn Zabala related: "The letter of Umar ibn al-Aziz was read out to us in Madinah, saying that the market was a *ṣadaqa* and that no rent (*kira*) should be charged by anyone for it."[27]

4) With no taxes charged on it (that is, charged to the trader):

> Ibrahim ibn Mundir related: "When the Messenger of Allah (S.A.W), wanted to set up a market in Madinah, he went to the market of Bani Qaynuqa' and then came to the market of Madinah, stamped his foot on the ground and said: " This is your market. Do not let any tax (*kharaj*) be levied on it."[28]

5) Where no reservations can be made (that is, no prebooking of space):

> Ibn Zabala relates: "Umar ibn al-Khattab (once) passed by the Gate of Ma'mar in the market and saw that a Jar had been placed by the gate and he ordered that it be taken away. . . . Umar forbade him to put any stones on the place or lay claim to it (in any way)."[29]

6) Where no shops can be constructed:

> The Prophet (PBUH) said: "This is your market. Do not build anything in stone (*La tataḥājjaru*) [in it], and do not let any tax (*kharāj*) be levied on it."[30]

Viewed against this humane and natural background, trade in the modern age appears trapped in precisely the opposite conditions. It has, furthermore, incorporated usury and monopoly as acceptable components of business activity. Trade has become the victim of the tyranny of overregulation and taxation. It therefore becomes necessary to reestablish the traditional free markets for the following reasons.

Justice

Pure trading remains a universal generator of wealth and prosperity. Trading is a commutative act of justice. It simultaneously and mutually benefits both parties, maintaining their absolute independence. No other human endeavor proves, like trading does, that only justice results in prosperity. No other human endeavor can so affect, when inhibited or corrupted, the freedom of the people.

Equity

Equity (*'adl*) in Islamic trading is part of worship. Equity demands equality of agreement and equality of value. Equity is based on trust; therefore, any exchange of goods is permitted as long as it does not involve forbidden commodities (wine, pork, drugs, etc.), usury (paper money or any increase with no corresponding counter value), uncertain transactions (sale of goods not in the possession of the seller; *al-gharār,* etc.), or fraud (charging higher prices to travelers not aware of local prices, or fixing prices in order to influence a bid *najsh*, etc.). No adulteration of the original goods is permitted. Speculation of goods or commodities is expressly forbidden in Islam.[31] Trade must at all times be transparent and conducted in public. Fundamental to an understanding of equity is that profit and liability (risk) go together.[32] Private ownership is intrinsic to labor, capital, the means of production, and the accruing of profit and loss.

The End of Monopolies

In Islam there is no monopoly business so, therefore, there is no cash price (lower) or credit price (higher).[33] There are no wholesale or retail prices because Islam does not reward capital for the mere possession of it; it rewards labor. Monopolies proliferate when capital is allowed to command price. The Prophet (PBUH) said: "The holder of a monopoly is a sinner and offender."[34]

Entrepreneurship can only have any meaning in an open market with open distribution. In defense of "small" traders, Justice Louis Brandeis observed of the emerging chain store industry during his time "that the chain store, by furthering the concentration of wealth and of power and by promoting absentee ownership, is thwarting American ideals; that it is making impossible equality of opportunity; that it is converting independent tradesmen into clerks; that it is sapping the resources, the vigor and the hope of the smaller cities and towns."[35] A free market without monopolies brings everybody along in growth. The more wealth people share, the more extensive their transactions among each other. Confucius wrote in his *Great Learning* (*Da xue*): "A country does not prosper by making profits; its equity is its profit."

Empowerment

Free and just trade breeds free and just people. A community, its possessions, its spirituality, and the environment are safe among free and just persons. The virtues of trade are exemplified in many sayings of the Prophet (PBUH): "Endeavoring for *ḥalāl* earning is a *jihād* (righteous effort), it is the duty after the duty"; "Righteous traders will be the first to enter paradise."[36] He told his successors, "I advise you for leniency to the business community. They are guards against calamities and are God's peace on earth."[37] Trade has always been viewed as the final arbiter between the state of well-being for the individual and poverty. Islam fosters trade within the prescribed limits of Allah and His Messenger (PBUH).

End of Unemployment

Unemployment is the result of restraining access to the business nexus, in order to guarantee cheap labor. Brandeis argued that "existing unemployment is the result, in large part, of the gross inequality in the distribution of wealth and income which giant corporations have fostered."[38] Unemployment is not the result of the replacement of the human workforce by machines. A machine can replace human work processes, but it still does not prove that the mechanization of production processes is creating unemployment.

It is a fallacy to assume that a person working for a salary as an "employed" person is the only way of gaining an income. Ibn Khaldun associates salaried work with the status of slavery. The great advocate of social credit, Eric Gill, asserts that "Modern finance imposes on us a totally unnatural privation . . . the wage system is really a slave system . . . man has been reduced to a sub-human condition of intellectual irresponsibility."[39]

However much we may ponder the value of labor, the fact of the matter, as C. H. Douglas pointed out, is that "We cling dogmatically to the work ethic and the labor theory of value when the truth is that labor has become a relatively small and rapidly diminishing factor in the production of material wealth."[40] From this it is apparent that industry has created a labor fallout called unemployment. Viewed against this background, the importance of the open market and the restoration of the guilds increases in relevance.

The Guilds

Open markets in Muslim cities, under the protection of an authority, gathered around them a population of traders and producers. Production was shaped in the form of guilds. The town was divided into radiating sections, each one of which was dominated by a guild. The guilds were also divided according to religious orders.[41] Today's corporate structures, especially mass-production factories, reveal themselves as anachronistic and inefficient forms of production. Modern cell production is a new force in manufacturing processes and is therefore viewed as one step in the reclamation of the guild system.[42]

The guilds in Islamic society were no mere economic units; they were directed by a master who was both a Sufi *shaykh* (spiritual guide) and a craftsman. *Futūwwa* principles exercised great influence over the guilds. According to *futūwwa* ethics, the perfect person is one who is generous, self-sacrificing, self-disciplined, obedient to his superiors, and sober.[43] This Sufi connection with the guilds is still evident among guild societies in North Africa, especially in Morocco.

Ḥisba regulations guided the guilds in pricing and quality standards. The *muḥtāsib*, or sheriff of the market, ensured that the regulations of *iḥtisāb* were met by all traders and guilds in the market. He would enforce the law and bring infringements to the notice of the *qāḍī*, or judge. This was the only real submission of the guilds to the authority of the sultan. Other than this, the guilds functioned as independent and self-regulatory units or societies.

The guilds were an instrumental component of the phenomenon of *jamā'at*, or community. The guilds in history permeated throughout all sections and classes of society and were a driving force behind industry and trade. Guilds were defined by the following features:

- Profits were shared. Among them there were no salaried workers.

• Partnership contracts such as the *shirkat* and *mudāraba* were common.

• They separated into masters and brought others in as apprentices.

• They established various *waqf*s (charitable endowments) for taking care of widows and families of deceased members, pensions, orphanages, production facilities, and caravanserais.

• They developed "insurance" facilities for their members and their families.

• They introduced statutes regulating work conditions, quality standards, partnership policy, and the like.

• They established embassies and ambassadors in their relations with state authorities, other guilds, towns, and cities.

• They had firmly based governing structures under the leadership of a Sufi *shaykh*. All guilds were closely bound to Sufism, and brotherhood was the cornerstone of their association.

• Guilds even empowered women in certain crafts.

• They organized their own security for their caravans and other facilities. Guilds themselves were marshaled and regimented for *jihād*.[44]

With the advent of modernity, guilds were not quick enough to absorb changes in technology into their production methods, and hence allowed capital to dictate the use and development of industrial technology.[45] Without the highly moral and regulatory nature of the guilds, the use of technology for industrial purposes was allowed to spiral out of control. One could say that, historically, the guilds died by assassination. The guilds disappeared when the market disappeared. The market disappeared with the arrival of the deadly symbiosis between the state and the monopolists.[46] The first offered legal privileges (the privilege to print money and create monopoly) in exchange for taxation. In this tandem of privileges and taxation, the modern corporation emerged. Venice, for example, arose as an open market against the feudal order, and decayed as a monopolistic feud against the open market. The emergence of the secular state resulted in the secularization of social security and services and the nationalization of the *waqf*s. The guilds thus lost the infrastructure that guaranteed their financial autonomy.

It is hoped that in this new century guilds will reemerge as a natural consequence of corporate downsizing and reengineering and the introduction of cellular production networks. Unemployment, furthermore, is forcing people to look at alternative financial, manufacturing, and distribution methods that bypass existing monopoly structures. These emerging trends are witness to increased activities in cooperative enterprises at communal levels, growing informal market sectors, decentralization of technologies and workstations, and decentralization of production and distribution networks.[47] The technology of the future, according to Toffler's optimistic view, will create an "explosive extension of freedom." "It will create, not identical 'mass men', but people richly different from one another, individuals, not robots . . . it will encourage a crazy-quilt pattern of evanescent life-styles."[48]

Guilds can ensure a more rational approach to production methods and techniques. They are part of the answer to the ever-increasing mediocrity of the mass-production market. To assist in this transition, professionals will have to take on the role of masters and help create wealth through the joining of assets and skills. This is the road to collective and individual self-empowerment. As Omar Vadillo put it: "Employment is the lowest form of economic activity. The guild is the end of the enforced employee."[49]

The *Imārat* System

The *imārat* was a traditional urban unit, which consisted of a market and a mosque, as well as many other social and welfare institutions. In ancient Rome this urban unit consisted of the forum (market) and the basilica (civic center and temple). In ancient Greece this took the form of the agora and the temple. Thus, this coming together of trade and worship was the heart of the city's public affairs.

The *imārat*s were created in order to populate a new area or to establish a new neighborhood in the town. Thus, new towns and new suburbs within cities emerged around the *imārat*s. *Imārat*, from the Arabic word *imāra*, means "construction." In the Ottoman language *imārat* meant "improving the land or country."[50] Thus, it signifies Islamic development. A significant aspect of the *imārat* was that it was completely *waqf*. It was established as a public service, which was developed alike by sultans, public officials, and people of wealth. It sustained the overall economic, spiritual, administrative, charitable, and cultural life of a community.

The *imārat* was an old near-eastern institution which the Ottomans had adopted in the building of Bursa and other cities.[51] It consisted of a diverse number of institutions, such as the mosque, market, hospital, caravanserai, water installations, *madrāsa*, soup kitchens, roads, bridges, and, in some cases, even large libraries. Most services, especially health care, drinking water, and education, were free. The socially dynamic form of the *imārat* gains in significance in our time. The development of *imārat*s can become important architectural features in our modern urban environments, creating independence for communities as self-sustaining and caring socioeconomic units. In fact, in the face of growing urban degeneration, they become necessary, both socially and economically.

The Islamic Currency

The development of alternate and tradition-based financial systems and mediums of exchange become necessary in an age plagued by inflation, currency speculation, and financial indebtedness. The monopolies of money and credit are mutually destructive forces that inhibit meaningful socioeconomic development. They restrict the very sovereignty of nations. Thomas Jefferson once remarked, "I sincerely believe that banking institutions are more dangerous to liberty than standing armies."[52] President John Adams concurred: "Banks have done more injury to the religion, morality, tranquility, prosperity and even wealth of the nation than they can have done or ever will do good."[53]

In Islamic law money is any "commodity" commonly used as a medium of exchange. From this we can discern that money is a commodity; it is freely and communally accepted, and it is a medium of exchange. Money has to conform to three basic qualities: it must have intrinsic value, value in exchange, and value in use.[54] Paper money has neither intrinsic value nor value in use; that is, unlike gold, it cannot be melted down for any other use; its value in exchange is symbolic. Money cannot be rented, yet paper money in the form of bank notes is rented.

According to most fractional reserve regulations, a commercial bank is generally only required to hold 4 percent of deposits as a reserve, whereas they are allowed to lend out 96 percent. Reserve banks are allowed to create money seventeen times its capitalization. Banks therefore lend out money they do not really possess. Money is created out of nothing tangible; it is created from debt. This is the usurious nature of banking.

Paper money derives its value on the basis of credit, in fact unlimited credit. It is a promissory note, a debt, no longer redeemable in gold. Governments have abandoned the gold standard,[55] and, by doing so, they opened the door to currency speculation. Today, money lives up to its root meaning, as the other, not so famous, Adam Smith succinctly put it: "All money is a matter of belief. *Credit* derives from Latin, *credere*, 'to believe.' Belief was there, the factories functioned, the farmers delivered their produce. The central bank kept the belief alive when it would not let even the government borrow further."[56]

The Islamic position on this matter is clear. If paper money is a debt representing a piece of merchandise (*dayn*), then the debt must have a definition of what is owed. Clearly, paper money today has no such corresponding definition. Even if it is defined as a proper debt, a debt cannot be used as a medium of exchange. If paper money is a tangible medium of exchange (*'ayn*, real/tangible wealth), its value corresponds only to its weight in paper.[57] Equally, we take the value of gold coins by its weight, not its nominal value.

This brings us to the crux of the matter: "Gold is the only commodity that has universal acceptance as money. . . . To restore the usefulness of currencies, they will need to be convertible into gold. If that convertibility is not restored, individuals will be forced to turn to gold as an alternative medium of exchange—outside the normal currency systems." The author of this statement, Harry Browne, goes on to say: ". . . gold's role in proposed monetary systems will determine the future of those systems—not the future of gold. Gold is needed badly as a basis for international exchange and soon it will be needed badly for domestic transactions as well."[58]

In Islam, gold and silver, the dinar and dirham as currency, are mentioned in the Qur'an. They offer stability, and avert the possibility of monetary manipulation. More significantly, Omar Vadillo asserts that "The question of money is primarily a question about freedom. When people were free to choose they universally chose gold and silver, therefore money freely chosen is the instrument of freedom. Money imposed is the instrument of servitude."[59]

The reclamation of the Islamic gold dinar and silver dirham becomes a moral imperative in our age. The dinar as currency does not on its own guarantee wealth; it merely guarantees equality. It is precisely this sense of equality that prevails over the just transactions between individuals. The Qur'an states: "But Allah has permitted trade and forbidden usury . . ." (2:275), and "O you who believe! Fear Allah, and give up what remains of your demand for usury, if you are indeed believers. If you do it not, take notice of war from Allah and His Messenger" (2:278–79).

The problem with the unlimited creation of money is that it needs investment in order to ensure its credibility as a means of exchange. Banking has an inverted bookkeeping logic; money loaned out, or the debtors' book, is regarded as an asset, while deposits—which are its capital base—are deemed a liability. Banks need to create credit in order to sustain themselves. However, the unlimited creation of money also implies the almost unlimited need to invest. In a finite world limited options will imply the extension of investments beyond the manageable or moral, creating unlimited want in a limited market environment. This insatiable desire to invest and consume has a powerful impact on the environment—a limited resource.

Inflation is the result of the insolvency of its issuers, who print more and more promises of payment while failing to pay them. Bimetal currency, such as the gold dinar and silver dirham, remains free of inflation.

Islamic Business Contracts

The above analysis clearly makes the concept of banking (including so-called "Islamic" banking) and the use of paper money inimical to Islam. Usury creates restrictions in the market and inequality in agreements, whereas equity ensures freedom of the market and equality in agreements. In order to restore justice and fair dealing in the business environment it is necessary to go back to those contractual instruments of trade, which were common to Islamic civilization and which are sanctioned in Islamic law.

There exist in Islam numerous partnership contracts which make reliance upon financial institutions, as we have them in modern times, quite unnecessary. The most prominent of the partnership contracts was the *qirād*, which is the "dormant partnership" and involves a business loan between the lender of capital and the trader. This contract entails mutual sharing of profit and loss by the contracting parties.

The *mudāraba*, a "co-partnership," entails property or stock offered by the owner to another party to form a joint partnership in which all parties will participate in profit. The *shirkat* is a joint trading enterprise in which the working capital, profit, and loss of each of the partners are proportionate. *Ijāra* entails the laws of hire on moveable property for remuneration.[60]

Cooperation in economic activities is emphasized by Ibn Taymiyya and Ibn Khaldun, both of whom consider it natural for human beings. They believe this cooperative nature between people confirms humans as social beings; it increases prosperity and it achieves good and removes injury.[61] Trading in partnership at once allows people to enter the trading environment as independent traders. It also removes from prospective traders and producers the anxiety normally associated with usurious debt. *Qirād* is an important business contract. It allows for the effective and rapid transfer of wealth within society. It initiates and stimulates business activity and opens up the possibilities for trading to many people who may lack sufficient capital to start their own business. At the height of the Ottoman caliphate, 90 percent of all trade within the lands of the caliphate was in the form of the *qirād* contract.[62] Its use as a convenient form of contracting reached Europe in the tenth century, under the name of *commendas*.[63]

Caravans

Caravans represented an open distribution network, which meant that everyone could sell anything, anywhere, within a specified trading network. Caravans served to acquire materials for production and new markets—directly, without barriers or intermediaries. It represented a natural transfer of goods, skills, and technologies, without the restrictions common in modern times.

Accessibility is the key to understanding the tremendous importance of commercial representatives or ambassadors linked to the caravans.[64] They established commercial routes from one emirate to another, thus allowing merchants, ordinary traders, and guilds free access to outside and foreign markets. The caravan was, in turn, the representative body of an entire network of traders and producers, who would, as individuals, not intend or desire to trade on their own. The caravans were never under command of capital; rather, they represented physical traders and producers, as individuals, agents representing other merchants and guilds who all traveled with their goods.

A caravan was therefore more powerful than the individual trader and obtained from the authorities of the lands or cities visited special privileges which could not be granted to the solitary merchant. Caravans hindered corruption, since they were anxious to build up and maintain a reputation for honesty and fair dealing. The caravan offered access to the services that it had already established over many years, such as storage and accommodation. It also protected its members against robbery, fraud, trickery, and deceit.

Islamic business and partnership contracts played an important role in terms of how the caravan was commercially constituted. It also determined the success of the caravan. According to Halil Inalcik, the most common forms of contract applied by the caravans during Ottoman times were the *mudāraba* and *qirād*.[65]

The trade barriers of modern times, the monopolization of goods and commodities, of their movement, of their price structures, the subservience of goods and products to global shares and futures markets (stock market economics), price dumping and price fixing, produce dumping, hoarding, the sanctioning of a nation's products to protect profits, and so on, are all radically different practices from the organic nature and movement of goods and services common to the caravans. Governments can significantly alter the nature of national and international trade by effecting changes in the laws and regulations that govern trading activities today. This would pave the way for the reemergence of the principles that articulated free trade and distribution as represented by the traditional caravans.

Muslim Personal Law: The Gender Issue

Muslim personal law constitutes a significant part of the *sharī'a*. The intention here is to highlight the role of women in terms of their economic rights. This is necessary since the gender issue is an important component of human ecology. In Islam the economic rights, duties, and responsibilities of women are best articulated within the legal prescriptions governing marriage, divorce, inheritance, and business activity. The issues of ownership of property and free choice are intrinsic to these categories of personal law. Any money, property, or business which a women owns or inherits is entirely her own; her husband has no right to any of it.[66] The marketplace is open to women as it is to men.[67] Islamic societies through the ages have many examples of wealthy women who were great business women and great builders of *waqf*s.

It is important to acknowledge the economic rights and obligations of women in Islam. The role that women assumed within the socioeconomic arena of Muslim civilization represents a rich historical texture of women and men in mutual enterprise without compromising acceptable religious codes of behavior or violating that which was sacrosanct to women, such as their lives, reputations, property, and families.

*Waqf*s

Waqf is a very simple institution of enormous social significance. *Waqf* is contained in the root of the Arabic word itself; that is, it refers to something which has been "stopped" or "restrained." In concrete terms it usually refers to a building or land donated by someone "in the way of God," to be used for the public good. The property itself or the rent derived from it can be used for the purpose intended. A *waqf* is a gift made by an individual or a family to a community. It includes any number of institutions, such as mosques, markets, caravanserais, clinics, hospitals, schools, colleges, bridges, wells, libraries, and other places of public welfare.[68]

There are five aspects specific to this institution: 1) *waqf* is generally based on and composed of real estate; 2) it is donated for use in perpetuity by a *wāqif* (the donor); 3) the *waqf* is effected as an act of worship, or *qurba*—coming closer to Allah—on the part of the *wāqif*, who stipulates that his donation be used for a social purpose; 4) the *waqf* is an institution with a specific aim, of local importance, and benefit of an independent nature; 5) although generally real estate, *waqf* may be based on anything, however insignificant, which is capable of yielding a benefit; thus, even a single tree whose produce is donated for a named purpose, an animal for its milk, land for grazing, a book for study are all valid subjects of *waqf*.[69]

We can see from Ottoman times that the *waqf* fulfilled far more efficiently the role that the modern state has taken upon itself today. As Shaykh ‘Abd al-Qadir has pointed out in his work *The Return of the Khalifate*, “there were only three thousand administrators in the Ottoman empire. This vast territory was able to function economically and socially by the existence of an intricate network of local *waqfs*, self-fulfilling, self-financing and self-governing.”[70] Only the institution of the *waqf* could and does afford a flexibility and spontaneity compatible with the needs of local communities.

*Waqf*s are naturally places of increase, whether they be of a social, economic, educational, or spiritual nature, unlike present-day state-run hospitals and schools, which are based on the initial impulse to control and the desire to produce a nation of consumers. The initial act of giving undertaken by a particular person determines the nature of the *waqf*s, and it lends them an intense and authentic individuality or coloring, which contrasts starkly with the impersonality and alienating quality of state-based, state-run institutions.

*Zawīya*s

One may well ask what Sufi *ṭarīqa*s have to do with *mu‘āmalāt*, or even matters of ecology. Yet, what must be understood about the Sufi orders is that they have been, at various times in history, either persecuted or socially ostracized. This was for no reason other than their refusal to submit to the project of the consumer society and their vigorous opposition to political tyranny. The Sufis are the countermeasure to the material worldview. Sufism (Arabic, *taṣawwuf*) can be understood as the science of the journey to the Lord of creation, Allah. This journey requires that the adept relinquish the world (*takhāllī*) because he recognizes it as an illusion. He is *faqīr* (poor), yet “his is a poverty in Allah, and Allah is enough for him in his poverty.”

The true Sufi hands over his affairs to guidance and illumination. This is *ṭarīqa*, a condition which maintains the fine balance between the *sharī‘a* and the *ḥaqīqa*;[71] the one is the science of the outward, and the other the science of the inward. *Ṭarīqa* is balance and harmony; it is beyond mere religious significance—it is also socially and politically significant.

The *zawīya*s are the homes of the *ṭarīqa*s. They were to be found in the cities and towns, on the outskirts of towns, in the hills and mountains, at every major route and highway that carried travelers, and on the frontiers of the Islamic empire. The *zawīya*s fulfilled their primary function, which was the performance of *dhikr* (calling upon the Divine Presence) and learning at the feet of the master:

> The whole educational system, commencing with the foundation of society as embodied in the craft guilds, moving up to the *madrāsa*, or college, and culminating in the *zawīya* itself as the center for spiritual training, is directly interwoven with the entire Islamic tradition, especially the esoteric dimension contained within Sufism.[72]

The *zawīyas* also served as hospices, offered hospitality to travelers, gave succor to the needy and to wayfarers, and served as sanctuaries for immigrants and the persecuted. They served as prototypes for the *imārat*s. These *zawīya*s were *waqf* endowments and they were financially self-sufficient. The adepts of the *shaykh*s would go out to work and contribute to the upkeep of the center. The *zawīya*s were fiercely independent institutions that would often clash with political and religious authorities. Their social role was indispensable, both in terms of its charitable nature and in terms of aiding development by fostering the growth of villages and towns.[73]

The Sufis are people who have the "inner technology" capable of coexisting in absolute harmony with the outer project of human existence. They are the personification of the ideal condition of *fiṭra*. History is rife with examples of Sufi orders that emerged in times when Muslim civilization had become weak and decadent, to restore the true faith and inspire a resurgence in civilized standards of existence. In the rich history of Sufism, we can discover valuable insights into a primal pattern of ordered existence. The Sufis have a knowledge, both esoteric and existential, that can recreate civilization.

Architecture and Urbanism

Our circle of the *mu'āmalāt* cannot be complete without the art of architecture laying its claim as one of the vital creative elements that sustains and mirrors the condition of human society. In the cycle of life, human civilizations are born and they die. Ibn Khaldun put the birth of civilizations in the urban environment, and the death of them in the sedentary nature of urban existence. Architectural forms mirror the various phases of civilization. Cities are universal, and urban civilization represents the highest degree of refinement and culture reached.

Neither the most sophisticated rational planning categories nor the most sophisticated technologies could create the same degree of inner harmony and social coherence of urban space and usage that is evident in many traditional cities. Social and economic space is part of the same whole, and traffic routes do not separate but, on the contrary, maintain the unity of the urban space. In the traditional urban environment one has the impression of moving inside a single continuous space.[74] Kropotkin believed that the essence of every city is a freely accessible market. The transformation of a village into a city has always been marked by the establishment of a weekly market.[75] Indeed, all traditional cities, both Islamic and European, have been founded on free trade zones, and the market was a vital part of the towns' growth.

In Islam these principle are evident in the architectural forms of its cities. Islam does not consist of a series of rituals only. Islam is a way of life, and the inward spiritual condition of humans and their external material environment are mutually dependent. Hence, this homogeneity between the body and soul—material and spiritual—has its own architectural expression. This expression is rooted in the tradition, or *sunna*, of the Prophet (PBUH). This architecture is determined by the simplest of human activities, such as how to wash, how to sit on the ground, how to eat from a single platter, how to behave in the family and toward the stranger, the receiving of guests, neighborliness, the multiple marriage, the extended family, and so on. Thus, the *sunna* indirectly fashions clothing, the home, and the town.

Muslim town planning responds, therefore, to material requirements, but never treats them apart from their spiritual character. This distinguishes it essentially from modern town planning, which tends to dissociate people's bodily, psychic, and spiritual needs. In traditional urban society, architecture is a life-form. The characteristics of traditional life are not only external; they also assume more profound inner meanings, as symbols of natural congruence of all expressions of life, ranging from spiritual to manual occupations by combining them through their related meanings.[76] The innermost reason for the city as living space is based on the deep-rooted belief in the elusiveness and transcendence of the Divine Being and the imperfect nature of human creation. Islam facilitates the rise of a comprehensive lifeform integrating economic, social, and religious activities into a new understanding of urbanism characterized by the solidarity between people and their buildings.

With the impact of electrotechnology and the need for microeconomic solutions to our economic woes, we will have to imbue tradition into the *zeitgeist* of our age. We will have to rethink our existential relationship to our social and urban space so that we are better prepared for the future needs of our ecological environment.[77]

The Way Forward

The restoration of the institutions and principles of the *mu'āmalāt* is the key to self-empowerment. The *mu'āmalāt* provides the necessary ingredients for the recreation of autonomous and integrative communal and social units found in traditional towns and cities. In a self-empowered society, people take on responsibility for their shelter, health, education, and security precisely because they have the incentives to manage themselves cooperatively.

Confucius concluded several thousand years ago that the wealth of nations is not to make profit, but to make equity. Adam Smith concluded two hundred years ago that the wealth of nations is to make profit. In the aftermath of the industrial revolution and at the edge of a new era, we have to wonder whether Smith was right. If profit was the norm for civilization, its achievements lie buried in the mass degradation and impoverishment of the human condition and the collapse of the natural environment. Perhaps Confucius was right after all, that economic success should be measured by the degree of equity that it produces.

To sum up, we can say that the ongoing shift from an industrial to an information-based society has opened up the socioeconomic nexus in a way that will facilitate the incorporation of traditional methods of living and contracting. It will also initiate a trend away from large centralized to smaller decentralized work environments. It has already initiated a trend away from large inflexible organizational structures to intelligent, self-controlled, and self-dependent work groups (the precursors to the guilds). These are geographically distributed and perform virtually integrated business processes, with the support of new information superhighways and global, large-bandwidth networks. To enable this historic shift in lifestyle, we will have to:

- Reverse an alarming trend toward unprecedented forms of long-term unemployment by restructuring our economic framework through the transformation of employees into entrepreneurs, traders, and independent professionals (empowerment through the guilds and open markets);
- Lessen our dependency on macroeconomic indicators as determinants of economic growth by reverting to microeconomic development models (open markets and the deconstruction of monopolies);
- Transcend artificial fiscal barriers by reverting to tangible, non-inflationary mediums of exchange representing real wealth (the bi-metal currency of gold and silver);
- Lessen the world's financial dependence on any single monopolistic and interest-bearing credit institutions in favor of a natural movement of capital (the traditional contracts of *qirād* and the *commendore*);
- Create a new breed of self-motivated professionals who take pride in their work and the constant refinement of their products through the common regulation of professional societies (guilds);
- Lessen the world's economic and financial dependence from any single national, geographic, or cultural source by the consequent decentralization of know-how and production and distribution facilities (the guilds, caravans, and open markets);
- Reengineer, through the effective use of future-oriented technology, the urban environment toward organic work and living and decentralized, independent, and fully integrated productive communities (traditional urban model);
- Recognize the disastrous consequences to the ecological and socioeconomic environment of the unremitting application of the principles that have motivated the industrial economy since the advent of the industrial revolution. (See diagrams in appendices B, C, and D.)

This shift in lifestyle offers the ecology movement a nondialectical and more rational approach to the needs of environmental sustainability. It begins by addressing the issues of human ecology at the most fundamental level of human activity, which is economic sustainability. Such an approach will demand a change in emphasis on how the ecology movement deals with ecological issues. The current method of spending large sums of donor monies for impact studies on the environment and the persistent war of attrition between ecologists and the "plunderers of the environment" is one that merely treats the symptoms and not the cause. The ecology movement is trapped by big finance. It is unable to steer away from its patronage. The subject of environmental awareness is hosted by "big business," while big business continues ravaging the earth under the guise of patrimony.

Furthermore, it is not the business of humankind to save the human species from extinction. The survival of the human species is God's business. Humankind's business is to ensure that the human condition is meaningfully sustained so that nature can be meaningfully sustained. Humans have to create those conditions that will allow us to regain our inner worth, to reclaim our generosity, and to act with responsibility as trustees of our environment. Humans need a "just contract" to maintain the "just balance." Humans need a model of existence that will ensure a healthy symbiosis between heart and mind, human and nature. This is, in essence, what Islam teaches about humankind's relation to our world.

Notes

1. Ibn Khaldun, *The Muqaddimah: An Introduction to History*, trans. Franz Rosenthal (London: Routledge and Kegan Paul, 1967), 24.

2. Fritjof Capra, *The Turning Point: Science, Society and the Rising Culture* (London: Fontana 1983), 1.

3. Eugene Linden, "What Have We Wrought?" *Time*, November 1997, 10.

4. Adam Smith, *Paper Money* (New York: Dell, 1981), 35.

5. Alvin Toffler, *Future Shock* (London: Pan Books 1981), 395.

6. Capra, *The Turning Point*, 13–19. Capra uses his concept of paradigm as a complete cultural pattern that includes our entire scientific, ideological, and economic worldview.

7. Eric de Maré, *A Matter of Life or Debt* (Bullsbrook, Australia: Veritas Publishing, 1986), 2.

8. The labor theory of value states that an article costs one dollar because the total human labor involved in obtaining the raw materials, designing, making, and selling the article amounts to one dollar. This is a fallacy which assumes that labor produces all wealth. In reality, production is 95 percent a matter of tools and process of which the "laborer" is not the legal administrator.

9. De Maré, *A Matter of Life or Debt*, 2.

10. E. F. Schumacher, *Small Is Beautiful: A Study of Economics as if People Mattered* (London: ABACUS Sphere Books, 1983), 35–36.

11. *Fitra* refers to the natural form of humans. It has both an inner and outer meaning in terms of humans as "beings" in existence.

12. Christopher Flavin, "How to Build a Society That Will Stand the Test of Time," *Time*, November 1997, 82.

13. Though fourteen centuries have passed since the inception of Islam, which is dated from the *hijra* (migration), I consider the end of the complete Islamic ethos as having occurred during the demise of the Ottoman caliphate in 1924. Political sovereignty, or *'amr* (divinely established authority), is implicit to the definition of the complete Islamic ethos, which derives its relevance only within the reality of the caliphate. The absence of a caliphate for the past three-quarters of a century is considered to be a short anti-Islamic interregnum.

14. Omar Ibrahim Vadillo, "The Workers Have Been Told a Lie," *Islamic Times* (Pretoria) 2, no. 4 (June 1998). This philosophy of Wagner is well explained in *The New Wagnerian* by Ian Dallas; see n. 15.

15. Ian Dallas, *The New Wagnerian* (Freiburg: Freiburg Books, 1990), 141–42. Martin Heidegger defines the five basic rubrics of Nietzsche's philosophy as follows: 1. Nihilism; 2. Transvaluation of all values; 3. Will to power; 4. Eternal recurrence of the same; 5. The Superman.

16. *Mu'āmalāt* refers to the zone of human transactions in the Islamic law. It stems from the word *'āmal*, meaning action, in particular the actions of the people who constituted the first three generations of Medina, the first city of Islam. *Mu'āmalāt* primarily covers those transactions dealing with trade, personal law, and governance. For the purposes of this paper, I removed governance from the zone of *mu'āmalāt*.

17. 'Abd al-Qadir as-Sufi, *Jihad: A Groundplan* (Weldon: Diwan Press 1978), 42.

18. I call this the Hashimi diagram because of the connotation it has with the family name of the Holy Prophet (PBUH) and also because Hashim is my first name. Omar Ibrahim Vadillo, whose works are referred to in this paper, is the real inspiration behind the formulation of this diagram.

19. Abdul Azim Islahi, *Economic Concepts of Ibn Taimīya* (Leicester, United Kingdom: Islamic Foundation 1988), 174. Accordingly, Ibn Taymiyya, Ibn Khaldun, al-Mawardi, and others recognize that the importance of the role of state and economic affairs in *sharī'a*, *tijāra*, *ḥisba*, and *imāra*, when put together, form the largest part of *fiqh*.

20. Omar Ibrahim Vadillo, *The End Of Economics* (Granada: Madinah Press, 1991), 48–72.

21. Hashim Ismail Dockrat, *Developing a Free Society* (Pretoria: Institute For Human and Environmental Development, 1996), 7.

22. Peter F. Drucker, *Post-Capitalist Society* (London: Harper Collins, 1994). Drucker says that the transition from nation-states to fiscal states came after, and as a result of, the two world wars.

23. *Ḥisba*, from its root *ḥ.s.b.*, means "arithmetical problem," "sum," or "reward." Its verb, *ḥasaba yasūba*, means "to measure." *Iḥtisāba* means "to take into consideration." *Ḥisba* connotes the state institution to promote what is proper and forbid what is improper—*'amr b'il-ma'rūf wa-n-nāhī 'an il-munkir'*—that is, an institution for supervision over economic and social conditions.

24. For the rules of *ḥisba*, see al-Mawardi, *al-Aḥkām as-sultaniya*; Ibn Taymiyya, *Public Duties in Islam*; and any general source on Islamic *fiqh*.

25. PBUH is an abbreviation for "Peace Be upon Him." This is a mark of respect shown to the honorable person of Muhammed, the Prophet of Islam and the seal of prophethood. It is normally recited in Arabic.

26. Al-Hindi, *Kanz al-'umāl*, vol. 488, no. 2688.

27. Ibn Shaba, *Tarīkh al-madīna al-munawwāra,* 306, no. 6. A *ḥadīth* narrated by Ibrahim ibn al-Mundir al Hizami, who took from Abdullah ibn Ja'far, who took from Muhammed ibn Abdullah ibn Hassan.

28. As-Samhudi, *Wafā al-wafā*, no. 747. Ibn Zabala related from Ilyas al-Adawi.

29. Ibn Shaba, *Tarīkh al-madīna al-munawwāra*, 304, no. 6.

30. As-Samhudi, *Wafā al-wafā*, no. 752. Ibn Zabala related from Hatim ibn Ismail, who related from Habib, who related from Umar bin al-Khattab.

31. As-Samhudi, *Wafā al-wafā*, no. 750. Ibn Shabba related from Salih ibn Kaysan.

32. S. M. Hasanuz Zaman, *Trade in Islam: Principles and Practices* (Karachi: Umma, 1985), 20–24.

33. Ibid., 18: This is a *ḥadīth* of the Prophet (PBUH), who said; "Profit goes with liability"; from Tirmidhi.

34. Ibid., 16: The Prophet (PBUH) said, "Do not fix two prices of a commodity, a cash price and a credit price." Jurists have treated such increase as *riba* (usury).

35. Alfred Lief, *Brandeis: The Personal History of an American Ideal* (New York: Stackpole 1936), 454.

36. Hasanuz Zaman, *Trade in Islam*, 11–13.

37. Ibid.

38. Lief, *Brandeis*, 455.

39. De Maré, *A Matter of Life or Debt*, 42.

40. Ibid., 36.

41. Halil Inalcik, *The Ottoman Empire: The Classical Age, 1300–1600* (London: Phoenix Books 1994), 151.

42. *The Johorbaru Proposal: Tomorrow's Technology-oriented Urbanism*, ed. H. Dahinden (Zurich: The Management Team, 1995), 15.

43. Inalcik, *The Ottoman Empire*, 151. See also Nader Ardalan and Laleh Baktiar, *The Sense of Unity: The Sufi Tradition in Persian Architecture* (Chicago and London: University of Chicago Press, 1973), 9.

44. The general principles that governed the traditional guilds in Islamic society can be found in many texts that deal with organized production in early times. Many of these principles were not unique to Islamic guilds but were intrinsic to the general nature of guild structures wherever they existed. For this information, see R. H. C. Davis, *A History of Medieval Europe: From Constantine to St. Louis* (Oxford: Longman, 1980), 193–94.

45. Omar Ibrahim Vadillo, *The Islamic Development Plan for the State of Kelantan* (Inverness: World Islamic Trading Organization, 1997). This proposal deals with guilds in economic development.

46. Giovanni Arrighi, *The Long Twentieth Century: Money, Power, and the Origins of Our Times* (New York: Verso, 1996), 102–3, 194. See also Inalcik, *The Ottoman Empire*, 156.

47. Dockrat, *Developing a Free Society*, 28–30. See also *The Johorbaru Proposal.*

48. Toffler, *Future Shock*, 275.

49. Omar Ibrahim Vadillo, "The Return of the Guilds," *Islamic Times* 1, no. 2 (1997).

50. Omar Ibrahim Vadillo, *The Wealth of Turkey* (Inverness: World Islamic Trading Organization, 1996), 8.

51. Inalcik, *The Ottoman Empire*, 140.

52. Anthony Sampson, *The Money Lenders: Bankers in a Dangerous World* (New York: Hodder and Stoughton, 1985), 608.

53. Ibid., 29.

54. Vadillo, *The End of Economics*, 78–81.

55. Harry Browne, *You Can Profit from a Monetary Crisis* (New York: Bantam Books, 1974), 200.

56. Smith, *Paper Money*, 72.

57. Omar Ibrahim Vadillo, *Fatwa on Paper Money* (Granada: Madinah Press, 1991), 26–27.

58. Browne, *You Can Profit from a Monetary Crisis*, 200.

59. Omar Ibrahim Vadillo, *The Return of the Gold Dinar: A Study of Money in Islamic Law* (Cape Town: Madinah Press, 1996), 65.

60. Ibn Rushd, *Bidayat Al-Mujtahid; The Distinguished Jurist's Primer*, trans. I. A. K. Nyazee and M. A. Rauf (Reading, United Kingdom: Centre For Muslim Contribution to Civilization, Garnet, 1996). See also Abdur Rahman Doi, *Shari'ah: The Islamic Law* (London: Ta-Ha Publishers, 1984).

61. Islahi, *Economic Concepts of Ibn Taimīyah*, 105.

62. Muhammed Fakir, "*Qirād*—Towards Freedom," *Islamic Times* (Pretoria) 1, no. 4 (1997).

63. Vadillo, *The End of Economics*, 105.

64. Vadillo, *The Wealth Of Turkey*, 25.

65. Inalcik, *The Ottoman Empire*, 161.

66. Aisha B. Lemu and Fatima Heeren, *Woman in Islam* (Leicester, United Kingdom: The Islamic Foundation 1978), 23.

67. Abdur Rahman Doi, *Women in Shari'ah* (London: Ta Ha Publishers, 1989), 148.

68. Doi, *Shari'ah: The Islamic Law*, 57.

69. Asadullah Yates, "The Waqf Returns," *Islamic Times* (Pretoria) 1, no. 1 (1997): 7.

70. Shaykh 'Abd al-Qadir as-Sufi, *The Return of the Khalifate* (Cape Town: Madinah Press, 1996), 60–65.

71. Shaykh 'Abd al-Qadir al-Murabit, *The Hundred Steps*, 2d ed. (Kuala Lampur: Madinah Press, 1998), 2–5.

Ṭarīqa (literally, "the path") can also be called *īmān* (acceptance, that is, acceptance of Allah and all that He has decreed.) It also means coming out of a safe place of ordinary existence into the alien existence of search. *Sharī'a* implies confirmation of the five pillars of Islam and recognition of the biological laws that function at every level of existence. *Ḥaqīqa* means the realities that are the inward illuminations of knowledge which flood the heart of the seeker. This is also called esoteric knowledge. To the Sufis, this is real knowledge. *Sharī'a* is submission, *ṭarīqa* is handing over, and *ḥaqīqa* is victory.

72. Ardalan and Bakhtiar, *The Sense of Unity*, 9.

73. Inalcik, *The Ottoman Empire*, 148–49.

74. Dockrat, *Developing a Free Society*, 57.

75. *Johorbaru Proposal*, 26.

76. Titus Burckhardt, *Arts in Islam* (Cambridge: Islamic Texts Society, 1992), 189.

77. Dockrat, *Developing a Free Society*, 61.

Appendix A: The Organic Islamic Society

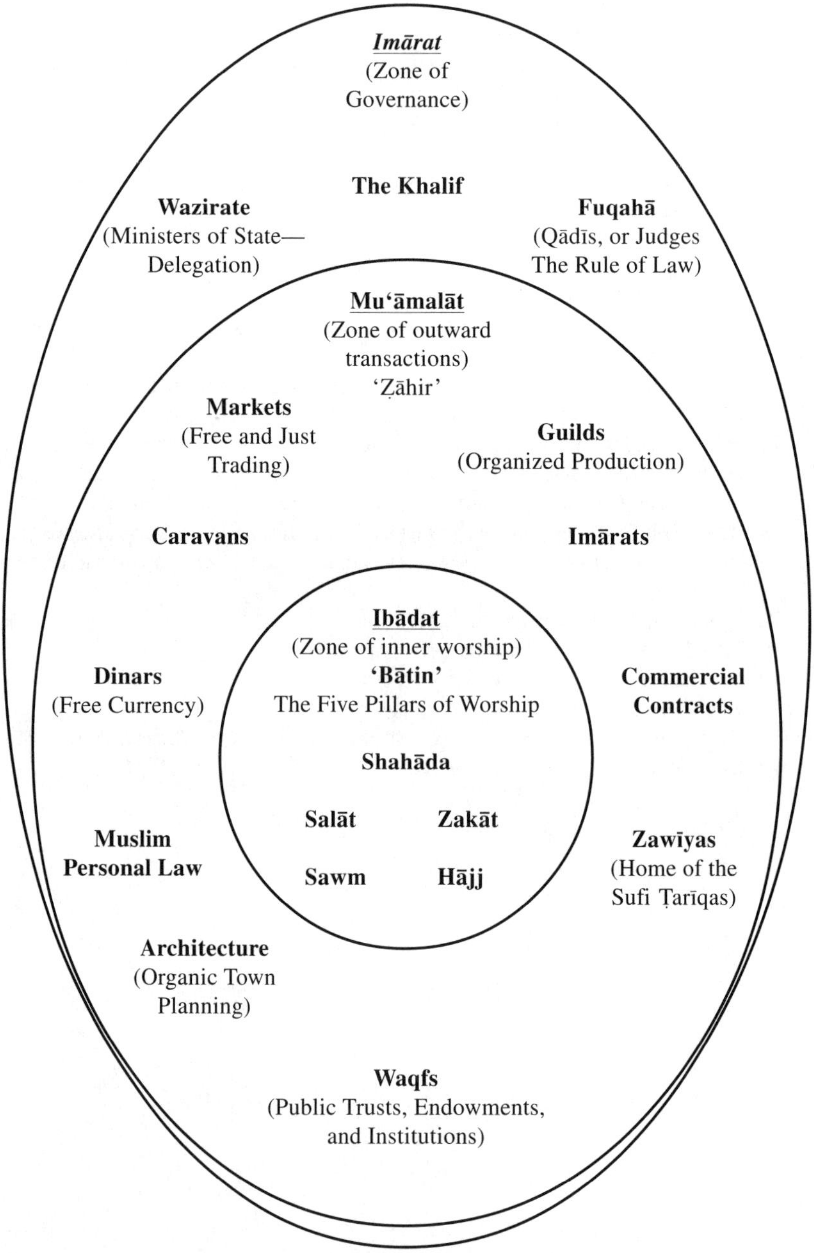

Appendix B

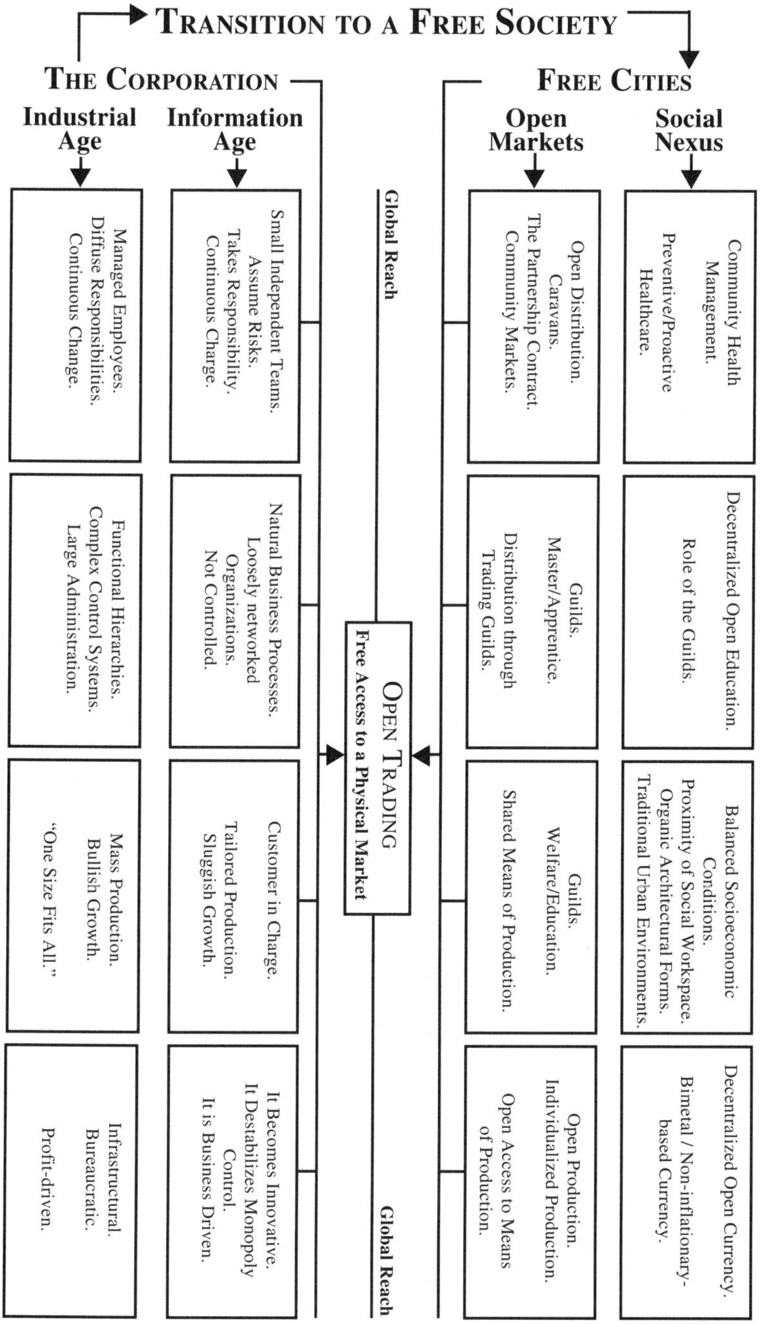
TRANSITION TO A FREE SOCIETY
THE CORPORATION
FREE CITIES
Industrial Age
Information Age
Open Markets
Social Nexus
Managed Employees. Diffuse Responsibilities. Continuous Change.
Functional Hierarchies. Complex Control Systems. Large Administration.
Mass Production. Bullish Growth. "One Size Fits All."
Infrastructural. Bureaucratic. Profit-driven.
Small Independent Teams. Assume Risks. Takes Responsibility. Continuous Charge.
Natural Business Processes. Loosely networked Organizations. Not Controlled.
Customer in Charge. Tailored Production. Sluggish Growth.
It Becomes Innovative. It Destabilizes Monopoly Control. It is Business Driven.
Global Reach
OPEN TRADING
Free Access to a Physical Market
Global Reach
Open Distribution. Caravans. The Partnership Contract. Community Markets.
Guilds. Master/Apprentice. Distribution through Trading Guilds.
Guilds. Welfare/Education. Shared Means of Production.
Open Production. Individualized Production. Open Access to Means of Production.
Community Health Management. Preventive/Proactive Healthcare.
Decentralized Open Education. Role of the Guilds.
Balanced Socioeconomic Conditions. Proximity of Social Workspace. Organic Architectural Forms. Traditional Urban Environments.
Decentralized Open Currency. Bimetal / Non-inflationary-based Currency.

Appendix C

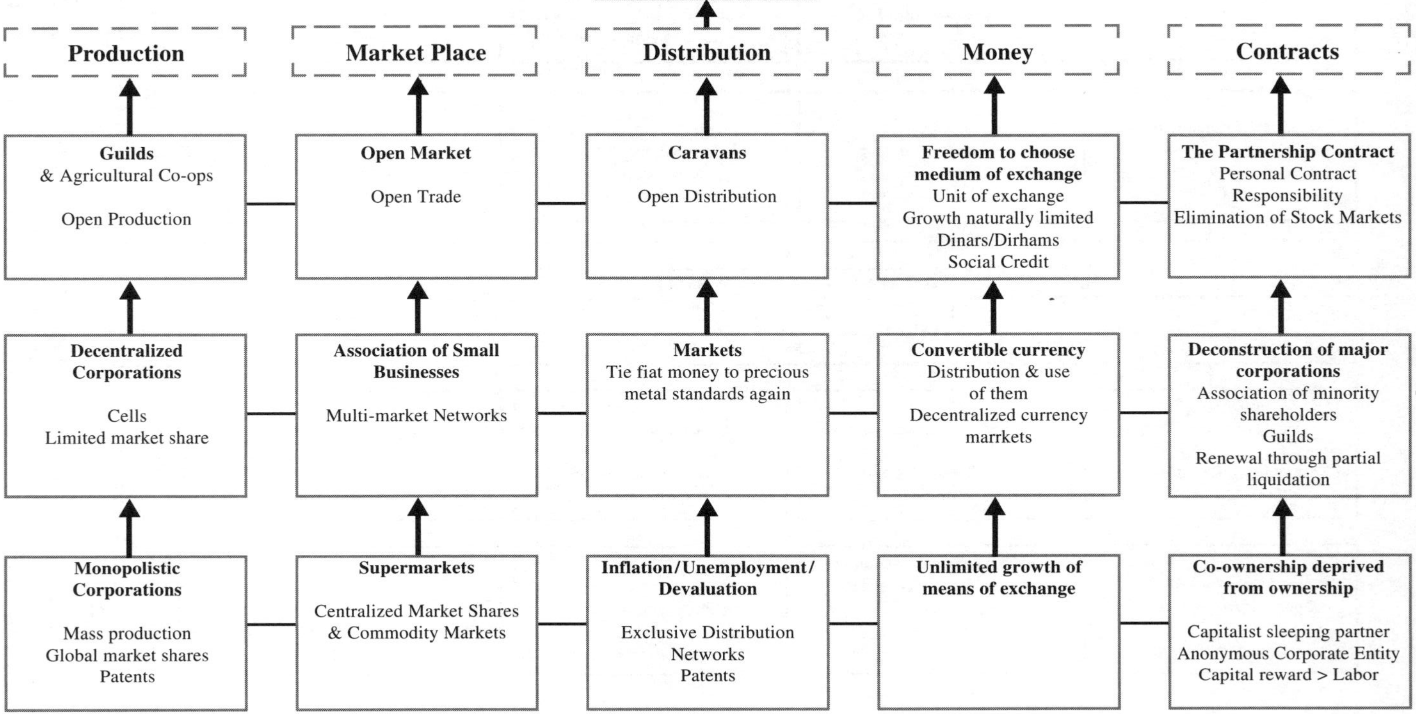
Open Trading
Production
Market Place
Distribution
Money
Contracts
Guilds
& Agricultural Co-ops
Open Production
Open Market
Open Trade
Caravans
Open Distribution
Freedom to choose medium of exchange
Unit of exchange
Growth naturally limited
Dinars/Dirhams
Social Credit
The Partnership Contract
Personal Contract
Responsibility
Elimination of Stock Markets
Decentralized Corporations
Cells
Limited market share
Association of Small Businesses
Multi-market Networks
Markets
Tie fiat money to precious metal standards again
Convertible currency
Distribution & use of them
Decentralized currency marrkets
Deconstruction of major corporations
Association of minority shareholders
Guilds
Renewal through partial liquidation
Monopolistic Corporations
Mass production
Global market shares
Patents
Supermarkets
Centralized Market Shares
& Commodity Markets
Inflation/Unemployment/Devaluation
Exclusive Distribution Networks
Patents
Unlimited growth of means of exchange
Co-ownership deprived from ownership
Capitalist sleeping partner
Anonymous Corporate Entity
Capital reward > Labor

Appendix D

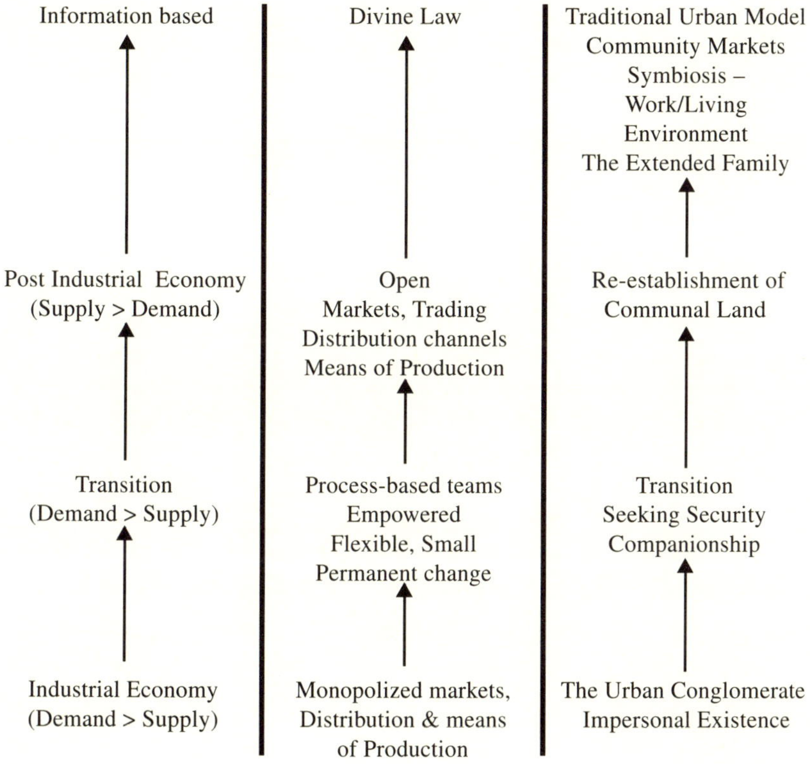
Information based
Post Industrial Economy
(Supply > Demand)
Transition
(Demand > Supply)
Industrial Economy
(Demand > Supply)
Divine Law
Open
Markets, Trading
Distribution channels
Means of Production
Process-based teams
Empowered
Flexible, Small
Permanent change
Monopolized markets,
Distribution & means
of Production
Traditional Urban Model
Community Markets
Symbiosis –
Work/Living
Environment
The Extended Family
Re-establishment of
Communal Land
Transition
Seeking Security
Companionship
The Urban Conglomerate
Impersonal Existence

Ecological Justice and Human Rights for Women in Islam

NAWAL AMMAR

At present, discussions on Muslim women and their relationship to the environment remain anchored in simplistic debates about population and reproduction (for example, family planning and abortion), as though these are matters connected only to technological fixes or to education. The discussions that one finds in the literature and other venues of the debate about Muslim women and the environment can be summarized in four ideas. The first idea emphasizes that central to reducing stress on environmental resources is the reduction of birthrates among Muslim women, and that this can be accomplished by making available to them certain methods of birth control. The second argument sees that reducing birthrates, and hence, reducing stress on environmental resources among Muslim women, requires empowering them through education and skill development. A third argument reiterates that family planning and the empowerment of women are neo-imperialist ideas that the West is imposing on the Islamic family and society. Finally, a fourth idea totally silences the feminine from the discussion, and instead examines the issue of Islam and ecology from the vantage point of resource management and banking.

The United Nations conferences on population in Cairo in 1994 and on women in Beijing in 1995 helped to further reinforce such views of the relationship between Muslim women and the environment. Hence, the issues of family planning and abortion emerged as highly explosive topics in both conferences, leading some Muslim countries to withdraw from or boycott the conferences altogether.

Elsewhere in the world, however, the past quarter of a century has seen the emergence of a variety of epistemes regarding the relationship between women and the environment, including ecofeminism. Ecofeminists view the domination of the earth as directly connected to a set of cultural, psychological, and economic factors that create hierarchies which in turn oppress women and other vulnerable segments of society. For ecofeminists, the characteristics of masculine-centered ideologies, violence, discrimination, and ethnocentric views, together with Western technology and science, have contributed greatly to the depletion of the "biological environment" and pose a threat to the continuation of life on earth.[1]

Hence, to ecofeminists, the earth crisis is neither a biological problem nor a variable connected solely to fertility rates or education. It is a *process* that needs to be perceived in a holistic manner with a focus on issues of justice, equity, accessibility to resources, and a recognition of human rights for women and other vulnerable animate and inanimate components of society.

In this paper I use the holistic framework of ecofeminism to examine the relationship between Muslim women and the environment, thereby extending the discussion beyond technological fixes and education as an isolated factor. I utilize Michel Foucault's idea, expressed in his book *The Order of Things*, that "humans inhabit a culture and not a planet,"[2] and ask questions such as: What are some of the cultural characteristics of Islamic society that impact women's role vis-à-vis environmental depletion? How does this culture manifest itself, and what are the complexities involved in its processes? How do we and can we impact or change the cultural variables that affect women's relationships to the environment?

To answer the above questions from an ecofeminist perspective I do two things. First, I recount, briefly, one Muslim woman's life history. I met this woman in 1986 while conducting anthropological research in a village in southern Egypt. In retelling her story I intentionally move away from the Western paradigm of "reliability" and generalizability into the realm of "validity," "empathy," and "understanding." In other words, I emphasize the "experience" rather than the "data" in this discussion.

My second strategy in this paper is to stay away from Qur'anic or other textual justification of everything I say. Unlike the previous work I have done on Islam, the environment, and women,[3] here I want to present Islamic culture in its composite reality of the "sacred" and the "profane," Islam as a religion and a way of life, especially as it relates to women. I aim here to underscore the fact that for Muslim women the depletion of our planet's environment should be extended beyond the Qur'anic text and into the holistic, dynamic cultural arenas of justice, equity, and human rights.

The United Nations' "State of the World Population Report" of 1989 had the title "Investing in Women: The Focus of the Nineties." In this report the director of the United Nations Fund for Population Activities (UNFPA), Dr. Nafis Sadik, explained that women are the key to the goal of sustainable development. Investing in women means widening their choice of strategies and reducing their dependence on children for status and support. Besides family planning, investment in women should also include access to health services and education, their rights to land and credit, rewards of employment, and personal and political rights.

The words of this report did not translate soon enough, however, for Nour, who lived in a village in southern Egypt. Nour died in 1995 from heart failure at the age of forty. A mother of three living children and one deceased, Nour's life typifies some of the cultural issues that relate to justice, equity, and the human rights of Muslim women that are connected with our planet's ongoing destruction.

Nour was not from the very poor, malnourished, uneducated, landless women of the village. To the contrary, she was relatively less poor than others. Her father was a school principal and her mother is the daughter of the last village *umdah* (village head).[4] She was the fourth of eight children.

At the age of nine Nour suffered from rheumatic fever. Rheumatic fever was a very prevalent illness in Egypt during the 1950s and 1960s, both in villages and cities. The climate, hygienic practices, and medical care services of Egyptian society allowed the epidemic to spread, and it was dubbed "the throat-like cold" because the initial symptoms were those of a sore throat and fever. In Nour's case both of her older brothers had the disease and they were cared for. The boys stayed in bed for weeks and rested. They saw the doctor as soon as they had a high fever. Nour, on the other hand, did not see a doctor initially. As her fever subsided she stayed at home and helped her mother and the other women in the house to bake, wash clothes, and fetch water. It was not until one day when she complained of "tied joints" and had a high fever again that her father took her to a doctor, who at that point diagnosed her with rheumatic fever.

Nour survived the episode. Though she suffered a damaged heart, the doctor told her she could expect a normal life if she did not exert herself and expend too much energy in play and work. Nour grew up, therefore, as a sedentary child. She graduated from high school and entered teacher's training college to become an elementary-school art teacher. At twenty she married, and she had her first child at twenty-one. During her first pregnancy her physician warned that her heart was weak and that she should think of having only one more child.

A few years later Nour's husband took a job as a teacher in one of the oil-rich Gulf countries, leaving his wife and daughter back home (something many Egyptians did during that time). This made it difficult for Nour to conceive, though she was able to become pregnant again six years later at the age of twenty-seven. Her second child, however, at the age of three months fell on a concrete floor and died a few days later from internal bleeding from a head injury. Nour was determined to have another child. While I was in the village, she said to me, "I have to erase this pain of losing a child, by having another. . . . I am hurting, but like everything I have had to do in my life I am hurting without exerting effort and energy, so you think I am not hurting." Against doctor's orders, at thirty, Nour had a third child. She took a three-month maternity leave prior to delivery, followed by three months of summer vacation. Her son was a healthy child, but Nour was tired for most of her postpartum rest period. She would sleep the whole day, and she took her meals in bed. Nour's husband was in the Gulf when the boy was born, and she stayed at her father's house.

After I completed my research, I was in touch with Nour on an irregular basis. Her sister and I communicated regularly by phone and in writing. I learned four years ago that Nour was pregnant for the fourth time. Nour had her fourth child the same time that I had my daughter, and at that point I lost regular contact with many people in her village. I also knew that Nour's youngest brother was giving the family trouble. At the age of sixteen, he was found to have had a double addiction to alcohol and to prescription pills. He was treated numerous times by doctors and in specialized clinics, but to no avail. In the summer of 1994, at the age of twenty-three, he died from an overdose of pills and alcohol. This, I was told, affected Nour especially, as she was living in her father's home at the time and was in the early stages of her fourth pregnancy.

Last year on the phone I learned that Nour had passed away. I was talking to her uncle, who lives in Cairo, as I had done several times in the past years, and I asked about everyone in the village. I named them one by one; when I came to Nour, the voice on the other side was silent. When I repeated the question, the uncle finally replied, "Nour—we did not want to tell you, but may you live (an expression denoting death)." Horrified, I said, "I'm asking you about Nour, not Shams (her aunt who is in her late seventies)." He said, "Yes, Nour gave you her years (another expression denoting a person's death)." In a flash, I realized that her heart must have given out after the last pregnancy. Indeed, three months after giving birth to her youngest daughter, Nour died. After the delivery Nour was having a very hard time breathing, so she and her husband traveled to Cairo to see a doctor. The doctor had no good words for them. Nour's body had given up on her. In addition to her heart, her kidneys were failing, and it was only a matter of time before her entire body gave up on her and surrendered to the inevitable, death. When I talked to her husband a year and half later, to give him my deepest condolences, he said, "I had no idea that she had a rheumatic heart . . . no one told me . . . even she didn't tell me. . . she wanted lots of kids and I didn't care."

Nour's story reveals to us how cultural practices of justice and human rights are intricately connected to women, the environment, and Earth's rights. Her story shows how reproduction—at least in cases such as Nour's—is more complicated than population growth, neo-imperialist arguments, or simply developing the skills of women. It is a holistic issue that includes disease, equal access to basic health services, poverty, drug addiction, educating beyond credentialing, internalization of cultural values, and informal socialization.

Nour was not taken, as a child, to the doctor when she was first ill, because girl children in many Muslim cultures are not treated as well as their brothers. The little research that has been conducted on socialization in Islamic cultures (including Morocco, Egypt, Pakistan, Turkey) indicates that there is preferential treatment of boys over girls. This preference is neither true to Qur'anic Islam, nor is it a consequence of individual parental discretion. It is actually a historic survival of old economic traditions when boys were economic assets in agriculture or service labor. It is reinforced in the contemporary culture by the new economic imperatives of the age: limited resources to be distributed among many children.

Nour's parents made a choice based on their limited resources, which needed to be distributed among eight children. In a country such as Egypt (typical of many of the countries and regions where Muslims live), in 1994–1995 more than 65 percent of infants died before the age of five, and less than onc-third of the population had access to clean water and sanitation; women earned one-fourth of men's income, the real GDP was US$3,846 per person, and public expenditure on health ranged between 1 and 2 percent of the GDP.[5] In the early 1960s, when conditions in the village were much worse, Nour's parents made a decision not to take their daughter to the doctor initially, based on their limited resources and within the cultural norms of giving boys preferential treatment.

The context of the decision to delay taking Nour to the doctor can be better understood in comparing her case to that of her cousin. Nour's cousin, whom I shall call Souma, had rheumatic fever at the same time as Nour. Souma, however, lived in Cairo, and her parents were highly educated. Souma was diagnosed with rheumatic fever very early and was kept on bed rest for two months. Souma continued to take preventive medicine until puberty. Souma's parents were among the well-to-do of Cairo and were thus empowered to make certain economic decisions that eliminated the imposition of the cultural norm of preferential treatment of male children.

In short, it is essential that the discussion of Muslim women's relationship to the environment shift its focus to include poverty and limited resources as factors that influence the rights of Muslim girl-children and women. Muslim women's connectedness to the environment ought to reflect ecological needs of social equity, including basic human needs and fundamental human rights.[6]

Child mortality and morbidity is one of the main reasons cited by many Muslim women for having many children. Today, in many Islamic societies children don't die from disease or lack of access to health services, but due to other causes. Nour's life story clearly illustrates one such cause, namely socialization patterns. The study conducted by Hamed Ammar in 1952[7] and my own restudy of the same village in 1988[8] both show that in one Egyptian village, childcare patterns are influenced by fatalistic and superstitious practices. Children before the age of four or five months are often treated as though they are expected to die rather than to live. Hence, neglect, rather than parental investment, characterizes this very early stage of infancy. Infants often are not given first names until the end of the first week of their birth, and after they are given a name it is not used until they are one or two years old. The infants are usually covered with white cloth on which blue stones and pendants with Qur'anic inscriptions are pinned, to protect them from the evil eye. Parental investment at this very early stage is not high, and infants are left unattended for prolonged periods of times, even if they are crying. In the past, infants at this age were known to die from reactions to scorpion bites because they were left on the floor where scorpions could reach them.

Today, due to these experiences with scorpion bites, caretakers leave young infants on elevated structures, such as beds, sofas, or sometimes tables. Between two and four months, infants begin to turn and move more frequently than before; unattended, they often fall if they have been placed on beds or high surfaces. This is what happened to Nour's second child: he fell from a bed while he was unattended, something that happens to many children in the village these days. Hence, the death of Nour's second child, which led her to have more children, ought to be understood within the context of early childhood socialization in this particular village.

Understanding the particularities and details of early childhood socialization patterns in Islamic communities, beyond depictions of preference for boys, is essential to comprehend the causes of child mortality and morbidity. Muslim women's reproduction rates ought to be examined more as an ecological need, based on self-realization due to lack of basic human needs and fundamental human rights, than as a simplistic biological exercise based on the intrinsic value of children. Now in many Islamic societies, children do not die from disease or lack of access to health services but because of social patterns that are hazardous to their health and survival.[9] Understanding the existing patterns can lead to more realistic programs that could reduce child mortality or morbidity, and hence the rate of population increase among Muslims.[10]

Nour's life story also points to another cause of death among village children that is not due to natural causes or disease, namely, drug addiction. Nour's brother, who was the youngest of eight children, suffered from an addiction for over seven years. This shows us how there are new emerging socialization issues that we need to focus on in Islamic cultures. While these issues were once associated mainly with the industrial world, today they have become part of the problems Muslims living in non-Western societies face.[11] We need to address questions such as: How early do our children start using these substances? Why are they using them? Is it only this generation that is suffering from the epidemic use of such substances? It is important to understand how, in communities where alcohol and other addictive substances are publicly absent, youth get introduced to their use and then become addicted. What are the factors that influence drug abuse and addiction? Is abuse only a male problem, or are there girls and women who are also users and are addicted? What are the consequences of addiction on the well-being of the family unit? Has it introduced more violence generally, and family violence in particular?

All these issues need to be included in the discussion of Muslim women and their relationship to the environment in order to gain a more realistic view of the factors affecting the depletion of the earth's resources. We need to understand these new forces as well as the old ones that affect early childhood and youth socialization patterns, because environmental destruction includes more than resource consumption. The context in which cultural reproduction takes place has a great impact on promoting basic human needs, fundamental human rights, self-realization, and connectedness with others; it is a context that permits a connection between humanity and nature.

Informal education, however, is not the only form of cultural reproduction that we need to understand and contextualize in the case of the relationship between Muslim women and the environment. The issue of formal education also needs to be reformulated and examined more clearly in this context. Population increase in many developing countries is not as pressing an environmental issue as in the developed world, due to the inequity in resource distribution and consumption.[12] The number of children an individual woman has, and their spacing, has an impact on her basic health and access to other resources. But also, beyond issues of social justice, although the rate of population increase in Muslim countries is not alarming, it is not an environmental myth. Muslim countries' natural increase rate (birthrate over death rate) exceeds that of the rest of the developing world by 1.6 percent. This rate requires attention in view of waste generation. Cairo in 1996 was declared the second most polluted city in the world after Mexico

City.[13] Hence the need to discuss issues of population growth, Muslim women, and the environment in terms of social equity of ecological needs and sustainable waste generation.

Research conducted on the effect of education on women's fertility rates shows that there is an inverse relationship between the level of education and the number of children a woman has.[14] In other words, the more education the woman has, the fewer the number of children. Statistics from the Islamic world raise questions about the generalizability of such research. It actually forces such questions as: What kind of education? And at what level? What quality of education? And education for what?

Statistics show that there has been a vast improvement in literacy rates in many Islamic countries. For example, in Saudi Arabia the literacy rate for women rose from approximately 30 percent in 1982 to 59 percent in 1997, while in Egypt the rates rose from approximately 34 percent in 1990 to 41 percent in 1995. Yet, the total fertility rate for the countries in the North African and Western Asian region (as designated by the U.N.—a region that has a large concentration of Islamic countries, though not the major proportion of the total world Muslim population) for the years 1990–1995 ranged from 3.4 percent to 7 percent. The average household size in the countries of the ESCWA (Economic and Social Commission of Western Asia) region ranged from five to eight between the years 1990 and 1995, with little variation between rural and urban households.[15]

One could argue that fertility has not declined in some Islamic countries because education has focused on increasing functional literacy and low-level skills. The rate of women obtaining a university degree in the ESCWA region, for example, is still less than 7 percent.[16] But even those who do receive a higher education, as in the case of Nour, receive instruction that conforms to Hegel's conception of "the need to educate the educator." In Egypt, issues of teacher/student ratio, teacher salary, cost of books, teacher training, and examination styles all work to reinforce rote memorization versus critical thinking in education. Such an education style merely produces credentialed individuals, not educated thinkers. Antiquated values and norms stay internalized and are reproduced from one generation to another.

In the case of Nour, the internalization that a good wife has many children is clear from her husband's comments to me after her death, that "she never told him about the doctor's warning against having more than two children and her rheumatic heart." Although her third child was a result of psychological compensation (because of the death of her second baby), the fourth child (which she had at thirty-nine) is a consequence of her internalization of the norm that her value is determined by the number of children she has. Unlike many married Muslim women, Nour used family planning methods.[17] However, she told me back in 1986 that she used contraception to regulate the timing of her pregnancies, not to limit them.

Again, it is essential to remember that in speaking about the impact of women's formal education about fertility on the environment, the issue is a matter of quality as well as level of education. We must understand that education needs to go beyond credentials and to include a change in the educational style and the development of critical thinking that will question existing norms and values.

The need for Nour to have more than two children ought to be understood as more complex than the reductionist views of technological population-control fixes, structural educational reforms, or ideological zealots' fears of Western imperialism. Nour's need for children, like that of other women in her community, her country, on her continent and her earth, relates directly to issues of equity, justice, and the rights of people. These issues in her case are inextricably related to those of health care, poverty, infant socialization, youth developmental patterns, and the quality and level of women's education. These issues are reiterated in the Earth Charter's articles 5 and 7 as universal needs for all people.[18] For a social scientist like myself, the problems of global warming, pollution, ozone depletion, loss of biodiversity, deforestation, and land degradation are but a reflection of social justice issues related to the diversity of Islamic cultures as a way of life.

For some readers, the question remains how different Nour's story is from that of a Maria in Guatemala, a Xi in China, or a Josna in India. My answer to this is twofold. First, Nour's case is different because at the theoretical level the discussion of eco-justice and Muslim women has lagged behind those of most other cultures—indeed, it is almost nonexistent. Nour's case is a humble contribution to, hopefully, a developing field of study. Second, at Nour's funeral and the various remembrance periods of her death, the following merciful words from the Qur'an were read:

> Allah commands justice, the doing of good and liberality to kith and kin, and He forbids all shameful deeds, and injustice and rebellion: He instructs you, that ye may receive admonition. Fulfil the covenant of Allah, when ye have entered it and break not your oaths after ye have confirmed them, indeed ye have made them. All your surety; for Allah knoweth all that ye do. And do not be like a spinner who breaks into untwisted strands that yarn she has spun after it has become strong. . . . Whoever works righteousness Man or woman and has faith, we will give then a new life and life that is good and pure and We will bestow on such their reward. (*Sūrat al-Naḥl*, verse 78)

It is this final moment, when Nour's spirit and body claimed their Islamic connection, that makes her case of particular concern for Muslims. It makes her death and the relationship between ecology and Muslim women the responsibility of every Muslim, and especially those who are empowered by prestigious positions, wealth, wisdom, and true faith.

Notes

1. Ynestra King, "Ecofeminism," in *The Reader's Companion to U.S. Women's History*, ed. Wilma Mankiller, Gwendolyn Mink, Marysa Navarro, Barbara Smith, and Gloria Steinem (Boston: Houghton Mifflin Company, 1998), 207; Noël Sturgeon, *Ecofeminist Natures: Race, Gender, Feminist Theory, and Political Action* (New York: Routledge, 1997); Val Plumwood, *Feminism and the Mastery of Nature* (New York: Routledge, 1993).

2. Michel Foucault, *The Order of Things*, trans. A. Sheridan (New York: Random House, 1972).

3. Nawal Ammar, "Islam and the Environment: A Legalistic and Textual View," in *Population, Consumption, and the Environment: Religious and Secular Responses*, ed. Harold Coward (Abany: State University of New York Press, 1995), 123–36; idem, "Islam and the Environment: Issues of Justice," in *Visions of a New Earth: Religious Perspectives on Population, Consumption, and Ecology*, ed. Harold Coward and Daniel C. Maguire (Abany: State University of New York Press, 2000), 131–44.

4. This position was abolished in the early 1960s.

5. ESCWA, *Compendium of Social Statistics and Indicators* (New York: Economic and Social Commission of Western Asia, 1997).

6. Ecological needs are composed of three levels: *physical sustainability* (i.e., meeting environmental imperatives in terms of resource consumption and waste generation); *social equity* (i.e., promoting fundamental human rights, starting from satisfying basic human needs [e.g., air, water, food, clothes, shelter, health, and education] and increasing citizens' political access to decision making that affects their future); and *ontological richness* (i.e., providing ample opportunity to realize oneself as one wishes, to achieve personal growth in many directions, and to appreciate and enjoy a spiritual web of intrinsic connections with other beings); Yuichi Inoue, "The Northern Consumption Issue after Rio and the Role of Religion and Environmentalism," in *Population, Consumption, and the Environment*, ed. Coward, 286.

7. Hamed Ammar, *Growing Up in an Egyptian Village: Silwa, the Province of Aswan* (London: Routledge and Kegan Paul, 1952).

8. Nawal Ammar, "An Egyptian Village Growing Up: Silwa, the Governorate of Aswan" (Ph.D. diss., University of Florida, Gainesville, 1988).

9. This is not very different from American children who die mostly (75 percent) from accidents rather than natural causes.

10. Islamic countries show a 4.1 percent annual rate of population increase, compared to 2.5 percent for the rest of the developing world.

11. Muslims living in Western societies, especially in the U.S., have encountered drug addiction as an epidemic. In many American juvenile detention centers, more than 90 percent of the African-American Muslim children there are serving time for drug-related crimes. A new emergent immigrant population is now in American prisons and jails for drug-related crimes, and a large number of the immigrant Muslim populations that work in inner-city grocery stores in the Midwest of the U.S. have lost their lives in drug-related "failed" deals.

12. Twenty percent of people who live in the richest countries receive 82.7 percent

of the world's income, and 20 percent of the world's people barely survive on 1.4 percent of the total income; quoted in David Korten, "Sustainability and the Global Economy: Beyond Bretton Woods" (opening plenary presentation to the Environmental Grantmakers Association, Fall Retreat, 13–15 October 1994, Bretton Woods, New Hampshire), 8. The United States, with only 5 percent of the world population, uses 25 percent of the world's energy and accounts for 25 percent of the world's GNP; quoted in Inoue, "The Northern Consumption Issue," 288.

13. "*Al-Qāhira akthār mudin al-'ālam talwītha*" (Cairo, One of the Most Polluted Cities in the World), *Al-Akhbār*, 6 June 1995, 3.

14. Susan Hill Cochrane, *Fertility and Education: What Do We Really Know?* (Baltimore: Published for the World Bank by Johns Hopkins University Press, 1979); Alaka M. Basu, *Culture, the Status of Women, and Demographic Behaviour* (New York: Oxford University Press, 1992); and Roger Jeffery and Alaka M. Basu, *Girls' Schooling, Women's Autonomy, and Fertility Change in South Asia* (Thousand Oaks: Sage Publications, in association with the Book Review Literary Trust, 1996).

15. ESCWA, *Compendium of Social Statistics and Indicators.*

16. Except for Lebanon, the countries of western Asia are all majority Muslim countries. Most of these countries have the highest women's gender empowerment indices among Muslim countries (ESCWA, *Compendium of Social Statistics and Indicators*).

17. On average, less than 25 percent of married Muslim women, with the exception of Indonesia, use some form of birth control; *Human Development Report* (New York: United Nations Development Program, 1997).

18. Articles 5 and 7 of the Earth Charter emphasize notions of the rights of people and equity and justice.

Toward a Sustainable Society

Scientific Innovation and *al-Mīzān*

MOHAMMAD ASLAM PARVAIZ

Our earth is a beautiful planet. It is the only planet which harbors life as we know, define, and understand it. It is endowed with living and nonliving components which constitute its very unique environment. These living and nonliving components are very distinct and different from one another. While the nonliving components, like atmospheric gases or air, temperature or water, can literally be counted on fingers, the living components of our environment run into millions. Even a layperson acknowledges the diversity of life-forms encountered in almost all groups of plants and animals. It is not surprising, therefore, that most of these creatures are not even known or recorded. This fact is mentioned in the Holy Qur'an:

> And He has created [other] things of which ye have no knowledge. (16:8)

As Allah is the creator of every thing, He has full knowledge about His creations:

> He created all things, And He hath full knowledge of all things. (6:101)

Ecological balance—that is, the balance that exists between the different components of our environment—is a relatively new concept, articulated as such only during the last fifty years. However, fourteen centuries ago the Holy Qur'an very lucidly described the phenomenon to which this term refers:

> Verily all things have We created in proportions and measure. (54:49)

The concept of measure, or balance (*al-mīzān*), among the various components of our environment dawned on us when we noticed some very disturbing phenomena in nature. One such phenomenon is the so-called greenhouse effect. The Swedish scientist Ahrrenius discovered in 1898 the causal link between carbon dioxide and global warming, but it was only in the 1970s that this began to be recognized as a serious environmental concern.

The temperature of the earth's atmosphere is maintained by a process in which the amount of energy the earth absorbs from the sun, mainly as high-energy ultraviolet radiation, is balanced by the amount radiated back into space as lower-energy infrared radiation. Playing a key role in regulating this temperature are the greenhouse gases, mainly carbon dioxide, water vapor, nitrous oxide, and methane. They are called "greenhouse gases" because, like a pane of glass in a green house, they let in visible light from the sun, but prevent some of the resulting infrared radiations from escaping and re-radiate them back to the earth's surface. The buildup of heat that results from this re-radiation raises the temperature of the earth's lower atmosphere, a process commonly known as the greenhouse effect. Over the past few decades human activity, especially the burning of fossil fuels like coal and petroleum and the use of chlorofluorocarbons (CFCs), has increasingly overloaded the earth's natural greenhouse system, slowing down the escape of heat into space and increasing the average temperature of the earth's atmosphere. In 1988, the United Nations Environment Program (UNEP) and the World Meteorological Organization established the Intergovernmental Panel on Climate Change (IPCC). In 1996 the IPCC published its second assessment report, written and reviewed by two thousand scientists and experts. It has established that:

> based on current emission levels, it is believed that the global temperature will rise by between 1^0C and 3.5^0C between now and the year 2100; that even after emission levels are stabilized, climate change will continue to occur for hundreds of years.[1]

The mean sea level will rise by fifteen to ninety-five centimeters between now and the year 2100, causing floods and threatening the existence of some island countries. All this disturbance in the climate is occurring because the proportion of certain gases has increased slightly in the atmosphere, thereby disturbing the natural balance that exists among all the creations of Allah. The Qur'an says:

> And the earth We have spread out [like a carpet], set there on mountains firm and immoveable; And produced therein all kinds of things in due balance. (15:19)

Global warming is also producing another catastrophic phenomenon, known as El Niño, which is not only disturbing the climate the world over, but is also spreading epidemics and reviving many fatal diseases in the affected regions. While global warming and El Niño are caused by disturbing the natural balance among the components of the environment, the ozone layer depletion has occurred because of the introduction of synthetic industrial chemicals—specifically CFCs—into the atmosphere.

These examples very clearly establish the importance of balance in nature. Since the onset of the industrial revolution we have created disturbances in physical or nonliving components of our environment. The consequences have been horrible. We are breathing poisonous air, water is polluted, loaded with toxic chemicals, the earth is parched, its soil is barren, contaminated by pesticides. The scenario needs no elaboration.

After doing what we should not have done to the physical components of our environment, we have now fixed our greedy eyes on the living components of this beautiful planet. Armed with selfish and utilitarian objectives, we are trying to modify different living organisms according to our needs. This is genetic engineering. Living organisms have details of their development, in special structures known as chromosomes, located in their nuclei. These chromosomes have efficiently packed and stacked long strands of DNA, the magic molecule of life. Each functional unit of this double-stranded DNA molecule is known as a gene. For every character, behavior, structure, or function of an organism, there is a separate gene or group of genes that bring about the desired effects in the organism at a specific time during the course of its development. Thus, how much milk a cow gives is determined by the concerned genes, and so too is the grain yield in a particular variety of wheat. Geneticists have identified genes and their respective functions for many organisms. Using various techniques of genetic engineering, they are trying to incorporate "useful" genes in those organisms where they are not found naturally. This is being done with utter disregard to the natural balance that exists among all the genes of a gene pool. It is totally illogical and unscientific to assume that the balance, which occurs among different nonliving components of this planet, does not also exist among life-forms or within their gene pools. In fact, Allah has created everything with due balance and He forbids us from disturbing this balance:

> "And the sky He hath uplifted; and He hath set the balance (measure). That ye exceed not the balance. But observe the balance strictly, nor fall short thereof. (55:7–9)

However, genetic engineers have brought out many innovations in Allah's creations. We have genetically engineered fish that grow much faster than wild and traditional aquaculture varieties. We have crops bioengineered for pest resistance, crops engineered to produce oil-derived chemicals, and recombinant bovine growth hormone (rBGH) that enables cows to produce more milk. To elaborate upon the risks, which are associated with our efforts to change Allah's creations, one may point out the case of transgenic fish.

Currently, about forty or fifty laboratories around the world are working on transgenic fish. About a dozen of them are in the United States, another dozen in China, and the rest in Canada, Australia, New Zealand, Israel, Brazil, Cuba, Japan, Singapore, Malaysia, and several other countries. Some of these labs are associated with companies that expect to commercialize their fish in a few more years. Many of the fish under development are being modified to grow faster than their wild or traditionally bred aquaculture siblings. Faster growth is usually accomplished by transferring a fish growth hormone gene from one species of fish into another. One example is the work of Robert H. Devlin, a research scientist with Fisheries and Oceans, Canada, in West Vancouver, British Columbia. He has modified the growth hormone gene in coho salmon by developing a gene construct in which all the genetic elements are derived from sockeye salmon.[2] The transgenic coho grew on average eleven times faster than unmodified fish and the largest fish grew thirty-seven times faster.

Transgenic fish are wild types, or nearly so, often created from eggs hatched from gametes collected in the wild, so they are fully capable of mating with wild fish. Consequently, one important risk associated with transgenic fish is that, if they escape to fresh water or to the ocean and mate with wild fish, they could destroy the diversity of the wild population gene pool. Such an event occurred in Norway, with framed salmon. Seals occasionally broke the net cages where the salmon were being raised in fjords and some of the salmon escaped and mated with Norway's wild salmon. Because the numbers of wild salmon had already been depleted as a result of acid rain on fresh water spawning grounds, the wild salmon were easily overwhelmed by aquaculture salmon. As a result, says Anne R. Kapuscinski, professor of fisheries and sea grant extension specialist at the University of Minnesota, the genes of the wild salmon were homogenized and Norway lost one of its most important resources—a tremendous amount of genetic diversity in its wild salmon—and the associated commercial and sport fishing industries.[3]

In addition, transgenic fish could also eliminate whole aquatic ecological systems by preying on and outcompeting native species, as many introduced exotic (nonindigenous) fish have done.

As for transgenic crop plants, so far we have the knowledge to engineer two varieties of tomato with delayed ripening; cotton resistant to the herbicide bromoxynil; an insect-resistant potato, insect-resistant corn, herbicide-resistant soybeans, and virus-resistant squash; a tomato engineered to have a higher solid content for easier processing into sauce; and canola with the oil composition altered to be high in lauric acid. Some experts warn that herbicide resistance, or insect-resistance genes, could spread from transgenic crops to their wild relatives and create new weeds that are especially difficult to control, or that the crop itself could become a weed. Jack Brown, a plant breeder geneticist at the University of Idaho, has been studying the spread of herbicide resistance genes from transgenic canola to its relatives in the mustard family. He has found that the resistance gene moved through pollination from the canola to a small fraction of one type of Brassica weed, and that gene then moved to wild mustard, a weed that is much more troublesome. Even though the fraction of weeds affected was low, so much herbicide resistant canola will soon be growing in the United States that a large number of herbicide resistant weeds could potentially be created in a few years.

Similarly, despite its advantageous yields, the virus-resistant squash is a subject of scientific controversy. Some experts worry that when the squash is infected with other viruses, recombinational events could occur that would generate new viral strains. Plant biologists Anne Green and Richard Allison of Michigan State University found that recombinational events occurred in transgenic cow pea plants modified with a virus coat protein. When the plants were inoculated with a different virus, viral RNA or DNA recombined with genetic material from the invading virus to form a new, more virulent strain.[4]

These few examples clearly indicate that it is very dangerous to modify or change Allah's creations. Allah says in the Holy Qur'an that His creations are perfect and flawless. They have been created in harmony and balance with the environment. As the Holy Qur'an states:

> No want of proportion wilt thou see in the creation. (67:3)

Those who change Allah's creations are said to be the followers of Satan, the Satan who spoke of misguiding humanity in different ways. The incident is narrated in the Holy Qur'an:

> And surely I [i.e., Satan] will lead them astray, and surely I will arouse desire in them, and surely I will command them and they will cut the Cattle's ears, and surely I will command them and they will change Allah's creation. Who so chooses Satan for a patron instead of Allah is verily a loser and his loss is manifest. (4:119)

While genetic engineering attempts at creating new life-forms, the technique of cloning reproduces a particular genome. We know that each and every individual is born with a unique set of genes. This genetic makeup, which appears in a particular organism, has been perfected by Allah, over thousands of years of screening and selection. Second, it is destined to live once. It passes on some of its modified portion to the next generation, and that is all. However, there are certain organisms in nature, particularly plants, which propagate asexually and thus retain and maintain their same genetic stock for several generations. But one should remember that they have evolved through a long course of time and have been perfected by Allah.

More important is the fact that this phenomenon is confined to plants only. We hardly find any such example among animals. In contrast, today's scientific efforts are directed toward the creation of animal clones. How these clones will disturb the balance on this planet remains to be seen, but one relevant example where humans tried to modify the natural course, to suit their needs, will help us gauge the possible consequences. I am referring to the so-called "mad cow disease," or bovine spongiform encephalopathy (BSE), which caused havoc throughout Europe during the 1990s. In fact, in Europe the general public and consumer organizations have yet to recover from the impact of the BSE crisis.

This disease first came to the attention of the scientific community in late 1986 with the appearance in cattle of a newly recognized form of neurological disease in the United Kingdom. By May 1995, around fifteen thousand cases of BSE were confirmed. Epidemiological studies in the United Kingdom suggested that the source of the disease was cattle feed prepared from carcasses of dead cattle. It is believed that the disease entered the food chain from the carcasses of sheep with a similar disease.

Normally, cows are vegetarian. To increase their growth rate and to make them fatter, we went against nature and tried to introduce a non-vegetarian component into their feed. The results are present for everybody to see. The outbreak of the disease not only resulted in the ruthless slaughter of thousands of cows, but also affected those people who consumed the infected beef. In fact, we helped this infection to cross the species barrier and move from sheep to cows and from cows to humans. The point to be noted here is that all this havoc occurred when we tried merely to modify the feed of one particular animal.

One can very well imagine what will happen when an attempt is made to change the most sacred of the sacreds, that is, the gene pool of an organism. These changes are deep seated and run through generations. There is no return pathway and no way out. Once a new gene or a new genetic combination has been introduced into a life-form, it is there to stay and take its own course. Interestingly, most of this manipulation work is being done with microorganisms, and this is the group about which very little is known. In fact, we do not even have full details of their diversity. Very few species are known to us and much remains to be characterized. How one would justify, even on scientific grounds, our attempts to alter such life-forms just to suit our needs, when we do not have the full knowledge of the components of the system, the interrelationships that exist, or the balance among different species? These piecemeal efforts are bound to create unknown, unforeseen disturbances on the planet. When even a slight change in the gaseous balance of our atmosphere has created such problems for us, it follows logically that changes in balance among various life-forms will produce catastrophic effects of at least similar magnitude, though perhaps not for one hundred years. In fact, when people started to harness the fruits of the industrial revolution, nobody imagined what havoc this would play on our environment. Similarly, today people are eager to reap the benefits of genetic revolution. They simply refuse to see the obvious. We must understand that Allah has created everything on this planet in order, with perfection, and with due balance. He forbids us to create disorder on the planet:

> Do no mischief on the earth, after it hath been set in order, but call on Him with fear and longing (in your hearts); For the mercy of Allah is (always) near to those who do good. (7:56)

Notes

1. United Nations Environment Program, *Second Assessment Report No. FCCC/SBSTA/1996/7/Add.1* (Nairobi: UNEP, 22 February 1996), 7–10.

2. Robert H. Devlin, Timothy Y. Yesaki, Carlo A. Biagi et al., "Extraordinary Salmon Growth," *Nature* 371, no. 6494 (1994): 209.

3. Anne R. Kapuscinski and E. M. Hallerman, "Implications of Introduction of Transgenic Fish into Natural Ecosystems," *Canadian Journal of Fisheries and Aquatic Sciences* 48 (1991): 99–107.

4. Anne Green and Richard Allison, "Recombination between Viral RNA and Transgenic Plant Transcripts," *Science* 263, no. 5152 (1994): 1423.

Capacity Building for Sustainable Development: The Dilemma of Islamization of Environmental Institutions

SAFEI-ELDIN A. HAMED

Introduction

As the world enters the first years of the twenty-first century, it confronts a challenge without precedent in human history, one that perhaps will determine the future of humankind as a species. In brief, the current patterns of production and consumption are unsustainable; the transition to sustainable development, therefore, is an imperative for the continued existence of the human race on this planet. In other words, this transition is not a matter of moral and ethical ideals alone, but is a matter of survival.

The adoption of sustainable development as a public policy by any society raises some key questions:

- What is required to attain that policy?
- How should a society build capacity for the task?
- Will the implementation of sustainable development principles impose the enactment of new or different legislation and regulations?
- Does pursuing sustainable development require a major adjustment of the administrative structure of the governments involved?
- Would it be necessary to establish new and specialized agencies?

These and other questions regarding the ethical implications of pursuing that policy have been debated and interpreted in different ways around the world. They often prompt an analysis, not only of the existing systems of governments, but also of the relationships and the sharing of responsibilities among neighboring countries. In the Muslim world, this discussion often extends to include two additional questions:

- How can Muslim environmentalists and other Muslim intellectuals respond to the global crises and the challenges of environmental pollution and natural resources depletion? and
- Are the traditional Islamic institutions of *ḥisba, ḥarām, ḥimā, waqf*, and *iḥyā* capable of providing the operational models for achieving sustainable development today?[1]

In this paper I address these questions and review the recent scholarly work that proposes the revitalization of traditional Islamic institutions. First, I survey the background of the emerging concept of sustainable development and clarify its definition. Second, I analyze the basic components for building the capacity of a society to achieve sustainable development. Finally, I reflect on the findings in an attempt to advance the dialogue regarding the validity and practicality of revitalizing the traditional, natural resource institutions of Islam in pursuit of achieving sustainable development.

Defining the Concept of Sustainable Development

The term sustainable development was made popular when the World Commission on Environment and Development—commonly known as the Brundtland Commission—used it in its report *Our Common Future*.[2] Certainly, the mission of sustaining the earth has proven to be a powerful stimulus in raising public awareness and focusing on the need for better environmental stewardship.

The Brundtland Commission's definition of sustainable development as "meeting the needs of the present generation without compromising the needs of future generations," has been strongly endorsed by political decision makers and bureaucrats the world over. For environmental scientists and scholars of international development, this newly coined term led to a wide range of investigations in an effort to make the concept both precise and operational. This has not been an easy task. In spite of the substantial work that has been undertaken to define the term and to draw out its operational implications, the concept of sustainable development continues to be interpreted in many different ways.

The definition used by the World Wide Fund for Nature (WWF) focuses on ecological concerns but leaves several questions unanswered.[3] By defining sustainable development as "improvement in the quality of human life within the carrying capacity of supporting ecosystems," the WWF opens up a wider debate regarding what constitutes the quality of human life.

Economist Herman Daly's definition of sustainable development is similar to the WWF's, but recognizes and adds the social dimension.[4] He refers to sustainable development as "development without throughput growth beyond environmental carrying capacity and which is socially sustainable."

A few years later, Robert Goodland expanded and advanced these two definitions by suggesting that "environmentally sustainable development implies sustainable levels of both production (sources), and consumption (sinks), rather than sustained economic growth. The priority for development should be improvement in human well-being, the reduction of poverty, illiteracy, hunger, disease, and inequity."[5]

Perhaps each of these definitions of sustainable development (as well as numerous others) has some validity. Given the diversity of lifestyles and preferences present in the world today, it may be that no single definition suffices to meet the needs and expectations of all societies.

Despite these differences in interpretation, there is growing consensus that sustainable development, however defined, is a goal worth striving for. In addition, some agreement regarding the basic elements that make a society sustainable is also beginning to emerge. Most experts suggest that a sustainable society should, on the one hand, balance and reconcile the often-competing interests of economic prosperity, environmental integrity, and social equity. On the other hand, it must also accommodate the satisfaction of basic human needs, the attainment of inter- and intragenerational equity, and the protection of the natural systems that sustain life.

Even major international development funding organizations are coming to the same realization. For example, Ismail Serageldin, a former senior official at the World Bank asserts:

> One thing is sure: we will fail in our efforts unless better progress is made to integrate the viewpoints of three disciplines:
>
> • Those of the economists, whose methods seek to maximize human welfare within the constraints of existing capital stock and technologies.
>
> • Those of the ecologists, who stress preserving the integrity of ecological subsystems viewed as critical for the overall stability of the global ecosystem.
>
> • Those of the sociologists, who emphasize that the key actors are human beings, whose patterns of social organization are crucial for devising viable solutions to achieving sustainable development.[6]

Finally, it should also be recognized that notions of what constitutes sustainability are constantly evolving, both because of the relative newness of the field and also because of the ever-changing nature of the world. Just in the past several years, the concept has been broadened from an almost exclusive focus on ecological concerns to include such social concerns as cohesion of community, cultural identity, diversity, solidity, civility, tolerance, humility, compassion, patience, forbearance, fellowship, fraternity, institutions, love, pluralism, and commonly accepted standards of honesty, laws, and discipline.[7]

Capacity Building for Environmentally Sustainable Development

Capacity building for environmentally sustainable development is a convenient and descriptive term covering both a long-term process and a wide range of specific activities that enhance the ability of individuals, organizations, and societies to manage their environment. There is enough evidence to suggest that capacity building for environmentally sustainable development cannot be considered in isolation from economic and social development. For example, investment in building the environmental management capacity of a country may be judged as poorly spent or totally wasted resources if the community has little respect for environmental laws or if the government has no appreciation of the value of biodiversity, soil conservation, and/or cultural heritage.

On the whole, certain conditions need to be met in order for any society to develop the capability of managing its environmental resources in a sustainable manner.[8] The key conditions are: organizations and institutions, human resources, an information base, and public involvement.

Organizations and Institutions

Organizations and institutions are often used interchangeably, and their purposes often converge, but they are distinct from one another.[9] An organization (for example, a government department, a ministry, or an agency) is only a major part of the institutional framework as it performs specific functions. When the utility or efficiency of an organization is questioned, it may be restructured, replaced, or eliminated. Institutions, on the other hand, are more deep-rooted and enduring. They incorporate the norms, rules, roles, and structures that people develop to organize and guide their individual or joint activities. The norms and rules of behavior that an institution embodies cannot be sustained without a network of organizations that promote, codify, enforce, and defend them.

Human Resources

People are the reason for and the means of development. Their efforts, beliefs, and aspirations provide the foundation on which any development program rests. The work needed to achieve or move toward sustainable development is multidisciplinary, as it encompasses a wide spectrum of issues. Although the needs may differ from one society to another, certain types of human resources are usually needed.[10] These types include:

- *Policymakers* to set policies and develop strategies.
- *Legal experts* to draft laws and prepare regulations.
- *Technical staff* to plan projects and implement the specialized work.
- *Managers* to administer the operations and coordinate various programs.
- *Educators* to teach and disseminate the body of knowledge related to sustainable development activities.
- *Opinion makers*, including community leaders, journalists, writ-

ers, artists, and other members of the mass media, to raise awareness and motivate the public.

Information Base

Information is essential to all human activities. Without information about their surrounding environment, different communities could make neither the necessary adaptations for their survival nor the rational decisions to advance their condition. Rational decisions always require two kinds of information: descriptive information to comprehend the existing situation, and prescriptive information to determine actions to be taken.[11] Both kinds are critical in improving the planning and management of natural resources and in attaining sustainable development.

Public Involvement

On the whole, public involvement represents the social dimension of sustainable development; therefore, it is considered an ingredient of no less importance than other dimensions. Failure to recognize the determinant role of the "social actors" has doomed many programs trying to induce development.[12] Since the environment is at risk not from extraterrestrial enemies, but from human beings, including both local and distant resource users, the centrality of people in the development process cannot be overstated.

Public involvement is a process through which both the concerned communities and other stakeholders influence and share control over development initiatives and over decisions and resources that affect them. Public involvement in sustainable development programs can be pursued on three different levels: information dissemination, mutual consultation, and direct participation.

The above-mentioned conditions—that is, organizations and institutions, human resources, an information base, and public involvement—are highly interactive, mutually dependent, and self-reinforcing. A significant synergy exists among them in such a way that improvements in one can often improve the effectiveness of the other conditions, and deterioration in one condition may erode the effectiveness of the others.[13] For instance, well-written environmental protection legislation will be ineffective unless people skilled in auditing and monitoring are available. Similarly, unless communities are well-informed and consulted during the development planning process, new projects and programs will not benefit from local knowledge and may never gain the support of the community.

In brief, movement toward environmentally sustainable development by any society involves more than establishing an environmental protection agency, raising environmental awareness, or providing technical training. It requires comprehensive efforts on all fronts to strengthen the sustainable development institution as a whole and to shift the priorities of the society at large.

Islamization of Environmental Institutions

The relationship between sustainable development and environmental ethics is an increasingly critical issue. As the world moves into a new millennium, certain trends are becoming evident: first, the gap is widening locally between the rich and the poor and globally between the North and the South; second, the conditions of the earth's ecosystems are deteriorating quickly on all fronts; and third, Western economic models and political systems have failed when they were applied in most developing countries. This last trend could have been predicted, since no significant progress in history was ever accomplished without an ethical emphasis, sincere loyalty, genuine affection, and authentic convictions.[14]

In the Muslim world, most of these factors were removed as the national regimes—which ruled these countries after the colonial period —abandoned their traditional ways and opted for borrowed secular systems of government. As a result, a number of contemporary Muslim scholars now advocate a major shift. Their proposed approach to achieving sustainable development in Muslim societies involves two tasks: implementing an Islamic economic system, and revitalizing the traditional resource management institutions of Islam, including *ḥisba, ḥarām, ḥimā, waqf,* and *iḥyā*. These scholars argue that their position is based on several substantive reasons. These are:

1) The spectacular economic progress of the twentieth century that

was led by the West has resulted in a gradual depletion and, in some cases, an outright destruction of scarce ecological systems and other natural resources.[15]

2) The existing ecological crisis is believed to be, in fact, a moral crisis and needs a moral solution.[16] The world needs a set of principles which simultaneously emphasizes ethical ideals and encourages improvement in material well-being.

3) Islam as a paradigm and a system of life provides a distinct view of the role of humans on Earth and of the ownership of resources. Associated with this view are sets of unique values that are different from those of the West and other world cultures. Also, Islamic jurisprudence (*fiqh*) provides specific laws and standards that govern the management of all environmental resources.[17]

4) There is an emerging consensus that every society needs to develop and adopt conservation ethics appropriate to its unique ecological content, and in keeping with its particular traditions. The records of past civilizations indicate that no significant progress in human history was ever accomplished without an ethical emphasis.[18]

5) It is now widely accepted that a single model of development is not likely to work for all developing societies. Development is above all a question of values. It involves an attitude and preferences, self-defined goals, and criteria determining what costs are tolerable to be borne in the course of change.[19]

6) Worldwide, nearly one person in five is a Muslim, or 1.2 billion people in more than seventy-five countries. Most live in developing countries, striving to improve their economic conditions while conserving their cultural heritage. Evidently, imported economic models and Western-style social institutions have not succeeded in any of these societies.

Considering all of the above factors, it is not surprising that some contemporary scholars advocate reviving traditional Islamic institutions and claim that implementing such ideas can provide the operational components needed for achieving environmentally sustainable development.[20] Others have gone into further detail and suggested an exhaustive research agenda in order to study the full implications of applying Islamic economic principles within our existing global economy.[21] Thus far, no systematic examination exists that verifies whether revitalizing the traditional institutions of Islam is economically feasible or not, or politically practical or not.

The Key Issues

Muslim intellectuals may receive as good news the emerging trends described above and the newly evolving recognition of what constitutes sustainable development. These phenomena indicate that the West has come a long way from early models of development, which were limited to economic growth and which viewed progress as no more than a simple process of increasing capital at a rate greater than that of population growth. Does this mean that one can expect an easier path toward building a new world economic order, a global environmental ethic, and a universal social system? Unfortunately not. One should recognize that although Western economists have moved a respectable distance from a strictly material approach to development, they are still not speaking from an Islamic paradigm. This is a critical issue, considering that the unique characteristic distinguishing Islamic development institutions from all other secular institutions is that they are primarily gleaned from and based on a revealed source, namely, the Qur'an and the tradition and sayings of the prophet Muhammad. As work toward implementing sustainable development moves to a greater depth and wider context, this contrast will become more and more pronounced.

Also, one should realize that many voices, both inside and outside the Muslim countries, still confuse growth with development and equate modernization with Westernization. More seriously, another group implies that Islam and development are incompatible. Daniel Lerner, for example, states: "The top policy problem of three generations of Middle Eastern leaders has been whether one must choose between Mecca and mechanization, or whether one can make them compatible."[22]

Considering this divergence in positions toward what constitutes development from an Islamic perspective, it seems that the duty still falls upon Muslim scholars to lay down guidelines for sustainable development institutions that are fundamentally Islamic in character.

This does not simply imply that all persons contributing to this effort should be Muslim or that the proposed policies and activities should be implemented by a Muslim government in a Muslim country. That would be a narrow and a misleading proposal. What is meant by "fundamentally Islamic" is that the objective of development is based on and motivated by the injunctions of *sharī'a* (Islamic law), such as fulfilling the requirement of commanding what is good and prohibiting what is wrong. This particular injunction is, in fact, the ultimate duty of the Islamic state and the essential basis for its legitimacy. Any attempt to intentionally segregate the religious and the secular components of development will lead to the erosion of its merits, as well as the violation of its fundamental attributes.

Is Sustainable Development Possible in the Muslim Countries?

The few proposals made by contemporary scholars to revitalize traditional Islamic institutions, such as the *ḥisba, ḥarām, ḥima, waqf, iḥyā*, and other institutions, are rather limited. Most of these efforts tend to be overly optimistic, focusing on spiritual ideals, such as *tazkīa*[23] (increased purification) and *khilāfa*[24] (trusteeship), but stop short of any substantive discussion of the practical problems and resistance that may confront these efforts in the Muslim countries. In this section I will explore that topic by assessing the situation of the four components needed by any society to develop the capacity of managing its environmental resources in a sustainable manner, namely, organizations and institutions, human resources, information base, and public involvement.

Although there is a risk in making broad generalizations, it is safe to say that, at least on paper, most Muslim countries have established their own environmental government agencies in the last three decades. This reflects considerable effort by these governments and a persuasive ability on the part of the various bilateral and international development organizations that have assisted them. As expected, each of these newly established environmental management agencies has been modeled after European or American systems of governance. And, not surprisingly, none of them have incorporated the ideals of the *sharī'a* or included elements of traditional Islamic institutions. Since the collective experience of the field of public administration indicates an unwillingness among governmental establishments to alter or change their earlier courses of action or their initial bureaucratic styles, one should not anticipate any major change in the near future.

Even if comprehensive and thoroughly detailed Islamic approaches for achieving sustainable development were available today, one would expect them to encounter considerable resistance. Government officials under authoritarian regimes are often hesitant to endorse or pursue goals that do not conform to the explicit interests or the implicit pressures of a country's most powerful constituencies, such as a royal family, a military elite, or an influential business lobby.

Regarding the legislation needed to pursue sustainable development policies, the secular environmental laws and regulations now in place will not be easily changed. Indeed, short of such a radical social change as was witnessed in Iran in the late 1970s or in Sudan in the mid-1990s, current policies will probably stand long after changing conditions have diminished their utility.

People's behavior is generally determined not only by their economic rationality and profit-seeking urge, but also by a host of cultural variables. These kinds of variables are intrinsic to sustainable development, and thus must be recognized and purposefully addressed to achieve the objectives of any development project or program under consideration. Unfortunately, very little relevant research has been conducted that surveys, analyzes, and documents the social norms and cultural variables present in Muslim societies or that assesses how close or distant these are from the Islamic environmental ethics articulated in the *sharīʻa*. Since people's views of their environment strongly influence how they manage it, it follows that only if development projects reflect local beliefs, values, and ideologies will the community support them.

Obviously, a greater challenge may result from conducting such research if one ultimately concludes that the prevailing practices of the community are in violation of the *sharīʻa* tenets. Such a situation will require broad-based efforts to educate and inform people both about principles of environmental management and about fundamentals of *sharīʻa* regarding sustainable development issues.

This may be easier said than done. For example, a World Bank officer suggested in 1995, as a component of a three-year capacity-building program, a training course in environmental issues for Muslim clergymen. Her suggestion was met initially by strong opposition, and it was ultimately rejected by none other than the official government representatives of several Muslim countries of the Middle East. This example suggests that it will be very hard for the current generation of Muslim environmental officials to adopt approaches other than the Western ones they have learned in a typically secular education system. Unfortunately, most academic and governmental institutions in Muslim countries today are either religious or secular.[25] These two components are rarely joined and, as a result, even such a basic tenet of *sharīʿa* as "enjoining good and forbidding evil" is no longer a part of the policy or the operation of contemporary institutions in the Muslim countries.

Another problem facing the efforts of Muslim countries to achieve sustainable development under their existing circumstances is related to information. The modern industrialized world is producing enormous quantities of information. This is transmitted through an explosive expansion of electronic media, mass communication, and the wide application of remote sensing in environmental planning and management. As a result, there is a real concern about information overload or intellectual drowning in the flood of readily available data that cannot now be easily assimilated and analyzed.[26] Another concern is related to financing a database. The costs of information needed for planning and managing development projects is becoming increasingly expensive, to the point of being prohibitive in most developing countries. Even when international development agencies provide this information base as a part of their financial aid or technical assistance to these countries, the tendency of most Muslim governments is to treat it as a national security matter or highly confidential data bank. Some political leaders perceive notions like the "Freedom of Information Act," which is a basic right for every citizen in the Western countries, as a means of gathering military intelligence about their respective governments. Attempts to share natural resources data with local nongovernmental groups are routinely rejected, suspected, or treated as acts of treason.

From a purely technical point of view, the process of advancing descriptive information to prescriptive information as a part of the decision making remains as challenging as ever. Development planners' real challenge is to provide their society with acceptable criteria by which to judge between conflicting objectives and to try to weigh environmental and societal benefits and costs. Such criteria have to be based on the needs and the value system of the community at large, and not only the narrow interest of the ruling class.[27] Taking such an independent and ethically responsible position is too dangerous in a political system that suffers from the typical ills of autocratic regimes, including monopoly of power and privileges, financial corruption, administrative incompetence, and a deformed judiciary system. In brief, although information is an essential ingredient in attaining sustainable development, it requires a political climate and social conditions that may not be readily available in most Muslim countries today.

Finally, development specialists agree today that most environmental problems cannot be solved without the active participation of local people.[28] This is why public involvement is considered one of the four cornerstones of the concept of sustainable development. Unfortunately, however, most Muslim countries are poorly prepared in that respect. For a long time, these societies have missed the opportunity to learn or practice the social ethics of Islam, and therefore have remained oblivious to the Islamic imperative of representative governance.[29] According to the *shūra* (mutual consultation) principle, the Muslim community is required to express concretely their values and positions on various issues that affect their life and influence their relationship with other communities in the world. Other essential guidelines fall under the *shūra* principle, including notions such as *riḍa al-awām* (popular consent), *ijtiḥād jāmī'ī* (collective deliberation), and *mas'ūlīyah jama'īyya* (collective responsibility), let alone universal human rights such as personal freedom, justice, equality, and dignity of each human being. Certainly, an honest and open articulation of one's views cannot come about under autocratic, authoritarian, or totalitarian governance, but only under democratic principles or a progressive and genuine system of *shūra*. However, it appears that none of the regimes currently ruling Muslim countries will transform voluntarily or take the initiative and stress the authentic Islamic principles of *shūra*. Essentially, the principle of *shūra* runs parallel to the principles of democracy in the Western political thought and is considered as a central principle of the Islamic system of governance.

In brief, the crucial connection between sustainable development and the principle of *shūra* seems somehow blurry, or is totally resented in the minds of the existing leaders of Muslim countries, and is yet to be sufficiently forged in the mind of Muslim peoples. Generally, the political climate in the Muslim world, from Indonesia in the East to Algeria in the West, is not favorable to citizens' involvement. It is suggested that implementing the kinds of political reforms that could enable local people to participate meaningfully in sustainable development decisions within their own communities is unlikely, at least in the near future. It may be that sustainable development has to wait.

Conclusions

A brief survey of the state of knowledge, the nature, and the process of pursuing sustainable development in the Muslim countries has led to the following conclusions:

Attaining sustainable development remains the greatest challenge facing humanity. Considerable disparity between the rich and the poor continues to widen both within local communities and among countries.

The term "sustainable development" means different things to different people. Currently it implies no universally accepted pattern of activities, components, or time frame. Given the diversity of lifestyles and preferences that are present in the world today, perhaps no single definition suffices to meet the needs and expectations of all societies. Notions of what constitutes sustainability are constantly evolving, both because of the relative newness of the field and because of the ever-changing nature of the development problems that face each nation.

Certain conditions need to be met in order for any society to build the capacity to attain sustainable development while managing its environmental resources. The key conditions are organizations and institutions, human resources, information base, and public involvement. These four conditions are highly interactive, mutually dependent, and self-reinforcing. Significant synergy exists among them. Improvements in one condition can often improve the effectiveness of the other conditions, while deterioration in one condition may erode the effectiveness of the others.

Evolution in defining what constitutes sustainable development brings it closer to the Islamic interpretation that is based on the *sharīʿa*, particularly in relation to its harmony with the Islamic concepts of *khilāfa* (trusteeship) and *istimār al-arḍ* (development of the earth). However, the duty of laying down guidelines for Islamic institutions for sustainable development will always fall upon the Muslim intelligentsia. Until now, efforts to achieve sustainable development in the Muslim countries have rarely capitalized on the cultural heritage of the *sharīʿa*. The programs implemented throughout these countries suggest an elitist bias. Their conceptual underpinning is rooted in Western values and/or serving foreign users. The proposals that have been presented by different scholars to revitalize traditional Islamic institutions (such as *ḥisba*, *ḥarām*, *ḥimā*, *waqf*, *iḥyā*, and others) are few in number, sketchy in content, and overly optimistic in spirit. All of these proposals have avoided any serious assessment of implementing their schemes under the political conditions that prevail in Muslim countries today.

A brief assessment of the situation in Muslim countries has been conducted here, based on an examination of the four conditions required in any society to build a capacity toward achieving sustainable development. It appears that a disappointing proliferation of weak and ineffective government agencies in the Muslim countries is behind the trend of advocating the application of the *sharīʿa* heritage in managing environmental resources. This assessment also suggests that most Muslim countries are less prepared than others in the world to achieve sustainable development with or without revitalizing their Islamic cultural heritage. The greatest obstacle facing them today is not environmental, but political. Political conditions are at the heart of the ecological destruction and resource depletion in the Muslim world.

In conclusion, it may be true that Islam as a religion and as a body of knowledge has provided its followers with a comprehensive system of environmental ethics and successful institutions to manage development wisely and equitably. This is history, but history alone will not influence or enhance the future of any community confronting the global environmental crises we are now facing. Sustainable development hinges on public involvement. This is rooted in what is commonly known in Western political thought as democracy and in Islamic jurisprudence as *shūra*. In the words of a contemporary political science scholar:

> No claim of commitment to Islam, no matter how many mosques are built or pious commentaries broadcast from the state-owned media, can be taken seriously where *shūra* is denied, ignored, distorted, or compromised. . . .[30]

In brief, ideals that do not give rise to practical actions on the part of those who hold them are sterile and possibly hypocritical.

Notes

1. *Ḥisba* (Office of Public Inspection) is based on the Qur'anic command of "promotion of good and the prevention of evil." This is the underpinning feature that makes *ḥisba* a purely Islamic institution. The Qur'an states: "And there may spring from you a nation who invite to goodness, and enjoin right conduct and forbid the reprehensible. Such are they who are successful" (Qur'an 3:104).

Just like many other institutions, *ḥisba* grew with society until it became a singularly complex system within the Islamic state. Noted scholars of *sharīʻa*, such as Mowardi, Ibn Ukhwwah, and Ibn Khaldun, considered *ḥisba* a religious office. Early in Islam, it was an integral part of the office of the *qāḍī* (judge), who had the right to appoint whomever he found suitable for carrying out the required tasks. Nevertheless, the functions of *muḥtāsib* were clearly distinct from those of a *qāḍī*. Both the secular and the religious sides of the *ḥisba* system continued from the eighth century until around the middle of the fourteenth century, when the religious side was discontinued. The secular side survived to some extent in Egypt until the middle of the nineteenth century. It was replaced in some parts of the Ottoman Empire by country councils.

Ḥarām (forbidden zone) has the primary function of limiting development in unique areas that could be damaged by human activities. These are usually areas of significant cultural or natural resources of great value to the individual and/or the whole community. According to the *sharīʻa,* the *ḥarām* of a private area belongs to its owner(s), and that of public areas is public property managed by the *muḥtāsib.* Historically, the three most inviolate places in Islam are the cities of Mecca, Medina, and Jerusalem. The prophet Muhammad declared Mecca and Medina *ḥarām* areas a few years before he died. The *ḥarām* of Mecca is believed to have been declared inviolate even earlier than the time of the Prophet. However, it was he who described its exact boundaries and declared that within the *ḥarām* of Mecca no wildlife could be killed or even disturbed, no native tree could be cut or uprooted, and no grass could be cut except that used for medicinal purposes. Similar guidelines were declared for Medina and were later applied to Jerusalem.

Ḥimā (preserve) is defined as a set of standards and guidelines designed to regulate the intensity and the location of the use of resources. Although the system of *ḥimā* existed before Islam, the prophet Muhammad prohibited the pre-Islamic tradition of establishing private reserves for the exclusive use of the elite, because they were used to oppress the common people. Five types of *ḥimā* existed in Arabia:

1) *Ḥimā* for forest trees in which woodcutting is prohibited or limited;

2) *Ḥimā* in which grazing was prohibited;

3) *Ḥimā* in which grazing was limited to certain seasons (such as the one for beekeeping during flowering period);

4) *Ḥimā* restricted to certain species and numbers of livestock;

5) *Ḥimā* managed for the welfare of a particular community which occasionally suffered from drought or other natural catastrophes.

Waqf (charitable endowment) is based on the Qur'anic declaration: "They ask thee O Muhammad what they shall spend in alms. Say: let the good ye spend go to parents, and kindred, and orphans and the poor, and the wayfarer; and whatsoever good ye do,

God is aware of it" (Qur'an 2:215). On the whole, Islam encourages every capable individual to support the cause of charity in all its forms. Giving charity to the poor or for public welfare is considered one of the highest and most important duties in Islam. Further, the concept of detaining the corpus from the ownership of any person and granting its income in perpetuity to some noble cause is highly praised in Islam.

The earliest governmentally organized agency of *waqf* was established during the time of Umar, the second caliph, who led the Islamic state after the death of the prophet Muhammad. Initially, the agency consisted of *Dār al-daqīq* (the flour house), to help the poor. Umar himself endowed some of his land for this purpose and bequeathed all incomes from that land to the *waqf* foundation fund. For more than ten centuries, the Muslim empire financed all its public works, bridges, roads, mosques, hospitals, and libraries through the institution of *waqf.*

Iḥyā (reclamation) is the Islamic institution that deals with *mawāt* (dead land), which included any land that is not farmed or built on, and which has not been declared as *ḥarām* or *ḥimā*. Whoever cultivates a *mawāt* that does not belong to anyone will acquire the right to possess it. *Iḥyā* is literally translated as "bringing new life" to the land. Accordingly, utilizing undeveloped land through *iḥyā* requires the introduction of a new use. Ultimately, however, the Islamic state maintained the right to repossess any land that was improperly utilized or was unutilized within a specified period.

2. World Commission on Environment and Development (WCED), *Our Common Future* (Oxford: Oxford University Press, 1987).

3. World Wide Fund for Nature (WWF), *Sustainable Use of Natural Resources: Concepts, Issues and Criteria* (Gland, Switzerland, 1993).

4. Herman E. Daly, "Toward Some Operational Principles of Sustainable Development," *Ecological Economics* 29 (1990): 1–6.

5. Robert Goodland, "The Concept of Environmental Sustainability," *Annual Reviews of Ecological Systems* 26 (1995): 1–24.

6. Ismail Serageldin, "Making Development Sustainable," *Finance and Development* 30, no. 4 (1993): 6–10.

7. Goodland, "The Concept of Environmental Sustainability."

8. Olav Kjørven et al., *Building Environmental Assessment Capacity in Sub-Sahara Africa* (discussion paper prepared by the World Bank, IUCN, and the World Conservation, 1996).

9. Aysha Kudat and S. Peabody, *METAP Capacity Building: A Renewed Commitment to Participation* (Washington, D.C.: World Bank, 1994).

10. Safei Hamed and Jose Furtado, "Capacity Building of EA Institution," *EDI Training Manual on Environmental Assessment*, volume 1, section 7 (Washington, D.C.: Economic Development Institute of the World Bank, 1996).

11. Melville Branch, *Comprehensive Planning* (Pacific Palisades, Calif.: Palisades Publishers, 1993).

12. Michael M. Cernea, "The Sociologist's Approach to Sustainable Development," in *Making Development Sustainable: From Concepts to Action*, ESD Proceedings Series, no. 2 (Washington, D.C.: World Bank, 1994), 7–9.

13. Kjørven et al., *Building Environmental Assessment Capacity*.

14. Aldo Leopold, *A Sand County Almanac* (New York: Oxford University Press, 1949).

15. Mohamed I. Ansari, "Islamic Perspectives on Sustainable Development," *American Journal of Islamic Social Sciences* 11, no. 3 (1992): 394–402.

16. Iqtidar Zaidi, "On the Ethics of Man's Interaction with the Environment: An Islamic Approach," *Environmental Ethics* 3, no. 1 (1981): 35–47.

17. Othman Llewellyn, "Desert Reclamation and Conservation in Islamic Law," *Muslim Scientist* 11, no. 9 (1982): 9–29.

18. Aldo Leopold, *A Sand County Almanac.*

19. Denise Goulet, "An Ethical Model for the Study of Values," *Harvard Educational Review* 41 (1979): 205–27.

20. S. Waqar Hussaini, *Islamic Environmental Systems Engineering* (London: Macmillan, 1980); Llewellyn, "Desert Reclamation and Conservation"; and Hesam A. Joma, "The Earth as a Mosque" (Ph.D. diss., University of Pennsylvania, 1991).

21. Monzer Kahf, "Contemporary Challenges to Islamic Economists," *Al-Ittiḥad* 15, no. 2 (1978): 25–30.

22. Daniel Lerner, *The Passing of Traditional Society: Modernizing the Middle East* (Glencoe, Ill.: Free Press, 1958).

23. *Tazkīa* derives from the *zakāt*, which means "increase" or "purification." Technically, *zakāt* is a fixed portion of one's wealth, which one is obliged to give annually for the benefit of the poor; the giving of wealth to the needy is thus regarded as bringing about its purification and increase. According to Khurshid Ahmed, the mission of all the prophets of God was to perform the *tazkīa* of humans in all their relationships—with God, with other humans, with the natural environment, and with society and the state. *Tazkīa* is a concept that addresses itself to the problem of human development in all its dimensions and is concerned with growth and expansion toward perfection through purification of attitudes and relationships.

24. *Khilāfa* (trusteeship) is an Islamic concept that explicitly answers the eternal question: "What is man's purpose on earth?" The Qur'an declares that humankind was created to be God's *khalīfa*, or steward, on Earth. The central role of humankind on Earth is included in several chapters of the Qur'an. The prophet Adam is mentioned as the first *khalīfa*: "And when thy Lord said unto the angels: Lo! I am about to place a vicegerent on earth" (Qur'an 2:30).

The same task was assigned to the prophet Noah and his followers after the flood: "But they denied him, so We saved him and those with him in the ship, and made Them viceroys (in the earth) while We drowned those who denied Our Revelations" (Qur'an 10:74).

The role of the steward of the earth and its attendant challenges have ultimately reached the followers of the new faith of Islam as stated in the Qur'an to the prophet Muhammad:

"We destroyed the generations before you when they did wrong; and their messengers came unto them with clear proofs of God's Sovereignty but they would not believe. Thus do We reward the guilty folk.

"Then We appointed you viceroys in the earth after them, that We might see how ye behave." (Qur'an 10:13–14)

As a *khalīfa*, a human is expected to interact with nature and its processes so as to transform the world from what it is into what it ought to be. God declared everything in creation subservient to humans, designed and/or redesignable to serve their happiness. However, the development or reconstruction of the earth is a pursuit that should be attained, not in a greedy and exploitative way, but through responsible and justly balanced means. It requires strength, vision, and discipline.

For a more detailed discussion of all these Islamic institutions, see *Kitāb el-Amou'al* (The Book of Finance; 1975); also *Iḥyā al-arḍ al-muwāt* (Developing Dead Lands; 1972).

25. Joma, "The Earth as a Mosque."

26. Branch, *Comprehensive Planning*.

27. Safei-Eldin A. Hamed, *Landscape Planning for the Arid Middle East: An Approach to Setting Environmental Objectives* (Lewiston, N.Y.: Edwin Mellen Press, 2002).

28. World Bank, *The World Bank Participation Sourcebook* (Washington, D.C.: World Bank, 1996).

29. Sadek J. Sulaiman, "The Shūra Principle in Islam," *Arab American Dialogue* 9, no. 2 (1997): 19–22.

30. Ibid.

Islam, the Environment, and Family Planning: The Cases of Egypt and Iran

NANCY W. JABBRA AND JOSEPH G. JABBRA

Introduction

Broadly speaking, Muslims believe that God created nature and its laws, that God established humankind as stewards of creation, and that environmental problems are caused by human irresponsibility.[1] Muslim scholars have brought to bear numerous texts from the Qur'an and the *sunna* to their reasoning on environmental issues. As social scientists we look at those texts and beyond them, to human behavior. Thus we hold that particular issues, including environmental pollution, population planning, and economic development, are subject to variable interpretation in the Islamic tradition. In other words, we must ask *which* Muslims, when, and where—that is, we must investigate the historical, cultural, political, social, and economic contexts—when we search for an Islamic perspective on a particular topic.[2] Moreover, Muslims have no central hierarchy comparable to that of the Catholic Church, so there is no final authority save that of consensus among scholars. Finally, as Joseph Chamie points out, the beliefs and practices of ordinary people might be quite at odds with views promulgated by religious leaders.[3] In Lebanon, for example, until quite recently Muslims were less likely than Christians (including Catholic Christians) to practice contraception, quite in contrast to the teachings of their religious leaders.

Because the environment is so broad a topic, because population issues affect both the environment and economic development, and because the issue of family planning lends itself to a consideration of both religious teachings and behavior, we decided to limit our discussion of the relationship between Islam and environment in the present context to a consideration of family planning policies in two specific Islamic environments.

Numerous instances show us that environmental problems are not necessarily related to population pressures. Simply recall, for example, the cases of Love Canal, Chernobyl, and Bhopal in modern times, or the water and air pollution caused by the dye industry in ancient Tyre. However, it is also true that population pressures exacerbate the deleterious effects of human activity upon the natural environment (and upon national efforts at economic development), as the following examples demonstrate.

For many decades, Egypt's already scarce resources of housing, arable land, and water have been stressed by its annual growth rate of 2.3 percent. Sewage, a rising water table, and air pollution threaten its antiquities, and thus the tourism industry so essential to national revenues. Urban expansion has crept to the margins of antiquities and swallowed up agricultural land. Cairo grows by about eight hundred people a day. Housing there is so scarce that people are living in shacks, on rooftops, and in cemeteries. Its infrastructure is so strained that sewage and solid waste threaten public health. The air pollution caused by dust and emissions from growing numbers of factories and motor vehicles is extremely serious. Efforts to raise agricultural production have resulted in salinization problems and polluted water; polluted water, in turn, affects not only the safety of people's drinking water, but also fishing in the Nile and along the Mediterranean and Red Sea coasts. Lastly, overpopulation threatens Egypt's capacity to educate and employ its people.[4]

The situation in Iran differs from that in Egypt mainly in that Iran depends more heavily upon petroleum revenues. Thanks to population growth and rural-urban migration, pressures for greater agricultural production have led to overuse and misuse of nitrogen fertilizers and pesticides. Attempts to expand the amount of arable land have led farmers to cultivate steeply sloping land, thus contributing to soil loss and erosion. In the effort to house new families, the number of brick factories has grown, and consequently the air pollution from the heavy fuel they use. That pollution is added to by lead from the growing numbers of motor vehicles, particularly in urban areas. As industries have expanded to meet Iran's growing needs for consumer goods, solid wastes have accumulated. So has the pollution of waterways, as factories discharge liquid wastes directly into rivers already polluted by agricultural runoff and improperly managed sewage. These rivers form a significant part of Iran's water supply.[5]

Because the topic of Islam and family planning is still very broad, and because as social scientists we believe that one must pay attention to the contexts in which believers live as well as to their beliefs, we decided to limit further our topic to the cases of Egypt and Iran. We chose these countries as our case studies for several reasons. First, they are both large, important, and predominantly Muslim states situated in the Middle East. Second, they differ in several interesting respects. Most significantly, the Islamic Republic of Iran today officially and effectively promotes family planning. Although Egypt has officially promoted family planning since 1965, the implementation of its programs remains ineffective, and the country's Islamist groups, as was evident at the time of the International Conference on Population and Development held in Cairo in 1994, remain opposed to family planning. Why do Egypt and Iran differ?

A number of possible variables can be noted: 1) the difference between mainly Arab (Egypt) and mainly Persian (Iran) cultures; 2) the differences in beliefs between mainly Sunnite (Egypt) and mainly Shi'ite (Iran); 3) differences in the nature of the bureaucracies in the two countries in that somehow greater charisma inheres in the Iranian bureaucracy, and in that the Egyptian bureaucracy is less well-organized, less committed, and less efficient than the Iranian one; and 4) the fact that the Islamists control the government in Iran, but remain in opposition in Egypt. It will be our position that the last two variables are the most likely explanations for the differences we have observed.

Marriage, Sexuality, Abortion, Contraception, and Family Planning in Islamic Tradition

It might initially be supposed that Islamic teachings forbid birth control. When the United Nations held its conference on population and development in Cairo in 1994, numerous Muslim spokesmen in Egypt reacted negatively to the conference draft document; some, in fact, were staunchly opposed to any kind of family planning. On the eve of the conference, members of Egypt's Gama'a al-Islamiyya fired on a tour bus, killing one person and wounding others. Several Muslim countries boycotted the conference, while others downgraded the level of their participation. After the final document was released some Muslim states, while declaring their overall acceptance, announced that they would implement it in accordance with their own religious values and culture.[6] In fact, Muslim scholars have addressed these topics since early in their history. Generally speaking, they agree on most issues. Human beings are meant to live in society and to marry. Sexual expression in marriage is viewed positively, and having children is thought to be one of the purposes and joys of marriage. The influential medieval scholar Abu Hamid al-Ghazali (1058–1111 C.E.), in his *Book on the Etiquette of Marriage* (part of a larger work called the *Iḥyā'*), not only supported such views, but also expounded upon proper Muslim behavior in marriage. He listed procreation as the main purpose of marriage.[7]

Medieval scholars also held that contraception is lawful. They extended the prophet Muhammad's permission of *coitus interruptus* to include all forms of contraception known to them.[8] Most of the permissible rationales for contraception involved either health or economic considerations. As Abdel Rahim Omran points out, al-Ghazali himself defended economic justifications for practicing contraception, even though the Qur'anic verse states, "There is not a creature on earth, but its sustenance depends on Allah."[9] Muhammad himself said that "The most grueling trial . . . is to have plenty of children with no adequate means" and "I seek refuge in Allah from the most grueling trial."[10] The point is that Islam is supposed to be a religion of ease rather than hardship; "God desires for you ease; He desires not hardship for you" (Qur'an 2:185). Contraception for the purpose of avoiding economic hardship does not imply a lack of trust in God.[11] During the medieval period, both medical scientists and writers of erotica devoted considerable attention to methods of contraception, and many of these, evidently, were practiced.[12]

Abortion, however, was another matter. Infanticide was forbidden in the Qur'an (for example, 17:31). But was abortion infanticide? Here the medieval jurists differed. They all agreed that after ensoulment (one hundred twenty days) abortion was forbidden except to save the health of the mother. Today, the Hanafi and Zaydi schools of jurisprudence permit it before one hundred twenty days, the Shafi'is are divided, while the remaining schools generally forbid it.[13] As Abul Fadl Mohsin Ebrahim points out, however, abortion is not equated with homicide.[14]

Sterilization, or the rendering of either men or women permanently infertile, is also viewed with much caution. Apart from surgical castration, which was forbidden in the tradition of Muhammad, means to induce permanent infertility were unknown until relatively recently, and thus Islamic tradition did not have much to say about them. In modern times Muslim theologians have tended to oppose any permanent method of sterilizing either men or women, except for medically indicated reasons.[15]

In sum, then, Muslim theologians and lawgivers have generally accepted the concept of family planning as being consistent with their belief that God is merciful and that Islam is a universal religion of moderation. On the other hand, they have not accepted all means of population control: abortion is, for most, unacceptable, as are permanent means of sterilization; but reversible means, adopted without coercion from public authorities, are legitimate.

Population Growth in Egypt and Iran: A Tale of Two Countries

Although we established in the previous section that Islam permits family planning, one may also find Islamic texts that encourage large families. Sexuality within marriage is viewed in a positive light. Following the example of Muhammad, early marriages of young women are permitted. Moreover, several verses in the Qur'an must be described as pronatalist, for example, "He brought you forth from the earth and delegated you to inhabit and develop it" (2:61), and "Your wives are your tilth, so go unto them as you will" (2:223). Moreover, generally pronatalist views have prevailed among ordinary people in both Egypt and Iran. Even today, in Iran newlyweds are greeted with "Next year we hope you have a child in your arms," and in Egypt with "We hope the firstborn will come soon." As in other Middle Eastern countries, young children are welcome at adult events, and generally are much petted and spoiled. Such attitudes are not surprising in countries which had, until recently, high infant and child mortality rates and negligible provision for old age security. In rural populations, too, children were economic assets rather than liabilities, and male children would grow up to fight, if necessary, for their families.[16]

Gender roles also support high fertility rates. In both Egypt and Iran, people consider it unnatural for a woman not to want children; the woman who is unable to bear children is treated as a deviant and is likely to be divorced. Women gain prestige through bearing children, particularly boys, and later on, gain both prestige and power through arranging marriages for their children and becoming mothers-in-law and grandmothers.[17] Given this pronatalist climate, then, what has happened to make the paths of Iran and Egypt diverge in the late twentieth century?

In our introduction to this chapter, we mentioned the possibility that the Shi'ite-Sunnite or Persian-Arab differences might somehow explain the differences in outcomes between Iran and Egypt. In many respects, the Shi'ite and Sunnite jurists and theologians did develop separate conclusions from the same basic texts and traditions. On the other hand, both groups vary internally, and on issues relating to population control and family planning there is no clear divide between Sunnites and Shi'ites.

Persian and Arab cultures, too, differ. Apart from the obvious linguistic gulf—Persian and Arabic belong to separate language families—the cultures differ in terms of traditional foods, styles of art, architecture, music, poetry, and in many other ways. But again, it is hard to see how these kinds of differences could have any effect upon public policies toward birth control or environmental issues in general in the late twentieth century. Following will be a treatment of population issues first in Iran, and then in Egypt.

Iran

The Reign of Shah Mohammad Reza Pahlavi (1944–1979)

During the early years of the twentieth century, Iran's population grew very slowly, fertility being balanced by mortality and migration having a negligible effect upon growth. Eventually, improvements in the standard of living and in public health reduced mortality rates and led to rapid population growth. The country's first modern census was taken in 1956, at which time the population was 18.9 million. By 1976, on the eve of the Islamic Revolution, the population had increased to 33.7 million.[18]

After the 1966 census, Iranian public officials realized that the country's population growth had to decrease so as to facilitate modernization. (Policymakers recognized the need to control environmental pollution at about the same time, but subordinated environmental concerns to development needs.)[19] Therefore, the Ministry of Health established the Family Planning Council of Iran in 1967. Its goal was to reduce the population growth rate from 3.1 percent in 1971 to 2.0 percent by 1978. They began by distributing contraceptives through public clinics. In 1973, new legislation created a loophole in Iran's previously strict laws against abortion and sterilization. Secondary school and university curricula began to include materials on family planning, and by the 1970s a mass media propaganda campaign was begun. About 11 percent of Iran's married women were practicing some form of contraception by the end of the Pahlavi period.[20]

Modernization and changes in gender roles had some effects on population growth as well. Women's access to education and to paid employment increased, particularly in urban areas. The Family Protection Laws of 1967 and 1975 limited divorce and polygyny and made some provisions for the support of divorced women and their children; these laws mainly benefited urban middle- and upper-class women. Women received the right to vote in 1963 and began to enter the professions.[21] Age at first marriage increased. Iranian fertility rates declined between 1966 and 1976, because of both modernization and the country's family planning program.[22]

However, neither the support of affluent Iranian women, nor the combined efforts of the Iranian army, the SAVAK, and the CIA were able in the end to save the regime of Shah Mohammad Reza Pahlavi. The government had become a cruel dictatorship, and the benefits of modernization were rather unevenly distributed among provinces and social classes. Western powers, mainly the United States, held political, cultural, and economic hegemony over Iran. Eventually, a religion-based movement developed in opposition to the Iranian government and its sponsor, the United States of America.

The Early Years of the Islamic Republic (1979–1986)

The early years of the new age were characterized by patriotic and religious zeal. Efforts were made to recreate Iran along more authentically Islamic lines; Western-style secularism was eschewed in favor of piety and religious guidance. When Iraq declared war on Iran in 1980, national defense motives were added to the nation's cultural and political agenda.

Family planning was not high on that agenda. Moreover, just as (middle- and upper-class urban) women had symbolized modernity under the regime of the shah, under the Islamic Republic women became the symbolic means through which the country's cultural authenticity was communicated. According to Valentine Moghadam's analysis, women were viewed as particularly vulnerable to *gharbzadegī* ("Westoxication"), and, in turn, their weakness could harm the entire nation.[23] The Family Protection Laws were abrogated, replaced by the *sharī'a*. The minimum age of marriage for women was lowered. Women were required to wear *hijāb* (modest dress) in public, and gender segregation was enforced in the workplace; indeed, women were barred from certain occupations on the grounds that these were unsuitable for them.

Motherhood was extolled as women's most precious gift to Islam and to the nation. It was not only women's nature to be first and foremost mothers, but it was their duty to raise committed Muslims and martyrs in the war with Iraq.[24] Abortions and the distribution of contraceptives were banned. Not only were the government's family planning clinics closed, but propaganda about the ill side-effects of many contraceptive methods was also disseminated.[25] Finally, despite Ayatollah Ruhollah Khomeini's 1980 *fatwa* (judicial opinion) permitting contraception, many religious and political leaders claimed that family planning was a Western plot to subjugate Third World nations and reduce the number of Muslims in the world. Echoing traditional beliefs, they even held that a high population was the sign of a strong country.[26]

Under the circumstances, it is not surprising that fertility levels increased. By 1986, Iran's population stood at 49.4 million, of whom approximately 1.8 million were refugees from Afghanistan. The annual population growth rate between 1976 and 1986 was about 3.8 percent. The crude birthrate increased from forty-three per one thousand in 1976 to forty-eight per one thousand in 1986, while the total fertility rate increased from 6.3 in 1976 to 7.0 in 1986.[27] At the same time, the continued fall in infant and child mortality rates further contributed to population growth.[28] The war with Iraq, which lasted from 1980 to 1988, was costly. Four hundred thousand Iranians lost their lives, and one million were wounded or disabled. Refineries, petrochemical plants, and factories were damaged or destroyed. Iran's main oil shipping terminal at Kharg Island was closed because of damage. Petroleum revenues fell precipitously. The city of Abadan and other cities, towns, and villages suffered severe material destruction. Refugees fled the war zones for Tehran and other places of safety. All in all, billions of dollars were lost.[29]

Recent Years under the Islamic Republic (1986–Present)

Although initially the 1986 population figures were viewed as a sign for rejoicing, by 1988 Iranian officials began to see that the combination of high birthrates, internal migration, and a damaged infrastructure would soon lead to difficulties. Among other things, a government committed to justice for the poor and oppressed could not afford to fail to deliver on its promises lest it risk severe popular reactions.[30] Once again, development issues took primacy over purely environmental concerns. It should be noted, however, that the Constitution of the Islamic Republic states that citizens have a duty to protect the environment for future generations.[31]

In 1988, the same prime minister, Hossein Moussavi, who had once viewed a large population as a sign of strength and who had welcomed the results of the 1986 census, reinstated population as a public policy issue. At a conference convened by government planners later that year, demographers urged the government to institute and implement a national family planning policy.[32] Shortly before he died, the still charismatic Ayatollah Ruhollah Khomeini endorsed the government's new policies, and Ayatollah Ali Khamene'i supported them in an important Friday sermon.[33] In April 1989, Prime Minister Moussavi, in a major public address, emphasized the country's urgent need for a strong family planning program.[34]

By December 1989, Iran's new population program finally began, with three primary goals: to encourage birth spacing of three to four years; to discourage pregnancies in women under the age of eighteen; and to limit family size to three children. In 1990, the Health Ministry created the Population Policy Board to implement its program. The government began to allocate money, amounting to over U.S.$17 million by 1991. They created clinics and health centers throughout the country. In rural areas family planning services are integrated with comprehensive primary health care programs; the workers in these centers are recruited and trained locally, so that they understand the mentality of the local people. Condoms and pills are available gratis, and a variety of newer methods are also offered. Sterilization of both men and women is encouraged.[35] Evidently, some *'ulamā'* (Islamic scholars), including Ayatollah Ali Khamene'i, have permitted both tubal ligation and vasectomies on the grounds that they might be reversible. Abortions, although technically illegal, are easy to obtain on grounds of preserving maternal health. In fact, in 1973 Ayatollah Mohammad Hossein Beheshti stated that they were licit before one hundred twenty days (or ensoulment).[36]

The government has instituted a powerful public information campaign. One important theme stresses the need for Iran to be independent in food resources. Another important theme emphasizes the issue of quality of children—the notion that it is better for a couple to have one or two well-fed, clothed, housed, and educated children than to have many who need more than their parents can provide. Yet another theme is that women should have only a few children, preferably when they are between the ages of twenty and thirty-five, in order to preserve their health.[37] These themes, as well as specifics about family planning, are promulgated on radio and television, on public billboards, and in Friday sermons. Couples planning to marry are required to attend family planning classes before obtaining a marriage license. University and secondary school students must take courses in family planning. Information is offered in adult literacy classes and in separate classes for men and women at their places of employment. Every July, Population Week is observed in conjunction with the United Nations Population Day on July 11. Indeed, it is the provision of public information and debate, and the close collaboration between political and religious leaders, that affords one of the major contrasts between the monarchy's family planning efforts and those of the Islamic Republic.[38]

The Republican government also established several disincentives to prevent large families. Since 1993, it has provided no subsidized day care for women employees, no paid maternity leave for women having a fourth or subsequent child, no further food coupons, and no subsidies for health insurance for fourth or subsequent children.[39] A last element of the government's population control program is the collection, analysis, and systematic use of information about population issues. On the eve of the program's inception in 1989, demographers collected data from a baseline survey, and they have carried out additional surveys since then.

From 1989 to 1992, the number of women using a contraceptive method had nearly doubled, from 36 percent to 65 percent. Predictably, more urban than rural women were practicing contraception. Nearly three-quarters of women with four or more children were practicing contraception. A 1991 population survey showed that Iran's population had reached 55.8 million, indicating that the population had increased by 2.5 percent between 1986 and 1991, a decline from the 1976–1986 rate of 3.4 percent. The country's family planning program is partly responsible for these changes, although other factors, such as higher levels of education and rising standards and costs of living, have also played an important role.[40] Unfortunately, much still needs to be done. A recent survey found that about one-third of all pregnancies were unwanted by one or both parents, and that about one-quarter of those pregnant women had been using oral contraceptives. Iran's population is expected to reach 90 million by 2025 or sooner.[41]

In 1992, at the Earth Summit held in Rio de Janeiro, Iran presented a detailed report which not only described the current state of its environment but also detailed ways for maintaining and improving it. Up to now, however, the links between population and development have been more evident to policymakers than the links between population and environment.[42]

Egypt

Under the Regime of Gamal Abdel Nasser (1952–1970)

Although demographers realized the need for population control in Egypt as far back as the 1930s, no policy favoring family planning was announced until 1953, when the revolutionary government of the Free Officers established a National Council for Population Affairs. Unfortunately, because politicians and experts were divided on the issue of whether national development would slow population growth, or whether rapid population growth would retard national development, the government adopted a neutral policy. It did, however, open a few experimental clinics with access limited to women whose husbands gave them permission to attend and who already had large families.[43] Environmental concerns seem not to have been a priority at this time.

The 1961 National Charter, announced after Nasser's government adopted a socialist orientation, forthrightly regarded a high population growth rate as a hindrance to development. During the 1960s the government opened more family planning clinics and removed the restrictions on access. In 1965, it established the Supreme National Council for Family Planning, headed by the prime minister and including other government ministers and the president of the central statistical office.[44] Basically, throughout the 1960s, policymakers operated on the assumption that married couples were already interested in family planning, and consequently all that needed to be done was to supply the means for contraception. Abortion services, however, were not provided. In other words, their approach was technology based and did not seek to address people's motivations for their reproductive behavior. This philosophy was consistent with that advocated at the time by international bodies such as the Population Council.[45]

However, Egyptian authorities did make some attempt to promote a positive view of family planning. Both the *shaykh al-azhar* (head of the al-Azhar seminary) and the grand mufti of Egypt published *fatwa*s permitting family planning. These and interviews with them were published in newspapers and religious magazines. Government preachers were instructed to follow the lead of the country's religious leaders, but most of them failed to cooperate, continuing to oppose family planning as against religion.[46]

Both the total fertility rate and the crude birthrate dropped from 1965 to 1972, from 6.8 percent to 5.5 percent and 41.7 per thousand to 34.4 per thousand, respectively. The rate of crude natural increase dropped from 27.6 per thousand to 19.9 per thousand during the same period. However, it seems that the rate of contraceptive usage increased only slightly during this period. Evidently, the fall in fertility owed more to the wars which took place in 1967 and in 1973, and to a severe recession, and less to any effects of government policy.[47]

During the Regime of Anwar al-Sadat (1970–1981)

Under Sadat's government, the philosophy of Egypt's family planning policies changed. Now the guiding concept was the belief that social and economic development would motivate couples to reduce their fertility. The government would play an essentially passive role in promoting birth control, although it would provide family planning services to meet the expected demand. The reason for this change in emphasis was political: Sadat needed the political support of conservative religious organizations, such as the Muslim Brotherhood, who opposed family planning.[48] The Muslim Brotherhood held that God would provide food for all Egyptians, advocated both patriarchy and polygyny, and called for women to return to the home as wives and mothers.[49]

During Sadat's tenure, birthrates in Egypt rose. The new laissez-faire policies may have had some effect on fertility, as did the end of the 1973 war. Also, the *infitāḥ* (open door) economic policy raised per capita incomes, emigrant remittances provided many families with new funds, and most women continued to be housewives rather than members of the labor force.[50] By 1985, shortly after Sadat's assassination, the rate of natural increase (births minus deaths) had risen to 30.4 per thousand; in 1983 the total fertility rate was 5.3, the same as in 1976.[51]

Although Sadat had originally cultivated the support of the Muslim Brotherhood and other religious groups, eventually the Islamists and the government broke over a number of issues: the peace treaty with Israel in 1979, political corruption, moral decadance, inflation, and political repression. Members of a small Islamist group, Takfir wal-Hijra, assassinated Sadat in 1981.

During the Regime of Husni Mubarak (1981–Present)

Thanks to the *infitāḥ* policy, the decline in oil prices and revenues, and a reduction in tourism, the Egyptian economy began to falter in the mid-1980s. It became evident to policymakers that the high fertility rates of the previous decade could not continue without bankrupting the country. Early in 1985, the government established the National Population Council. It gave highest priority to family planning on the national level. Demographic research, sponsored by the council, became important. Policies continued to emphasize the provision and expansion of family planning services, just as they had during Sadat's regime. Also, policies favored the provision of modern contraceptive technology, such as pills or IUDs, rather than promoting traditional contraceptive methods, such as prolonged lactation, which have been effective in other Muslim countries.[52] However, determined efforts were now made to induce couples to limit the number of offspring.[53]

These efforts, while noncoercive in nature, included the following: widely publicized and broadcast speeches by President Mubarak and other high government officials which emphasized the need for family planning; articles by journalists describing the negative results of too-rapid population growth; sermons by government preachers and *fatwa*s, interviews, and articles by Muslim and Christian religious leaders which emphasized the compatibility of religion and family planning; newspaper cartoons, posters and billboards; and short films and commercials on television.[54] They did not, however, address the all-important issue of the age of women at marriage, which continues to be low.[55]

In contrast to Iranian policies, however, Egyptian family planning policies lacked strong incentives. President Mubarak and his ministers resisted suggestions to offer bonuses to men for sterilization or to withhold education and health services to fourth or higher order children. Partly this was because they believed that such proposals would contradict the constitution. Also, they did not want to lose political support among the poor and working-class masses. Finally, there were many contradictions and loopholes in Egyptian laws and social policies which either rewarded large families or tolerated deviance from the law; for example, laws against underage brides and the employment of child labor were widely ignored with impunity.[56]

Several bureaucratic factors have contributed to the ineffectiveness of Egyptian population policies. One is budgetary: for example, for 1988–1989, the government's share of the family planning budget was only 0.5 percent of its total social services budget and 3.1 percent of its public health budget (the remaining family planning expenses were paid by NGOs, international agencies, and the like).[57]

Jurisdictional conflicts among government agencies responsible for implementing family planning programs have seriously impeded implementation. The Ministry of Population has no authority over the other agencies involved with population issues. Moreover, the Ministry of Population, the Ministry of Health, and the Ministry of Social Affairs have long been involved in power conflicts, and these extend to the grassroots level. Generally speaking, in fact, so many agencies are involved in family planning that any sense of accountability is nowhere to be found.[58]

Additionally, from the president[59] on down, government officials have tended to minimize the importance of family planning.[60] In 1993, nearly seven hundred individuals involved in family planning policy-making and implementation were surveyed in a research project designed to explore the limited success of Egypt's family planning initiatives. In interviews with cabinet-level executives, only four out of twenty-two spontaneously mentioned population issues as major national problems. When queried, few put them toward the top of the list, and some even claimed that population issues were only an excuse for the failure of other state policies.[61] Executives responsible for the implementation of population policies on the governorate level were more likely than national-level executives spontaneously to mention the importance of family planning, but over half of them, even when specifically asked, denied that population issues were important. They may comply with directives from Cairo, but do not support or accept national policies.[62]

Finally, physicians and social workers from local family planning units were interviewed; these individuals, younger than their superiors in Cairo or the governorate capital, are the ones who are actually responsible for delivering family planning services to couples and individuals. Three-fourths of the physicians failed to mention population as a problem, although three-fourths of the social workers did. Even when prompted, few of the physicians put population problems on their lists of national issues. Interviewers noted that many of the young physicians wore Islamic dress, and that many put issues such as corruption, lack of moral values, and Western conspiracies high on their lists of problems facing Egypt.[63] Although medical training in Egypt, as elsewhere, tends to emphasize technical problems rather than social issues, it should also be noted that the Muslim Brotherhood—and probably other Islamist groups as well—recruits heavily among physicians and other professionals.[64] The result is that well over half of those directly responsible for delivering family planning services do not believe that population issues are important.

In the population issues survey, local *imāms* (preachers) in both government and private mosques in middle-class and working-class areas tended not to support government family planning policies, which they equated with birth control and believed to be incompatible with Islam. The nongovernmental *imāms* in fact preached against birth control and suggested compassion on the part of others and patience on the part of parents as the only acceptable solutions to the problems of couples with large families. On the positive side, local community leaders were much more supportive of family planning, although often critical of government efforts. Women, too, the primary targets of family planning efforts, were supportive of family planning. Nearly all of the women in their reproductive years (fifteen to forty-nine) who were surveyed had heard of family planning methods and supported them; about 85 percent had used family planning methods, and about 40 percent were regular users of contraceptive methods. More than any other group surveyed, they believed that overcrowding and other population problems were significant issues for the country.[65] In fact, women tend to desire fewer children than do their husbands, although the latter have more influence on the final decision.[66]

Despite the weakness of Egypt's population policies and the many significant problems with their implementation, it is encouraging that in the past decade Egyptian fertility rates have been declining. The total fertility rate was 5.3 in 1979–1980, 3.9 in 1990–1992, and then 3.6 in 1991–1993. Predictions for future total fertility rates made by Egyptian demographers range from 2.0 to 2.6 children per woman by the period 2016–2021. On the basis of these, plus continuing changes in mortality rates, they project a total population for 2021 ranging from 83,290,000 to 91,695,000.[67]

A number of reasons have been adduced to explain the decline in Egyptian fertility. One of these is the state of the Egyptian economy. Since the mid-1980s, inflation, declines in national revenues, declines in wages and emigrant remittances, and liberalization of the economy have all made large families a much heavier burden on parents. As Philippe Fargues has shown, birthrates since 1970 have closely tracked wages, emigrant remittances, and construction activity (a measure of prosperity).[68]

Another important factor appears to be women's education, which generally is inversely associated with their fertility. By the mid-1980s, most Egyptian women of reproductive age were literate, and many were university graduates.[69] A number of reasons associated with the women themselves may explain that negative correlation. Educated women are more likely to be employed and hence valued for reasons in addition to their roles as mothers; their income gives them more power in family decision making. They are more likely to know their rights, and more likely to be in control of many aspects of their lives.

A number of reasons may be associated with the children who are being educated: reduction of the child's potential as a worker; increased schooling costs; the child becomes a dependent; schooling speeds cultural change (including adopting the ideal of smaller families); and schooling introduces Western values (including secularism and individualism versus familism).[70] All of these are likely to create societal trends toward smaller family size. When Kimberly Faust and her colleagues surveyed secondary school students in Cairo, they found that all of these, except the acceptance of Western values, were true of their sample. Although their respondents had many nontraditional values, they still valued motherhood very highly, thought that love would grow after marriage, and believed that their parents had more influence on them than did their teachers or other nonrelatives. Faust and her colleagues concluded that, because Egyptian public schools in recent years have included a strong Islamic curriculum, many traditional values will continue to be inculcated rather than challenged in the schools; these values might well retard the diminution of family size.[71]

Government and Islamists in Contention

And so we return to politics in contemporary Egypt. Today, the two major political forces are the government and the Islamist opposition, both contending for political power and control of public opinion. The government, since Sadat's break with the Muslim Brotherhood and other Islamist groups, has tried to contain the Islamist challenge through two major ways: concession and repression. In 1976, the constitution was amended to state that the *sharī'a* was one of the sources of Egyptian legislation, and in 1981 to state that it was the only basis for legislation.[72] The Muslim Brotherhood was once more accepted in the political arena. In publications and on state television, it and other religious organizations began to call yet more publicly for a return to Islamic values. More and more women, including university and secondary school students, began to wear *hijāb*. New mosques, including some seventy thousand private mosques, have been established throughout the country. State television now broadcasts the call to prayer five times a day.[73] Al-Azhar, the state Islamic university, became more prestigious and powerful culturally. And, religion was added to the curriculum in the elementary and secondary schools; some schools, in fact, were more or less taken over by the Islamists.[74]

Repression has been the other means pursued by the government in its attempts to weaken the Islamist challenge. Groups other than the Muslim Brotherhood—which, having eschewed violence and illegal means of changing the government is considered to be both moderate and legitimate—are put down ruthlessly; this is especially true of violent groups such as the Gama'a al-Islamiyya, which has been responsible for attacks on tourists, United Nations personnel, and police. Militants have been imprisoned, tortured, and executed by government forces, and even their families have been harassed.[75]

Thus far, the Egyptian government remains in charge. Whether it will remain so, as Fouad Ajami asserts, or whether it will follow the shah's path into defeat through Islamic revolution, remains uncertain.

As we saw above, the government's family planning policies and their implementation have been severely weakened by lack of conviction and will on the part of government ministers, executives, and physicians, inadequate budgets, and interagency rivalries. However, since the time of Nasser the government has been on record as supporting family planning, has delivered a variety of programs, and has obtained support from high religious authorities. These include Shaykh Jād al-Haqq (1979), then grand imam of al-Azhar; Shaykh Sayyid al-Tantawi (1988), then mufti of Egypt; and even the very conservative Shaykh Muhammad Sha'arawi (1980), scholar, television star, and minister of *awqāf* (religious foundations) under Sadat.

The Islamist opposition considers the government to be un-Islamic and hence illegitimate. Central to its project of cultural authenticity are women, who should act in all ways as proper Muslims, accepting their God-given differences from men, remaining home as good wives, and above all passing on the "straight way" to their children.[76] Islamists, in Egypt and elsewhere, are very concerned about Western economic, political, and cultural hegemony; this includes the still acceptable (to the Egyptian government) Muslim Brotherhood. Thus, if Western-dominated institutions, such as the United Nations or the Population Council are concerned about population growth in Egypt, it is because they want to weaken the Muslim nation by reducing the number of Muslims. Moreover, it is blasphemous to suggest that couples should limit the size of their families, because God will provide; one should not doubt His mercy and benevolence.

Given these beliefs, it is not surprising that members of Islamist groups and representatives of conservative Muslim governments often reacted negatively to the initial draft of the 1994 United Nations Conference on Population and Development held in Cairo, and even to the very fact of the conference itself. A leading member of the Muslim Brotherhood said, "What is wrong with big families? My own opinion is this: A big family is much better than a small family. It gives a very good chance to bring up children well, to give them a good education in traditions, to reduce selfishness." "All the family-planning policy here in Egypt is planned and financed by the Americans." "The responsible way to stop the population problem is to make development and create jobs. So we can welcome the newcomers, not kill them."[77]

Saudi Arabia, Lebanon, Sudan, and Iraq boycotted the conference altogether; neither Lebanon nor Iraq is known for its official religious conservatism, but both had to deal with complex internal situations. Pakistan's and Turkey's prime ministers, both women under pressure from conservative forces, did not attend, although their countries still sent delegations.[78] The objections religious conservatives, Muslims as well as the Catholic Church, had with the conference draft document were in part that it seemed to condone extramarital sexuality and promote sex education for adolescents outside of the family; sex education evidently was viewed as teaching young people both to desire sex and how to practice it.[79]

Summary, Discussion, and Conclusion

Both Egypt and Iran have long traditions of pronatalist attitudes and practices. For centuries, nearly everyone married, women married young, and large numbers of children were eagerly desired. High infant and child mortality rates offset high birthrates, so that populations remained stable. Families were able, barely, to meet their political and economic labor needs. Means of contraception were known, and condoned by religious scholars, but not generally practiced.

Well before the middle of the twentieth century, mortality rates began to fall, thanks to improved public health and nutrition. The result was that population growth began to pose a threat both to national development and to the environment. It was not until the 1960s, however, that the Egyptian and Iranian governments began, rather cautiously, to declare and implement family planning policies.

During the 1970s, conservative Muslim movements began to be significant political forces in both Egypt and Iran. In Iran, they were able to overthrow the government in 1979, but they have not succeeded in doing so in Egypt. Initially, the Islamists in Iran opposed family planning, but by the late 1980s the twin realities of rapid population growth and a badly damaged economic infrastructure required them to embrace family planning. To their credit, they have done this with commitment and competence. Moreover, although the Islamist forces in Iran continue to control the government, a split has become evident between older, more conservative forces and younger, more liberal forces; the rapid population growth occasioned by the Islamic Republic's original policies not only created a population which was very youthful but also one which knew only the Islamic Republican system. In this context young Islamic feminists challenge hegemonic interpretations of gender roles.[80]

The Islamists in Egypt, on the other hand, continue to oppose family planning. Even though leading Egyptian muftis and shaykhs have condoned family planning, Islamist spokesmen believe that family planning is a Western device to reduce the number of Muslims in the world, and that national development will solve any problems that might be caused by overpopulation.

As we have seen, Egyptian married women in their reproductive years are more likely than other segments of the population to support family planning. They are, of course, the ones who have to deal with the day-to-day practical family issues. Women of all ages, not excluding students and young working women, have also been drawn to the Islamists. Zaynab al-Ghazali, a leading figure in the Muslim Brotherhood and its women's auxiliary since the 1930s, advocated a model of family life and gender relations not unlike that promulgated by the

Christian Right in the United States—a model characterized by husband-wife intimacy, patriarchy, and devotion to motherhood and housekeeping.[81] Such a model might entail a large family, but not necessarily so.

A survey of veiled and unveiled students at Cairo University found that, as expected, the veiled students were more traditional and less feminist than the unveiled students. However, both groups had a lot in common, supporting women's rights to education, labor-force participation and professional work, and political equality. Even in marriage, a substantial number of the veiled women believed in equality of rights. The veiled students often had a rather vague idea of what was entailed by the *sharī'a* they advocated, but clearly were drawn to Islam's call for justice and equality.[82] Like their Iranian counterparts, young Egyptian women Islamists are challenging traditional interpretations of Islamic teachings on gender roles.

Despite the many similarities Egypt and Iran share as Middle Eastern Muslim countries, when it comes to family planning a real difference exists. Iran's Islamist government today is committed to family planning in word and deed. Egypt's government has officially proclaimed a family planning policy, but its commitment and implementation have been weak and erratic. The Islamist opposition is officially opposed to family planning. Why do Egypt and Iran differ?

The answer, we conclude, is twofold. First, and most significantly, the Islamists control the government in Iran. They are the opposition in Egypt. In Iran they are responsible and accountable for the consequences of policies and their implementation. They have to deal with the results of their actions. In Egypt, on the other hand, the situation is different. While it is true that many of the Islamist critiques of the Egyptian government are just, it must also be said that many ideas advocated by Egyptian Islamists are vague and utopian. After all, they are only criticizing the government; they are not running it. That makes all the difference.

Second, there appear to be more bureaucratic problems associated with the implementation of family planning policies in Egypt. First, Presidents Nasser, Sadat, and Mubarak all have evinced a rather weak commitment to family planning. Nasser believed that socialism and national development would solve any problems caused by overpopulation and would induce couples to want fewer children. Sadat and Mubarak tried to appease the Islamists; by doing so they weakened numerous policies, laws, regulations, and government activities relating to gender and family. As Saad Eddin Ibrahim found, the lack of commitment at the top spread to the very grassroots of the family planning agencies.[83]

Although both Egypt and Iran have many of the bureaucratic problems common to Third World countries, such as corruption and lack of accountability,[84] it would appear that Egypt's bureaucratic problems are even worse. For many years, Egypt has not only admitted all qualified secondary school graduates to university, but has later on given them employment in the civil service.[85] Thus, its bureaucracy has far too many employees, making accountability problems even more severe. The tasks of coordinating multiple agencies charged with delivering family planning services, interagency rivalries, and the lack of commitment at all bureaucratic levels combine to produce a serious weakness in Egypt's family planning programs.[86] The post-revolutionary Iranian bureaucracy, despite its weaknesses, is committed to equality, justice, and service to the poor and oppressed. Citizens are free to criticize the bureaucracy. Government agencies are overseen by a variety of bodies, including local Islamic societies. Prime Minister Moussavi has attempted to make the civil service more efficient and better organized.[87] It would seem that the Iranian national bureaucracy is more accountable to the citizens it is supposed to serve than is the Egyptian civil service.

One might argue, too, that greater charisma inheres in the Iranian bureaucracy, and thus citizens are more likely to comply with government policies than might be the case in Egypt. Our logic, very briefly, is this: for Shi'ites, Ali and the *imāms* (in this case, not preachers but leaders of the entire Muslim community) who succeeded him inherited Muhammad's charisma. With the disappearance of the last *imām* in 874 C.E., that authority eventually devolved upon the *'ulamā'*. By the nineteenth century, the Shi'ite *'ulamā'* in Iran had not only established a centralized hierarchy, but they also legitimized the monarchy. With the Islamic revolution of 1979 and the institutionalization of the *velāyat-e faqīh* (state guided by a supreme religious authority), religious leaders and local Islamic councils came to oversee all levels of the Iranian bureaucracy. In a sense, then, Muhammad's charisma may be said to extend across the entire state.[88]

Sunnite Islam historically developed a very different relationship between the religious establishment and the state. Four distinct legal traditions developed; although all are equally legitimate, one tends to dominate in a given region or country. Most of the clergy and jurists became government functionaries, at least in areas under control by the state. Since the nineteenth century, Sunnite Muslim states, including the Egyptian one, have gradually extended their control over religious education, jurists, preachers, and pious foundations. However, government management of the religious establishment never led to the creation of any centralized religious hierarchy comparable to the one that developed in nineteenth-century Iran. Thus, in modern Egypt, alongside the system of government schools, preachers, and mosques, there exist private mosques, religious schools, and preachers. Added to this we see the growing role of religion as critic of government since the October War of 1973. Thus, it is not possible for religion to be a source of legitimacy or charisma for Egyptian government agencies and their policies, even when leading religious figures issue *fatwa*s or make public pronouncements of support.

It is our conclusion that one cannot discuss Islam and family planning, Islam and the environment, or indeed Islam and any other topic without taking into account the larger political, social, cultural, economic, and historical contexts. The divergent courses of family planning policies and programs in Egypt and Iran show us that most plainly.

We further conclude that we need more empirical case studies of the relationships among population, environment, and economic development in Muslim countries. If development is to be sustainable for future generations, then quality of life must be assured by attention both to the environment and to the number of people who live in it.[89] In these case studies, we must not only examine and apply Islamic precepts, but we must also scrutinize policies and behaviors to see whether they adhere to those precepts, or exist independently of them. Up to now, evidence[90] suggests that not only have development needs taken priority over environmental issues in Muslim countries, but that both Muslim scholars and Muslim policymakers have not studied carefully economic development and environmental issues within the framework of Islamic beliefs.

Notes

1. Al-Hafiz B. A. Masri, "Islam and Ecology," in *Islam and Ecology*, ed. Fazlun Khalid with Joanne O'Brien, (London: Cassell, 1992), 1–24.

2. Carla Makhlouf Obermeyer, "Religious Doctrine, State Ideology, and Reproductive Options in Islam," in *Power and Decision: The Social Control of Reproduction*, ed. Gita Sen and Rachel C. Snow (Cambridge, Mass.: Harvard School of Public Health, 1994), 59–75; and idem, "Reproductive Choice in Islam: Gender and State in Iran and Tunisia," *Studies in Family Planning* 25, no. 1 (1994): 41–51.

3. Joseph Chamie, *Religion and Fertility: Arab Christian-Muslim Differentials* (Cambridge: Cambridge University Press, 1981).

4. Mahasen M. Mostafa, *Population, Development and Environmental Policies in Egypt*, CDC Series on Population and Development, 4 (Cairo: Cairo Demographic Center, 1994); Miriam Horn, "The Vanishing Past: Soot, Water, and War are Costing the World Its Treasures," *US News and World Report* 113, no. 11 (21 September 1992): 80–87.

5. Seid Zekavat, "The State of the Environment in Iran," in *Challenging Environmental Issues: Middle Eastern Perspectives*, ed. Joseph G. Jabbra and Nancy W. Jabbra (Leiden: E. J. Brill, 1997), 56–66.

6. Kim Murphy, "180 Nations Adopt Population Plan," *Los Angeles Times*, 14 September 1994, A13; idem, "Conference Safety a Priority in Cairo," *Los Angeles Times*, 3 September 1994, A9.

7. Madelain Farah, *Marriage and Sexuality in Islam: A Translation of al-Ghazālī's Book on the Etiquette of Marriage from the Iḥyā'* (Salt Lake City: University of Utah Press, 1984), 47–77.

8. See the extended discussion of this point in Abdel Rahim Omran, *Family Planning in the Legacy of Islam* (London: Routledge, 1992), 113–42).

9. Ibid., 171.

10. Ibid., 171–72.

11. Ibid., 59–69.

12. Basim F. Musallam, *Sex and Society in Islam: Birth Control Before the Nineteenth Century* (Cambridge: Cambridge University, 1983).

13. Omran, *Family Planning in the Legacy of Islam*, 190–93.

14. Abul Fadl Mohsin Ebrahim, *Abortion, Birth Control, and Surrogate Parenting: An Islamic Perspective* (Indianapolis: American Trust Publications, 1989), 95–100.

15. Omran, *Family Planning in the Legacy of Islam*, 187–90; Ebrahim, *Abortion, Birth Control, and Surrogate Parenting*, 28–33.

16. Muhammad Faour, "Fertility Policy and Family Planning in the Arab Countries," *Studies in Family Planning* 20, no. 5 (1989): 254–55.

17. Haleh Afshar, "Women and Reproduction in Iran," in *Woman—Nation—State*, ed. Nira Yuval-Davis and Floya Anthias (New York: St. Martin's Press, 1989), 117–18; Marcia C. Inhorn, "Population, Poverty, and Gender Politics: Motherhood Pressures and Marital Crises in the Lives of Poor Urban Egyptian Women," in *Population, Poverty, and Politics in Middle East Cities*, ed. Michael E. Bonine (Gainesville: University Press of Florida, 1997), 193–203.

18. Akbar Aghajanian, "Family Planning and Contraceptive Use in Iran, 1967–1992," *International Family Planning Perspectives* 20, no. 2 (1994): 66.

19. Zekavat, "The State of the Environment in Iran," 51.

20. Aghajanian, "Family Planning and Contraceptive Use," 66.

21. Hamideh Sedghi, "Women, the State, and Development: Appraising Secular and Religious Gender Politics in Iran," in *The Gendered New World Order: Militarism, Development, and the Environment*, ed. Jennifer Turpin and Lois Ann Lorentzen (New York: Routledge, 1996), 115–17; Afshar, "Women and Reproduction in Iran," 114–16.

22. Aghajanian, "Family Planning and Contraceptive Use," 66–67; Ali A. Paydarfar and Reza Moini, "Modernization Process and Fertility Change in Pre- and Post-Islamic Revolution of Iran: A Cross-Provincial Analysis, 1966–1986," *Population Research and Policy Review* 14, no. 1 (1995): 79–80.

23. Valentine M. Moghadam, *Modernizing Women: Gender and Social Change in the Middle East* (Boulder, Colo.: Lynne Rienner Publishers, 1993), 88–91, 141–43.

24. Afshar, "Women and Reproduction in Iran," 118–23.

25. Homa Hoodfar, "Population Policy and Gender Equity in Post-Revolutionary Iran," in *Family, Gender, and Population in the Middle East: Policies in Context*, ed. Carla Makhlouf Obermeyer (Cairo: American University in Cairo Press, 1995), 108–9; Moghadam, *Modernizing Women*, 175.

26. Hoodfar, "Population Policy and Gender Equity," 108; Aghajanian, "Family Planning and Contraceptive Use," 67.

27. The crude birthrate represents the number of births per thousand of population as counted at the year's midpoint. The total fertility rate is a much more refined measure. It is basically an estimate of the number of children one thousand women would bear throughout their reproductive years (that is, ages fifteen to forty-nine). It is based upon the actual numbers of children born in a single year to all women across the reproductive age span. The figures in the text have been divided by one thousand to yield the average per woman.

28. Aghajanian, "Family Planning and Contraceptive Use," 66–67.

29. James A. Bill and Robert Springborg, *Politics in the Middle East*, 4th ed. (New York: Harper-Collins, 1994), 386; Hooshang Amirahmadi, "War Damage and Reconstruction in the Islamic Republic of Iran," in *Post-Revolutionary Iran*, ed. Hooshang Amirahmadi and Manoucher Parvin (Boulder, Colo.: Westview Press, 1988), 130.

30. Hoodfar, "Population Policy and Gender Equity," 109.

31. Zekavat, "The State of the Environment in Iran," 53.

32. Aghajanian, "Family Planning and Contraceptive Use," 67.

33. Hoodfar, "Population Policy and Gender Equity," 109.

34. Aghajanian, "Family Planning and Contraceptive Use," 68.

35. Ibid.

36. Hoodfar, "Population Policy and Gender Equity," 111–12; Robin Wright, "Iran's Population-Control Programs are User-Friendly," *Los Angeles Times*, 10 May 1998, A1, A20; Yasmin L. Mossaver-Rahmani, "Family Planning in Post-Revolutionary Iran," in *Women and Revolution in Iran*, ed. Guity Nashat (Boulder, Colo.: Westview Press, 1983), 258–59.

37. Hoodfar, "Population Policy and Gender Equity," 110–13.

38. Ibid., 113; Wright, "Iran's Population-Control Programs"; Aghajanian, "Family Planning and Contraceptive Use," 68.

39. Aghajanian, "Family Planning and Contraceptive Use," 68.

40. Ibid.

41. Wright, "Iran's Population-Control Program," A20.

42. Zekavat, "The State of the Environment in Iran," 55–56, 69–70.

43. Philippe Fargues, "State Policies and the Birth Rate in Egypt: From Socialism to Liberalism," *Population and Development Review* 23, no. 1 (1997): 115–18.

44. Ibid.

45. Gad Gilbar, *Population Dilemmas in the Middle East: Essays in Political Demography and Economy* (London: Frank Cass, 1997), 117–18.

46. Ibid., 118.

47. Ibid., 118–19.

48. Ibid., 119; Abd al-Monein Said Aly and Manfred W. Wenner, "Modern Islamic Reform Movements: The Muslim Brotherhood in Contemporary Egypt," *Middle East Journal* 36 (1982): 342–48.

49. Raymond A. Hinnebusch, Jr., *Egyptian Politics under Sadat: The Post-Populist Development of an Authoritarian-Modernizing State*, updated ed. (Boulder, Colo.: Lynne Rienner Publishers, 1988), 201.

50. Fargues, "State Policies and the Birth Rate in Egypt," 121–26; Youssef Courbage, "L'imprévisible fecondité égyptienne," *Population* 44, no. 1-3 (1994): 214–16.

51. Gilbar, *Population Dilemmas in the Middle East*, 120.

52. Youssef Courbage, "La politique démographique en Égypte et son évaluation: Que nous apprenent les enquêtes récentes?" *Population* 49, no. 4-5 (1994): 1052–53.

53. Gilbar, *Population Dilemmas in the Middle East*, 120.

54. Ibid., 121–28.

55. Courbage, "La politique démographique," 1053–54.

56. Gilbar, *Population Dilemmas in the Middle East*, 128–29; Courbage, "L'imprévisible fecondité égyptienne," 216.

57. Gilbar, *Population Dilemmas in the Middle East*, 129–30.

58. Saad Eddin Ibrahim, "State, Women, and Civil Society: An Evaluation of Egypt's Population Policy," in *Family, Gender, and Population in the Middle East: Policies in Context*, ed. Carla Makhlouf Obermeyer (Cairo: The American University in Cairo Press, 1995), 75.

59. Since the early 1990s, President Mubarak has shown more interest in population issues, thanks to publicity from the 1994 United Nations Conference on Population and Development, which was held in Cairo, and to pressures from the IMF and various international agencies and organizations. Whether and how his greater interest will be translated into stronger and more effective policies remains to be seen (Ibrahim, "State, Women, and Civil Society," 65–67).

60. Courbage, "L'imprévisible fecondité égyptienne," 213–14; Georgia Lee Kangas, *Population and Survival: The Challenge in Five Countries* (New York: Praeger, 1984), 162–63.

61. Ibrahim, "State, Women, and Civil Society," 64–67.

62. Ibid., 67–68.

63. Ibid., 68–69.

64. Aly and Wenner, "Modern Islamic Reform Movements," 353.

65. Ibrahim, "State, Women, and Civil Society," 72–74.

66. Hassan H. M. Zaky, "Profile of Men's and Women's Fertility Preferences in Egypt," in *Perspectives on Fertility and Family Planning in Egypt: Results of Further Analysis of the 1992 Egypt Demographic and Health Survey* (Cairo: National Population Council, 1995), 59–64.

67. Hesham Makhlouf, Saad Zaghloul, and Ferial A. Ahmed, *Population Projections for Socioeconomic Development in Egypt* (Cairo: Cairo Demographic Center, 1994), 14–15.

68. Fargues, "State Policies and the Birth Rate in Egypt," 125–28.

69. Ibid., 126; Courbage, "La politique démographique," 1049–51.

70. Kimberly Faust et al., "Mass Education, Islamic Revival, and the Population Problem in Egypt," *Journal of Comparative Family Studies* 22 (1991): 333–37.

71. Ibid., 337–39.

72. Mervat Hatem, "Secularist and Islamist Discourses on Modernity in Egypt and the Evolution of the Postcolonial Nation-State," in *Islam, Gender, and Social Change*, ed. Yvonne Yazbeck Haddad and John L. Esposito (New York: Oxford University Press, 1998), 91–92.

73. Murphy, "180 Nations Adopt Population Plan," 30.

74. Fouad Ajami, "The Sorrows of Egypt," *Foreign Affairs* 74, no. 5 (1995): 72–89.

75. Kim Murphy, "Martyr, Schoolgirl, Soldier, Terrorist: The Battle for Egypt," *Los Angeles Times Magazine*, 17 November 1994, 30, 34; Ajami, "The Sorrows of Egypt."

76. Hatem, "Secularist and Islamist Discourses," 92–97.

77. Kim Murphy, "Summit's Family-Planning Strategies Worry Muslims," *Los Angeles Times*, 27 August 1994, A1.

78. Christine Gorman et al., "Clash of Wills in Cairo," *Time*, 12 September 1994, 56.

79. Kim Murphy, "U.N. Delegates Tackle Tough Issue of Youth, Sex," *Los Angeles Times*, 11 September 1994, A10.

80. Afsaneh Najmabadi, "Feminism in an Islamic Republic: 'Years of Hardship, Years of Growth,' " in *Islam, Gender, and Social Change*, ed. Yvonne Yazbeck Haddad and John L. Esposito (New York: Oxford University Press, 1998), 59–84.

81. Hatem, "Secularist and Islamist Discourses," 95–97.

82. Leila Ahmed, *Women and Gender in Islam: Historical Roots of a Modern Debate* (New Haven: Yale University Press, 1992), 222–30.

83. Ibrahim, "State, Women, and Civil Society."

84. Joseph G. Jabbra, "Public Service Accountability in the Arab World: The Cases of Lebanon, Egypt and Saudi Arabia," in *Public Service Accountability: A Comparative Perspective*, ed. Joseph G. Jabbra and O. P. Dwivedi (West Hartford, Ct.: Kumarian Press, 1988), 181–200.

85. Monte Palmer, Ali Leila, and El Sayed Yassin, *The Egyptian Bureaucracy* (Syracuse, N.Y.: Syracuse University Press, 1988), 38–41.

86. Ibrahim, "State, Women, and Civil Society."

87. Ali Farazmand, *The State, Bureaucracy, and Revolution in Modern Iran: Agrarian Reforms and Regime Politics* (New York: Praeger, 1989), 166–96.

88. Hamid Dabashi, *Authority in Islam: From the Rise of Muhammad to the Establishment of the Umayyads* (New Brunswick, N.J.: Transaction Publishers, 1989), 1–16, 95–120; Said Amir Arjomand, "Introduction: Shi'ism, Authority, and Political Culture," in *Authority and Political Culture in Shi'ism*, ed. Said Amir Arjomand (Albany: State University of New York Press, 1988), 3–7.

89. Zekavat, "The State of the Environment in Iran," 66–69; Mona A. Khalifa, *Family Planning and Sustainable Development in Egypt* (Cairo: Cairo Demographic Center, 1994), 1–3.

90. Joseph G. Jabbra, and Nancy W. Jabbra, eds., *Challenging Environmental Issues: Middle Eastern Perspectives* (Leiden: E. J. Brill, 1997).

An Ecological Journey in Muslim Bengal

MOHAMMAD YUSUF SIDDIQ

There is a popular story in the Islamic east that tells of five wise brothers who were traveling together. They arrived in a place where, all of a sudden, each one of them found he had lost inner consciousness and perception. Utterly confused and disappointed, they started wondering why this had happened. The wisest one among them, by his power of meditation and spiritual wisdom, finally found that the place itself had lost its inner life after being severely exploited for years. Thus, after becoming dead itself, it could no longer offer any spiritual enrichment or instill any life into the souls of its inhabitants.

From an Islamic point of view, the whole environment—the universe—is a living organism in its own way, every element of which is deeply engaged in worshiping the Creator.[1] There exists a strong relationship between the Creator and the creation, which achieves its perfection only when developed properly, in harmony. The Creator is manifested everywhere through His creation, a concept often expressed by Sufi saints as *waḥdat al-shuhūd* (lit., evidence of Divine Unity). A true believer, then, constantly finds testimony of divine presence everywhere in the universe. For a believer, every element of time and space reminds one of the greatness of Allah, which evokes a great sense of awe and an excitement deep within the heart that leads the believer to a peak spiritual experience and to communion with the Creator. At that point, the believer spontaneously exclaims with great wonder and surprise the glory of God by proclaiming *subḥān-Allāh* (Glory be to Allah).

In a deeper sense, Allah is the ultimate universe, being the All-Encompassing (in the Qur'an, *al-Muḥīṭ*).[2] He surrounds everything and is present everywhere (in the Qur'an, *al-Mawjūd*, meaning ever-present, a divine attribute). The ultimate reality (*al-ḥaqq*,[3] another divine attribute) of existence (*al-wujūd*) lies in the essence of divine unity, or *tawḥīd* (lit., the oneness of God)—the pivotal message of Islam—best explained in the sufi concept of *waḥdat al-wujūd* (lit., the unity of existence). Thus, in Islam, all is unity, and *al-dīn* (lit., the religion), in essence, is the return to primordial unity.

The role of natural phenomena in the Qur'an and their place in Qur'anic theology is very prominent, although this has been seldom explored as a topic in its own right.[4] According to the Qur'anic view, all the elements of the universe follow natural laws which are divine and henceforth Islamic. The Qur'an declares: "everything that exists glorifies Allah" (17:44). Pious acts and worship (*'ibāda*) help human beings come closer to nature and nurture human understanding of the delicate ecological balance and their intimate relationship with it.

The earth thus has a sacred aspect in Islam. The Prophet declared the whole of it as sacred and as clean as a mosque.[5] Therefore, the whole universe is uniquely created as a place of worship; and Muslims, wherever they may happen to be—in the jungle, on a mountain, in the desert or at sea, are bound by their religious duty to remember their Creator at least five times daily in the form of *ṣalāt* (prayer). While the mosque plays a very important role in different spheres of life in Islam, it has never been meant as the only place of worship or prayer, nor does it have any liturgical center.[6]

It is humankind which has been entrusted with the sacred responsibility of caring for the environment (*al-dunyā'* in Arabic). In the Qur'an, humankind has been made *khalīfa* (vicegerent) of the earth (Arabic, *al-arḍ*). For believers, it becomes a sacred commitment and a religious duty (Arabic, *al-amāna*) to accomplish this very important task. To every single particle of divine creation, the human being owes graciousness according to the teaching of the Prophet.[7] In the Islamic tradition, there is a popular saying: "Work for your worldly life as if you are going to survive forever, prepare for the hereafter as if you are going to die tomorrow."[8] While the final goal of *sharī'a* (the Islamic code of life) is to ensure felicity for both the individual and the community in a healthy environment and natural ecological setting in both worlds, the ultimate reward of a true believer is *janna* (garden)—the eternal peak experience of happiness—symbolically expressed as a garden that is full of life, plants, flowers, rivers, and waters in a most harmonious setting.

Beauty is a cherished quality because of its relationship with truth. The concept "beauty is truth and truth is beauty"[9] thus finds an important place in the Islamic tradition. Aesthetic perception in the ecological expression is considered an essential quality for a *mu'min* (believer) in order to understand divine beauty. The prophet Muhammad's saying, "Allah, being beautiful Himself, loves beauty,"[10] signifies the importance that Islam attaches to aesthetic perception. The origin of beauty thus has its reality in the existence of Allah, which is so magnificent that a naked human eye can not bear it. When manifested in a simpler form in divine creation, this beauty can be perceived by those who are pious, who have deep spiritual vision. Exploring this divine beauty in the universe is an integral part of religious piety, which finally leads a believer to form a close relationship with nature.

The Islamic ecological message is wonderfully expressed in Islamic art, which draws its motivation from the endless beauty in the divine creation scattered in nature. Imagining the process of creation, the rhythmic yet contrasting patterns in nature, and the uniqueness of elements in the cosmic system, is an essential duty for a believer. Lack of interest in these is compared to mental blindness (Qur'an 22:46). According to the Qur'an, it is the foremost duty of every human being to contemplate the uniqueness of the cosmic order (3:190). In Islamic culture, an artist's perception is considered a divine gift. It enables him to look minutely at nature and to see its beauty in a more comprehensive way.[11] During the course of his artistic efforts, he expands his vision of truth and soon realizes the limitations of his imaginative power and creativeness. In this process, he discovers that the origin of every form has its reference in the creation of Allah. Every creation in its original form carries the essence of pure beauty (Qur'an 32:7), which loses its original character when being copied. As the artist's perceptions grow, he realizes that the origins of every color, motif, form, and design have their realities only in the divine creation.[12] Therefore, no matter the degree of perfection the artist achieves in his art, he cannot create anything new, or of his own in a true sense. Thus, a true work of art helps a believer come closer to the cosmic truth. In the course of his artistic endeavor, he perceives his Creator with greater intimacy.

While a Muslim enjoys considerable freedom in his creative work, his Islamic objectivity means he has a positive and useful goal in his creativeness, so that it serves humanity positively. Islamic art ideally should express truth, supreme beauty, true human values, and virtuous life. In a way, it means the rejection of anything that does not lead toward positive creativity. Henceforth, Islamic life cannot be divided into profane and sacred domains. As a Muslim artist strives to reach his Islamic goal, his work of art turns into an act of devotion (expressed as *'ibāda* in the Qur'an). In his pursuit of artistic creativity, a Muslim is not supposed to cross the boundaries of natural law (*dīn al-fiṭra*). Furthermore, he is not allowed to cause any disturbance (*fasād*)[13] to the divine setting of nature (*al-fiṭra*) through excessive or unwise exploitation of natural resources or by harming the delicate ecological balance.

One of the basic teachings of Islam is the establishment of justice (*al-'adl*),[14] and a true believer is not supposed to violate the laws of justice, whatever the reason. The Islamic concept of justice is not limited to humankind, the animal world, or nature; it encompasses all spheres of life and existence. Economic justice is particularly emphasized, as it plays a central role in creating harmony and well-being in society and affects human relations with the environment and nature. A just distribution of global wealth is the key to the Islamic economic philosophy. The deprived or impoverished, who are denied basic needs, such as food, shelter, and education, are less likely to act with responsibility in caring for the ecological balance, since they will not hesitate to do anything for their own survival. Someone in a poverty-stricken village in a rural area of the Islamic world chopping trees for fuel consumption, and thus deforesting the environment, does so solely to survive. Ecological preservation is thus directly connected with economic justice on which Islam places great emphasis.

Ecological concerns thus forms an important message in Islamic culture. There are a number of basic Islamic principles that govern Islamic environmental ethics and ecological views, derived essentially from the Qur'an and the sayings of the Prophet. Some of them are:

1) There should be neither harming nor reciprocating harm.[15]

2) No damage can be put right by a similar or greater damage.[16]

3) Prevention of damage takes preference over the achievement of interests or fulfillment of needs.

4) False excuses leading to damages should be repudiated.

5) The merit of utilization lies in the benefit it yields, in proportion to its harm.[17]

6) Afforestation is highly encouraged. According to a saying of the Prophet, even if the day of judgment begins and one finds a palm shoot in his hand, one should plant it.[18]

7) While human beings are encouraged to be active and produce, consumerism as a way of life, particularly as it creates false needs, is strongly discouraged.

8) The animal world should be treated as a silent partner (*ḥaywān ghayr nāṭiq*) of humankind (*ḥaywān nāṭiq*) in this world. Animals communicate among themselves, understand each other, and even worship Allah in their own unique way and with their own capacity, which Allah has given them, though we may not comprehend that. Any act of cruelty toward animals is strongly forbidden.

9) While *jihād* (pious struggle against injustice) is permitted, imposing indiscriminate war over others is forbidden. However, in a given situation where a war cannot be avoided, civilian populations (most particularly old people, children, women, and monks) and natural resources (e.g., plants, trees, cornfields) particularly should be protected. Since weapons of mass destruction are a particular menace to all life, ecology, and the environment, they should be eliminated from the earth without any discrimination toward a particular nation or group.

10) Misuse, excessive exploitation, overconsumption (*isrāf*) and waste (*tabdhīr*) of resources are not permitted. To cite an example, the Prophet said that a person should not use more water needed, even if the source of supply is a flowing river.

Deeply imbued with these ecological messages, Islam reached the riverine deltaic region of Bengal—the gateway to rice culture—at the beginning of the thirteenth century. This was a time when Bengal was still sparsely populated, with natural forests and wilderness covering a large part of its fertile soil.[19] Although the penetration of the Aryan race and Vedic culture had begun almost fifteen hundred years earlier, a majority of the population of Bengal was still non-Aryan (called *mleccha*, or unclean barbarians, by the invading Aryans) and many of the indigenous people had not yet adopted a settled agrarian life. In addition to the Vedic religious tradition and local animistic cults, Buddhism also spread in the region prior to Islam and survived for a long time, in spite of numerous onslaughts, particularly from the Hindu ruling classes.

Much of the consolidation of Islam in the region was possible because the Islamic message was conveyed in the popular language and often used indigenous religious imagery, though not necessarily in a syncretistic form. Bengal experienced great prosperity during the rule of some of the independent Muslim sultans, whose far-reaching welfare works, such as public roads and *siqāya* (water tanks, wells), helped spread Islam to the furthest corners of the region. Institutions such as *waqf* and *madād-i-ma'āsh* (special endowment in support of living expences) benefited all commoners regardless of their religion. During the subsequent Mughal period (seventeenth and eighteenth centuries), Bengal also witnessed sustained growth in the positive utilization of its natural resources, without losing its ecological balance, and came to be considered the granary of the empire.

Islam finally emerged as the primary faith, as well as the dominant culture, of Bengal during the eighteenth century. Although there has been much speculation about the factors that led to the spread of Islam in this region, it is perhaps not an exaggeration to say that Islam entered the region as a religion close to nature (*dīn al-fiṭra*). Thus, it appealed profoundly to rural Bengalis, whose traditional lifestyle had remained very close to nature for centuries. Bengal's wonderful ecological balance and natural harmony left a strong imprint on its popular literature, art, architecture, culture, and folklore during the Sultanate and Mughal periods.

One fascinating aspect of natural harmony can be found in the traditional architecture of the Bengali mosque, which is seen as fitting within a natural setting rather than forcing itself on its surroundings. The monumental mosque architecture of the fabulous capitals—such as Gaur, Pandua, Dhaka, Murshidabad and Rajmahal—gives us a different message, as this architecture represents royal patronage and majestic taste. However, the overall nature of Islamic art and architecture in Bengal is not imposing; rather, it belongs to the natural background in its basic character. In the vast rural areas of the Bengal, simple forms of vernacular mosques are used for daily prayers—mosques that draw their architectural vocabularies from local traditions and natural settings. Typical examples are the Bengali village mosques that have thatched roofs and mud walls, somewhat similar to the original Masjid al-Nabawī (the Prophet's mosque), one of the earliest mosques in Medina. Often, natural ponds are attached to these Bengali mosques. These serve as a place of *wudhū* (ablution). These simpler places of prayer also contributed to the easy acceptance of Islam by the rural population. The vernacular architecture of the Muslim villages reminds us that the focus of Islamic architecture should not be solely on building; rather, it should be about people and their environment and ecology.

Monumental calligraphy in Muslim Bengal is another example where nature has come very close to the Islamic artistic goals. This is particularly true of Bengali *ṭughrā* decorative writings that flourished and dominated architectural calligraphy during the fourteenth, fifteenth, and early part of the sixteenth centuries (see fig. 1). In monumental Bengali *ṭughrā*, the convoluted uprights (*muntaṣibāt*) of the vertical letters are highly stylized, often bearing the characteristics of the letter *alif* of *thulth* with distinctive features of *zulf*, *badn*, and *sayf* (see shape A). While the crescent-like undulating curves represented by the oval letters, such as *nūn* (see shape B) and *yā*, and in some cases the upper horizontal stroke (*shākila*) of the letter *kāf* (see shape C) and the word *fī* (see shape D), are superimposed on the extended uprights of the vertical letters, the main body of the text clusters very thickly at the bottom, rendering an extremely intricate pattern of writing (see fig. 2).[20] The calligraphers thus ranged freely, using their creative imaginations in producing different forms and patterns of *ṭughrā*. However, it is not difficult to find in Bengali *ṭughrā* a rhythmic pattern in the movement of the letters and in the flow of lines, which often contained metaphorical expressions of life, nature, and the environment of Bengal in abstract forms ranging from the bow and arrow of Bengali hunting life to the swan and reeds of riverine rural Bengal (see fig. 3).[21]

This symbiotic relationship between humankind and nature was thwarted during the colonial period of the late eighteenth, nineteenth, and early twentieth centuries because of the excessive exploitation of human resources and natural wealth. The only interest the colonial power had in the farmers of rural Bengal, who formed the bulk of the population, was as potential tax-payers. Both the East India Company and its successor, the British Raj, continuously practiced various oppressions, such as the forced labor on indigo plantations that created horrors in the land and finally resulted in a series of man-made disasters never witnessed before. During this period alone, Bengal faced twenty-two recorded famines. The tragedy of the 1770 famine was

Fig. 1. Bengali ṭughrā *decorative writing in an Arabic inscription dated 884/1479, found at Darsbari Masjid and Madrasa in ʿUmarpur, Gaur, from the reign of Sultan Yusuf Shah, now in the Indian Museum, Calcutta.*

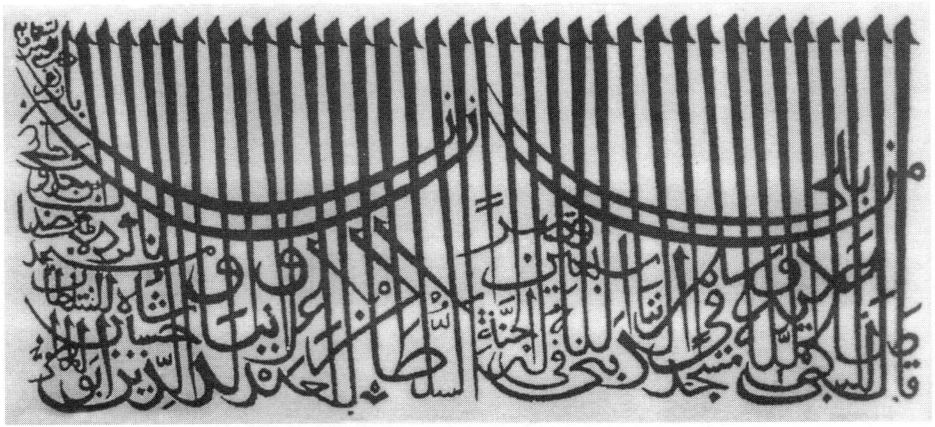

Fig. 2. The bow-and-arrow variety of ṭughrā *in the Babargram mosque inscription in Murshidabad, West Bengal, dated 905/1500, from the reign of Sultan Husayn Shah of Gaur, Bengal.*

Fig. 3. The swan-reed variety of ṭughrā *in a mosque inscription in Sylhet, dated 869/1465, from the reign of Sultan Barbak Shah of Bengal.*

Shape A. The letter alif *in the Barsbari Masjid inscription, with distinctive features of* zulf, badn, *and* sayf.

Shape B. The letter nūn *that looks like a cresent in the bow-and-arrow variety of tughra in an inscription dated 905/1500.*

*Shape C. The upper horizontal stroke (*shākila*) of the letter* kāf *superimposed on the elongated uprights of the vertical letters in the Darsbari Masjid inscription dated 884/1479.*

Shape D. The Arabic preposition fi *in a stylized form that looks like a swan, in the Sylhet inscription dated 869/1465 (fig. 3).*

depicted by John Shore, an East India Company official in Bengal at that time, in his verse:

> Still fresh in memory's eye the scene I view,
> The shriveled limbs, sunk eyes, and lifeless hue.

It was during this period that large-scale deforestation for cultivation started, in order to generate more and more revenues from farming. This left a profound and adverse impact on the proverbially rich flora and fauna of Bengal. The world's largest mangrove forest, the Sundarban, also started shrinking during this period because of massive forest clearing efforts by land-hungry peasants. The killing of wild beasts, particularly elephants, was one of the most important duties for the collector of revenues in rural Bengal. The widespread introduction of firearms for hunting added to the mass killing of wild animals in their natural habitats.

The legacy of this massive disruption in the ecological balance is still evident in this most densely populated region of the world. During the twentieth century alone, the region lost more than a dozen important animal species, including the marsh crocodile, pinheaded duck, nilgai, swamp deer, and rhinoceros, while thirty-five endangered species are threatened with extinction. Many species of fish that were recorded in the late nineteenth and early twentieth centuries in the district gazetteers (e.g., *District Gazetteer of Rajshahi*) have already become extinct. Faced with a series of man-made famines, pollution, epidemics, overpopulation, and numerous other ecological disasters, certain parts of the region seemed at one point unfit to accommodate its huge population. Its ecological balance was further affected by the construction in India of the Farrakkha barrage, a huge artificial dam that changed the natural flow and direction of the water.

This region must be saved from further ecological destruction before it is too late. While intellectual theorizing may provide insight into certain remedies, it is popular awareness and the understanding of environmental issues by common people that will ultimately produce the most effective and far-reaching results. An example of how this goal can be achieved is BANI (Baitulmal Prokolpo), a relatively small but highly successful nongovernment rural welfare project near the city of Kushtia in Bangladesh. The goal of the project is to alleviate the conditions of the poor in Chowrhash, Kamlapur, and a few villages in the Kushtia district of Bangladesh through its Islamic microcredit program. While working on ecological issues, BANI realized that, unless some concrete steps were taken to eradicate poverty from the disadvantaged villagers, no ecological program would ever be successful. Through its Islamic microcredit program, BANI has extended small loans, based on Islamic financial concepts, to the most deprived sections of the population. Three examples of their microenterprise projects are raising cattle, providing rickshaw-pullers with new rickshaws, and setting up small rice mills—all of which will eventually be owned by the participants of the program after paying back their interest-free loans on easy terms. Several hundred families have already benefited from this program. To publicze its environmental awareness program, BANI used local mosques as its centers of activity and local *imām*s and *mu'adhdhin*s as proselytizers of ecological concerns. The impact was very effective and far-reaching. The time has come for similar programs to be introduced in other rural areas of the Muslim world. To effectively carry this out, the following measures are recommended:

1) Mosques, whose numbers far exceed even the total number of primary schools in many Muslim countries, should be used as centers for mass education and for creating environmental awareness.

2) Small libraries should be added to these mosques, which must include books on environmental issues in the local vernacular, with messages from the Qur'an and *ḥadīth* on Muslims' responsibilities to preserve the ecological balance and natural harmony.

3) *Imām*s and *mu'adhdhin*s should be provided with some sort of stipend to support them in receiving training in how to educate common people about environmental issues and as recompense for participation in actual programs on the preservation of nature.

The popular voice of Islam should once again carry an ecological message and bring environmental awareness to the millions of rural Muslims spread over many thousands of villages across the Islamic East.

Notes

1. As the Qur'an says, in a profound and meaningful way, in the chapter *al-Isrā'* [17:44]: *wa in min shay' in illā yusabbiḥu bi-ḥamdihi* (Everything that exists glorifies Allah).

2. One of the one hundred most beautiful Divine Names that appear in the Qur'an (*al-Nisā'*, 4:126).

3. The Qur'an, chapter *Yūnus* (10:32).

4. William A. Graham, "The Winds to Herald His Mercy," in *Faithful Imagining Essays in Honor of Richard R. Niebuhr*, ed. Sang Hyun Lee et al. (Atlanta: Scholars Press, 1995), 22.

5. Al-Qurṭtubī, *al-Jāmi' li Aḥkām al-Qurān*, vol. 3, chapter *al-Baqara*, verse 253. The Arabic text of the *ḥadīth* is as follows: *Ju'ilat lī 'l-arḍ masjid wa ṭuhūr*.

6. Titus Burckhardt, *Mirror of the Intellect* (Albany: State University of New York Press, 1987), 224.

7. 7 The Arabic text of the *ḥadīth* is: *Inna Allah kataba al-iḥsān 'alā kulli shay* (*al-Saḥiḥ al-Muslim*, chapter *al-Ṣayd* [hunting]).

8. Imām al Manāwī, *Fayḍ al-Qadīr Sharḥ Jāmi' al-Ṣaghīr*, vol. 2, s.v. *I'mal*; see also Imām al Sakhāwī, *Maqāṣid al-Ḥasana*, chapter one, s.v. *mīm*.

9. Burckhardt, *Mirror of the Intellect*, 216. This concept can be found in the work of Plato, the English poet John Keats, and many others.

10. *al-Ṣaḥiḥ al-Muslim, Kitāb al- Īmān* [The Book of Faith], chapter *al-taḥrīm al-kibr* [the prohibition of pride].

11. Titus Burckhardt, *Sacred Art in the East and West* (Albany: State University of New York Press, 1987), 101–19.

12. Ibid.

13. A verse in the Qur'an says: "When he turns away from divine message, he attempts to terrorize the earth through destroying agriculture and human civilization; and Allah does not like terrorism" (*al-Baqara*, 2:205).

14. The Qur'an, *al-Naḥl* (16:90).

15. al-Qurṭubī, *al-Jāmi' li Aḥkām al-Qur'ān*, vol. 8, chapter *al-tawba*, verse 107. The text of the *ḥadīth* is "*la ḍarara wa la ḍirāra*."

16. "*al-ḍararu la yuzal*."

17. *al-Tirmidhī*.

18. *Masnad Aḥmad ibn Hanbal*, 5:440; al-Muttaqī al-Hindī, *Kanz al-'Ummāl*, vol. 3, chapter 4, on the virtue of farming and plantation.

19. The wilderness, swamps, and the natural setting of the region have found an expression in a popular Bengali proverb: *Jale Kumir Dangay Bagh*, which means "The lands are full of tigers while the marshes are full of crocodiles."

20. Mohammad Yusuf Siddiq, "An Epigraphical Journey to an Eastern Islamic Land" *Muqarnas* 7 (1990): 83–108.

21. *The Encyclopaedia of Islam*, 2d ed., s.v. "ṭughrā in Muslim India."

Islam in Malaysia's Planning and Development Doctrine

ABU BAKAR ABDUL MAJEED

Malaysia's economy, population, and urbanization have increased dramatically in recent years. This suggests a strong need to formulate a comprehensive and dynamic planning and development policy that focuses on an enduring and balanced spiritual and material development. It would seem that in order to achieve the status of a truly developed nation, it will be necessary for Malaysia not only to sustain its good economic performance, but also to retain the positive aspects of the Malaysian social and cultural fabric.

The Malaysian government has formulated a plan called Vision 2020 to this end.[1] Through the implementation of Vision 2020, Malaysia is dedicated to achieving a greater unity for all her diverse peoples, to maintaining a democratic way of life, to creating a just society in which the wealth of the nation shall be equitably distributed, to ensuring a liberal approach to her rich and diverse cultural traditions, and to building a progressive society oriented to modern science and technology.

The Problem

When Malaysia speaks of becoming a developed nation, it is not referring to industrialization and per capita income only. Wealth and success have a way of undermining the moral fiber of the society. It would be gratifying to be able to say that Malaysia is totally free of any evidence of societal decay. But the fact remains that there are signs that the country is moving toward the inevitable. Drug trafficking and abuse have continued despite tough antidrug laws. The young generation of Malaysians is taking to loafing and the mindless pursuit of fun and pleasure. Loyalty to the establishment is evidently eroding. Cases of vandalism are becoming more serious. Commercial crime is on the rise. The remnants of corrupt practices are still in evidence.

A degraded environment, including the breakdown of natural life-support systems, is also becoming widespread. Depletion of the land and soil, destruction of water catchment areas, and deforestation of green belts are Malaysia's outstanding environmental problems. Despite determined efforts by the local authorities, some of the more common negative effects of urbanization still refuse to go away. For example, pockets of squatter communities which lack basic sanitation, clean water supply, waste-disposal facilities, and adequate recreational services still persist. Traffic congestion, overcrowding, flash floods, inefficient waste disposal service, and stress-related diseases still loom in some major cities. It has been argued that one of the root causes of these societal and ecological problems is the inadequacy of Malaysia's planning and development policy.

Current Planning and Development Policy

Thus far, Malaysia's planning and development policy has mimicked that of its former colonial masters, the British. However, the British concept of planning does have certain limitations and drawbacks. For example, the "Garden City" concept put forth by Ebenezer Howard (who is sometimes referred to as the "Father of Modern Town Planning"), in his 1902 book entitled *Garden Cities of Tomorrow*, stresses "the beauty of nature, social opportunity, fields and parks of easy access, low rents, high wages, low rates, plenty to do, low prices, no sweating, field for enterprise, flow of capital, pure water, good drainage, bright homes and gardens, no smoke, no slums, freedom, co-operation."

Howard's vision led to widespread support among the British middle class for the "Garden City" concept. The "Garden City" movement propagated the idea of comprehensive planning, where business ventures could be harmoniously mixed with the development of suburbs while effecting a general plan to control growth. The most notable characteristic of this movement was that it maintained the idea of open spaces, green belts, and parks as core to its utopia. It was hoped that such an idea would help solve the workers' housing problems and improve their substandard living conditions.

Howard's noble idea, however, achieved very little success because of the realization that building houses for the working class was an uneconomical venture. The number of houses built was not enough to meet the demand. Attempts at rebuilding slum areas in the town centers met with limited success. Further failure of the idea was because the working class never championed it. Consequently, when this "middle-class" idea was incorporated into the various housing and town planning acts, the working class became the losers. Not only did members of this class lose their right to the claim of equal distribution of wealth, they also lost their prospective houses. Not surprisingly, the "Garden City" movement alone was not able to satisfy the changing societal needs of the time.

In Malaysia's case, as in other colonized societies, imperialist planning and development ideas and policies were often applied without much regard for the local environment. The indigenous parts of the environment tended to be contained, ignored, or even slighted. Thus, the imperialist facilities bore the marks of their sponsor's architecture and symbolic associations of building techniques and forms.[2] After independence, Western professionals returned to the former colonies to dictate planning and development strategies under the guise of consultants. They firmly believed that planning was an independent expertise, and that the indigenous social systems had no bearing whatsoever on it—hence the tendency to divide cities into zones, based on the model of Western industrial cities. Buildings were constructed in the extroverted Western style, which proved to be unsuitable both for climatic reasons, where protection from the sun was a must, and for cultural purposes, where religion and domestic prescriptions required seclusion.

Consequently, many people have taken exception to the imperialist concept of planning and development. Thus arose the normative, human-centered approach, which consists of two relevant features.[3] First, planning and development is recognized as being value-laden, involving human attitudes and preferences, self-defined goals, and criteria for determining what are tolerable costs to be borne in the course of change. These issues are far more important than better resource allocation, the upgrading of skills, or the rationalization of administrative procedures. Second, planning and development is seen to be a multifaceted concept best expressed as a human ascent in integral humanity, including the economic, biological, psychological, social, cultural, ideological, spiritual, mystical, and transcendental dimensions.

In short, in any form of development, apart from economic growth, there must also be social justice, since people prefer to live in a society where one's sense of well-being is influenced by the way others in the same society live.[4] Similarly, the well-being of others is somewhat dependent on one's own way of life. This interdependency cannot be ignored by a society aiming for a meaningful and sustainable development.

Nevertheless, the interdependency between producers and consumers has ecological implications, which, if not properly governed, may result in an environmental crisis. Today's global environmental impasse is a case in point. It has become a concern for all mankind. Failure to address this issue through the various programs implemented thus far signifies the need to have a deeper understanding of the malaise. It also strikes out at the root values where religion is most potent. There is a need to recognize the role of religion in establishing guidelines in efforts to protect the environment, as we move gracefully forward toward economic success. The intensity of religious commitment and the growing prevalence of religion in the world, despite modernization and globalization, are indeed healthy signs.

One particular dimension of planning and development stands out from other phenomena in history: this is the ability of Islamic civilization to produce, shape, and maintain citizens of a high intellectual and moral caliber, bound only by their complete submission to their religious precepts. This may possibly be the key to the problems of planning and development. While modern planning and development tend to address physical, economic, social, and environmental problems, either in isolation or in total, the Islamic approach looks at the whole person (*insān*).

As for the physical world, Islam subscribes to the "design earth" concept, which states that the world has been created by God, who provides a profound spiritual relationship toward all aspects of nature. There exists a strong link which binds God, humans, and nature. God created both humankind and nature, the former being given total jurisdiction over the latter.

The Islamic precept is based on an Islamic way of life that implies living in peace and harmony with oneself, with fellow beings, and with everything else that God has created, including the environment. The misuse of God's creation may be interpreted as a transgression of the absolute authority of God. This is in line with the concept of the ordained role of humankind as God's trustees on earth, which is reflected in various verses of the Qur'an, such as the following:

> And remember how He made you inheritors after the 'Ad people and gave you habitations in the land: ye build for yourselves palaces and castles in open plains, and carve out homes in the mountains; so bring to remembrance the benefits ye have received from Allah, and refrain from evil and mischief on the Earth. (Qur'an 7:74)

Total Planning and Development Doctrine

Islam calls for the adoption of theocentric strategies for planning and development. Malaysian planners find it imperative to free themselves from foreign-based concepts that have little or no relevance to the country's specific problems. In 1994, a group of planners gathered to ask the question: "Is there a way out?" Looking at the tradition of sound city planning evident during the period of Islamic dominance in the world, they tried to draw lessons that would be relevant to solving the current problems faced by the developing Malaysia.

The result of this effort is the Total Planning and Development Doctrine (TPDD), proposed by the Town and Country Planning Department of Malaysia's Ministry of Housing and Local Government. The most important aspect of this doctrine is its emphasis on the integration of spiritual and moral values into planning and development. These values should reflect the relationships between humans and their Creator, between human and human, and between human and the environment.

The TPDD requires that, as far as planning and development are concerned, all micro-urban decisions of the public and all macro-urban decisions of the planners and policymakers must be guided by theocentric (that is, God-centered and revelation-based) principles, rather than anthropocentric ones (based purely on human intellect and rationality). The universal values and development principles embedded within the doctrine are aimed at achieving and maintaining *al-salām (*security, peace, and tranquility) and *al-falāḥ* (victory, prosperity, and profit).

The Relationship between Humans and Their Creator

Theocentric relationships are vital, as they determine how one relates to other aspects of creation. Values pertinent to this relationship include the following.

Iḥsān

Iḥsān refers to a higher level of love and care. A person imbued with *iḥsān* truly believes that his actions are constantly monitored by the Creator. This feeling of God-consciousness will persuade a person to carry out her duties in a careful and responsible manner. *Iḥsān* also means "beauty" and "virtue"; more exactly, it relates to the inner beauty, the beauty of the soul or the heart which necessarily emanates outward, transforming every human activity into an art and every art into the remembrance of God (*dhikrallah*). The Qur'an enjoins Muslims to "Serve Allah and join not any partners with Him, and do good (*iḥsān*) to parents, kinfolk, orphans . . ." (4:36).

With *iḥsān*, the criteria for deciding what is good and what is bad are not based on humans' meager thought processes, but rather on the prescriptions of the Creator. These alone will determine that whatever actions taken by humans will be beneficial, and not otherwise. Thus, *iḥsān* will produce not only morally upright individuals, but also buildings and infrastructure of beauty and quality. This corresponds to the comment of Muhammad (PBUH) that "God is beautiful and loves beauty."

Some of the physical manifestations of the concept of *iḥsān* are calligraphy, sculptures of flora and fauna, shapes of geometry and arabesque, arches and signposts depicting words of praise of the Creator, and gardens and lakes with beautifully maintained landscapes. These can invoke an aura of tranquillity and sublimity, leading to an enhanced appreciation of the Creator.

Amāna

The concept of *amāna*, or trusteeship, envisages that humankind, as the vicegerent, or *khalīfa*, of the Creator on Earth, is given the trust of government and governance. But human rule must be based on God's will and pleasure. This "rule" also implies rule over oneself, since the trust refers to the responsibility and freedom of the self to do justice to itself. This, in a way, is the driving force of Islamic ethics and morality.

Each of us, as individuals, in accordance with our latent capacity and the power bestowed upon us by God to fulfill and realize our responsibility and freedom, must strive to achieve and realize the ideal for ourselves in the way manifested by the revealed law. As the Qur'an says: "Allah does command you to render back your trusts to those to whom they are due" (4:58).

This concept, when applied to planning, also relates to the willingness to accept opinions, ideas, and even criticisms from the public whenever these can contribute toward the betterment of the society.

'Adl

'Adl can mean justice or fairness. Justice is about putting the right thing or person in the right place, at the right time, and in the right manner. In the context of planning and development, any decision taken must be just, so that the public can accept it calmly and with an open heart. Otherwise, it will surely invite opposition and protest. Justice is not merely for one's own self or toward fellow humans, but encompasses the whole environment. The Qur'an proclaims: "Allah commands justice, the doing of good, and liberality to kith and kin, and He forbids all shameful deeds, and injustice and rebellion. He instructs you, that you may receive admonition" (16:90).

Tawḥīd

The concept of *tawḥīd* (unity) aims at integrating the various parts and components into a single purposeful entity. For example, in planning, buildings such as houses and infrastructure, like roads and parks, need to be laid out to enhance interactions between the dwellers and users. Writings, symbols and drawing should reflect the local culture, its mission and vision, and move toward achieving unity. If it is a city, then this city is to be like a human body, consisting of millions of tiny parts bonded together in one cooperative purpose. There is a civic sense of unity in purpose, but diversity in process. This particular concept is highly pertinent to the diverse ethics and cultures of Malaysian society.

Among the Muslim community, the concept of unity is exemplified in the performance of the congregational and Friday prayers, pilgrimage and the *qurbān*, or sacrifice, where collective efforts are required. Similarly, every Muslim prays toward the Ka'aba located in the holy city of Mecca. As in the Qur'an: "We see the turning of thy face for guidance to the heavens, now shall We turn thee to a *qibla* that shall please thee. Turn then thy face in the direction of the Sacred Mosque, wherever ye are, turn your faces in that direction" (2:144). Indeed, in the three Malaysian states of Kedah, Kelantan, and Trengganu, traditional houses have been built with Mecca as the reference point.

Knowledge

The possession of the right knowledge is vital for such professionals as administrators, planners, and developers. This means knowledge of how to design buildings and facilities that can invite dwellers and visitors to appreciate and spontaneously relate to the greatness of God, the ultimate source of all knowledge. The strong desire to develop the environment must be complemented by an even stronger desire to seek knowledge. Abuses, shortcomings, flaws, sore points, and the like can thus be avoided.

Using knowledge as the central theme in the planning and development of new areas can contribute to the growth of an improved society. With knowledge, humankind's dependency on the Creator will be enhanced. Instead of letting ourselves loose to the whims of the animal instinct within us, we can learn to acquire self-control through the use of thoughts and wisdom. As stated in the Qur'an: "Say, are those equal, those who know and those who do not know? It is those who are endowed with understanding that receive admonition" (39:9).

Libraries or mosques-cum-libraries have been the centers for knowledge development in traditional Islamic cities. Under present-day circumstances, libraries can also serve as information centers with educational aids presented in various forms: books, videos, audio, and multimedia. These public centers should be able to cater to all age groups, whether preschoolers, young children, adolescents, or adults.

The Relationship between Human and Human

Privacy

Privacy is of primary importance in the design of dwellings. This includes protection from any form of physical or visual trespass. Ethics as to how to enter the host's residence are also to be taken into considerations in the design.

Privacy in the house is a kind of virtue. The Qur'an states: "O ye who believe, enter not houses other than your own, until ye have asked permission and saluted those in them. That is best for you, in order that ye may heed" (24:27). Thus, the Islamic principle of asking respectful permission and exchanging salutation ensures privacy without exclusiveness and friendliness without undue familiarity.

Interactions

Semipublic and public spaces are provided for to ensure proper and positive interactions between neighbors and members of the society. Public areas, such as community halls, sporting arenas, and places of worship, should be built at strategic locations, to encourage meetings and social gatherings with the aim of molding a united and harmonious society. The Qur'an declares: "O mankind! We created you from a single pair of a male and a female, and made you into nations and tribes, that you may know each other, not that ye may despise each other. Verily the most honored of you in the sight of Allah is he who is the most righteous of you. And Allah has full knowledge and is well-acquainted with all things" (49:13).

Peace and Security

These concepts are based on the *maqāsid al-sharī'a*, that is, the fundamental purposes of Islamic law, which are the protection of the mind, religion, soul, heir, and property. Thus, in planning for a new township, for example, factors that may jeopardize the peace and security of future inhabitants, such as floods, pollution, and even diseases, need to be taken into account. The Qur'an states: "And remember, Abraham said, My lord, make this a city of peace, and feed its people with fruits, such of them as believe in Allah and the last day" (2:126).

Tolerance

In Malaysia this concept is of major importance in considering the appropriateness of erecting new buildings or opening new residential areas. In keeping with the principle of *la dharār wa la dhirār* ("One should not harm others or be harmed by others"), trespassing is disallowed regardless of whether it is beneficial or otherwise. Therefore, the citizens of Malaysia, irrespective of their faith, have the right to build their places of worship and maintain them, as long as they follow the laws of the country. Clause 3 of Article 11 in the Federal Constitution of Malaysia states that: "Every religious group has the right to (a) manage its own religious affairs; (b) establish and maintain institutions for religious or charitable purposes; and (c) acquire and own property and hold and administer it in accordance with the law."

Consultation

Everyone concerned with planning and development has to have an open mind in accepting and considering input from the different stakeholders. Comments and criticism need to be looked into with empathy. Whenever decisions are made, these must be transmitted to the stakeholders, so as to have a transparent form of administration. The Qur'an emphasizes this: "those who hearken to their Lord, and establish regular prayer; who conduct their affairs by mutual consultation; who spend out of what We bestow on them for sustenance" (42:38).

The Relationship between Humans and the Environment

Cleanliness and Aesthetics

This concept implies both the intrinsic and extrinsic forms. Thus, the onus is upon humankind to protect and beautify the environment. Pollution and destruction must be stopped at all costs. At the same time, purity of heart and mind is important in ensuring that humans fulfill their role as representatives of the Creator in this world. The Qur'an states: "For Allah loves those who turn to Him constantly and He loves those who keep themselves pure and clean" (2:222).

Conservation

Humans should live in symbiosis with the environment. Equilibrium must be maintained and sustained. The welfare of future generations who will inherit the environment has to be considered. The Qur'an states: "He has Created man. He has taught him speech and intelligence. The sun and the moon follow courses exactly computed. And the herbs and the trees both alike bow in adoration. And the firmament has He raised high, and He has set up the balance of justice, in order that ye may not transgress due balance. So establish weight with justice and fall not short in the balance" (55:3–9).

Conclusion

The Total Planning and Development Doctrine has been adopted by the Federal Cabinet. Since it was first introduced in 1994, the TPDD has been refined and specialized into planning guidelines referred to as the Total Planning and Development Guidelines.[5] In fact, it has already been implemented in the planning and development of new sites, such as the Federal Administrative Center of Putrajaya and Cyberjaya, the information technology city within the Multimedia Super Corridor, or MSC.[6] The MSC will be the main development hub of the nation in the twenty-first century, where the major industries will be multimedia- and information technology–based. These facilities are expected to operate within an environment specially designed to facilitate their activities, while at the same time providing ample and appropriate living conditions for the workforce and their dependants.

Although the TPDD appears to be based on Islamic precepts, it has in fact been discussed in various committees consisting of representatives from all the major religious groups in Malaysia. Because the doctrine's concepts relate to universal values, it has been unanimously accepted.

As for the TPDD's implementation, it has the potential to be workable. This is due to the fact that the ecosystems in Malaysia are still reasonably well preserved. There remains a vast area of natural and virgin forest. Urbanization is still manageable and has not yet reached the point of being uneconomical. And last but not least, universal values are still very much in evidence in the daily practices of Malaysians. The potential for the TPDD to be successful is therefore tremendous.

Notes

1. M. Mohamad, "Imperatives of a Fully Moral and Ethical Society," in *Perspectives on Islam and the Future of Muslims* (Kuala Lumpur: Institute of Islamic Understanding Malaysia, 1993), 18–23.

2. A. Ravetz, "Values and Built Environment: A Case Study of British Planning and Urban Development," in *Touch of Midas: Scientific Values and the Environment in Islam and the West*, ed. Ziauddin Sardar (Manchester: Manchester University Press, 1984), 134–49.

3. D. Goulet, "An Ethical Model for the Study of Values," *Harvard Educational Review* 41 (1971): 205–27.

4. M. I. Ansari, "Islamic Perspective on Sustainable Development," *American Journal of Islamic Social Sciences* 11 (1995): 394–402.

5. Z. Muhammad, "Planning Towards Sustainable Urban Development" (paper presented at the Second National Conference on Healthy Cities, Kuala Lumpur, 14–15 July 1998).

6. JPBD, *Guidelines for the Multimedia Super Corridor (MSC)*, volume 1, *Federal Department of Town and Country Planning* (Kuala Lumpur: Ministry of Housing and Local Government, 1997).

The Aga Khan Development Network: An Ethic of Sustainable Development and Social Conscience

TAZIM R. KASSAM

> The Earth Community stands at a defining moment. The biosphere is governed by laws that we ignore at our own peril. Human beings have acquired the ability to radically alter the environment and evolutionary processes. Lack of foresight and misuse of knowledge and power threaten the fabric of life and the foundation of local and global security. There is great violence, poverty, and suffering in our world. A fundamental change of course is needed.[1]

Introduction

Mary Evelyn Tucker and John Grim have stated: "Ours is a period when the human community is in search of new and sustaining relationships to the earth amidst an environmental crisis that threatens the very existence of all life-forms on the planet."[2] The focal purpose of these conferences on religion and ecology is to mine the symbolic capital of the world's religions for ethical, theological, and imaginative resources which embody, inspire, and require an attitude of respect and care toward the earth. However, one hopes that, apart from mining symbolic capital, these intellectual discussions will also mobilize much needed dormant energies to create measurable positive change.

Although scientists, environmentalists, policymakers, and economists have extensively documented, analyzed, publicized, and proposed solutions to the environmental crisis for many decades, real progress has been negligible. Daniel Maguire starkly sums up the situation: "If current trends continue, we will not."[3] Tucker and Grim attribute this lag between abstract discourses and actual realization to a lack of pragmatic leadership that can transform "rhetoric in print to realism in action."[4] His Highness the Aga Khan III Sir Sultan Muhammad Shah, former Imam, or spiritual leader, of the Ismai'li Muslims, had a motto that was displayed on the bulletin boards of many Isma'ili community centers at the turn of twentieth century: Work Not Words! It is for this reason that instead of addressing the topic of Islam and ecology from a theological standpoint, I have chosen to focus on a nongovernmental organization which is dedicated to that maxim, namely, the Aga Khan Development Network (AKDN).

Theoretical and theological approaches to environmental problems are important and can be invaluable, but they are also susceptible to turning into ideological debates and inaction. Thought gets embroiled in polarized positions of the rich against the poor, socialism versus capitalism, faith versus secularism, North versus South.[5] Energy is consumed in defending ideological, theological, or policy positions. This is visible in the ecopolitics of the environmental movement, which has expressed itself in radical positions that sometimes demand untenable legal, business, and policy reforms that could adversely affect the livelihoods of people.[6] What often gets lost in the abstract debates and doomsday rhetoric of ecocentrism is the enormous potential that lies untapped in individual human beings to alter positively their destiny and environments. Moreover, the environmental crisis has been calculated primarily in terms of biodiversity—its preservation and restoration—without giving due regard to the well-being of human culture. Just as the earth today, in all its organic diversity, suffers unprecedented destruction and depletion, so too does a vast majority of the human population exist in an unacceptable state of hunger, poverty, disease, illiteracy, degradation, and despair. As aptly described by His Highness Prince Karim Aga Khan IV in a speech made during the inauguration ceremony of a housing project in Bombay, India:

> There are those who enter the world in such poverty that they are deprived of both the means and the motivation to improve their lot. Un-

> less these unfortunates can be touched with the spark which ignites the spirit of individual enterprise and determination, they will only sink back into renewed apathy, degradation and despair. It is for us, who are more fortunate, to provide that spark.[7]

In its quest for an earth-centered rather than a human-centered ecology, the environmentalist movement at times risks losing sight of the key agent and champion of effective change: the individual person or community. If the human being is a microcosm of the macrocosm, as many religions affirm, then neglecting the one cannot but be detrimental to the other. An eco-sensitive world that respects and cares for the natural resources of the earth must presume the genuine participation of human beings within that ecosystem. However, how can such conscience and responsibility be expected of peoples whose own perilous conditions of misery identify them with an ailing earth? It seems, therefore, that one of the first problems to address globally is the quality of life of those who live in hunger, disease, and destitute poverty. This would, with proper education, restore to them and their children their dignity, hope, and self-reliance and release incalculable human potential and commitment to protect and restore the natural habitat upon which their lives depend. According to His Highness the Aga Khan IV, "Development is ultimately about people, about enabling them to participate fully in the process and to make informed choices and decisions about their futures."[8]

This paper will focus on the Aga Khan Development Network and its ethic of sustainable development and social conscience. It will describe the humanitarian principles and pragmatic strategies which have inspired the agency's work during the last three decades. Headed by His Highness the Aga Khan IV, the Aga Khan Development Network has devoted itself to addressing a number of pressing needs in the developing nations of Asia and Africa—problems such as abject poverty, degradation of natural resources, disease control, economic self-sufficiency, and the preservation of cultural and natural habitats. The lessons and experiences acquired by the institutions and programs of AKDN may be of interest to policymakers in government agencies, intellectuals in academe, and religious leaders of various communities, since they are of a replicable nature. The pragmatic, humanitarian, and ethical underpinnings of the AKDN represent an approach to the human and environmental problems faced by our planet today that deserves close and serious scrutiny.

The Isma‘ili Muslims

The Isma‘ilis are a community of Shi‘a Muslims numbering about fifteen million and residing in over twenty-five countries. They trace their history back to the lifetime of Prophet Muhammad. The Islamic world is composed of many communities of interpretation of the faith, the two major ones being the Sunni and the Shi‘a. The Sunni assert that the Prophet did not designate a successor before he died, whereas the Shi‘a maintain that he did. According to the Shi‘a, whereas Qur'anic revelation ceased at the Prophet's demise, the need for spiritual and temporal guidance and for the interpretation of Qur'anic revelation continued. The authority for this guidance and interpretation devolved on Hazrat ‘Ali, the Prophet's cousin and son-in-law. It was subsequently to be passed on in an unbroken line of authority to the direct male descendant designated by the previous Imam. His Highness Prince Shah Karim al-Husseini Aga Khan IV is the forty-ninth direct lineal descendant of Imam Ali and is the present living Imam, or guide, of the Shi‘a Isma‘ilis.

While Islam encompasses all aspects of life, the present Imam, His Highness Prince Karim Aga Khan IV, repeatedly emphasizes the nonpolitical character of his Imamate and its institutions. "Nonpolitical," however, does not mean indifferent or uninvolved. In the words of the Aga Khan:

> Islam is not passive. It does not admit that man's spiritual needs should be isolated from his material daily activities. A Muslim must play an active role in helping his family and the brotherhood of believers. The object is not to achieve status, wealth, and power, but to contribute to society's overall development. This implies a moral responsibility to help its weaker, less fortunate members.[9]

Rather than interfering in politics, Isma‘ilis are urged to contribute actively to their nation's social, cultural, and economic progress and to work toward the well-being of all its citizens. The Imamate is thus conceived not as a theocratic office but as a locus of inspired leadership and timely guidance broadly defined to secure the overall welfare and happiness of the Isma‘ili community, the Muslim *umma*, and humanity as such.

Accordingly, the modern Isma‘ili *imāmat* is not rooted within a specific geographic region, but derives its character from and expresses its efficacy through a network of institutions that are service-oriented and international in scope, as opposed to being governmental, ideological, or theological. Thus, while the diverse Isma'ili Muslim communities around the world are united by a common bond of faith and allegiance to a living Imam, they do not constitute a political entity. Instead, each Isma'ili community pledges its allegiance and loyalty as citizens to the country in which it resides.

The Aga Khan and Sustainable Development

As their spiritual leader and guide, the Aga Khan IV is thus eager to see that each country in which his followers live is healthy, stable, and secure and has clear development horizons that offer to all its citizens a promising future of peace and prosperity. Both the previous Imam, Sir Sultan Muhammad Shah, and the present Imam have sought to support the integrity of the states where their followers live and to contribute to improving the overall quality of life for all its communities, not just their own. Apart from expecting the fundamental right of all people to freedom of faith, liberty, and security, the Aga Khan, his Network, and his followers are committed to achieving broad social objectives without political connotations. He says:

> When I assumed the responsibilities of the Imamate in 1957 I was eager—as I still am—to see that the countries where my followers live are sound and stable; that they are countries with clear development horizons; countries where, following my grandfather's example, I could help to underwrite the integrity of the State and to contribute to improving the quality of life for all communities, not just my own. I hoped to help bridge the gulf between the developed and the developing worlds. This aspiration, I felt, was particularly appropriate to the Imamate because of its commitment to broad social objectives without political connotations, save in its concern for the fundamental freedom of its followers to practice the faith of their choice.[10]

This explains why His Highness the Aga Khan IV, a religious leader, has been working in development for the last three decades. As the Imam of the Isma'ili Muslims, the responsibilities of his office entail not only interpreting matters of faith, but also relating that faith to the present environments in which his followers find themselves. Pluralism and diversity of race, language, cultural heritage, and socioeconomic levels are primary features of the Isma'ili Muslim community, most of whose members live in the developing world. Hence, to address their needs, the Aga Khan IV has had to become deeply involved in welfare and development. He says:

> You may wonder why I am involved in welfare at all. As the Imam of an Isma'ili Muslim Community spread over twenty-five countries, I have necessarily become a student of social problems. Islam is an all encompassing faith and it gives direction to every aspect of one's life. It urges the individual to lead a balanced life, one that strives to accommodate both material progress and spiritual well-being. But no man, woman or child can hope to achieve this balance in sickness, illiteracy or squalor . . . [Thus] I have become deeply involved in the provision of basic health and education, which I believe are crucial stepping stones towards mankind's self-realization and growth.[11]

The Aga Khan Development Network

In 1967 the Aga Khan IV established the Aga Khan Foundation in Geneva as a private, noncommunal, nongovernmental, social welfare institution to build upon and consolidate the health, education, and economic services launched in the 1880s by his grandfather, the previous Imam Sir Sultan Muhammad Shah. Sir Sultan Muhammad Shah was a pioneer of immunization and preventive health care in the nineteenth century. In 1897 he played a major role in stemming the spread of bubonic plague in Bombay by having himself inoculated in public to convince the general populace not to be afraid of vaccinations. When the present Aga Khan IV became Imam in 1957, many countries where Isma'ilis lived were emerging from colonial rule, and these newly independent nations were rebuilding themselves into independent nation-states. His Highness the Aga Khan IV directed the various health, welfare, and economic institutions founded by Sir Sultan Muhammad Shah to focus their energies on advancing the overall development of these emerging nations. Furthermore, their activities were to benefit all communities in the area, irrespective of race, religion, and culture.

His Highness the Aga Khan IV felt that the best way to build civil society in the modern age was through the creation of strong private institutions that were materially self-sufficient, had the capacity to renew themselves and to cultivate the people who worked within them, and which were capable of multiplying their impact by serving more people and wider needs. As he explains:

> To create a pluralistic, civil society, private institutions must be established that meet the needs of their constituent groups. Integral to the creation of good governance . . . is the establishment of indigenous non-governmental institutions custom-made to solve local problems. The state cannot do it all. To be successful, these private institutions must meet two conditions: their members must have a sense of common purpose; and those members must be organized so as to achieve that purpose. . . . Moreover, good governance is likely to be achieved only by organizations nurtured by an enabling environment, where the laws of State encourage private enterprise, a diversity of initiatives, and voluntary not-for-profit organizations.[12]

The Aga Khan Foundation was officially recognized by the United Nations Development Program in 1980. Today, it has affiliates in several countries and has accumulated more than four decades of development experience from wide-ranging projects in Asia and Africa.[13] Under the direction of His Highness the Aga Khan IV, the welfare institutions created by his grandfather in the 1880s have evolved into a complex array of institution-building agencies that identify and attempt to solve specific needs in the developing world, including health, housing, rural development, education, economic growth, and the proper use and care of natural resources. This collection of agencies is now organized under the rubric of the Aga Khan Development Network, which represents one of the largest international, nongovernmental social and economic development agencies in the world (see fig. 1, the AKDN organization chart). What is particularly noteworthy about the AKDN projects and activities is their inclusive scope and multidisciplinary nature, which manifests the fundamental principle that human cultures and their varied natural environments, despite their diversity and differentiation, are essentially and necessarily an integrated, organic, and interdependent whole.

Ineffective Development

The ultimate objective for development has been to improve the living conditions of ordinary people in poor countries. In the 1950s and

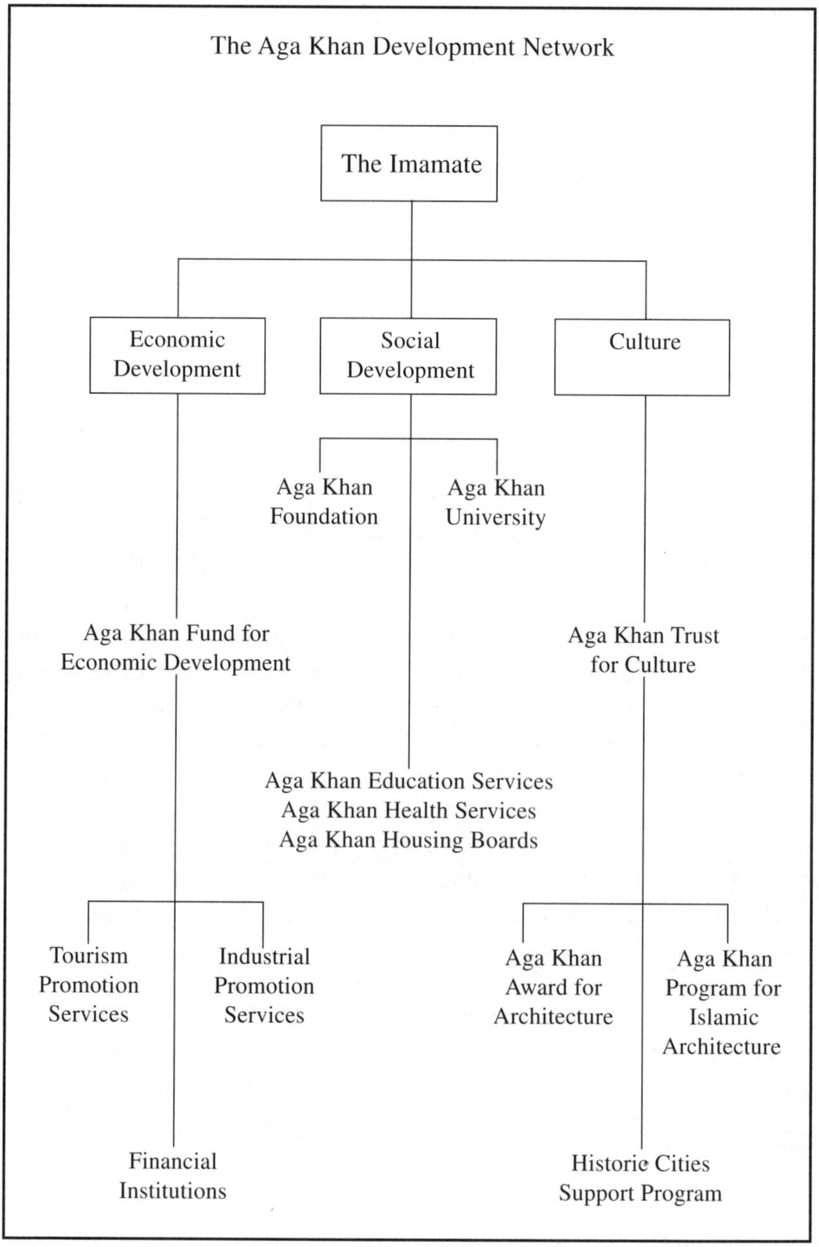
The Aga Khan Development Network
The Imamate
Economic Development
Social Development
Culture
Aga Khan Foundation
Aga Khan University
Aga Khan Fund for Economic Development
Aga Khan Trust for Culture
Aga Khan Education Services
Aga Khan Health Services
Aga Khan Housing Boards
Tourism Promotion Services
Industrial Promotion Services
Aga Khan Award for Architecture
Aga Khan Program for Islamic Architecture
Financial Institutions
Historic Cities Support Program

Fig. 1

1960s, development agencies and government officials believed improvement of life meant replicating the large-scale industrialization and megaprojects that were more suited to Western urbanized economies. Leaders of developing nations were eager to promote such gigantic industrial projects because they thought mass industrialization would accelerate the growth and prosperity of their budding nations.[14] Thus, international aid agencies pumped large sums of money into the governments of the developing world that were then invested in huge projects, such as oil refineries, complex highways, factories, and hydroelectric plants. Too many aid programs were capital intensive and insensitive to the fragile national economies and demographics of rural populations who could ill-afford them and who began an inevitable downward spiral into large national debt. International development agencies and governments failed to recognize that the provision of capital to import industrial technologies would not address the development problems of poorer nations, which lack the very basic necessities of life that are taken for granted in Western economies.

Many developing countries are primarily rural economies without the complex and stable infrastructure of sanitation, roads, communications, and primary health care that already exists in the developed world. Developed countries do not have the same population growth problems of the developing world. Nor are they as dependent on basic commodity prices for their economy. Western developers also mistakenly presume that rural populations should desire the same types of goods and services that urban citizens require, such as electric stoves and refrigerators, cars and skyscrapers. Resolving the most fundamental needs of the rural population, however, such as sufficient food and water, proper clothing, decent shelter, basic education, and primary health care, does not need large capital expenditures but a judicious balance of capital, new technologies, and human resource training and management skills. To be sure, these very basic needs have not been met by investments in glamorous megaprojects.

Such white elephant schemes of development have embarrassed governments and aid agencies, for they have not resulted in the rapid and significant progress that was promised to their constituencies. Building symbols of prosperity has not created local wealth and, since the 1970s, the capital-intensive, big-is-better view of development has been severely critiqued. Nonetheless, this approach is not yet obsolete. Increasingly, however, development workers and policymakers are recognizing that simpler, decentralized schemes that are sustainable and that rely on and efficiently manage local human and material resources and technologies offer superior results and have a measurable impact on quality-of-life indicators. Apart from providing capital, international aid agencies and policymakers are realizing the need to be more sensitive to the specific economic, environmental, and cultural facets of development. Through a profound and intimate understanding of the factors that retard improvements to the quality of life of rural peoples, agencies can plan to give support at multiple levels, but most especially in the transference of scientific know-how, management skills, and training of voluntary human resources. Outside planners are beginning to appreciate the importance of sparking the spirit of hope, self-help, and opportunity—once absent from their vocabulary—within grassroots communities.

The Aga Khan IV has cautioned that, apart from contributing further to the ecological crisis, if the developed world fails to uplift the developing world with relevant material and technical and intellectual resources, poorer nations through sheer frustration will return to brute political tactics and violent conflict and pose a threat to global security. During a recession in the early 1980s, in a speech made in Toronto to an audience consisting of members of Canadian aid agencies, including the Canadian International Development Agency, CARE, OXFAM, and UNICEF, His Highness the Aga Khan IV said:

> If the industrialized world does not do this [give the Third World increasing access to its know-how and make available increasing material support] in the relatively near future, but builds barriers to protect itself against any recurrence of economic crisis, then the world recession will do even more damage than it has already to Third World economies. The pragmatists will be overtaken by failure of performance and their countries will return, through sheer frustration, to the strident conflicts of the past, and rational reflection will once again become endangered.[15]

Hence, to protect the earth and its inhabitants, development must succeed, because successful development that genuinely improves the lives of poorer peoples will prevent political ideologies from replacing hard-nosed pragmatism, not only within the developing nations of

Asia and Africa, but also in the industrialized world where the problems of hunger, poverty, illiteracy, crime, and mental disease are growing.[16]

Pragmatism: AKDN Development Strategies

Meeting Urgent Needs with Limited Resources

To achieve effectiveness in health and education services, or in welfare generally, the Aga Khan IV has taken a pragmatic approach to the realities at hand. Sadly, although resources are scarce in developing countries, there is still duplication and waste. Thus, one of the major challenges is to maximize the effective use of these meager resources. Although the AKDN's activities are wide in scope, they cannot possibly address the total spectrum of needs of developing nations. Thus, the Network has set priorities, which are periodically reviewed. It has identified four strategic and thematic areas on which to focus:

1) To seek cost-effective ways to improve the quality of basic education in the developing world;

2) To establish community-centered health services at the village level which provide primary health care;

3) To generate employment and income opportunities in rural areas through economic support programs; and

4) To improve the effective management, use, and renewal of human and natural resources.[17]

Often, all these themes interlock, as in the case of the Northern Areas of Pakistan where the Aga Khan Rural Support Program, which was instituted in 1982 with the support of UNICEF and the Government of Pakistan, offers all four services.

As the Isma'ili Muslim community's demography is both urban and rural, the Network has been particularly well placed to assess the living conditions found in the two different settings through the community's own daily encounters and experiences. These grass-roots-level connections amplify and supplement the detailed surveys that AKDN offices carry out independently to evaluate the precise development needs of a specific region. Projects are undertaken only after substantial research and analysis of root causes and conditions is conducted and after available resources have been weighed against projected cost, risk, and benefit factors. The rigorously intellectual approach of AKDN institutions in seeking solutions for problems of development is methodical, rational, and analytical. Its agencies make full use of all that current scientific knowledge and best practices have to offer. Through a combination of intellectual effort and enlightened self-interest, the premise of the AKDN's work is that it is possible to evolve a social vision that is beneficial to the many rather than just the few, irrespective of culture, race, religion.

Integrated, Multidisciplinary Approach

It is difficult to point out which of the many elements in the development program, namely, health care, education, economic incentives, housing projects, rural development, and so on, will ultimately catalyze improvements in the quality of life of people in developing areas. Hence, the AKDN works on the prudent assumption that by providing an integrated variety of social and economic services, the impact of its manifold activities will have a compounding effect and will maximize the chances of success. As the needs in rural areas are so extensive, the AKDN has taken a multipronged approach as, for instance, in the Northern Areas in Pakistan, to offer a variety of programs and services. Such an all-encompassing approach promises that at least one, if not more, of these interventions will eventually have the greatest impact on the largest number of people.

Building Bridges and Partnerships

The hallmark of the AKDN's approach to solving the problem of limited resources is building bridges and partnerships that pool resources and point constituencies in the same direction. This includes forming partnerships between developed and developing nations, government and nongovernmental bodies, rural populations and national policymakers, the private and public sectors, and community volunteers and professional managers. His Highness the Aga Khan IV eschews the language of dualisms, such as North versus South, religious versus political, socialist versus capitalist, because speaking in terms of ideological positions creates deadlock and is thus counterproductive and inefficient. His primary objective is to create bridges and alliances between these so-called polarities in such a manner that there are beneficiaries on both sides. The obvious practical consequence is that the transfer of material, scientific, and managerial resources that are desperately required for advancing development is facilitated. In his view, successful development requires creative and synergistic partnerships between government, private enterprise, and the nonprofit and voluntary sectors.

Pooling Resources with Other NGOs—In addition to raising funds from the Isma'ili Muslim community and the corporate sector, the Aga Khan Foundation teams up with major international development and aid agencies to support various development projects, including the World Food Program, the World Health Organization, UNICEF, the Ford Foundation, the Canadian International Development Agency, Alberta Aid, and the World Bank. This pooling of resources with other international aid agencies and private nongovernmental organizations has enabled the AKDN to push forward substantially its development agenda in but a few decades of operation.[18]

Partnerships with Governments—AKDN has also signed accords with the Governments of Kenya, Tanzania, Uganda, Pakistan, Tajikistan, and other states to pursue development objectives that concur with the national objectives of their countries. All AKDN projects are guided by the purpose of aiding or complementing national policy objectives for a country's progress and welfare. Since governments of most developing countries are concerned about health care, education, and economic incentives, NGOs can advance shared goals by working together with governments. In working with the governments of developing nations, the Aga Khan IV has found that sometimes they need to be reminded of the importance of a clear political commitment to welfare services and of the advantages of working closely with private NGOs. NGOs are in a position to transfer essential knowledge and skills to local populations by bringing in technical, scientific, and management expertise as well as the foreign exchange required to establish such services as health care centers, dispensaries, and mobile clinics and to train volunteers as paramedics and nurses. Since developing countries always face the problem of how to allocate their meager resources between the competing demands of illiteracy, poverty, disease, lack of sanitation, utilities, and infrastructure, such infusion of resources, information, and skills is vital.

Working with the Private Sector—Many international aid agencies have channeled their funds into government and large public sector projects. Given the Aga Khan Development Network's limited assets, the Aga Khan IV concluded that it would be more beneficial to put these resources in the private sector, which is vital to a nation's growth.

> While most of the international aid agencies were channeling finance to governments and large public sector projects, I felt that in the face of such vast needs, we could best place our comparatively meager resources with the private sector. This strategy has met with some success. . . . The market place, not government, is beginning to be seen as the key mechanism in promoting development.[19]

The private sector is the engine that generates the productivity that governments and citizens need in order for them to reinvest profits back into their country's communities, services, and infrastructure. Although in a global capitalist economy pro-market policies are in favor, Western entrepreneurs are generally less attracted to invest in developing areas of the world such as Africa and Asia. Through the agency AKFED, the Aga Khan Fund for Economic Development, the Aga Khan has made an effort to direct investors' attention to the economic opportunities and potential in the developing world. The Aga Khan feels that the key mechanism by which to promote development and generate income is not via the government, but through the market. As this realization penetrates the policy process, he hopes it will offer new opportunities "not only to the people of the underdeveloped South, but to those of the industrialized North whose own enlightened self-interest should encourage them to seek income opportunities in the developing zones of our interdependent world."[20]

The private sector is vital to a nation's economy. It cultivates the mass of small enterprises, skills, and professional services that build a productive society. Apart from providing needed capital, private enterprise also introduces healthy competition, stimulates productivity, and develops key managerial skills and organizational structures necessary for economic growth. However, governments need to create an enabling environment for private sector initiatives to flourish, "that is to say the combination of confidence, of security and a philosophy and application of law which will enable commerce to flourish."[21]

Creating an Enabling Environment—His Highness the Aga Khan IV has urged at various times that it is in the interest of governments to create an enabling environment to ensure the success of the economic, social, and political development of their nations. This means constructing a legislative and policy framework that would allow private enterprise and the voluntary sector to work effectively. Often, governments fail to provide the incentives, laws, and policies that sustain a climate of economic, social, and political stability. If the legal and political environment is disabling, inevitably standards of quality and probity will weaken or fail in different sectors of human endeavor. Skilled professionals will despair and leave the country in the hands of the unqualified. The Aga Khan IV defines the enabling environment as follows:

> The enabling environment is created by various things. Confidence in the future. Reliance on the rule of law and a system of laws which itself encourages enterprise and initiative. Democratic institutions. Protection of the rights of citizens. These are what encourage investment, encourage good managers to remain, encourage doctors and nurses and teachers to want to serve their country rather than to emigrate as soon as they are skilled. The creation and extension to all areas of the nation's life of this enabling environment is the single most important factor in Third World development. It is as critical to national growth as sunlight is to the growth of plants.[22]

Importance of the Voluntary Sector—A major and largely untapped resource in developing countries is the voluntary sector, which can bring people together to serve a wide range of social needs. Effectively harnessing the energies of voluntary associations to work toward a common goal is a key strategy of the Aga Khan Development Network. The sheer size of the voluntary sector gives it immense potential to empower people and create lasting social change. Volunteers display virtues of dedication, self-reliance, and personal initiative, key ingredients of strong and imaginative social institutions. In fact, the lifeblood of the AKDN agencies and institutions is its legion of volunteers. Without the involvement of grassroots-level volunteers, few of the sophisticated strategies that managers and planners like to devise would have any momentum or impact. Thus, a key lesson learned by the AKDN is that true performance and changes of any lasting value cannot be achieved without locating hardy and dedicated community volunteers who can provide leadership, management skills, and public-spirited service.

Cultivating Grassroots Management—To put their altruism and energies to good use, however, volunteers need to be trained to perform their tasks effectively. Unfortunately, social institutions often lack the upper-level professional management talents that are imperative in corporations. To be effective, the same standards of operation and services are needed and should be expected from social organizations. Thus, the Aga Khan insists that it is critical to develop prudent and strategic management of social services and that the right balance has to be struck between local grassroots autonomy and expatriate professional oversight. This entails designing programs to train local people as managers, with the long-term goal of creating professional management skills within grassroots volunteer organizations.

Institutions within the AKDN rely on the talents of lawyers, teachers, accountants, doctors, and other professionals who donate their time, knowledge, and ability to train voluntary workers. This cross-fertilization of the professional's competency and the volunteer's enthusiasm goes a long way to ensuring higher professional standards of service and accountability of welfare institutions. AKDN institutions learned very early the need for professional levels of management of social welfare projects. A central factor that makes one NGO more effective than another is governance. The Aga Khan IV says, "Integral to the creation of good governance . . . is the establishment of indigenous non-governmental institutions custom-made to solve local problems."[23] The success of a development agency thus depends on its ability to mobilize local populations to address their own needs by creating social welfare organizations that are self-sustaining, both financially and in terms of effective leadership. In this respect, virtually all programs have self-reliance as their primary goal.

Conclusion

In its official statement, the Aga Khan Development Network describes itself as "a contemporary endeavor of the Isma'ili Imamate to realize the social conscience of Islam through institutional action."[24] This paper began with the assertion by Grim and Tucker that what is urgently needed to address the ecological crisis is pragmatic leadership that can transform theory and rhetoric into realism and action. His Highness the Aga Khan's development network suggests that he is, among other things, a pragmatic environmentalist. He can be ranked alongside other international philanthropists and eco-pioneers. Steve Lerner describes the latter as "modern path finders who create specific maps towards a sustainable future. . . . Doers rather than talkers, they are practical visionaries and backyard mechanics who are going into the field to put sustainable development into practice. . . . Each has taken on a discrete environmental dilemma and immersed himself or herself in the mechanics of solving it."[25]

The Aga Khan Development Network is one model created by a contemporary Muslim leader on how to give concrete manifestation to the social conscience of Islam and to pivotal Islamic concepts, such as responsible stewardship of the planet and all life within it (*khalīfa*) and the striving for a life of balance and integrity between the material (*dunyā*) and the spiritual (*dīn*). The AKDN's goal of relieving ignorance, disease, and deprivation is profoundly relevant to environmental issues. As Prince Sadruddin Aga Khan, the president of the Bellerive Foundation states, "Poverty, ignorance, oppression, and war are major causes of environmental degradation."[26] Viewed in terms of a health model, hunger, ignorance, and deprivation are forms of moral illness in those societies which allow these preventable conditions to persist. In addition, development is related to fundamental injustices in society. In his classic work *Development as Freedom*, Amartya Sen precisely states that "Development requires the removal of major sources of unfreedom: poverty as well as tyranny, poor economic opportunities as well as systematic social deprivation, neglect of public facilities as well as intolerance or overactivity of repressive states."[27]

The ADKN is based on an ethical framework. Although it draws its inspiration from Islamic concepts, these ethical principles are rational, rigorous, and humanistic in scope. Ethics bridges *dīn* and *dunyā* in Islam through the *khalīfa* ideal, which demands that human beings act as stewards of the biosphere which includes plants, animals, and human beings. However, this concept of human accountability can be derived independently of religious premises from the perspective of enlightened self-interest in preserving the beauty of the planet and the welfare of this and future generations of all life species. Under the Aga Khan's supervision, trusteeship and leadership of his institutions is not an abstract ideal but is measured through established protocols of accountability, probity, and independent external evaluations of AKDN personnel and projects. To squander and exploit the resources of the earth, which are limited and which are priceless gifts, is to "sin" or transgress against the limits embedded in life systems, and thus to fail in one's trusteeship.

Notes

1. "The Earth Charter," *Earth Ethics: Evolving Values for an Earth Community* 8, no. 2-3 (1998), 1.

2. Mary Evelyn Tucker and John Grim, "Series Foreword," in this volume, xv.

3. Daniel Maguire, *The Moral Core of Judaism and Christianity: Reclaiming the Revolution* (Philadelphia: Fortress Press, 1993), 13.

4. Tucker and Grim, "Series Foreword," xix.

5. Excellent discussions of these issues can be found in Tom Athanasiou, *Divided Planet: The Ecology of Rich and Poor* (Boston: Little, Brown, 1996), and Hazel Henderson, *Building a Win-Win World: Life beyond Global Economic Warfare* (San Francisco: Berrett-Koehler Publishers, 1996).

6. For a discussion of the apparent trade-off between the health of the environment and that of the community, see Malcolm G. Scully, "The Rhetoric and the Reality of 'Sustainability,'" *Chronicle of Higher Education*, 28 January 2000, B9.

7. Aga Khan IV, speech delivered at the inauguration ceremony of the Aga Khan Baug, Versova, India, 17 January 1983. The full text of speeches of the Aga Khan IV quoted in this paper can be found at the following web site: <http://www.ismaili.net/speeches.html>.

8. Aga Khan IV, speech delivered at The Royal Society for Asian Affairs, 6 February 1992.

9. Aga Khan IV, speech delivered at a dinner hosted by the *Globe and Mail*, Toronto, Canada, 14 May 1987.

10. Aga Khan IV, speech delivered at a dinner hosted by the president of Tanzania, Dar as Salaam, 21 November 1982.

11. Aga Khan IV, "Social Institutions in National Development: The Enabling Environment," speech delivered at the Enabling Environment Conference held in Nairobi, Kenya, 7 October 1982.

12. Aga Khan IV, 6 February 1992.

13. The Aga Khan Development Network (AKDN) maintains an in-depth web site at which can be found the vast array of projects which it oversees under its various agencies together with other development partners and donors. The Network includes the Aga Khan Education Services (AKES), the Aga Khan Foundation for Economic Development (AKFED), the Aga Khan Health Services (AKHS), the Aga Khan Trust for Culture (AKTC), and the Aga Khan University (AKU). The web site includes program briefs, Aga Khan Foundation annual reports, speeches of the Aga Khan, and news about the Network. See http://www.akdn.org.

14. For a lively discussion of this problem, see Rashmi Mayur and Bennett Davis, "How NOT to Develop an Emerging Nation," *The Futurist*, January-February 1998, 27–31.

15. Aga Khan IV, speech delivered at a luncheon hosted by the Aga Khan Foundation Canada, Toronto, Canada, 27 April 1983.

16. A study released by Second Harvest in 1998 revealed that 21 million Americans relied on emergency food assistance at least once during the year. Of these, two-thirds were women, 8 million were children, and 3.5 million were the elderly. See

"Hunger Persists in U.S. despite Economic Boom," *Christian Science Monitor*, 29 April 1998.

17. For a more detailed treatment of these foci, see *International Strategy: 1991–1999* (Geneva: Aga Khan Foundation, 1992), 25–72.

18. AKDN's institutional partners exist all over the world. A full list can be found at the AKDN web site. They include the Governments of India, Pakistan, and Japan; the Swiss Agency for Development Cooperation; Médecins sans Frontières; the Norwegian Agency for International Development; the British Council; the Ford Foundation; USAID; the European Commission; The World Bank; and the United Nations Development Program.

19. Aga Khan IV, Toronto, 14 May 1987.

20. Ibid.

21. Aga Khan IV, speech delivered at a luncheon hosted by Industrial Promotion Services, Tourism Promotion Services, the Diamond Trust, Jubilee Insurance, and Nation Printers, Nairobi, Kenya, 7 October 1982.

22. Aga Khan IV, "Social Institutions," 7 October 1982.

23. Aga Khan IV, 6 February 1992.

24. The document can be found at <http://www.akdn.org/imamat/imamat_akdn.html>.

25. Steve Lerner, "The New Environmentalists," *The Futurist*, May 1998, 36.

26. Prince Sadruddin Aga Khan, "Spirituality and Science: The Need for Togetherness," speech delivered at the Symposium on Trade, Environment and Animal Welfare, The European Parliament, Brussels, 26–27 September 1996.

27. Amartya Sen, *Development as Freedom* (Oxford: Oxford University Press, 1999), 3.

The Islamic Garden as Metaphor for Paradise

Nature in Islamic Urbanism: The Garden in Practice and in Metaphor

ATTILIO PETRUCCIOLI

The word "landscape" has various, often ambiguous meanings. It is used differently, for example, in the contexts of Romanticism, Impressionism, or human geography. In this paper, "landscape" refers to the mutual relationship between humankind and nature over time—a dialogue where nature challenges humans, to which humans respond by progressively shaping and transforming the environment. Today, the ever-worsening environmental situation demands complex answers—solutions calling for clearly articulated social systems and sophisticated technologies.

Landscape is far from being detached from human processes. On the contrary, it is the mirror of a dialectic relationship producing permanent transformations of the environment. The contemporary landscape contains, in more or less evident form, all traces of its evolution. It is constantly transformed according to new necessities, but at each stage the preceding stages are never completely erased. Thus, the landscape is a palimpsest—a complete database of civilization. It represents human intervention on a large scale, while containing within it all changes occurring on the small scale as well. Any discourse on landscape simultaneously implies and includes a discourse on architecture.

If the landscape is a palimpsest of the layering of human action over time, it is difficult to talk about Islamic architecture and Islamic landscape as two separate entities. The present-day notion of space and landscape—whether in Iran, Turkey, or East Asia—was, in general terms, already present in the social subconscious and in the territorial structure of the seventh century C.E. The Persian, the Arab, and the Ottoman mosque each belong to radically different concepts of space. The first, based on the layout of perpendicular axes, aims to be an earthly replica of sacred cosmological constructions. The second is a serial, open scheme in which one module can be theoretically repeated an infinite number of times. The third, influenced by the Byzantine culture, is by contrast a finite organic entity based on a clear spatial hierarchy. Within this general classification, the difference is even more evident between urban and rural mosques. It is important to understand the evolution of these concepts of space from the seventh century onward, as well as which and how external cultural influences transformed preexistent notions to generate new spatial syntheses.

We may start from the interpretation given to the first term of this dialectic relationship—nature. Based on the descriptions of nature in religious literature, I believe that attention should be given to what Aristotle defines as *natura naturaliter formata*—the anthropic appropriation of nature—rather than to *natura naturata*—the object of modern natural sciences. In the Qur'an, every description, from crops to the geometric pattern of water sources, refers to natural phenomena as divine signs.[1] According to Ibn Sina (Avicenna), nature is the place where everything acquires meaning and God's will is manifested. Therefore, any manifestation of nature tends toward the perfect and the divine. However, if Islamic culture longs for transcendental meaning, it doesn't pursue it by imposing human action on "profane" nature [as is often argued for the West—RCF]. Nature is not in the least regarded as a separate entity opposed to the supernatural and the divine, but as the very element mirroring heavenly perfection.[2]

I suggest that, although with a few exceptions,[3] Islamic speculation on nature lies between immanence and transcendence which, whether considered as a whole or not, reflects the right relationship between God and nature.

In contrast to the devotional aspect of Christianity—a religion that implicitly tends to keep faith and rationale separate—Islam pursues gnosis. The central issue in Islam is to remove the obstacle of human passion from intelligence in order to reach absolute and true faith. In Islam, natural phenomena do not induce mystical abandonment (like Saint Francis talking to the birds), but rather rational wonder for a marvelous and complex mechanism. Natural phenomena also often carry didactic meaning. For instance, when an excited Muhammad describes the life of bees, it is not the "marvelous mystery" of nature that moves him, but rather the perfect organization of a community he would like to transpose to the human Islamic *umma*.

Muslim travelers and geographers, on the other hand, often wrote about the miracle of man-made "nature": earth transformed and labored, earth seen as the Mother. Ibn Hawqal left us an idyllic description of Samarkand's surroundings:

> In the whole region of Samarkand there is no place healthier, with more generous crops, with more beautiful fruit, with stronger people. . . . Here high plains are more salubrious and beautiful than anywhere else; fields perpetually bring abundant crops that never turn bad. . . . Coming from Bukhara along the Sogdiana river, we look left and right at endless crops until the Buttam mountains. Here vegetation is perfect, and there is no interruption to the splendid sequence of gardens, fields and orchards cut by perpetual rivers. . . . It is the most magnificent of God's places.[4]

There is no enthusiasm here for nature in its virgin form. Only greenery and water make Ibn Hawqal think of Paradise. Fertile crops, counterpart of the hostile desert, are seen as a precious green textile. Earth has no value if not covered by continuous greenery.

Locus amoenus coincides with *locus ferax*. As a consequence, we deduce two important corollaries. The first is that Islamic civilization is not attracted by the proposals of the Western ecological movement, whose fundamentalist outlook envisages the preservation of a virgin, untouched nature or the restoration of nature back to a golden age, when humans had a more "natural" relationship with the earth. To those familiar with the level of pollution that plagues most of the Islamic world's urban settlements, it might seem ironic to think that traditional Islamic civilization could hold the potential for a balanced relationship with nature and the creation of sustainable landscapes. In reality, the religious Islamic literature favors the protection of nature either as an expression of the Divine or in support of human behavior.

The second corollary offers new perspectives in the scholarly research on Islamic gardens. Until recently, the Islamic garden has been studied through its literary aspects as a place of delight and love, through its religious aspects as a replica of the Qur'anic Paradise, through its formal aspects of artistic achievement (for example, the balance between nature and artifice, and forms of expression such as carpet weaving), and through its social aspects as a manifestation of power. But it is important to recognize that, first and foremost, the Islamic garden is the aesthetic distillate of agricultural practice, its geometric pattern showing a relationship between rationality and nature in which rationality does not become overpowered. Topiary art, for instance, is unknown in the Islamic garden design.

The coming of Islam in the seventh century C.E. did not change the territorial structures of the lands conquered, but supplemented and increased the quality of agriculture either in the great basins, where agri-managerial societies already existed, or in geographical enclaves like Yemen and the Ghouta of Damascus that had established rural traditions. It is in the meadows, however, and most specifically in the urban periphery where the culture becomes intensive and the property fragmented, that the rural ideal of Islam has been fully realized. It is in the *huertas* of Valencia, Spain, and in the suburban orchards of Bam (Iran)—where the principle of rigorous subdivision in small, geometric plots is still in use—that Islam made its original contribution to landscape, introducing exotic plants and improving traditional techniques of irrigation.

The following two examples, more than any abstract discussion, illustrate the appropriation and adaptation of a landscape by Islam. The first is an excellent example of a creation ex nihilo in an Islamic community and of landscape as an expression of integrated, indivisible unity mirroring Divine rationality versus harsh nature. The second is an example of reinterpretation and appropriation of a landscape with the recodification of its gardens and monuments.

The M'zab Valley (Algeria)

In a narrow valley, cut into a limestone plateau six hundred kilometers south of Algiers, the Islamic Kharijite sect settled in the eleventh century. After the first settlement at the mouth of the valley, al-Ateuf (1011), others soon followed. Such settlements included Bou Noura (1048) and then Melika, as well as Beni Izguen. The last settlement along the bed of the river was Gardaia (1054), after which the Pentapolis is named.

Along the curvilinear form of the valley, located on the peaks and irrigated palm groves (which, up until a century ago, constituted its main economic resource), there is a continuous sequence of settlements with cemeteries and open spaces for collective prayer. Along the ridges, there is a parallel system of watchtowers, whose main function was military, but which was also used to monitor and control damage by floods from the river.

The brilliant white of the cities and cemeteries is contrasted with the tan coloring of the lateral cliffs along the valley and the dark green of the palms, occasionally revealing patches of lighter green from the orchards. Under the palms within these orchards grow lemon, orange, fig, and pomegranate trees. Behind the mud walls, gardens, orchards, and summer houses lie one after the other. It is a hidden city, an "alternative" city where the Mozabites (as the inhabitants are called) seek refuge from the heat of the summer months.[5]

In the valley of M'zab, unlike other oases of the Sahara Desert, the aquifer has no possibility of natural replenishment. The only external agent that can serve this function is the flooding of the river—a unique and violent event that happens only periodically every several years. Inflated by the rains of the northern region, the streams rush into the dry riverbeds and, within a few hours, destroy whatever they meet. The destructive action of the waters has a cathartic function, because the water then filters through the sands alimenting the water-bearing stratum.

Along the river is a series of dams—the dam at Beni Izguen measuring longer than four hundred meters. Their function is that of easing the pressure of the spate. Connected to the dams is an ingenious system of openings, which have the form of an inverted comb and are further connected to underground channels. In the palm groves, a network of little channels runs along the streets at different levels. The channels cross over each other and finally branch out into openings that stretch from the walls of the gardens. These thirsty garden mouths intercept the water that is stored in the private underground tanks. The withdrawn water is proportional to the section of the mouth, calculated by a hydraulic specialist under the control of the *qāḍī*.[6]

The Vale of Kashmir (India)

Including the surrounding mountains, the Vale of Kashmir is about one hundred seventy kilometers long and sixty kilometers wide, with an approximately oval shape. It has always corresponded to the basin of the river Vitasta, today the Jhelum. The region owes its political and linguistic unity to its isolation, due to its peculiar geographical position—a fertile plain surrounded by a chain of very high mountains dominated by Mount Mahades and large enough to support a kingdom and nourish an advanced civilization.

Srinagar, the capital, occupies the heart of the valley in a magnificent position along the course of the Jhelum. It is a lively center for the trading of wares transported by boat, possessing a broad, fertile hinterland in the lakes Dal and Anchar.

The canvas plan kept in the City Palace Museum in Jaipur[7] evidences the structure of Srinagar, incised by numerous canals as opposed to a slender collar of terra firma on which rises the hill of Haraparbat.[8] The city is protected on three sides by the waters of the river—by the marshes where Anchar Lake expands to the west, and by the shores of Dal Lake to the east. Down below, one can see the knee-shaped Tsunth Kul, or Mar, the canal that links the river to Dal Lake, protected by a continuous dyke (*setu*). Beyond the canal, we find in succession the districts of Bardimar, Balandimar, and Khandabavan, where the ancient Skandabavana *vihāra* (Hindu or Buddhist monastery) used to stand and where today rises the *ziārat* (Islamic sanctuary) of Pir Muhammad Basur. Ancient ruins of the monastery were venerated until the nineteenth century as a *tīrtha* (sacred crossing, which came to mean a place of pilgrimage). The confluence of the Mar with the river, level with the Shergarhi Palace, has always been a *tīrtha* as well (called Marisamgana), used for funeral ceremonies.

On the left bank, a canal starts toward the district of Khatul and reaches the river after the last bridge, enabling boats to shorten the route. Further west, the city is protected by the Dudhganga River, which flows down from the Pir Pantsal chain and creates a confluence with the Jhelum, a river held sacred by the Hindus. On the right bank in the center of the built area, we can see the quadrangular form of the Jami Masjid—the congregational mosque around which numerous ancient remains bear witness to the earlier existence of Hindu temples.

To Hindu eyes, this bird's-eye description[9] makes it clear that Srinagar is a *kṣetra*—a complex hierarchical system of holy places linked by pilgrimage circuits (*yātrā*).[10] In fact, the whole Indian subcontinent is structured by similar privileged spaces which form an ensemble, where the practice of ritual movement generates a hierarchy of pilgrimages linked with a hierarchy of places. India is covered by this mesh of places and roads, divided, in its turn, into subsystems.

Starting from the largest scale, which marks the four corners of the Indian subcontinent, and going down to the single cities, this sacred landscape system is divided into zones structured by complex configurations and governed by symmetrical references, and by ritual movements which reflect the beginning of the largest scale. These hierarchical systems become more elaborate as one progresses. The smaller the area covered, and the more nonspatial, the more social and ideological factors become prevalent; it is a mental construction that could be depicted as a series of small concentric rings—the smallest ring being the city. Srinagar is no exception to the South Asian rule, located in such a way that the topographic landmarks all around it suggest and strengthen the sacrality of the place.[11]

We now have to identify the sacred areas of largest scale around Srinagar, or rather, those significant points that define its lines. To the south, the most important topographic element is the Takht-i-Sulaiman, with the remains of an ancient Hindu temple atop it—its pyramidal shape probably connected with the cult of Śiva, Jyesthesvara. A *liṅga* known by the same name is today venerated at the spring of Jyether, less than two kilometers to the east at the foot of the hill.[12]

Going eastward, amid vegetable gardens and vineyards, we reach the village of Thid. This is the Theda quoted in the *Rajaratangini*; the Mughal emperor Akbar's court chronicler Abu'l Fazl describes it as an enchanting spot, "where seven springs meet around sandstone buildings, reminders of bygone days."[13]

Further on, the little conurbation of Bran can be identified as the ancient Bhinadevi. The *tīrtha* has disappeared, but may be placed alongside the spring at Dampor, where later a Muslim shrine was established. Great fame and importance is attached to the village of Isabar, situated beside the Mughal garden of Nishat. Sacred to the Hindu goddess Durgā, it has numerous places of pilgrimage along the cliffs that sweep down to the lake.[14]

Passing the garden of Shalimar, we reach the village and spring of Ranyil in the Sind plain, and Zukur is also situated among the branches of the river north of Dal Lake. Muslim and Hindu shrines and tombs in the village are probably made with remains of an ancient Buddhist *vihāra*. Further on in the village of Amburher, the *ziārat* of

Farrukhzad Sahib covers an old temple of Śiva. Three kilometers lower down toward Srinagar, the large village of Vicar Nag dwells in the midst of walnut plantations. Here, the image of a sacred snake (*nāga*) is the goal for popular pilgrimage in the month of Caitra. To the west of the village, the ruins of three Hindu temples stand today, transformed into Muslim *ziārat*s and tombs.[15] Situated on a deep inlet of Dal Lake is the village of Sudarabal, where the Sodara spring was formerly located. Beside the village mosque are two basins fed by perennial springs. A few hundred meters further west, the Muslim shrine of Hazrat Bal, the most popular in all of Kashmir, where a hair from the beard of the Prophet is religiously preserved, is built upon the foundations of a previous, probably Muslim-era garden.[16]

Joining up all the points mentioned above, we can perceive a broken line upon the map. Surprisingly, the lines of this sacred space do not follow the crest of the hills overlooking the Jhelum valley, but rather mark the edge of the cultivated lands, separating the artificial world of the vegetable gardens, the vineyards, the floating gardens of Dal Lake and the canals, from the swamps of the forests. It is, after all, not by chance that in Hindu images the *kṣetra* is always represented as an enclosed garden! We are thus led to imagine along this boundary a continuous range of gardens of varied layouts, at times merging with the pattern of productive gardens, floating on the lake.[17] Its total synthesis of water and crops is the worthy response of a civilization which, in contrast to lands further West, has not established a dialectic or oppositional relationship with nature, but instead one of total devotion and belonging.

The preceding reconstruction, however, brings to light another interesting phenomenon, namely, the coincidence of the topography of Hindu and Muslim holy places [which is characteristic of the Indian subcontinent—RCF]. Lacking any confirmation coming from written sources, we may imagine that, initially, the appropriation of the territory of the Islamic dynasties from Shams al-din to Akbar took place by the mere substitution and reconsecration of the existing venerated springs. Continuity, for that matter, is borne out by the modern-day place-names, with their unmistakable Sanskrit origins.[18]

The Mughal emperor Akbar (r. 1556–1605) visited the valley only three times after Kashmir was added to the crown possessions. He built his palace in the fort of Haraparbat. The walls and two gates at the foot of the hill still exist, but the small garden which Akbar inserted is no more. The other garden attributed to Akbar, Nasim Bagh, is now a wood of plane trees planted in straight rows by his grandson Shah Jahan and facing Dal Lake. Of the original plantation, there remain some relics of terraces along the lake, while no trace remains of the hydraulic plants (an indispensable element for any Mughal garden).

It is, above all, in the basin around Srinagar that Jahangir (r. 1605–1627) and his son Shah Jahan (r. 1628–1658), imitated by the dignitaries of the empire, strove to transform the territory to reflect their image.[19] The monumental complexes reflected their imperial duty as Grand Protectors of Islam, but these rulers dedicated their more assiduous construction activities to the building of gardens. According to the sources, this construction fervor produced no fewer than seven hundred gardens throughout the valley.

Within the "sacred enclosure" of Srinagar, a systematic design activity was carried out that can only superficially be interpreted as an attempt at secularization. Gardens and parks are regarded as "services" only in the West, from the Enlightenment onward. In the case of the Mughals, we have instead an organic attempt to create a third branch of the sacred, with the figure of the king as the protagonist.

Wayne Begley's well-known article on the Taj Mahal has shown that emblems of power were an everyday obsession of the Mughals, and that the equation between architectural forms and celestial prototypes, always viewed in terms of the celebration of the deified image of the king, was the real spur for any architectural enterprise.[20] What could not be stated by the orthodox Muslim ruler as vicar of Allah was left to the metaphor of stone. Playing continually on the ambiguity between divine throne and royal throne, an unbridled vanity—urged on by adulatory court poetry—transformed tombs and monuments into symbols of glory and called for the laying out of gardens—replicas of the Qur'anic Paradise—to exalt the figure of the (holy) demiurge. "The garden is the place of illusions," says Pierre Grimal, "where the king is adulated and where the (wholly imaginary) evidence of his power has accumulated."[21]

Another original aspect of the Mughal period was the great mobility of the whole court [which was regularly packed up and transported between the various capitals of the Gangetic plain and the cooler summer climate of the Kashmir valley—RCF]. This mobility certainly had its origin in the distant nomadic tradition of the Turkish Chagatai [from whom the Mughal elite were descended—RCF], but was dictated also by the need for an ubiquitous presence of the royal image throughout the country in order to control the public conscience and intimidate rebels.

During the royal summer stays in Kashmir, this mobile tradition manifested itself in the coming and going of flotillas of *sikara* (local gondolas), taking the king on a "pilgrimage" from palace to garden and back in naturalistic explorations—"In those two or three days, I frequently went aboard boats and it was pleasant to go around admiring the flowers of Phak or of Shalimar"[22]—and on more distant expeditions up secondary branches of the Jhelum. This would appear to be an analogue to *tīrthayātrā*; in the gardens, the springs are harnessed and water flows under the king's throne (*chabūtra*), "a distillate of the emanation of the Divine Being—a ray of sunshine illuminating the Universe, the subject of the book of perfection, the repository of all the virtues."[23] Thus, the *tīrtha* has been rededicated.

Notes

1. In the Qur'an, the Latin *natura* and the Greek *physis* often translates as *tabī'a.*

2. Ibn Sina, *Le livre des directives et remarques*, trans. A.-M. Goichon (Beirut: Commission internationale pour la traduction des chefs-d'oeuvre, 1951), 302.

3. 'Asharite theology stresses the discontinuity between "finite" and "infinite." On the contrary, the Sufis emphasize the relationship between Divine Principle and its manifestation: they argue that, since two separate realities cannot exist, the "finite" must somehow coincide with the "infinite." On the subject, see Seyyed Hossein Nasr, *An Introduction to Islamic Cosmological Doctrines* (London: Thames and Hudson, 1978), 9 ff.

4. Ibn Hawqal, *Kitāb surāt al-arḍ*, in *Bibliotheca geographorum arabicorum*, ed. J. H. Kramers, (Leiden: E. J. Brill, 1938), 2:498–99.

5. M. Mercier, *La civilisation urbaine au M'zab* (Alger: E. Pfister, 1922); Henriette Didillon and Jean-Marc Didillon, *Habiter le désert: Les maison mozabites* (Brussels: P. Mardaga, 1977).

6. A. Berrien, "Gardaia, le miracle de l'eau," in *Renseignements coloniaux et documents du Comité d'Afrique Française* 47 (1933): 311–16.

7. Catalog no. 120 of the museum. It measures 280 x 223 cm. In the center of the plan is Dal Lake, at the top of the city with a fort. Countless gardens of the Mughal era are reproduced, but the author did not transcribe their names. The drawing, stressing the position of the waters, visualizes an aquatic microcosm.

8. Where the demons, according to legend, showed King Pravaresvara the site for the new foundation. At the foot of the hill there is a rock, long venerated as a physical manifestation of Gaṇeśa, a *svayambhū*. Nearby is the *ziārat* of Bahā' al-dīn Sāḥib, built with materials recovered from an ancient temple. Also not far away is the Jami Masjid.

9. A scientific but partial reconstruction of the *tīrtha* of Srinagar and environs has been attempted by Stein. See M. A. Stein, "Memoir on Maps Illustrating the Ancient Geography of Kashmir," in *Journal of the Asiatic Society of Bengal* 2 (1899): 147 ff.; Abu'l Fazl lists for the whole region forty-five shrines dedicated to Mahādeva, sixty-four to Viṣṇu, three to Brahma, and twenty-two to Durgā. In seven hundred localities he notes carved images of snakes, an object of devotion. See Abu'l Fazl 'Allami, *A'īn-i Akbārī*, trans. H. S. Jarrett (reprint, Delhi: Oriental Books, 1978), 2:352. Two hundred and fifty plans representing *tīrtha* are kept in the Srinagar museum, belonging to a manuscript of Pandit Sahibram, who died in 1872.

10. *Tīrthayātrā*, in Sanskrit, is a visit to the sacred places according to a prescribed itinerary. An interesting parallel could be made with the Kathmandu Valley, the great majority of whose population is Hindu and Buddhist. According to Niels Gutschow, who made a study of religious festivals in Kathmandu and Bhaktapur, processional rites tend to give significance to the spaces they touch. There is stated to be a mutual strengthening of significance between the rite and the place. Conversely, the circumambulatory rite is said to "group together" scattered places into a single concept. See Niels Gutschow, "Functions of Squares in Bhaktapur," in *Ritual Space in India: Studies in Architectural Anthropology*, ed. Jan Pieper (London: AARP, 1980), and idem, "Katmandu: Simbolik einer Stadt in Raum und Zeit," in *Stadt und Ritual*, ed. Niels

Gutschow and Thomas Sieverts, 2d ed. (Darmstadt and London: AARP, 1978). The concept of grouping is sometimes extended to the idea of delimitation of a sacred space, on a par with the illustrations described in the Gubbio tablets. See R. Herdick, "Stadt und Ritual: Am Beispiel der Newarstadt Kirtipur," in Gutschow and Sieverts, eds., *Stadt und Ritual*.

11. According to tradition, this also has a basis in the Islamic world: the *ḥarām* around Mecca; or, in the West, the Sacred Hills of Varese, for example.

12. The distance of the *tīrtha* from the temple is no greater than that of the temple of Lalitaditya at Martand from the sacred spring, to which it is dedicated. From this it may be inferred that the two structures at Takht-i-Sulaiman are associated with the same cult.

13. See Abu'l Fazl, *A'īn-i Akbārī*, 2:361.

14. The *tīrtha* of Isabar is quoted in all Kashmiri texts as exceptionally holy, and is sought by pious men before their death. The main attraction of the place is a spring known as Guptagariga, which fills an ancient tank in the center of the village.

15. On these ruins see Henry Hardy Cole, *Illustrations of Ancient Buildings in Kashmir* (London: India Museum, 1869), 31.

16. See C. M. Villiers-Stuart, *Gardens of the Great Mughals* (London: A. and C. Blake, 1913), 160.

17. The "floating gardens" of Dal Lake are artificial gardens consisting of a layer of soil and humus on broad water lily leaves, fixed to the bed by a stake transfixing them like a large pin. Like rafts, they can be moved and are therefore liable to be stolen by neighbors.

18. This is demonstrated by the recurrence of the terms ending in -pur, -mar, and -khot in village names; -sar, nambal, and -nag in the names of lakes and marshes; and -kul and -khan in the names of rivers and torrential streams.

19. See Attilio Petruccioli, "La citta come teatro: Note in margine all'urbanistica delle grandi capitali moghul dei secoli XVI e XVII," in Dalu Jones, ed., *Lo specchio del principe. Mecenatismi paralleli: Medici e Moghul* (Rome: Edizioni dell'Elefante, 1991), 63–75.

20. See Wayne E. Begley, "The Myth of the Taj Mahal and a New Theory of Its Symbolic Meaning," *Art Bulletin*, March 1979, 7–37.

21. See Pierre Grimal, "Jardin des hommes, Jardin des rois," *Traverses* 5/6 (1976): 71–72.

22. See *Tuzūk-i Jahāngīrī*, 2:150.

23. See Abu'l Fazl, *Akbarnāma* (Calcutta: Royal Asiatic Society of Bengal, 1877–86), 1:18.

From the Gardens of the Qur'an to the "Gardens" of Lahore

JAMES L. WESCOAT, JR.

Introduction

Mughal gardens evoke images of religious paradise and dynastic pleasure.[1] The religion is Islam, and the dynasty is a Central Asian military society that gained control over most of what is now India, Pakistan, Bangladesh, and Afghanistan.[2] During the sixteenth and seventeenth centuries, the Mughal nobility built spectacular gardens in the vicinities of Agra, Delhi, Lahore, Kashmir, and Kabul. These gardens served a wide range of functions, including palace-fortresses, suburban pleasure retreats, military encampments, and tomb complexes.

It has often been suggested that Mughal gardens symbolized the celestial paradise that awaits faithful Muslims on the day of judgment. The Qu'ran describes paradise gardens as having beautiful fountains, fruits, shade trees, and companions. Although Mughal gardens had many of these physical qualities, did they also embody the meaning of Islamic conceptions of paradise?

To interpret Mughal gardens as religious symbols is to imply that they effectively synthesized aesthetic and theological attributes of paradise. But few landscape researchers have focused on the relations between aesthetics and theology. Garden historians have examined the correspondence between Mughal gardens and descriptions of paradise in the Qu'ran.[3] Art historians have concentrated on garden elements, functions, and social contexts.[4] Scholars of religion have dealt with theological issues, but rarely in the context of specific places.[5]

A handful of studies have focused on the religious meaning of Mughal architecture. Wayne Begley and Z. A. Desai have compiled calligraphic passages at the Taj Mahal, many of which were drawn from the Qur'an.[6] Earlier, Begley interpreted the Taj Mahal as a physical representation of Sufi cosmologic concepts.[7] However, Ebba Koch argued that: ". . . a typical plan of Mughal residential architecture was used as a setting for the [Taj Mahal] tomb thus indicating that it was meant to represent an earthly replica of one of the houses of the heavenly paradise. . . ."[8] Juan Campo explored the religious dimension of residential architecture in Egypt. Paradise garden imagery also played a role in Carl Ernst's study of the sacred geography of a Sufi shrine in southern India.[9]

These works indicate the importance of paradise symbolism in Muslim environmental design, but they raise questions about its association with garden sites. Did historic gardens have theological as well as aesthetic associations with paradise? Were those theological meanings more, or less, important in other types of places (for example, mosques or shrines)? Have religious interpretations of Mughal gardens exaggerated their "Islamic" character?[10]

These questions may be addressed by comparing garden imagery of the Qur'an with selected sites in the city of Lahore, Pakistan, the "Mughal City of Gardens." Part one surveys garden references in the Qur'an, including passages that deal with the gardens of this world as well as those of the hereafter. Part two assesses the religious and secular character of selected sites in Lahore. To understand how gardens compare with other types of places, the selection includes shrines and mosques as well as gardens. Comparing historic places with Qur'anic meanings provides a basis for understanding the religious character of those places.

The Gardens of the Qur'an

The first step toward understanding the religious symbolism of gardens is to go beyond the most frequently cited descriptions of paradise in the Qur'an to the full corpus of garden references. The Qur'an contains 166 references to gardens, all but nineteen of which use the word *janna*, which connotes both "garden" and "paradise."[11] Fifteen of the remaining nineteen references use words that have dual connotations of gardens and afterlife—*'adn* (Eden), *firdaws* (paradise), *rawḍa* (tomb).

These passages may be grouped under three headings: 1) the gardens of the creation: 2) gardens of the hereafter; and 3) gardens of this world. All three groups serve the primary aim of the Qur'an, which is to guide human faith and conduct. In the sections below, passages are cited by chapter and verse, set within parentheses, as in: "Enter thou My Garden!" (89:301).

Gardens of Creation

The gardens created at the beginning of time have limited theological significance in Islam. The word "Eden" *('adn)* refers more frequently to gardens of the hereafter than to the creation. Several passages describe the expulsion of Adam and Eve from the garden (*janna*) of creation.

> O Adam! Dwell thou and thy wife in the garden and eat ye freely. . . . (2:35 and 7:19–36)

> O Adam! This is an enemy . . . so let him not drive you out of the garden (20:117–23)

But the brevity of these passages indicates that Islam is less concerned with paradise lost than with the path toward salvation.[12]

Gardens of the Hereafter

Most verses refer to paradise gardens that await the faithful on the day of judgment. They focus on two interlocking themes: the qualities of those who will be admitted to the gardens, and the experience of those gardens. Mughal garden studies have given more attention to the physical attributes of paradise than to the moral qualities of those admitted: the emphasis in Islamic theology is just the opposite. The theological meaning of paradise gardens is best discerned from the types of conduct they reward. Persons admitted to paradise will be those who "believe and do good works" (2:82; 20:75; 30:15; 42:22). They "control their wrath and are forgiving toward mankind" (3:134).

Despite hardships where they ". . . fled and were driven forth from their homes and suffered damage for My cause, and fought and were slain" (3:195), still they, "keep their duty" (3:198), "obeyeth Allah and His Messenger" (4:13), "humble themselves before their Lord" (11:23), "persevere" (13:24), and "repent" (19:60). One important passage makes an analogy between righteous persons and a "garden high upon a hill"—both are beautiful, productive, and favored by Allah (2:265). When admitted to paradise, they humbly say: "The praise to Allah, Who hath guided us to this. We could not truly have been led aright if Allah had not guided us" (7:43). At which time, they will be told: "Peace be unto you. You are good, so enter ye My Garden" (39:73–74). The gardens of the hereafter have a beauty almost beyond description. Some are peaceful and subdued, while others are sumptuous. The most common descriptions emphasize lush, well-watered "gardens, underneath which rivers flow" (many passages). These gardens are "wide as are the heavens and earth" (3:133), where the righteous are "safe forever" (3:198), residing like "brothers" in their "final home" or "dwelling," where "toll cometh not unto them" (many passages).

They will have riches and enjoyment beyond their imagination. They will "be given armlets of gold and will wear robes of finest silk and gold embroidery reclining on thrones therein" (18:31). They will "hear therein no idle talk, but only peace" (19:62). One of the most sumptuous passages describes the experience as follows:

> In the gardens of delight, on couches facing one another; a cup from a gushing spring is brought round for them. White, delicious to the drinkers, wherein there is no headache nor are they made mad thereby. And with them are those of modest gaze, with lovely eyes. (Pure) as they were hidden eggs (of the ostrich). (37:43–49)

As for the garden itself, it has "rivers of water unpolluted and rivers of milk whereof the flavor changeth not, and rivers of wine delicious to the drinkers, and rivers of clear-run honey . . ." (47:15). The most frequently quoted description of paradise is in a chapter titled "The Merciful" (*al-Raḥmān*):

> But for him who feareth the standing before his
> Lord, there are two gardens.
> Which is it, of the favors of your Lord,
> that ye deny?

Of spreading branches.
Which is it, of the favors of your Lord,
that ye deny?
Wherein are two fountains flowing.
Which is it, of the favors of your Lord,
that ye deny?
. . . .
And beside them are two other gardens.
Which is it, of the favors of your Lord,
that ye deny? (55:46–78)

The repeated question underscores the point that every element of paradise reflects the beneficence of Allah.

The unfaithful face eternal torment in a fiery hell (*jahannam*). These hypocrites will experience unquenchable thirst, boiling water, and roasting heat. They will have to watch those admitted to paradise, which will worsen their punishment and deepen their regret.

In the Islamic resurrection there are two alternatives—the garden and the fire. But there are many debates about how literally these descriptions of paradise and hell should be taken.[13] As in many religious traditions, conservative theologians argue for literal interpretation, while modernists urge a metaphorical interpretation of rewards and punishments that lie beyond the scope of imagination. Both groups agree that the greatest reward is acceptance by Allah, and the greatest punishment is rejection by Allah (7:72). These themes of rewards and punishments are closely connected with one another, and with analogies to the gardens of this world.

Gardens of This World

The gardens of this world (*dunyā*) provide signs (*āyāt*) for those who have the sense to recognize them. The signs are of three sorts. First, gardens on earth are signs of Allah's beneficence and sustaining power. It is Allah ". . . who produceth gardens trellised and untrellised and the date-palm, and crops of diverse flavor, and the olive and the pomegranate . . ." (6:142). He provides the resources that sustain gardens and make them productive: "He it is who sendeth down water from the sky, and therewith We bring forth buds of every kind . . . gardens of grapes . . ." (6:100). These are the signs for "people who believe" (6:100) and "people who have sense" (13:4). The key question raised by these signs is, "Will they not, then, give thanks?" (36:35).

Indeed, many people of the world do not give thanks, and a second set of verses refers to unbelievers who arrogantly demand gardens as proof of Allah's revelation to Muhammad: ". . . they say: We will not put faith in thee till thou . . . have a garden of date-palms and grapes and cause rivers to gush forth therein abundantly" (17:91). They ask: ". . . why hath he [the Prophet] not a paradise [garden] from whence to eat?" (25:5).

A third set of garden events presages the consequences of human arrogance: "Would any of you like to have a garden of palm-trees . . . [destroyed]? Thus, Allah maketh plain his revelations . . ." (2:226). The fruits of gardens can only be harvested if Allah wills it (68:17–20). Those who fail to recognize that Allah, not the gardener, creates gardens on earth receive warnings when those gardens are destroyed (2:226; 18:32–43). Gardens of the unfaithful are dried up and flooded (34:15–16). Grandiose gardens, palaces, and tombs on earth—like those of the Mughal kings—were vain displays (26:128). When a proud man said to his companion, "I am more than thee in wealth . . . his fruit was beset with destruction" (18:32–43). And of the wicked who were destroyed, the Qur'an asks: "How many were the gardens and water springs they left behind?" (44:25).

In summary, the central garden themes in the Qur'an are: the beneficence of Allah, dependence upon Allah, and moral prerequisites for admission to paradise in the hereafter. These themes provide the criteria for assessing the meaning of historical gardens and garden-like places in Lahore.

The "Gardens" of Lahore

The literature on Mughal gardens tends to oversimplify garden form and meaning. Garden form is invariably portrayed as a rectangular enclosure, symmetrically laid out with water channels, pavilions, and plantings. Recent research has shown that a wide range of garden forms developed during the Mughal period, and that these forms were associated with various dynastic rituals, historical situations, and environmental contexts.[14] But the religious meaning of Mughal gardens has not been explored.

This section of the paper assesses the religious character of historical places in Lahore, which lies on the left bank of the Ravi River in the broad semiarid plains of the Indus River basin. Besides the fortress-citadel, walled city, and suburbs, the city includes three main types of gardens built by Mughal rulers in the seventeenth century: 1) palace gardens in Lahore Fort; 2) a suburban pleasure-garden known as Shalamar; and 3) tomb-gardens of the emperor Jahangir and his family at Shahdara across the river from the citadel. These are some of the finest Mughal gardens in South Asia. But to what extent were they "paradise gardens" in the Qur'anic sense of the term? To address this question, brief comparisons are made with shrines, mosques, and a nineteenth-century Sikh garden built "in the Mughal style." These comparisons broaden our perspective on the places that have "garden-like" qualities, in the religious sense of the term.

The Mughal Gardens of Lahore

Only a handful of historical gardens survive in a city renowned for scores of gardens that lined the roads from Lahore Fort to the furthest suburbs. Suburban pleasure-gardens have been converted to public functions or subdivided for urban development. Gardens in the citadel have been altered by colonial barracks and commercial projects. Although tomb-gardens have been relatively protected, they too were taken over for private residences, schools, churches, and offices.

Three sites offer a perspective on the religious meanings associated with Mughal gardens. The suburban pleasure-garden known as Shalamar comes closest to the sumptuous descriptions of paradise gardens in the Qu'ran. During the fifteenth century, at the outset of the Mughal Empire, suburban gardens had served as military headquarters, territorial markers, and pleasure spots. The latter function was clearly dominant by 1643 when Shalamar was built by the fifth Mughal emperor, Shah Jahan.[15] The garden consists of three large rectangular terraces divided into quadrants by formal water channels, water chutes, tanks, and hundreds of fountains. Pavilions and shade trees sheltered the royal family from the blazing summer sun and monsoon rain. Feasts were held, dignitaries received, and poetry composed on moonlit nights. But notwithstanding these allusions to the pleasures of paradise, Shalamar has no overt references to the theology of paradise. In formal terms, Shalamar fulfilled the denotation, but not the connotation, of the Islamic paradise garden.

Garden quadrangles in Lahore Fort resembled Shalamar in many, but not all, respects. They served as private residential and reception areas for the royal family. They had exquisite pavilions and waterworks. But their association with the architecture of centralized authority (that is, fortifications, halls of public audience, imperial treasury, etc.) indicates the Mughal claim to be the vicegerents of Allah on earth. This conjunction of garden and fortress reflects longstanding ideas about divine kingship in Islamic societies.[16] Fortress-gardens synthesized the religious and political meanings of gardens.

Ideas about paradise and kingship are also reflected in the tomb-gardens of Shahdara, across the river from Lahore Fort.[17] Shahdara includes the tomb-gardens of the fourth emperor, Jahangir (1605–27), his wife Nur Jahan (d. 1645), and brother-in-law Asaf Khan (d. 1642). These places display the classic "Islamic" garden form—a square enclosure divided into four quadrants by elegant water channels, pools, and walks with the tomb set exactly in the center (this is often called the *chahār bāgh* pattern). The tombs stand on square or octagonal plinths, decorated with red sandstone and marble inlay. Although few inscriptions survive at Shahdara, other tomb-gardens in Lahore, Delhi, and Agra have inscriptions from the Qur'an referring to the gardens of paradise, the ninety-nine most beautiful names of God, and the pious hopes of their patrons.[18] Mughal kings and queens, including Jahangir and Nur Jahan, allegedly requested modest tombs, open to the sky, in accordance with Islamic law.[19] These single-storey royal tombs at Lahore sought to combine the monumentality required for dynastic glory and the religious expectations of Islam. Provisions were made for the recitation of the Qur'an and ritual circumambulation of the tomb by dynastic successors.

The political significance of tomb-gardens outlived their religious significance. They still inspire an occasional prayer, but they are more apt to be the destinations of school children, tourists, picnickers, designers, and state officials than of religious pilgrims. Because the latter group is most concerned with the theology of paradise, it is useful to compare the places they regard as sacred with Mughal gardens.

Sufi Shrines as Paradise Gardens

When asked, "What is the most sacred place in Lahore today?" most Lahoris will mention a specific shrine or mosque. Of the hundreds of shrines in Lahore the most famous is that of the eleventh-century Sufi saint known as Dara Ganj Bakhsh ("Bestower of Treasures") who wrote an important treatise on Sufism titled *The Unveiling of the Veiled*.[20] In contrast with Sufis who advocated ecstatic "intoxication," he portrayed Sufism as an unfolding synthesis of mystical experience and sober piety.

His shrine stands on an old river terrace south of the walled city. A marble grave lies at the center of the shrine, surrounded by a carved marble screen and covered with a green shroud and fresh rose petals. Outside the shrine are a large modern mosque, shops for pilgrims' needs, an open kitchen that provides free food, offices for shrine officials, and a bustling commercial area.

In contrast with the archaeological approach to conserving Mughal monuments, Sufi shrines are active religious sites that are frequently rebuilt with modern and pop architectural features. The shrine of Dara Ganj Bakhsh attracts thousands of pilgrims who offer prayers, make vows, and touch or kiss the grave. Shrines stimulate intense religious experience with allusions to the gardens of paradise.

In the popular religion of Muslim shrines, saints have the power (*baraka*) to intercede on behalf of their devotees on practical matters and also to help gain admission to the gardens of paradise on the day of judgment.[21] This power is spatially concentrated at the grave of the saint, which explains the activities of pilgrims at the grave. In addition to the popular belief that saints can help one gain admission to paradise, many also believe that saints have the spiritual character of a garden, and that their shrines have a sacredness resembling paradise. In contrast with Mughal gardens, shrines have the connotations, but rarely the physical form, of paradise gardens. A prominent Sufi saint in Shergarh, a town south of Lahore, is said to have pulled up his garden so his followers would not confuse an earthly garden with paradise.

One major site in Lahore, known as Mian Mir, did combine Sufi shrines with Mughal gardens. Mian Mir was a seventeenth-century saint revered by the Mughal prince Dara Shikoh (d. 1659 C.E.). Mian Mir's grave lies in the center of the area surrounded by the graves of his followers. A tomb-pavilion surrounded by a square water tank and garden, built for Dara Shikoh's wife Nadira Begum, lies on an axis with the shrine. Mian Mir's most important spiritual disciple, Mulla Shah, instructed Dara Shikoh in spiritual matters, and when Mulla Shah died, Dara Shikoh ordered a rectangular garden to be built around his tomb in the Mughal style. The shrine-garden of Mulla Shah represents an exceptional synthesis of spiritual and dynastic garden traditions in Lahore.

Mosques and Paradise Gardens

Although widely patronized for centuries, Sufi shrines generate intense theological controversy among Muslims, in part related to conflicting theologies of paradise. Orthodox Sunni Muslims believe in a direct relationship between human beings and Allah. They regard prayers to saints and worship at shrines as misdirected, and they reject all notions of intercession for admission to paradise. Persons will be admitted on the basis of their individual faith and actions.

When asked, "What is the most sacred place in Lahore?" such persons mention either mosques in general or a specific mosque like the Badshahi mosque built by the last great Mughal emperor Aurangzeb (r. 1658–1707 C.E.). Aurangzeb is remembered today for his orthodox beliefs, in contrast with the Sufism of his brother Dara Shikoh. Aurangzeb was the only Mughal emperor to be buried in strict accordance with Islamic law in a modest grave rather than a monumental tomb-garden. His architectural patronage emphasized mosques over other building types.[22]

The Badshahi mosque was, until a few years ago, the largest mosque in the world. It has three magnificent white marble domes surrounded by simple red sandstone walls and minarets. Its majestic yet simple beauty is unmatched in the monumental mosque architecture of South Asia. Despite Aurangzeb's pious reputation, some orthodox Muslims are put off by the dynastic pretensions of the Badshahi mosque and argue that it is no more or less sacred than any other mosque in the city, or any place where a person prays.

The sacredness of mosques differs from that of shrines by virtue of their role as places for collective community prayer directly with Allah, with no intercession by saints. They are in close accord with the

Qur'anic theology of paradise because they provide a space for actions that lead toward paradise. Some mosques have calligraphic inscriptions from the Qur'an and decorative vegetal motifs of carved stone, tilework, and painting that allude to the beauty of paradise gardens. But mosques rarely have planted gardens that focus attention on the gardens of this world rather than on the paradise gardens that should be foremost in the minds of the faithful.

Whereas Mughal gardens exemplified the description of paradise gardens and Sufi shrines their mystical experience, mosques embody the theological meaning of paradise. To appreciate the continuing significance of these differences, it is useful to consider a place constructed after the decline of Mughal rule that has elements of all three traditions.

After the Mughals

After Aurangzeb died in 1707 C.E., Lahore experienced rapid decline. A series of invasions culminated in the ascendence of a Sikh empire centered politically at Lahore and spiritually at Amritsar. This shift in religious control did not slow down the construction of gardens "in the Mughal style."[23] The Sikh ruler Ranjit Singh occupied garden quadrangles in Lahore Fort. His nobles built gardens along the roads from the fort to Shalamar. They scavenged marble and other materials from Shahdara tomb-gardens for pleasure gardens and their own funerary sites.

The best surviving Sikh garden is known as the Hazuri Bagh, built by Ranjit Singh in the open space between Lahore Fort and the Badshahi mosque. The Hazuri Bagh is rectangular in shape, divided into four equal parts by fountains, water channels, and plantings, with a marble pavilion in the center where cooling beverages were consumed during hot summer evenings in Lahore. The Hazuri Bagh follows the physical conventions of Mughal garden design closely, but it has little religious significance. The Sikhs shut down the Badshahi mosque and used it as an ammunition depot. They lived in the garden quadrangles of Lahore Fort but eschewed the lavish dynastic symbolism of the Mughals. Eventually, Ranjit Singh's ashes were commemorated in a beautiful structure (*samādhi*) next to the garden.

After the British took over Lahore in 1848, they built barracks in the fortress quadrangles and public works in the garden suburbs. Although they returned the Badshahi mosque to the Muslim community and renovated the Hazuri Bagh with modern archaeological techniques, the original fabric of garden symbolism continued to fade.

Modern Pakistani leaders have also built and rebuilt gardens in the Mughal style, though these gardens lack the physical refinement and symbolic association with gardens of the Qur'an. In 1988, an early Mughal garden situated in the middle of the Ravi River was completely reconstructed under the orders of a powerful politician and over the legal objections of the Pakistan Department of Archaeology. The resulting site has a modern park-like character and little of its original form or meaning.

A partial exception to this trend occurred at the tomb built for Allama Iqbal (1873–1937 C.E.), poet-philosopher and author of the idea of Pakistan, which stands in a corner of the Hazuri Bagh next to the Badshahi mosque. Iqbal sought to map out the future of Islam in the modern world and to explore its spiritual possibilities.[24] His jointly political, cultural, and religious mission bears comparison with the meaning, if not the physical form, of Islamic garden design. The secular Hazuri Bagh was thus surrounded by Mughal fortress-gardens, the Badshahi mosque, Ranjit Singh's grave, and Allama Iqbal's tomb. It stands at the intersection of, and perhaps mediates among, the diverse religious and cultural "gardens" of Lahore.

Conclusion

The historical places of Lahore have a wide array of associations with paradise gardens. Mughal gardens exemplified the descriptive imagery of the Qur'an but little of its meaning. They had more in common with pre-Islamic traditions of divine kingship than the message of the Qur'an. Places directly associated with religious life—for example, shrines and mosques—more closely approximated the theological meanings of paradise.

These findings suggest three lines for future research on landscape and religion in the Indo-Islamic realm. First, the paradise-like beauty of Mughal gardens deserves more detailed attention. Surprisingly, there have been no detailed studies of the aesthetics of Mughal gardens as envisioned by their builders and designers. Such studies might lead beyond simple associations between beauty and sacredness to a deeper understanding of the spiritual nature of landscape beauty.

A second line of research would focus on places that exemplify the religious meanings of paradise. This paper found that although few gardens are religious, many religious places have garden-like qualities. Research on these qualities might shed further light on the patterns and prospect of religious meaning in the built environment.

These two lines of inquiry could be combined to address a third, fundamentally practical, set of issues on synthesis and conflict in landscape design. If it is true that historical gardens achieved the form, but not the meaning, of paradise gardens, are there paths toward a deeper synthesis of form and meaning? This question has relevance for all cultures. Places like Mian Mir, which did combine the form and meaning of the paradise garden, deserve detailed study. It is important to understand when gardens have functioned as spaces of cultural contact (like the Hazuri Bagh) as well as conflict.[25] Integrating the roles of gardens as places of moral action, environmental beauty, and spiritual harmony is a vital challenge for the pluralistic societies of South Asia and of the world at large.

Notes

An earlier version of this paper was published in *Landscape Research* 20 (1995): 21–36, in a special issue guest edited by Professor Amita Sinha, and reproduced here with the generous permission of Taylor and Francis, http://www.tandf.co.uk/.

1. John Brookes, *Gardens of Paradise: The History and Design of the Great Islamic Gardens* (London: Weidenfeld and Nicholson, 1987); S. Crowe, S. Haywood, S. Jellicoe, and G. Patterson, *The Gardens of Mughal India* (London: Thames and Hudson, 1972); Jonas Lehrman, *Earthly Paradise: Garden and Courtyard in Islam* (Berkeley: University of California Press, 1980); C. M. Villiers-Stuart, *Gardens of the Great Mughals* (London: A. and C. Black, 1913); James L. Wescoat, Jr., "The Islamic Garden: Issues for Landscape Research," *Environmental Design: Journal of the Islamic Environmental Design Research Centre* 1986, no. 1, 10–19; and idem, "Picturing an Early Mughal Garden," *Asian Art* 2 (1989): 59–79.

2. John F. Richards, *The Mughal Empire*, New Cambridge History of India, 1.5 (Cambridge: Cambridge University Press, 1993).

3. E. B. Moynihan, *Paradise as a Garden in Persia and Mughal India* (New York: George Brazillier, 1979).

4. Catherine B. Asher, *Architecture of Mughal India*, New Cambridge History of India, 1.4 (Cambridge: Cambridge University Press, 1992); Ebba Koch, *Mughal Architecture* (Munich: Prestel Verlag, 1991); Attilio Petruccioli, *Fathpur Sikri: Città del sole e delle acque* (Rome: Carucci, 1988); James L. Wescoat, Jr., "Gardens of Invention and Exile: The Precarious Context of Mughal Garden Design during the Reign of Humayun," *Journal of Garden History* 10 (1990): 106–16; and idem, "Gardens vs. Citadels: The Territorial Context of Early Mughal Gardens," *Garden History: Issues, Approaches, Methods*, ed. J. D. Hunt (Washington, D.C.: Dumbarton Oaks, 1992), 331–58.

5. L. Gardet, "Djanna," *Encyclopedia of Islam*, 2d ed. (Leiden: E. J. Brill, 1983), 447–52; J. MacDonald, "Paradise: Islamic Eschatology, VI," *Islamic Studies* 5 (1966): 331–83; Annemarie Schimmel, "The Celestial Garden in Islam," in *Islamic Gardens*, ed. E. B. MacDougall and Richard Ettinghausen (Washington, D.C.: Dumbarton Oaks, 1976); and Jane I. Smith, *The Islamic Understanding of Death and Resurrection* (Albany: State University of New York Press, 1981).

6. Wayne E. Begley and Z. A. Desai, *Taj Mahal: The Illumined Tomb. An Anthology of Seventeenth-Century Mughal and European Documentary Sources* (Cambridge, Mass.: Aga Khan Program for Islamic Architecture; Seattle: University of Washington Press, 1989).

7. W. E. Begley, "The Myth of the Taj Mahal and a New Theory of Its Symbolic Meaning," *Art Bulletin* 61 (1979): 7–37.

8. Koch, *Mughal Architecture*, 99.

9. Juan Campo, *The Other Side of Paradise: Explorations into the Religious Meanings of Domestic Space in Islam* (Columbia: University of South Carolina Press, 1991); Carl Ernst, *The Eternal Garden: Mysticism, History, and Politics at a South Asian Sufi Center* (Albany: State University of New York Press, 1992).

10. For a range of skeptical, appreciative, and hybrid perspectives, see D. F. Ruggles, "What's Religion Got to Do with It?" A Skeptical Look at the Symbolism of

Islamic and Rajput Gardens," *DAK: The Newsletter of the American Institute of Indian Studies* 4 (autumn): 1, 5–8; James L. Wescoat, Jr., "Waterworks and Landscape Design at the Mahtab Bagh," in *The Moonlight Garden: New Discoveries at the Taj Mahal,* ed. Elizabeth B. Moynihan, 59–78 (Washington, D.C.: Smithsonian Institution; Seattle: University of Washington Press, 2000); and idem, "Mughal Gardens: The Re-emergence of Comparative Possibilities and the Wavering of Practical Concerns," in *Perspectives on Garden Histories*, ed. M. Conan (Washington, D.C.: Dumbarton Oaks, 1999), 107–26.

11. Gardet, "Djanna"; Hanna E. Kassis, *A Concordance of the Quran* (Berkeley: University of California Press, 1983).

12. There are, however, many references to the creation in the Qur'an and large literatures on cosmology in Islamic theology and philosophy.

13. Gardet, "Djanna"; MacDonald, "Paradise: Islamic Eschatology; and Smith, *Islamic Understanding.*

14. Elizabeth B. Moynihan, "The Lotus Garden of Zahir al-Din Muhammad Babur," *Muqarnas* 5 (1988): 134–52; James L. Wescoat, Jr., "Gardens, Urbanization, and Urbanism in Mughal Lahore: 1526–1657," in *Mughal Gardens: Sources, Representations, Places, Prospects*, ed. James L. Wescoat, Jr., and Joachim Wolschke-Bulmahn (Washington, D.C.: Dumbarton Oaks, 1996); and Mahmood Hussain, Abdul Rehman, and James L. Wescoat, Jr., eds., *The Mughal Garden: Interpretation, Conservation, and Implications* (Lahore: Ferozsons, 1996).

15. M. Baqir, *Lahore Past and Present: Being an Account of Lahore Compiled from Original Sources*, 2d ed. (Lahore: Panjabi Adabi Academy, 1984); and S. Kausar, Michael Brand, and James L. Wescoat, Jr., *Shalamar Garden: Landscape, Form, and Meaning* (Karachi: Ministry of Culture, Department of Archaeology, 1991).

16. John Renard, *Islam and the Heroic Image: Themes in Literature and the Visual Arts* (Columbia: University of South Carolina Press, 1993).

17. James L. Wescoat, Jr., Michael Brand, and N. Mir, "The Shahdara Gardens of Lahore: Site Documentation and Spatial Analysis," *Pakistan Archaeology* 25 (1993): 333–66.

18. Begley and Desai, *Taj Mahal.*

19. James L. Wescoat, Jr., "The Scale(s) of Dynastic Representation: Monumental Tomb-gardens in Mughal Lahore," *Ecumene: Journal of Environment, Culture, Meaning* 1 (1994): 324–48.

20. 'Ali bin Uthman al-Hujwiri, *Kashf al-Mahjūb*, trans. Reynold Nicholson (1911; Lahore: Islamic Book Foundation, 1982).

21. Christian W. Troll, ed. *Muslim Shrines in India: Their Character, History, and Significance* (Delhi: Oxford University Press, 1989).

22. Royal garden construction continued, however, under the patronage of his sisters, including the pious Jahanara Begum, underscoring the changing meaning of gardens from their early role in territorial conquest toward increasingly idealized places for women dwelling in the image and anticipation of paradise; for example, see Ebba Koch, *Mughal Art and Imperial Ideology: Collected Essays* (Delhi: Oxford University Press, 2001).

23. S. R. Dar, *Historical Gardens of Lahore* (Lahore: Aziz Publishers, 1982); S. Rasool, "From Private Gardens to Public Parks: A Study of Transformation in

Landscape of Lahore. Pakistan from Seventeenth Century to Present" (Masters thesis, Department of Landscape Architecture, University of Illinois, Urbana-Champaign, 1994).

24. Muhammad Iqbal, *The Reconstruction of Religious Thought in Islam* (Lahore: Institute of Islamic Culture, 1986).

25. James L. Wescoat, Jr., Michael Brand, and N. Mir, "Gardens, Roads and Legendary Tunnels: The Underground Memory of Mughal Lahore, *Journal of Historical Geography* 17 (1991): 1–17; Wescoat, "Gardens vs. Citadels."

Trees as Ancestors: Ecofeminism and the Poetry of Forugh Farrokhzad

FARZANEH MILANI

In her pioneering article "The Power and the Promise of Ecological Feminism," Karen J. Warren underscores the interconnectedness between feminism and environmentalism. "Ecological feminism," she writes, "is the position that there are important connections—historical, experiential, symbolic, theoretical—between the domination of women and the domination of nature, an understanding of which is crucial to both feminism and environmental ethics."[1]

The work of contemporary Iranian poet Forugh Farrokhzad delves into this complex interconnectedness. She is not only interested in our relationship with the natural world. She also explores the ways in which that pattern replicates itself in our interpersonal relationships. Ecologiçally aware, Farrokhzad was concerned about an environmental crisis that is too often ignored, justified, blamed on the "other," or simply explained away. This alertness went beyond the love of nature. It also called for action and warned against complacency and silence.

Born in Tehran in 1935, Forugh Farrokhzad was a gifted woman with many claims on her talent. In her tragically short life, she wrote five poetry collections, a few short stories, a travelogue, a number of critical pieces, two film scripts, and an anthology of contemporary poetry. She directed an internationally acclaimed, prizewinning documentary, *The House Is Black*. She also painted, acted, and translated. As a relentless explorer of new domains, she ceaselessly outgrew herself, transgressed her limits, and trespassed boundaries. Farrokhzad's whole body of work is a struggle against the institutions of both literature and society. It is an oasis of the conventionally forbidden—cultural, sexual, textual, or cinematic. From the very beginning of her literary career, this poet was a daring, often irreverent, explorer of taboo topics. Hers was the subversive, the innovative text, not only in its subject matter, technique, or point of view, but also in its simple, lucid, and unpretentious language. Farrokhzad died in a car accident on 13 February 1967 at the height of her creativity. She was thirty-two years old.

Over twenty years ago, I wrote my dissertation on Farrokhzad. Although my reading of her poetry has radically changed over the years, I still find myself fascinated by her work. Although I have continued to work on various aspects of her poetry, never before had I appreciated or even noticed her multifaceted concern with ecology. It is thanks to the conference on Islam and ecology that a whole new layer of her work has been made visible to me. For this gift of expanded vision, I am grateful to the organizers of this conference. What I see now and had not seen earlier is how Farrokhzad's reevaluation of gender relations is deeply connected to and closely mirrors relationships to nature. Her poem "I Feel Sorry for the Garden" is a case in point:

> No one worries for the flowers
> no one worries for the fishes
> no one wants to admit the garden is dying,
> its heart is swollen under the sun
> its mind is drained of green memories,
> its feelings are rotting in desolation.
>
> Our garden is lonely
> our garden yawns in hope of a new cloud
> and the pool in our yard is drying up.
>
> Innocent little stars fall from treetops
> and at nights
> the sound of coughing can be heard
> from the pallid windows of the houses of fishes
> our garden is very lonely.
>
> My father says:
> "It's over for me
> It's over for me
> I've paid my dues
> I've done my share."

From dawn to dusk
my father reads his *Book of Kings*
and *Nasekh ol-tavarikh.*
My father tells my mother:
"To hell with all the birds and the fishes
why should I care
if there is a garden or not when I die?
My retirement pension is all I need."

My mother's life is a prayer rug
spread at the threshold of hell's terror.
My mother traces the footprint of sin in everything.
My mother believes
the blasphemy of a plant has polluted the garden
and she prays all day long.
My mother is a born sinner.
She prays for the flowers
and she prays for the fishes
and she prays for herself.
My mother waits for a second coming
and the forgiveness
that will descend upon the earth.

My brother calls the garden a graveyard
my brother mocks the rioting weeds in the garden
and keeps count of dead fishes
who decay and decompose beneath the sick skin of the water.
My brother is addicted to philosophy.
He believes destruction is the only cure for the garden.
My brother gets drunk
and he bangs on the doors and the walls
and he tells everyone
he is tired, dejected and very, very sad.
My brother carries his sorrow
like his identity card, his calendar,
his lighter, and his pen
to the street and to the bazaar.
My brother's sorrow is so small, so very small that every night
it gets lost in the crowd at the bar.

And my sister who was a friend to the flowers
and every time my mother spanked her
took her heart's simple words

to the kind and quiet company of flowers
my sister,
the one who treated the whole family of our fishes
to a party of sun with cookies
lives now on the other side of the city.
In her plastic home
with her plastic goldfishes
protected by the love of her plastic husband
and under the branches of plastic apple trees
my sister sings phony songs
and makes real babies.
Whenever my sister visits us
and the hem of her garment
touches our garden's destitution
she takes a perfumed bath.
Every time she comes to visit us
my sister is pregnant again.

Our garden is lonely, O, so very lonely
all day long
the sound of breaking and explosions
can be heard behind the door.
Instead of flowers
our neighbors have planted
mortars and machine guns in their gardens.
Our neighbors cover their tiled pools
which become hidden reservoirs of explosives.
All the children in our neighborhood
fill their backpacks with little bombs.
Our garden is confused.
And I fear.
I fear an age that has lost its heart
I fear the futility of so many hands
and the alienation on so many faces.
Like a student, madly in love with geometry
I feel lonely.

But I believe the garden can be taken to the hospital
I am convinced
I am convinced
I am convinced
And the garden's heart lies swollen under the sun
its mind slowly draining out of green memories.

"I Feel Sorry for the Garden" is one of the most anthologized and most popular of Farrokhzad's poems. To the best of my knowledge, all those who have written about the poem—and that includes myself in previous writings—have taken the garden to be a political metaphor in its narrowest sense. We metaphorized the garden, allegorized it, politicized it, analyzed it over and over again, but never understood it to be simply a garden. Farrokhzad's ecological concerns evaded us.

Gardens have always held a privileged position in Iran's national imagination. They have played an amazing inspirational role and permeated various arts. Whether on carpets, on canvas, in literary texts, or in films, gardens kept the heat, the cold, the dust, and unwelcome intrusions out. With their cascading waterways and tall trees, they created fields of delight within their walled spaces.

Iranians visualize Paradise as a garden. Classical and modernist poets and painters have found a world of refuge, meditation, metaphors, and pleasure in gardens. From poets like Ferdowsi, Rumi, Sa'di, and Hafiz to Sepehri and Farrokhzad, from the painters Mani and Behzad to Kamal-el-molk, all have celebrated gardens and their beauty. "In the Persian imagination, the garden is an all-pervasive image, so central to inner vision for so many centuries that it is a kind of cultural memory. Shaped by landscapes, by the circumstances of history, by religion, and especially by a deep rooted tradition of mystic thought and poetry, aspects of this inner garden appear on every side and at every level of life."[2]

Gardens appear frequently in Farrokhzad's poetry. At times, they have metaphorical significance. The poem titled "Fath-e Bagh" (Garden Conquered), for instance, is an eloquent and engaging portrayal of the primordial garden.[3] The title, as well as several other obvious references and parallels, alludes to the Garden of Eden. In this poem, Farrokhzad deconstructs and then reconstructs the story of Adam and Eve.[4] Without a guilty figure to mediate between innocence lost and sin accomplished, both man and woman voluntarily pick the forbidden apple. Here, however, there is no need for a temptress, a docile dunce, a scapegoat. In this landscape of bliss, where death dies and the ephemeral joins the eternal, man and woman conquer time and finiteness. Neither the man nor the woman is committed to the preservation of a false innocence. They do not blame each other.

Two individuals, two individualities, are the enchanted inhabitants of this terrestrial paradise—two individuals who have assumed responsibility for their needs and deeds, who enjoy a reciprocal and egalitarian relationship. Liberated from conventional sex-stereotyped modes of thoughts and emotions, committed to each other, and in communion with nature, man and woman celebrate reciprocity in this poem. In the utopic space of this garden, man and woman console, delight, and strengthen one another. This garden is a place of trust where both partners can lower their defenses, revel in the nonutilitarian quality of their partnership, receive the full force of love, and welcome intimacy and dialogue. In this garden, hierarchical relationships have no place. There is no domination of women or of nature. Together, the man and the woman bask in their love of and concern for each other and nature.

> Everyone knows
> everyone knows
> we found our way into the cold and silent repose
> of phoenixes
> we found truth in the little garden
> in the bashful look of a nameless flower
> and eternity in the never-ending moment
> when two suns gaze at each other.
>
> It is not a matter of fearful whispers in the dark
> it is a matter of daylight, open windows, and fresh air
> and an oven where useless things are burnt
> and an earth pregnant with a new crop.
> It is a matter of our amorous hands
> connecting the nights
> with perfume's messages of breeze and light.
>
> Come to the meadow
> come to the large meadow
> and call me from behind acacia blossoms
> like a deer calling its mate.

Erosion of the assumptions concerning gender relations proves to be fundamental in "Garden Conquered." Norms inherited from the past are no longer operative. Loving and loved, undeceived and undeceiving, the man and the woman in this poem neither assume guilt nor cast blame. They live in harmony and friendship with each other and with nature.

By contrast, "I Feel Sorry for the Garden" depicts a garden that is neglected and decrepit. The poet subtly but forcefully portrays the failings of the members of her family and, by extension, all the members of her society, in taking care of it. She brings into focus the apathy inherent in their attitude and their detrimental passivity. The entire family is aware of the deplorable state of the garden, yet they are unwilling to do anything about it. The father takes refuge in his books and in past glories. The mother, who believes the blasphemy of some plant has blighted the garden, awaits a divine savior. She prays all day long. The brother, addicted to philosophy, sees the garden's cure in its destruction. The sister, who formerly befriended the flowers and the goldfishes, now lives on the wealthier side of the city, and does not care a fig for the garden. It is no wonder that the garden is dying a slow death, its heart bloating under the baking sun, its mind emptied of green memories. This garden is paradise-turned-inferno. The poet who had proudly announced, "the trees are my ancestors,"[5] and was in communion with "wild rabbits," "shells full of pearls," and "young eagles,"[6] the woman who wanted "to press clusters of unripe wheat to her chest / and breastfeed them,"[7] laments the desolation of the garden.

Few poets in the history of Persian literature have challenged the nature of male/female relationships with as much vigor and conviction as Farrokhzad. Even fewer have established a close correlation between the domination of women and the domination of nature.

Notes

1. Karen J. Warren, "The Power and the Promise of Ecological Feminism," in *Ecological Feminist Philosophies*, ed. Karen J. Warren (Bloomington: Indiana University Press, 1996), 19.

2. Mehdi Khansari, M. Reza Moghtader, and Minouch Yavari, *The Persian Garden: Echoes of Paradise* (Washington, D.C.: Mage Publishers, 1998), 147.

3. Forugh Farrokzad, *Tavalodi digar* (Another Birth) (Teheran: Morvarid, 1963), 125–29.

4. For an analysis of this poem, see Farzaneh Milani, "Nakedness Regained: Farrokhzad's Garden of Eden," in *Forugh Farrokhzad: A Quarter-Century Later,* ed. Michael Hillmann, *Literature East and West*, 24 (1988): 91–104.

5. Forugh Farrokhzad, *Īmān biyāvarīm be āghāz-e fasl-e sard* (Let Us Believe in the Dawning of a Cold Season) (Tehran: Morvarid, 1974), 79.

6. Farrokhzad, *Tavalodi dīgar*, 80.

7. Farrokhzad, *Īmān biyāvarīm*, 80.

Glossary of Arabic Terms

ʿālam	world
amāna(t)	trust, trusteeship
āya (pl. *āyāt*)	miraculous sign (i.e., of God)
baraka(t)	divine blessing
bīʿa(t)	environment
dīn	"true" religion
fatwa (pl. *fatāwā*)	an opinion by a qualified legal scholar
fiqh	Islamic jurisprudence
fiṭra(t)	the true (i.e., primordial) nature of things
ḥadīth	a report of the sayings or deeds of the prophet Muhammad
ḥalāl	ritually pure, acceptable (especially in reference to food)
ḥarām	protected (lit., "forbidden") area
ḥimā	protected area
īmān	faith
jihād	struggle
khalīfa	vicegerent, steward
khilāfa	stewardship
mawāt	undeveloped (lit., "dead") lands
mīzān	balance
mufsid fi' l-arḍ	"corrupter on earth" (applied in the Qur'an to those who commit grievously evil acts)
muḥīṭ	environment (lit., "that which encompasses")
ribā	interest-taking (forbidden in Islam)
ṣaḥīḥ	"sound," as in the most reliable form of *ḥadīth*
sharīʿa(t)	the (idealized) Islamic way of life, understood as represented by classical Islamic law
sunna(t)	lit., "tradition," often specifically understood as the example of the prophet Muhammad as attested in the *ḥadīth*s
ṭabīʿa(t)	nature
ṭarīqa	Sufi order

taṣawwuf	Sufism, i.e., Islamic mysticism
tawḥīd	oneness (i.e., of God)
umma	community
uṣūl al-fiqh	the science of Islamic jurisprudence
waḥdat al-wujūd	"unity of being," a concept associated with the monist philosophy of Ibn 'Arabi
waqf (pl. *awqāf*)	charitable public endowment, inalienable and untaxable
zakāt	annual charitable donation of 2.5 percent, required of every Muslim

Bibliography on Islam and Ecology

RICHARD C. FOLTZ

Abdel Haleem, Harfiyah, ed. *Islam and the Environment*. London: Ta-Ha Publishers, 1998.

Abdel Haleem, M. "Water in the Qur'an." In *Islam and the Environment*, ed. Harfiyah Abdel Haleem, 103–17. London: Ta-Ha Publishers, 1998.

Abdu, Katende. "The Relationship between God, Man and Mother Nature: An Islamic Perspective." In *God, Humanity and Mother Nature*, ed. Gilbert E. M. Ogutu, 151–64. Nairobi: Masaki Publishers, 1992.

Abu-Sway, Mustafa. "Towards an Islamic Jurisprudence of the Environment (*Fiqh al-Bi'ah f'il-Islam*)." Lecture given at Belfast mosque, February 1998. <http://homepages.iol.ie/~afifi/Articles/environment.htm>.

Ackerman, Denise, and Tahira Joyner. "Earth-Healing in South Africa: Challenges to Church and Mosque." In *Women Healing Earth: Third World Women on Ecology, Feminism and Religion*, ed. Rosemary Radford Ruether, 121–34. Maryknoll, N.Y.: Orbis, 1996.

Afrasiabi, K. L. "Toward an Islamic Ecotheology." *Hamdard Islamicus* 18, no. 1 (1995): 33–49. Reprinted in *Worldviews, Religion and the Environment: A Global Anthology*, ed. Richard C. Foltz (Belmont, Calif.: Wadsworth Thomson, 2002), 366–75.

Agwan, A. R. *The Environmental Concern of Islam*. New Delhi: Institute of Objective Studies, 1992.

_______. "Toward an Ecological Consciousness." *American Journal of Islamic Social Sciences* 10, no. 2 (1993): 238–48.

Ahmad, Akhtaruddin. *Islam and the Environmental Crisis*. London: Ta-Ha Publishers, 1997.

Ahmad, Ali. *A Cosmopolitan Orientation of International Environmental Law: An Islamic Law Genre*. Lanham, Md.: University Press of America, 2001.

_______. "Islam and Environmental Law." In *Encyclopedia of Religion and Nature*, ed. Bron Taylor and Jeffrey Kaplan. New York: Continuum, 2004.

_______. "Islam and Modern Transformation of Environmental Thoughts." *American Muslim Quarterly* 2, no. 1 (1998): 129–36.

_______. "Islam and Nature in Nigeria." In *Encyclopedia of Religion and Nature*, ed. Bron Taylor and Jeffrey Kaplan. New York: Continuum, 2004.

_______. "Islamic Water Law as an Antidote for Maintaining Water Quality." *University of Denver Water Law Review*, summer 1999, 170–88.

Ahmad, Ali, and Carl Bruch. "Maintaining Mizan: Protecting Biodiversity of Muslim Communities in Africa." *Environmental Law Reporter* 32, no. 1 (2001): 20–37.

Ajmal, Mohammed. "Islam and Ecological Problems." In *Quest for New Science*, ed. Rais Ahmed and S. Naseem Ahmed, 215–20. Aligarh: Centre for Studies on Science, 1984.

Akbar, Khalid Farooq. "Environmental Crisis and Religion: The Islamic View." *Islamic Thought and Scientific Creativity* 3, no. 1 (1992): 23–29.

Albert, Jeff, Magnus Bernhardsson, and Roger Kenna, eds. *Transformations of Middle Eastern Natural Environments: Legacies and Lessons*. Yale School of Forestry and Environmental Studies Bulletin Series, no. 103. New Haven, Ct.: Yale University, 1998.

Alhilaly, Tajuddin H. "Islam and Ecology." Trans. Keysar Trad. 1993. <http://www.speednet.com.au/keysar/ecology.htm>.

Ammar, Nawal H. "Islam and Deep Ecology." In *Deep Ecology and World Religions: New Essays on Sacred Ground*, ed. David Landis Barnhill and Roger S. Gottlieb, 193–211. Albany: State University of New York Press, 2001.

_______. "Islam and Eco-Justice." In *Encyclopedia of Religion and Nature*, ed. Bron Taylor and Jeffrey Kaplan. New York: Continuum, 2004.

_______. "Islam and the Environment: A Legalistic and Textual View." In *Population, Consumption, and the Environment: Religious and Secular* Responses, ed. Harold Coward, 123–136. Albany: State University of New York Press, 1995.

_______. "An Islamic Response to the Manifest Ecological Crisis: Issues of Justice." In *Visions of a New Earth: Religious Perspectives on Population, Consumption, and Ecology*, ed. Harold Coward and Daniel C. Maguire, 131–46. Albany: State University of New York Press, 2000. Reprinted in *Worldviews, Religion and the Environment: A Global Anthology*, ed. Richard C. Foltz (Belmont, Calif.: Wadsworth Thomson, 2002), 376–85.

Ansari, M. I. "Islamic Perspective on Sustainable Development." *American Journal of Islamic Social Sciences* 11 (1995): 394–402.

Asmal, Abdul Cader, and Mohammed Asmal. "An Islamic Perspective." In *Consumption, Population and Sustainability: Perspectives from Science and Religion*, ed. Audrey Chapman, Rodney Peterson, and Barbara Smith-Moran, 157–65. Washington, D.C.: Island Press, 2000.

Aydüz, Davud. "The Approach to the Environment Question of the Qur'an and Its Contemporary Commentary, the *Risale-i Nur*." Paper delivered at the Fourth International Symposium on Bediuzzaman Said Nursi: A Contemporary Approach towards Understanding the Qur'an: The Example of *Risale-i Nur*, Istanbul, Turkey, 20–22 September 1998.

Ba Kader, Abou Bakr Ahmed, Abdul Latif Tawfik El Shirazy Al Sabagh, Mohamed Al Sayyed Al Glenid, and Mawil Y. Izzi Deen. *Islamic Principles for the Conservation of the Natural Environment*. Gland, Switzerland: International Union for Conservation of Nature and Natural Resources, 1983. 2d edition online: <http://www.islamset.com/env/index.html>.

Bakhashab, Omar A. "Islamic Law and the Environment: Some Basic Principles." *Arab Law Quarterly*, 1982: 287–98.

Ba Ubaid, Ali Yeslam. "Environment, Ethics and Design: An Inquiry into the Ethical Underpinnings of Muslim Environmentalism and Its Environmental Design Implications (Saudi Arabia)." Ph.D. diss., University of Pennsylvania, 1999.

Bousquet, G. H. "Des animaux et de leur traitement selon le Judaïsme, le Christianisme et l'Islam." *Studia Islamica* 9 (1958): 31–48.

Brookes, J. *Gardens of Paradise: The History and Design of the Great Islamic Gardens*. London: Weidenfeld and Nicolson, 1987.

Callicott, J. Baird. "The Historical Roots of Western European Environmental Attitudes and Values: Islam." In *Earth's Insights: A Multicultural Survey of Ecological Ethics from the Mediterranean Basin to the Australian Outback*, 30–36. Berkeley and Los Angeles: University of California Press, 1994.

Canan, Ibrahim. *Environmental Ethics in the Light of the Hadiths* (in Turkish). Istanbul: New Asia Press, 1995.

________. "Environment in Islam." *Yeni Türkiye* 5 (July-August 1995): 27–38.

Canatan, Kadir. "The Paradigmatic Background to the Ecological Crisis and Said Nursi's Cosmological Teachings." Paper delivered at the Fourth International Symposium on Bediuzzaman Said Nursi: A Contemporary Approach towards Understanding the Qur'an: The Example of *Risale-i Nur*, Istanbul, Turkey, 20–22 September 1998.

Chelhod, J. "Ḥimā." *Encyclopedia of Islam*, 2d ed., 3:393. Leiden: Brill, 1971.

Chittick, William. "God Surrounds All Things: An Islamic Perspective on the Environment." *The World and I* 1, no. 6 (June 1986): 671–78.

Clarke, L. "The Universe Alive: Nature in the Philosophy of Jalal al-Din Rumi." In *Thinking About the Environment: Our Debt to the Medieval Past*, ed. Thomas Robinson and Laura Westra, 159–81. Lexington, Mass.: Lexington Books, 2002.

Damad, Mostafa Mohaghegh. *A Discourse on Nature and Environment from an Islamic Perspective*. Tehran: Department of the Environment, 2001. <http://www.ir-doe.org/hamaiesh/publication.htm>.

Denny, Frederick M. " Islam and Ecology: A Bestowed Trust Inviting Balanced Stewardship." *Earth Ethics* 10, no. 1 (1998).

Dutton, Yasin. "Islam and the Environment: A Framework for Inquiry." *Faiths and the Environment: Conference Papers* (*Faith in Dialogue*, no. 1), 46–70. London: Centre for Inter-Faith Dialogue, 1996. Reprinted in *Islam and the Environment*, ed. Harfiyah Abdel Haleem (London: Ta-Ha Publishers, 1998), 56–74.

_______. "Natural Resources in Islam." In *Islam and Ecology*, ed. Fazlun Khalid and Joanne O'Brien, 51–67. New York: Cassell, 1992.

Eaton, Charles Le Gai. "Islam and the Environment." *Islamica: The Journal of the London School of Economics and Political Science* 1, no. 2 (1993): 18–21.

Erdur, Oguz. "Reappropriating the 'Green': Islamist Environmentalism." *New Perspectives on Turkey* 17 (fall 1997): 151–66.

Findly, Ellison Banks. "Jahangir's Vow of Non-Violence." *Journal of the American Oriental Society* 107, no. 2 (1987): 245–56.

Foltz, Richard C. "Environmental Initiatives in Contemporary Iran." *Central Asian Survey* 20, no. 2 (2001): 155–65.

_______. "Iran's Water Crisis: Cultural, Political and Ethical Dimensions." *Journal of Agricultural and Environmental Ethics* 15, no. 4 (2002): 357–80.

_______. "Is There an Islamic Environmentalism?" *Environmental Ethics* 22, no. 1 (2000): 63–72.

_______. "Is Vegetarianism Un-Islamic?" *Studies in Contemporary Islam* 3, no. 1 (2001): 39–54.

_______. "Islam and Environmentalism in Iran." In *Encyclopedia of Religion and Nature*, ed. Bron Taylor and Jeffrey Kaplan. New York: Continuum, 2004.

_______. "Islamic Environmentalism in Theory and Practice." In *Worldviews, Religion and the Environment: A Global Anthology*, ed. Richard C. Foltz (Belmont, Calif.: Wadsworth Thomson, 2002), 358–65.

_______. "Nasr, Seyyed Hossein." In *Encyclopedia of Global Environmental Change*, 5:412. London: Wiley, 2001.

_______. "Pure Brethren." In *Encyclopedia of Religion and Nature*, ed. Bron Taylor and Jeffrey Kaplan. New York: Continuum, 2004.

_______. Review of *The Environmental Dimensions of Islam*, by Mawil Izzi Dien. *Journal of the American Academy of Religion* 69, no. 1 (2001): 241–44.

_______. "Vegetarianism—in Islam." In *Encyclopedia of Religion and Nature*, ed. Bron Taylor and Jeffrey Kaplan. New York: Continuum, 2004.

_______. "Water—in Islam." In *Encyclopedia of Religion and Nature*, ed. Bron Taylor and Jeffrey Kaplan. New York: Continuum, 2004.

_______. "Water—in Zoroastrianism." In *Encyclopedia of Religion and Nature*, ed. Bron Taylor and Jeffrey Kaplan. New York: Continuum, 2004.

Foltz, Richard C., ed. *Environmentalism in the Contemporary Muslim World.* Forthcoming.

_______, ed. *Worldviews, Religion and the Environment: A Global Anthology.* Belmont, Calif.: Wadsworth Thomson, 2002.

Forward, Martin, and Mohamed Alam "Islam." In *Attitudes to Nature*, ed. Jean Holm and John Bowker, 79–100. London: Pinter, 1994.

Ganai, Gh. Nabi. "Nature Conservation in Islam." *Islam and the Modern Age* 26, no. 4 (1995): 280–92.

Gürsel, D. *Çevresizsiniz* (You Are Environmentless) (in Turkish). Istanbul: Insan Yayincilik, 1989.

Haleem, Harfiyah Abdel. Review of *The Environmental Dimensions of Islam*, by Mawil Izzi Dien. *Journal of Islamic Studies* 12, no. 2 (2001): 179–82.

Hamed, Safei El-Deen. *Landscape Planning for the Arid Middle East: An Approach to Setting Environmental Objectives.* Lewiston, N.Y.: Edwin Mellen Press, 2001.

_______. "Paradise on Earth: Historical Gardens of the Arid Middle East." *Arid Lands Newsletter* 36, no. 2 (1995): 5–10.

_______. "Seeing the Environment through Islamic Eyes: Application of Shariah to Natural Resources Planning and Management." *Journal of Agricultural and Environmental Ethics* 6, no. 2 (1993): 145–64.

Haq, S. Nomanul. "Islam." In *A Companion to Environmental Philosophy*, ed. Dale Jamieson, 111–129. London: Blackwell, 2001.

_______. "Islam and Ecology: Toward Retrieval and Reconstruction." *Daedalus* 130, no. 4 (2001): 141–78.

_______. "*Ṭab'īa*." *Encyclopedia of Islam*, 2d ed., 8:25–28. Leiden: Brill, 1998.

Helmy, Mustafa Mahmud. *Islam and Environment 2: Animal Life* (in Arabic, English, and French). Kuwait: Environment Protection Council, 1409/1988–89.

Hope, Marjorie, and James Young. *Voices of Hope in the Struggle to Save the Planet*, 153–89, 292–94. New York: The Apex Press, 2000.

Hopkins, Nicholas S., et al. *People and Pollution: Cultural Constructions and Social Action in Egypt*. Cairo: American University in Cairo Press, 2001.

Husaini, S. Waqar Ahmad. *Islamic Environmental Systems Engineering*. London: Macmillan, 1980.

Ibrahim, F. *Ecological Imbalances in the Republic of Sudan*. Bayreuth: Druckhaus Bayreuth Verlagsgesellschaft, 1984.

Idris, Jafar Sheikh. "Is Man the Viceregent of God?" *Journal of Islamic Studies* 1 (1990): 99–110.

Ikhwan al-Safa (The Pure Brethren). *The Case of the Animals versus Man Before the King of the Jinn*. Trans. Lenn Evan Goodman. Boston: Twayne Publishers, 1978.

International Union for the Conservation of Nature (IUCN)–Pakistan. *The Pakistan National Conservation Strategy*. Karachi: IUCN, 1992.

Izzi Dien, Mawil Y. *The Environmental Dimensions of Islam*. Cambridge: Lutterworth, 2000.

_______. "Islam and the Environment: Theory and Practice." *Journal of Beliefs and Values* 18, no. 1 (1997): 47–58.

_______. "Islamic Environmental Ethics, Law, and Society." In *Ethics of Environment and Development: Global Challenge and International Response*, ed. J. Ronald Engel and Joan Gibb Engel, 189–98. Tucson: University of Arizona Press, 1990.

_______. "Islamic Ethics and the Environment." In *Islam and Ecology*, ed. Fazlun Khalid and Joanne O'Brien, 25–35. New York: Cassell, 1992.

Jabbra, Joseph G., and Nancy W. Jabbra, eds. *Challenging Environmental Issues: Middle Eastern Perspectives*. Leiden: Brill, 1997.

Jazayery, Hashem Najy. *Hemayat az heyvanat dar eslam* (The Importance of Animals in Islam) (in Persian). Qom: Dar al-saqalin, 1379/2000.

Johnson-Davies, Denys. *The Island of Animals, Adapted from an Arabic Fable*. Austin: University of Texas Press, 1994.

Joma, Hesam A. "The Earth as a Mosque." Ph.D. diss., University of Pennsylvania, 1991.

Jumah, Salwa Sharawi. *Environmental Policy Making in Egypt*. Gainesville: University Press of Florida, 1997.

Kaplan, Jeffrey. Review of *The Environmental Dimensions of Islam*, by Mawil Izzi Dien. *Worldviews: Environment, Culture, Religion* 5, no. 1 (2001): 110–12.

Kayani, M. S. *Love All Creatures*. 1981. Reprint, Leicester: The Islamic Foundation, 1997.

Khalid, Fazlun. "The Disconnected People." In *Islam and Ecology*, ed. Fazlun Khalid and Joanne O'Brien, 99–110. New York: Cassell, 1992. Reprinted in *Worldviews, Religion and the Environment: A Global Anthology*, ed. Richard C. Foltz (Belmont, Calif.: Wadsworth Thomson, 2002), 385–91.

_______. "Guardians of the Natural Order." *Our Planet* 8, no. 2 (August 1996).

_______. "Islam and the Environment." *Encyclopedia of Global Environmental Change*, 5:332–39. London: Wiley, 2001.

_______. *Qur'an: Creation and Conservation*. Birmingham, U.K.: IFEES, 1999.

Khalid, Fazlun, and Joanne O'Brien, eds. *Islam and Ecology*. New York: Cassell, 1992.

Khan, Inayat. *The Nature Meditations of Hazrat Inayat Khan*. Lebanon Springs, N.Y.: Sufi Order Publications, 1980.

Kılıç, Sadık. "The Message of the *Risale-i Nur* in the Ecological Context." Paper delivered at the Fourth International Symposium on Bediuzzaman Said Nursi: A Contemporary Approach towards Understanding the Qur'an: The Example of *Risale-i Nur*, Istanbul, Turkey, 20–22 September 1998.

Kula, Erhun. "Islam and Environmental Conservation." *Environmental Conservation* 28, no. 1 (2001): 2–9.

_______. Review of *The Environmental Dimensions of Islam*, by Mawil Izzi Dien. *Environmental Conservation* 28, no. 3 (2001): 286–87.

Lau, Martin. "Islam and Judicial Activism: Public Address Litigation under Environmental Protection in the Islamic Republic of Pakistan." In *Human Rights Approaches to Environmental Protection*, ed. Alan E. Boyle and Michael R. Anderson, 285–302. New York: Clarendon Press, 1996.

Lehrman, J. *Earthly Paradise: Garden and Courtyard in Islam*. Berkeley: University of California Press, 1980.

Llewellyn, Othman. "Desert Reclamation and Conservation in Islamic Law." *Muslim Scientist* 11, no. 9 (1982): 9–29. Edited version reprinted in *Islam and Ecology*, ed. Fazlun Khalid and Joanne O'Brien (New York: Cassell, 1992), 87–97.

_______. "Islamic Jurisprudence and Environmental Planning." *Journal of Research in Islamic Economics* (Jeddah) 1, no. 2 (1984).

_______. "Shari'ah Values Pertaining to Landscape Planning and Design." In *Islamic Architecture and Urbanism*. Dammam, Saudia Arabia: King Faisal University, 1983.

MacDougall, E. B., and R. Ettinghausen, eds. *The Islamic Garden*. Washington, D.C.: Dumbarton Oaks, 1976.

Majmu 'e-ye maqalat-e avalin hamayesh-e eslam va mohit-e zist (Papers from the First Conference on Islam and the Environment) (in Persian). Tehran: Department of Environmental Protection, 1378/1999.

"Man and His Environment." In *Islam: A Challenge.* Lahore: Tolu-e-Islam, 2000. <http://www.toluislam.com/pub_online/islam_a_challenge/chapter17.htm>.

Manzoor, S. Parvez. "Environment and Values: An Islamic Perspective." In *Touch of Midas: Scientific Values and the Environment in Islam and the West*, ed. Ziauddin Sardar, 150–70. Manchester: Manchester University Press, 1984.

Masri, Al-Hafiz. "Animal Experimentation: The Muslim Viewpoint." In *Animal Sacrifices: Religious Perspectives on the Use of Animals in Science*, ed. Tom Regan, 171–98. Philadelphia: Temple University Press, 1986.

_______. *Animals in Islam.* Petersfield, Harts, England: The Athene Trust, 1989.

_______. "Islam and Ecology." In *Islam and Ecology*, ed. Fazlun Khalid and Joanne O'Brien, 1–23. New York: Cassell, 1992.

_______. *Islamic Concern for Animals.* Petersfield, Harts, England: The Athene Trust, 1987.

Meier, Fritz. "The Problems of Nature in the Esoteric Monism of Islam." Trans. R. Mannheim. In *Spirit and Nature: Papers from the Eranos Yearbooks*, ed. Joseph Campbell, 149–203. New York: Pantheon, 1954.

Morewedge, Parvez. "Islamic Ecology: The De-Alienation of Persons from Nature." In *Thinking about the Environment: Our Debt to the Medieval Past*, ed. Thomas Robinson and Laura Westra, 143–58. Lexington, Mass.: Lexington Books, 2002.

Moynihan, E. B. *Paradise as a Garden in Persia and Mughal India.* New York: Braziller, 1979.

Nasif, Abdullah Omar. "The Muslim Declaration of Nature." *Environmental Policy and Law* 17, no. 1 (1987): 47.

Nasr, Seyyed Hossein. "The Ecological Problem in Light of Sufism: The Conquest of Nature and the Teachings of Eastern Science." In *Sufi Essays*, 2d ed., 152–63. Albany: State University of New York Press, 1991.

_______. "Islam and the Environmental Crisis." *MAAS Journal of Islamic Science* 6, no. 2 (1990): 31–51.

_______. "Islam and the Environmental Crisis." *Islamic Quarterly* 34, no. 4 (1991): 217–34.

_______. "Islam and the Environmental Crisis." In *Spirit and Nature*, ed. Steven C. Rockefeller and John C. Elder, 83–108. Boston: Beacon Press, 1992.

_______. *Man and Nature: The Spiritual Crisis in Modern Man.* Rev. ed. Chicago: Kazi Publishers, 1997.

_______. "The Meaning of Nature in Various Intellectual Perspectives in Islam." *Islamic Quarterly* 9, no. 1-2 (1965): 25–29.

_______. *Religion and the Order of Nature*. New York: Oxford University Press, 1996.

Nursi, Bediuzzaman Said. "On Nature." In *The Flashes Collection*. Trans. Sukran Vahide. Istanbul: Sözler Nashriyat, 1995.

Özdemir, Ibrahim. "Bediuzzaman Said Nursi's Approach to the Environment." Paper delivered at the Fourth International Symposium on Bediuzzaman Said Nursi: A Contemporary Approach towards Understanding the Qur'an: The Example of *Risale-i Nur*, Istanbul, Turkey, 20–22 September 1998.

_______. *Çevre ve Din* (Environment and Religion) (in Turkish). Ankara: Ministry of Environment, 1997.

_______. *The Ethical Dimension of Human Attitude[s] toward Nature*. Ankara: Ministry of Environment, 1997.

_______. "Muhammad." In *Encyclopedia of Religion and Nature*, ed. Bron Taylor and Jeffrey Kaplan. New York: Continuum, 2004.

_______. "Rumi, Jalal al-Din." In *Encyclopedia of Religion and Nature*, ed. Bron Taylor and Jeffrey Kaplan. New York: Continuum, 2004.

_______. "Said Nursi." In *Encyclopedia of Religion and Nature*, ed. Bron Taylor and Jeffrey Kaplan. New York: Continuum, 2004.

Özdemir, Ibrahim, and Münir Yükselmis. *Çevre Sorunları ve Islam* (Environmental Problems and Islam) (in Turkish). Ankara, 1995.

Parvaiz, Muhammad Aslam. "Man, Nature and Islam." In *Encyclopedia of Religion and Nature*, ed. Bron Taylor and Jeffrey Kaplan. New York: Continuum, 2004.

_______. "Nature in Hadith and Shari'a Law." In *Encyclopedia of Religion and Nature*, ed. Bron Taylor and Jeffrey Kaplan. New York: Continuum, 2004.

Peirone, Federico. "Islam and Ecology in the Mediterranean Muslim *Kulturkreise*." *Hamdard Islamicus* 5, no. 2 (1982): 3–31.

Pusch, Barbara. "The Ecology Debate among Muslim Intellectuals in Turkey." *Les Annales de l'Autre Islam* 6 (1999): 195–209.

al-Qaradhawi, Yusuf. *Ra'it al-bi'at fi sharī'at al-islam* (in Arabic). Cairo: Dar al-Shuruq, 1421/2001.

Rafiq, M., and Mohammad Ajmal. "Islam and the Present Ecological Crisis." In *World Religions and the Environment*, ed. O. P. Dwivedi, 119–37. New Delhi: Gilanjal Publishing House, 1989.

Rahman, M. K. "Environmental Awareness in Islam." *MAAS Journal of Islamic Science* 2 (1980): 99–105.

Raskhy, Fruzan. "Ertebāt-e ensān va tabi'at az negāh-e eslām va Ayin-e Dā'o" (The Relationship between Man and Nature in Islam and Daoism) (in Persian). *Haft Āsmān* 1, no. 2 (1387/1999): 87–117.

Rizvi, Ali Raza. "Pakistan." In *Environmental Education in the Asia and Pacific Region: Status, Issues and Practices*, ed. Bishnu B. Bhandari and

Osamu Abe, 171–91. Hayama, Japan: Institute for Global Environmental Strategies, 2001.

Sabarini, Rashid Al-Hamd, and Muhammad Sa'id. *Al-bi'at wa mushkilātuha* (The Environment and Its Problems) (in Arabic). 3d ed. Kuwait: Almajlis al-watani lil-thaqāfah wa al-funūn wa al-adāb, 1986.

Sardar, Ziauddin. "Towards an Islamic Theory of the Environment." In *Islamic Futures: A Shape of Ideas to Come*, 224–37. London: Mansell, 1985.

Sardar, Ziauddin, ed. *An Early Crescent: The Future of Knowledge and the Environment in Islam*. London and New York: Mansell, 1989.

_______. *Touch of Midas: Scientific Values and the Environment in Islam and the West*. Manchester: Manchester University Press, 1984.

Saritoprak, Zeki. "Fethullah Gulen and Nature." In *Encyclopedia of Religion and Nature*, ed. Bron Taylor and Jeffrey Kaplan. New York: Continuum, 2004.

_______. "The Qur'an and Nature." In *Encyclopedia of Religion and Nature*, ed. Bron Taylor and Jeffrey Kaplan. New York: Continuum, 2004.

Shafi, Mohd. "[The] Ecosystem in Light of [the] Quran." *Abstracts of the First All India Seminar on Islam and Scientist* [sic]. Aligarh, India, 1980.

Shirazi, Muhammad Husayni. *Al-fiqh al-bi'at* (in Arabic). Beirut: Mu'assasat al-wā'i al-islāmī, 1420/2000.

Stewart, Philip J. "Islamic Law as a Factor in Grazing Management: The Pilgrimage Sacrifice." *Proceedings of the First International Rangeland Congress*, 119–20. Denver: Society for Range Management, 1978.

Swearington, Will D., and Abdellatif Bencherifa, eds. *The North African Environment at Risk*. Boulder, Colo.: Westview Press, 1996.

Uslu, I. *The Environmental Problems: From Transformation in the Conception of Cosmos to the Ecological Catastrophe* (in Turkish). Istanbul: Insan Press, 1995.

Taylor, Bron, and Jeffrey Kaplan, eds. *Encyclopedia of Religion and Nature*. New York: Continuum, forthcoming 2004.

Timm, Roger E. "The Ecological Fallout of Islamic Creation Theology." In *Worldviews and Ecology*, ed. Mary Evelyn Tucker and John A. Grim, 83–95. Lewisburg, Pa.: Bucknell University Press, 1993.

Wersal, Lisa. "Islam and Environmental Ethics: Tradition Responds to Contemporary Challenges." *Zygon* 30 (1995): 451–59.

Wescoat, James L., Jr. "From the Gardens of the Qur'an to the Gardens of Lahore." *Landscape Research* 20 (1995): 19–29.

_______. "Muslim Contributions to Geography and Environmental Ethics: Challenges of Comparison and Pluralism." In *Philosophy and Geography I: Space, Place, and Environmental Ethics*, ed. Andrew Light and Jonathan M. Smith, 91–116. Lanham, Md.: Rowman and Littlefield, 1997.

_______. "The 'Right of Thirst' for Animals in Islamic Law: A Comparative Approach." *Environment and Planning D: Society and Space* 13 (1995): 637–54.

Wilber, Donald Newton. "Persian Gardens and Paradise." In *Persian Gardens and Garden Pavilions*, 3–21. Washington, D.C.: Dumbarton Oaks, 1979.

Wilkinson, John C. "Islamic Water Law with Special Reference to Oasis Settlement." *Journal of Arid Environments* 20 (1978): 87–96.

_______. "Muslim Land and Water Law." *Journal of Islamic Studies* 1 (1990): 54–72.

Winder, Jonathan, and Haleh Esfandiari, eds. *Persian Lion, Caspian Tiger: The Role of Iranian Environmental NGOs in Environmental Protection in Iran*. Washington, D.C.: Search for Common Ground, 2000.

Yahya, Hafiz S. A. *The Importance of Wildlife Conservation from an Islamic Perspective*. Delhi: Author's Press, 2003.

Zaidi, Iqtidar H. "On the Ethics of Man's Interaction with the Environment: An Islamic Approach." *Environmental Ethics* 3, no. 1 (1981): 35–47.

Notes on Contributors

Abu Bakar Abdul Majeed holds a Bachelor of Pharmacy from al-Zagazig University, Egypt, a Ph.D. in Neuroscience from Sheffield University, United Kingdom, and a Masters in Business Administration from Science University of Malaysia. He was a senior fellow at the Institute of Islamic Understanding, Malaysia, dealing with issues on Islam and science and technology and the environment. Currently, he is Profesor and Dean, Faculty of Pharmacy, MARA University of Technology, Malaysia. His recent publications include *Bioethics: Ethics in the Biotechnology Century*; *Making the Best of Both Worlds*, volume 1, *Faith and Science*; and *Making the Best of Both Worlds*, volume 2, *Heaven and Earth.*

Kaveh L. Afrasiabi is an Iranian scholar residing in the United States. Afrasiabi received a Ph.D. in political science from Boston University in 1988 and has done graduate studies in theology at the Andover-Newton Theological School. He is the director of Global Interfaith Peace. Afrasiabi is the author of, among others, *After Khomeini* (Westview Press, 1994) and *Dialogue of Civilizations/ Dialogue of Theologies* (Global Publication Press, forthcoming). Afrasiabi's articles have appeared in numerous scholarly journals, including *Harvard Theological Review*, Brown's *Journal of World Affairs*, *UN Chronicle*, *Mediterannean Quarterly*, *Middle East Journal*, *Telos*, and *Hamdard Islamicus*.

Adnan Z. Amin is the Director of the New York Regional Office of the United Nations Environment Programme. He has been with UNEP for twelve years where he has served in several capacities. Mr. Amin is an economist specializing in environment and sustainable development. He has a background and substantive experience in a multidisciplinary approach to development, having worked extensively on development issues at the Institute of Development Studies of the diversity of Sussex in the United Kingdom and at the World Bank.

Nawal H. Ammar, Ph.D., is Associate Dean and Associate Professor of Justice Studies and Anthropology at Kent State University. Her work has focused on issues of women and justice, most recently on Islam and punishment, women in prison, and immigrant battered women in the U.S. She has been an Open Society Institute Fellow (1997–2000) and a Ford Foundation Scholar (1987–1988). She has been entered in the newly published *Encyclopedia of Who Is who among Egyptian Women*. Professor Ammar has served as a nongovernmental organization delegate and consultant to various U.N. functions. In 2001 she was one of eight experts who wrote the United Nations Basic Principles of Restorative Justice. The Principles were adopted in April 2002 by more than seventy-five member states.

Azizan Baharuddin is the Director of the Centre for Civilisational Dialogue, the University of Malaya, Kuala Lumpur, and Professor in the Department of Science and Technology Studies where she teaches, researches, and publishes in the areas of environmental ethics, biothics, the interactions and relationships between religion and science, the impact of science on society, and dialogue between civilizations.

Saadia Khawar Khan Chishti holds an M.Sc. and Ph.D. in education from Cornell University and two other master's degress and diplomas in other disciplines. She is currently a member of the Higher Education Commission of Pakistan and represents it as a member of the syndicate of five universities. The commission has entrusted her with a project entitled "Islamization of Higher Education." She is also an advisor to the Government of Azad Kashmir for writing text books for teaching English. She has authored a home economics text book for English-medium schools and has edited a book for teaching Urdu to foreigners. She is coauthor of the *Encyclopaedic History of World Spirituality: The Quest for the Divine* and author of a work on Judeo-Christian-Islamic perspectives on environment and sustainable development (Future Generations Foundation, Malta). Chishti is the Founding President of CHEC-Pakistan, a chapter of CHEC-London-International. She was the only woman member of the Council of Islamic Ideology, Government of Pakistan, for two terms and was an ex-officio member of the Federal Council of Pakistan. She served the Ministry of Education of Pakistan in various key positions and she was the first woman to be the Director of Public Instruction Colleges and Chairperson of the Commission for Women's University. She has been a visiting fellow of Oxford University, a visiting professor at Villanova University, and a senior fellow at Harvard University.

L. Clarke (Ph.D., Institute of Islamic Studies, McGill University) is Associate Professor of Religion in the Department of Religion, Concordia University, Montréal, with previous appointments at Bard College, N.Y., and the

University of Pennsylvania. She conducts research principally in Shiism, Persian Sufism, and gender and Islam. Recent publications include "The Rise and Fall of Esoterism (*taqiyah*) in Shiite Islam," in *Mystical Thought in Islam: New Research in Historiography, Law, Sufism and Philosophy in Honor of Hermann Landolt* (London: I. B. Tauris, 2003); "*Hijāb* According to the *Hadīth*: Text and Interpretation," in *The Muslim Veil in North American: Issues and Debates* (Scholars' Press, 2003); and the chapter on women in Islam in *Women in Religious Traditions*, ed. Pamela Dickey Young (Oxford University Press, 2003).

Frederick M. Denny is Professor of Religious Studies at the University of Colorado at Boulder. A University of Chicago Ph.D. with previous teaching appointments at Yale College and the University of Virginia, he has conducted field research on Qur'anic recitation, Muslim popular ritual, and characteristics of contemporary Muslim societies in Egypt, Indonesia, and Malaysia. His current research includes Muslim community formation in North America and Muslim human rights discourses. His college-level textbook *An Introduction to Islam* (2d ed., Macmillan, 1994) is widely used and his University of South Carolina Press series "Studies in Comparative Religion" published pioneering books on Islamic subjects. He served on the editorial boards of *The Muslim World, Teaching Theology and Religion*, and *Journal of Ritual Studies*. He recently published (with John Corrigan, Carlos M. N. Eire, and Martin S. Jaffee) *Jews, Christians, Muslims: A Comparative Introduction to Monotheistic Religions,* together with a related anthology, *Readings in Judaism, Christianity, and Islam* (Prentice-Hall 1998).

Hashim Ismail Dockrat is the Founder and Director of the Institute for Human and Environmental Development. He is also the chief editor of *The Islamic Times* and Director of Peoples Alliance for Nature. Dockrat obtained his B.A. at the University of South Africa, went to the Cadet School for the Department of Foreign Affairs, and is a graduate member of the Foundation for Business Leaders. He is author of *Developing a Free Society* (1996).

Yasin Dutton was educated at Jesus College, Oxford, where he received both his first degree, in Arabic and Urdu, and his doctorate, in early Islamic law. Having taught at the Oriental Institute, Oxford, he is currently Senior Lecturer in Arabic and Islamic Studies at the University of Edinburgh. In addition to specific research interests in early Islamic law and the textual history of the Qur'an, he is also particularly interested in Islam and the environment. He has published several articles on these topics, and is also the author of *The Origins of Islamic Law: The Qur'an, the* Muwaṭṭa' *and Madinan 'Amal* (RoutledgeCurzon).

Richard C. Foltz is Associate Professor of Religion, History, Natural Resources, and Asian Studies at the University of Florida. He holds a Ph.D. in History and Middle Eastern Studies from Harvard University. Foltz is the author of *Religions of the Silk Road* and *Mughal India and Central Asia*, and editor of *Worldviews, Religion, and the Environment: A Global Anthology*. He has recently written a religious history of Iran which is due to be published in 2004.

Nathan C. Funk is Visiting Assistant Professor of Political Science and International Affairs at George Washington University's Elliott School of International Affairs. He received his B.A. from Gustavus Adolphus College (St. Peter, Minnesota) and his Ph.D. in international relations from American University. He has authored or coauthored writings on international conflict resolution, the contemporary Middle East, Islam, and United States foreign policy. With Abdul Aziz Said and Ayse S. Kadayifci, he coedited *Peace and Conflict Resolution in Islam* (University Press of America).

Safei-Eldin A. Hamed is an environmental planning consultant and international development scholar who practices in North America and the Middle East. He holds a B.Arch. from Cairo University, an M.L.A. from the University of Georgia, and a Ph.D. from Virginia Tech. He has taught at the University of Guelph and the University of Nova Scotia in Canada, King Faisal University in Saudi Arabia, the University of Georgia, Virginia Tech, and the University of Maryland in the United States. From 1994 to 1997 he worked as an environmental assessment specialist for the World Bank. He is currently on the faculty of Texas Tech University, and is a fellow of the International Center of Arid and Semi-Arid Lands. He has also served as consultant for several national and international organizations, including the Aspen Institute for Humanistic Studies, Smithsonian Institute, Parks Canada, U.S. Fish and Wildlife Service, U.S. Agency for International Development, Aga Khan Award for Architecture, and U.S. Information Agency. Dr. Hamed's research activities cover a wide range of studies, including best practices in landscape architecture, environmental strategies and management, Islamic architecture and urbanism, Arab-Muslim cross-cultural issues, and sustainable tourism development.

S. Nomanul Haq is on the faculty of Rutgers University and is a Visiting Assistant Professor at the University of Pennsylvania. For several years until 1996, he was Assistant Professor of Religious Studies at Brown University. His research interests lie in Islamic intellectual history, religion, and Sufism.

Mawil Izzi Dien is a British citizen of Arabic origin. He is a Senior Lecturer in Islamic Studies at the University of Wales. Izzi Dien is author and coauthor of many articles on Islam and the environment including the first work on Islam and the environment (IUCN, 1982) and a forthcoming book entitled *Islamic Law and Environment* (Lutterworth–Cambridge).

Joseph G. Jabbra is Academic Vice President and Professor of Political Science at Loyola Marymount University in Los Angeles. He is a member of fifteen professional societies, the recipient of several grants and awards, and the author or coauthor of over nine books and twenty-nine articles. His specific areas of expertise are the Middle East, international law, and higher education. His latest publication is entitled *Where Corruption Lives*. Prior to his appointment at Loyola Marymount University, he served as Vice President (Academic and Research) at St. Mary's University in Halifax, Nova Scotia.

Nancy W. Jabbra, an anthropologist, is Professor and Director of Women's Studies at Loyola Marymount University. She previously was a member of the Department of Sociology and Social Anthropology at Dalhousie University in Halifax, Nova Scotia. She is the author, coauthor, or coeditor of numerous publications on women and gender roles, politics, and the environment in the Middle East, and on gender, the family, and politics among Lebanese immigrants in North America. Her books include *Voyageurs to a Rocky Shore: The Lebanese and Syrians of Nova Scotia*, *Challenging Environmental Issues: Middle Eastern Perspectives*, and *Women in the Middle East and North Africa*. She is a member of numerous professional organizations.

Tazim R. Kassam is Associate Professor of Islamic Studies and Director of Graduate Studies in the Department of Religion at Syracuse University and has also taught at Middlebury College and Colorado College. She received her Ph.D. at McGill University in the history of religions and specialized in the Islamic tradition with a focus on South Asia. Her research and teaching interests include gender, ritual, devotional literature, syncretism, and the cultural heritage of Islam. Her book *Songs of Wisdom and Circles of Dance* (SUNY, 1995) explores the origins and creative synthesis of Hindu-Muslim ideas expressed in the song tradition of the Isma'ili Muslims of the Indian Subcontinent. She has cochaired the Study of Islam section of the American Academy of Religion, served as president of the AAR Rocky Mountain–Great Plains Region, is a Lilly Teaching Scholar, and is on the editorial board of the *Journal of the American Academy of Religion*.

Fazlun M. Khalid is the Founder Director of the Islamic Foundation for Ecology and Environmental Sciences. He was the Director of Training of the Alliance of Religions and Conservation, 1995–2002, and is an advisor and consultant to numerous international agencies and academic institutions, including the World Wide Fund for Nature International, the World Bank, and CARE USA. He is coeditor of *Islam and Ecology* and author of *Qur'an, Creation and Conservation* and of major essays and articles on Islamic environmentalism. He sees his main task as working toward the revival of Islamic environmental norms through programs designed to reeducate Muslims in *Sharī'a*-based conservation practice.

Othman Abd-ar-Rahman Llewellyn is an environmental planner in Saudi Arabia's National Commission for Wildlife Conservation and Development. His responsibilities include planning and design of protected areas, environmental restoration, and habitat enhancement. He studied environmental planning and landscape architecture with Ian McHarg in the Masters Program at the University of Pennsylvania and took courses in Islamic law at the University of Pennsylvania, Temple University, and the University of Michigan. He has written articles on a variety of subjects pertaining to conservation in Islamic law, and revised and expanded the World Conservation Union (IUCN) publication *Environmental Protection in Islam*. He is a member of IUCN's World Commission on Protected Areas and its Commission on Environmental Law.

Farzaneh Milani is Professor of Persian and Women's Studies at the University of Virginia. She is the author of *Veils and Words* (Syracuse University Press, 1992), *A Cup of Sin: Selected Poems of Simin Behbahani* (with Kaveh Safa), and numerous articles and book chapters in Persian and English. Currently she is working on a book, tentatively titled *Remapping the Cultural Geography of Iran: Women, Mobility, and Power*. Milani is the past President of the Association of Middle Eastern Women's Studies and the current Director of Studies in Women and Gender at the University of Virginia.

Seyyed Hossein Nasr was born and received his early education in Iran. He later studied in the United States where he received his B.S. degree with honors in physics from the Massachusetts Institute of Technology and his M.S. and Ph.D. degrees in the history of science and learning with a concentration in Islamic science, from Harvard University. From 1958–79, he was Professor of Philosophy at Tehran University and is presently University Professor of Islamic Studies at the George Washington University. He is the author of many works on Islamic science and religion and the environment, including: *An Introduction to Islamic Cosmological Doctrines*, *Science and Civilization in Islam*, *Islamic Science: An Illustrated Study*, *Man and Nature*, *The Need for a Sacred Science*, and *Religion and the Order of Nature.*

İbrahim Özdemir is Professor of the History of Philosophy, Ankara University, Divinity School. He received his M.A. and Ph.D. in philosophy from the

Middle East Technical University. He has held visiting professorships in the United States (University of Hartford and Hartford Seminary) and has traveled widely in the Muslim world and the West. He is associate faculty at the Macdonald Center for the Study of Islam and Christian-Muslim Relations, Hartford Seminary. He has addressed different audiences on topics related to the philosophy of religion, world religions, religion and the environment, and Islamic studies. He has published six books and over fifty articles. His books include *The Ethical Dimension of Human Attitude Towards Nature* (1997), *Çevre ve Din* (Environment and Religion; 1997); *Yalnız Gezegen* (Lonely Planet: Essays on Environmental Ethics and Philosophy; 2001), and *Postmodern Dusunceler* (Postmodern Thoughts; 2001).

Mohammad Aslam Parvaiz, who has a doctorate in plant physiology from Aligarh Muslim University, is currently Senior Reader of Botany at Zakir Husain College of Delhi University. His research and teaching experience is spread over twenty years. He is a science communicator and has four books and more than 350 popular science articles to his credit. He heads the Islamic Foundation for Science and Environment (India), a voluntary, nonprofit organization. Through this platform, he spreads scientific and environmental awareness and aptitude to the population in general and to students of *Madarsa*s (Islamic theology schools) in particular. He is founder and editor of *Urdu Science*, India's first and only popular science monthly magazine published in Urdu. He was awarded an "International Visitorship" by the U.S. Government in 1995.

Attilio Petruccioli, Aga Khan Professor for Islamic Architecture at M.I.T. (1994–1998), is at present Full Professor of Landscape Architecture in the Faculty of Architecture, Polytechnic of Bari, Italy. A specialist in typological study of Islamic and European urbanism, he was trained in architectural practice in Europe and northern Africa. Since his initial appointment at Rome in 1973, Petruccioli has taught in the Rome programs of both Pratt Institute and the Catholic University of America and at the University of Maputo in Mozambique, and has an ongoing commitment to the Ecole Polytechnique d'Architecture et d'Urbanisme in Algiers. He was the founder of the Islamic Environment Research Center in 1983 and has been chief editor of its journal, *Environmental Design*, since that time. He is the author of numerous studies of Islamic and Italian urbanism and landscape, most recently a major edited volume of Islamic gardens published by Electa of Milan in 1994. The theoretical framework developed from his studies of the Islamic environment was published as *Dar al Islam: L'architectura del territorio nei paesi islamici* in 1985 and as *Fathpur Sikri: Città del sole e delle acque* in 1988.

Abdul Aziz Said (Ph.D., American University, 1957) is the senior ranking professor at the School of International Service, American University, where he is Mohammed Said Farsi Professor of Islamic Peace and Director of the Center for Global Peace. Dr. Said was a member of the White House Commission on the Islamic World during the Carter Administration, has served as a consultant to the U.S. Information Agency and Department of State, and has played an active role in Arab-Israeli dialogues. His work *Concepts of International Politics in Global Perspective* is now in its fourth edition. With Nathan C. Funk and Ayse S. Kadayifci, he coedited *Peace and Conflict Resolution in Islam* (University Press of America).

Mohammad Yusuf Siddiq is a faculty member at the University of Sharjah in U.A.E., where he teaches Islamic civilization and culture. Previously, he was the chair of the Department of Arabic and Islamic Studies at Zayed University in Dubai and Abu Dhabi, where he played a key role in establishing a vibrant Arabic and Islamic studies program. Prior to that, he was Associate Professor of Islam at Islamic University in Kushtia, Bangladesh. He also spent several years at Harvard University in various academic programs from 1987 to 1994 and from 1996 to 1998. During 1991–92, he was a visiting fellow at the Oxford Centre for Islamic Studies, Oxford University. A cultural historian of Islam, he has written extensively on the history, civilization, and culture of Muslim Bengal, both in Arabic and English, including a dozen entries in the *Encyclopedia of Islam*. He is now working on the Arabic and Persian inscriptions of Bengal dating to the period 1205–1707. He is also the Founding President of BANI (Baitulmal Association for Needy People's Improvement), a rural welfare project based on Islamic economic concepts and principles successfully engaged in a number of poverty eradication programs in the villages and slums of Kushtia.

James L. Wescoat, Jr., is Professor and Head of the Department of Landscape Architecture at the University of Illinois at Champaigne-Urbana. He conducts research on water in environmental design in South Asia and the United States. From 1985 to 1995 he supervised the Smithsonian Mughal Gardens Project in Lahore with colleagues from the Pakistan Department of Archaeology and University of Engineering and Technology-Lahore. That project yielded numerous publications, including two books that won the Allama Iqbal prize, and an overall research merit award from the American Society of Landscape Architects. He is currently conducting research on water management in Mughal, Rajput, and Sultanate gardens in India; serving as advisor for the Taj Mahal Conservation; and writing about the modern relevance of Indo-Islamic waterworks, planting design, and culture.

Index